North Florida & the Florida Panhandle

North Florida & the Florida Panhandle

Sandra Friend & Kathy Wolf

The Countryman Press ✳ Woodstock, Vermont

SECOND EDITION

DEDICATION

To my sister Sally, for our years of St. Augustine memories and our travels across the globe—may there be many more! S.F.

"A journey is best measured in friends, rather than miles."—Tim Cahill

Interior photographs by the author unless otherwise specified
Maps by Erin Greb Cartography, © The Countryman Press
Book design by Bodenweber Design
Composition by PerfecType, Nashville, TN

Published by The Countryman Press, P.O. Box 748, Woodstock, VT 05091

Distributed by W. W. Norton & Company, Inc., 500 Fifth Avenue, New York, NY 10110

Printed in the United States of America

No entries in this book have been solicited or paid for.

North Florida & the Florida Panhandle
978-0-88150-965-6

10 9 8 7 6 5 4 3 2 1

Also by Sandra Friend
Explorer's Guide Orlando & Central Florida
Explorer's Guide South Florida (with Trish Riley)
50 Hikes in North Florida
50 Hikes in Central Florida
50 Hikes in South Florida
Along the Florida Trail (with Bart Smith)
Exploring Florida's Botanical Wonders
Florida
Hiker's Guide to the Sunshine State
The Hiking Trails of Florida's National Forests, Parks, and Preserves
    (with Johnny Molloy)
Sinkholes

EXPLORE WITH US!

Welcome to the second edition of *Explorer's Guide North Florida & the Florida Panhandle*, the first comprehensive travel guide to this diverse region. No paid advertisers are included in this guide. All attractions, accommodations, restaurants, and shopping have been included by your author on the basis of merit and personal experience. The following points will help you understand how the guide is organized.

WHAT'S WHERE

The book starts out with a thumbnail sketch of the most important things to know about traveling in Florida, from where the waterfalls are (yes, waterfalls!) to which beaches you should head to first. I've included important contact information for state agencies and advice on what to do when you're on the road.

LODGING

All selections for accommodations in this guide are based on merit; most of them were inspected personally or by a reliable source known to me. No businesses were charged for inclusion in this guide. Many B&Bs do not accept children under 12 or pets, so if there is not a specific mention in their entry, ask them about their policy before you book a room. Some places have a minimum-stay requirement, especially on weekends. Please note the warnings about booking vacation rentals and condo hotels, which I found necessary to include throughout the book due to reader feedback. While most visitors are satisfied with their selections, I certainly hear from the ones who aren't! Quality does vary from unit to unit because of private ownership of each unit.

RATES

Rates quoted are for double occupancy, one night, before taxes. When a range of rates is given, it spans the gamut from the lowest of the low season (which varies around the region) to the highest of the high season; a single rate means the proprietor offers only one rate. Rates for hotels and motels are subject to further discount with programs offered through such organizations as AAA and AARP, and may be negotiable depending on occupancy.

RESTAURANTS

The distinction between *Eating Out* and *Dining Out* is based mainly on price, secondarily on atmosphere. Dining in Florida is more casual than anywhere else in the United States—you'll find folks in T-shirts and shorts walking into the dressiest of steak houses. If a restaurant has a dress code, it's noted. Destinations farther from the beach tend to have dressier clientele, especially in city centers.

Smoking is no longer permitted within restaurants in Florida, if the bulk of the business's transactions are in food rather than drink. Many restaurants now provide an outdoor patio for smokers.

KEY TO SYMBOLS

🏵 **Special value**. The special-value symbol appears next to lodgings and restaurants that offer quality not usually enjoyed at the price charged.

🐾 **Pets**. The pet symbol appears next to places that accept pets, from B&Bs to bookstores. All lodgings require that you let them know you're bringing your pet; many will charge an additional fee.

✎ **Child-friendly**. The crayon symbol appears next to places or activities that accept children or appeal to families.

♿ **Handicapped access**. The wheelchair symbol appears next to lodgings, restaurants, and attractions that provide handicapped access, at a minimum with assistance.

💍 **Weddings**. The wedding-rings symbol appears beside facilities that frequently serve as venues for weddings.

((ᵠ)) **WiFi**. Locations that offer wireless Internet.

↬ **Ecofriendly establishments**. In the case of lodgings, this symbol denotes certified participants in the Florida Green Lodging Program. In the case of other businesses and non-certified lodgings, these properties have been noted by the author as taking special initiatives to reduce, reuse, and recycle.

Your feedback is essential for subsequent editions of this guide. Feel free to write me at Countryman Press, P.O. Box 748, Woodstock, Vermont 05091.

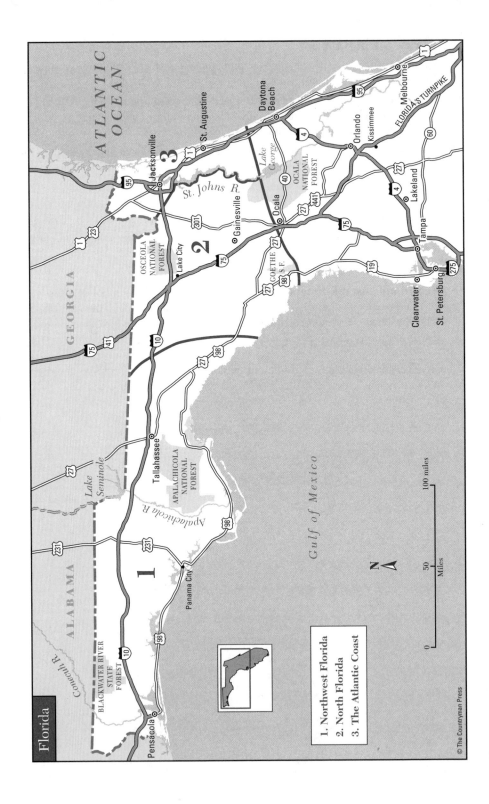

Florida

ALABAMA

GEORGIA

ATLANTIC OCEAN

Gulf of Mexico

Conecuh R.

Lake Seminole

BLACKWATER RIVER STATE FOREST

Pensacola

APALACHICOLA NATIONAL FOREST

Apalachicola R.

Panama City

Tallahassee

OSCEOLA NATIONAL FOREST

Lake City

Jacksonville

St. Johns R.

St. Augustine

Gainesville

Ocala

OCALA NATIONAL FOREST

Lake George

Daytona Beach

Orlando

Kissimmee

Melbourne

FLORIDA'S TURNPIKE

Lakeland

Tampa

Clearwater

St. Petersburg

GOETHE S.F.

1

2

3

N

0   50   100 miles

Miles

1. Northwest Florida
2. North Florida
3. The Atlantic Coast

© The Countryman Press

CONTENTS

MAPS

INTRODUCTION

Welcome to the quiet side of Florida, the oldest part of Florida, the region where life goes on at a mostly unhurried pace. In North Florida and the Florida Panhandle—known better within our state as Northwest Florida—you can still swim in a spring and hear the frogs croaking from the shore, search for waterfalls along rugged tributaries, glide down a crystalline stream on an inner tube, and in general have yourself a great time. North Florida feels like the Old South, and it's never more evident than in towns like White Springs, Madison, Marianna, and Milton, places that retain vital historic downtowns where people still go to work and sip a cup of coffee. Genteel culture remains intact: You'll hear a lot of "yes, ma'am" and "no, sir" up here, where live oaks and magnolias thrive and rolling acres of cotton and wheat dance off into the distance. In the early-morning sun, Spanish moss casts shadows on centuries-old antebellum mansions, and a light mist rises from the cotton fields.

It is across this swath that Florida's history runs deepest. Spanish missionaries traced trails west from St. Augustine to found missions among the Apalachee in the 1600s. The French, British, and Spanish fought for control of the deep-water port at Pensacola. Florida's capital, Tallahassee, was founded in 1824 as a halfway meeting point between the state's only truly populous cities, St. Augustine and Pensacola.

Jacksonville, a modern metropolis both vibrant and historic, anchors the eastern corner of this canvas along with Amelia Island, where the city of Fernandina still shows its colonial character, and St. Augustine, Florida's oldest European settlement and one of my favorite places to get in touch with art and history. Our coverage follows the languid flow of the St. Johns River upstream to the historic centers of Green Cove Springs and Palatka, and swings across the state to encompass the university city of Gainesville and the laid-back coastal communities of Cedar Key and Steinhatchee.

STARFISH PILED IN A BASKET AT A SHOP IN FERNANDINA BEACH

VIEW OF THE APALACHICOLA RIVER FROM NEAL LANDING, BLOUNTSTOWN

As you move west, you step back in time—literally. The Central Time Zone begins at the Apalachicola River and extends west to Pensacola. Along the Gulf of Mexico, the shrimpers come in at dawn after a hard night's work harvesting the sea. Time moves slowly here; the farther you stray from the interstate, the more relaxed you'll find the pace. In Northwest Florida—the Florida Panhandle—agriculture and fishing are still a way of life for many. But tourists now flock to the shore as well, soaking up color along the powdery quartz beaches that extend west from Panama City through South Walton, Destin, Fort Walton, Navarre, and Pensacola. This is a region of natural wonders, where rugged clay cliffs rise high above clear, sand-bottomed rivers; where rhododendron, azalea, and mountain laurel bloom in profusion along streams that seem straight out of the Appalachians; and where vast savannas of pitcher plants shake their draping lemon-yellow blooms in an April breeze.

Welcome to the best that Florida has to offer. Slow down and savor the views.

ACKNOWLEDGMENTS

For my assisting with my research on this edition, I'd like to thank Harvey Campbell, Columbia County Tourism; Susan Estler, Panama City Beach Tourism; Dean Fowler, Steinhatchee Landing; Holly Germano-Wolfrath, Amelia Island Tourism; Anita Grove, Gulf County Tourism; Jay Humphreys and Richard Goldman, St. Augustine, Ponte Vedra, and the Beaches; Art Kimborough, Jackson County Tourism; Katie Kole and Kerri Post, Visit Tallahassee; Katie Kurycki, Visit Jacksonville; Jaffy Lee and Peggy Heiser, Flagler County; Laura Lee, Visit Pensacola; Marcheta Keefer and Roland Loog, Visit Gainesville; and the many museum docents, shopkeepers, restaurateurs, outfitters, and other folks I spent time with in revisiting old favorites and learning about new places.

I couldn't have explored such a large region—seven hours' driving end to end—without help, so many thanks to my many friends who pitched in with lodgings, personal recommendations, research, and good meals, with a special call-out to Linda and Jerry Benton, Lee Berger, Herb Hiller, Howard and Carolyn Pardue, Linda Patton, Denise Rains, Tom and Susan Schmidt, Robert Seidler, Jeff Smith, Elam Stoltzfus, Georgia Turner, Susan Turner, and Jeff and Marti Vickery.

Lodging assistance also came from Linda Larsen, 44 Spanish Street, St. Augustine; Richard Germano, Amelia Island Hotel on the Beach; Michael Setboun, La Maison de Lucy, Alford; Bay Point Marriott Resort, Panama City Beach; Gibson Inn, Apalachicola; Herlong Mansion, Micanopy; Hilton Garden Inn, Pensacola; Toni and Mark Treworgy, Island Cottage Villas, Flagler Beach; Janet Chernoff, Wakulla Lodge; and the good folks at Stephen Foster Memorial Folk Culture State Park, White Springs.

Thanks to my mom, Linda Friend, for joining me in many travels around the region. My brother, Scott Friend, and my sister Sally White, along with their families, participated in scouting locations and providing feedback. Other traveling companions and essential helpers included Morena Cameron, Amber Friend, Phyllis Malinski, and Kathy Wolf. Thanks, Kathy, for helping get the original series off to a big start.

WHAT'S WHERE IN NORTH FLORIDA & THE FLORIDA PANHANDLE

ADMISSION FEES If an admission fee is $7 or less, it's simply listed as "fee." Those greater than $7 are spelled out. Although fees were accurate when this book went to press, keep in mind that yearly increases are likely, especially for the larger attractions and theme parks.

AIR SERVICE Major international airports in the region covered by this book include **Jacksonville International Airport** (904-741-4902; jaa.aero), 2400 Yankee Clipper Dr, Jacksonville, and the **Northwest Florida Beaches International Airport** (850-763-6751; iflybeaches.com), 6300 West Bay Pkwy, Panama City Beach. Smaller regional airports served by commuter flights are listed in their respective chapters.

ALLIGATORS No longer an endangered species, the American alligator is a ubiquitous resident of Florida's lakes, rivers, streams, and retention ponds. Most alligators will turn tail and hit the water with a splash when they hear you coming—unless they've been fed or otherwise desensitized to human presence. Do not approach a sunning alligator, and never, ever feed an alligator

(it's a felony, and downright dangerous to do) in the wild. Nuisance alligators should be reported to the **Florida Fish and Wildlife Conservation Commission alligator hotline** (866-FWC-GATOR; myfwc.com).

AMTRAK Two daily Amtrak (800-USA-RAIL; amtrak.com) trains make their way from New York and Washington, DC, to Florida: the **Silver Service/Palmetto**, ending in either Tampa or Miami, and the **AutoTrain**, bringing visitors (and their cars) to Sanford. Since Hurricane Katrina, rail service through Northwest Florida has been suspended. Stops in North Florida are noted in *Getting There*.

ANTIQUES While **Micanopy** is my favorite North Florida destination for antiques, you won't want to miss the great finds in **Havana**, **High Springs**, **Lake City**, and **Fort Walton Beach**, each worth an afternoon for antiques browsing. St. Augustine boasts a don't-miss antiques row on San Marcos Ave. Since 1985, the free magazine *Antiques & Art Around Florida* (352-475-1336; aarf.com) has kept up with the trends throughout the Sunshine State; pick up a copy at one of the antiques stores you visit, or browse their website to do a little pretrip planning. No matter what you're collecting, it's out there somewhere!

ARCHAEOLOGY Florida's archaeological treasures date back more than 10,000 years, including temple mound complexes such as those found near Tallahassee at **Letchworth Mounds** and **Lake Jackson Mounds**, and thousands of middens (prehistoric garbage dumps) of oyster shells found along the state's rivers, streams, and estuaries. Of the middens, the most impressive in size and area are those at **Timucuan Preserve** in Jacksonville, **Mount Royal** in Welaka, and **Shell**

Mound near Cedar Key. More recent archaeological finds focus on the many **shipwrecks** found along Florida's coasts and in its rivers, protected by underwater preserves. For information about archaeological digs and shipwrecks, contact the Florida Division of Historical Resources, Bureau of Archaeological Research (flheritage .com/archaeology).

ART GALLERIES Florida is blessed with many creative souls drawing their inspiration from our dramatic landscapes, working in media that range from copper sculpture and driftwood to fine black-and-white photography, giclee, and watercolor. Many artists gravitate into communities, so you'll find clusters of art galleries in places like **Apalachicola**, **Cedar Key**, and **St. Augustine**; I'd happily drop a bundle in any of them for the beautiful Florida paintings and photography I found there.

ARTS COUNCILS The **Florida Division of Cultural Affairs** (florida -arts.org) offers resources, grants, and programs to support the arts throughout Florida; its Florida Artists Hall of Fame recognizes great achievements in the arts.

BEACHES Where to start? Florida's 2,000-mile coastline means plenty of beaches for every taste, from the busy social scene at **Atlantic Beach** to the remote serenity of **St. Vincent Island**. In the Panhandle, resorts and condos cluster around the beaches at **Fort Walton–Destin**, **Pensacola Beach**, and **Panama City Beach**; if you want a quieter experience on the same brilliant white sands, seek out **Mexico Beach**, **Cape San Blas**, and **St. George Island**. On the peninsula, **Amelia Island** offers beautiful strands with luxurious resorts. Public lands are your best places to enjoy pristine dunes and uncluttered beachfronts. My personal favorites in this region include **St. Joseph Peninsula State Park**, **St. George Island State Park**, **Little Talbot Island State Park**, and **Anastasia State Park** as well as the **Fort Pickens Unit of Gulf Islands National Seashore**.

BED & BREAKFASTS Given the sheer number of B&Bs throughout Florida, this book doesn't list every B&B in the regions it covers, but it does give you selections from what I feel are the best I've encountered. There is a mix of historical B&Bs, rustic lodges, and easygoing family homes. Some of my choices, but not all, are members of associations such as **Superior Small Lodging** (superiorsmalllodging.com) or the **Florida Bed & Breakfast Inns** (877-303-FBBI; florida-inns.com), both of which conduct independent inspections of properties. All of the B&B owners I stayed with were eager to tell their story; most have a great love for the history of their home and their town. I find B&B travel one of the best ways to connect with the real Florida and strongly encourage you to seek out the experiences listed throughout the book. Some motels and hotels that offer breakfast list their establishments as B&Bs. Since websites can be deceiving, be assured that the B&Bs listed here are, in fact, traditional bed & breakfast accommodations.

BICYCLING Regional clubs and nonprofit organizations have done a great job of establishing and maintaining both on-road bike routes and off-road trails suitable for mountain biking, and information on these routes and trails is listed in the text. Check in with the **Office of Greenways and Trails** (see

Greenways) for information on dedicated bike trails throughout the state.

BIRDING As the home to millions of winter migratory birds, Florida is a prime destination for bird-watching. The **Great Florida Birding Trail** (floridabirdingtrail.com), supported by the Florida Fish and Wildlife Conservation Commission, provides guidance to birders on the best overlooks, hiking trails, and waterfront parks to visit and which species you'll find at each location. Sites listed in the regional Great Florida Birding Trail brochures are designated with brown road signs displaying a stylized swallow-tailed kite. Certain sites are designated "Gateways" to the Great Florida Birding Trail, where you can pick up detailed information and speak with a naturalist. In the region covered by this guidebook, these sites include **Fort Clinch State Park** for the East Section, **Paynes Prairie Preserve State Park** for the West Section, and **Big Lagoon State Park** for the Panhandle.

BOAT AND SAILING EXCURSIONS Exploring our watery state by water is part of the fun of visiting, from the blasting speed of an airboat skipping across the marshes to the gentle toss of a schooner as it sails across Matanzas Bay. Many ecotours rely on quiet, electric-motor pontoon boats to guide you down Florida's rivers and up to its first-magnitude springs. I greatly recommend a sail on the **Schooner** *Freedom* in St. Augustine and on the **narrated cruises at Wakulla Springs**, but you'll find almost any boat tour you take a delight.

BOOKS To understand Florida, you need to read its authors, and none is more important than **Patrick Smith**, whose *A Land Remembered* is a landmark piece of fiction tracing Florida's history from settlement to development. A good capsule history of Florida's nearly 500 years of European settlement is *A Short History of Florida*, the abbreviated version of the original masterwork by **Michael Gannon**. To see through the eyes of settlers who tried to scratch a living from a harsh land, read the award-winning books of **Marjorie Kinnan Rawlings**, including *The Yearling*, *Cross Creek*, and *South Moon Under*. For insights into the history of African American culture in Florida, seek out novelist **Zora Neale Hurston**; her works *Their Eyes Were Watching God* and *Jonah's Gourd Vine* touch the soul. For the feel of life in North Florida, **Connie May Fowler** sets powerful characters against these landscapes in her novels *How Clarissa Burden Learned to Fly*, *The Trouble with Murmur Lee*, *Remembering Blue*, and *River of Hidden Dreams*.

The nonfiction classic *Palmetto Leaves* from **Harriett Beecher Stowe** captures life during Reconstruction along the St. Johns, and to understand Florida culture, read *Palmetto Country* by **Stetson Kennedy**, a Florida icon who worked to compile Florida's folklore with the 1940s WPA project and went on to fight for civil rights throughout the South. For a glimpse of Florida's frenetic development over the past century, *Some Kind of Paradise: A Chronicle of Man and the Land in Florida* by **Mark Derr** and *I Lost It All to Sprawl: How Progress Ate My Cracker Landscape* by **Bill Belleville** offer serious insights. All visitors to Florida who love the outdoors should read *Travels* by **William Bartram**, a botanist who recorded his adventures along the St. Johns River during the 1700s, as well as *A Thousand-Mile Walk to the Gulf* by **John Muir** and *A Naturalist in Florida: A Celebration of Eden* by **Archie Carr**. *River of Lakes: A Journey on Florida's St. Johns River* by Bill Belleville is a wonderful celebration of our state's mightiest river. When you plan your outdoor activities, don't forget that Florida has more than 2,500 miles of hiking trails—and I walked most of them while compiling my many hiking books, including *50 Hikes in North Florida*; *The Hiking Trails of Florida's National Forests, Parks, and Preserves*; and *Hiker's Guide to the Sunshine State*, essential for hikers visiting this region.

BUS SERVICE Greyhound (800-229-9424; greyhound.com) covers an extensive list of Florida cities; see their website for details and the full schedule. Stops are noted in the text under *Getting There*.

CAMPING & CABINS Rates are quoted for single-night double-occupancy stays; all campgrounds offer discounts for club membership as well as weekly, monthly, and resident (six months or more) stays, and often charge more for extra adults. If pets are permitted, keep them leashed. All Florida State Parks now use **Reserve America** (800-326-3521; floridastateparks.reserveamerica.com) for all campground reservations, but sometimes a handful of sites are kept open for drop-ins or remain unreserved. Ask at the gate. Many Florida campgrounds belong to the **Florida Association of RV Parks & Campgrounds** (campflorida.com), which you can become a member of to receive discounts to campgrounds statewide.

CHILDREN, ESPECIALLY FOR

The crayon symbol ✎ identifies activities and places of special interest to children and families.

CITRUS STANDS, FARMER'S MARKETS, AND U-PICKS

Citrus stands associated with active groves are typically open seasonally Nov–Apr. I've listed permanent stands as well as places you're likely to see roadside fruit and vegetable sales (often out of the backs of trucks and vans) from local growers. All U-pick is seasonal, and Florida's growing seasons run year-round with citrus in winter and spring, strawberries in early spring, blueberries in late spring, and cherries in early summer. If you attempt U-pick citrus, bring heavy gloves and wear jeans: Citrus trees have serious thorns. Also, don't pick citrus without permission: It's such a protected crop in Florida that to pluck an orange from a roadside tree is a felony. For a full listing of farmer's markets around the state, visit the **Fresh From Florida** (florida-agriculture.com/marketing /state_markets.htm) website, presented by the Florida Department of Agriculture.

CIVIL WAR

As the third state to secede from the Union, Florida has a great deal of Civil War history to explore, particularly in the region covered by this book. Civil War buffs shouldn't miss **Olustee Battlefield**, site of Florida's largest engagement,

and should check out **Florida Reenactors Online** (floridareenactors online.com) for a calendar of reenactments held throughout the state.

CRABS

Florida's seafood restaurants can lay claim to some of the freshest crabs anywhere; blue crabs and stone crabs are caught along the Gulf Coast. October is Crab Festival time in **St. Marks**, and you'll find them celebrating the seafood harvest down at **Cedar Key** that month, too. Eat your crab legs with melted butter for optimum effect.

DIVE RESORTS

Dive resorts cater to both open-water and cave divers, and feature on-site dive shops. They

tend toward utilitarian but worn accommodations—wet gear can trash a room! Lodgings categorized under this header will appeal to divers because of their location, not because of their quality.

DIVING Certification for open-water diving is required for diving in Florida's rivers, lakes, and streams; certification in cave diving is required if you plan to enter the outflow of a spring. Expertise in open-water diving does not translate to cave diving, and many experienced open-water divers have died attempting to explore Florida's springs. Play it safe and stick with what you know. A DIVER DOWN flag is required when diving. Open-water diving is popular offshore in the Gulf between Panama City and Pensacola, as there are many wrecks. Go with a knowledgeable outfitter; there are many listed in this guide.

THE DIXIE HIGHWAY Conceptualized in the 1910s by Carl Graham Fisher and the Dixie Highway Association as a grand route for auto touring, the Dixie Highway had two legs that ran along the East Coast of the United States into Florida, both ending in Miami. Since it ran along both coasts of Florida, you'll find Old Dixie Highway signs on both US 1 and US 17 on the east coast and along US 19, 27, and 41 on the west coast, and even US 441 in the middle—the highway ran through places as diverse as **Jacksonville**, **Tallahassee**, and **Micanopy**.

EMERGENCIES Hospitals with emergency rooms are noted at the beginning of each chapter. Dial 911 to connect to emergency service anywhere in the state. For highway accidents or emergencies, contact the Florida Highway Patrol at °FHP on your cell phone or 911.

FACTORY OUTLETS You've seen the signs, but are they really a bargain? Several factory outlets offer brand and designer names for less, but you may also get great deals at smaller shops and even the local mall. I've listed some factory outlets that I found particularly fun to shop at that also had a nice selection of eateries and close access to major highways.

FERRIES Florida has only a few remaining ferryboats. In the region covered by this book, you'll find FL A1A crossing the St. Johns River on the **Mayport Ferry**, and the **Fort Gates Ferry** crossing from the Ocala National Forest to Welaka.

FISH CAMPS Rustic in nature, fish camps are quiet retreats that allow anglers and their families to settle down along a lake or river and put in some quality time fishing. Accommodations listed under this category tend to be older cabins, mobile homes, or concrete-block structures, often a little rough around the edges. If the cabins or motel rooms at a fish camp are of superior quality, I list them under those categories.

FISHING The **Florida Fish and Wildlife Conservation Commission** (myfwc.com) regulates all fishing in Florida, offering both freshwater and saltwater licenses. To obtain a license, visit any sporting goods store or call 888-FISH-FLORIDA for an instant license or apply online at fl.wildlife license.com, choosing among short-term, annual, five-year, or lifetime options. No fishing license is required if you are on a guided fishing trip, are fishing with a cane pole, are bank fishing along the ocean (varies by county), or are 65 years or older.

FLORIDA GREEN LODGING PROGRAM Established in 2004 by the Florida Department of Environmental Protection, this innovative program recognizes lodgings that go the extra mile to protect Florida's natural resources by lessening their environmental impact. The program is entirely voluntary and encompasses not just linen reuse but energy efficiency, waste reduction, clean air, and communications. There are several levels of achievement for which lodgings earn one-, two-, or three-palm ratings. **Designated Green Lodgings** are marked with a [⊕] symbol in this guide; to date, 680 lodgings statewide have earned this honor. To learn more about the program, visit the Florida Green Lodging website (dep.state.fl .us/greenlodging).

FLORIDA TRAIL The **Florida Trail** is a 1,400-mile National Scenic Trail running from the Big Cypress National Preserve north of Everglades National Park to Fort Pickens at Gulf Islands National Seashore in Pensacola. Construction started in 1966 and is ongoing, but you can follow the orange blazes from one end of the state to the other. Most of Florida's best backpacking is along the Florida Trail. It is managed by the USDA Forest Service and maintained by volunteer members of the nonprofit Florida Trail Association (877-HIKE-FLA; floridatrail.org), 5415 SW 13th St, Gainesville 32608, your primary source for maps and guidebooks for the trail.

FORESTS, NATIONAL There are three national forests in Florida (Apalachicola, Ocala, and Osceola), all of which are found in the regions covered by this book. These forests are administered by the **USDA Forest Service, National Forests in Florida** (850-523-8500; fs.usda.gov/florida) offices in Tallahassee. Established in 1908 by President Theodore Roosevelt, the Ocala National Forest is the second-oldest national forest east of the Mississippi River. A little-known fact is that Choctawhatchee National Forest was established at the same time in Florida's Panhandle. But in the 1940s, the military took it over as a reservation and renamed it Eglin Air Force Base. Recreational users visiting the base have the opportunity to enjoy the old-growth trees preserved by the original national forest designation.

FORESTS, STATE The **Florida Division of Forestry** (fl-dof.com) administers Florida State Forests, encompassing thousands of acres of public lands throughout North Florida. Each offers an array of outdoor activities from hiking, biking, trail riding, and camping to fishing, hunting, and even motocross and ATV use. Most (but not all) developed state forest trailheads charge a per-person fee of $2 for recreational use. For $30, you can purchase an annual day-use pass good for the driver and up to eight passengers: a real bargain for families! If you're a hiker, get involved with the **Trailwalker** program, in which you tally up miles on hiking trails and receive patches and certificates; a similar program, **Trailtrotter**, is in place for equestrians. Information on both programs can be found at trailhead kiosks or on the Florida State Forests website.

GAS STATIONS Gas prices fluctuate wildly around the state—and not in proportion to distance from major highways, as you might think. You'll find your best bargains for filling your tank along US 19 in Crystal River; it's always painful to top off the tank in Gainesville. If you're traveling near the

Georgia border, it may be worth the drive across to tank up.

GENEALOGICAL RESEARCH In addition to the excellent resources found at the **Florida State Archives** (dos.state.fl.us) in Tallahassee and local genealogical libraries, check the **Florida GenWeb project** (sites.google .com/a/flgenweb.net/official) for census data, vital records, pioneer families, and links to the state's many historical societies.

GOLF Golfing is a favorite pastime for many Florida retirees, and there are hundreds of courses across the state, impossible for me to list in any detail; a good resource for research is Visit Florida's section on golf (visitflorida .com/golfing), the state's official golf course website. I've covered courses that are particularly interesting or feature exceptional facilities. Florida is home to both the PGA and LPGA headquarters, with Ponte Vedra Beach home to the acclaimed TPC Sawgrass, home of **The Players Championship** (pgatour.com/theplayers).

GPS COORDINATES Since the first edition of this book, GPS units have become popular additions to vehicles.

Some readers have written in saying they needed more complete directions to certain locations, especially listings in *Green Space*, *Birding*, and other outdoor pursuits. For destinations that aren't especially easy to find, I've added GPS coordinates in decimal degrees, designated in brackets [ ].

GREENWAYS Florida has one of the nation's most aggressive greenway programs, overseen by the **Office of Greenways and Trails** (877-822-5208; dep.state.fl.us/gwt), which administers the state land acquisition program under the Florida Forever Act and works in partnership with local agencies in identifying crucial habitat corridors for preservation and developing public recreation facilities.

HANDICAPPED ACCESS The wheelchair symbol ♿ identifies lodgings, restaurants, and activities that are, at a minimum, accessible with minor assistance. Many locations and attractions provide or will make modifications for people with disabilities, so call beforehand to see if they can make the necessary accommodations.

HERITAGE SITES If you're in search of history, watch for the brown signs with columns and palm trees that mark official Florida Heritage Sites— everything from historic churches and graveyards to entire historic districts. According to the **Florida Division of Historical Resources** (flheritage .com), to qualify as a Florida Heritage Site a building, structure, or site must be at least 30 years old and have significance in the areas of architecture, archaeology, Florida history, or traditional culture, or be associated with a significant event that took place at least 30 years ago.

HIKING I note the best hiking experiences in each region in the *Hiking* section—from my own personal experience—and you can find additional walks in places mentioned under *Green Space.* The most comprehensive hiking guides for this portion of Florida include my *50 Hikes in North Florida* (Countryman Press), *The Hiking Trails of Florida's National Forests, Parks & Preserves* and *Hiker's Guide to the Sunshine State* (University Press of Florida), and Florida Hikes! (florida hikes.com), my online resource for hikers.

HISTORIC SITES With nearly five centuries of European settlement in Florida, historic sites are myriad, so this book's coverage of Florida history is limited to sites of particular interest. For the full details on designated historic sites in Florida, visit the state-administered **Florida's History Through Its Places** website (flheritage .com/facts/reports/places). Historic sites that belong to the **Florida Trust for Historic Preservation** (850-224-8128; floridatrust.org), P.O. Box 11206, Tallahassee 32302, honor Florida's Historic Passport program, in which your membership of $35 ($50 family) includes a passport that offers special access to member sites—some for free, others for discounted admissions.

HOTELS, MOTELS & RESORTS In general, chain hotels and motels are not listed in this guide because of their ubiquitous nature. I've included a handful that are either the only lodging options in a particular area or happen to be outstanding places to stay due to some special facet of their property.

HUNTING Hunting is regulated by the **Florida Fish and Wildlife Conservation Commission** (myfwc.com), with general gun season falling between October and February in various parts of the state. Check the website for specific dates, the wildlife management areas (WMAs) open to hunting, and hunting license regulations.

HURRICANES Hurricane season runs June through November, and when the big winds from Africa start moving across the Atlantic, it pays to pay attention. Follow public announcements on what to do in the event of a tropical storm or hurricane.

INFORMATION Roadside billboards will taunt you to come in for vacation deals. Most are tied to time-shares or are operating in their own interest. True visitors centers will offer information without trying to sell you something. At the beginning of each chapter under *Guidance* I have listed the visitors bureaus and chambers with no commercial affiliation.

INSECTS Florida's irritating insects are myriad, especially at dawn and dusk during summer months. We love our winters when they get chilly enough to kill the little buggers off. If you don't like DEET and you can't stand citronella, you'll spend 99 percent of your time indoors. Flying annoyances include the **mosquito** (which comes in hundreds of varieties), gnat, and no-see-um; troublesome crawling bugs are the **chigger** and the **tick**, which you'll find in deeply wooded areas, and **red ants**, invaders that swarm over your feet leaving painful bites if you dare step in their nest. Florida has had confirmed cases of both Lyme disease and malaria. Bottom line: Use insect repellent when playing outdoors, and carry an antihistamine with you to counter any reaction you have to communing with these native residents.

JELLYFISH At almost any time of the year you will find jellyfish in the ocean and washed up on the shore. Take particular care with the blue man o' war jellyfish; the sting from this marine creature is excruciatingly painful. Do not touch the dead ones on the beach; their venom is still potent. Contrary to popular belief, they won't chase you down, but in case you get stung, consider carrying a small bottle of white vinegar in your beach bag; this seems to help alleviate some of the pain. Then seek medical attention. Just as with bee stings, reactions vary.

THE KINGS HIGHWAY Established between 1763 and 1819 to connect coastal communities south from Brunswick through Cow Ford (Jacksonville) and St. Augustine to New Smyrna, this military trail is now approximated by the route of US 1; you will see KINGS HIGHWAY signs on historic sections of the road that are not part of US 1, most notably from Dupont Center south.

MARITIME HERITAGE In a state where many still pull their living from the sea, it's only appropriate that we have a **Florida Maritime Heritage Trail** (flheritage.com/archaeology /underwater/maritime) that ties together the elements of our maritime

heritage: working fishing villages such as Cedar Key, Steinhatchee, and Apalachicola; coastal fortresses built to defend Florida from invasion; lighthouses; historic shipwrecks; and our endangered coastal communities such as the coastal pine flatwoods and coastal scrub. Visit the website for a virtual travel guide.

MUSEUMS Explore our centuries of history: The **Florida Association of Museums** (850-222-6028; flamuseums .org) provides a portal to more than 340 museums throughout the state, from the small Heritage Museum of Northwest Florida in Valparaiso to the high-tech Florida Museum of Natural History in Gainesville. Their website also provides a calendar of exhibits in museums around the state.

OYSTERS Nowhere in the United States can compare to **Apalachicola** and its oysters, pulled fresh from the Gulf estuary. A lack of industrial pollution and a small population mean the waters are clean and the oysters prime; eat them locally, where the steamed or fried oysters melt like butter in your mouth, and you'll be hooked for life.

PADDLING Canoeing and kayaking are extraordinarily popular activities in Florida, especially during the summer months. Most state parks have canoe livery concessions, and private outfitters are mentioned throughout this guide.

PETS The dog-paw symbol 🐾 identifies lodgings and activities that accept pets. Always inform the front desk that you are traveling with a pet, and expect to pay a surcharge.

POPULATION According to the 2010 federal census, Florida's population is closing in on **19 million people**. What's scary to those of us who live here is that our governor's office reports a net gain of 1,000 people moving into Florida every day—which means an increasingly serious strain on our already fragile water resources.

RAILROADIANA Florida's railroad history dates back to 1836 with the **St. Joe & Lake Wimico Canal & Railroad Company**, followed shortly by the 1837 opening of the mule-driven **Tallahassee & St. Marks Railroad** bringing supplies from the Gulf of Mexico to the state capital. Railroad commerce shaped many Florida towns,

especially along David Yulee's **Florida Railroad** (circa 1850), which connected Fernandina and Cedar Key, and the later grandiose efforts of Henry Plant and the **Plant System** (later the Seaboard Air Line) on the west coast and Henry Flagler's **Atlantic Coast Line** on the east coast. Sites of interest to railroad history buffs are noted throughout the guide under this heading; this region is especially rich in railroad heritage.

RATES The range of rates provided spans the lowest of low season to the highest of high season (which varies from place to place) and does not include taxes or discounts such as those enjoyed by AARP, AAA, and camping club members.

RIVERS For recreation on the Suwannee River and its tributaries, contact the **Suwannee River Water Management District** (386-362-1001; srwmd.state.fl.us), 9225 CR 49, Live Oak 32060, for a map that indicates boat ramps; you can also download their recreational guide from their website. The **St. Johns Water Management District** (386-329-4500; sjrwmd.com), 4049 Reid St, Palatka 32177, can provide similar information for the St. Johns River and its tributaries, and has an excellent free guidebook to recreation on their public lands. The **North Florida Water Management District** (850-539-5999; nwfwmd.state.fl.us), 81 Water Management Dr, Havana 32333-4712, oversees major rivers in the Panhandle, such as the Apalachicola and Blackwater.

SCENIC HIGHWAYS The Florida Department of Transportation has designated scenic highways throughout the state, some of which are also federally designated Scenic Byways. Both are numerous in this region. Along the Atlantic Coast, the **A1A Scenic and Historic Coastal Byway** (scenica1a.org) stretches from Fernandina Beach to Flagler Beach and beyond. The **William Bartram Scenic & Historic Highway** (bartramscenichighway.com), FL 13, follows the eastern shore of the St. Johns River south from Mandarin to Hastings, and the **Florida Black Bear Scenic Byway** (floridablackbearscenicbyway.org) crosses the St. Johns River on the Fort Gates Ferry. The **Old Florida Heritage Highway** (scenicus441.com), includes 48 miles of back roads around Gainesville. In Northwest Florida the **Big Bend Scenic Byway** (floridabigbendscenicbyway.com) is the biggie,

looping over 250 miles between Apalachicola and Tallahassee. **Scenic 30A** (30a.com) is a seaside county road in Walton County, and the **Pensacola Scenic Bluffs Highway** (floridascenichighways.com/pensacola-scenic-bluffs) provides some excellent and unusual views for Florida. You'll also find local designations, such as the **Apalachee Savannahs Scenic Byway**, and county-designated canopy roads in places like Tallahassee and Alachua County, where the dense live oak canopy overhead makes for a beautiful drive.

SEASHORES, NATIONAL Encompassing large portions of Santa Rosa Island and Perdido Key, **Gulf Islands National Seashore** provides vast unbroken stretches of white quartz beaches near Pensacola, perfect for sunning and swimming.

SEASONS Florida's temperate winter weather makes it ideal for vacationers, but we do have a very strong tropical delineation of wet and dry seasons, which strengthens the farther south you venture. Winter is generally dry and crisp, with nighttime temperatures falling as low as the 20s in the Panhandle and the 30s in North Florida.

SHARKS Yes, they are in the water. At any given time there are a dozen or more just offshore, but for the most part they will leave you alone. To avoid being bitten, stay out of the water if there is a strong scent of fish oil in the air, which means that fish are already being eaten and you may be bitten by mistake. You will also want to avoid swimming near piers and jetties, which are active feeding zones.

SHRIMP You'll find different types of shrimp fried, broiled, sautéed, and blackened up and down the coast, from Pensacola to Cedar Key. The most sought-after are red, white, pink, rock, "brownies," and "hoppers." When you dine, ask for fresh Gulf shrimp and support Florida shrimpers! To learn more about Florida's commercial shrimp species, visit wildflorida shrimp.com.

STATE PARKS Florida State Parks (850-245-2157; floridastateparks.org) is one of the United States' best and most extensive state park systems, encompassing more than 160 parks. All Florida State Parks are open 8 AM–sunset daily. If you want to watch the sunrise from a state park beach, you'll have to camp overnight. Camping reservations are centralized through **Reserve America** (800-326-3521; floridastate

parks.reserveamerica.com), and can be booked through the Florida State Parks website (floridastateparks.org). Walk-in visitors are welcome on a first-come, first-served basis. An annual pass is a real deal if you plan to do much in-state traveling: Individual passes are $80 plus tax, and family passes are $160 plus tax, per year. The family pass is good for up to eight people in one vehicle. These passes are honored at all state parks except the Sunshine·Skyway Fishing Pier, where they are good for a 33 percent discount. Pick up a pass at any state park ranger station, or order through the website. If you need geo-located park information on-the-go, you can download my Florida State Parks app for your smartphone.

THE SUNSHINE STATE The moniker *Sunshine State* was an effective 1960s advertising slogan that was also required on motor vehicle tags; it became the state's official nickname in 1970 by a legislative act.

TAXES Florida's base sales tax is 6 percent, with counties adding up to 1.5 percent of discretionary sales tax. In addition, a tourist development tax of up to 10 percent may be levied on hotel accommodations in some cities and counties.

THEME PARKS You could say Florida is the birthplace of the theme park, starting with glass-bottomed boats drawing tourists to enjoy **Silver Springs** in 1878 and to gawk at alligators in the **St. Augustine Alligator Farm** in 1893. But the real heyday came with Dick Pope's water-ski and botanical garden wonder called **Cypress Gardens**, circa 1932, soon followed by **Weeki Wachee Springs**, the "Spring of Living Mermaids," in 1947. The 1960s saw an explosion in

range of destinations, from the sleepy hamlets of the Big Bend to snazzy new hotels along the beach at Destin. Utilize their website resources to plan your trip, from the interactive map that lets you explore destination possibilities to the vast amount of editorial content that tells the story of each experience.

WATERFALLS Yes, Florida has natural waterfalls! They flow into deep sinkholes (such as the ones at **Falling Waters State Park** and **Devils Millhopper Geologic State Park**) or drop over limestone ledges along creeks and rivers (**Steinhatchee Falls**, **Falling Creek**, and others). Florida's highest concentration of waterfalls is along the Suwannee River and its tributaries, with many seen along the Florida Trail.

WEATHER Florida's weather is perhaps our greatest attraction. Balmy winters are the norm, with temperatures dropping into the 50s for daytime

roadside attractions and zoos like **Gatorland**, while fancier parks like **Rainbow Springs** and **Homosassa Springs** showed off Florida's natural wonders. But when Walt Disney started buying up Osceola County in the 1950s, Florida changed forever. After Walt Disney World opened in 1971, most of the old roadside attractions that made Florida so much fun in the 1960s folded. Many, thankfully, have become state parks, like Wakulla Springs. But the St. Augustine Alligator Farm is still going strong!

TRAIL RIDING Bringing your own horses? You'll find working ranches and B&Bs with boarding stables listed in this guide, and believe it or not some hotels will put up your horse. Remember, under state law riders utilizing trails on state land must have proof with them of a negative Coggins test for their horses. If you're interested in riding, hook up with one of the many stables listed in the text. Under state law, equine operators are not responsible for your injuries if you decide to go on a trail ride.

VISIT FLORIDA The state's official tourism bureau, Visit Florida (visit florida.com) is a clearinghouse for every tourism question you might have. Their partners cover the full

and 30s at night. When it snows (which is rare), it doesn't stick for long. Our summers are predictably hot and wet, with thunderstorms guaranteed on a daily basis and temperatures soaring up to the 80s in North Florida and the Panhandle. Florida thunderstorms come up fast and carry with them some of the world's most violent and dangerous lightning. It's best to get indoors and out of or off the water should you see one coming.

WHERE TO EAT I've limited choices to local favorites and outstanding creative fare, generally avoiding the chains seen everywhere across America. However, several Florida-based chains deserve a mention; you'll enjoy their cuisine when you find them. **Harry's**, a Cajun restaurant found in many cities, delights with tasty seafood and steaks; **R. J. Gators** appeals to the sports-bar crowd. **Too Jays**, a New York–style deli, shines with big breakfasts, stellar sandwiches, and their yummy Mounds Cake. **Woodies** has consistently excellent barbecue at reasonable prices.

WINERIES Florida's wineries run the gamut from small family operations to large production facilities, and some partner to provide a storefront in a high-traffic region while the growing, fermenting, and bottling is done in an area more favorable for agriculture. Native muscadine grapes are the cornerstones of the state's wines. For an overview of Florida wineries, contact the **Florida Grape Growers Association** (941-678-0523; fgga.org), 343 W Central Ave, #1, Lake Wales 33853.

Northwest Florida

1

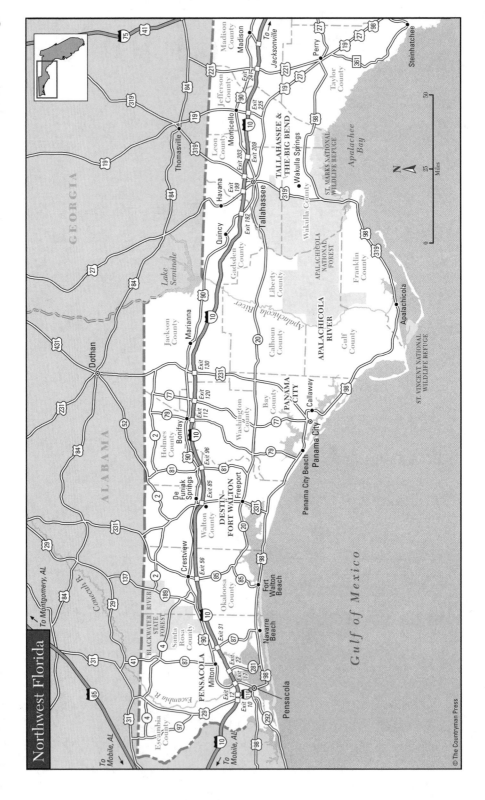

Northwest Florida

PENSACOLA

PENSACOLA BAY AREA (PERDIDO KEY, PENSACOLA, PENSACOLA BEACH) & SANTA ROSA COUNTY (MILTON AND NAVARRE BEACH)

With its powdery white beaches, lush pine forests, broad open prairies, rugged riverside bluffs, and clear sandy-bottomed rivers attracting outdoors enthusiasts, the region around **Pensacola** has a deep and rich history. While this unusually deep bay first attracted Spanish explorer Juan Ponce de León, it was Don Tristán de Luna y Arellano who settled on its shores in 1559, founding the first European settlement in what is now the continental United States. A devastating hurricane struck soon after, and within two years, the 1,400 colonists were scattered far and wide. The second Spanish settlement, in 1686, stuck. Over the next two centuries, five flags flew over Pensacola. Spain had three reigning periods, 1698–1719, 1722–1763, and 1781–1819, with France taking control in 1719, only to be driven out by a hurricane in 1722. At the end of the French and Indian War in 1763, England held the city until 1781, when the United States became the governing body. In January 1861 Florida became the third state to secede from the Union. Shots were fired by Confederate militia at the Federal encampment in Fort Barrancas hours before the cannonade opened on Fort Sumter in South Carolina. In 1868, Florida was readmitted to the United States.

Because of its strategic military importance as a deep-water port, Pensacola has always had a significant military presence, with three major forts flanking the entrance to the bay. Two are now significant historic sites. A vibrant military presence continues today, with Pensacola Naval Air Station the home of the Blue Angels and Whiting Naval Air Station an important helicopter training facility.

To the east of Pensacola, **Milton** began as an early-1800s trading post along the Blackwater, a river deep enough to navigate up from the Gulf of Mexico for trade with the indigenous peoples. The bluffs made it tough to get from ships to land, resulting in the town's early names of "Scratch Ankle" and "Hard Scrabble." Thanks to its lush canopy of live oaks and vast longleaf pine forests, Milton became an important shipbuilding and repair center. In 1842 Santa Rosa County was created from parts of Escambia and Walton counties. Milton became the county

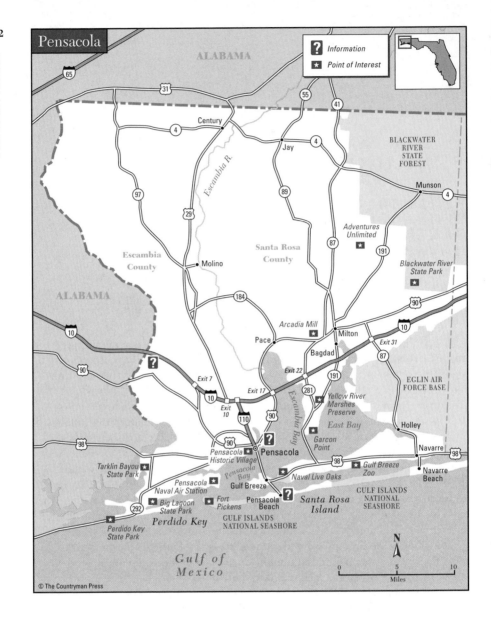

seat and applied to be an official port of entry. Adjacent **Bagdad** developed as a company town for a new lumber mill in 1840 and grew with the size of the enterprise. As you drive north from Milton on FL 87 you can see a series of ridges off in the distance, giving the sense of ascending into the mountains, something you'll experience nowhere else in Florida.

GUIDANCE **Pensacola Bay Area Convention & Visitors Bureau** (800-874-1234 or 850-434-1234; visitpensacola.com), 1401 E Gregory St, Pensacola 32502.

THE BLACKWATER RIVER AT MILTON

For activities east of the Escambia River, contact the **Santa Rosa County Tourist and Development Council** (800-480-7263 or 850-748-7317; floridabeach estorivers.com). Not to confuse Santa Rosa County with the beach of the same name, you'll find Santa Rosa Beach located in Walton County west of Destin (see the *Destin–Fort Walton* chapter) and Santa Rosa Island shared by Navarre Beach and Pensacola Beach. In Milton, stop at the **Santa Rosa County Chamber of Commerce**, at the corner of FL 87 and Berryhill, for local information.

GETTING THERE *By air:* **Pensacola Gulf Coast Regional Airport** (850-436-5000; flypensacola.com), 2430 Airport Blvd, Pensacola 32504, is served by a broad range of carriers with commuter flights.

By bus: **Greyhound** (850-476-4800; greyhound.com), 505 W Burgess Rd, Pensacola 32503.

By car: **I-10**, **US 90**, and **US 98** run east–west through the Panhandle. **US 90** stays north of I-10 through Milton. As it heads west to Pensacola, it dips south of I-10 into the city and continues west into Alabama. **US 98** is the east–west coastal route and will take you along the Gulf from Navarre Beach to downtown Pensacola and to Alabama. From I-10 follow **FL 87** south to Navarre Beach or north to Pace; **FL 191** north to Bagdad and Milton or south to Navarre Beach (toll bridge). **FL 292** heads west from downtown Pensacola to Perdido Key.

GETTING AROUND **ECAT** (850-595-3228; goecat.com), Escambia County's public transportation system, runs 285 miles throughout the Pensacola area ($1.75 adults, 85¢ seniors and disabled; children shorter than the fare box ride free). The seasonal **Beach Trolley**, operating Fri–Sun from Memorial Day to Labor Day, is free for everyone.

PARKING Pensacola has two-hour metered slots throughout downtown, free on weekends. Milton has free two-hour parking throughout downtown. Ample free beach parking is available at Pensacola Beach and Navarre Beach along CR 399 and Fort Pickens Rd.

MEDICAL EMERGENCIES In Pensacola, **Baptist Hospital** (850-434-4011; ebaptisthealthcare.org), 1000 W Moreno St, West Pensacola; **Sacred Heart Hospital** (850-416-7000; sacred-heart.org), 5151 N 9th Ave, Pensacola; **West Florida Hospital** (850-494-4490; westfloridahospital.com), 8383 N Davis Hwy, Pensacola. For the eastern beaches, there is **Gulf Breeze Hospital** (850-934-2000; ebaptist healthcare.org/GulfBreezeHospital), 1110 Gulf Breeze Pkwy, and **Baptist Medical Park** (850-939-4888; ebaptisthealthcare.org/BMPNavarre), 8888 Navarre Pkwy, with a walk-in clinic Mon–Sat in Navarre. In Milton visit **Santa Rosa Medical Center** (850-626-7762; srmcfl.com), 6002 Berryhill Rd. Always call 911 for life-threatening emergencies.

✳ To See

ARCHAEOLOGICAL SITE ✄ & The **Arcadia Mill Archaeological Site** (850-628-4438; historicpensacola.org/arcadia.cfm), 5709 Mill Pond Ln, Milton, interprets the first and largest industrial complex built in Northwest Florida, circa 1830. Excavation of the site began in 1990 under the auspices of the University of West Florida. It included a silk cocoonery, along with a water-powered sawmill, gristmill, cotton mill, and textile mill, all of which turned local resources into trade goods. Now that the land surrounding it has been preserved, it is open to the public and can be explored along a interpretive boardwalk above the digs and at a small outdoor museum. Hiking trails meander upstream over swinging bridges. Open Tue–Sat 10–4, with guided tours at 11, 1, and 2:30. Free.

ART GALLERIES A Means of Expression (850-232-4369; ameansofexpression .com), 215 E Zaragoza St, Pensacola, offers original works of art and high-quality reproductions in additions to fine crafts such as art furnishings and art glass, pottery, and jewelry. Open Mon–Fri 11–4, Sat 11–5. The **Quayside Gallery** (850-438-2363; quaysidegallery.com), 17 E Zaragoza St, is the artists' co-op in downtown. Founded in 1973 and serving more than 60 member artists, it's one of the largest co-ops in the Southeast. Housed in the historic Germania Steam Fire Engine and Hose Company Building, it has both expansive spaces and small niches to showcase everything from large acrylics and fiber arts to delicate art glass and turned wood. Open Wed and Sat 10–5, Sun 1–5.

In the historic Faircloth-Carroll House, the **Dragonfly Gallery** (850-981-1100; thedragonflygallery.org), 5188 Escambia St, Milton, showcases the creativity of local artists—stained glass, photography, folk art, natural wood sculptures with stone accents, and fine paintings in acrylics and oils. A co-op staffed by the artists of the Santa Rosa Arts & Culture Foundation, it's open Tue–Sat 10–4.

Pensacola Museum of Art (850-432-6247; pensacolamuseumofart.org), 407 S Jefferson St, Pensacola. The museum's permanent collection is of 19th-, 20th-, and 21st-century artists, including John Marin and Salvador Dalí, with rotating exhibits by world-renowned artists such as George Rodriguez. The museum also has a superb collection of European and American glass, and African tribal art. From

1910 to the mid-1940s the building was used as a jail. Note original fixtures and hardware on many of the doors and windows. Open Tue–Fri 10–5, Sat and Sun noon–5. Fee.

HISTORIC SITES

Bagdad

At one time, everything you needed to build a house was created in Bagdad, so it's no surprise that so many fine homes remain. Stop in at the Bagdad Village Museum (see *Museums*) for a walking tour brochure and to visit the **1867 post office** and **New Providence Missionary Baptist Church** as well as an original shotgun cottage. The imposing **Thompson House**, 4620 Forsyth St, can't be missed—it's a Greek Revival home that was built in 1847 for timber baron Benjamin Thompson; Union troops camped on the front lawn in October 1864. You'll find it along FL 191, but it is a private residence, so enjoy it from a distance.

Harold

Paralleling US 90 between the Harold Store and CR 87, the Old Pensacola Highway is a stretch of historic roadway. Completed in 1921, this early brick highway known as **Florida Highway 1** connected Pensacola with Jacksonville, enabling Model Ts to putter across the state. It is now used as a footpath for the Florida Trail.

Milton

Milton boasts 117 buildings of historic significance, from 1850s Victorians to Spanish Mission–style homes erected during the 1920s boom. Listed on the National Register of Historic Places, the Bungalow/Craftsman, Late Victorian, Greek, Gothic, and Colonial Revival styles are evident in structures such as the 1872 **St. Mary's Episcopal Church and Rectory**, 300–301 Oak St, built in the Greek and Gothic revival styles, respectively. The church is also known as the **McDougall**

DOWNTOWN MILTON

House, because the town's physician, Dr. Charles E. McDougall, who was also the rector, built it. A little-known fact shared by one of my homeowner friends in Milton pertains to the city's Ringling legacy: In one of his many ventures during the 1920s Florida boom, circus magnate John Ringling built a grand hotel in Milton that never opened. Rather than let the costly materials go to waste, resourceful residents recycled portions of the hotel into their home construction, including doors, mantels, and decorative elements. Pick up *Tour of Milton's Historic Sites and Murals*, a brochure, to discover the city's many landmarks, among them the 1872 **Milligan-Kilmartin House**, 6820 Berryhill St, a gingerbread Victorian from 1872 built by a Confederate veteran who later went on to rename the town of Chaffin, up the road, to Milligan. The steamboat-style **Williams Shields House**, 6810 Berryhill St, dates back to 1887. The **Santa Rosa County Courthouse**, 6865 Caroline St, was dedicated on July 4, 1927, and the Gothic **Olliner-Cobb-Tilghman House**, 6829 Pine St, is a large Gulf Coast cottage dating from 1871. A simple cottage, the **Ollinger-Cobb House** (circa 1870), 302 Pine St, includes Gothic elements. The home was built by Joseph Ollinger, a ship's carpenter and

PENSACOLA FORTS

After Pensacola was selected to be a federal naval yard in the early 1800s, four forts were built (or shored up) to protect it. Originally built by the British Royal Navy as a log redoubt in 1763, **Fort Barrancas** sits on a hill above the western shore of Pensacola Bay. The Spanish added their touches in 1797, and the fort went through another update between 1839 and 1844, supervised by Major William H. Chase. The nearby **Advanced Redoubt of Fort Barrancas** was built between 1845 and 1859 to protect the Pensacola Naval Yard but was never used. **Fort McRee** on Perdido Key dated back to 1834, with 128 cannons trained on the entrance to Pensacola Bay. It succumbed to erosion by wind and waves over the decades; only a single battery built in 1942 remains. But of the four forts, **Fort Pickens** on Santa Rosa Island has the most storied history. Chase supervised construction between 1829 and 1834. Construction materials came from all over the world, including copper from Switzerland for the drains and granite from Sing-Sing; the fortress contains 21.5 million locally made bricks. The night before Florida seceded from the Union (January 10, 1860), Federal commander Lieutenant Adam J. Slemmer moved his men from the mainland to Fort Pickens to hold what President Lincoln considered a key position in coastal defenses. Confederate troops attempted to rout the entrenched Federals on September 2, 1861, during the Battle of Santa Rosa Island but failed, and subsequently turned the city over to the Union forces. In 1886 the Apache chief Geronimo was imprisoned at the fort as a tourist attraction. Fort Pickens came into play during World War I with new defensive batteries constructed to protect Pensacola, but no shots were fired. All of Pensacola's forts are part of Gulf Islands National Seashore (see *Beaches*); fee.

OLD CHRIST CHURCH IS PENSACOLA'S OLDEST PLACE OF WORSHIP

immigrant from Luxembourg. The historic **Milton Depot** is now a museum (see *Railroadiana*).

Pensacola

The stucco on the circa-1932 **Crystal Ice Company Building**, 2024 N Davis St, conveys the impression of a block of ice. The one-story building is one of the few remaining examples of vernacular roadside commercial architecture in Pensacola.

🐌 At the center of the **Pensacola Historic District**, the **Old Christ Church** (850-595-5985), 405 S Adams St, is one of the older churches in Florida, circa 1832. When the church isn't otherwise busy with weddings (and it often is), this is one of the stops along the walking tour of Historic Pensacola Village (see *Museums*), which encompasses 27 buildings on the National Register of Historic Places. Among the highlights of the historic district are the **Charles LaValle House**, built in 1805 with a French-Creole influence; the **Clara Barkley Dorr House**, a post–Civil War two-story home from 1871; the **Barkley House**, which, built in 1825, is the oldest remaining "High House" in Pensacola; and the very Victorian **Lear-Rocheblave House** from the 1890s.

First lit in 1859, the **Pensacola Lighthouse** (850-393-1561; pensacolalighthouse .org), 2081 Radford Blvd, stands on a 40-foot hill above Fort Barrancas at the Pensacola Naval Station. Climb to the top of the 177-step ascent to see the first-order Fresnel lens, which was removed during the Civil War for safekeeping. In the restored light keeper's quarters, the Richard C. Callaway Museum provides an overview of the region's earliest settlements. For a different take on history, try the "Light of the Moon Tour" offered monthly on full-moon nights to learn the legends of "one of America's most haunted lighthouses." Open Mon–Sat 10:30–5:30, Sun 12:30–5:30. Fee.

THE MILTON RIVERWALK

MEMORIALS The **Florida Vietnam Veterans Memorial** on Bayfront Pkwy near Ninth Ave, Pensacola, is the nation's only full-name, permanent replica of the Vietnam Veterans Memorial in Washington, DC. The historic **St Michael's Cemetery** (stmichaelscemetery.org), at the corner of Alcaniz and Chase streets in Pensacola, dates back to 1822, with 3,200 marked burials. Open daily.

One of the more moving memorials I've encountered is the **Veterans Memorial** at the Riverwalk in Milton. Reflective slabs of black granite hold relief images of warfare, with a roll call of all American wars and their key dates, each with a sidebar of the population of the United States at that time, the commander in chief, number of service members, combat deaths, and casualties. It was a history lesson that gave me the chills—especially when I saw the blank panels remaining to be inscribed.

BAGDAD VILLAGE MUSEUM, BAGDAD

MURALS Large murals decorate the sides of historic buildings in downtown Milton. Pick up *Tour of Milton's Historic Sites and Murals* (see *Historic Sites*) to track them down.

MUSEUMS The **Bagdad Village Museum** (850-983-3005; bagdadvillage .org), 4512 Church St, Bagdad, showcases artifacts of the early logging and shipping history that shaped this riverside town, as well as local architecture and domestic life in the 1920s. The complex includes a shotgun cottage and the original town post office. Open 9–noon Tuesday and on the first Saturday of each month.

The Santa Rosa Historical Society manages the **Museum of Local History** (850-626-9866; santarosahistoricalsociety.com), 5234 Willing St, Milton. Showcasing artifacts and photos from the early days of Milton, it's a volunteer effort that is expected to reopen in 2011; a fire in the historic Imogene Theater forced its closure several years ago. Free. Meanwhile, the organization offers a **Ghosts of Milton Walking Tour** during the Halloween season, $10 adults, $5 children.

✐ も Exhibits of the navy's role in the nation's defense are found at the **National Naval Aviation Museum** (850-452-3604; navalaviationmuseum.org), 1750 Radford Blvd, Pensacola, with more than 140 beautifully restored aircraft from U.S. Navy, Marine Corps, and Coast Guard aviation. You'll see wood-and-fabric biplanes, an NC-4 flying boat, and a Douglas "Dauntless" bomber in Hangar Bay. Then fly an FA-18 flight simulator on a mission in Desert Storm. See *The Magic of Flight* on the seven-story-high IMAX screen. If the Kennedy Space Center is the place to be on the east coast, then this is the place to be on the west. Open daily 9–5; free.

Pensacola Historical Museum (850-438-1559), 405 S Adams St. Learn about the city of five flags through extensive exhibits on and artifacts from Pensacola's colorful history—from the clay deposits that provided the city's brick streets through the "Gallant capture of a lady's wardrobe" Civil War–era cartoon poking fun at Florida's troops. Open Mon–Sat 9–4:30; free.

✐ Built as Pensacola's city hall in 1907, the **T. T. Wentworth Jr. Florida Museum** (850-595-5990), 330 S Jefferson St, holds the vast collection of Florida-related artifacts that Theodore Thomas Wentworth Jr. (1898–1989) amassed over his lifetime, more than 100,000 items—and that was before eBay! To showcase his collection a bit at a time, there are three floors with changing exhibit galleries, and a special Discovery Gallery for children under 8. Open 10–4 Mon–Sat; purchase tickets at the Historic Pensacola Village. Free.

RAILROADIANA ✐ Housed in the historic Milton Depot, the **West Florida Railroad Museum** (850-623-3645; wfrm.org), 206 Henry St, focuses on the railroad history of the historic logging districts of Northwest Florida and Southern Alabama, particularly the L&N Railroad. Volunteers continue active restoration of rolling stock, some of which dates back to 1911. See the live coal-burning miniature steam engine, walk through the Museum of Railroading History, and come for the annual open house, their big event, in October. Open Fri and Sat 10–3, or by appointment.

ZOO ✐ も Ride the Safari Line train through 50 acres of free-ranging wild animals at the **Gulf Breeze Zoo** (850-932-2229; gulfbreezezoo.org), 5701 Gulf Breeze Pkwy, Gulf Breeze, where you'll see wildebeests, pygmy hippos, capybaras, and more—over 900 species in all. Then walk along the perimeter enclosures and boardwalk to get an up-close look at lions, tigers, and bears. Oh my! Open daily 9–6 with extended summer hours, closed Thanksgiving and Christmas. Admission rates range $7–13 for various ages and discounts, plus an extra $3 for the train.

HISTORIC PENSACOLA VILLAGE

One of the more expansive outdoor museums in Florida, **Historic Pensacola Village** (850-595-5993; historicpensacola.org) spans several blocks between downtown and Seville Square and includes 27 properties on the National Register of Historic Places in the Pensacola Historic District. Eleven of these buildings are interpreted and open for viewing. You are welcome to roam the village anytime to see these furnished period homes, which span in age from the earliest Spanish settlements to the Florida real estate boom of the 1920s. The best way to experience the charm of this village, however, is on a guided walking tour, which starts at the **Tivoli High House**—home to the ticket office and gift shop—and proceeds through a parade of home museums. Starting around a well in a practical household garden, the tour proceeds to one of the oldest buildings in the complex, the **Charles Lavalle House**, built in 1805. Inside, you can see the stark simplicity of the era, with a rope bed occupying a simple bedroom next to a kitchen room, complete with fireplace and clever devices to ward off insects and vermin from food storage. The adjoining **Julee Cottage** is a simple saltbox of the same vintage, home later to an African American family during the difficult period of Reconstruction. If there isn't a wedding going on, you'll walk through the **1832 Christ Church** overlooking Seville Square, which is filled with ancient live oaks and interesting pieces of art. At the **Dorr House**, circa 1871, see the spaces upstairs that their daughters shared (the sons ended up in the attic) and Victorian furnishings downstairs. The tour ends at the grand Victorian **Lear-Rocheblave House**. Built in the 1890s, it is filled with the finery you would expect in a captain's residence of the era, including a china cabinet, a vanity, a canopied bed, and a thicket of furniture that fills the broad hallway.

Flanking Zaragoza Street, two historic warehouses have been converted into stand-alone museums that you can roam at your leisure after the

✳ To Do

BICYCLING Love the salt air in your lungs while pedaling? You've come to the right place. The **Pensacola Bicycle Path** extends through the commercial district out to the entrance to Fort Pickens, where you can continue biking down the narrow scenic highway to the end of the island. To the east, the Pensacola Bicycle Path offers more oceanfront views, and now scoots along the edge of the University of West Florida Dunes Preserve on its way to meet the **Navarre Bicycle Trail**, which will take you all the way to the bridge in Navarre Beach. Sunscreen and plenty of water are a must on these rides.

🐾 The **Blackwater Heritage State Trail** (850-983-5338; dep.state.fl.us/gwt/state /black), 5533 Alabama St, Milton, is the region's premier forested cycling venue, a

formal tour. The **Museum of Commerce** feels like a movie set, complete with a full-sized retired streetcar amid storefronts of classic Pensacola businesses that are no longer found downtown. A museum-within-a-museum sponsored by the local newspaper showcases printing presses of yesteryear and explains to Internet-age kids what fonts are all about. Inside the **Museum of Industry**, massive displays and larger-than-life dioramas evoke the sounds and smells of the past. Discover the many different types of bricks that were created in the region, learn the ongoing importance of fishing as a regional industry, and find out how many items came from the great forests that once surrounded Pensacola. Historic Pensacola Village is open Mon–Sat 10–4, with tours at 11, 1, and 2:30; fee.

THE PFEIFFER HOUSE IS ONE OF SEVERAL STOPS ON THE HISTORIC PENSACOLA VILLAGE TOUR

paved rail-trail on the old Whiting Naval Railway. It stretches 8.5 miles, following the Blackwater River north from Milton.

DIVING For underwater exploration of an aircraft-carrier-sized artificial reef, **Dr. Dive** (850-932-6602; drdive.com), 600 S. Barracks St, Pensacola, leads tours to the **USS Oriskany**, sunk in 2006 a good 25 miles offshore from Pensacola Bay. This combat naval vessel, built in the 1940s and in service in Vietnam, now provides a tableau for barracuda, amberjack, sharks, and reef fish. Depths range from 80 to 170 feet, so diving this site requires technical skills and advanced certification, including experience in open-water dives. Dive trips and scuba certifications are also offered by **Dive the Mighty O** (814-680-0015; divemightyo.com), 4771 Bayou Blvd #107, Pensacola, and **MBT Dive and Surf** (850-455-7702; mbtdivers.com),

3920 Barrancas Ave, Pensacola, which also leads snorkeling trips and dives to historic shipwrecks in as little as 15 feet of water.

FAMILY FUN ⵦ Hit **Fast Eddie's Fun Center** (850-433-7735; fasteddiesfunctr .com), 505 W Michigan St, for go-carts, mini golf, and video games. One of Pensacola's oldest family-fun parks, it features four different go-cart tracks—including one gentle enough for four-year-olds—and a serious competition speedway for mature racers. Open daily.

ⵦ At **Sam's Fun City** (850-505-0800; samsfuncity.com), 6709 Pensacola Blvd, Pensacola, you stay dry or get as wet as you like. At Surf City you'll be soaked on four thrilling waterslides, two interactive children's pools with mini slides, and a 750-foot winding lazy river, and then dry off at Fun City, which features go-carts, mini golf, and more than a dozen amusement rides. Fun City also has bumper boats if you want to get a bit of a splash. The only park of its type in the area, it's open daily year-round, 11–10. Fee. Passes available.

ⵦ Strap on a pair of skates at **Skateland** (850-623-9415; skatelandmilton.com), 6056 N Stewart St, Milton, a massive roller rink that's popular with the younger set.

ⵦ For laid-back family fun, head to **Tiki Island Golf and Games** (850-932-1550), 2 Via Del Luna Dr, Pensacola Beach, where you can spread out a picnic and play a round of mini golf at the tropically landscaped entertainment center. The 18-hole course dotted with palm trees and waterfalls will ensure the fun lasts a long time. When your game is over, head into the arcade for a game of Skee-Ball. It's located right on the beach, so you can take a nice stroll with one of their famous ice creams or rent a family-sized bicycle. Open daily year-round with extended hours on weekends and in summer. Fee.

FISHING At **Brown's Inshore Guide Service** (877-981-6246; brownsinshore .com), Captain David Brown will customize your charter trip, even an excellent fly-fishing trip, around Perdido Bay and vicinity. Day or night fishing on four- to six-hour trips including licenses for Florida and Alabama fishing, bait, and tackle. $350–500 for two passengers, $50 each additional passenger.

Go fishing for the big one with **Captain Wes Rozier** (850-982-7858 or 850-457-7476; captwesrozier.com); Captain Wes will regale you with a number of fish tales and local lore. Search out trout hidden in the grass flats or flounder in the mud-flats; these are just some of the many species of fish you'll catch. Trips from four to six hours. Rates run $240–400 depending on length.

For fly-fishing the Gulf of Mexico, **Gulf Breeze Guide Services** (850-934-3292; gulfbreezeguideservice.com) connects you with Captain Baz, whose passion for fly fishing, especially for false albacore and redfish, is infectious. An expert who knows the seasons and the species, he'll plan a memorable trip for you. Inshore, $400–500 for one to three anglers, four to six hours; offshore, $600 for six hours.

GOLF Tee off at the spectacular 18-hole, par-72 course at **Hidden Creek Golf Club** (850-939-1939; hiddengolf.com), 3070 PGA Blvd, Navarre, designed by Ron Garl. Or lose yourself at the legendary 18-hole, par-72 Arnold Palmer **Lost Key Golf Club** (888-256-7853; lostkey.com), 625 Lost Key Dr, Perdido Key. The heavily wooded course is so challenging that golf carts with a GPS yardage system are mandatory. Established in 1926, Pensacola's most historic course is the **Osceola Municipal Golf Course** (850-453-7599; osceolagolf.com), 300 Tonawanda Dr. It has green fees as low as $15 (not including cart) for the 18-hole, par-72 course and a long and storied history with the PGA Tour. Home of the Pensacola Open for a decade, the **Perdido Bay Golf Club** (850-492-1223; perdidobaygolf.com), 1 Doug Ford Dr, Pensacola, offers an extensive practice facility in addition to its greens. A dress code applies. The par-36 and par-72 courses at the **Tiger Point Golf and Country Club** (850-932-1330; tigerpointclub.com), 1255 Country Club Rd, Gulf Breeze, feature views of Santa Rosa Sound. The East Course is the favorite, designed in the Scottish style.

HIKING The **Florida Trail** (see *What's Where*) is the country's only National Scenic Trail to traverse a beach—and not just any beach, but the sparkling white-sand strands of Santa Rosa Island, right up to the trail's western terminus at **Fort Pickens**. An alternate northern terminus is at the Alabama border inside **Blackwater River State Forest** (see *Wild Places*), where portions of the **Juniper**

PITCHER PLANTS

If you're as obsessed with pitcher plants as I am, you've found Nirvana. This portion of the Gulf Coast has the most diversity of pitcher plant species that you'll find in Florida, and if you arrive between late March and mid-April, you'll catch them in their showiest finery. Among the easier places to find them are along the trails of **Tarkiln Bayou State Park**, home of the Perdido Pitcher Plant Prairie; at **Garcon Point Preserve** along Blackwater Bay; and at adjacent **Yellow River Marsh Preserve State Park** (see *Wild Places* for all three). More are hidden within the wild spaces of Blackwater River State Forest. However, the mother lode of beauty is along the **Clear Creek Nature Trail** at Whiting NAS [30.710586, -87.032572], which leads to a boardwalk surrounded by thousands upon thousands of blooms.

PITCHER PLANTS BLOOM AT GARCON POINT EACH SPRING

Creek section burst into a colorful tunnel of pink mountain laurel in early spring. Now, normally you can't walk on sand dunes, but the Florida Trail also traverses several miles of undulating dunes inside the **University of West Florida Dunes Preserve** along CR 399, adjoining the Pensacola Bicycle Path (see *Bicycling*). For more dune climbing, do the loop trail at Big Lagoon State Park (see *Parks*).

PADDLING Adventures Unlimited Outdoor Center (800-239-6864 or 850-623-6197; adventuresunlimited.com), 12 miles north of Milton off CR 87, has offered canoeing, tubing, and kayaking down Coldwater Creek, Juniper Creek, and the Blackwater River since 1975. You'll also enjoy land activities such as the ropes course, hiking, biking, and hayrides. Founder Jack Sanborn was stationed at Whiting Field and decided he wanted to start a business that kept him outdoors. He's parlayed his original 12 canoes into a complex where guests can stay in relocated, renovated historic cabins, a campground, and even a schoolhouse (see *Lodging*), and has earned Milton the title "Canoe Capital of Florida." Paddling excursions start at $25 per person and can run from 4 to 18 miles for a day trip. The staff can also arrange overnight trips of up to three days.

Whether you want a short or long canoe or kayak trip or just want to go tubing, **Blackwater Canoe Rental** (850-623-0235; blackwatercanoe.com), 10274 Pond Rd, Milton, has several options to enjoy the pristine Blackwater River. The snow-white sandbars are graced on each side by magnolias and river cedar. Can't you just smell the fresh air? Consider a multiday trip with camping on the sandbars, a day trip at your own pace, or a lazy tubing trip down the shallow, clear river.

At **Bob's Canoe Rental** (850-623-5457), FL 191, rent tubes, canoes, and kayaks for a paddle down Coldwater Creek, one of the most beautiful of the Blackwater River's tributaries; shuttles included in price.

SCENIC DRIVES The city park on the **Pensacola Scenic Bluffs Highway** offers an outstanding view of Escambia Bay. Designated a Scenic Byway in April 1998, the road leads you beneath moss-draped oaks and stately magnolias with scenic vistas along the way. At one point you'll reach the highest point along the entire coastline of Florida. Then continue through freshwater and tidal wetlands down to the Escambia River. Two spectacular coastal drives await on Santa Rosa Island. Follow **Fort Pickens Drive** west through Gulf Islands National Seashore to Fort Pickens (see *Historic Sites*) for broad views of beaches and dunes on both sides of the rebuilt highway. **CR 399** offers a sweep of sparkling sands and dunes in all directions as you head east from Pensacola Beach to Navarre Beach through a string of public lands that protect these fragile, windswept landscapes. Pull-offs on both drives provide places for you to enjoy the beach.

SCENIC TOURS Captain Kirk at **Condor Sailing Adventures** (850-637-SAIL; condorsailingadventures.com) offers two-hour dolphin cruises on Pensacola Bay and sunset cruises each evening. Multiple trips daily, departing from the Palafox Pier Yacht Harbor at the end of Palafox St, downtown Pensacola, $59 per person.

At Navarre Beach, a guided tour with **Navarre Beach Eco Tours** (850-939-7734; navarrebeachkayaks.com/eco-tours) at the Navarre Pier gets you out on the gentle waters of Santa Rosa Sound for four hours of exploration in a small-group setting, $45 and up. Kayak rentals available.

TUBING Coldwater Creek in Blackwater River State Forest (see *Wild Places*) is *the* destination for floating down a lazy creek in an inner tube. Check with the outfitters listed under *Paddling* for logistics.

WALKING TOURS Talk a stroll along the beautiful banks of the Blackwater River in historic **Bagdad Village** (bagdadvillage.org). Listed on the National Register of Historic Places with 143 buildings, the Village's frame vernacular and Greek Revival architecture dates back to the mid-1800s. Built with Creole elements by former slaves, Bagdad Village is located just north of Milton. Maps and guided tours are available by calling 850-623-8493 or through the Santa Rosa County Tourist and Development Council (see *Guidance*).

The **Milton Historic District**, also listed on the National Register of Historic Places, contains a day's worth of exploring, with homes and structures dating from 1850 to 1945 (see *Historic Sites* and *Museums*).

ZIPLINE One of the newest attractions at Adventures Unlimited (see *Paddling*) is their extensive zipline and canopy walk course, **Zip Adventures** (850-613-6197; floridaziplineadventures.com), which encompasses three separate routes through the forests surrounding Coldwater Creek. You must do them in sequence, since each one is progressively more difficult. Forest Flight soars over the historic Spring Hill Dam and other scenic spots on nine ziplines and takes three hours, $89. Soaring Stream has two 6-foot towers, a skybridge, and 5 ziplines, including a sharp dive over Coldwater Creek. It takes two hours; $89. The "Ultimate Zip Adventure" includes nearly a mile's worth of ziplines over Wolfe Creek and Big Coldwater Creek, and takes five hours to complete; $129, two-person minimum.

✳ Green Space

BEACHES Public beaches along the Gulf of Mexico are a major draw for this region, with powdery white sands and emerald waters, and for good reason. They abound along the entire sweep of coastline across Santa Rosa Island and Perdido Key. Access points are clearly marked along the coastal highways, CR 399 on Santa Rosa Island and FL 292 on Perdido Key. Parking is free except within certain public lands listed below. This region has borne the impact of several years of hurricanes and tropical storms in the past decade, topped off with the *Deepwater Horizon* oil spill in 2010. Extensive beach cleanups went on for many months after the flow of oil ceased beneath the Gulf, including removal of tarballs and oil-soaked sands. No oil was visible during my 2011 visit to the region. If you're worried about the aftereffects of the spill, check water quality reports from the State of Florida before your visit. These are available on an interactive map at the bottom of this website: myfloridaeh.com/BEACHnames.html.

✦ ⅙ **Gulf Islands National Seashore** (850-934-2600; nps.gov/guis), 1801 Gulf Breeze Pkwy, Pensacola Beach. Broken into seven segments along Florida's coast, this expansive seaside park includes Pensacola's historic forts, as well as great swimming beaches on Santa Rosa Island and Perdido Key. Some accessible crossovers provided. The **Fort Pickens Unit** (see *Historic Sites*) has the most extensive and lonely stretches of beaches in the region, as well as a campground where you can hear the waves; fee.

VACATIONERS RELAX ALONG PENSACOLA BAY ON SANTA ROSA ISLAND

At the east end of Santa Rosa Island, a former state park is now **Navarre Beach Park** (santarosa.fl.gov/parks/navarrebeach.html), 8579 Gulf Blvd, Navarre Beach. Crossovers from the ample parking areas provide beach access, and seaside picnic pavilions are surrounded by sand drifts white as snow. Free.

✍ **Perdido Key State Park** (850-492-1595; floridastateparks.org/perdidokey), 12301 Gulf Beach Hwy, Pensacola, the coastal scrub and beaches preserved here are home to the tiny, federally endangered Santa Rosa beach mouse.

GREENWAY ♿ **Blackwater Heritage State Trail** (850-245-2052), 5533 Alabama St, Milton, is a paved, linear 8.5-mile biking and hiking trail following the historical route of the Florida & Alabama Railroad, with nice views of the Blackwater River. Free.

PARKS ✍ One of the best places in the region for birding (see *Birding*), **Big Lagoon State Park** (850-492-1595; floridastateparks.org/biglagoon), 12301 Gulf Beach Hwy, Pensacola, surrounds its namesake lagoon. Kayak the shallow waters of several linked lagoons, camp in the middle of a coastal scrub forest, or meander miles of trails across the dunes. A tall observation tower provides a bird's-eye view from which you can see the distant whitecaps of the Gulf of Mexico. Fee.

Blackwater River State Park (850-983-5363; floridastateparks.org/blackwater river), 7720 Deaton Bridge Rd, Holt. Bask on a sandy freshwater beach, hike the Chain of Lakes Trail along ancient oxbows in the floodplain, or drop your kayak in for a scenic trip along one of the purest sand-bottomed rivers in the world. The park offers a campground with electric and water hookups, plus primitive camping for backpackers along the Juniper Creek Trail, part of the Florida Trail System. Fee.

Just east of the Seville Historic District along the bay, the **Hawkshaw Lagoon Memorial Park** (850-434-1234), part of the Habitat Restoration, is a perfect location for spotting cormorants, pelicans, and great blue herons. The pedestrian bridge spanning the lagoon serves as a platform for the memorial sculpture *The Sanctuary*, the National Memorial for Missing Children.

🐾 With at least a mile of very strenuous boardwalks and staircases swarming up and down bluffs that tower as much as 85 feet above the water below, **Bay Bluffs Preserve** (850-436-5510; playpensacola.com), 3400 Scenic Hwy, Pensacola, makes a good personal training ground for hill-climbing stamina, with beginner, intermediate, and advanced routes. The views across Escambia Bay are nice, too. Several parking areas along the Scenic Highway (US 90) east of downtown provide access. Dogs are welcome off-leash on a dedicated beach provided for them.

PENSACOLA BAY BLUFFS PRESERVE

WILD PLACES 🐾 At **Blackwater River State Forest** (850-957-6140; fl-dof.com/state_forests/blackwater _river.html), 11650 Munson Hwy, Milton, immerse yourself in the largest state forest in Florida—190,000 acres surrounding the Blackwater River and its tributaries. Fingers of red clay seep down from Alabama, exposed in outcroppings like the tall cliffs above Juniper Creek. With high ground topped with longleaf pine and wiregrass, the undulating landscape seems to stretch on forever. Paddling, hiking, and hunting are the major draws to this vast wilderness. Enjoy backpacking 38 miles of the Florida Trail, drop your kayak in at Red Rock, or utilize one of three reservoirs built especially as fish management areas—Karick, Hurricane, and Bear Lakes. With six campgrounds and recreation areas to choose from, you won't run out of things to do! Fees apply at some recreation areas.

Just outside the gates of Whiting Naval Air Station north of Milton off FL 87, **Clear Creek** is protected by military and conservancy lands. Follow the Clear Creek Nature Trail for one of the most spectacular scenes in natural Florida when you arrive in late March–early April in time to see thousands of pitcher plants in bloom along the boardwalk. Open sunrise–sunset; free.

🐾 **Garcon Point Preserve** (850-539-5999), FL 191 just north of the Garcon Point Bridge tollbooth, offers more than 4 miles of trails through open prairies and pine flatwoods, providing panoramic views of Blackwater Bay and close encounters with carnivorous pitcher plants. Open sunrise–sunset; free.

🐾 🦴 ♿ Part of Gulf Islands National Seashore, the **Naval Live Oaks Area** (850-934-2600; nps.gov/guis/planyourvisit/naval-live-oaks.htm) straddles US 98 in Gulf Breeze. It has secluded beaches for fishing on both Santa Rosa Sound and Escambia Bay, accessible through a network of hiking trails. The visitors center explains the strategic and historic significance of this site: It was established as the country's first federally protected forest. Not to protect the trees, mind you, but to ensure they'd be there for future shipbuilding. Yes, it was a tree farm, established in 1828 by President John Quincy Adams, and was overseen by Henry Breckenridge, our first federal forester. Ancient live oaks were felled to make wooden sailing ships to ensure the fledgling United States would have a strong navy. It's been a while since warships were made of wood, so the live oaks that have survived centuries of hurricanes are a very impressive sight. Open daily 8–sunset; free.

🐾 ♿ Walk through wild wet pine flatwoods on a mild paved pathway at **Tarkiln Bayou State Park** (850-492-1595; floridastateparks.org/tarkiln bayou), CR 293 south of US 98, Pensacola, or jump off the easy route and explore the soggy forest on 7 miles of old jeep trails. At the end of the paved path, the Emma Claire Boardwalk of Hope stretches across a colorful pitcher plant bog and ends at a scenic overlook on the bayou. Fee.

🐾 Florida's largest pitcher plant prairie is protected at **Yellow River Marsh Preserve State Park** (850-983-5363; floridastateparks.org/yellowriver), FL 191 south of Bagdad at Dickerson City Rd [30.484300, -87.071500]. There are no formal trails, but there is a parking area as well as plenty of colorful blooms to see in April—bring your GPS to find your way back. Open sunrise–sunset; free.

FOLLOWING AN INTERPRETIVE TRAIL AT NAVAL LIVE OAKS AREA, GULF BREEZE

✴ Lodging

BED & BREAKFASTS

Pensacola 32501

(📶) Located in historic North Hill, the **Noble Manor Bed & Breakfast** (850-434-9544; noblemanor.com), 110 W Strong St, is a Tudor Revival home designed by Charlie Hill Turner in 1905. Classy contemporary decor and furnishings, cable, and WiFi bring these spacious historic guest rooms up to date. The Carriage House Suite, with its own separate entrance, sits in the yard. Guests can enjoy a heated pool and outdoor hot tub. $125–160.

🐾 ♿ (📶) Overlooking the sweep of Pensacola Bay, the **Lee House Bed and Breakfast Inn** (850-912-8770; lee housepensacola.com), 400 Bayfront Pkwy, is an elegant inn across from Seville Square. It captures the essence of place while providing modern accommodations downtown. Each suite features its own unique contemporary decor; some have two beds, sleeping up to four guests. Business travelers will appreciate the work desks in each room. $195–225, including breakfast, parking, and numerous on-site amenities.

(📶) The Queen Anne Victorian **Pensacola Victorian Bed & Breakfast** (800-370-8354 or 850-434-2818; pensacolavictorian.com), 203 W Gregory Ave, was once a ship captain's home. Awaken each morning to fresh fruit, waffles, omelets, or quiche; you'll also be treated to complimentary fresh-baked treats and beverages throughout your stay. $85–125.

HOTELS, MOTELS & RESORTS

Milton 32570

🎵 (📶) In the 1930s it served as a working schoolhouse in Fidelis; now it provides a retreat in a most restful setting. Tucked away in the forest at Adventures Unlimited (see *Camping & Cabins*), the **Old School House Inn** showcases original bead board walls and ceiling and hardwood floors in each of its literary-themed rooms: Poets, Audubon, Faulkner, Dr. Seuss, Hemingway, Mitchell, Rawlings, Twain. My room, Margaret Mitchell, boasted a set of related books on the mantel, photos from the Civil War period, and a framed image of Tara above the bed. I enjoyed being able to sit in a rocking chair on the porch while sipping my morning coffee and reading a novel. No phones and no television—but you'll appreciate the coffeemaker, microwave, and small fridge. Rates run $79–129 per night with a three-night minimum during the summer.

Pensacola 32504

🛁 ♿ (📶) ❧ Among the many chain hotels found around Pensacola, jazz aficionados seek out the **Hilton Garden Inn** (850-479-8900; hiltongarden innpensacola.com), 1144 Airport Blvd, since their Sunday brunch buffet features live jazz and has for many years. Locals enjoy coming in for the music; if you stay, you'll be able to grab a table early and savor a mimosa with those smooth sounds. The hotel, located near the airport and medical centers, has a pool, business center, and fitness center, plus all the amenities you'd expect under the Hilton banner. Rates start at $99; Sunday jazz brunch, $22.

Pensacola 32502

🐾 (📶) Updated, cozy rooms and suites that feel just like home make the **New World Inn** (850-432-4111; newworld landing.com/newworldinn.htm), 600 S Palafox St, an appealing and historic destination for downtown accommodations, positioned nicely near the best

museums, restaurants, and shopping. $129–149, includes deluxe continental breakfast and free downtown parking. The New World Landing complex also caters to wedding parties with a large event venue on site; relax after a busy day with a martini at the 600 Palafox Wine and Tapas Bar.

♿ (📶) A fine example of urban revitalization, **Sole Inn and Suites** (850-470-9298; soleinnandsuites.com), 200 N Palafox St, is a former Travelodge reincarnated as a hip boutique hotel. I've seen before and after, and this transformation rates a huge "wow" from me. The rooms have crisp, sleek, urban decor in tasteful black and white, with extras you appreciate in a walkable downtown, like a microwave, mini fridge, coffeemaker, and free parking. Rates start at $89, include continental breakfast and Happy Hour each evening 5–7.

Pensacola Beach 32561

🛁 ♿ (📶) Jimmy Buffett hasn't forgotten his roots here along the Gulf Coast, opening the **Margaritaville Beach Hotel** (850-916-9755, margaritaville hotel.com), 165 Fort Pickens Rd,

ONE OF THE ROOMS AT THE OLD SCHOOL HOUSE INN

Pensacola Beach. Kick back and relax with one of Jimmy's margaritas at the rooftop pool, or soak in the sun along the sparkling sands. The sleek, spacious rooms have a colonial Caribbean feel and ample space for kicking back and enjoying the view. Several eateries are on site, making it an easy, laid-back destination with the beach, the drinks, the tunes, and the eats right here. You'll be humming "Creola" before you know it. $179–399.

VACATION RENTALS Take in the breathtaking view of the emerald-green waters at **Eden** (850-492-3336; edencondominiums.com), 16821 Perdido Key Dr, Perdido Key 32507. The resort features a lush, tropical landscape with heated 176-foot Gulf-side pool complete with waterfalls. On cold or rainy days you'll love the heated indoor solarium with pool and gardens.

THE MARGARITAVILLE BEACH HOTEL IS ONE OF THE NEWEST ACCOMMODATIONS ON PENSACOLA BEACH

Other amenities include indoor/outdoor hot tubs, an exercise club, and lighted tennis court for night play. One-, two-, and three-bedroom units come with full kitchens and washer/dryer. Rentals start at $140 for a one-bedroom in the off-season and rise to $570 for a three-bedroom during the summer months. Weekly and monthly rates available.

One of the largest suppliers of fully furnished homes in Perdido Key, Pensacola Beach, and Navarre Beach, **Resort Quest** (888-909-6807 or 850-275-5060; resortquestperdidokey vacations.com) can select which will be right for you—from condos in resort-style settings to portfolio homes with private pools, by the day, week, or month.

For all vacation rentals and condo resorts, quality of accommodations can vary widely from unit to unit. Be aware that cleaning and maintenance fees may be added atop your room fee. Ask before booking.

CAMPING & CABINS

Century 32535

Off the beaten path at the northern end of Escambia County, **Lake Stone Campground** (850-256-5555; co.escambia.fl.us), 801 W FL 4, is a 100-acre county-run campground centered on Lake Stone. The 77 broad, mostly shaded campsites are ideal for large RVs and can handle tent campers as well. Bring your fishing poles and enjoy a weekend in the woods with the family. Sites are first come, first served, but general reservations for camping are accepted with advance payment. $13–15, including electric and water hookups.

Milton 32570

⚓ **Adventures Unlimited** (800-239-6864 or 850-623-6197; adventuresun limited.com), 12 miles north of Milton off CR 87, offers a wide variety of accommodations, including cabins, motel rooms, and camping. Stay in the Old School House Inn (see *Hotels, Motels & Resorts*) or choose from a variety of fully equipped cottages with country charm and sizes to fit every family, from Granny Peadon's Cottage with period furnishings and a back porch overlooking Wolfe Creek ($119–149) to the Fox Den Bungalow ($79–109) with its fireplace. For something more basic, try the rustic one- and two-room camping-style cabins with air-conditioning and bunk beds ($39–59), some of which are along the creeks; restrooms are a short walk away. Primitive campsites are $20 ($25 with hookup).

Blackwater River State Forest (see *Wild Places*) has six campgrounds amid its sweep of 190,000 acres between Milton and Alabama. My favorite is **North Hurricane Lake**, a scenic site along the Florida Trail, but the bath-house at **North Karick Lake** can't be beat. Each campground is centered on a recreation area along one of the "lakes" (reservoirs, really) and offers electric and water at sites tucked beneath the forest canopy, as well as direct access to hiking trails, paddling, and fishing. The other campgrounds are **South Hurricane Lake** (tents only), **Krul Recreation Area**, **South Karick Lake**, and **Bear Lake Recreation Area**. Primitive camping is permitted along the Florida Trail (see *Hiking*), with several camping shelters along the route.

At **Blackwater River State Park** (see *Parks*), 30 campsites (800-326-3521; floridastateparks.reserveamerica.com) with electric and water hookups offer easy access to paddling and hiking expeditions. The sites book up every weekend, so reserve well in advance. Similarly, **Big Lagoon State Park** (see *Parks*) has a popular campground that can handle RVs, although the sites—unlike Blackwater River—are in full sun in the scrub forest.

Navarre Beach 32566

Park your rig under the pines at the **Navarre Beach Campground** (888-639-2188 or 850-939-2188; navbeach.com), 9201 Navarre Pkwy, where amenities include a fishing pier on Santa Rosa Sound, a heated pool and hot tub, a playground and game room for the kids, and a dog walk for your pooch. Sites come in 30- and 50-amp flavors ($49–69 depending on location), plus a couple 20-amp sites for tent campers ($49). No camper? No problem! Cabin rentals range from simple sleeping spaces with cold water to a big three-bedroom family units, $69–164.

Pensacola Beach 32561

Now that Fort Pickens (see *Historic Sites*) has reopened its campground, you can again sleep outdoors within sound of the rumbling surf. The 200-site **Fort Pickens Campground** (877-444-6777 or 850-934-2656; recreation.gov) is on the bay side of the island, but it's an easy walk on dune boardwalks over to the beach. The campground has bathhouses and a camp store, but little shade. Tents, trailers, and RVs welcome. Sites are $20 per night with water and electric (50 percent discount for seniors with Golden Age Pass), but must be reserved in advance.

✳ Where to Eat

DINING OUT

Milton

A gas station revitalized as bistro dining—that's the **Mainstreet Café** (850-626-3376), 6820 Caroline St, the upscale spot in downtown Milton, featuring "fine dining in a casual atmosphere." Lunch includes gourmet-style deli sandwiches, wraps, and a classic cheeseburger or grouper sandwich. Their dinner menu changes weekly. On my visit, I encountered crabcakes with fried green tomatoes, amberjack, grouper, and duck, $16–21. It's a popular hangout for locals, not just for the food but for live music Thu–Sat nights.

Pensacola

Jackson's Steakhouse (850-469-9898; jacksons.goodgrits.com), 400 S Palafox St, sits in the heart of downtown Pensacola's historic district, cozy in an 1860s mercantile building overlooking historic Plaza Ferdinand. Notable as one of Florida's top 25 restaurants, it features grain-fed beef from the Midwest served up in five different grilled cuts, from a 6-oz. petite filet to a 24-oz. porterhouse. Fresh Maine lobster is always on the menu. Chef Irv's menu sports creative creations beyond these classics, which on any given night might include treats like Irv's Coast Crab Cakes, dressed with homemade sweet cream corn, sautéed spinach, portobello mushrooms, cherry toma-

toes, and fried slab bacon topped with sweet potato hay, or gnocchi with Port St. Joe shrimp, Cedar Key clams, and blue gold mussels. Half portions available on some entrées, $16–35/market price.

Don't miss the **Pensacola Fish House** (850-470-0003; fishhouse.goodgrits.com), 600 S Barracks St, a local institution with a menu that leans toward Asian fusion. My favorite is Grits à Ya Ya—jumbo spiced Gulf shrimp atop a sauté of spinach, portobello mushroom, applewood-smoked bacon, garlic, shallots, and cream atop a heaping bed of smoked Gouda grits. For those wanting something lighter, try the sushi, or the cashew-and-Vidalia-crusted soft-shell crab salad. Save room for a piece of Florida key lime pie, served naturally yellow. Entrées $18–28; sushi starts at $8. Stop in on Sunday for the "Southern Sunday Supper," featuring tasty farm-to-table treats like chicken and dumplings or Cracker-Friend Catfish for $14, including classic southern sides.

With a classy fusion menu sprinkling southern favorites like fried pickles and

PLAZA FERNDINAND IS A GREEN SPACE IN THE HEART OF HISTORIC DOWNTOWN PENSACOLA

a fried green tomato BLT among more upscale offerings including seared beef carpaccio, Asian duck salad, and Black Angus filet mignon, **Vic and Ike's** (850-912-8569; vic-and-ikes.com), 104 S Palafox St, is both upscale and down-home, an American bistro that embraces the cultural diversity we so love in our food. In the heart of the downtown district, it's a smart choice for a fine evening meal.

Pensacola Beach
Featuring inspired creations and presentations of seafood with a menu that changes daily to reflect the freshest sources—yes, the source of your dinner is noted, so you don't have to ask, as I do at many restaurants, if they use Gulf shrimp or Apalachicola oysters—**The Grand Marlin** (850-677-9153; thegrandmarlin.com), 400 Pensacola Beach Blvd, is the hot spot for fine dining at the beach. Typical dinner selections from Chef Gregg might include horseradish-crusted grouper with whipped potatoes, seasonal vegetables, orange vinaigrette, and balsamic reduction, or "simply grilled" market fresh sea scallops from Georges Bank, Massachusetts, and cobia from Pensacola. A selection of grilled steaks and chops are available for those not so fond of the seafood that is this restaurant's forte. Entrées $17–32, lighter fare $6–14.

EATING OUT
Gulf Breeze
The savory smokehouse aroma of Carolina barbecue greets you at the door at **Billy Bob's Beach BBQ** (850-934-2999; billybobsbarbecue.com), 911 Gulf Breeze Pkwy, a just-plain-good barbecue joint on the way to the beach. Try the big burgers or the pig pudding, and don't forget a side of fried squash. Drive through to grab your 'que for a seaside picnic, or settle back into the Blue Angels niche for a family meal. Open daily 11–9.

Milton
At **Bass' Kwik Burger Cafe** (850-623-6942), 5173 Stewart St, Mama Bass set the standard for good food, big portions, and homemade pies (apple and egg custard are favorites), along with fresh veggies that keep a regular clientele coming back. True southern food in generous portions in a setting that's nothing fancy but feels like family. Open for breakfast, lunch, and dinner; closed Sun.

The aromas from **Bodacious Pies & Bakery** (850-450-9398), 4537 Willing St, drew me in, but it was the wall of whoopie pies that I marveled at. Not content with just chocolate, they whip up unique flavors like pumpkin. Brownies, cookies, and other sweets, too.

Fried mullet? Fresh local oysters plucked from nearby East Bay? You know where to go. **Nichol's Seafood** (850-623-3410), 3966 Avalon Blvd, is the local favorite, where whatever's fresh from local fisherman—cobia, amberjack, flounder—shows up as the special of the night. $3 a dozen (yep, you read that right) for fresh-shucked raw oysters, and satisfying seafood for $9–15, lunch and dinner.

Munson
Ruth's Country Store (850-957-4463), corner of FL 4 and CR 191. Established in the 1940s in a onetime timber industry boomtown, this rustic and quaint country store has deep local roots—Bobby (Ruth's son) grew up sleeping under the cash register, and his wife, Patty, offers a great little breakfast in the back room. Gather around the picnic table and order up fresh pancakes, omelets, and eggs and bacon, or stop in for burgers and dogs at lunch on your way to Blackwater River State Forest. Pop in, and you might catch a bluegrass jam in session!

Navarre Beach

For fresh baked breads and hot coffee, start your mornings at **Sailors' Grill & Bakery** (850-939-1092; juanaspagodas .com/restaurant.htm), 1451 Navarre Beach Blvd (corner of Gulf Blvd), with tasty treats like cinnamon raisin French toast. Breakfast served 8–11 Mon–Sat, 8–noon Sun. Pizza, nachos, and other "Galley Grub" go on until closing. Cold beer and wine coolers can be found next door at **Juana's Pagoda** (850-939-2130). This meet-and-greet spot is best around sunset, with live music Wed–Sun.

Pensacola

More than a baker's dozen of flavors awaits at **Bagelheads** (850-444-9661), 916 E Gregory Ave, a busy breakfast stop between the bluffs, beach, and downtown. Overlooking Pensacola Bay, it's a place to settle in with their cinnamon-dressed mocha latte and a helping of steel-cut oatmeal with a variety of toppings. Open 6–2 week-days, 7–2 weekends.

Stop for lunch at the colorful **Hip Pocket Deli** (850-455-9319), 4130 Barrancas Ave, Warrington, featuring world-famous gyros, calzones, sand-wiches, and more. Open 10–2:30 Mon–Sat.

(((•))) Kick back at the **Leisure Club** (850-912-4229, tlcdowntown.com), 126 S Palafox St, a trendy downtown meet-up spot within walking distance of entertainment venues, museums, and the Palafox Market. The art on the walls evokes the weirdness of Edward Gorey, as do the funky furnishings. Come early for coffee, late for wine, and anytime for WiFi.

Lively Irish folk music and traditional fare are found at **McGuire's Irish Pub** (850-433-6789; mcguiresirish pub.com), 600 E Gregory Ave. Sing-alongs are encouraged; if you don't learn the words, you'll have to kiss the moose, and that's no blarney. The sen-ate bean soup is still only 18 cents, but if it's your only purchase, they'll charge $18. The extensive drink menu includes the full-on "Irish Wake," which you'll have to try to believe.

After a strenuous walk on the Pensa-cola Bluffs, a stop at the **Scenic 90 Cafe** (850-433-8844; scenic90cafe .com), 701 Scenic Hwy, soothed my hunger. It's a cute diner with a 1950s feel, but you can skip the cute and relax out on the big covered patio if it's cool enough to catch a breeze. What's important here is the food, classic diner comfort food like big breakfasts (the Greek omelet and Stack of Jacks get a big thumbs-up), juicy burgers, ice cream sundaes, chocolate malts, and root beer floats. $3 and up.

At the **Tuscan Oven** (850-484-6836; thetuscanoven.com), 4801 N 9th Ave, the flicker of an authentic Italian wood-fired pizza oven reflects in the front window, drawing you in with the promise of warmth and that tantalizing smoky aroma. Pasta is made fresh, and the antipasto is a vibrant mix of arti-chokes with Italian meats and cheeses. Cheery acrylics of peppers, eggplants, and tomatoes take center stage until the food appears, and then you won't be looking up again until you're done. Save some room for dessert, which includes chocolate mousse cake, tiramisu torte, raspberry gelato, and dressy cannolis. Pizza $9–24; pasta, $8–11, includes one of my favorite dishes, pasta al forno, baked to a finish in the aromatic oven.

Pensacola Beach

⚓ **Flounder's Chowder House** (850-932-2003; flounderschowderhouse .com), CR 399 at Fort Pickens Rd. Since 1979 this casual beach bar has been a Pensacola favorite, set in a play-ful tropical atmosphere befitting its setting on Santa Rosa Sound—right down to a lively pirate ship playground for the kids. From their award-winning flounder chowder ($3) to "Floyd Flounder's Flawless Full Flavored Florida Flash Fried Fish" ($14), you won't go wrong with the fresh seafood cramming the menu. Here for the band? Hoist a "dirty old Mason jar" full of "Diesel Fuel" while you toast your buddies over platters of Baked Oysters, Pensacola Beach Style ($11), and seafood nachos ($15). Add speedy, friendly service for lunch and dinner daily, and this one's a winner.

With a real Florida Cracker atmosphere, **Peg Leg Pete's** (850-932-4139; peglegpetes.com), 1010 Ft Pickens Rd, remains a favorite getaway. Settle back and enjoy a constant sea breeze from over the dunes while savoring baked oysters (pick your style, from Parmesan to Rockefeller) or a plate of crab legs; entrées $14–21.

Perdido Key
Flora-Bama Lounge (850-492-3048; florabama.com), 17401 Perdido Key Dr, on the state line, prides itself on being the "last authentic American Roadhouse." Stop in for a brew and a stack of oysters, and you might stumble upon Jimmy Buffett playing acoustic out on the porch, unannounced. It's a laid-back, rambling beachside bar and grill serving burgers, seafood baskets, and fresh seafood platters for lunch and dinner, $5–20; it also hosts the Annual Interstate Mullet Toss, first full weekend of April, with prizes for successful tosses across the river from Florida to Alabama (you have to see it to believe it!). Cover charge for bands and special events.

✳ Entertainment
Between Pensacola and Milton, the **Panhandle Community Theatre** (850-221-7599; panhandlecommunity theatre.com), 4636 Woodbine Rd,

Pace, showcases local talent with live performances, dinner shows, and special community events.

The **Pensacola Little Theatre** (850-434-0257; pensacolalittletheatre.com), 400 Jefferson St, Pensacola. The community theater puts on main-stage and children's shows throughout the year. Note the remnants of the old county jail in the courtyard. The 1936 building is also home to the Pensacola Cultural Center and **Ballet Pensacola** (850-432-9546; balletpensacola.com).

Sno-cones, Skee-Ball, and beer? You betcha, at **Play** (850-466-3080; iplay pensacola.com), 16 Palafox St, Pensacola, a different kind of sports bar downtown. Arcade games and big-screen televisions compete for attention. Happy hour daily 4–7, and free Skee-Ball on Tue.

The **Saenger Theatre** (850-595-3880; pensacolasaenger.com), 118 S Palafox St, Pensacola, hosts top acts like Hal Holbrook's one-man show as Mark Twain in a grandly renovated and expanded Spanish baroque/rococo theater that debuted in 1925. Once again, it's the place to see and be seen during its busy slate of comedy, drama, and symphony performances.

Inside a Masonic Lodge more than a century old, the hip **Vinyl Music Hall** (877-435-9849; vinylmusichall.com), 2 S Palafox St, is the hot place for music in downtown Pensacola, featuring both major acts on tour and top local artists.

✳ Selective Shopping
Bagdad
Just off the I-10 exit for Bagdad, **Stuckey's** (850-623-2522), 3675 Garcon Point Rd, is one of the last of its breed. Back in the 1960s, I saved up my allowance to buy pecan pralines whenever we'd stop at Stuckey's on a road trip, and I still have an old

brochure that shows more than a dozen stores in Florida in the 1970s. But today this is the state's only honest-to-goodness Stuckey's in sparkling shape in its original building (shared with a Dairy Queen). It retains the kitschy ambience and southern charm—not to mention all the classic candy I remember as a kid.

Gulf Breeze

Vintage art and furnishings, collectible glassware, books, and home decor fill the shelves of **Magnolia Antiques Mall** (850-932-2992), 4390 Gulf Breeze Pkwy. Open Mon–Sat 10–5, Sun noon–5.

Milton

With dozens of dealer booths spaciously spread out beneath one roof, **The Copper Possum** (850-626-4492), 7060 US 90, is a pleasure to explore. First, it's fully air-conditioned. The booths contain all sorts of treasures, from a 1963 Chevy owner's guide to chewing tobacco molds, quilts, artifacts for historic home restoration like windows and sinks, fine antique furniture, and Floridiana.

Pensacola, downtown

Artesana (850-433-4001; artesana imports.com), 242 W Garden St, in a historic gingerbread-trimmed cottage, pulls together beauty and function. Browse through their extensive selections of wooden tableware, handcrafted pottery, and bespeckled German enamelware. If that's not enough, they delve into many more of the finer things that make a house a home, along with stationery, fragrances, and gift items. Mom–Sat 10–5, plus Sun in Dec.

For the freshest seafood in the region, head to **Joe Patti's** (800-500-9929 or 850-432-3315; joepattis.com), South A St and Main St on the waterfront. Drawing clients from around the world, this frenetic fish house has been in business since 1931, offering the best from local fishermen and shrimpers. Open daily at 7:30, closes 7 on Sat, 6 on Sun, and for major holidays.

Pensacola

Delicate angels in porcelain and glass. Inspirational figurines by Willow Tree. At **Angel's Garden Unique Gifts** (850-435-9555), 1208 N 12th Ave, you'll find the perfect expression of faith, hope, or love for a wedding, confirmation, or baby shower gift.

Along US 29 north of I-10, **Dixie's Antiques & Collectibles** (850-484-6899; dixies-antiques.com), 10100 Pensacola Blvd, brings together 50-plus dealers under one roof." Expect to find Fenton and Vaseline glass, antique clocks, colorful old bottles, record albums, folk art, and much more. Open Mon–Sat 10–5, Sun noon–5.

Pick the finest pecans at **J. W. Renfroe Pecan Company** (800-874-1929 or 850-432-2083; renfroepecan.com), 2400 W Fairfield Dr. In business since 1957—when it was all strictly nuts— this family operation has expanded to include related food items such as pecan fudge, fresh pralines, divinity, pecan logs, and nut mixes. Coffee, too. Select from plenty of fancy gift packages online or pop in the store to make up your own. Open Mon–Fri 9–5.

Look for folksy stuff for your home at **Shabby Chic Antique Boutique** (850-457-7537), 2601 Gulf Beach Hwy between Pensacola NAS and Big Lagoon State Park.

Near Gary Park just northwest of downtown, the crowds pack in at **T&W Flea Market** (850-433-4315; tandwfleamarket.com), 1717 North T St at W St, "Pensacola's Largest Flea Market." Open Sat–Sun.

FARMER'S MARKETS On Saturday 8–2, the **Palafox Market** (palafox market.com) is a sprawling farmer's-and-arts market in the heart of downtown Pensacola, with a dash of antiques for good measure. Pick up local produce at the **Riverwalk Farmer's Market** (850-626-6420; mainstreetmilton.org/Market.htm), intersection of Berryhill, Willing, and Broad streets north of Riverwalk Park in Milton on Tue, Thu, and Sat 7–1. Handmade crafts and green products are a part of the mix.

✳ Special Events

January: Don't miss the popular **Polar Bear Dip** at the Flora-Bama Lounge (see *Eating Out*). This annual splash in Santa Rosa Sound on New Year's Day isn't as cold as its New England counterparts, but it can be chilly by Florida standards! Afterward, join in the southern tradition of eating black-eyed peas. Whoever finds a dime in their peas has good luck for the year.

January–March: **Pensacola Mardi Gras** (850-434-1234; pensacolamardi gras.com) encompasses celebrations during the traditional Lenten season with numerous parades. Just like in New Orleans, beads and treats are tossed from floats decorated and manned by creative krewes that keep the annual tradition colorful and vibrant. Perdido Beach flaunts a street party, while the celebrations in Pensacola and Pensacola Beach cater to families.

March: At the **Gulf Coast Renaissance Fair** (877-429-8462; gcrf.net), expect madrigals and magicians, storytellers and jesters, for an anachronistic mix of family entertainment.

Pensacola Bay International Film & Television Festival (866-611-9299; pensacolafilmfestival.com) takes place over four days. Submissions come from the United States, Britain, France, and Spain and include indie feature films, series and documentary television, and student shorts.

April: The **Annual Interstate Mullet Toss** (850-492-6838; florabama.com) at the Flora-Bama Lounge (see *Eating Out*), first weekend, is not to be missed. This wacky tournament is a local tradition, with real mullet tossing, live music, food, and drinks throughout the weekend.

Historic Bartram Park is host to the **Annual Pensacola Crawfish Festival** (850-433-6512; fiestaoffiveflags .org/CrawfishFestival), celebrating the Cajun influence in Northwest Florida. The three-day crawfish boil is one of the largest in the state, with Cajun fare like spicy chicken and red beans and rice. Held the last weekend of April.

✐ In early April, the **Festival on the Green** (850-474-2610, uwf.edu /festival) gives families a chance to roam the grounds of the University of North Florida and enjoy fine arts, arts and crafts, live music, and children's activities.

Pour another tasting: The **Pensacola Wine Festival** (850-434-5371, pensacolawinefestival.com), mid-April, is the region's biggest event for oenophiles, with varietals from around the world.

Milton's own **Scratch Ankle Festival** (850-626-6246; mainstreetmilton.org /ScratchAnkle.htm) in mid-April is more than 40 years old and features a nice slice of Americana, including bake-offs, live music, craft vendors, carnival rides, and the "Little Mr. and Miss" pageant.

April–May: Catch the Caribbean spirit at the Annual **Goombay Gulf Coast** (850-748-1728, goombaygulfcoast .com), a celebration of island music with steel drum bands, international reggae, calypso music, and African song and dance.

June: Pensacola's biggest and oldest annual bash is the **Fiesta of Five Flags** (fiestaoffiveflags.org), held for 10 days in mid-June to commemorate the landing of Don Tristán de Luna in 1559 and the founding of the first settlement of Pensacola. Events during the Fiesta include a boat parade, airplane meet, coronation ball, and the Fiesta Parade.

June–July: One of the country's largest billfish tournaments, the annual **Pensacola International Billfish Tournament** (850-453-4638; pbgfc.com) drew in more than 600 anglers last season competing for prizes. It's hosted by the Pensacola Big Game Fishing Club.

July: The **Pensacola Beach Air Show** (850-932-2257; visitpensacolabeach.com) features the aeronautic talents of the famous Blue Angels, stationed here at Pensacola Naval Air Station.

September: If you love seafood, you won't want to miss the **Pensacola Seafood Festival** (fiestaoffiveflags.org/SeafoodFestival), centered on Seville Square in late September. Now more than 35 years running, it showcases the best that local fisherman and chefs have to offer, with samples of delicacies like oyster croquettes, bang bang shrimp, and grilled conch available at vendor booths.

October: For more than 77 years, the Annual **Pensacola Interstate Fair** (850-944-4500; pensacolafair.com)—bigger than a county fair and smaller than a state fair—has brought farmers and city families together to enjoy exhibits, competitions, fair food, and midway rides.

Jay Peanut Festival, first weekend, Gabbert Farms, Jay. A true farmers' festival, this annual event began more than 20 years ago and continues to delight large crowds that return each year for live music, pig chases, tractor pull, pet parade, and peanuts every way you can dream of eating them. Free.

November: One of Florida's must-see aviation events, the **Blue Angels Homecoming Air Show** (850-452-2583; blueangels.navy.mil) showcases naval aeronautics and acrobatics above the home of the Blue Angels as they finish out their touring season.

Creek Indian Tribe Indian Day Celebration (850-994-9633), held late November, is a powwow in Pace featuring traditional dancing and Native American crafts and foods, open to all.

⚓ The family-friendly **Depot Days Arts and Crafts Festival** (850-623-3645; wfrm.org), 206 Henry St, is held the second weekend at the L&N Train Depot/West Florida Railroad Museum (see *Railroadiana*).

December: Santa comes to the seashore with a beachy touch, arriving in early December with the **Lighted Boat Parade** (850-932-1500; visit pensacolabeach.com) and presiding over the **Surfing Santa Parade** a few days later. Look for him at the **Downtown Christmas Parade** (coxchristmasparade.org) as well.

Ring in the New Year with the **Pelican Drop** (850-435-1603; pensacolapelicandrop.com), a new Pensacola tradition where a 10-foot, half-ton illuminated pelican is dropped 100 feet at midnight while fireworks illuminate the skies.

DESTIN–FORT WALTON

OKALOOSA, HOLMES & WALTON COUNTIES/ EMERALD COAST/SOUTH WALTON

When southerners head for the beach, they head for the "Number One Beach Towns in the South," acclaimed by *Southern Living* magazine—this stretch of sugary white sand sweeping east through Okaloosa and Walton counties from Okaloosa Island to Seaside, a place of emerald waters, fine museums, historic towns, and outdoor adventure. This is one of Florida's top tourist destinations, and the main attraction is the beach, covered in pure Appalachian quartz. The tiny crystals resemble powdered sugar, are baby-powder soft, and are surprisingly cool to walk on with bare feet. You'll want to keep your sunglasses handy when collecting the plentiful seashells; the sand is as white and bright as newly fallen snow.

The history of the region is showcased at the Indian Temple Mound and Museum in **Fort Walton Beach**, where you'll discover a unique ceremonial mound and artifacts from five distinct Native American periods. European settlers arrived in 1538, Spanish explorers who first surveyed the land. Many pioneers tried to settle here, but it wasn't until 1845 that the first permanent settler, Connecticut shipmaster Captain Leonard Destin, took hold of the land. Instrumental in creating a rich and prosperous fishing community, Captain Destin, for whom **Destin** is named, laid the groundwork for the present-day town, which is now home to Florida's largest charter fishing fleet. Chartered in 1916, Crestview is the county seat for **Okaloosa County**, 30 miles north of Fort Walton Beach. In the late 1800s, **Crestview** was a stop on the Pensacola & Atlantic Railroad, a trading center for farmers, timbermen, and ranchers on a crest between the Yellow and Shoal rivers near Florida's high point, Britton Hill. At 345 feet, it's the *lowest* high point in the United States.

In 1931 **Eglin Air Force Base** was built on 137 acres north of Destin to test non-nuclear weaponry. Today the base covers 384,000 acres of the former Choctawhatchee National Forest (established in 1909 and ceded to the military during World War II), wrapping around Fort Walton Beach and Destin to the north, thus restricting further development. Hikers will enjoy nearly 50 miles of trails through the ancient forests of the base. A favorite pastime of tourists and residents alike is sitting on the beach or at a local waterfront eatery watching pods of dolphins greet a variety of seafaring craft—it's almost impossible to look out on the

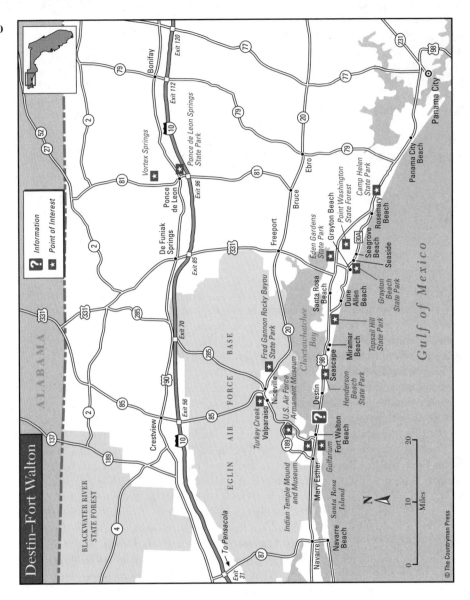

Destin–Fort Walton

water without seeing one. There are more than 100 vessels moored at the Destin Marina, so you'll be sure to find just the right charter boat to fish the open waters of the Gulf of Mexico or the backwater flats of Choctawhatchee Bay. Paddlers will especially love exploring the bay's calm backwater, where they can pull up on isolated sandy beaches and bask in the solitude. From Destin, a drive east along US 98 will take you through areas teeming with shops, restaurants, attractions, beaches, and coastal natural areas.

South Walton covers the region east of Fort Walton Beach along 26 miles of coastline in **Walton County**, with 14 diverse hamlets along the oceanfront connected by Scenic 30A. In Destin, you'll find luxury resorts; in quaint towns such as

WESTERN LAKE AT GRAYTON BEACH IS ONE OF WALTON COUNTY'S MANY COASTAL DUNE LAKES

Grayton Beach, great opportunities for antiquing or finding an eclectic piece of art; and in **Seaside**, where the movie *The Truman Show* was filmed, you'll find a beachside movie set of Victoriana dotted with white picket fences. For a unique paddling experience, head to one of 17 coastal dune lakes along the Gulf: These rare natural features are found only here and in parts of Africa and Australia, freshwater lakes that flush into the sea. A full marina is located at the popular 220-acre Western Lake in Grayton Beach State Park.

Founded in 1881 as a railroad town along the Louisville & Nashville Railroad, **DeFuniak Springs** is the county seat of Walton County, its historic residential district clustered around a perfectly round spring-fed lake exactly a mile in circumference. The town is named for Fred R. DeFuniak, general manager of the railroad, and it truly came to life when the Florida Chautauqua association organized and held its first assembly here in February 1885, establishing one of the first grand cultural centers of the Southeast. After the 1920s post-boom crash, the town retreated into a quiet rural community with a grand Victorian heart and the oldest continually operating library in Florida. The historic district surrounding Lake DeFuniak is a delight to visit, its classical architecture evoking old New England.

In adjacent rural **Holmes County**, **Ponce de Leon** has no traffic light, but it's a center of summer fun thanks to its three major springs—Ponce de Leon, Vortex, and Morrison—open for swimming and diving.

GUIDANCE For vacation planning in towns in Okaloosa County, including Crestview, Destin, Okaloosa Island, and Fort Walton Beach, contact the **Emerald Coast Convention & Visitors Bureau** (800-322-3319 or 850-651-7131; destin -fwb.com), which has a welcome center at 1540 Miracle Strip Pkwy SE, Fort Walton Beach. You'll also find valuable resources at the **Greater Fort Walton Beach Chamber of Commerce** (850-244-8191; fwbchamber.org), 34 Miracle Strip Pkwy

SE, the **Destin Chamber of Commerce** (850-837-6241; destinchamber.com), 1021 US 98 E, Suite A, and the **Crestview Chamber of Commerce** (850-682-3212), 502 S Main St.

For tourism information on the 15 beachside towns of Walton County, **Grayton Beach**, **Rosemary Beach**, **Santa Rosa Beach**, and **Seaside** among them, contact **Visit South Walton** (800-822-6877; visitsouthwalton.com). The **Walton County Chamber of Commerce** (850-892-3191; waltoncountychamber.com), with visitors centers at 95 Circle Dr, DeFuniak Springs, and 63 South Centre Trail, Santa Rosa Beach, covers all of Walton County. For explorations of **Ponce de Leon** and **Bonifay**, see the **Holmes County** website (holmescountyonline.com).

GETTING THERE *By air:* **Northwest Florida Regional Airport** (850-651-7160; flyvps.com), 1701 FL 85 N, Eglin Air Force Base, is served by five major carriers, including Continental, Delta, and US Airways. Delta and Southwest serve the new **Northwest Florida Beaches International Airport** (850-763-6751; iflybeaches.com), 6300 West Bay Pkwy, Panama City Beach.

By bus: **Greyhound** (800-231-2222).

By car: **I-10** and **US 90** run east–west through this region. **FL 85** will take you from Crestview down past Eglin AFB and into Fort Walton Beach; **US 331** connects DeFuniak Springs, Freeport, and Santa Rosa Beach. **US 98** runs east–west from Panama City Beach through Santa Rosa Beach, Destin, and Fort Walton Beach. **Scenic 30A** connects the small beach towns of South Walton.

GETTING AROUND ♿ **Okaloosa County Transit/The WAVE** (850-833-9168; rideoct.org) is the local public transportation service in and around Destin and Fort Walton. The Wave operates only in Fort Walton and connects to the **Okaloosa Island and Destin Beach Shuttle**, which runs in sections along US 98 from Fort Walton to the Silver Sands Factory Stores. All vehicles are equipped with wheelchair lifts. No charge to bring a bicycle, which gets loaded on the front rack. The Wave operates Mon–Fri 6–6. The Beach Shuttle operates seven days, 7 AM–10 PM. Full fare for both is $1–1.50, 25–75¢ for seniors, and free for children under 12 traveling with an adult and for military personnel.

PARKING **DeFuniak Springs** offers ample free parking in the downtown shopping district and in the historic district around the lake.

MEDICAL EMERGENCIES **Fort Walton Beach Medical Center** (850-862-1111; fwbmc.com), 1000 Mar-Walt Dr, Fort Walton Beach; **Sacred Heart Hospital on the Emerald Coast** (850-278-3000; sacredheartemerald.org), 7800 US 98 W; Miramar Beach; and **Twin Cities Hospital** (850-678-4131; tchospital.com), Niceville. Always call 911 for major emergencies.

✳ To See

ARCHAEOLOGICAL SITE A National Historic Landmark, the **Indian Temple Mound** (850-243-6521; fwb.org/index.php/museums.html), 139 Miracle Strip Pkwy, built between AD 800 and 1400, was a major ceremonial center for the Mississippian culture. Climb 15 feet to the top of the ceremonial mound, which measures 223 by 220 feet at the base and 90 by 150 foot at the top. Next door, in the museum, more than 6,000 artifacts, some as much as 10,000 years old, describe the history of the peoples who once lived on these shores. Open Mon–Sat 10–4:30; fee.

ART GALLERIES At the **Arts and Design Society of Fort Walton Beach** (850-244-1271; artsdesignsociety.org), 17 1st St SE, enjoy the creativity of member artists showcased in the historic city hall complex.

View international and national exhibitions at the **Mattie Kelly Fine & Performing Arts Center** (850-729-6000; mattiekellyartscenter.org), 100 College Blvd, Niceville. The center houses two galleries: the Holzhauer and the McIlroy. Between the two sits *The Sculpture of the Seven Dancers*, an exquisite example of the creative talents of internationally famous sculptor Esther Wertheimer. Open Mon–Thu 9–4, Sun 1–4.

AQUARIUM ✔ The **Florida Gulfarium** (800-243-9046 or 800-247-8575; gulfarium.com), 1010 Miracle Strip Pkwy SE, Fort Walton Beach, is the oldest continuously operated marine show aquarium in the world. A true gem of the Emerald Coast, the facility has been teaching the general public about marine life since 1952, and in the process has undergone a great deal of growth and renovation, today featuring a 400,000-gallon dolphin tank and 60,000-gallon living sea aquarium. Despite several hurricanes that pummeled the coast, the dedicated staff and supporters have continued to keep the facility in great shape with extensive rebuilding. Visit places like Dune Lagoon, which has a large variety of marine fowl, or Fort Gator, where you'll see a pair of American alligators; compare seals and sea lions at the Seal and Sea Lion Rookery; watch the unique eating habits of lemon and nurse sharks; and enjoy colorful tropical birds and unique tropical penguins, which are native to near-equatorial regions in South America. You'll keep cool under the comfortably shaded exhibits and from occasional splashes from playful dolphins. Open daily 9–4, last admission at 2; $20 adults, $18 age 55 and over, $12 age 4–11.

HISTORIC SITES

Crestview
Built in 1947, the **Fox Theatre**, 382 Main St, premiered the movie *12 O'Clock High*, filmed in and around the area with Gregory Peck. It is presently undergoing restoration.

DeFuniak Springs
The city of **DeFuniak Springs** boats more than 250 buildings on the National Register of Historic Places, most clustered around circular Lake DeFuniak. They are privately owned but can be enjoyed from Circle Drive or the sidewalk on a walking tour (see *Walking Tours*). You'll find the **DeFuniak Springs Historic District** roughly bounded by Nelson and Park avenues and 2nd and 12th streets.

The 1890 **St. Agatha's Episcopal Church**, with its beautiful stained-glass windows, is the oldest church building in the city.

Several notable homes include **The Verandas**, 262 Circle Dr, a 1904 "steamboat"-style folk Victorian with wraparound porches; the **Dream Cottage**, 404 Circle Dr, built in 1888 for poet Wallace Bruce, former U.S. consul to Scotland; and the turreted **Thomas House**, 188 Circle Dr, an elaborately decorated 1895 three-story Queen Anne.

Florida's oldest continually operating library, the **Walton-DeFuniak Library**, 3 Circle Dr, opened in 1887. It has many rare books as well as a medieval armor collection.

Built in 1909, the **Chautauqua Hall of Brotherhood**, 95 Circle Dr, remains an imposing structure along Lake DeFuniak. Seating more than 4,000, it attracted visitors for its broad slate of cultural programs, which were discontinued during the Great Depression. In 1976 and again in 1993, local citizens revived the Chautauqua tradition (see *Special Events*), and this hall is once more used for major events.

Fort Walton Beach

Inside the **Heritage Park and Cultural Center** (850-833-9595; friends ofthemuseums.org), 139 Miracle Strip Pkwy SE, you'll find several historic sites of note for the region, most significantly the **Indian Temple Mound** (see *Archaeological Site*). The 1912 **Camp Walton School House** was in use until 1936 and is now restored, fully furnished with desks, chairs, and chalkboards of the period, even a dunce cap! The **Garnier Post Office & Civil War Museum** is a

ESTABLISHED IN 1886, DEFUNIAK SPRINGS LIBRARY IS FLORIDA'S OLDEST CONTINUOUSLY OPERATING PUBLIC LIBRARY

BUILT IN 1909, CHAUTAUQUA HALL WAS THE CULTURAL CENTER FOR FLORIDA'S CHAUTAUQUA MOVEMENT

restored 1918 post office with Civil War exhibits. These two smaller sites are open Mon–Sat 1–3; fee.

Point Washington

Tour the antebellum **Wesley House** and gardens at Eden Gardens State Park (see *Garden*). The seven-bedroom mansion, built in 1898, showcases different time periods, cultures, and the second-largest collection of Louis XVI furniture in the United States. Guided tours through the home begin on the hour, Thu–Mon 10–3, and are an additional fee above park admission.

MEMORIALS Although many North Florida towns have monuments to honor their Confederate soldiers, the **Confederate Monument** at the Walton County Courthouse in DeFuniak Springs was the first such memorial in the state, installed in 1871.

MUSEUMS The Baker Block Museum (850-537-5714; bakerblockmuseum .org), 1307 Georgia Ave (corner of FL 189 and CR 189), Baker, provides a pictorial history of rural Okaloosa County's cotton and lumber heritage with a dramatic mural; inside, browse through artifacts and archives, including extensive genealogical records. Historic farm buildings brought in from their original rural settings surround the museum. Open Tue–Fri 10–3:30 and third Sat of the month. Free; donations appreciated.

AIR FORCE ARMAMENT MUSEUM

(850-882-4062, afarmamentmuseum.com), 100 Museum Dr, Eglin Air Force Base. A century's worth of aviation warfare history is on display here. You'll find an impressive selection of U.S. aircraft and weaponry, along with similar items from around the world. Outside, walk or drive on a tour past two dozen aircraft, including a SR-71A Blackbird and a Soviet MIG-21. Inside the museum you can walk around carefully restored planes representing several war periods, such as the P-51 Mustang and F-105 Thunderchief. The history of Eglin AFB is shown throughout the day in a 32-minute movie. Don't miss the balcony exhibits; at one point you'll step inside the Airborne Battlefield Command Control Center (ABCCC) for a rare view of the high-tech, automated facility. On a side wall, an exquisite watercolor by Val Williamson was created in memory of the crew of the AC-130H Spectre gunship lost in action during Desert Storm on January 31, 1991. The Shipman Model Collection, showcasing more than 105 1:72 scale model planes, was painstakingly and accurately detailed by Major Ernest Shipman. A fighter pilot, Major Shipman was a POW from 1944 to 1945 in Germany's Luftwaffe Prison Camp. His dedication to this project has spanned nearly two decades. In the gift shop you can purchase a wide variety of model planes to take home and assemble yourself. Open Mon–Sat 9:30–4:30; donations welcome.

⌀ For rainy-day activities, head to the **Emerald Coast Science Center** (850-664-1261; ecscience.org), 139 Brooks St, Fort Walton Beach, where you can learn about tropical birds, Florida snakes, and more in the Critter Room or watch a model airplane fly through a wind tunnel in the Electricity Room. Lots of hands-on activities. Mon–Sat 9–6, Sun noon–4. Fee.

You'll find the **Walton County Heritage Museum** (850-951-2127 or 800-822-6877; waltoncountyheritage.org), 1140 Circle Dr, DeFuniak Springs, inside an 1882 L&N Railroad depot. The museum provides a great overview of the history of the area along with a vignette showcasing Allison's Grocery. The exhibit includes songs and memorabilia of Feenie Allison, the woman who owned it for 61 years, retiring in 1992 at the age of 89. You'll also enjoy the collection of general-store items from the 1930s and 1950s.

RAILROADIANA Along Crestview's Main Street, watch for the **railroad mural** fronting the railroad tracks that cross the street.

An L&N caboose sits on a siding adjoining the **DeFuniak Springs Depot**, where trains still fly through on an adjacent working track. Built in 1882, the depot was expanded in 1909 and once hosted more than 4,000 passengers a day.

WINERIES Learn about grape growing and winemaking at **Chautauqua Vine-yards** (850-892-5887; chautauquawinery.com), 364 Hugh Adams Rd, DeFuniak Springs, just off I-10. Planted in 1979 and opened in 1989, the winery has the largest vineyards in Florida and has won more than 140 awards internationally for its vintages. One of their specialties is a barrel-aged port. Take the tour and enjoy the tasting, and then browse their gift shop for goodies like grapeseed cooking oil, made right on the premises. Harvesttime is late Aug through early Sept, but the shop and tasting room are open year-round.

The master winemakers at the unique **Destin Winery** (850-654-0533; destin winery.com), 36150 Emerald Coast Pkwy, Destin, take tropical fruits and marry them to unusual ingredients with award-winning expertise. Sample a unique wine, maybe the Chardonnay-like 40 Karat, made with Florida carrots, the refreshing Category 5 Florida sangria, or the distinctive Cocoa Beach, which marries choco-late with Florida orange juice. Located 1 mile east of Destin Commons (see *Selective Shopping*) in the City Market Shopping Plaza; open Mon–Sat 10–6.

✳ To Do

BICYCLING The **Eastern Lake Bike/Hike Trail** in Point Washington State Forest (see *Wild Places*) offers up to 10 miles of doubletrack riding through natural areas accessed via Grayton Beach State Park; the trailhead is on CR 395 (see *Beaches*).

The **Timberlake Mountain Bike Trail System** (850-882-4164; eglin.af.mil), 107 FL 85 N, Niceville, is located in the Eglin Air Force Base Recreation Area (see *Wild Places*), where you can travel through 21 miles of narrow rolling trails to ele-vations up to 50 feet. Before using the trail, you must stop by the Eglin Natural Resources office to get a permit.

BIRDING ⌀ ♿ Little **Laird Park** [30.50162, -86.145784] just west of downtown Freeport along FL 20, is a pretty spot for a picnic lunch and a bit of birding along boardwalks above a clear, shallow creek. Walk the nature trail in **Eden Gardens State Park** (see *Garden*) to slip within sight of herons and egrets along the bayou. ⚓ ♿ **Turkey Creek Park** (see *Tubing*) is another pleasant boardwalk along a winding waterway, an excellent spot for songbirds.

DIVING In Ponce de Leon, spring diving awaits. At Vortex Spring (see *Dive Resort*), diving classes and certifications are offered at all levels, from PADI to cavern. The 25-million-gallon spring is a beautiful place for open-water divers to explore. If you're cavern-certified, you can go deep to see the spring basin 50 feet down, lit well through the crystalline water. Gear rentals are available, and off-site excursions to other springs are offered. Non-diving visitors are welcome to snorkel the spring and lengthy spring run. Open 7–dusk daily except Christmas.

ECOTOURS ⚓ Family fun can be found on the glass-bottomed boat at **Boogies** (850-654-4497; boogieswatersports.com), 2 Harbor Blvd at the foot of Destin Bridge, Destin, which features dolphin encounters, bird feedings, and a narrated cruise ($29 adults, $16 ages 2–12). A new addition are Waverunner tours to follow the dolphins; $145 for up to three passengers, based on weight.

FAMILY ACTIVITIES ⚓ Part water, all adventure, **Big Kahuna's Adventure Park** (850-837-8319; bigkahunas.com), 1007 US 98 E, Destin, offers days of activities. The tropical setting touts the world's largest man-made waterfall, with clear water descending 250 feet. There's something for everyone, with high-adrenaline pipeline speed slides, spectacular splash fountains, a lazy river, and a pirate ship splash zone for the little ones. At the adventure side of the park you can race in Grand Prix go-carts, play mini golf on a tropically landscaped course, or try your skill on a wide variety of arcade games. One-day admission $56; water park only, $30–37.

⚓ You won't break your wallet at the original 1950s **Goofy Golf** (850-862-4922), 401 Eglin Pkwy NE, Fort Walton Beach, where mini golf is only a few bucks on a classic course.

⚓ At the **Track Recreation Family Fun Center** (850-654-5832; destintrack .com), 1125 US 98 E, Destin, you'll find thrill rides like the skyflyer and bungee jumping, along with mini golf, bumper cars, and go-carts. They even have mini go-carts for five-year-olds. At Kids Kountry, little ones will want to ride the Rio Grande Train and Red Baron Plane Ride over and over.

⚓ On rainy days, get a blast from the past while watching today's movies at the 1940s **Tringa's Theatre** (listed under Cinema Plus, 850-302-0129; cinemaplusinc .com), 174 Miracle Strip Pkwy SE, Fort Walton Beach. And dine on beer and pizza! Daily shows at 4:30 and 7; movie tickets $4; beer and pizza extra.

FISHING Captains Paul and Cathy Wagner of **Backcountry Outfitters** (850-654-5566) at Harborwalk Marina, Destin, will take you into the shallow flats to fish for speckled trout, redfish, and tarpon day or night on their four-, six-, or eight-hour charters.

Go bottom fishing for snapper, triggerfish, sea bass, flounder, and grouper aboard the ***American Spirit*** (850-837-1293) with Captain Jim Green.

Drop a line from the "ultimate fishing machine," the **Swoop** (850-337-8250; swooppartyboat.com), Harborwalk Marina, Destin. This 65-foot-long fishing boat, with air-conditioned cabin, takes up to 49 passengers for half- or full-day charters, $55 and up.

If bottom fishing is your game, Captain Jim Westbrook on the 85-foot **New Florida Girl** (850-837-1293; newfloridagirl.com) brings in the catch. They're docked behind AJ's (see *Eating Out*).

For those wanting a private deep-sea charter with only a few people, **Harbor-Walk Charters** (850-837-2343; harborwalkfishing.com), located at Harbor Walk, Destin, will match you with up to eight passengers for half-or full-day excursions. $100–300 per person, six to eight people on a boat.

GOLF You'll enjoy the scenery at Fred Couple's signature par-72, 18-hole golf course at **Kelly Plantation** (800-811-6757 or 850-650-7600; kellyplantation.com), US 98 just west of Mid Bay Bridge, covering a challenging, 7,099-yard course complete with satellite yardage system. At **Indian Bayou Golf Club** (850-837-6192; indianbayougolf.com), 1 Country Club Dr, tee off on the 18-hole par-72 course or play a quick game on the 9-hole, par-36 course.

HIKING Pick up an Annual Recreation Pass ($10) at the Jackson Guard Station, Eglin Air Force Base, to enjoy more nearly 50 miles of the **Florida Trail** (florida trail.org) complete from DeFuniak Springs at US 331 to Crestview at FL 85, with beautiful backcountry campsites set in old-growth forests.

Unusual scenery and salt breezes make for pleasant hikes at **Topsail Hill Preserve State Park** (see *Beaches*), where more than 11 miles of hiking along the Campbell Lake and Morris Lake trails leads you to hidden freshwater lakes behind the dune line. At **Grayton Beach State Park** (see *Beaches*), the nature trail loops through a variety of coastal habitats, while at **Eden Gardens State Park** (see *Garden*), a short trail leads you to a hidden bayou. The **Seven Runs Trail**, starting along FL 81 at Seven Runs Park, follows Seven Runs Creek for 7 miles to its confluence with the Choctawhatchee River. **Ponce de Leon Springs** (see *Springs*) offers an excellent short nature trail through lush hardwood river bluff habitat.

PADDLING Follow scenic **Holmes Creek** as it flows from Alabama to the Choctawhatchee River, edged by ancient cypresses. An easy 12-mile route runs from Cypress Springs (3 miles north of Vernon) to Live Oak landing off CR 284.

Go paddling with **The Kayak Experience** (850-837-1577 or 850-837-1579; kayak experience.com), 600 US 98 E, Destin, where you can rent a open kayak and launch right into the blue-green waters of Destin Harbor for fun in the surf. Then explore the calm waters of Choctawhatchee Bay. Rentals from two hours to all day include all safety equipment.

PARASAILING At **Sun Dogs Parasail** (850-259-1898; sundogsparasail.com), 1310 Miracle Strip Pkwy, Okaloosa Island, you can float effortlessly high—at the end of 1,200 feet of line!—above the Gulf or the bay on single, double, or triple parasails. Rent out a 24-foot pontoon boat or go on a guided dolphin excursion. Three-seater Waverunners are also available for rent. A second location is directly

ALONG THE GULF OF MEXICO AT TOPSAIL HILL

across from the Emerald Coast Convention & Visitors (see *Guidance*). **Boogies Watersports** (see *Ecotours*) also offers parasailing.

SCENIC DRIVES Take a drive along **Scenic CR 30A** for a great view of rare coastal dunes lakes, an ecosystem that only exists here and in Africa and Australia. When these freshwater lakes become too full, they naturally dump runoff into the ocean. At that time seawater seeps back into the lakes, creating a unique, biodiverse ecosystem. There are 17 dune lakes along this route, starting at the western end with Stalworth Lake, the focal point in Dune Allen. Oyster Lake, also in Dune Allen, once filled with oysters, is actually named for its oyster-like shape. At Deer Lake in Santa Rosa Beach, you'll discover rare pitcher plants. The highest point on the Gulf of Mexico in the United States is at Blue Mountain Beach at 62 feet above sea level. It is named for the beautiful, rare blue Gulf lupine.

SURFING/SAILBOARDING Located away from the Gulf in downtown Fort Walton Beach, **Liquid Surf & Sail** (888-818-9283 or 850-664-5731; liquidsurf andsail.com) is the tops for all your surfing and sailing needs for beginner or experienced water lovers. Lessons by qualified instructions will get you up surfing, sailing, or kiteboarding in no time. Rentals by the half or full day: windsurfers, foam and glass surfboards, sit-on-top kayaks, and Hobie Mirage pedal kayaks.

TUBING ✐ Bring-your-own-tube family fun awaits at **Turkey Creek Park** (850-729-4062; cityofniceville.org/turkey.html), 340 John Sims Pkwy W, Niceville, where during daylight hours you can walk the ¾-mile boardwalk out to any of several launch points and float down the chilly, clear stream to the final take-out. Swimming, snorkeling, and paddling are part of the fun, too, and it's a pleasant, breezy walk on a warm day. Open from 6:30 AM; closes before sunset. Free.

WALKING TOURS Check in with the **Fort Walton Beach Main Street** (850-664-6246; fwbmainstreet.org), 12 SE Miracle Strip Pkwy, for information on architectural and archaeological sites on the **Fort Walton Historic Walking Tour**.

Take a nice leisurely stroll through **Grayton Beach**, one of the oldest towns on the Emerald Coast. Dating back the turn of the 20th century, the main street area is flush with quaint shops and eateries. Take note that driving on the beach is for residents only.

Pick up *A Walking Tour of Historic Circle Drive* at the visitors center in DeFuniak Springs (see *Guidance*) for an appreciation of the architecture found around Lake DeFuniak, and follow the mile-long route to enjoy the historic homes (see *Historic Sites*).

✽ Green Space

BEACHES The rare coastal flatwoods ecosystem in **Deer Lake State Park** (850-231-0337; floridastateparks.org/deerlake), 357 Main Park Rd, on CR 30A just east of Seagrove Beach in Santa Rosa Beach, provides many opportunities to view Gulf Coast lupine and stately magnolias. The dune crossovers at this park provide sweeping views of tall sand dunes.

& Reserve beach wheelchairs in advance at the Emerald Coast Convention & Visitors welcome center for a view of the Gulf from **Beasley Park**, 1550 Miracle Strip Pkwy (US 98), and **Fort Walton Beach**, located next door to the welcome center (see *Guidance*).

& **Grayton Beach State Park** (850-231-4210; floridastateparks.org/graytonbeach), 357 Main Park Rd, Santa Rosa Beach. With more than 2,000 acres of coastal dunes, coastal scrub, pine flatwoods, and beachfront, this is one of Northwest Florida's most beautiful state parks. Resembling a romantic scene from *Lord of the Rings*, it is a great place for hiking, with a nature trail winding through dunes and pines to end up along a scenic stretch of beach. Canoeists and kayakers find this lake especially appealing, and the campground (see *Camping & Cabins*) offers access to it all. Fee.

& ✑ **Henderson Beach State Park** (850-837-7550; floridastateparks.org/henderson beach), 17000 Emerald Coast Pkwy, Destin, is a coastal oasis amid the sprawl of condos; you can get back to nature on more than a mile of scenic shoreline backed by coastal dunes topped with scrub vegetation. Fish for pompano, camp in the full-service campground, or walk the nature trails. A handful of beach wheelchairs are available on a first-come, first-served basis. Fee.

A favorite of locals, the quiet **James Lee County Park** (850-689-5772), 3510 Scenic Hwy 98, Destin, features 300 feet of waterfront along emerald-green seas. Free.

& ❦ ✑ **Topsail Hill Preserve State Park** (877-232-2478; floridastateparks.org /topsailhill), 7525 W CR 30A, Santa Rosa Beach. Explore rare coastal dune lake habitats along the Campbell Lake Nature Trail and the Morris Lake Nature Trail, or swim along more than 3 miles of beautiful beaches. The campground is a destination in itself (see *Camping*), with 156 sites near the ocean. Fee.

GARDEN ❦ ✑ & ✑ **Eden Gardens State Park** (850-231-4214; floridastate parks.org/edengardens), CR 395, Point Washington. A century ago this grand plantation belonged to the William Henry Wesley family. Tour the manor—which holds the second-largest collection of Louis XVI furnishings in the United States—by candlelight, picnic at the old mill, or come out and enjoy the fragrant camellia

THE ANTEBELLUM WESLEY HOUSE IS
DECORATED FOR CHRISTMAS AT EDEN
GARDENS STATE PARK

blooms each spring. Walk under a canopy of moss-draped oaks and pause for a moment by a tranquil reflection pool. Gardens surrounding the home include a rose garden, azalea garden, camellia garden, and a "hidden garden" in the forest. Note the unusual monkey puzzle trees near the ranger's office; they are native to Patagonia.

PARKS 🐾 🐾 **Fred Gannon Rocky Bayou State Park** (850-833-9144; floridastateparks.org/rockybayou), 4281 FL 20, Niceville. Scenic nature trails and great fishing on the tidal bayou draw visitors to this beautiful park on an arm of Choctawhatchee Bay; enjoy camping in one of their 42 spacious, shaded sites (see *Camping & Cabins*). Fee.

🐾 🐾 You'll love **The Landing Park**, 139 Brooks St SE, Fort Walton Beach, for quiet picnics after your visit at the Emerald Science Center. Enjoy the cool breeze from the Intracoastal while the kids play on jungle gyms under shady trees. In summer free movies are shown every Fri night.

SPRINGS Surrounded by the town that bears its name, **DeFuniak Springs** is a perfectly circular spring-fed lake more than 60 feet deep. Privately owned Vortex Spring (see *Dive Resort*) is surrounded by lush forests; fee.

South of I-10 off FL 81 and CR 181, **Morrison Springs** was purchased by the state in 2004 and turned over to Walton County to manage. The 161-acre county park is a destination for divers, with three major vents in the spring descending to 50 feet; cave diving extends 300 feet underground. For the less adventuresome, the clear water makes this second-magnitude spring pleasant for swimming and snorkeling as well. Fee.

Ponce de Leon Springs State Park (850-836-4281; floridastateparks.org/ponce deleonsprings), 2860 Ponce de Leon Springs Rd, Ponce de Leon. Chalky blue 68-degree water tempts swimmers in for a chilly dip in this first-magnitude spring, gushing forth 14 million gallons of water daily. Fish, picnic, or walk the nature trails through the lush hardwood forest. Fee.

WILD PLACES Established as the Choctawhatchee National Forest in 1909 by Theodore Roosevelt, **Eglin Air Force Base** encompasses 300 square miles between Crestview, DeFuniak Springs, Niceville, and Freeport, and offers public recreation along its fringes. Check with the Jackson Guard Natural Resources Facility (850-882-4164; eglin.af.mil) for permit information and a full roster of outdoor activities, from camping and hunting to backpacking and fishing, permitted on this military reserve.

Between Ebro and DeFuniak Springs, **Nokuse Plantation** (nokuse.org) is one of Florida's largest privately owned conservation efforts, part of a million-acre landscape-level conservation project creating a vast biodiversity corridor from Blackwater River State Forest (see the *Pensacola* chapter) to the Apalachicola River. Created for regional environmental education, the E. O. Wilson Biophilia Center opens occasionally for public events. You may explore the plantation, which is undergoing active restoration from former farms and pine plantations to longleaf pine forest, along a segment of the Florida Trail (see *What's Where*) stretching from FL 77 north of Bruce to US 331 south of DeFuniak Springs.

Point Washington State Forest (850-231-5800; fl-dof.com/state_forests/point _washington.html), 5865 E US 98, Santa Rosa Beach. Sea breezes filter through the pines in this state forest protecting a vast swath of southern Walton County; access the forest for nature study, biking, and hiking via the Eastern Lake Bike/Hike Trail. Fee.

✳ Lodging

BED & BREAKFASTS

DeFuniak Springs 32433

🍴 (𝗉) In the heart of downtown, the **Hotel DeFuniak** (850-892-4383; hoteldefuniak.com), 400 E Nelson Ave, dates back to 1920 and was painstakingly restored to its original glory in 1997, evoking the rich ambience of the Florida boom years, with 19th-century antique furnishings throughout. Centrally located for your exploration of the historic downtown and residential districts, it offers three large suites and seven standard railroad-hotel-sized rooms, each uniquely themed. A massage therapist on staff can see you in a private massage room, and there is WiFi throughout the building. Rates start at $89; a full breakfast is included with your stay.

Grayton Beach 32459

🍴 🐾 ✐ ♿ Off the beaten path, the **Hibiscus Coffee & Guesthouse** (850-231-2733; hibiscusflorida.com), 85 DeFuniak St, is a slice of Old Florida with a room for everyone ($120–365). Lovers will want to check into the Romance Room with king-sized bed and supersized Jacuzzi for two. In the Hibiscus Room, you'll find an antique clawfoot tub in the bathroom.

Those with special needs will feel right at home in the Big Easy cabin. Formerly the home's kitchen, the room is equipped with a small refrigerator, microwave, and coffeemaker. The Woodpecker Cottage is a mini suite, which also has a small refrigerator and microwave. And unlike most other B&Bs, a crib or cot can be provided if you have a small child. Five of the rooms are child-friendly, and one is pet-friendly, too. A hot breakfast is included each morning 7:30–11:30, with the coffeehouse also open to general public. Check out the BE sign posted out front. Each day it has a different saying. The day I was there it said BE CHEERFUL.

Santa Rosa Beach 32459

🍴 ♿ (𝗉) The antebellum-style **Highlands House Bed & Breakfast** (850-267-0110; ahighlandshouse.com), 4193 W Scenic CR 30A, is in fact a modern home with classic flourishes. It's situated west of Destin directly off the sugar-sand beach. It's private and peaceful, and you'll enjoy sitting on the porch overlooking the beautifully landscaped lawn, sand dunes, and emerald-green water. Their healthful breakfast includes warm home-cooked breads, and since there are only seven bedrooms, tranquility is assured. Queen- and king-sized beds in most rooms; one room has two double beds, $150–250. Seaside weddings are their specialty.

Seagrove Beach 32459
The cheerfully decorated **Sugar Beach Inn** (850-231-1577; sugar beachinn.com), 3501 E Scenic CR 30A, is only a short walk from the picturesque town of Seaside. Its spacious rooms have queen and king brass canopied and poster beds; some offer Jacuzzi and fireplace ($169–249).

HOTELS & MOTELS

Destin 32541
Two chain accommodations in Destin stand out due to their extra friendliness and close proximity to the beach and golf courses. (ᵗᵖ) & **Country Inn & Suites** (850-650-9191 or 800-456-4000; countryinns.com), 4415 Commons Drive E, is the best choice for those wanting to be near the greens at Kelly Plantation Golf Course (see *Golf*). The home-style motel offers both guest rooms and suites with a wet bar and mini fridge ($89 and up). High-speed Internet access is free, so you can plan your activities around town or to destinations beyond.

(ᵗᵖ) & ✎ At the **Comfort Inn Destin** (850-654-8611; comfortinn.com), 19001 Emerald Coast Pkwy, Henderson Beach State Park (see *Beaches*) is located directly across the street. Or sit out by the pool where palm trees sway in warm Gulf breezes. Enjoy the complimentary breakfast in the bright and cheery breakfast room. Standard rooms have two queen beds; king and family suites also available ($89 and up).

CONDO RESORTS ✎ Centrally
located between Pensacola and Panama City, the resort destination **Sandestin**

Golf and Beach Resort (877-622-1038 or 850-267-8000; sandestin.com), 9300 Emerald Coast Pkwy W, is only 8 miles east of downtown Destin. Pools, lakes, beaches, golf, tennis, shopping, and dining can all be found within the boundaries of the resort. Kids will enjoy parks and playgrounds throughout the property, with the three-and-a-half-story Sooper waterslide and the beachside rock-climbing wall always favorites. Choose from several types of accommodations grouped in five unique "neighborhoods": beachside condos, villas overlooking a picturesque lake, cottage-style homes just off the fairways, and penthouse suites overlooking the Gulf and Choctawhatchee Bay; one will surely suit your taste and budget ($125–900). On the bay side, the Grand is their signature luxury hotel with hotel rooms and condos decorated in the Old South style. Shoppers will want to be near the restaurants and boutiques in the village of Baytowne Wharf. Nature lovers can nestle in to quiet cottages overlooking the saltwater marshes of the 5-acre Jolee

SANDESTIN RESORT IS A LARGE COMPLEX IN DESTIN WITH BOTH HOTEL AND CONDO ACCOMMODATIONS

Island Nature Park. Gulf-side, you'll find Mediterranean-inspired townhomes and villas in a quaint neighborhood setting or towering condos overlooking the beach. A free trolley links the resorts, beaches, and village shopping.

Situated directly on the Gulf, all condo accommodations face the ocean at the **Inn at Crystal Beach** (800-336-9669 or 850-650-7000; destinresorts.com), 2996 US 98. While each room is decorated by individual owners, all decor is governed by strict guidelines. You'll find each unit uniquely decorated, typically with a tropical theme. The resort website allows you to virtually tour most rooms, so you'll know what to expect before you get there. And the 24-hour front desk ensures a pleasant greeting if you're arriving late. My favorite unit is the tastefully decorated 1607, with a South Seas Island theme. The owner of this three-bedroom condo has artistic talent; many walls are covered in stylish murals and accents complementing the furnishings. Another fine unit is 1410, furnished in white wicker throughout. The floor-to-ceiling mirrored walls in the Florida-themed two-bedroom unit

makes the already spacious abode seem even larger. You'll find that all units have washers and dryers along with Jacuzzis in most master suites. For resort-quality amenities, what better way to exercise than by looking out over the Gulf from the state-of-the-art fitness center, or taking a dip in the heated pool? Condos have two to six bedrooms, and rates range seasonally $191–970 daily or $1,000–6,500 per week. Expect a housekeeping fee in addition to the regular room taxes. All reservations are booked through Dale E. Peterson Vacation Resorts, not through the property.

VACATION RENTALS Ocean Reef Resort Properties (850-837-3935; oceanreefresorts.com) and **Dale E. Peterson Vacation Resorts** (800-336-9669; destinresorts.com) both offer furnished cottages, beach homes, condos, townhomes, luxury homes, and resorts by the day, week, or month. One of the largest suppliers of fully furnished homes, the folks at **Resort-Quest** (800-GO RELAX; resortquest .com) can select which home will be right for you—from condos in resort-style settings to portfolio homes with private pools. Rent by the day, week, or month.

For all vacation rentals and condo resorts, quality of accommodations can vary widely from unit to unit. Be aware that cleaning and maintenance fees may be added atop your room fee. Ask before booking.

CAMPING & CABINS

DeFuniak Springs 32433
🐾 ♂ (ᵗ⁰) **Sunset King Lake RV Resort** (850-892-7229 or 800-774-5454; sunsetking.com), 366 Paradise Island Dr, with direct access to King Lake, is a favorite of folks seeking big bass from their boat. Campsites are set

AT SANDESTIN RESORT, SHOPS ARE CLUSTERED AROUND BAYTOWNE WHARF

THE CAMPGROUND AT ROCKY BAYOU STATE PARK IS ONE OF FLORIDA'S FINEST

in a forested area, with all hookups (including cable) and pull-through sites available ($36). Rental units include beautiful log cabins and cottages, fully furnished, for $80 (two-night minimum for weekends). Discounts for military, Good Sam, and Coast to Coast members. Weekly and monthly rates available. Enjoy the clubhouse with pool and WiFi, playground, game room, and general store.

Niceville 32578

✎ My favorite Florida State Park campground (800-326-3521; florida stateparks.reserveamerica.com) is at **Fred Gannon Rocky Bayou State Park** (see *Parks*), which balances amenities, settings, and distances in a perfect mix. A cool breeze off the bayou combines with the low sand live oak canopy to keep the 42 well-shaded campsites naturally pleasant. Walk in either direction, and you'll find trails. Fish right off the beach, or take the kids over to the playground on the bluffs. Add a camp chair and a good book to relax and enjoy.

Santa Rosa Beach 32459

✎ & ↬ At **Grayton Beach State Park** (see *Beaches*), camp with a sea breeze in the 37-site campground (800-326-3521; floridastateparks .reserveamerica.com) or rent one of 30 fully furnished cabins. Either way, you'll have early access to sunrise watching over the dune lakes.

✎ & ↬ **Topsail Hill Preserve State Park** (see *Beaches*) offers one of the top RV campgrounds in the nation— the Gregory E. Moore RV Campground (800-326-3521; floridastate parks.reserveamerica.com) off CR 30A. The 156 sites have 30- or 50-amp electric, water, sewer, and cable, and are set in a diminutive coastal scrub forest and pine flatwoods. Amenities include a heated swimming pool, shuffleboard, and private tram access to the beach. If you don't have a big rig, consider renting one of their modern bungalows, each with living room, dining room, bedroom, screened porch, and carport (by week or month).

DIVE RESORT

Ponce de Leon 32455

Vortex Spring (850-836-4979; vortex spring.com), 1517 Vortex Spring Ln, opened in 1972, is the largest privately owned diving facility in Florida, owned and operated by active divers. The complex includes the 68-degree spring, a campground, and three lodges. The Pinewood Lodge has male and female dorms, each with 26 bunk beds, and eight four-person rooms ($64 per room) upstairs with private bath and television. Otter Creek Lodge offers six kitchenettes ($96) and a variety of large rooms sleeping up to six, with private baths. The Grandview Lodge has rooms with queen beds, full kitchens, and dive gear lockdown cages, $104–145. All three lodges are nestled in lush woods and require that you bring your own linens (sleeping bag or sheets, pillow, towels). There are also camping cabins with no plumbing (campground bathhouse nearby), $50–70, and campsites for tents and RVs, $20–27.

✳ Where to Eat

DINING OUT

Destin

🍴 A 12-foot giraffe greets you at the door at **Harry T's** (850-654-4800; harryts.com), 46 Harbor Blvd, a souvenir from his circus days. Harry loves to make kids laugh, so every Tuesday is Kids Night, with lots of clowns and balloons. But don't be misled: Harry also has grown-up food, like grouper beurre blanc—a char-grilled grouper topped with shrimp, crabmeat, and creamy beurre blanc sauce—along with filet mignon kebabs and classic seafood steamers. Entrées $17–49. Open for lunch, dinner, and Sun brunch.

At the **Lucky Snapper Grill & Bar** (850-654-0900; luckysnapper.com), 76 US 98 E, go ahead and spoil your appetite with one of their signature drinks, such as the Snapper Sensation, which blends tropical rum with cool and creamy raspberry ice cream. The open-air restaurant caters to an upscale crowd without all the stuffiness. It overlooks Destin Harbor, and you'll sit inside at comfortable wood-grained booths or high-top tables and stools on the deck, watching dolphins swim by. For hungry appetites, dig into the Crystal Beach grouper, a house favorite, stuffed full of crabmeat and blanketed with a creamy white cheese sauce. If you can't decide between sea and shore, order it with a half rack of ribs smothered in honey-glaze barbecue sauce for a few dollars more. Open daily 11–10; entrées $18–38.

A must-stop for any Irish gal, the lively Irish folk music and traditional fare at **McGuire's Irish Pub and Brewery** (850-654-0567; mcguiresirishpub.com), 33 US 98, will keep you going till after midnight. You'll find healthy portions of traditional Irish pub fare along with a wide selection of seafood, steaks, and chops ($10–27); the senate bean soup is still only 18¢. Sing-alongs are encouraged, and at times mandated. Daily 11–11; light fare served until 1:30 AM.

Fort Walton Beach

🐾 Enjoy great gumbo in a historical 1910 Florida home at **Magnolia Grill** (850-302-0266; magnoliagrillfwb.com), 157 Brooks St. The house was one of many of the period that were mail-ordered and shipped by train in a complete kit ready for assembly, bricks for the chimneys and cupboards for the kitchen. The home is still in pristine vintage condition with many original components, such as the brick fireplace and left and right bookcases, windows that still open with ropes and pulleys, and cupboards still containing the wavy glass typical of that period. You'll also want to take note of the board marked DR. G. G. FRENCH, CAMP WALTON, FLA., which was the mailing label for the assembly kit. The fine-dining eatery features dishes such as Steak Magnolia, served with green peppercorn and mushroom sauce, and blackened amberjack, a local fish, served with rice on a crawfish étouffée ($12–32). You'll also find more than a dozen Italian entrées on the menu. Lunch 11–2 weekdays; dinner Mon–Thu 5–8, Fri and Sat 5–9.

🐾 Established in 1913, **Staff's** (850-243-3482; staffrestaurant.com), 24 Miracle Strip Pkwy SE, is a true Florida treasure, the second-oldest continually operating restaurant in Florida. Founder "Pop" Staff was one of the

SEAFOOD DINNER AT STAFF'S, FORT WALTON BEACH

top 20 restaurants. Founded by a couple of surfing buddies, it's now the top local hangout in the area. The views from the rooftop bar are phenomenal, but the casual atmosphere and top-notch food seal the deal. Shrimp and grits, Bud and Alley's crabcakes with candied pecans, and grilled fish of the day served with field peas and succotash ($8–15) make the lunch menu pop. Dinner is meant to be savored with the sunset, featuring entrées like seared diver scallops with creamy grits and sugar snap peas, and free-range chicken breast with truffled risotto and roasted pearl onions ($25–33). Looking for something more laid-back? Check out their Taco Bar and Pizza Bar, extensions of the restaurant complex that are lighter on the wallet and sure to please the picky eaters in your family.

EATING OUT

Bruce

☙ **Bruce Café** (850-835-2946), corner of FL 20 and FL 81. Generals and lumberjacks rub elbows at this great family café, where Lillie Mae serves up inexpensive specials like beef tips, fried chicken, and barbecued pork with three country-style veggies on the side. Seat yourself and look over the menu board, which includes burgers and a pork chop sandwich. Save room for one of the 10 choices of cakes and pies! Open 6 AM–7 PM; closed Sun and Mon.

Crestview

A 1950s-style lunch counter with a loyal following, **Desi's Restaurant** (850-682-5555), 197 N Main St, offers up a buffet laden with southern favorites like roast chicken, ribs, fried fish, cheese grits, greens, and three kinds of peas—black-eyed, zipper, and field, all for $8 daily. Open for lunch only until 2.

area's first pioneers, supplying the Gulfview Hotel with fresh-caught fish and vegetables from his family garden. The tradition continues, with family members serving up fish purchased right off the boat, from amberjack to triggerfish; soft-shell crabs, scamp, and shrimp several ways. Meat eaters will appreciate six choices of fine steaks, and the soups are savory. All entrées ($16–44) include salad, fresh-baked wheat bread, German potato salad, corn on the cob, new potatoes, and dessert. Most of the recipes have been handed down from generation to generation, and that's something you rarely encounter these days. Their seafood-okra gumbo recipe is a family secret, and the crabmeat-stuffed green chiles will get your mouth warmed up for the main dish. While you can order a fine steak or a chicken breast, why bother—the heart of this restaurant's business is great seafood, served your way, broiled or fried. Open for dinner daily at 5.

Seaside

☙ The oldest restaurant in this newish town, **Bud and Alleys** (850-231-5900; budandalleys.com), 2236 CR 30A E, consistently rates as one of Florida's

(((ɯ))) A pretty downtown bistro, **Not Just Cakes** (850-398-6650; notjustcakes bakery.com), 290 N Main St, is where the stacks of thin-sliced. fresh-sliced deli meat look as appealing as the creative cookies, cakes, and pastries. Love pancakes? So do they. Order them in blueberry, pecan, banana, chocolate chip, peanut butter, strawberry, or cherry. Mon–Fri 7–5, Sat 8–3.

DeFuniak Springs

A 1916 landmark in the historic downtown district, **Busy Bee Café** (850-951-2233; busybeecafe.net), 35 S 7th St, offers an array of entrées sure to please any palate, from grouper amandine to a grilled New York strip smothered in grilled onions, mushrooms, and melted provolone. Open for lunch (10:30–2:30) Tue–Sat and dinner (5–9) Fri and Sat.

🐾 🐾 Since 1947, tiny **H&M Hot Dog** (850-892-9100), 43 S 9th St, has been a place where you can walk right up to the lunch counter window and place your order. The hot dogs and hamburgers are cooked to order, and the sides are carefully handmade, with the Bodiford family carrying on the tradition that Harley & Margaret Broxson started. Enjoy your meal at the picnic table underneath the adjacent arbor. Open Mon–Fri 9–5:30, Sat 10–4.

After a tiring day hiking and four-wheeling, I adjourned with friends to 🐾 **McLain's Family Steakhouse** (850-892-2402), 622 Hugh Adams Rd, just north of I-10. You can order from the menu or take the buffet, and given the wide range of foods you'll find on it—good traditional southern foods, of course—the buffet is your best bet.

You'll find homespun goodness at **Murray's Café** (850-951-9941), 660 Baldwin Ave, where a mile-high cake turned my head and lured me in. I started off with whisper-thin fried green tomatoes, some of the finest I've ever had, and delighted in my fresh fried grouper, green beans cooked southern-style, and perfect sweet tea. Yum! Their adjacent gift shop carries china and whimsical gifts, baked goods, gourmet cookies, and ice cream.

BOATING IN DESTIN

VISIT FLORIDA

Destin

Shucking fresh oysters since 1984, **AJ's Restaurant & Bimini Bar** (850-837-1913; ajs-destin.com), 116 US 98 E, is the place to go for great food, beer, and fun. Try the baked Oyster AJ made with fresh jalapeños, Monterey Jack, and bacon. Sensational seafood entrées are broiled, baked, and fried. The broiled seafood platter always includes oysters. The fresh-air restaurant also serves food for landlubbers. And for fun, AJ's charter fleet will take you on their Sea Blaster at speeds up to 55 mph. If fishing is your game, their charter fleet will help you land coastal favorites, such as grouper, amberjack, and wahoo.

Locals travel hours for **Ali's Ciao Bella Pizza** (850-654-9815), 29 US 98 E, with the #10, Ortolana Pizza, a favorite choice. The crunchy thin-crust pizza allows you to really enjoy all the toppings. The menu has more than 70 items, so you'll want to go back again and again, but you'll want to put the Toscana salad, chicken cacciatore sandwich, and portobello mushroom ravioli at the top of your list. Open daily 11–9:30.

❦ **Another Broken Egg** (850-650-0499; anotherbrokenegg.com), 104 US 98 E, delights with its ambience of pure country comfort. You wouldn't expect gourmet items such as the Pontchartrain, an open-faced croissant covered with scrambled eggs, broccoli, tomatoes, mild green chiles, onions, and melted Jack cheese. Dainty appetites will want order the yogurt, fruit 'n' granola parfait—strawberries, bananas, kiwi, and granola layered between low-fat vanilla and strawberry yogurts, and served with muffins—or the house specialty, Blackberry Grits. The presentation of each dish is worth admiring before you dig in. While the menu reads like a gourmet magazine,

you'll find the prices very reasonable. Burgers, salads, and sandwiches available during lunch hours. Get there early or plan to patiently wait in line. Open Tue–Sun 7–2; closed Mon.

❧ **The Candymaker** (888-654-6404 or 850-654-0833; thecandymaker.com), 757 US 98 E. The "Grouchy Old Candymaker," Tom Ehlke, isn't so grumpy after all. Once he decided there had to be a better saltwater taffy, he set his sights and shop up in Destin, and since 1992 he's been satisfying locals and tourists alike with not only his saltwater taffy but other confections as well. You'll find sumptuous delights like crunchy, rich, South Georgia–style pralines; creamy, buttery fudge; and chewy caramels. So you're never too far from the chocolate, he's got other locations in Sandestin (850-351-1986) and Mystic Port (850-534-0030).

Just 1 mile east of the Destin Bridge is the world-famous **Hog's Breath Café** (850-837-5991; hogsbreath.com), 541 US 98. Established in 1976, this is the original café to its porcine cousin in Key West. The saloon features live music, restaurant and raw bar, great beer, and even fishing charters. Open daily for lunch and dinner.

❧ For a cool treat on a hot summer day, or even a rainy day, **Shake's Frozen Custard** (850-269-1111; shakesfrozencustard.com), 1065 US 98 E (tucked a bit back from the roadway), is the place to be. Made fresh every hour, the smooth and creamy frozen concoction contains no fillers or preservatives and is never fluffed up with air. Any hey, it's 90 percent fat-free! The Pink Poodle dips up the creamy custard and smothers it with pineapples, bananas, and strawberries. The signature Shake's Bopper contains a monstrous three scoops of creamy frozen custard, caramel, and hot fudge. Open 10 AM–midnight during the summer and 11 AM–close during the winter months.

Fort Walton Beach

A great photo op can be found right at **Angler's Beachside Grill** (850-790-0260; anglersbeachside.com), 1030 Miracle Strip Pkwy SE, located next door to Florida Gulfarium and the Okaloosa Pier. Kids, who are always welcome here, can crawl through a partially submerged sand shark's belly and out through the mouth—definitely one for the scrapbooks. They offer cool drinks, burgers, sandwiches, and baskets, and you'll want to try the Anglers Elizabeth, a dish made with mahimahi with a shrimp, crabmeat, and pine nut topping, entrées $10 and up.

Grayton Beach

❦ At **Picolo's & The Red Bar** (850-231-1008; theredbar.com), 70 Holz Ave, capture the pre-condo past of this coastline when this strip was all about surfing, fishing, and hanging out at the beach. Listen to live music—the Red Bar Jazz Band—while lounging in the red velvet living room. This comfy and eclectic restaurant serves some of the best burgers around along with treats like baked eggplant, shrimp and crawfish, smoked salmon salad, and Belgian waffles, $8–18. Cash only, open daily for lunch and dinner.

Ponce de Leon

Kay's Restaurant (850-836-4008), 2972 N FL 81 is a popular stop for breakfast just south of I-10, where you can pick up the breakfast special for under $4. She serves a lunch buffet and big burgers, too, country cooking at reasonable prices. Open Sun–Wed 6–2, extended hours Thu–Sat for dinner.

Santa Rosa Beach

✎ Soak up the local buzz at **Miss Lucille's Gossip Parlor** (850-267-2522; thegossipparlor.com), 45 Town Center Loop in Gulf Place. This artsy boutique serves great desserts, ice cream, and coffee.

✳ Entertainment

You'll enjoy Broadway shows at the two-tiered, 1,650-seat Mainstage Theater at the **Mattie Kelly Fine & Performing Arts Center** at Northwest Florida State College (mattiekellyartscenter.org), 100 College Blvd, Niceville. Take particular note of the walls in the lobby, which are covered with fossilized Mexican limestone. The deep theater seating ensures that everyone is within 100 feet of the stage. For smaller performances on the square, 195-seat Sprint Theater offers options—show seating on two or three sides of the theater or an intimate theater in the round. Outside, the OWC Amphitheater houses up to 4,000 on sloping grounds for concerts and shows.

✳ Selective Shopping

Crestview

Downtown Crestview is a charming place to browse, with a smattering of boutiques, antiques, and resale shops among the restaurants on historic Main Street. I couldn't help but notice the full-sized traffic light in the window of **Pappy T's Antique Uniques & Collectibles** (850-689-2323), a small shop stuffed with jewelry, gifts, and collectibles, including dolls, fine china, artwork, glassware, kitchen items, and home decor. Looking like it plopped down here from Durango, **Ron's Antiques** (850-305-2441), 213 N Main St, draws you in with its Wild West facade to examine the wares, from beaded lamps and large advertising signs to a vintage stove, cuckoo clocks, and a watch repair counter.

Put your fancy on at the **Jewelry Garden Boutique** (850-689-7676), 267

Main St, where there's unique jewelry, interesting gifts, and formal wear for the next big shindig.

Walk the aisles at **Emerald Coast Book Haven** (850-682-1956; ecbooks .com), 801 W James Lee Blvd (US 90), and you're bound to find something you're looking for. With more than 50,000 books (mostly used, some new) in stock, it's quite the collection!

DeFuniak Springs

The Book Store (850-892-3119), 640 6th Ave, carries a large selection of used books, with trades welcome. Look for new titles near the front, and freebie paperbacks on the bench outside. Open Mon–Sat 10–5.

Don't let the bygones be at **Buy Gones Antiques** (850-520-4641), 5315 US 331, a delightful shop with country primitives and furnishings from around the world. Open Wed–Sun 10–5.

The **Little Big Store** (850-892-6066), 35 S 8th St, is one of those places I can spend a long time browsing. With local books and postcards, old-fashioned country store candies and foods, country goodies and gifts, it's the one place in town you'll be sure to find something to take home for the kids.

Destin

There's much to uncover in **Abrams Destin Harbor Antique Mall** (850-650-9005), 37B Harbor Blvd, as it's packed with more than 12,000 square feet of dealer space. You'll spend hours browsing the tcotchkes and home decor items, and this is the place to look for antique fishing gear in the world's luckiest fishing village.

The shoe fits everyone but Cinderella at **Allen Edmonds Shoes** (850-654-4790; allenedmonds.com), 10406 US 98 E. The fine footwear establishment has sizes 5–18, widths AAA–EEE, but only for the men.

Designer home decor packs **Antiques on Holiday** (850-837-0488; antiques onholiday.com), 105 N Holiday Rd, a warehouse full of vintage direct-from-Europe elegance in 40 dealer booths.

The atmosphere for casual shopping at **Destin Commons** (850-337-8700; destincommons.com), 4300 Legendary Dr, will satisfy everyone in your family. The small-town "village" layout makes it easy to walk among a bevy of upscale shops, boutiques, galleries, and eateries. Kids will love to ride the mini train that winds its way through the town past the interactive fountain. Open daily.

Fudpucker Trading Company (850-654-4200; fudpuckers.com/dining .destin.loca.htm), 20001 Emerald Coast Pkwy, features "fudnominal" shopping and the world-famous Fudpucker merchandise. You'll also enjoy the eclectic mix of Clay Works pottery, Cow Parade cows, Maryhoonies, raku pottery, neon clocks, and kids' toys.

Pick up a CD by artist Nancy Veldman at **Magnolia House Lifestyle Store** (850-460-2005 or 888-272-3250; magnoliahouse.com), 600 Grand Boulevard, Suite M10 in the Shops of Grand Boulevard at Sandestin. This incredible, inspirational woman can be found playing selections of her own music on a white baby grand piano. In her shop you'll find a phenomenal selection of her watercolor art among that of other local artists, custom-designed Diane Katzman jewelry, and unique gifts. A fine selection of inspirational books, her writings on beauty, insight, and inspiration will open your awareness of provide a sense of purpose.

Potagers Gardens & Verandas (850-269-3211; potagers.net), 9755 W Emerald Coast Pkwy, is a family business with a classy display of French and Italian pottery, European linens and toiletries, garden elements, and a few select antiques.

Didn't catch the big one? Or can't take the rolling seas? Just want to cook your own? Then you'll want to stop by **Sextons Seafood** (850-837-3040), 601 US 98 E, Destin, for the freshest catch of the day. Open daily 8–7.

To visit the **Shoppes of Baytowne Wharf** (850-267-8000; baytownewharf .com), 9300 Emerald Coast Pkwy, you'll first need to pass through the Sandestin Resort guard gate. Tell them you are heading to Baytowne Wharf. Intermingled with restaurants that cater to folks staying at the resort, the boutiques are centered on a lagoon off the bay and offer a variety of interesting themes, from children's toys to seashells, upscale pet supplies, and resort wear.

At **Silver Sands Factory Stores** (850-654-9771; silversandsoutlet.com), 10562 Emerald Coast Pkwy, you'll find more than 100 designer-name stores in one of Florida's largest designer outlet complexes.

Wyland Paradise Gallery at Harborwalk (850-650-1800; wylandgalleries .com), 51 US 98 E, features limited-edition prints, sculptures, jewelry, and collectibles from the famous marine artist who painted his Whaling Wall #88 in Destin.

Fort Walton Beach
The historic downtown district is noted for its Antique Row, where you'll find treasures galore; most shops are closed Sun.

Grab some booty at the **Buccaneer Gift Shop** (850-244-5002; buccaneer giftshop.com), 152 Miracle Strip Pkwy, where Betty Boop lives and advertising collectibles are fun to peruse.

De'France Indoor Fleamarket Antiques & Collectibles (850-314-7500), 244 SE Eglin Pkwy, isn't fancy,

but it's busy with furnishings and home decor that graced many a home during my childhood, and has a devout following for its ever-changing stock.

Childhood toys and classic advertising is all a part of the mix at the busy **Fort Walton Beach Flea Market** (850-301-3729), 125 SE Eglin Pkwy SE. Don't let the name fool you; this place is like flea markets were when I was a kid, full of great discoveries including collectible coins, vintage clothing, and 45 rpm records.

At **Marilyn & Company Antique Mall** (850-243-4991), 151 SE Eglin Pkwy, dig through stacks of books or look for fine glassware atop the many antique furnishings.

Classy collectibles await at **Southern Belle Antiques** (850-243-0878; southernbelleantiques.com), 119 Perry Ave (one block off the Row), including fine armoires, quilt racks, dining room sets, and dressers of the highest-quality craftsmanship. Period antique furniture is the cornerstone of this multi-dealer business, but they also delve into vintage linens, silver, and 18th-century porcelain.

✐ For the kids, check out **Hugs & Hissyfits** (850-796-4847; hugsandhissy fits.com), 184-2 Miracle Strip Pkwy. It's loaded with cute little girls' dresses. The sweet **Little Bo Feet Boutique** (850-314-7400), 184 Miracle Strip Pkwy, has unique shoes and accessories for kids.

Next door to the Indian Temple Mound Museum is **One Feather** (850-243-9807), 159 Miracle Strip Pkwy SE, an authentic Native American shop housing an impressive selection of authentic Native American goods from 40 different tribes. Ask to see the tiny kachina dolls. The removable headdress reveals a carefully painted face about the size of a grain of sand. Open Tue–Sat 10–7.

Grayton Beach

Phil Kiser, who's earned accolades as the Walton County Artist of the Year, displays his dimensional mosaics created using recycled materials, including vintage plates and glass, at **Big Mama's Hula Girl Gallery** (850-231-6201; bigmamashulagirlgallery.com), 1300B CR 283 S. Laura Holthoff's colorful folk art is also worth close inspection. Exhibiting a wide range of local creative talent, this eclectic gallery is one of the best in the state.

At the **Shops of Grayton** at 26 Logan Ln (2 blocks north of CR 30A), you'll find home decor, art, antiques, and unique clothing in eight colorful cottages, plus a "dog wall" with paintings of local pooches. While walking around the old town, note the buildings on Hotz Ave, which date back to the early 1900s. Here you'll find the eclectic home and garden store, **Zoo Gallery** (850-231-0777; thezoogallery.com), 89 Hotz Ave, founded in 1979 to showcase contemporary American arts and crafts.

Ponce de Leon

A whimsical little shop, **Flutes & Vegetables** (850-836-9996), 2831 N FL 81, has everything from fresh produce and local honey to bamboo poles, natural stone for landscaping, handmade soaps, rock albums, and of course bamboo flutes. Closed Sun–Mon.

Old Town Trading Post (850-865-0810), 2988 FL 81, welcomes you to browse its selection of western-themed collectibles, including carved Native American figurines, dream catchers, and architectural accents; they also sell saddles and other tack.

Seaside

Follow CR 30A to the quaint "New Urbanism" village that served as the backdrop for *The Truman Show*, starring Jim Carrey. More than 40 shops, quaint cafés, and eateries line the storybook streets, some of which are cobblestoned. At the heart of town is the **Ruskin Place Artist Colony** (Ruskin, Quincy, and Central Square area), 120 Quincy Circle, where you'll find a nice collection of arts, crafts, and galleries, such as superior blown glass at **Fusion Art Glass Gallery** (877-231-5405; fusionartglass.com), 63 Central Square. Pieces by Josh Simpson are especially mesmerizing, with entire planetary scenes inside each globe. Open daily 10–7.

SEASIDE

VISIT FLORIDA

The local grocer, **Modica Market** (877-809-0994 or 850-231-1214; modicamarket.com), 109 Seaside Central Square, has everything to outfit your cottage while staying in the area, from fine foods to the dishes from which you eat. And if the market looks vaguely familiar, it might be because you saw it in a scene from the movie. A few doors down, Sundog Books & Central Square Records (850-231-5481; sundogbooks.com), 89 Central Square, is a great place to browse, with something for all ages.

The beachside open-air market, **Perspicasity** (850-231-5829), 2236 E CR 30A, has something fun for everyone. Just say the name three times fast! Celebrating 25 years in business, it started as a produce stand and now is a collection of cottages with clothing, decor, and art that celebrates the beach lifestyle.

✳ Special Events

January: **Florida Chautauqua Assembly** (florida-chautauqua-center .org), DeFuniak Springs, is a southern companion to the original New York Chautauqua, offering workshops and classes, lectures and activities in the original Victorian setting established as a learning center in 1885. Classes continued through the 1920s. Revitalized and reborn in 1993, the Chautauqua tradition continues during this annual four-day event.

February: Don your favorite costume or penguin suit at the annual **Mardi Gras Ball** (850-244-8191; fwbchamber .org), Fort Walton Beach. The fun continues throughout the weekend with the Island Festival and Parade. Destin-area restaurants compete at the **Great Southern Gumbo Cook-Off** (850-267-8092), with live Cajun music and door prizes.

April: ✍ Go fly a kite at the annual **Beach Kite Festival** (850-796-0102), a two-day event at the boardwalk on Okaloosa Island. Free kite making, and exhibitions of stunt and giant kite flying.

At **Musical Echoes** (850-243-4405; musicalechoes.com), held at The Landing (see *Parks*) in Fort Walton Beach, you'll experience an authentic Native American flute gathering. This cultural event is weekend-long festival of music, food, and performances presented by the Muscogee Nation of Florida.

May: Now held during the spring, the **Biggest All-Night Gospel Sing in the World**, Bonifay, has been held by the Kiwanis Club (bonifaykiwanis.org /gospel.htm) for more than 50 years. Nationally known singers entertain from sundown to sunup for more than 8,000 appreciative fans; buy tickets ($7–15) in advance online or at the gate. Onsite camping is available.

June: If you love wine, you're in the right area for the annual **Chautauqua Wine Festival** (chautauquawinery.com) in DeFuniak Springs (see *Wineries*).

The Billy Bowlegs (Bowles) Pirate Festival (billybowlegspiratefestival .com) in Fort Walton Beach is not to be missed, featuring a torchlight parade with "Captain Billy" and "Queen and the Krewe of Bowlegs" throwing goodies to the kids. The charismatic scoundrel, from 1779, was one of this region's earliest settlers, capturing the shipping lanes and creating a band of pirates out of runaways and renegades. Only one other—the independent Republic of Texas— outlives Captain Bowles's governing body, the Independent State of Muskegee. Three days of activities involve a mock battle between the captain and city militia, which often includes the

Fort Walton Beach mayor. Food, fun, music, and unique performances are celebrated in a festival atmosphere for all ages. Contact the Fort Walton Beach Chamber for more information (see *Guidance*).

August: **Grit & Grace** (gritandgrace .org), the official folklife production of Walton County, runs during the beginning of August annually in Freeport.

September: Volleyball is big in Destin, as evidenced by the **Emerald Coast Volleyball Fall Classic** (850-243-2555; emeraldcoastvolleyball.com/ffc .htm), which, as part of its schedule, encompasses one of the top five beach volleyball events in the United States, the **Fudpucker's Fall Classic Beach Volleyball Tournament** (800-447-7954; fudpucker.com/volleyball.htm).

October: ✔ There's fun for all at the **Boggy Bayou Mullet Festival** (850-678-1615; mulletfestival.com), Niceville, a seafood and down-home country festival held in late October celebrating the roots of the town founded as Boggy Bayou. Enjoy smoked mullet, baked mullet, and mullet chowder . . . mullet every way you can think of. It's a fish that eats only plants, so it's always tasty. Major country music stars perform and everyone has a fine old time.

A monthlong fishing frenzy goes on at the **Destin Fishing Rodeo** (850-837-6734; destinfishingrodeo.org), one of the most prestigious fishing events in the world. It began in 1948 as a way to attract anglers to Destin, and it worked! The first prizewinner won a kitchen full of appliances; today's prizes lean more toward exotic fishing vacations, fast boats, and fast cars. Learn how the "luckiest fishing village in the world" can boost your luck on the water by booking a tournament charter or registering your boat for the event.

🐾 How could you miss doggy square dancing at the annual **Dog Daze** (850-244-8191; fwbchamber.org), Fort Walton Beach Landing? Field events and other doggy delights take place throughout this one-day event.

✔ Held in and around Munson, sometimes in the Blackwater River State Forest (see the *Pensacola* chapter), the **Munson Heritage Festival** (src chamber.com) highlights traditional folkways of Northwest Florida, with storytelling and folksingers, traditional crafters and history displays.

Northwest Florida Championship Rodeo (bonifayrodeo.org), Bonifay, is a major event put on by the Kiwanis Club. It's been a staple of Walton County life since 1944 and has been voted one of the best rodeos in Florida. More than 25,000 enthusiasts attend each year, and ample camping is provided on site. Tickets $7–15, can be purchased locally in advance.

✔ More than 40 years old, the **Northwest Florida Fair** (850-862-0211; nwffair.com) encompasses the agricultural bounty and country fun of several surrounding counties. It takes place at the Northwest Florida Fair Grounds in Fort Walton Beach late Oct–early Nov.

November: ✔ The **Thunderbird Intertribal Powwow** (850-822-1495; thunderbirdpowwow.org) has been a tradition for more than 25 years, celebrating regional Native American culture during the first weekend of Nov with storytelling and dancing, Niceville.

December: ✔ **Christmas Reflections**, DeFuniak Springs. More than three million lights bring a storybook Christmas to the Victorian residential district along Circle Drive between Thanksgiving and Christmas; free.

PANAMA CITY & REGION

BAY, GULF & WASHINGTON COUNTIES
PANAMA CITY BEACH, PORT ST. JOE,
MEXICO BEACH, ROSEMARY BEACH
& CHIPLEY

I t all started with fishing around St. Andrews Bay, deep waters protected by a
sweep of barrier islands along the coast. More than 2,500 years ago, coastal tribes
roamed these placid shores, discarding their oceanic bounty in middens and later
building temple mounds along the shores. When the Spanish reached these shores
in the mid-1500s, they found the Chatot peoples, who vanished soon after. The village of **St. Andrews** emerged in the 1820s, with a handful of people working year-
round at fishing and salt making and housing the occasional visitor from "up
north." The population swelled during the summer months, reaching up to 1,500
in the mid-1800s. Around the same time, the settlement of Harrison, a commercial
shipping port, developed just up the road. It became known as **Panama City**,
established 1906, and St. Andrews, still growing, incorporated as a town in 1908.
As the 1920s Florida land boom swept through the region, residential neighborhoods filled in and the two communities met; Panama City, now the county seat,
annexed St. Andrews along with several other towns in 1927. It is now the largest
municipality between Tallahassee and Pensacola.

Panama City became an important port for shipbuilding and repairs during
World War II, as up to 30,000 workers the Wainwright Shipyard constructed 102
Liberty ships and six tankers. After the war ended, the shipyard stayed open, dis-
mantling warships for scrap metal. Built in 1941, Tyndall Air Force Base brought
many servicemen and their families to the region for training during the war. After
the base was demobilized, it became part of the USAF Tactical Air Command.
Today it is home to the 325th Fighter Wing, focusing on air education and training. Over the years many service personnel who served at Tyndall returned to the
sugary sand beaches and emerald-green waters to make Bay County their home.
The shipyards, bought by the county in the 1960s, became the Port of Panama
City and today continue to be an important shipping and receiving complex for
industry.

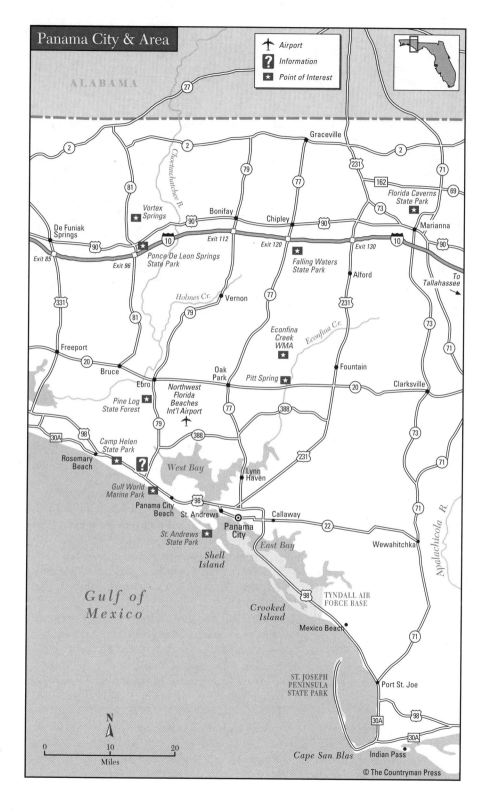

Panama City & Area

Airport
Information
Point of Interest

ALABAMA

Graceville

Vortex Springs

Bonifay

Chipley

Florida Caverns State Park

Marianna

De Funiak Springs

Exit 112

Exit 120

Exit 130

To Tallahassee

Ponce De Leon Springs State Park

Falling Waters State Park

Alford

Exit 85

Exit 96

Holmes Cr.

Vernon

Econfina Creek WMA

Freeport

Oak Park

Pitt Spring

Fountain

Clarksville

Bruce

Ebro

Northwest Florida Beaches Int'l Airport

Pine Log State Forest

Camp Helen State Park

Rosemary Beach

West Bay

Lynn Haven

Gulf World Marine Park

Panama City Beach

St. Andrews

Callaway

Panama City

St. Andrews State Park

Shell Island

East Bay

Wewahitchka

Gulf of Mexico

Crooked Island

TYNDALL AIR FORCE BASE

Mexico Beach

ST. JOSEPH PENINSULA STATE PARK

Port St. Joe

N

0   10   20

Miles

Cape San Blas   Indian Pass

© The Countryman Press

SURFS UP ALONG PANAMA CITY BEACH

Over on the barrier island at the mouth of St. Andrews Bay, **Panama City Beach** came into being in 1936, incorporated after developer Gideon Thomas built the Panama City Hotel, "to grow people" to the region. Since then, the beach community—a separate municipality—has filled in rapidly, especially over the past decade, when the remaining dunes gave way to a skyscraper skyline not unlike that seen in Southeast Florida above Miami Beach. This 7-square-mile vacation mecca draws crowds from Alabama, Georgia, Tennessee, and Kentucky, especially during the summer and spring break seasons. The draw has always been the gorgeous white sands and turquoise-blue waters of the Gulf of Mexico, of course, with plenty of man-made attractions for family fun. **Rosemary Beach**, established in 1995, was named for the wild Florida rosemary, which is native to the endangered coastal scrub habitats. Lush and plush, this self-contained resort village on the western edge of Bay County offers a quaint town center and vacation rentals. On the eastern side of the county, beyond Tyndall Air Force Base, you'll find **Mexico Beach**, which is so small that you may drive through it without taking notice. The 35–45 mph speed limit should help. Felix DuPont, who used the local pine trees for turpentine production, bought the land around 1900. Incorporated in 1966, at a time hotels were springing up all along the coast, Mexico Beach vowed to stay small. Its first mayor, Charlie Parker, was a developer who wanted his town to remain a small, quiet, getaway destination. Ordinances, zoning, and town owner-ship of the entire beach secured the charm that remains today. Building height is restricted to four stories, and you'll find that the shops, eateries, and lodgings are owned locally.

A little farther east along US 98, **Gulf County** touches the Apalachicola River but offers little river access, with much of its lands in farming and timber. Vacation destinations here are mainly along the coast, centered around the historic county seat of **Port St. Joe**, one of the first cities established in Northwest Florida. Its

marvelous beaches are found along the arc of **Cape San Blas** out to the tip of the
St. Joseph Peninsula, which forms the large, shallow St. Joseph Bay. The county is
also known as Florida's home of tupelo honey, which you'll find in **Wewahitchka**.

In 1825 frontier farmers created **Washington County**, north of Panama City,
growing pears, watermelons, sweet potatoes, and cotton. By 1882, the Pensacola &
Atlantic Railroad was completed near present-day **Chipley**, 60 miles north of
Panama City, and the small community was renamed to honor Colonel W. D.
Chipley, the builder of the railroad. In 1927 Chipley became the county seat; its
first post office was located in one of the boxcars. With just a few hundred residents, **Ebro**, just 16 miles northwest on FL 79 from Panama City Beach, provides
a quiet natural area for camping, hiking, and canoeing. **Vernon**, friendly but noto-
rious thanks to a 1981 documentary about the town, sits along beautiful Holmes
Creek. Since 1899, the entire county has prohibited the sale or manufacture of
alcohol. The close-knit farming community welcomed the revivalist influence that
spread the nation in 1916, holding one of the largest religious revivals in Northwest Florida. Today the religious influence remains strong, with Baptist, Methodist,
and Presbyterian churches found countywide. You'll find more than two dozen
churches dating from the turn of the 20th century in Chipley alone.

GUIDANCE Stop by the **Panama City Beach Convention and Visitors
Bureau** (850-233-5070 or 800-PCBEACH; visitpanamacitybeach.com), 17001
Panama City Beach Pkwy, 8–5 daily, for brochures, attraction information, and
hotel bookings. The **Bay County Chamber of Commerce** (850-785-5206;
panamacity.org/visitor) offers general information about visitors services in the
county. For information on Mexico Beach, contact the **Mexico Beach Visitor
Center** (888-723-2546; mexicobeach.com/cdc), 102 Canal Pkwy. **Rosemary
Beach** (888-855-1551; rosemarybeach.com) is an independently owned community within the county. For Port St. Joe, Indian Pass, Cape San Blas, and Wewahitchka in Gulf County, your resource is **Visit Gulf County** (800-482-GULF or
850-233-5070; visitgulf.com), 150 Captain Fred's Place, Port St. Joe, a nice new
visitors center near the marina. To learn more about Chipley, Ebro, and Vernon,
contact the **Washington County Tourist Development Council** (850-638-6013;
visitwashingtoncountyfl.com), 672 5th St, Chipley, in a historic firehouse.

GETTING THERE *By air:* Delta and Southwest serve the new **Northwest Florida Beaches International Airport** (850-763-6751; iflybeaches.com), 6300
West Bay Pkwy, Panama City Beach, the first new international airport built in
the United States in more than a decade.

By bus: **Greyhound** (800-231-2222).

By car: **I-10** and **US 90** run east–west along the Panhandle. Chipley is at the
intersection of **US 90** and **FL 77**. A few miles west of Chipley, take **FL 79** south
to reach Ebro and Panama City. **US 231** will take you from **I-10** south to Panama
City, passing through the towns of Alford (see *Apalachicola River*) and Fountain
en route, about a 45-minute drive. **US 98** runs east–west along the coast, connecting Port St. Joe with Mexico Beach, Panama City, Panama City Beach, and Rosemary Beach, continuing west toward Destin–Fort Walton. **CR 30A west** of
Panama City Beach leads to Rosemary Beach; **CR 30A east** of Port St. Joe leads
to Indian Pass and Cape San Blas.

GETTING AROUND The **Bay Town Trolley** (850-769-0557; baytowntrolley.org), 1116 Frankford Ave, Panama City, is the local public transportation service in and around Panama City and Panama City Beach, covering hundreds of stops for shopping, dining, and fun in the sun. Buses are equipped with bicycle racks and wheelchair lifts. The trolley operates Mon–Fri 6 AM–6:30 PM. Full fare for bus or trolley is $1.50; 75¢ for seniors, persons with disabilities, and students; children under 5 ride free, day pass $3. During special events, a free beach trolley runs along the 3-mile stretch of Mexico Beach. On New Year's Eve, the shuttle transports you across Eastern and Central time zones so you can ring in the New Year twice.

MEDICAL EMERGENCIES In the Panama City area, **Bay Medical Center** (850-769-1511; baymedical.org), 615 N Bonita Ave, and **Gulf Coast Medical Center** (850-769-8341; gcmc-pc.com), 449 W 23rd St. For Gulf County, **Sacred Heart Hospital on the Gulf** (850-229-5600; sacred-heart.org/gulf), 3801 E US 98, Port St. Joe. Washington County is served by **Northwest Florida Community Hospital** (850-638-1610; nfch.org), 1360 Brickyard Rd, Chipley. The center of the region in between the state line and the coastal communities (north to south) is quite rural. Always call 911 for major emergencies.

✷ To See

AQUARIUM ✐ ♿ Spend a day exploring the creatures of the sea at **Gulf World Marine Park** (850-234-5271; gulfworldmarinepark.com), 15412 Front Beach Rd, Panama City Beach, where you can see a wide variety of shows. Marvel as spectacular bottlenose dolphins leap and flip, and streamlined rough-toothed dolphins display great speed; laugh at the comical California sea lion shows; and learn about loggerhead and sea turtles at the reptile show. Wander through the lush tropical gardens where colorful macaws greet you with a loud squawk, or touch slippery stingrays in the petting pool. The well-kept facility, open since 1969, exhibits a variety of sharks, alligators, sea turtles, flamingos, and even penguins. Later on see the colorful and musical Splash Magic Laser Show with 16 fountains reaching sky-high and laser lights projecting on 50-foot screen. Open daily 9 AM–sunset. The admission price of $27 adults, $11 ages 5–11, includes all shows. As an add-on adventure you can swim with a dolphin ($150) or be a trainer for a day ($199).

ART GALLERIES The **Visual Arts Center of Northwest Florida** (850-769-4451; vac.org.cn), 19 E 4th St, Panama City. The building itself is a piece of art. Built in the 1920s, the Spanish Revival facility also reveals art deco influences, combining neoclassical, Gothic, and baroque features. Inside, it's the only museum of its kind for more than 100 miles. Permanent and rotating exhibitions from local and nationally acclaimed artists in a variety of media are shown in the Main, Higby, and Permanent galleries. The Impressions Gallery is a hands-on experience for children. Tue/Thu 10–8, Wed/Fri–Sat 10–6; fee. ＇

In Port St. Joe, the **Studio on 4th** (850-227-1910; studioon4th.com), 521 4th St, is both a woodturner's working studio and an art gallery showcasing local artists in media like stained glass, ceramics, acrylics, and photography. Open Fri–Sat 11–6.

HISTORIC SITES Take a walk through the **South 3rd Street Historic District** (circa 1887–1938), Chipley, and reminisce about the old days. The affluent neighborhood contains 16 private residences of historical interest, built in the Frame Vernacular style. The 1857 Moss Hill Church at the corner of Vernon and Greenhead Rd is another fine Frame Vernacular construction. The one-story church is the oldest unaltered building in Washington County and is an excellent example of local preservation efforts.

Established in 1827, **St. Andrews** (historicstandrews.com), now part of Panama City, is the oldest waterfront community along the coast. A stroll around its original downtown, including beautiful Oaks by the Bay Park (see *Parks*), will give you a taste of its history. The **Robert L. McKenzie House** (also known as the Belle Booth House) features one and a half stories under a gabled roof. The private residence at 17 E 3rd Court, Panama City, is not open to the public, but you can gaze at the Frame Vernacular architecture circa 1909.

LIGHTHOUSE A climb to the top of the **Cape San Blas Lighthouse** (850-229-1151; capesanblaslighthouse.com) will get your heart pumping. This is the third lighthouse for the cape, built in 1885 and moved inland to this spot so it wouldn't be demolished by yet another hurricane. From the top, I could see the sweep of Cape San Blas, a fair distance across St. Joseph Sound, and straight across into the pines where a bald eagle was looking back at me. The light keepers' residences contain some restored rooms, offices, and a gift shop with a museum upstairs recounting the history of the lighthouses on the cape. Wed–Fri 11–5, Sat 10–4; fee charged for lighthouse climb. Special tours provided on full-moon nights.

THE CAPE SAN BLAS LIGHTHOUSE IS OPEN FOR TOURS

MUSEUMS

Panama City

Once the home of Panama City's first newspaper, circa 1920, the **Panama City Publishing Museum and Visitor's Center** (historicstandrews.com), 1134 Beck Ave, is devoted to telling the early history of the region, with a special emphasis on St. Andrews, where the museum is located. Exhibits from local artists are also featured. Open Tue/Thu 2:30–6, and the first Saturday of each month 10–2. Free.

✐ You'll have hands-on fun and learn about science, history, and culture at the **Science & Discovery Center of Northwest Florida** (850-769-6128; scienceanddiscoverycenter.org), 1731 Jenks Ave, Panama City. See Northwest Florida pioneer life portrayed through a gristmill, cabin, barn, smokehouse, and 1943 Bay Line Engine. The nature boardwalk winds through 12 acres of hardwood swamp. Tue–Sat 10–5, Sun noon–5; fee.

Panama City Beach

Divers (and those who are fascinated with submarines and submersibles) will want to visit the **Museum of Man in the Sea** (850-235-4101; maninthesea.org), 17314 Panama City Beach Pkwy, which showcases the history of diving and work in the ocean. This fascinating museum includes artifacts like SEALAB-1, the first-ever underwater living environment, early submarines and both human-powered and remote submersibles, antique diving equipment from 1837 and 1913, and other items that illustrate the long and storied history of underwater exploration. Open daily 10–4; fee.

Port St. Joe

&. At the **Constitution Convention Museum State Park** (850-229-8029; florida stateparks.org/constitutionconvention), 200 Allen Memorial Way, interpretive exhibits and artifacts put a face on Florida's frontier days, with a special focus on St. Joseph. Established by homesteaders who were kicked out of Apalachicola, thanks to a sneaky 1830 land deal called the Forbes Purchase, St. Joe was Florida's first real tourist destination, a deep-water port that was the Las Vegas of its day. Some said the hand of God wiped out Sin City in 1841 with a triple whammy of yellow fever, hurricane, and wildfire. A stone marker, cemetery, and this museum are all that's left. In 1838 St. Joe hosted Florida's Constitutional Convention. A replica meeting room has bios of all of the delegates and gives a nice glimpse into a time when Mosquito County took up most of the southern peninsula. Thu–Mon 9–noon, 1–5. Fee.

RAILROADIANA Chipley owes its existence to the Pensacola & Atlantic Railroad circa 1882. The main line still divides the town in two and is busy with modern-day train traffic. The historic **Louisville & Nashville Depot** (850-638-6180), 685 7th St, sits half a block away from the current tracks and houses the local historical museum. Within the same grassy block, you'll find the small white **Bill Lee Station**, an Amtrak stop until service was shut down on the Sunset Limited after Hurricane Katrina, and an **L&N caboose** sitting by itself on a piece of track.

Inside the **Constitution Convention Museum** (see *Museums*) you'll find a scale replica of Florida's first steam engine, which ran on an 8-mile route, the St. Joseph & Lake Wimico Canal & Railroad, between St. Joseph and Depot Creek in 1836. Outside the

DOWNTOWN CHIPLEY HAS ALWAYS BEEN DOMINATED BY THE RAILROAD

museum, look for a 1915 steam engine that belonged to the St. Joe Lumber Company. It sits at the terminus of the Port City Trail (see *Bicycling*).

93

PANAMA CITY & REGION

ZOO ✎ ⟐ At **ZooWorld Zoological and Botanical Park** (850-230-1243; zoo worldpcb.net), 9008 Front Beach Rd, Panama City Beach, you'll get closer to the animals at than at any other zoo. With more than 260 critters, including big cats, giraffes, and orangutans, this zoo is also one of the cleanest. Through the glass windows at the Tilghman Infant Care Facility you can view the care and feeding of newborn baby animals. Your little ones will enjoy the friendly Gentle Jungle Petting Zoo. Mon–Sat 9:30–5, Sun 11–5; adults $15, seniors $12, ages 4–11 $10.

✳ To Do

ATTRACTIONS ✎ The **Miracle Strip at Pier Park** (850-230-5200; miracle-strip .com) keeps the spirit of the old amusement park, which was demolished to build the mall, alive. The rides here are historic originals, all a part of the park, and are perfect for young riders. They include the park's 1964 Alan Hershel Carousel, a 1985 Zamperalla Balloon Race, 1975 Big Eli Ferris Wheel, 1952 Alan Hershel Red Baron Planes, 1975 Eli Bridge Scrambler, and my favorite, the 1991 Selner Tilt-A-Whirl. This gentle attraction also features a butterfly house. Each ride costs one ticket, which is $3.50; $29 for a book of 10 tickets, season passes available.

✎ ⟐ The curious and weird can be found at cartoonist's **Robert Ripley's Believe It or Not! Museum** (850-230-6113; ripleyspanamacitybeach.com), 9907 Front Beach Rd, Panama City Beach. The pirate ship counterpart to the original in St. Augustine will have you walking through spinning tunnels and displays of the bizarre. On the new 4-D movie ride you'll experience a mine shaft or cosmic galaxy—a great roller-coaster experience for those wanting a virtual thrill without the physical dips and turns. Open daily 8 AM–1 AM; museum admission $15 adults, $10 ages 4–12; theater admission $11 adults, $10 for children; combo passes available.

You've seen dolphins at the parks; you may have even taken a dip with them in the constraints of a pool or lagoon. Now you want to swim in the open water with them—because this is what true dolphin lovers really want to do. At **Water Planet** (850-230-6030; waterplanetusa.com), 5605 Sunset Ave, Panama City Beach, your dream is realized. One-day, three-day, and weeklong programs teach you about ecology, dolphin physiology, and how to interact with wild dolphins both socially and legally. Only six guests per excursion; you'll travel on a 24-foot pontoon boat around Shell Island for an unforgettable experience with wild bottlenose dolphins. Later the team will take you on a walk in the shallows for a marine ecology wet lab, where you'll learn about crustaceans and local fish. A one-day excursion is $98; three days $430; weeklong trip $750 (five days, plus one replacement day if needed). Snorkeling equipment is available to rent for $5.

✎ ⟐ An upside-down building. A rollicking family funhouse. If it rains, you'll want to stay dry in **Wonderworks** (850-249-7000; wonderworkspcb.com), where your kids won't even realize they're learning about science as they're having fun. Hang out in the Hurricane Shack to learn what Category One is all about. Let the kids (and yourself, if you dare) try the three-story indoor ropes course. Lie down on a bed of nails, or design your own roller coaster and ride it in a simulator. Heck, it's so tempting you might even slip in here on a *sunny* day! $23 adults, $19 for ages 4–12 and 55+, extra for Lazer Tag.

Other attractions are listed under *Family Activities* and *Aquarium.*

BICYCLING The winding singletrack 9-mile **Crooked Creek Trail** in Pine Log State Forest (see *Wild Places*) was built with mountain bikers in mind; access the trailhead off FL 79, 1 mile south of the main entrance of the forest's recreation area. For 4 miles, the new **Port City Trail** provides a paved biking surface for bicyclists through Port St. Joe, connecting the downtown restaurant and shopping district with the Constitutional Convention Museum State Park (see *Museums*) on the east side of town.

BIRDING The wetlands along the edge of **St. Andrews Bay** is one of the better places to watch for wading birds. Public access is via Oaks by the Bay (see *Parks*) or St. Andrews State Park (see *Beaches*). On the upper **Choctawhatchee River**, noted ornithologist Dr. Geoffrey Hill from Auburn spotted an ivory-billed woodpecker in 2006. Local sightings persist, and Cornell University (birds.cornell.edu /ivory) volunteers make regular trips into the ancient cypress floodplain to capture a clear video of the birds; audio is available on the Auburn website.

BOAT SHUTTLES To get to the barrier islands, you'll need a shuttle, such as **St. Vincent Island Shuttle Services** (850-229-1065; stvincentisland.com) at Indian Pass or the **Shell Island Shuttle** (850-233-0504; shellislandshuttle.com) at St. Andrews State Park (see *Beaches*).

BOATING **Marquardt's Marina** (850-648-8900), 3904 US 98, Mexico Beach, has been around since 1977. Whether you need fuel for yourself or your craft, the knowledgeable staff will help you stock up on supplies for your day of fishing or cruising the emerald-green waters of the Gulf of Mexico. You can also get bait, tackle, licenses, diesel, and gasoline at the **City of Mexico Beach Public Boat Ramp/Hide-A-Way Harbor Marina** (850-648-5407), 3700 US 98.

Located at the Port St. Joe Marina, **Seahorse Water Safaris** (850-227-1099; seahorsewatersafaris.com), 340 Marina Dr, rents everything from a kayak to a 23-foot pontoon boat. Boat rentals and fishing guides are also available at **Presnell's Bayside Marina & RV Resort** (see *Cabins & Camping*).

If you love marinas, you should take the time to walk around the **St. Andrews Marina** (850-872-7240), 3151 W 10th St, Panama City, the hub around which the historic district grew. Live-aboards abound, but charter captains dock here, too (see *Fishing*).

BOAT TOURS ♿ **The Shell Island Glass Bottom Boat Cruise** (800-409-3173; panamacitytours.net), 3605 Thomas Dr at Treasure Island Marina, Panama City Beach, takes you to Shell Island, where you can swim or search for shells along the sugar-sand beach. This unique three-hour trip also explains shrimp nets and crab trap operations. $20–22 adult, $10 child.

Swashbucklers will want to step back in time aboard authentic 85-foot pirate ship the *Sea Dragon* (850-234-7400; piratecruise.net), 5325 N Lagoon Dr, Panama City Beach. You'll enjoy cruising the Gulf for two hours while pirates blast can-

VISIT FLORIDA

AHOY, MATEYS! CRUISING ON THE *SEA DRAGON*

nons, hang from the rigging, and then have a sword fight, which you might be asked to join! Reservations recommended. $24 adults, $20 seniors and juniors ages 13–17, $18 ages 3–12, $12 ages 1–2.

DIVING The waters off Panama City Beach are known as the **Wreck Capital of the South**. You can swim among sea turtles, rays, catfish, flounder, grouper, and curious puffer fish in half a dozen historic wrecks in natural reefs reaching 100 feet a few miles offshore, or in 50 artificial reefs set just offshore. The famous 465-foot *Empire Mica* is there; dive down 75 feet to reach a 184-foot-long naval mine sweeper. Or inspect a 100-foot aluminum hovercraft, also sitting under 75 feet of water. A favorite dive is the Black Bart. The intact 185-foot oil-field supply ship offers an abundance of fish and turtles and is a great spot for underwater photography. Explore cargo holds, wheelhouse, galley, and even the heads. Sitting in 75 feet of water, the bridge is at 40 feet; the main deck at 66. Certified divers have several charter options: You'll never feel crowded with **Wild Goose Diving Charters** (850-896-3304), 3304 Treasure Circle, Panama City Beach, where, for more than 20 years, Coast Guard–licensed captain Terry "Captain Cranky" McNamer has taken small parties to natural reefs at secret dive spots in search of spiny lobsters. His inshore dives, 5–6 miles out, take you to 60–80 feet for $70; offshore dives, 10–12 miles out, take you to depths of 80–120 feet for $80–90.

Whether diving inshore or offshore on wrecks or natural and man-made reefs or in the crystal-clear waters of a natural spring, **Dive Locker/Panama City Dive Charters** (850-230-8006; divelockerpcb.com), 106 Thomas Dr, Panama City Beach, takes you on an unforgettable dive. Dives 5 to 6 miles offshore take you to 60–80 feet for $79; dives 10–12 miles offshore take you from 80–120 feet for $89–109. A three-day dive class in a freshwater spring certifies you for up to 60 feet ($285). Rental equipment available.

FAMILY ACTIVITIES

Panama City Beach

⚓ One of the country's most challenging mazes is at the **Coconut Creek Family Fun Park** (850-234-2625; coconutcreekfun.com), 9807 Front Beach Rd. Longer than a football field, the Gran Maze has doors that are changed often so you can never really memorize the routes. When you've completed it, head over to the South Pacific Island–style mini golf park and bumper boats for more family fun.

⚓ Play a game of mini golf at **Barnacle Bay Mini Golf** (850-234-7792), 11209 W US 98, Panama City Beach, which has two tropically landscaped 18-hole golf courses with rope bridges, waterfalls, and dark caves. Swashbuckling golfers will want to head for **Pirate's Island Golf** (850-235-1171; piratesislandgolf.com /panama-home), 9518 Front Beach Rd, for a pirate-themed adventure. Or for a retro evening on the mini-golf course, head for the original **Goofy Golf** (850-234-6403), 12206 Front Beach Rd, a beachfront classic built in 1959.

✐ At **Race City** (850-234-1588; racecitypcb.com), 9523 Front Beach Rd, there's fun for everyone, including the only haunted house on the beach, a drag strip where you go from 0 to 70 mph (driver's license required!) in mini dragsters, a massive indoor arcade, mini golf by blacklight . . . the list is exhaustive, the fun exhausting and exhilarating.

Drive extreme go-carts at **Cobra Adventure Park** (850-235-0321), 9323 Front Beach Rd, where 9-horsepower go-carts race up and down three-story coils.

✐ Race on the longest go-cart track in North Florida at **Hidden Lagoon Super Racetrack & Super Golf** (850-233-1825; hiddenlagoongolfandracetrack.com), 14414 Front Beach Rd.

✐ Experience the Alien Arcade, bungee bounce, and bumper boats at **Emerald Falls Family Entertainment Center** (850-234-1049), Thomas Dr at Joan Ave.

FISHING Panama City is a fishing village all grown up, but it's still a fishing village at heart. You'll find plenty of guides here to let you fish to your heart's content, whether you're looking for deep-sea action, bay fishing, or inshore trolling. For deep-sea—and I'll warn you, it can get rough out there—**Tomcat Fishing Charters** (850-303-2210; tomcatfishingcharters.com) represents a group of captains who run trips from half a day to several days on the water. Rates are per hour ($125–150) for up to six passengers, and you can review the boats online before you book. Departing from **Captain Anderson's Marina** (captandersonsmarina .com/deep-sea-fishing), 5550 N Lagoon Dr, Panama City Beach, Captain B. J. Burkett runs **Hook 'em Up Charters** (850-774-8333; pcbeachfishingcharters.com), focused on taking the whole family out fishing, as does Captain Don Williams with **Cynthia Lynn Charters** (850-249-5813; cynthialynncharters.net), 825 Linda Ln, Panama City Beach. For more recommendations, tune in to local legend Jim Wilson, WMBB-TV 13 in Panama City—he'll point you in the right direction—and he'll guide your trip, too. **Fishin' With Jim** (850-769-2536; fishinwithjim.com).

Want to keep your feet on the ground, not in a boat? Head for the **Russell-Fields Pier** (850-233-5080; pcbgov.com/visitors_citypier.htm), Front Beach Rd, Panama City Beach, open 24/7; fee.

Bay Point Marina at the Bay Point Marriott Resort (see *Lodging*) is the home of the **Bay Point Invitational Billfish Tournament** (baypointbillfish.com), drawing top anglers from around the world. All proceeds from the tournament go to disadvantaged youth in the region.

A quiet place to drop a line is off the **Mexico Beach Fishing Pier** at 37th St. Bait, licenses, and gear can be purchased nearby at Cathey's Ace Hardware (850-648-5242), 3000 US 98, which also rents some equipment.

Inland, trophy-sized lunkers lurk along the **Dead Lakes** at Dead Lakes Park (see *Parks*).

GOLFING Always at the top of any golfer's list, Panama City offers five challenging courses with green fees averaging $50 or less. The area's first golf course, built in 1962, is **Signal Hill** (850-234-3218; signalhillgolfcourse.com), 9615 N Thomas Dr, originally designed on dunes. Starting at $28 for an 18-hole public course, it's the best value in the area. One of the most challenging courses in the United States is the intimidating par-72 **Nicklaus Course at the Bay Point Resort Golf Club** (850-235-6397; baypointgolf.com), 4701 Baypoint Rd at Bay Point Marriott Resort (see *Lodging*). Measuring more than 7,100 yards and with a slope rating of 152, the first Nicklaus course in the Florida Panhandle was completely overhauled in 2005. If the Nicklaus Course is too much to handle, you'll never be bored at the **Meadows Course** in the same complex. Easy enough for beginners, the course still offers enough challenge for experienced golfers. The 18-hole, par-72 course at **Holiday Golf Club** (850-234-1800; holidaygolfclub.com), 100 Fairway Blvd, is only 1 mile from the beach and is the only night 9-hole executive course in the county. At **Hombre Golf Club** (850-234-3673; hombregolfclub.com), 120 Coyote Pass, wetlands and water holes are favorites.

HIKING ✔ 🐾 **St. Andrews State Park** (see *Beaches*) offers two excellent nature trails through coastal scrub and pine flatwood habitats. The 0.6-mile Pine Flat-woods Trail starts at a replica of an old-time turpentine processing plant and loops through scrub and coastal flatwoods along the bay side of the park, while the Gator Lake Nature Trail offers a 0.4-mile loop with views of both a freshwater pond and the distant dunes.

One of the most intriguing walks in Florida is the Sinkhole Trail at **Falling Waters State Park** (see *Parks*), a boardwalk that carries you above and between a series of deep sinkholes leading to the state's highest waterfall.

As it crosses this region, the statewide **Florida Trail** (see *What's Where*) provides opportunities for backpacking and day hiking on two distinct segments. The 18-mile stretch paralleling scenic **Econfina Creek** can be accessed from FL 20 and off Scott Rd in Fountain; another 6.1-mile segment passes through the Sand Pond Trailhead at **Pine Log State Forest** (see *Wild Places*). This trailhead is the nexus of three hiking trails on which you can explore the cypress-lined ponds and dense pine flatwoods of Florida's oldest state forest.

HORSEBACK RIDING Cape San Blas is one of the few places in Florida where you can go horseback riding on the beach with an approved outfitter. Your ride starts at Salinas Park, near the beginning of the sweep of the cape. Outfitters include **Two Bit Stable** (850-227-4744; twobitstable.com) and **Broke a Toe** (850-899-RIDE; brokeatoe.com). Rates start at $50 per hour. Private inland rides can also be arranged with Broke a Toe.

OFF-ROADING Bring your dirt bike or ATV to the new **Hard Labor Creek Off-Road Park** (850-527-0615; hardlaborcreekoffroadpark.com), 2009 CR 277, Chipley.

PADDLING Follow scenic **Holmes Creek** as it flows from Alabama to the Choctawhatchee River, edged by ancient cypresses. An easy 12-mile route runs from Cypress Springs (3 miles north of Vernon) to Live Oak landing off CR 284. **Holmes Creek Canoe Livery** (850-210-7001; holmescreekcanoelivery.com), 2899 A FL 79, rents canoes, $30 for two to four hours, $45 for four hours or more, and will shuttle to various points on the creek for $15 and up.

Econfina Creek is one of Florida's most spectacular places to paddle. From high clay bluffs with splashing waterfalls to gentle floodplains where springs bubble up along the sides of the creek, it is a beautiful waterway well worth your exploration. Plan your trip with **Econfina Creek Canoe Livery** (850-722-9032; canoeeconfina creek.net), Strickland Rd, Youngstown. $40 kayak, $50 canoe for the three-to-four-hour trip. Bring your own craft and pay $15 to launch or $25 for shuttle service. Cash only.

Explore the needlerush marshes along **St. Joseph Bay** by launching at St. Joseph Peninsula State Park (see *Beaches*) or at the public launch. Rent kayaks at **Happy Ours** (850-229-1991; happyourskayak.com), 775 Cape San Blas Rd, $30 half day, $40 full day. Guided excursions available.

SCALLOPING St. Joseph Bay is Scalloping Central on the coast. In fact, the Florida Department of Environmental Protection says, "St. Joseph Bay has one of the healthiest populations of bay scallops in Florida." The season runs July 1–Sept 10. You can wade in at any of the bayside public beaches and sift through the shallows for free, or book a charter—check in at **Port St. Joe Marina** (850-227-9393; psjmarina.com), 340 Marina Dr, or drop in at **Scallop Cove** (850-227-7557; scallopcove.com), 4310 Cape San Blas Rd, where they also rent canoes and kayaks and run ecotours.

SHELLING Shelling can be good on any beach, especially after a storm. Several tours will take you to **Shell Island** across from St. Andrews State Park (see *Boating* and *Beaches*). Paddling across is not recommended due to rough open water, submerged rocks, and treacherous shipping lanes. **Mexico Beach** offers a quiet place to search for sand dollars, fragile paper fig shells, and the rare brown speckled junonia. Removal of live shells is prohibited.

SURFING Surf's often up at **St. Andrews State Park** (see *Beaches*), where wave action is almost guaranteed along the zone between the jetty and fishing pier.

WATER PARK ✔ Families will love swimming around the Great Shipwreck or riding the White Knuckle Rapids at **Shipwreck Island Waterpark** (850-234-3333; shipwreckisland.com), 12201 Middle Beach Rd, Panama City Beach. Little ones will delight at Tadpole Hole, where they can slide down a toad's tongue into a few inches of water, while the thrill seekers will scream as they descend the 65-foot Tree Top Drop. Those needing to relax can float on tubes down the scenic Lazy River. For the most part, fees are measured in inches, not age. Guests 50 inches and above $33, 35–50 inches $28, under 35 inches free. Seniors over age 62 get in for $22, regardless of height.

✳ Green Space
BEACHES

Cape San Blas
 ♿ **Rish Park** (850-227-1876; apdcares.org/rish-park), Cape San Blas Rd, deserves special note as Florida's only state park designated specifically for and limited to wheelchair-bound residents and their families. Barrier-free boardwalks and tunnels allow access to swimming, cabins, the beach, fishing piers, and nature trails on both sides of the highway. Only Florida residents with developmental disabilities may utilize the facilities; call in advance of your visit.

A BOATER COMING IN TO DOCK
AT ST. JOSEPH PENINSULA STATE PARK

🐾 🐾 A longtime local park and beach access point, **Salinas Park**, 240 Cape San Blas Rd, provides a picnic grove with small wooden pavilions in a pine forest. It's the primary access point for equestrians headed to the beach. Although the sands here aren't as lovely as at St. Joseph Peninsula State Park, the beach is busy since access is free and leashed pets are welcome. Across the street, a new bayside adjunct to the park offers a playground, fire pit, screened rooms for picnicking, and a long pier for fishing and dropping your kayak into the sound.

🐾 🐾 ⅙ **St. Joseph Peninsula State Park** (850-227-1327; floridastateparks .org/stjoseph), 8899 Cape San Blas Rd, is far and away my top choice for a beach destination vacation. This slender peninsula offers everything you could ask for: big dunes protecting the most stunning undisturbed white-sand beaches on the coast, with no homes or towering condos to sully the view; two campgrounds that accommodate RVs, trailers, and tent campers; a sweep of coastline along St. Joseph Bay, perfect for scalloping, snorkeling, and sea kayaking; nature trails that showcase the fragile coastal habitats; a backpacking trail that lets you head out into the wilderness area at the tip of the peninsula and pitch your tent on a lonely beach; and A-frame cabins (see *Camping & Cabins*) nestled in the coastal scrub forest on high bluffs with a sweeping view. Bring a week's worth of food and drinks, a few books, beach towels, and an easel and paints. Relaxation is assured. Fee.

Panama City Beach

🐾 ⅙ 🐾 On a peninsula that served as a vacation getaway for factory workers in the 1940s, **Camp Helen State Park** (850-233-5059; floridastateparks.org/camphelen), 23937 Panama City Beach Pkwy, borders the Gulf of Mexico, Phillips Inlet, and Lake Powell, and is an excellent site for birding. Hike along the trails and beaches, or cast your line from the shore. Employees of an Alabama textile mill enjoyed the lodge and cottages from 1945 until 1987 as their getaway; the structures are in the process of being restored. A new accessible nature trail on the north side of US 98 showcases coastal habitats. Don't miss the story of the sea monster of Lake Powell! Fee.

🐾 ⅙ 🐾 **St. Andrews State Park** (850-233-5140; floridastateparks.org/standrews), FL 392, Panama City Beach, is the one pristine getaway on the coast that you won't want to miss; in fact, it's Florida's most visited state park. Encompassing 1,200 acres of undisturbed forests and sand dunes, the park has miles of beaches; you can swim and snorkel in the protected pool behind the jetty or cast a line off one of two fishing piers. It's the only place along Panama City Beach where condos won't be crowding your ocean views. Two beautiful natural campgrounds under the pines have sea breezes as a bonus, and two hiking trails introduce you to the splendor of one of Florida's most threatened habitats, the coastal scrub. The nature trail through the coastal pine flatwoods is a delight, and I was surprised to see an alligator in a freshwater pond less than a quarter mile from the beach. This is Surfer Central, too—catch big waves near the jetty. Camping, fishing, and picnicking round out the activities at this park at the end of FL 392. Fee.

🐾 The one **pet-friendly beach** at Panama City Beach (850-233-5045) is just west of the Russell-Fields Pier (see *Fishing*) and at the south end of Pier Park (see *Shopping*). Download a map and find out more about pet-friendly parks from Bay Families with Dogs (bayfwd.org).

VISIT FLORIDA

SNORKELING AT ST. ANDREWS STATE PARK

PARKS ♂ ♿ A visual landmark just south of I-10 at Chipley, **Blue Lake Park**, 1865 FL 77, has picnic tables with grills along the edge of a very pretty lake. The park includes a fishing pier and boardwalk, small swimming beach, and playground area for the kids.

Along the Choctawhatchee River, **Cedar Tree Landing**, 4985 Cedar Tree Landing Rd, Ebro, provides a place to slip a boat or canoe into the cypress-lined river where researchers have been searching for the ivory-billed woodpecker for several years—and yes, they've been spotted upriver from here by experts searching the ancient cypress floodplain forests, although audio and video proof of this thought-to-be-extinct bird is still being sought.

🐾 ♂ **Dead Lakes Park** (850-639-2702), This strangely beautiful 6,700-acre lake, its with dark tannic waters and wizened ancient cypresses, was formed when a dam was placed across the Chipola River in 1960 near Wewahitchka. The creation of a Chipola Cutoff diverted the river's main flow away from the cypress swamp to the Apalachicola River. After much of this massive cypress swamp in the flooded river floodplain died back and fishing declined, the dam was removed between 1987 and 1989. Without the dams, fish populations and species diversity have risen every year. For anglers, this destination has an excellent reputation for its bluegill (bream) and redear (shellcracker) fishing in spring. The lake is accessible off FL 71 just north of Wewahitchka on State Park Rd and south off Land Rd. In addition to this county park—a former state park that has a campground (see *Camping & Cabins*), boat ramp, fishing ponds, and nature trails—you can access the Dead Lakes from fish camps (see *Fish Camps*) located along its shores. Care should be taken when operating a motorboat in this lake—it's filled with cypress snags and stumps.

♂ **Falling Waters State Park** (850-638-6130; floridastateparks.org/fallingwaters), 1130 State Park Rd, Chipley. On my first visit to the park, I was disappointed that Florida's tallest waterfall wasn't falling—it drops 67 feet into a perfectly cylindrical sinkhole. But the Sinkhole Trail, on boardwalks over the rugged fern-lined karst, was a delight. Stop by in the rainy season to get the full feel of this unusual geological site. The park offers camping, hiking, and picnicking; fee.

✄ ⚬ 🏕 **Oaks by the Bay Park** (pcgov.org/residents/leisure-services), 1000 Beck Ave, Panama City. Along the waterfront in St. Andrews, this 5-acre community park protects a quiet shoreline and the massive live oaks for which it's named. Among the surprises you'll find walking around the park are a four-headed pindo palm, historic exhibits on salt making along this coast, and a boardwalk that leads down to the edge of St. Andrews Bay, where you can walk along the shore and watch for wading birds plucking fish from the shallows. Free.

SPRINGS Along FL 20 at Econfina Creek between Ebro and Fountain, the entrance to **Pitt Spring** is clearly marked. It's a swimming hole in the creek, and at first glance doesn't look especially inviting. A nature trail leading away from the parking area showcases springs big and small along the edges of the creek, leading, eventually, to a vast and beautiful chalky blue spring known as **Williford Spring**, which is much more tempting for a dip. It is surrounded by a small recreation area also accessible via Strickland Rd off FL 20.

WILD PLACES Florida's oldest state forest is **Pine Log State Forest** (850-872-4175; fl-dof.com/state_forests/pine_log.html), FL 79, Ebro. Established in 1936, it covers 6,911 acres of sandhills, flatwoods, cypress-lined ponds, and titi swamps, with several extensive trail systems introducing you to this variety of habitats; the Florida Trail passes through here as well. A campground with electric and water hookups, showers, and restrooms provides respite beneath the pines. Bring your

A HIDDEN TREASURE NEAR ECONFINA CREEK: WILLIFORD SPRING

canoe and paddle across East Lake, or fish in the natural streams and ponds. Trail riding is permitted on numbered forest roads.

Offshore from Indian Pass, **St. Vincent National Wildlife Refuge** (fws.gov/saintvincent) is one of Florida's wilder barrier islands, encompassing over 12,000 acres of forests, marshes, and coastal habitats. Most visitors roam the lonely beaches, where shelling is fantastic. Rustic trails lead into the lesser-visited interior of the island, where you might encounter one of its more unlikely inhabitants, a sambar deer. Imported here from Asia over a century ago for a hunting reserve, these larger-than-expected

ST. VINCENT NWR CAN ONLY BE REACHED BY FERRY, KAYAK, OR PRIVATE BOAT

deer have propagated to the point that there is an annual hunt on the island; call for permit details. The island is also home to a colony of red wolves, which, as they mature, are sent to other refuges to help reestablish the species in the wild. One creature you will absolutely encounter: an ungodly quantity of mosquitoes. Be prepared. The refuge hosts an annual Open House, providing free trips to the island; the rest of the year, you can kayak over from Indian Pass, take your own boat to the dock, or use the shuttle service from Indian Pass (see *Boat Shuttles*). Overnight stays are not permitted.

THE CAPE SAN BLAS INN IS A RELAXING CHOICE FOR A BEACH GETAWAY

✳ Lodging

BED & BREAKFASTS

Panama City Beach 32413

🦴 🐾 (📶) Bring your pups along to the **Wisteria Inn** (850-234-0557; wisteria-inn.com), 20404 Front Beach Rd, where you might just find homemade dog biscuits in the lobby. The pool—where mimosas are served at noon—and oversized hot tub are set inside a private courtyard with lush landscaping and a koi pond. The garden behind the property is for pets and their owners to enjoy. Guests meet up in the evenings over wine and in the mornings for breakfast before heading out to the beach. You'll spend more time indoors than out, but each of the cozy rooms has its own specialized decor and unique flair; some offer two doubles. $69–149, depending on season; minimum stay required on certain weekends.

Port St. Joe 32456

Along a tiny finger of St. Joseph Bay, the **Cape San Blas Inn** (800-315-1965; capesanblasinn.com), 4950 Cape San Blas Rd, offers five spacious guest rooms ($150–235) with DVD players, phones, small refrigerators, and extraordinarily comfortable beds. Stroll down to the dock and put in your kayak for a paddle, or head up the road to one of the top beaches in the United States. The private courtyard out back is a perfect place for relaxation, but the rooms are roomy enough you might just stay in on a lazy day. Minimum stays required for weekends and holidays.

♂ (📶) � Along a relaxing stretch of remote Gulf beachfront at Indian Pass, the **Turtle Beach Inn & Cottages** (850-229-9366; turtlebeachinn.com), 140 Painted Pony Dr, features four comfy modern rooms ($165–195) and several cottages; enjoy a full break-fast with an ocean view. The large wooden sea turtles set amid the pines and palms remind you that in the proper season you can watch logger-heads nesting or hatching. Walk by moonlight—no lights, please!

Rosemary Beach 32461

♿ You can't miss the carnelian-red stucco as you drive up to the Italianate **Pensione Inn** (866-348-8952; rosemarybeach.com/pensione-rosemary-beach.aspx), 78 Main St. The eight rooms are decorated in contemporary simplicity with many furnishings from local artisans. Take notice of the tiniest details, such as the tiles in the bathroom, which not only look like a sparrow's speckled egg, but feel like one, too. Located directly across the street from the Gulf of Mexico; each room offers one queen-sized bed and breathtaking views of the emerald-green water. Nightly rates $150 and up, depending on season, includes a light continental breakfast buffet. The Onano Neighborhood Cafe (see *Dining Out*) is on the main floor.

HOTELS, MOTELS & RESORTS

Mexico Beach 32456

🐾 ♂ (📶) You'll find a simpler way of life at the **Driftwood Inn** (850-648-5126; driftwoodinn.com), 2105 US 98, where relaxation is the number one activity. The Victorian-style inn is more like a bed & breakfast, without the food and with a beachy twist. You'll note the grand architecture, spacious verandas, and luscious lawns and think you have gone back in time. Families will enjoy the slower pace as they barbecue on back decks that overlook the Gulf of Mexico. Stay in the main house or the spacious duplex and quad-plex cottages next door. Each air-conditioned room comes with fully equipped kitchen and cable TV. If you'd like more privacy, you can stay at one of their Victorian houses located across the road behind the inn. The two-bedroom, one-and-a-half-bath homes will accommodate six guests. This is a pet-friendly establishment; your own pets are welcome with prior arrangements. Rooms start at $110–140, homes at $130–175, depending on season. Weekly and monthly rates available.

♂ (ᵢᵢ) ⌀ Every room at the beachfront **El Governor Motel** (850-648-5757; elgovernormotel.net), 1701 W US 98, overlooks the blue-green waters of the Gulf of Mexico. Breathe in the fresh air from your own private balcony, curl your toes in the sugary sand, take a dip in the ocean or pool, and then sip a

cool drink at the beachside pool bar. The not fancy but spacious rooms ($129 and up), with double or king-sized beds, offer cable TV and kitchenettes. Daily and monthly rates available. RVs park across the street (see *Camping & Cabins*).

🦞 Across from the beach, the **Gulf View Motel** (850-648-5955), 1404 W US 98 and 15th St, offers an affordable option at a pleasant 1950s Old Florida mom-and-pop motel, simple and clean. Rates start around $69 a night, with weekly rates available.

Panama City Beach 32408

&. (ᵢᵢ) ↦ Having stayed at the **Bay Point Marriott Resort Golf Resort and Spa** (800-874-7105 or 850-236-6000; marriottbaypoint.com), 4200 Marriott Dr, for both conferences and pleasure, I've enjoyed the relaxed atmosphere and scenic views. The extensive complex sits within its own 1,100-acre wildlife sanctuary along the bay, looking out to the bay side of St. Andrews State Park (see *Beaches*) and wrapping you in a marsh-fringed forest. Notable for its size and amenities—including a luxury spa, two championship golf courses (one designed by Jack Nicklaus), and four on-site restaurants—it's a destination within a destination. Rooms within the main hotel complex are pleasant and typical for the brand. Golf-side and waterfront one-, two-, and three-bedroom condo rentals are available in other parts of the complex and are managed separately, although guests in those units share all amenities with hotel guests, including complimentary shuttles to Shell Island (see *Shelling*). Package details and promotions bring rates as low as $89; more typical rates are $169 and up.

Panama City Beach 32413

⌀ &. (ᵢᵢ) Right on the beautiful Gulf of Mexico, the **Driftwood Lodge** (800-

LOOKING OUT OVER THE POOL AND BAY AT THE BAY POINT MARRIOTT

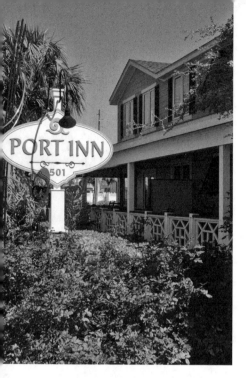

THE PORT INN IN PORT ST. JOE

your choice of kitchenettes or suites. $99 and up.

🦐 🌊 ♿ (📶) **Palmetto Inn & Suites** (850-234-2121; palmettomotel.com), 17255 Front Beach Rd, is one of the more popular non-chain, non-condo properties on the beach, with a big thumbs-up from families who stay here. Rooms include kitchenettes as well as traditional-sized hotel rooms; all of the Beachside rooms in the seven-story hotel include balconies. $75–95 and up. A pool, kiddie pools, and hot tub are right above the beach. The original motel is now the Northside, on the opposite side of the street, and has its own indoor pool and solarium; $55–75 and up.

Port St. Joe 32456

🦐 ♿ (📶) ⤴ **Port Inn** (850-229-PORT; portinnfl.com), 501 Monument Ave. This snazzy little hotel honors the memory of the original, circa 1913, with 20 spacious rooms ($69–149) reflecting modern sensibilities such as cable TV, Internet access, and a sparkling pool. But you can still sit on the front-porch rocking chairs and dine on the complimentary breakfast while watching the fishing boats on St. Joseph Bay.

CONDO HOTELS & RESORTS

Panama City Beach 32408

♿ ♂ (📶) On the beach, overlooking the Gulf of Mexico, the **Boardwalk Beach Resort** (850-914-8484; boardwalkbeachresort.com), S 9450 Thomas Dr, features a tropical paradise with lots of water activities. Relax as you float down the lazy river pool, lounge around the lagoon pool, or let the kids splash in the kiddie pool. Then head to the beach, where you can splash in the surf or hunt for shells. Simple hotel rooms ($59 and up) and efficiencies to deluxe one-, two-, and three-bedroom suites ($94 and up) are all uniquely

442-6601 or 850-234-6601; driftwood pcb.com) 15811 Front Beach Rd, is an older perennial favorite for families looking for a laid-back place to stay. The sparkling rooms in this refreshingly low-rise hotel rate highly and come in sizes from a simple double to a 900-square-foot Cabana Suite. The pool deck looks out right on the beach and provides direct access to the beach. Both the pier and Pier Park are nearby. $79–108 and up.

🌊 ♿ (📶) A stay at **Osprey on the Gulf** (800-338-2659 or 850-234-0303; ospreyonthegulf.com), 15801 Front Beach Rd, keeps you in the middle of the action while off to the west of the party crowd you'll find certain times of year (especially spring break) along this beach. Parents and kids love the beachfront playground and planned children's activities. A sister property to the Driftwood Lodge, it's 25 years old but still in excellent shape, with

decorated according the taste of the unit's owners. Weekly and monthly rates available.

&. ♂ (((•))) You can spend your entire vacation on site at the **Edgewater** (800-331-6338 or 850-235-4977; edge waterbeachresort.com), 11212 Front Beach Rd, where you'll find everything from water sports, such as windsurfing, banana boats, Jet Skis, parasailing, tropically landscaped pools, and a lazy river, to land sports, such as tennis on 11 all-weather Plexicushion-surfaced courts and golf on the nine-hole executive course at the 18-hole Hombre Golf Club (see *Golf*). One-, two-, and three-bedroom suites ($99 and up) are located oceanside and across from the beach. An on-site trolley takes you all over the property.

VACATION RENTALS Rent a beach-front home from **Anchor Vacation Properties** (800-624-3964; florida -beach.com), an agency based in Apalachicola that manages oceanfront home rentals between Carrabelle and Mexico City. Properties range from old-fashioned beachfront cottages to mega mansions.

Ocean Reef Resort Properties (850-837-3935; oceanreefresorts.com) offers furnished cottages, beach homes, condos, townhomes, luxury homes, and resorts by the day, week, or month. The folks at **Resort-Quest** (resortquest .com)—one of the largest suppliers of fully furnished homes—can select which home will be right for you, from condos in resort-style settings to portfolio homes with private pools.

🐾 In the village of **Rosemary Beach** (888-855-1551; rosemarybeach.com), you can rent upscale cottages and carriage houses by the night or week. Some even allow pets. Carriage Houses are 400–1,000 square feet with

rates from $155 a night to $2,100 a week. Cottages run 1,000–5,000 square feet, with rates from $250 a night to $8,000 a week.

For all vacation rentals and condo resorts, quality of accommodations can vary widely from unit to unit. Be aware that cleaning and maintenance fees may be added atop your room fee. Ask before booking.

CAMPING & CABINS

Chipley 32428

✿ At **Falling Waters State Park** (see *Parks*), 24 campsites are nestled in the campground (800-326-3521; florida stateparks.reserveamerica.com) in a dense pine forest and offer easy access to all of the park's amenities. Each site offers a picnic table, ground grill, and clotheslines; electric and water are available, and there is a dump station on site.

Ebro 32437

Twenty campsites await beneath the pines at **Pine Log State Forest** (see *Wild Places*), each with electric and water hookups. No reservations accepted; sites are first come, first served.

Mexico Beach 32456

For those with their own campers, the **El Governor Campground** (850-648-5432; elgovernormotel.net), 1701 W US 98, is just across from the El Governor Motel (see *Hotels, Motels, & Resorts*) and the sugar-sand beach. The full-service campground offers spacious shady sites with full hookups ($31), showers, and laundry.

Panama City Beach 32408

Catch a sea breeze through the windows of your RV at **St. Andrews State Park** (see *Beaches*), where 176 campsites (800-326-3521; floridastateparks .reserveamerica.com) with water and

STAY ALONG ST. JOSEPH BAY AT THE OLD SALTWORKS CABINS

electric hookups give you the opportunity to park your rig or pitch your tent within walking distance of the beach.

Port St. Joe 32456

🦐 At the end of CR 30A, **Indian Pass Campground** (850-227-7203; indianpasscamp.com), 2817 Indian Pass Rd, encompasses a small peninsula surrounded by estuary, with sites set under gnarled oaks. There's plenty to do, with the newly renovated pool, fishing charters (they'll set you up with a local guide), excursions to St. Vincent Island, canoe and kayak rentals, and bike rentals. Choose from RV sites with water and electric for $32–42, waterfront tent camping for $25, or the Stewart Lodge camping cabins (I love 'em!) for $95 and up.

At **Presnell's Bayside Marina & RV Resort** (850-229-9229; presnells.com), 2115 CR 30A, their RV sites are right on the rim of St. Joseph Bay. Bring your boat and launch here for scalloping expeditions and flats fishing. RV sites $32; add $8 for your boat.

🦐 🐾 𝒮 If you loved to play "fort" as a kid or are a history buff, don't miss the **Old Saltworks Cabins** (850-229-6097; oldsaltworks.com), 1085 Cape San Blas Rd. Hidden in a pine forest at the historic St. Joseph Saltworks, the cabins share a big play fort and a nice slice of St. Joseph Bay. Look for artifacts and Civil War dioramas at the office—the Confederates produced salt here, after all. Eleven cabins "better than sleeping in a tent" with various configurations of bedrooms, perfect for families. Rates start at $59 in winter, $89 summer, with two- or three-night minimums at busy times of year.

𝒮 ♿ 🔌 **St. Joseph Peninsula State Park** (see *Beaches*) has a perfect perch for its two-story cabins atop a bluff looking out over the bay. With two campgrounds and the popular cabins, it's a top state park destination (800-326-3521; floridastateparks.reserveamerica.com). Sites $24 and up, cabins $100.

Wewahitchka 32465

𝒮 Formerly a state park, the county-run **Dead Lakes Park** (see *Parks*) offers pleasant campsites for trailers and tents in the pine woods around a small pond with easy access to a playground, hiking trails, and bank fishing. Anglers will want to trailer in a boat to explore the vast Dead Lakes, a natural river oxbow cut off from the river's flow.

KIDS WILL LOVE THE PLAY FORT AT THE OLD SALTWORKS CABINS

NORTHWEST FLORIDA

Wewahitchka 32465

Fish camps are clustered around Dead Lakes (see *Parks*), catering to anglers looking for peace and quiet amid the cypresses. Choices include **Gate's Fish Camp** (850-639-2768), FL 71; **Lakeside Lodge** (850-639-2681), just 1 mile north of Wewahitchka on FL 71; and **Dead Lakes Sportsman Lodge** (850-639-5051) at the old Dead Lakes Dam, 2001 Lake Grove Rd.

✻ Where to Eat

DINING OUT

Mexico Beach

Their tag line—"The Freshest Seafood from the Gulf of Mexico!"—is what they stand behind at the **Fish House Restaurant** (850-648-8950; fishhouse mexicobeach.com), 3006 US 98, where you can feed your family great seafood at reasonable pieces. Their array of seafood options include grouper, bay scallops, oysters, mahimahi, crab, and shrimp several ways ($15–20), with half orders an option. A hearty shrimp basket with fries and slaw is only $7 from 11 to 4 daily. Open for lunch and dinner, and for breakfast on weekends.

Panama City

Right on the waterfront at the historic St. Andrews Marina (see *Boating*), **Uncle Ernie's Bayfront Grill & Brew House** (850-763-8427; uncle erniesbayfrontgrill.com), 1151 Bayview Ave, treats diners to an excellent view and the sparkle of history—this restaurant is in a home built in the late 1800s and moved here from nearby. Seafood is the primary focus, with soft-shell crab, scallops Florentine, Grouper Imperial—a lovely creation in which shrimp and sea scallops topped with Crab Imperial sauce adorn a grouper fillet—and the St. Andrews Seafood Combo (shrimp, sea scallops, grouper, and stone crab claws), prepared your way, among the many delights on the menu. It's easier to grab a table at lunchtime, but dinner ($18–32) is worth the wait. Tue–Sun 11–10.

Panama City Beach

Since 1978 the Old English–style **Boars Head Restaurant & Tavern** (850-234-6628; boarsheadrestaurant .com), 17290 Front Beach Rd, has been serving up great prime rib and fresh Gulf seafood. They're proud to feature "wild" Florida shrimp—caught by Florida shrimpers—on the menu, along with an array of signature fish dishes such as Paneed Grouper (pan-fried, topped with lump crabmeat and béarnaise) and Grouper Sonoma (with creamy sauce flavored with Chardonnay, mushrooms, and king crab meat). Their char-grilled steaks include a mouthwatering "Greek" Petite stuffed with feta cheese, smoked bacon, and chopped Greek peppers. Venison and quail are on the menu, too. Entrées $18–32. Open daily at 4:30 PM.

The Boatyard (850-240-9273; boat yardclub.com), 5323 N Lagoon Dr. Executive chef Konrad Jochum has stepped up the range and quality of the beloved Key West–influenced menu here, and like his predecessor picked up the Key West flavor while working on the island. Lunch options ($7–17) pull in Keys faves like hearts of palm and roasted pepper chopped salad, black beans and yellow rice, and the Cuban Mix, a sandwich recipe straight from the M&M Laundry in Key West. Dinner showcases entrées ($12–27) like key lime garlic shrimp, with colossal pink shrimp broiled in garlic butter and fine herbs, topped with garlic and cilantro sauce, and served with black beans, yellow rice, and sweet plantains. Creative sushi is featured Thu–Sun with rolls that will surprise and delight. Add in an extensive martini selection, special Sunday brunch (11–3), and the monthly "Little Sun Dress Party," and this is a happening hangout.

Port St. Joe

Sunset Coastal Grill (850-227-7900; sunsetcoastalgrill.com), 602 Monument Ave. Settle back and watch the sun set over the bay in this New Orleans–influenced restaurant, where fresh, local seafood has a twist of Cajun spice and hand-cut steaks sate the hungry land-lubbers. Dinner served nightly, $16–25.

Rosemary Beach

For fine seafood dishes, head to **Blue by Night** (850-231-6264; oceanreef resorts.com/summer-kitchen-cafeblue -night), 60 N Barrett Square, which is also Summer Kitchen (see *Eating Out*) by day. As night falls, the menu shifts to fine seafood preparations such as pan-fried grouper with stone-ground Gouda grits, grilled asparagus, and saffron butter sauce; or blackened mahimahi with tropical fruit salsa, buttermilk-chive mash, and butter sauce. Entrées ($20–28) change frequently, depending on what's fresh; their meats and fish come from top-class sources.

Onano Neighborhood Cafe (850-231-2436; onanocafe.com), 78 Main St, Rosemary Beach, is located in Pensione Inn (see *Lodging*). Delight in their northern Italian cuisine, which features local seafood served with Tuscan flair. Pair a classic Caprese salad with a crab polpette—a crab "cake" grilled and served with tarragon-caper aioli and greens—for a light meal, or enjoy the chef's choice cioppino, fresh seafood braised in a light tomato broth with a grilled crostini. Entrées $15–35.

EATING OUT

Chipley

Gloria's 1901 Gallery & Cafe (850-638-8463), 803 Main St, is a part of Chipley's history, with its Victorian atmosphere and comfort cooking. Try the sausage and chicken gumbo, or a light Gloria's Plate with three small salads. Kids can get peanut butter and jelly sandwiches! Lunch $5–7. A long display counter runs down one wall, showcasing jewelry and gifts for sale. Open Tue–Fri 9–2.

Home Town Diner (850-638-9960), 709 7th St, keeps hopping during the morning hours—they open at 5:30 AM, so you can grab a bite on your way to go fishing. Menu changes daily.

Mexico Beach

Ever have a seafood or fish taco? The folks at **Killer Seafood** (850-648-6565; killerseafood.net), 820 US 98, will be happy to introduce you to this treat; landlubbers can stick with the tasty burgers. Choose from plenty o' po'boys, Killer Shrimp (simmered in their own special "Killer Seafood Simmerin' Sauce"), a bunch of baskets, or the combo platters, $6–18.

((ツ)) On hot days, head to the local ice creamery, **Scoops Up** (850-648-5118), 2802-A US 98, which riffs off a surfer theme. You can cool down with a quick cone while you shop in their cute gift shop, or savor a banana split as you check your email.

Locals love **Sharon's Café** (850-648-8634), 1100 US 98, a mom-and-pop place at the beach, for breakfast: Kids of all ages are delighted with their fluffy pancakes, which come decorated with a Happy Face. And yes, those are real blueberries in your pancakes, a tough thing to find these days! Cash only.

Relax after a long day of fishing or sightseeing at **Toucan's Restaurant** (850-648-8207; toucansmexicobeach fl.com), 812 US 98, enjoying a breath-taking view of the Gulf of Mexico. Fresh local seafood comes prepped steamed, broiled, or fried. You're close enough to the famed bay for a mouth-watering plate of Apalachicola oysters baked several ways—I'd go for Monterey, with lump crab, sherry, and Monterey cheese. She-crab soup, fresh peel-'n'-eat shrimp, grouper, it's all good. Entrées $15–25. If you like your seafood fried, go for a basket. Happy hour 4–6 at the Tiki Bar.

Panama City

Bayou Joe's Marina Grill (850-763-6442; bayoujoes.com), 112A E 3rd Court, serves all three meals daily—homemade jam in the morning, Cajun cookin' in the evening—with a side order of a blissful view of Massalina Bayou. Hearty breakfast options include the Bayou Omelet, Tom's Trash with Class, Garbage Potatoes, and Catfish & Eggs; dinner brings out the house favorite Pecan Encrusted Fillet O' Fish (cod or grouper, your choice) and a dozen other temptations, $16–22. Yes, they have fried green beans and fried pickle chips in case you need some down-home veggies, but the Bayou Blue Chips—freshly made potato chips with blue cheese crumbles—are my appetizer of choice. Sun–Mon 7–7, Tue–Sat 7–9.

The top dog in town is at **Tom's Hot Dogs** (850-769-8890), 555 Harrison Ave, which is consistently voted best hot dog year after year, and is always bustling at lunchtime. Get your dog topped with "Tom's Sauce" for the authentic taste.

(ᵂⁱ-ᶠⁱ) Take a break from shopping at the charming English tea shop **Willows British Tea Room** (850-747-1004; willowstea.com), 461 Harrison Ave, where British favorites like the Ploughman's Lunch and Shepherd's Pie join the delicacies you'd expect in a tearoom—scones with cream and jam, finger sandwiches, and crumpets,

$3–8. Of course, a Royal Afternoon Tea ($14) is offered. Tue–Sat 10–4.

Panama City Beach

Craving a blueberry waffle? Seafood omelet? Granted, most of the accommodations along the beach have their own kitchenettes or continental breakfast, but **Mike's Diner** (850-234-1942; eatatmikes.com), 17554 Front Beach Rd, is worth a venture out of your room for a sit-down meal, $3–6. And their Beach Lover's Lunch hits the high notes on diner classics such as beef tips over rice, country-fried Steak, and chop steak, $7–8, served with fresh corn bread and grits, two veggies, and a dessert.

✍ Sitting across from the dunes since 1971, **Thomas' Donut and Snack Shop** (850-234-8039), 19208 Front Beach Rd, has a long line at the take-out window at sunrise; the breakfast room is packed, too. The family has been serving food up on this beach since 1948—the same folks who own Mike's Diner—so this is an institution. Grab a hot fresh sack of long johns if you're in a hurry, but better if you have the time to wait for their hot country biscuits ($2), all dressed up with your choice of sausage, ham, chicken, steak, pork chops, eggs, or gravy. Open at 6, breakfast until 10:30 AM. Lunch served all afternoon, including hot dogs, pizza, subs, burgers, and an oyster burger, $2–5. Closed Wed.

Port St. Joe

Anchored just outside the gates of St. Joseph Peninsula State Park, **Cone-heads** (850-229-5252), 8020 Cape San Blas Rd, has tasty "world famous burgers," hand-pattied and seasoned. Plunk down and enjoy yours inside a little niche indoors or outdoors with a sea breeze. Other lunch treats include fried or grilled shrimp salad, chef salad, seafood chowder, $5–12. Don't forget the ice cream, including a big banana split for $8. Open for lunch only, closed Sun.

Dockside Café (850-229-5200; docksidecafe.net), 340 Marina Dr at the marina, offers a nice selection of local seafood—or bring your own catch and they'll prepare and cook it your way. Lunch and dinner, $9–28.

Indian Pass Raw Bar (850-227-1670; indianpassrawbar.com), 8391 CR 30A, Indian Pass, looks like an old general store, where folks hang out drinking cold beer while chowing down on some of the freshest seafood in these parts. Grab oysters and shrimp by the dozen, steamed crab legs, or get the kids a corn dog. Lunch and dinner Tue–Sat.

A downtown favorite, **Sisters Restaurant** (850-229-7121), 236 Reid Ave, serves up tasty lunches like the Port Special, a turkey-bacon-Swiss BLT mash-up, and Carolina Chicken Salad, with slices of southern fried chicken atop fresh garden veggies. Lunch, $4–7.

Rosemary Beach
((♥)) Take your laptop to the **Courtyard Wine & Cheese** (850-231-1219), 66 Main St, where you can connect to WiFi while enjoying wine by the glass from more than 50 varietals. Add a nice piece of imported and domestic gourmet cheese and enjoy the fresh air of the open courtyard. Daily 11–11.

Grab breakfast or a healthy lunch of wraps, salads, or sandwiches at **Summer Kitchen** (850-231-6264; thesk cafe.com), 60 N Barrett Square, a delightful eatery open 7:30–3:30 and boasting the best burgers around. For dinner, the restaurant turns into Blue by Night (see *Dining Out*).

At the **Wild Olives Market** (850-231-0065; wildolivesmarket.com), 29 Canal St, you can shop for specialty groceries or order lunch salads, sandwiches, pizza, and hot meals to go. The tapas menu is a great for a late-afternoon snack.

✳ Entertainment

The art-deco-style **Ritz-Martin Theatre** (850-763-8080; martintheatre .com), 409 Harrison Ave, Panama City, first opened in 1936 as part of a movie house chain. During the 1950s, the Martin family purchased the aging facility and operated it for more than 20 years. It then sat dormant for more than a decade; only in the late 1980s were major renovations brought about by the Panama City Downtown Improvement Board. With the historic theater gracefully restored to

THE RITZ-MARTIN THEATRE, DOWNTOWN PANAMA CITY

life, the state-of-the-art facility now serves the community as an intimate venue for comedy, plays, and musical performances.

The **Spanish Trail Playhouse** (850-638-9133; spanishtrailplayhouse.com), 680 2nd St, Chipley, offers community theater productions. First established in 1962, the playhouse was shuttered for many years but reopened in 2008.

✳ Selective Shopping

Chipley

Set a few miles north of town, **Anomaly** (850-638-1009), 506 Main St, can't be missed—Elvis has left the building and is standing roadside. Poke around in this fully stuffed store to find a little bit of everything, from old LPs to pennants, vintage books, and furnishings.

Give in to temptation at **The Chocolate Gallery** (850-638-9393), where tasty coffee complements the selection of hand-dipped specialties. Tue–Fri 9–5.

At the **Historic Chipley Antique Mall** (850-638-2535), the groaning floorboards of this beautiful building hold stacks of treasures from numerous local dealers. In addition to handmade dulcimers and 1940s advertising art, I found vintage glass and the only cigar shop in this part of the state. Tue–Fri 4:30–8 PM, Sat 10–5.

Farm-fresh produce is a highlight of the **Main Street Market** (850-638-7755; chipleymarket.com), 1251 Jackson Ave, a family business with roots going back five generations on a local farm. Their Amish imports, from homemade soaps to jams and apple butter, make great gifts.

Mexico Beach

A nice selection of gifts and beachwear can be found at **Beachwalk** (850-648-4200; mexicobeachgifts.com), 3102 US 98, featuring some of the top casual names like Life is Good, Columbia, Santiki, and Teva.

SHOPPING AT MEXICO BEACH

A great place to pick up beach and fishing supplies, **Cathey's Ace Hardware** (850-648-5242), 3000 US 98, also rents some equipment.

You'll enjoy browsing antiques and fine gifts at the **Driftwood Inn** (see *Lodging*) as much as you'll enjoy the ambience of this grand Victorian Inn.

Kitschy souvenirs and beach necessities can be found at the beachside gift shop inside the **El Governor Motel** (see *Lodging*).

Inside **Toucan's Restaurant** (see *Eating Out*), the Gift Shop carries a great line of beachwear, including bathing suits—in case you forgot yours.

If you are into nautical decor, then head to **The Grove** (850-648-4445; thegroveofmexicobeach.com), 2700 US 98, where you'll find fine furnishings and accessories for both inside and outside the home.

Whether beachy or preppy, ladies will be sure to find just the right ensemble at **Ladyfish** (850-648-4847), 2802 US 98, which features such boutique wear as Lacoste and Lilly Pulitzer. Open Wed–Sun.

Named for fruit native to the area, a must-stop is **Prickly Pears Gourmet Gallery** (850-648-1115; pricklypears .net), 101 S 36th St (set back off US 98), where owners Arlene and Mike offers up a unique collection of gourmet food, organic spices, coffee, hand-dipped chocolates, and exotic cheeses, such as the Drunken Goat Cheese from Spain, or (my favorite) the blueberry Stilton from England. The eclectic gallery also exhibits a wide variety of art crafted by local artisans. Barbecue is now on the menu, too! Tue–Sat 10–5:30.

You'll find great shelling on the beach, but fabulous shells and shell jewelry are also at **The Shell Shack** (850-648-8256; shellshackmexicobeach.com), 3800 US 98, where you can also buy fresh seafood.

The chic shopper will enjoy **Two Gulls at the Beach** (850-648-1122), 2802 US 98, which offers resort wear for both men and women along with a nice line of Brighton jewelry.

Panama City

Downtown, Harrison Avenue is the hot spot for shopping. The **Main Street Gallery of Art** (850-785-7110; main streetgallerypc.com), 537 Harrison Ave, showcases original art, sculpture, and pottery by local artists. You'll find an extensive selection of antiques, jewelry, and collectibles at the **Olde Towne Antique Mall** (850-763-9993), 437 Harrison Ave, along with a nice art collection. Grab a new or used book to read on the beach at **Books by the Sea** (850-784-8100; booksbythesea .com), 571 Harrison Ave, an independent bookstore with character. Fine women's clothing, including plus sizes, can be found at **DeHerberts** (850-769-0592), 550 Harrison Ave, while **Elegante Heirs** (850-769-0245), 314 Harrison Ave, has nice clothing and gifts for your little ones.

🐾 Don't forget Fluffy and Rover while you're on vacation. They'll want to go to the **Downtown Pet Salon** (850-769-9786), 547 Grace Ave, for conditioning and grooming after the dog days of summer.

The gallery and studio of internationally known watercolor artist **Paul Brent** (850-785-2684; paulbrent.com), 413 W 5th St, features originals and prints of coastal scenes and wildlife art, along with pottery, jewelry, and glassware from other talented artists.

Learn some new recipes and then pick up a fine wine to complement your new culinary skills at **Somethin's Cookin'** (850-785-8590; somethinscookin.com),

93 E 11th St, or just stop in for a tasty lunch.

Vision Quest Gallery and Emporium (850-522-8552), 230 W 15th St, displays art, antiques, and jewelry and offers classes.

Panama City Beach

Once upon a time, Pier Park was a classic amusement park with one of the oldest wooden roller coasters in Florida. I'm glad I had a chance to ride that coaster, since **Pier Park** (850-236-9974; simon.com/mall/?id =1204), 600 Pier Park Dr, is now a hot open-air Caribbean-themed shopping mall for the beach crowd. Pop into Jimmy Buffett's Margaritaville for a bite, catch a movie at the Grand 16, or check out Chico's for cute resort wear. Dillards, JCPenney, and Target anchor the mall complex. Mon–Sat 10–9, Sun noon–6.

Port St. Joe

Bay Artiques (850-229-7191), 301 Reid Ave, displays classy coastal art from local and Panhandle artists, interspersed with antiques. Thu–Sat 10–5.

The **No Name Café** (850-229-9277), 306 Reid Ave, may highlight the café on their sign, but I know a bookstore when I see one. This is the "everything" shop of Port St. Joe, from toys to new fiction and Floridiana, art by local artists, a big space in which art classes are held, and the namesake coffee shop—which serves up lunch as well.

Find tons of tiny treasures inside **Persnickety** (850-227-7194), 210 Reid Ave, including sweet clothes for tots, treats for your favorite pooch, classic toys, and local art.

Portside Trading Company (850-227-1950), 328 Reid Ave, has home decor and goodies with a nautical flair—painted stemware, glass sea

horses, and gourmet foods from the Blue Crab Bay Company. Closed Sun.

St. Patrick's Seafood Market (850-229-0070) along FL 71 packs your shrimp, oysters, and other seafood treats for travel.

Rosemary Beach

Take the little tykes to **Gigi's Fabulous Kids Fashions and Toys** (888-353-6161 or 850-231-0110; gigisfab kids.com), 62 Main St, for fun toys and cool clothes. You'll also find educational and craft supplies to keep the little ones busy on rainy days.

Tuck into the **Hidden Lantern Bookstore** (850-231-0091; thehiddenlantern .com) 84 N Barrett Square, to browse through thousands of books to find just the right read for relaxation.

Breathe in aromatic scents at **Pish Posh Patchoulis** (850-231-2005; patchoulis.com), 82 S Barrett Square, where you'll find beach essentials, fragrant decor, and organic indulgences.

Shabby Slips (850-231-4164), 58 Main St, is known mainly for its custom slipcovers and pillows, but you'll also enjoy their fine collection of original abstract art.

You'll want to remember your beach vacation; your best bet for Rosemary Beach logo items is at the **Rosemary Beach Trading Company** (850-231-2410; rosemarybeach.com), Lofts East, 34 N Barrett Square, which also features other nifty souvenir items.

✳ Special Events

February: Chefs from all over the United States compete annually at the Mardi Gras–style **Mexico Beach Gumbo Cook Off** (888-723-2546; mexicobeach.com); proceeds subsidize the town's Independence Day celebration.

May: ✒ **The Mexico Beach Spring Fling and Fishing Tournament** (888-723-2546; mexicobeach.com) offers thousands of dollars in cash prizes. Families will enjoy the children's fishing tournament and live entertainment in a wholesome party atmosphere.

The **Gulf Coast Triathlon** (850-282-8573; gulfcoasttriathlon.com) kicks off in Panama City Beach, where athletes from all over the United States and 15 countries compete in a celebratory weekend.

Tupelo Festival (850-227-1223), mid-May. They've been making tupelo honey in Wewahitchka for more than a century, and the town celebrates this heritage with food, crafts, and entertainment at Lake Alice Park. Free.

July: ✒ The **Best Blast on the Beach** (888-723-2546; mexicobeach.com). Expect a fun beach party for the Fourth of July with lots of entertainment for the kids. A beach trolley runs up and down the 3-mile stretch of town for easy transportation from your hotel or campground.

In Panama City Beach, the **Bay Point Invitational Billfish Tournament** gives anglers top dollar awards for fishing billfish, dolphin, wahoo, and tuna, such as the 998.6-pound billfish that landed Barry Carr the $100,000 prize in 2006. Invitations are by nomination or by application to Bay Point Marina Company (850-235-6911; baypointbillfish.com).

Vernon 4th of July Extravaganza offers an authentic slice of Americana and apple pie, with Little Miss and Mister Firecracker presiding over the downtown parade.

August: ✒ A family favorite! Anglers of all ages will want to compete in the largest kingfish tournament in the area. Sponsored by the Mexico Beach Artificial Reef Association, the annual **King Mackerel** event (888-723-2546; mbara.org) is held the weekend before Labor Day. There's lots of music, fun, and food, including a fish fry. Cash prizes awarded for the largest king mackerel, Spanish mackerel, and wahoo. Proceeds benefit artificial reef and fisheries habitat education and research and local fishery habitat improvements.

Now more than 15 years old, the **Florida Scallop & Music Festival** (850-227-1223; gulfchamber.org /scallopfestival), Port St. Joe, last weekend, is educational and entertaining—learn all about scallops and scalloping along the bay. Free.

October: Don't miss the annual **Mexico Beach Art & Wine Festival** (888-723-2546; mexicobeach.com), when the tiny town presents juried artists, fine wines, unusual beers, and live jazz and blues at the Driftwood Inn.

December: A highlight of the holiday season, the **Holly Fair**, features crafts, choirs, and culinary delights at the Boardwalk Beach Resort (850-785-7870; boardwalkbeachresort.com) in Panama City Beach, benefiting the Junior Service League.

APALACHICOLA RIVER

APALACHICOLA, MARIANNA, QUINCY/CALHOUN, FRANKLIN, JACKSON, LIBERTY & WESTERN GADSDEN COUNTIES

The superhighway of the region, the meandering 108-mile Apalachicola River, begins at the confluence of the Flint and Chattahoochee rivers, where Georgia and Florida meet. Over millennia it's been the dynamic force that shaped ecology, wildlife, and human settlement, and it marks the divide between Eastern and Central time zones—except for the town of **Apalachicola**, which is rooted, as the seat of Franklin County, in Eastern Standard Time. Along the lower Apalachicola River, nearest the city that bears its name, are remains of aboriginal sites, where the first peoples of this area gathered oysters and clams and left mounds called middens, building high ground with their refuse amid the swamps. The Creek Indians followed the river's course and settled here in the 1700s, coining the name, which means "the people on the other side." Fighting the British in the War of 1812 and the Creeks during the Creek War of 1813–1814, Andrew Jackson moved his interests into Western Florida to fight the British and their Indian allies. In 1816, under Jackson's command, American colonel Duncan Clinch led a force to take the fort upriver from Apalachicola at Prospect Bluff. A single cannonball hit the ammunition pile inside, causing a massive explosion that blew apart the fort and instantly killed most of its defenders. Now known as Fort Gadsden, it's a significant historic site along the river.

River traffic grew tremendously from 1829 onward, with upward of 200 river boats making the 262-mile journey between the towns of Columbus, Georgia, and Apalachicola, with more than 240 docks and landings between them. As plantations rose on the bluffs above the river, commerce kicked into gear, with shipments of cotton and produce bound for distant ports. As the port city incorporated in 1829, Apalachicola thrived. Shipping cotton, it became the third-largest port on the Gulf Coast by 1836, after New Orleans and Mobile. The bustling city attracted enterprising folks of all types, including the celebrated Dr. John Gorrie, one of only two historic Floridians represented with a statue in the U.S. Capitol Building in Washington, DC. An inventive man, Gorrie applied his engineering know-how to keeping his recovering malaria patients cool by using compressed air, condensation

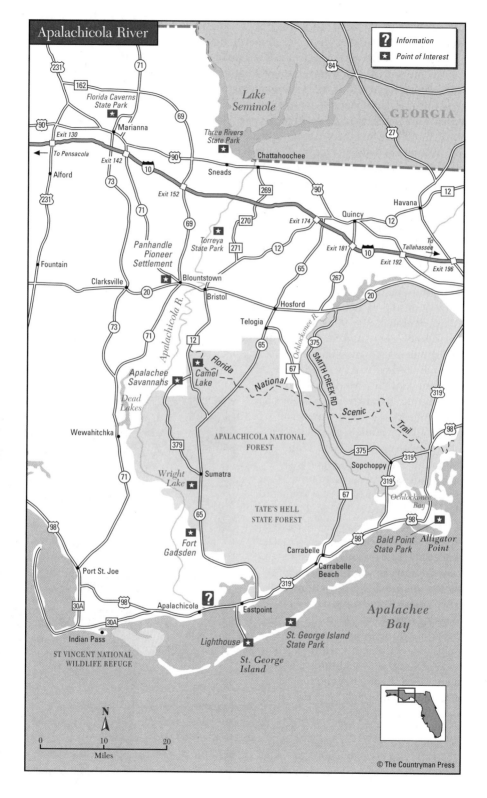

Apalachicola River

? Information
★ Point of Interest

GEORGIA

Lake Seminole

Florida Caverns State Park ★

Three Rivers State Park ★

Chattahoochee

Marianna
Exit 130
To Pensacola
Exit 142
Alford
Sneads
Exit 152
Quincy
Havana
To Tallahassee
Exit 174
Exit 181
Exit 192
Exit 196
Fountain
Torreya State Park ★
Panhandle Pioneer Settlement ★
Clarksville
Blountstown
Bristol
Hosford
Telogia
Apalachicola R.
Ochlockonee R.
SMITH CREEK RD
Florida
Camel Lake ★
National
Apalachee Savannahs ★
Dead Lakes
Scenic
Trail
Wewahitchka
APALACHICOLA NATIONAL FOREST
Sopchoppy
Wright Lake ★
Sumatra
Ochlockonee Bay
TATE'S HELL STATE FOREST
Fort Gadsden ★
Carrabelle
Bald Point State Park ★
Alligator Point
Port St. Joe
Carrabelle Beach
Apalachee Bay
Apalachicola ?
Eastpoint
Indian Pass
Lighthouse ★
St. George Island State Park
ST VINCENT NATIONAL WILDLIFE REFUGE
St. George Island

N

0   10   20
Miles

© The Countryman Press

and a fan. By doing so, he developed the world's first system for mechanical refrigeration, patented in May 1851: forerunner to the air conditioner.

During the Civil War, Apalachicola was under heavy siege by the Union Blockading Squad. The river's strategic importance to the Confederacy was key to Confederate naval efforts, since shipbuilding for the fleet occurred in Columbus. Timbering, especially of the ancient cypress found in the swamps along the river, became the mainstay of trade after the war. The boom in oyster harvesting hit its stride by 1896, when three canneries were shipping more than 50,000 tins of oysters nationwide daily, and a sponge industry rivaling that of Tarpon Springs took hold. But as railroads started carrying more commercial freight than ships, commerce in Apalachicola declined, and by 1927 steamboat traffic had ceased due to increasingly unpredictable water levels. Between 1935 and 1946, efforts by the Army Corps of Engineers to manage water levels meant upstream dams and dredged navigational channels as well as piles of spoil dumped on fragile habitats, which led to a decline in the fisheries.

Today 246,000 acres at the sweep of the river mouth are under state and federal protection and named a United Nations Biosphere Reserve, surrounding **Apalachicola**, the vibrant heart of the region; **Eastpoint**, a community defined by its working shrimpers and oystermen, who provide the bounty enjoyed in local restaurants and elsewhere—90 percent of Florida's oysters are harvested from Apalachicola Bay—and **St. George Island**, with its white-sand beaches and rolling dunes separating the bay from the Gulf of Mexico. As you drive the gorgeous shoreline bends of the Big Bend Scenic Byway from Apalachicola to Carrabelle, watch for other small barrier islands in the Gulf shallows, Little St. George Island and **Dog Island** among them. The public lands along these shores mean an immersion into authentic Old Florida as you enjoy the beauty of the "Forgotten Coast."

In the northerly counties along the Apalachicola River watershed, expect pine-topped ridges and high bluffs above the rivers, where rural life thrives in settlements like **Blountstown**, **Bristol**, and **Chattahoochee**. Working downtowns characterize these small towns—islands in a sea of cotton fields, pine plantations, cattle ranches, and dairy farms. **Marianna** anchors the northwest corner of the region, with genteel historic homes and outstanding outdoor recreation.

The Apalachicola River region is a friendly place, where you can share small talk with shopkeepers and innkeepers, or hoist a beer with the

DOWNTOWN MARIANNA

locals down at the waterfront. And don't be surprised to see the sheriff wave hello as he drives past on US 98!

GUIDANCE **Riverway South Apalachicola/Choctawhatchee** (www.rwsfl.org) is a new umbrella tourism organization representing the many rural communities of the region. You can also find information at local chamber offices. You'll easily find the **Apalachicola Bay Chamber of Commerce** (850-653-9419; apalachicolabay.org), 122 Commerce St, Apalachicola, right in the shopping district. Similarly, it's hard to miss beautifully restored Russ House in Marianna (see *Historic Sites*), where the **Jackson County Chamber of Commerce** (850-482-9633; jacksoncounty.com), 4318 Lafayette St, is housed and can help you with local tourism and accommodation information. Stop in the **Gadsden County Chamber of Commerce** (850-627-9231; gadsdencc.com), 208 N Adams St, Quincy, or the **Calhoun County Chamber of Commerce** (850-674-4519; calhounco.org), 20816 Central Ave E, Suite 2, right in the heart of the commercial district of Blountstown. The **Carrabelle Chamber of Commerce** (850-697-2585; carrabelle.org) and **Liberty County Chamber of Commerce** (850-643-2359; libertycountyflorida.com) are best contacted in advance.

GETTING THERE Four major highways run east–west through this region, which is taller than it is broad. **US 90** connects Quincy, Chattahoochee, Sneads, and Marianna; **FL 20** crosses the Apalachicola River between Bristol and Blountstown; **US 98** runs along the scenic coastline between Carrabelle, Eastpoint/St. George Island, and Apalachicola; and **I-10** has exits for Quincy, Chattahoochee/Bristol, Grand Ridge, and Marianna. On the west side of the river, **US 231** heads south from Dothan, Alabama, through Jackson County—Campbellton, Cottondale, and Alford—toward Panama City Beach; **FL 71** will get you to Apalachicola from I-10 at Marianna via Blountstown, and **US 98** east from Port St. Joe (see the *Panama City* chapter); **FL 65** is the scenic route through Liberty County to US 98 between Carrabelle and Eastpoint (head west for Apalachicola), and **FL 67** the scenic direct route from FL 20 to Carrabelle. Virtually every route through the region will delight you with rural scenery or forested landscapes.

MEDICAL EMERGENCIES Emergency treatment can be received at **George E. Weems Memorial Hospital** (850-653-8853; weemsmemorial.com), 135 Ave G, Apalachicola, and at **Jackson Hospital** (850-526-2200; jacksonhosp.com), 4250 Hospital Dr, Marianna. Most of this region is very remote, and cell phone service isn't guaranteed in the vast rural areas and forests between I-10 and US 98.

✳ To See

ART GALLERIES

Apalachicola
The **Alice Jean Art Gallery** (850-653-3166), 29 Ave E, showcases Alice Jean Gibbs's haunting coastal scenes, Jane Tallman's pastels, and the photography of Alecia Ward. Mon–Fri 11–5 and some Saturdays.

Inside the beautifully restored Fry-Conter House, built in 1845 by Captain Daniel Frye, the **Apalachicola Museum of Art** (850-653-2090; apalachicolamuseumofart.org), 96 5th Ave, showcases changing exhibitions of the visual arts.

Florida landscapes, especially watercolors and acrylics of the iconic Apalachicola River, will draw you in the door at **Artemis Gallery** (850-653-2030; artemisgallery online.com), 127 Commerce St. Their shop competes with the gallery space, with handmade soaps, racks of colorful women's resort wear, and unique gifts from local artists.

🐾 The place for fine arts and crafts, the **Bowery Art Gallery** (850-653-2425; boweryartgallery.com), 149 Commerce St, is a collaborative effort among local artists who work in a variety of media, including fiber, pottery, and wood. You can tell their love of pets by the fun sculptures within (by Leslie Wallace-Coon) and the water bowl on the porch. Open Tue–Sat 10–5, by appointment on other days.

Inside a restored historic commercial building adjoining Scipio Creek, **Gallery 75** (850-653-6279; gallery-75.com), 317 Water St, showcases the abstract art of Charles S. Chapin and sculptures by his son, Samuel Chapin. Open by appointment.

Richard Bickel Photography (850-653-2828; richardbickelphotography.com), 81 Market St, is the showcase for this outstanding photographer's haunting black-and-white images of daily life that capture the soul of this region.

Blountstown

It was a pleasure to be there for the grand opening night at the **Preble-Rish Gallery** (850-674-4519; calhounco.org), 20684 Central Ave E, where two dear friends paid homage through their work to the beauty of the Apalachicola River—noted black-and-white landscape photographer Clyde Butcher and local filmmaker Elam Stoltzfus. Expect future installations to showcase the talents of regional artists and others who make the Apalachicola River a part of their artistic vision.

St. George Island

Sea Oats Gallery (850-927-2303; forgottencoastart.com), 128 E Pine St, has four rooms filled with scenes of Apalachicola and the Panhandle, featuring artists like Ellen Sloan and Roger Leonard, who deftly capture the coastal light. The sculptures of Cass Allen Pottery are joyful figures of angels in flight. Don't miss this gallery!

DAIRY FARM 🐾 At Shady Nook Farm's **Ocheesee Creamery** (850-674-8620; ocheeseecreamery.com), 28367 NE FL 69, Grand Ridge, the Jersey cows—which roam the pastoral landscape until milking time—provide the natural goodness that goes into every old-fashioned recyclable glass bottle of Ocheesee milk (remember milk bottles?), which comes in whole, skim, chocolate, and cream-top. You can watch the pasteurized milk being bottled; they make their own butter and cheese, too.

GHOST TOWNS Off FL 65 in the Apalachicola National Forest at New River, **Vilas** has little more to note its passing than some scattered building materials and a long-unused railroad siding; the Florida Trail (see *What's Where*) meanders through the remains of this turn-of-the-20th-century turpentine town.

HISTORIC SITES Driving through this rural region, you'll uncover Florida's pre–Civil War plantation history, where cotton grows on lands handed down through the generations. Most of the small towns have an old-time county courthouse, and sometimes the entire downtown district is a Florida Heritage Site. Here are a few of the most significant stops along the way.

Apalachicola

Downtown Apalachicola is a Florida treasure, with more than 900 homes and buildings on the National Register. Pick up a walking tour map at the chamber of commerce (see *Guidance*) and explore the many unique sites, such as the 1836 Greek **Sponge Exchange**, the 1831 **Chestnut Street Cemetery**, the Greek-built shrimp boat *Venizelos*, and this port city's **Customs House** from 1923, now a U.S. post office. One of only five surviving two-masted schooners in the United States, the 1877 Schooner *Governor Stone* (governorstone.org) is moored at the City Dock in Apalachicola. The 66-foot-long wooden-hulled vessel has masts made of longleaf yellow pine.

&. On a high bluff above the river, **Orman House** (850-653-1209; floridastate parks.org/ormanhouse), 177 5th St, was built by early settler and shipping magnate Thomas Orman with wood shipped from Syracuse, New York, in 1838. A tour through the mansion, which served as a B&B for some years and is now furnished with non-original period antiques, evokes the period in which cotton was king in Apalachicola. The dining area has a small alcove with exhibits about Orman. Ranger-led tours are offered periodically, or you can take a self-guided tour. Open Thu–Mon 9–5; fee.

The city-owned **Raney House** (850-653-1700), corner of Market St and Ave F, is a Greek Revival home built for prominent cotton merchant David Raney in 1825. Docents with extensive knowledge of the Raney family and the city of Apalachicola during their lives guide you through the rooms of the home, which is furnished with many original pieces on both stories. Free, donations appreciated. Open Tue–Fri 1–4, Sat 9–5.

Blountstown

Circa 1904, the old **Calhoun County Courthouse**, 314 Central Ave, is a pictur-esque sight along FL 20 as you drive into town from the river, especially in spring when the cherry trees around it are covered in blossoms. An excellent example of Romanesque Revival archi-tecture, it is on the National Register of Historic Places.

Carrabelle

Although the police force has out-grown its old digs, the **World's Small-est Police Station**, a phone booth downtown, remains, with a squad car always parked next door. It dates back to 1963, and I was going to ask the officer on duty about it, but he was busy giving a ticket to a speeder.

Chattahoochee

Since the early 1900s, the historic **Chattahoochee Arsenal**, site of Florida's first military arsenal in 1839,

CHERRY BLOSSOM TIME IN DOWNTOWN BLOUNTSTOWN

has been part of the grounds of the Florida State Hospital, a sanitarium.

Greenwood

Established in 1869, **Pender's Store** near the junction of FL 71 and FL 69 on Bryan St is one of the oldest continuously operated stores in Florida, retaining its original shelving and heart pine floors. On the way there, you'll pass stately **Great Oaks**, known as Bryan Plantation during the Civil War. The **Erwin House** on Fort Rd, east of FL 71, is perhaps the oldest structure in Jackson County, circa 1830. All three structures are on the National Register of Historic Places.

Marianna

First settled in the 1820s, Marianna formed the commercial center for a hub of busy plantations, including **Sylvania**, the home of Civil War–era governor John Milton, near what is now

THE WORLD'S SMALLEST POLICE STATION, CARRABELLE

the grounds of Blue Springs Park (see *Springs*). During the war, Marianna was a target because it was the governor's hometown. On September 17, 1864, the **Battle of Marianna** pitted the Home Guard (a militia of old men and teenagers) against invading Union troops. They fought in and around **St. Luke's Episcopal Church**, which was burned during the conflict. A Union officer preserved and returned the Holy Bible to the church, where it remains on display. Faced with surrendering the state to the Union army, Governor Milton returned home on April 1, 1865, and shot himself, eight days before Lee surrendered the Confederacy. Milton is buried at St. Luke's.

Down the street, the distinctively rounded **Russ House**, built in 1895 by prominent merchant Joseph W. Russ, had its fancy neoclassical pillars added in 1910. It now houses the Jackson County Chamber of Commerce (see *Guidance*), where you can pick up a walking tour guide to Marianna's many other historic structures.

Sumatra

One of the more significant historic sites along the Apalachicola River, **Fort Gadsden** in the Apalachicola National Forest (850-643-2282; fs.usda.gov/apalachicola) is tricky to find but worth the effort for the detailed historic interpretation on site. Two forts stood at this strategic location along the river. Constructed during the War of 1812 to defend British colonial interests, the original fortress encompassed a 7-acre tract along the Apalachicola River as a base to recruit runaway slaves and Indians to the British cause of wresting control of Florida from the Spanish. In 1815 the British abandoned the effort but left behind a force of 300 former slaves and Seminoles to watch over the river from what was then dubbed the "Negro Fort." When American colonel Duncan Clinch sailed upriver in 1816, the inhabitants of the fort fired on his gunboats. Clinch returned fire. A single cannonball hit the ammunition pile inside the fort, causing a massive explosion that blew apart the fort and its defenders. Only 30 survived, and Clinch had several of them executed. General Andrew Jackson ordered a new fortress erected on the spot as a base of operations for his missions during the First Seminole War. Lieutenant James Gadsden and his men held the fort until Florida became a U.S. territory in 1821. The fort fell into disrepair, although it was briefly occupied by Confederate troops guarding the gateway to the Apalachicola River. It's reached by dirt roads from FL 65 south of Sumatra—follow the signs. A mile-long interpretive and nature trail showcases the key points. Open sunrise–sunset; fee.

LIGHTHOUSES ⚓ Built in 1895 to replace a lighthouse destroyed in a hurricane on Dog Island, the newly restored **Crooked River Lighthouse** (850-697-2732; crookedriverlighthouse.org) along US 98 west of Carrabelle is the centerpiece of a pretty park with a pirate ship playground. Decommissioned from service in 1995, the lighthouse is now on the National Register of Historic Places and is adjoined by the Keeper's House Museum and a gift shop, open Thu–Sun noon–5. Depending on the weather, you can climb up the very narrow staircase to the top of the lighthouse, Sat–Sun, 1–4, if you are 44 inches or taller. Fee.

⚓ The **St. George Lighthouse** (850-927-7744; stgeorgelight.org) now sits prominently in the center of St. George Island, moved and reconstructed from its original components after a hurricane toppled the historic structure into the Gulf in 2005. Dating back to 1852 and rebuilt with a sturdy broad interior staircase, the lighthouse no longer has a lens inside, but that means you can crawl right up into the top (dexterity on a narrow ladder required) and look out across the island below. Adjoining structures illustrate the light keeper's quarters and provide a museum of artifacts from the lighthouse. Tours Mon–Wed, Sat 10–5, Sun noon–5; fee.

MURALS Local history is illustrated through the use of murals in several downtowns throughout the region. In Chattahoochee, the prominent **J. W. Callahan Riverboat Mural** by Von Tipton, gracing a brick building at Heritage Park, 400 W Washington St, reminds westbound travelers on US 90 of the importance of riverboats to the history of the Apalachicola River. Blountstown sports several showy murals, the work of my talented friend, local artist Jeff Vickery. The **Snowden Land Surveying Mural** near FL 20 and Pear St, behind the Preble-Rish Building (see *Art Galleries*), greets visitors driving through downtown with historical surveying scenes and a detailed map of the city; the **Diamond Corner Mural** on the northeast corner of FL 20 and FL 71 focuses on historic architecture from around the area; and the **Lake House Restaurant**, FL 20 W, shows a wilderness scene from the nearby Chipola River.

MUSEUMS

Apalachicola
Apalachicola Maritime Museum (850-653-2500), 103 Water St. Learn about the Gulf Coast's long and storied maritime history through the permanent and changing exhibits at this museum, including the fully restored 1877 schooner *Governor Stone* (see *Historic Sites*), moored along the waterfront. It's considered the oldest operating sailing vessel in the American South.

John Gorrie Museum State Park (850-653-9347; floridastateparks.org/john gorriemuseum), 46 6th St. Living in malaria-stricken Florida in the 1850s, Dr. John Gorrie had a problem: How to keep his recovering patients cool? With a great deal of engineering savvy, Gorrie found a way to use compressed air and condensation to make ice, then ran a fan across the ice to keep his infirmary cool. By doing so, he developed the world's first system for mechanical refrigeration, patented in May 1851: an icemaker. At the time, ice for refrigeration was cut from frozen northern lakes and packed in sawdust for transport. Gorrie died in obscurity, his achievement too "far out" for his time. It wasn't until the 1890s that ice

BLOUNTSTOWN'S PANHANDLE PIONEER SETTLEMENT

In 1966 Willard Smith got a gleam in his eye every time he saw the Yon Farm House. This 1897 wood frame pioneer home had a certain appeal, and when Willard finally took possession of it, it wasn't for him and new bride Linda, but to create the centerpiece of a personal mission to preserve Florida Panhandle history, the **Panhandle Pioneer Settlement** (850-674-3050; ppmuseum.org), 17869 NW Pioneer Settlement Rd, Sam Atkins Park, Bloustown. "It's a lifestyle worth preserving for future generations," said Willard, a fifth-generation Bloustown native, "and these buildings were disappearing." Together with Linda, who learned to write grants for historic preservation, they kicked off Calhoun County's prime tourist attraction in 1995. More than 20 structures now surround the Yon Farm House, all donated, all carefully restored by volunteers. The care shows in the presentation, too—in every building, it looks as if someone just stepped out for the moment, leaving behind whatever they were in the middle of, be it knitting, making dinner, or repairing a cane seat. Volunteer docents lead informative tours of this living history museum, which also has a farmstead and holds annual festivals (see *Special Events*). Open 10–2 Tue/Thu–Sat.

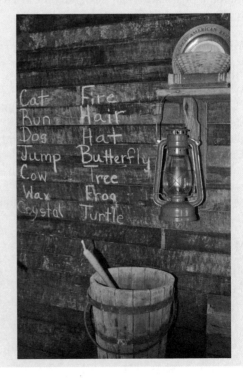

INSIDE THE PIONEER-ERA SCHOOLHOUSE AT THE PANHANDLE PIONEER SETTLEMENT

merchants discovered the magic of Gorrie's system, which led to the design of air-conditioning. Across the street, Gorrie is buried in Gorrie Square. In 1911 he was honored with a statue as one of two representatives of Florida history in the U.S. Capitol in Washington, DC. Open Thu–Mon 9–5; fee.

Carrabelle

Bet you didn't know that the first amphibious landing craft didn't land at Utah Beach on D-Day: They tried them out in Carrabelle first! From 1942 to 1946, the Gulf Coast from Ochlockonee Bay to Eastport was Camp Gordon Johnston, a training facility for more than 250,000 amphibious soldiers as they practiced storming beaches. The **Camp Gordon Johnston Museum** (850-697-8575; campgordon johnston.com), 302 Marine St, honors the World War II troops who trained here and preserves the history of that important effort, which clinched the Allied liberation of France, via artifacts and archives of special interest to vets and history buffs. Mon–Tue, Thu–Fri 1–4; Wed 10–4; Sat 10–1. Donation.

RAILROADIANA In downtown Bluntstown, you can't miss their railroad history at ✺ ✹ **Depot Park**, with the big M&B steam engine, tender, and caboose on what used to be the main line between N Pear St and N Main St (FL 71), in the middle of, fittingly, Railroad Ave and along the Bluntstown Greenway (see *Greenway*). On the opposite side of N Pear St, Depot Park includes the original Bluntstown Depot, restored by the local historical society to house the M&B Railroad Museum, open Mon–Wed 9–3, Thu 9–4, Fri–Sat 8–5, Sun 9–5. It's a city park with a railroad-themed playground and direct access to the greenway.

In Marianna, the **L&N Railroad Depot** was the eastern terminus of the railroad line when it was built. It dates back to 1881 and has been used for various functions since, including a bank. In Chattahoochee, Heritage Park has a **red caboose** parked next to a beautiful mural of the John W. Callahan steamboat on the Apalachicola River.

✳ To Do

BICYCLING A dedicated bicycle path runs down the middle of **St. George Island**; rent bikes at Island Outfitters (see *Paddling*). The **Bluntstown Greenway** (see *Greenway*) offers a paved path from the Panhandle Pioneer Settlement (see *Museums*) to the Apalachicola River. The region's scenic rural roads lend themselves to long-distance excursions as well.

BIRDING Along nearly 100 miles of back roads in the **Apalachicola River Wildlife and Environmental Area** (see *Wild Places*) look for hundreds of bird species, including swallow-tailed and Mississippi kites roosting in tall cypresses. Shorebirds abound on the tidal flats of the barrier islands.

BOAT EXCURSIONS To get to the remote barrier islands, you'll need a shuttle, such as **Dog Island Water Taxi** (850-697-3989), Carrabelle, or **Journeys of St. George Island** (see *Ecotours*), where you can rent your own boat to putter around Apalachicola Bay. Or kick back and enjoy a pleasurable sail on a 1950s sloop with **Wind Catcher Sailing Charters** (850-653-3881), which offers daily trips and can be chartered out to the islands.

BOATING As the quickest way between two points along this coast might be by boat, there are marinas and boat ramps along the way. In Apalachicola, the **City Marina** hides well beneath the big bridge depositing drivers westbound on US 98 into downtown, adjoining Battery Park. The **Scipio Creek Marina** (850-653-8030; scipiocreekmarina.com), 301 Ave B, has slips, dockage, showers, gas/diesel, and a ship's store, and is within walking distance of downtown. In Eastpoint, **Wefing's Marine** (850-670-8100; apalachicolaboatrentals.com), 131 US 98, offers boat rentals, which they'll meet you with at a boat ramp right on Apalachicola Bay. Choose from cats, skiffs, and flats boats starting at $275 a day, plus launch fees and fuel. Proof of boating experience required.

The **Moorings at Carrabelle** (see *Lodging*) provides dockage and onshore amenities in a hotel/condo complex.

DIVING Go diving with **Carrabelle Charters** (850-528-1926; scubadivecharters .com) to explore artificial reefs and wrecks off the Forgotten Coast; trips start at $650 for up to six divers.

ECOTOURS For a closer look at the estuary, a guided tour will give you a sense of place amid the vastness of this watery wilderness. Cruise with **Book Me A Charter** (850-653-2622, bookmeacharter.com) for an overview of oystering and the culture of the watermen, or head out with them for some fishing on the bay. Tours start at $300 for a four-client maximum.

⌀ Departing from the Water Street Hotel (see *Lodging*), **Wheelhouse Tours** (850-653-6032; wheelhousetours.com/tours.htm) runs relaxing tours for up to six people along the Apalachicola River. One-hour trip, $15; longer journeys available on request, including shelling trips.

⌀ **Journeys of St. George Island** (850-927-3259; sgislandjourneys.com), 240 E 3rd St, has a complete menu of tours, ranging from guided paddling trips, to ecotours to St. Vincent and Dog islands, to deep-sea and bay fishing. They also rent sailboats, motorboats, and kayaks, and run environmental summer camps and special kid-oriented trips. Kayak-based ecotours start at $30.

FAMILY ACTIVITIES ⌀ **Putt-N-Fuss Fun Park** (850-670-1211), 236 US 98, Eastpoint. Mini golf, bumper boats, and an arcade clustered around a miniature mountain at the gateway to St. George Island. Open daily, hours vary by season; fee.

FISHING No matter whether you prefer deep-sea excursions or casting a line off a bank, the entire Apalachicola River watershed is a huge destination for sport fishing, with tournaments held nearly every month. In Carrabelle ask about fishing guides at the **C-Quarters Marina** (850-697-8400; c-quartersmarina.com), 501 St. James Ave (US 98). **Top Knot Charters** (800-446-1639) is one of the long-established services in Carrabelle. Ask around Apalachicola for top guides like the **Robinson Brothers Guide Service** (850-653-8896; floridaredfish.com), or **Boss Charters** (850-853-8055; bosscharters.com), 150 Bay City Rd, for inshore light-tackle bay fishing, or offshore fishing on the *Miss Emily*. Depending on the guide, length of trip, and location, you'll pay $350 and up for a trip.

To fish the Apalachicola River on your own, put your boat in the river at any of many ramps along FL 71 or FL 67; you can rent a fishing boat from **Wefing's Marine** (see *Boating*). Stop in at **Forgotten Coast Outfitters** (850-653-9669), 94 Market St, Apalachicola, for fly-fishing tackle and homespun advice.

✐ For more than 15 years, the **Big River Roundup Flathead Catfish Tournament** (see *Special Events*), sponsored by the Blountstown Rotary, has drawn anglers from all over down to the banks of the Apalachicola River with prizes for the top cats. Fish from your boat or from the bank; family participation encouraged. Pre-register starting in March for a discount; registration fees of $25–55.

Lake Seminole is the hot spot for bass fishing in the region, splitting the state line between Georgia and Florida as the Flint and Chattahoochee rivers come together to form the Apalachicola. My friends tend to head for **Seminole Lodge** (see *Fish Camps*), a storied institution along the southern shore. For day trips with your own boat, **Three Rivers State Park** (see *Parks*) provides access as well. To its west, you won't want to miss the serenity of cypress-lined **Merritts Mill Pond** along US 90, Marianna, and **Spring Creek** for fly fishing.

GOLF Built by the Civilian Conservation Corps in the 1930s, the hilly **Florida Caverns Golf Course** (850-482-4257), 3309 Caverns Rd, has nine holes under the tall pines adjoining the state park and is managed by a local club, not the state park. Off US 90 east of Marianna, **Indian Springs Golf Club** (800-587-6257; indianspringsgolfcourse.net), 5248 Club House Dr, offers 18 holes, par 72.

HIKING The **Florida Trail** (see *What's Where*) passes through true wilderness in the Apalachicola National Forest between Porter and Camel lakes, with rare pitcher plant savannas (best seen during their blooming period in March) west of Camel Lake and around Memery Island. For more pitcher plants, hike the **Wright Lake Trail** around Wright Lake Recreation Area, Sumatra.

Florida Caverns State Park (see *Parks*) is a don't-miss locale for day hiking, thanks to its rugged geology and beautiful spring wildflowers. Speaking of rugged, the **Garden of Eden Trail** at the Apalachicola Bluffs and Ravines Preserve (see *Wild Places*) is one of the toughest little day hikes in Florida—up and down and up again to a prominent bluff above the Apalachicola River along a balloon-shaped trail less than 4 miles long. Backpackers won't want to miss the challenges of **Torreya State Park** (see *Parks*), where during the winter months you have ridgeline views from the 14-mile double-loop trail system. A primitive campsite perched in a quiet spot well above the river is worth the hike—in fact, the hike itself, physically challenging and visual diverse, is worth the trip to this lushly forested park.

HORSEBACK RIDING **Broke-A-Toe** (850-229-WAVE; brokeatoe.com) offers horseback riding on the shifting sands of St. George Island, $50 per hour.

PADDLING The **Chipola River Canoe Trail** starts at Florida Caverns State Park (see *Parks*) and flows 50 miles south to Dead Lake at Wewahitchka (see the *Panama City & Region* chapter), a three-day trip with a stretch of whitewater (portage recommended) near the FL 274 bridge. For canoe rentals and shuttling, check with **Scott's Ferry Landing** (see *Camping & Cabins*) or **Bear Paw**

Adventures (850-482-4948; bearpawescape.com), Magnolia Rd off FL 71, which runs half-day, full-day, and overnight trips daily. For day trips on the Upper Chipola, rent a canoe at Florida Caverns State Park.

Nonprofit guardians of the health of the river and bay, **Apalachicola Riverkeeper** (850-653-8936; apalachicolariverkeeper.org), 232-B Water St, runs guided paddling trips the fourth Saturday of every month in the Apalachicola watershed. The trips are free to members and $30 for non-members.

Along FL 65 you'll find numerous put-ins for paddling adventures into **Tate's Hell** (see *Wild Places*) and on the Apalachicola River; watch for the yellow-and-black signs at places like Graham Creek. Eleven such routes are outlined in the free **Apalachicola River Paddling Trail System** map available from the Apalachicola River Wildlife and Environmental Area office (850-488-5520; myfwc.com/viewing /recreation/wmas/lead/apalachicola-river/recreation/paddling).

For saltwater adventure, **Island Outfitters** (850-927-2604; sgioutfitters.com), 235 E Gulf Beach Dr, St. George Island, rents kayaks—single and tandem—and stand-up paddle boards. **Journeys of St. George Island** (see *Ecotours*) runs guided kayaking trips and rents and sells kayaks.

SCENIC DRIVES One of Florida's best scenic drives was once a little-known treasure through Liberty and Franklin counties, and is now a part of the nationally acclaimed **Florida Big Bend Scenic Byway** (floridabigbendscenicbyway.com). Start at FL 20 in Bristol; head south on CR 12 into the Apalachicola National Forest. This designated scenic route merges with FL 65 and continues south through nearly 50 miles of unspoiled old-growth longleaf pine forest as the road parallels the Apalachicola River. When the road ends, turn left. Atop a high sand bluff, US 98 offers sweeping views of St. George Sound for the next 22 miles. At Carrabelle, head north on FL 67 through the national forest to return to FL 20 at Hosford. Total drive time: three hours. Alternatively, CR 379 south of Bristol is the Apalachee Savannahs Scenic Byway, which dovetails into the above route onto FL 65 at Sumatra. Along this route, you'll see vast pitcher plant savannas blooming each spring.

SWIMMING In addition to the region's many beaches (see *Beaches*), swimmers head for **Blue Hole** at Florida Caverns State Park (see *Parks*) and to **Blue Springs** in Marianna (see *Springs*).

TUBING **Bear Paw Adventures** (see *Paddling*) sets up 4-mile tubing trips down crystal-clear, cypress-lined Spring Creek; Mar–Sep, $15 and up.

WALKING TOURS Stop at the Apalachicola Bay Chamber of Commerce (see *Guidance*) for a copy of their historic walking tour booklet that highlights 34 sites, most within seven blocks of Market St. In Marianna, pick up a 44-page self-guided tour of historic sites in Jackson County (see *Guidance*), which you can use to explore downtown on foot.

WATER SPORTS Check on the beach in front of the Blue Parrot (see *Eating Out*) on **St. George Island** for summer-season stands with Hobie Cat rentals and parasail rides, and at **Island Outfitters** (see *Paddling*) for water sports rentals.

✳ Green Space

BEACHES ✍ **Bald Point State Park** (850-349-9146; floridastateparks.org/bald point), 146 Box Cut Rd, provides Alligator Point with a quiet sweep of sandy beach along a peninsula of scrub oaks and pines. It's perfect for kids thanks to the lack of waves and the gentle shallow slope. Nature trails and bicycle paths following old roads wind through the coastal hammocks of the park; fee.

✍ Used for D-Day invasion practice in 1942, **Carrabelle Beach**, US 98 west of Carrabelle, tends to be busy because of its easy-to-reach location along this scenic stretch of coastal highway. It has restrooms, shaded picnic shelters, and a panoramic view that includes Dog Island in the distance. Free.

✍ ♿ Occupying the purely natural eastern end of St. George Island, **St. George Island State Park** (850-927-2111; floridastateparks.org/stgeorgeisland), 1900 E Gulf Beach Dr, has a pleasant campground nestled in among the pines at the east end of the island, and primitive camping for folks who hike the Gap Point Trail. A new wheelchair-accessible trail connects beach to bay. But the big draw here is the miles and miles of unspoiled white-sand beaches with a backdrop, behind the scenic park road, of tall dunes. Fee.

GARDEN Now a part of Orman House Historic State Park (see *Historic Sites*) and accessed from the same parking area, the **Chapman Botanical Garden** honors Dr. Alvin Wentworth Chapman (1809–1899), a medical doctor and botanist who spent most of his life in Apalachicola and defined 144 plant species during his research of regional botanicals. In 1860 he published *Flora of the Southern United States*. He is buried at the nearby Chestnut Street Cemetery, surrounded by some of the many plants named for him. Volunteers have made the park into a pleasant place to take a walk or read a book, with gazebos, benches, and quiet nooks. Free.

CHAPMAN BOTANICAL GARDEN, APALACHICOLA

GREENWAY 🐾 ✎ ♿ Park your car at the Blountstown Depot or the Panhandle Pioneer Settlement and walk, bike, or in-line skate the scenic and historic **Blountstown Greenway**, a 5-mile paved trail that connects the community to Apalachicola Landing along the Apalachicola River.

NATURE CENTER ✎ Recently moved to Eastpoint, the **Apalachicola National Estuarine Research Reserve Visitor Center** (850-670-7700), 108 Island Dr, is open Tue–Sat 9–4:30. See aquariums with aquatic life, including turtles and fish, from the Apalachicola estuary and river basin, and learn about the habitats and wildflowers common to this region. Free.

PARKS

Apalachicola

Home to the annual Florida Seafood Festival (see *Special Events*), **Battery Park** (850-653-9319), Bay Ave and 6th St, sits at the foot of town, in front of the Gibson Inn and beneath the big US 98 bridge into downtown. Bring a picnic lunch and enjoy it by the water. It is adjoined by the City Marina.

🐾 **Dog Park**, Ave L and 17th St, will give your furry friends a place to race around. It's divided into sections for large and small dogs, along with a special section for visitors with small children. Shaded rest areas and water keep your pups happy.

♿ Unless you go for a stroll in the historic residential district to the west of Apalachicola's downtown, you might miss **Lafayette Park** (850-653-9319), 13th St and Ave B, and that would be a shame. Dating back to 1832, this waterfront park is on a bluff well above the bay, with a long fishing pier that stretches out over the placid waters. Period lamps and an old-fashioned gazebo remind you of a bygone era, as do the many beautiful Victorian homes around the park's edges.

LAFAYETTE PARK PIER, APALACHICOLA

Riverfront Park, at the base of Ave E and along Water St, encompasses the historic docks in downtown Apalachicola. New additions of more dockage, outdoor seating, and unencumbered views make this a pleasant place for birding and watching boats go by on the river.

At the base of the bluff below the Orman House (see *Historic Sites*), the new **Veteran's Memorial Plaza**, 230 Market St, honors area servicemen and -women. This landscaped space features a Circle of Freedom walkway and the bronze *Three Servicemen Statue*, a tribute to Vietnam veterans by Fredrick Hart.

Blountstown
Sam Atkins Park, 19th St off FL 20 west of downtown, hosts regional powwow events and has the Panhandle Pioneer Settlement (see *Museums*) at the far edge of the park. The Blountstown Greenway (see *Greenway*) has a terminus here.

Chattahoochee
Tucked away in a residential area on the bluffs south of downtown, **Angus Gholson Nature Park** (850-663-2123), 400 Park St, is best visited in early spring for its delightful array of rare and unusual wildflowers. Its trails connect with the 107-acre **River Landing Park** (850-663-2123), 269 River Landing Rd, which has access to the Apalachicola River for anglers and boaters alike, as well as a playground and a large midden along the river. On the upper portion of River Landing Park you'll find a county-run campground, the Chattahoochee RV Campground & Fishing Resort (see *Camping & Cabins*).

Marianna
✧ ♿ **Citizens' Lodge Park** (850-718-0437; jacksoncountyfl.com/citizens_lodge .htm), 4577 Lodge Dr off Caverns Rd, is a great place to bring the kids to let off some steam. There's a duck pond where you can feed the ducks, and a playground with boulders to climb on. Paved trails wind through the open parkland, and a hiking trail heads for the hills on one side of the park.

♿ Along US 98 near Merritt's Mill Pond, tiny **Spring Creek Park** provides a wheelchair ramp right down to the water for fishing.

Bristol
From the 150-foot bluffs above the Apalachicola River at **Torreya State Park** (850-643-2674; floridastateparks.org/torreya), 2576 NW Torreya Park Rd/FL 271 between Bristol and Greensboro, you can see for miles. An 1849 mansion, the Gregory House, dominates the skyline. The star attraction, however, is the 14-mile hiking trail system, offering one of the most rugged backpacking experiences in the state as you pass earthen battlements built during the Civil War and climb through deep ravines and the tops of ridges. It's getting harder to find the namesake of the park, the torreya tree—also known as the stinking cedar—as a blight keeps the young trees from maturing. But they are along the trails. Enjoy the peaceful, scenic, developed campground (see *Camping & Cabins*), where you can try out Florida's only state park yurt!

Sneads
♿ **Three Rivers State Park** (850-482-9006; floridastateparks.org/threerivers), 7908 Three Rivers Park Rd, Sneads. Defined by the confluence of the Chattahoochee and Flint rivers creating the Apalachicola, this expansive recreation area includes Lake Seminole, a top-notch bass fishing destination, as well as a large

FLORIDA CAVERNS STATE PARK

(850-482-9598; floridastateparks.org/floridacaverns), 3345 Caverns Rd, Marianna. A dip into this, Florida's only show cave, brings on an instant sense of cool. Built by the Civilian Conservation Corps' "Gopher Gang" from 1938 to 1942, the tour route wraps through more than a dozen rooms with their own distinct landscapes. It's a live cave, dripping water on us from the stalactites above. Volunteer tour leader Dana Haynes used to work in mines, so he's comfortable in an environment where places have names like Fat Man's Squeeze, the Wedding Room, and the Cathedral. "If you'll follow me please, single file," he says, and we work our way down the well-worn paths deep into the earth. After spotlighting shimmering rimstone pools, translucent soda straws, and rippling cave bacon, he shines his light down a darkened passage. "Duck down and look to the left," he says, and we do, and he recounts the discovery of the cave in 1937, followed by a shadow-puppet version of the sinking of the *Titanic*. "And yes, I spend a *lot* of time down here." Everyone laughs. The passageways through the Catacombs get tighter before we emerge, but the splendors are worth the wriggle. For the claustrophobic, a video tour plays constantly in a big theater at the visitors center, where informative exhibits explain the unique habitats found in the park.

Above the caverns, hikers enjoy rugged limestone bluffs along the 1.5-mile Caverns Trail System, where the Bluff Trail goes right through Tunnel Cave, once used for shelter by ancient peoples. It's one of the most interesting day hikes in Florida, especially in spring when columbine and trillium bloom profusely. A drive along the park's very scenic main road will take you

lakeside campground (see *Camping & Cabins*) with a wheelchair-accessible rental cabin, picnic pavilions, hiking trails, and canoe rentals.

SPRINGS Marianna's **Blue Springs Park** (850-482-9637; jacksoncountyfl.com), 5461 Blue Springs Hwy, offers a sandy beach, diving boards, and playground fringing a 70-degree, first-magnitude spring bubbling more than 64 million gallons of water daily. Open Memorial Day–Labor Day. Fee. **Blue Hole**, at Florida Caverns State Park (see *Parks*), is also spring-fed; it's open to swimmers when water conditions permit.

WILD PLACES **Apalachicola Bluffs and Ravines Preserve** (850-643-2756; tnc.org), CR 12, Bristol, provides hikers with a look at unique natural areas along the bluffs of the Apalachicola River along the extremely rugged 3.5-mile Garden of Eden Trail, where the world's most endangered conifer, the torreya tree, grows along with rare varieties of magnolias and the showy Florida anise—look for bright red blooms in spring. The hike has a big payoff beyond the botanical wonders here: You'll enjoy great views from Alum Bluff above the Apalachicola River.

to other outposts within its boundaries. Stop at the Chipola River, where you can borrow a canoe (arrange the rental beforehand at the entrance station) to paddle this cypress-lined waterway, which vanishes underground before reemerging at this point. The camp-ground (see *Camping & Cabins*) is deeply shaded by forest and is within walking distance of Blue Hole, a spring that is open, when clear enough, for swimming. The parking area at Blue Hole accesses picnic pavilions and is the saddle-up point for equestrians and mountain bikers headed out on the Upper Chipola Trail System. Open 8 AM–sunset, the park charges a per-carload entrance fee with additional per-person fee for cavern tours. Call ahead to ensure tour availability.

BLUE HOLE IS A BEAUTIFUL SPRING AT FLORIDA CAVERNS STATE PARK

The **Apalachicola National Forest** (850-643-2282; fs.usda.gov/apalachicola) encompasses more than half of Liberty County, with some of the world's finest pitcher plant savannas on its western edge, surrounding Sumatra. This is the most rugged and wild portion of Florida's largest national forest, best enjoyed at its recreation areas—Camel Lake and Wright Lake (see *Camping & Cabins*)—as well as along its very scenic highways, including the Apalachee Savannahs Scenic Byway, which branches south from CR 12 south of Bristol. During the spring pitcher plants bloom in profusion in the wet flatwoods along the byway and around Sumatra. The forest offers many quiet primitive getaways for anglers and hunters; four-wheel drive is recommended on most unpaved forest roads. The Florida Trail (see *Hiking*) traverses the northern portion of this part of the forest, which is also home to the Fort Gadsden Historic Site (see *Historic Sites*).

South of Sumatra, the **Apalachicola River Wildlife and Environmental Area** (myfwc.com/viewing/recreation/wmas/lead/apalachicola-river) along FL 67 protects thousands of acres of floodplain forests and marshes along both sides of the river, with more than 10 boat ramps and an interpretive trail at Sand Beach Recreational

Area. Primitive camping (no permits, no fees required) is permitted in the upland areas of the preserve.

&. **Tate's Hell State Forest** (850-697-3734; fl-dof.com/state_forests/tates_hell .html), 1621 US 98, Carrabelle. With nearly 150,000 acres of mostly wetlands, this is one helluva swamp. It's an important chunk of land, a giant natural filtration system for water flowing out of the swamps of the Apalachicola National Forest and into the bay and estuaries. Hunting, fishing, and paddling are the main recreation here, but hikers have two spots to explore: the short wheelchair-accessible Ralph G. Kendrick Dwarf Cypress Boardwalk (look for signs on FL 67) leading out over a rare (for North Florida) dwarf cypress swamp, and the High Bluff Coastal Nature Trail along US 98.

Several of the region's wild places are barrier islands, accessible only by boat. **Cape St. George Island**, a 9-mile stretch of beach sheltering Apalachicola Bay, has a historic lighthouse and plays host to families of red wolves being acclimated to the wild, as does adjacent **St. Vincent National Wildlife Refuge** (see the *Panama City* chapter). Off Carrabelle, **Dog Island Preserve** can only be reached by boat. Coastal scrub and coastal pine forests are the predominant ecosystems on these barrier islands, where day-use visitors are welcome to roam the beaches and watch for birds; no overnight visits are permitted.

✳ Lodging

BED & BREAKFASTS

Apalachicola 32320

🐾 ☀ (ᵞᵖ) **Bryant House** (888-554-4376; bryanthouse.com), 101 6th St. European elegance infuses this grand 1897 home, where Brigitte (enjoying her dream job) brings a touch of Germany to Florida, and Einstein, the resident blue and gold macaw, will call out a cheery greeting on your arrival. Period antiques embellish each of the three lavish rooms: Blue, Gold, and Red. Business travelers will appreciate the WiFi and spacious downstairs sitting room, while the romantically inclined will fall in love with this very grand setting. A new addition is the pet-friendly Sadie Ford Cottage, dressed in more modern furnishings with two bedrooms, a dining room, a living room, and a full kitchen. You won't want to use it, though, as Brigitte's traditional German breakfast of thinly sliced smoked meats, cheeses, fresh fruit, homemade jam and biscuits, and a soft-boiled egg is simply superb. $87–249.

♂ (ᵞᵖ) **Coombs House Inn** (850-653-9199; coombshouseinn.com), 80 6th St. One of the grandest restored mansions in the South (circa 1905) and one of the nation's top inns, the pride of lumber baron James Coombs will amaze you. Step inside the doorway into a grand hall lined with black cypress walls and a high-beamed ceiling. Each room offers spacious Victorian elegance with careful restorative touches, such as the gleaming colored tile on the coal-fired fireplaces (a relic of the days when ships from Liverpool swapped coal ballast for cotton) and built-in cabinets moved into the bathrooms. You'll feel like royalty amid the lush furnishings and art, and the aroma of home-baked breads will ensure you come to the breakfast table. Eight rooms, each with en suite bath, $109–249.

The **Witherspoon Inn** (850-653-9186; witherspooninn.com), 94 5th St, was the home of a 19th-century sea captain—now it's yours. Settle in under the oaks and relax in your comfortable room or suite, $105–119.

♂ (•ꜛ•) An oasis of hospitality off the stretch of US 231 from I-10 to Panama City, **La Maison de Lucy** (850-579-0138; lamaisondelucy.com), 2388 Park Ave 32420, immerses you in the romance of exotic travel. It took hard work and artistic flair to transform this historic elementary school into a series of massive suites, each themed around a different country, but owner Michael Setboun poured his passion into restoration. Emigrating from France, he sought a creative project in the hospitality field, and found a canvas to work with in this small rural town. Centered on a pool and patio, the compound includes the restored gymnasium, now a 5,500-square-foot meeting and reception space, a fitness center with sauna and massage room, and the main brick building itself. Where children once sat at desks, you'll relax in the luxurious fantasy of a night in Morocco, a morning in Mexico, or any of 12 different destinations complete with furnishings, music, books, and fine art that evokes a sense of place. A talented chef, Michael cooks gourmet dinners upon request, and prepares a savory breakfast each morning; my delicately scrambled eggs had a hint of rosemary and other fragrant herbs. The suites, $175 and up, range from 400 to nearly 800 square feet in size; some have multiple beds, wet bars, and microwaves. A delightful romantic getaway, it's the perfect perk-me-up for couples and a dream-come-true for armchair world travelers.

LUXURIATE IN MORROCO AT LA MAISON DE LUCY B&B, ALFORD

Carrabelle 32322

🐾 The **Old Carrabelle Hotel** (850-697-9010; oldcarrabellehotel.com), 201 Tallahassee St, circa 1890, is a former railroad hotel, lovingly restored by Skip and Kathy Frink in 2000. Like a sea captain's home (which it once was), it's filled with treasures from abroad, fine art from the tropics and from Florida's coasts, reflecting the owners' exotic and artistic tastes. Kick back and read the morning paper in the Monkey Bar, or curl up with a good book in the Hemingway Room, which certainly appealed to me with its literary theme and decor evoking dreams of Africa. Each room is a quiet, private retreat, or you can mingle with your fellow guests in the parlor or on the veranda and watch the sunset shimmer on the Carrabelle River, $77–107.

🐾 The **Winchester Cottage** (850-697-9010; oldcarrabellehotel.com /Winchester), 506 Tallahassee St, is a restored 1933 coastal cottage made of tongue-and-groove pine. A breezy screened porch fronts the cottage, which has three bedrooms, a bath, and a full kitchen. $350 for a three-night weekend, or $500 per week, just 2 miles from Carrabelle Beach.

BRYANT HOUSE B&B, APALACHICOLA

Marianna 32446

🐾 ♂ ♿ (ᵞ) It's always Christmas at the **Hinson House** (800-531-4786; phonl .com/hinson_house), 4338 Lafayette St, a classic 1922 bungalow in Marianna's historic residential district. Choose from two regular rooms or three spacious suites (including the Home Guard Suite, which overlooks the site of the Battle of Marianna), with your choice of multiple beds—great for friends and relatives traveling together. $69–89; Judy welcomes well-behaved children.

GUESTHOUSES

Apalachicola 32320

As the historic hub of the region, Apalachicola is blessed with several guesthouses, where you're left to your own devices after checking in. The settings are just as comfy as the B&Bs, with rates to match. Your selections include the 1835 **Raney Guest Cottage** (850-653-9749; apalachicola -vacation.com), 46 Ave F, at $140; and the **House of Tartts** (850-653-4687; houseoftartts.com), Ave F and 4th St, $105–135.

HOTELS, MOTELS & RESORTS

Apalachicola 32320

🐾 At the **Apalachicola River Inn** at Oystertown (850-653-8139; apalachicolariverinn.com), 123 Water St, all of the pleasant, large newly remodeled rooms come with a river view, breakfast at adjoining Caroline's Restaurant, and a happy-hour drink at the Roseate Spoonbill Lounge. Kick back on your riverfront balcony and watch the shrimpers come in. $129–149.

Perhaps the most private rooms in town, **The Consulate** (800-341-2021 or 850-927-2282; consulatesuites .com), 76 Water St, consists of four apartment-sized suites above the J. E.

THE OLD CARRABELLE HOTEL, CARRABELLE

Grady & Company Market. The brick walls, 10-foot-high tin-plated ceilings, and heart pine floors remind you you're in a historic building; in the early 1900s, this was the French consulate in Florida. The artistic touches and views remind you you're in Apalachicola. The complex has a private garden entrance off Commerce St and private balconies for each suite, which range in size up to 1,300 square feet. Amenities include washer/dryer, fully equipped kitchen, and cable TV. Right in the heart of downtown, this classy choice lets you wander down the staircase and into the action in moments. A minimum two-night stay starts at $350; weekly rates available.

🦐 😺 🐾 (ᵂⁱᶠⁱ) At the **Gibson Inn** (850-653-2191; gibsoninn.com), 51 Ave C, the hallways and doorjambs are a little out of kilter and the solid wood floors creak a bit underfoot, but it's all part of the charm of this meticulously restored hotel in the heart of downtown. Known as the Franklin Hotel when it

opened in 1907, it was constructed by James Fulton Buck, who hand-selected the tongue-and-groove paneling used as wainscoting throughout the structure. Built of heart pine and black cypress three stories tall with wraparound porches, it offers exterior halls and doors on upper floors, which are put to good use as pet-friendly rooms. On the National Register of Historic Places, the inn has 31 rooms and suites, restored in 1985 and decked out in antique furnishings, with full bath, cable television, window-unit a/c, and WiFi. Some rooms are cozy, others spacious; my pick: Room 209. Opt for a corner room to throw your windows open and catch the cool salt breezes, or settle down in a rocking chair on the shaded broad wraparound porch to watch the world go by. $60-119.

😺 (ᵂⁱᶠⁱ) All rooms are on the Apalachicola River at the **Water Street Hotel** (850-653-3700; waterstreethotel.com), 329 Water St. Decked out in Caribbean colonial style, these apartments are big enough to move in for the season, with a full kitchen and full-sized appliances, a screened deck overlooking the river, and accents like shiny hardwood floors and wall-mounted flat-screen televisions. A dock runs along the front of the hotel, but doesn't obstruct your view of the river and its vast estuary; on the back side of the complex, a pool with sunning deck is surrounded by the marsh that wraps around the property. $129–199.

Carrabelle 32322

🦞 🐾 ♿ (ᵞ) A new hotel along US 98, the **Franklin Inn at Carrabelle** (850-697-4000; franklininncarrabelle .com), 1589 US 98 W, is between downtown and the beach. One peek in the window and you can tell they're friendly from the big friendly pooch in the breakfast rooms. The sparkling-clean rooms have flat-screen TVs, a fridge, microwave, and coffeepot. Relax just moments from a free boat launch, dining, hiking trails, and pretty Carrabelle Beach. Rates start at $69.

🐾 The **Moorings at Carrabelle** (850-697-2800; mooringsatcarrabelle.com), 1000 US 98. This popular full-service marina overlooking the Carrabelle River offers large waterfront condos (one, two, and three bedrooms) with

THE NEW FRANKLIN INN ALONG US 98, CARRABELLE

docking slips just outside your door, $89–225; or standard large hotel rooms, $70–80. Smoking and non-smoking units; weekly rates available. Swimming pool, dive shop, and charter captains on site.

Marianna 32446

Chain motels (ᵞ) ♿ 🐾 such as **Holiday Inn Express** (850-526-2900), **Micro-tel** (850-526-5005), **Hampton Inn** (850-526-1006), and **Comfort Inn** (850-526-5600) cluster around I-10, exit 142, at FL 71.

St. George 32328

♿ (ᵞ) **St. George Inn** (850-927-2903; stgeorgeinn.com), 135 Franklin Blvd. Built to look like a turn-of-the-20th-century hotel, this pleasant, modern inn is a short walk from both beach and bay. Each of the rooms is large and well appointed, with French doors opening onto the porch or balconies and a mini kitchen (refrigerator, microwave, coffeepot) to help with your morning wake-up. $90–170, discounts for weekly stays.

VACATION RENTALS Anchor Vacation Properties (800-624-3964; florida-beach.com) manages classy properties like Casablanca, a well-appointed two-story beach home that tips its hat to Bogey. Traveling solo, I felt a little lonely kicking around this four-bedroom rental on St. George Island, but borrowing someone's lifestyle is the fun of a beach rental. You'll find it cost-effective if you split the tab with enough people to fill the house. Anchor's properties run from Carrabelle to Mexico Beach. Other rental agencies in the region include **Ochlockonee Bay Realty** (850-984-0001; obrealty.com), with a focus on Alligator Point; and **Collins Vacation Rentals** (800-423-7418; collinsvacation rentals.com) and **Prudential Resort Realty** (800-332-5196; stgeorgeisland

.com), both covering St. George Island.

For all vacation rentals, quality of accommodations can vary widely from unit to unit. Be aware that cleaning and maintenance fees may be added atop your rental fee. Ask before booking.

CAMPING & CABINS

Blountstown 32424

Scott's Ferry Landing and General Store (850-674-2900), 6648 FL 71, offers a back-to-nature campground under the pines along the Chipola River, with RV and tent sites ($18 and up), and cabins ($55) built on stilts above flood level. They also rent canoes (see *Paddling*), and there's a fish-cleaning station and boat launch.

Bristol 32321

🌳 In the Apalachicola National Forest, **Camel Lake Recreation Area** (850-643-2282; fs.usda.gov/apalachicola), FR 105 off CR 12 south of Bristol, offers a quiet retreat along its namesake lake. Tent and RV sites, $10–15, give you direct access to hiking trails, fishing, and swimming along the lakeshore.

✍ ↬ Along with hiking, camping is a big reason to spend your hard-earned vacation time at **Torreya State Park** (see *Parks*). There are three primitive campsites along the hiking trails, and the campground (800-326-3521; floridastateparks.reserveamerica.com) has a tepee-like yurt, $16–40.

Carrabelle 32322

🌳 📶 **Ho Hum RV Park** (888-88-HO-HUM or 850-697-3926; hohumrvpark.com), 2132 US 98, offers free cable and WiFi with their sites, many of which face right out on the Gulf of Mexico. Full hookups, pull-throughs for RVs, recreation hall, and laundry facilities. $29–37, discount for Good

Sam, FMCA, AAA, Escapee. Weekly and monthly rates available. No credit cards.

Chattahoochee 32324

✍ County-run **Chattahoochee RV Campground & Fishing Resort** (850-663-4475; cityofchattahoochee.com/rv&fishing.html), 269 River Landing Rd, has an RV park and cabins within walking distance of the Apalachicola River at River Landing Park (see *Parks*), offering anglers another inexpensive option for fishing the Apalachicola, or teaching the kids how to fish in fishing ponds right on site. Campsites include full hookups, $15–17, and tent sites $7. Facility has a dump station, bathhouse, laundry, and clubhouse. Cash or check only.

✍ 📶 A spin around the **KOA Chattahoochee** (850-442-6657; koa.com/campgrounds/chattahoochee), 2309 Flat Creek Rd, convinced me it's a worthwhile place to stay when you're headed down I-10 and looking for a shady campground. Kids will appreciate the pool and playground while you check your email with WiFi included. Tent and RV campsites, $23–35, and cabins, $42 (A/C, no bath, bring your own linens).

Marianna 32446

✍ On beautiful, cypress-lined Merritts Mill Pond, **Arrowhead Campground** (850-482-5583; arrowheadcamp.com), 4820 US 90, has several rental cabins with baths ($50–60, bring your own linens) in addition to its full-hookup spaces ($26 and up) shaded by tall pines. Swimming pool and general store; canoe rentals available. The sites at **Dove Rest RV Park & Campground** (850-482-5313), FL 71 S, are nicely tucked under the pine trees, $15 and up. 🌳 **Florida Caverns State Park** (see *Parks*) has one of the more beautiful campgrounds (800-326-3521; floridastateparks.reserveamerica.com) in our state park system, deeply shaded by a canopy of hardwood trees and feeling like a getaway in the Appalachians, without the radical grades, $20.

Sneads 32460

🐾 ♿ ⌁ The campground (800-326-3521; floridastateparks.reserveamerica.com) at **Three Rivers State Park** (see *Parks*) has a rental cabin ($65) and accessible bathhouse in addition to its 30 shaded sites ($16) within a short walk of Lake Seminole.

Sumatra

🐾 Quiet **Wright Lake Recreation Area** (850-643-2282; fs.usda.gov /apalachicola), Wright Lake Rd off FL 65 in the Apalachicola National Forest (see *Wild Places*), is set on a cypress-lined spring-fed lake in the pine woods above the Apalachicola River. In springtime, photographers will delight in rambling these woods, on and off the trail, in search of picturesque stands of trumpet pitcher plans in bloom. Pitch a tent or bring your trailer, $10.

FISH CAMPS

Eastpoint 32328

🐾 Offbeat and Old Florida, the funky **Sportsman's Lodge Motel** (850-670-8423), 99 N Bayshore Dr, caters to the get-off-the-beaten-path and fish crowd. It sits directly on the bay across from downtown Apalachicola but worlds apart, a small complex with a tropical exterior and basic rooms inside. Smoking and pets permitted.

Sneads 32460

🐾 The legendary **Seminole Lodge** (800-410-5209 or 850-593-6886; seminolelodge.com), 2360 Legion Rd, is an angler's getaway along the shores of Lake Seminole, the best place for bass fishing in Northwest Florida. The complex includes a nine-room waterfront motel ($45–58, some units with kitchenettes), marina with full-service fuel ($5 a day for slips), campground ($15–20), and bait-and-tackle shop/ store.

✳ Where to Eat

DINING OUT

Apalachicola

The she-crab soup at **Caroline's Dining on the River** (apalachicolariver inn.com/carolinesdining.html) at the Apalachicola River Inn (see *Hotels, Motels & Resorts*) was a delicious delight, especially when coupled with the gorgeous view of the river through the picture windows in this upscale dining room. Don't plan to hurry through dinner, especially while the sun is setting. Fresh local oysters come in several preparations, and the dinner menu has its own vegetarian section, including a Vegetarian Curry made with edamame, roasted garlic, and baby spinach simmered in an aromatic spicy Indian curry and coconut milk, served over grilled Napa cabbage and tomatoes with a side of rice. Yum! Entrées, $9–31, range from pastas to a grilled filet mignon, with many seafood choices on the menu. Open daily for breakfast, lunch, and dinner.

The Owl Cafe & Wine Room (850-653-9888; owlcafeflorida.com), 15 Ave D, treats your taste buds upstairs with fun dishes like Apalachicola Bay deep-fried oyster salad; Brie, berries, grapes, and pecan salad; and lump blue crab cakes with spicy tartar sauce. Richard Bickel's scenes of Apalachicola add moodiness to the room. Savor fine wines downstairs in The Wine Room. Lunch and dinner, $12–17.

Tamara's Cafe Floridita (850-653-4111; tamarascafe.com), 71 Market St, serves up funky fusion foods orchestrated by its South American owner. Look for tapas (on Wednesday evenings), paella, pecan-crusted grouper, and grouper tacos with fresh cilantro sauce. Trust me, they're fabulous! Lunch and dinner, most entrées under $25, and now open for breakfast, too. Closed Mon.

Smooth jazz hooks you into noticing **Verandas Bistro and Wine Bar** (850-653-3210; verandasbistro.com),76 Market St, Suite G, a snazzy second-story restaurant, and one look at the menu will have you headed upstairs to this romantic getaway. Dine on the porch and savor the live music, or slip into the interior to savor specialties such as fried oysters with a Creole rémoulade (corn-dusted Apalachicola oysters, of course), roasted red pepper and artichoke polenta, or homemade jambalaya. The ample portions, $11–27, include crisp, fresh vegetables with spices that bring on a warm glow. Peruse the fine wines for a bottle to take back to your room. Sun–Thu 11–9, Fri–Sat 11–10.

EATING OUT

Apalachicola

☙ With the best people-watching view in town (big picture windows and an unobstructed view down to the shrimp boats) and fabulous fresh fish, the **Apalachicola Seafood Grill** (850-653-9510), 100 Market St, is a century-old (yes, century) landmark in a city best known for its seafood. I sampled the oysters and of course they were perfect, but you won't go wrong with shrimp, grouper, or "the world's largest fried fish sandwich." In a nod to local beekeepers and film trivia, the menu includes a "Ulee's Gold" gold tequila with tupelo honey, and you can sip it in the same seat Peter Fonda took during the making of the movie. Lunch and dinner; closed Sun.

Dolores Sweet Shop (850-653-9081), 48 Ave D, bakes up fluffy muffins and

croissants for breakfast treats, and a bit of quiche, too. Enjoy eating on the expansive porch of this historic home, the 1908 Hays House.

☙ The **Old Time Soda Fountain** (850-653-2606), 93 Market St, is arguably the state's oldest, in business since 1905. Sit at the 1940s-style luncheonette counter (from the days when this still was a drugstore with a soda fountain) and slurp down an egg cream or a big chocolate milk shake, or order up a giant ice cream sundae, hand-scooped and prepared right in front of your eyes. Touristy gifts like T-shirts and coconut monkeys fill the remainder of the shop, which is open daily.

☙ At **Papa Joe's** (850-653-1189; papa joesoysterbar.com), 301-B Market St, a down-home place along the riverfront at Scipio Marina, there are always oysters on ice behind the bar and they serve them up 14 different ways, including baked and topped with capers and feta cheese. Order them fried and they come southern-style with a big bowl of cheese grits and hush puppies. Shrimp, scallops, crab, and grouper are fresh choices, or opt for some beef; the steak-and-shrimp

TRY A PO'BOY AT THE APALACHICOLA SEAFOOD GRILL

combo is the best of both worlds. Mon–Sat lunch and dinner.

If you have a family member who isn't a big seafood buff, don't bring them to Apalachicola! But if you must, head for the **Red Top Cafe** (850-653-8612; redtopcafe.com), 238 US 98, where there are plenty of choices on the casual menu to take care of their tastes. Since 1946, these folks have served up country fare like pork chops, roast beef, and hamburger steaks. And yes, they have seafood, too, so you won't miss out. I've enjoyed hearty breakfasts here at value prices.

Blountstown

For breakfast, **Connie's Kitchen** (850-674-1988), 20737 Central Ave E, is the happening place downtown, feeding the folks along the river since 1998. Come in for a hearty "Trash Plate," a stack of huge blueberry pancakes, or some delicious French toast, $2–7. Lunch ($3–7) includes chicken and dumplings, shrimp salad, and burgers. Mon–Fri 5 AM–"until," Sat 5 AM–noon.

The hopping spot downtown after dark, **El Jalisco** (850-674-3411), 16919 Pear St, fills a former IGA supermarket. A festive Mexican restaurant with authentic dishes and a menu that goes on and on and on, they'll fill you up—and still keep the chips and salsa coming. Entrées include grilled rib-eye steaks prepared Mexican-style, mole and adobe chicken, and platters with half a dozen delights, $7–12.

Homemade cakes tempt at the **Country Creamery** (850-674-4663), 20755 Central Ave E, where lavender sprays decorate the ceiling and watercolors by Anna Gitera lend a splash of color. Stop in for a hearty Navajo Wrap, with grilled chicken, tomato, romaine, banana peppers, onions, provolone, and chili mayonnaise—it's a

handful! The kids will appreciate this downtown ice cream stop, too. Mon–Fri 9–5, Sat 10–4, lunch items $2–8.

For railroad buffs, **Main Street Station** (850-237-1500), 17415 Main St N, lets you sit at big picture windows and stare at a historic steam engine (see *Railroadiana*) while chowing down on fish tacos, authentic Cuban sandwiches, and burgers, $6–7. A small ice cream parlor in the back caters to folks right off the Blountstown Greenway.

Carrabelle

Offering up a triple scoop of nostalgia: old-fashioned soda parlor, quirky Florida memorabilia and postcards, and recollections of when this was Camp Gordon Johnson, **Carrabelle Station** (850-697-9550), 88 Tallahassee St, has that time-travel feel, thanks to Ron Gempel's eye for antique signs and ephemera adding to the original 1940s soda fountain decor. Grab a sundae or a sandwich ($3–6), or enjoy one of his nicely done salads or made-from-scratch soups ($3–5).

Eastpoint

It was a joy to find **The Hut** (850-670-8024; facebook.com/hut.restaurant), 315 US 98, reborn in this new location—the original, west of Apalachicola, was wiped out by a hurricane. With the same staff, family atmosphere, and excellent inexpensive local seafood as they've been known for since 1941, it was a pleasure to drop in for lunch and find the restaurant packed. Daily specials like homemade meat loaf, baked chicken, and the Gulf Shrimp basket for under $6; fresh seafood, from grouper to clams and local oysters, $6–12.

You can't get oysters fresher than at **Captain Snooks** (850-670-1515), 500 US 98, since it's owned by the same family that also goes out and collects the oysters processed next door at their shucking house and sold at Barber's Seafood. Sit on the porch along an oyster-shell-strewn shoreline to see an oyster boat up close and a great view of Apalachicola Bay; enjoy the breeze and the laughing gulls. Pick your preparation: I supped on the Hagan's Cove, my oysters baked with Parmesan, bacon, and chives, as I sat and watched bags of oysters being off-loaded from oyster skiffs into the warehouse on a busy Monday. Open daily for lunch and dinner.

Marianna

✎ (ᵂⁱᶠⁱ) Enjoy your gourmet panini with a side of smooth jazz at **Bistro Palms** (850-526-2226), 2865 McPherson St, a downtown lunch favorite serving up generous portions of soups, salad, and sandwiches, $4–7. Watch the world go by while dining out on the deck, but save room for their peanut butter pie! Mon–Fri 10:30–2.

Bobbie's Waffle Iron (850-526-5055), 4509 Lafayette St, a little country diner with home cooking, is your best bet for a cheap, hearty breakfast, starting at $3. Don't miss the home-cooked hash browns! Open 6–3 daily, with a $6 Blue Plate Special at lunch.

🍴 The **Gazebo Coffee Shop & Deli** (850-526-1276), 4412 Lafayette St, is a popular downtown coffee and lunch stop. Here in farm country, their eggs are farm-fresh, so order up an omelet or wait for lunch for one of their famed sandwiches, like the Flying Floss—a scoop of shrimp salad with garlic mayonnaise, melted Swiss cheese, and tomato slices atop a croissant. Breakfast $2–3, lunch $5–8; open Mon–Fri 7–3.

(ᵂⁱᶠⁱ) At the **Riverfront Restaurant and Grill** (850-482-1002), 4829 US 90, I dined on catfish while watching an egret spear his dinner along cypress-lined Spring Creek. Housed in the original icehouse circa 1900, it's a simple family restaurant that draws a big crowd for inexpensive Apalachicola oysters in-season, plus burgers, wings, and classic southern entrées, $7–17. It's also the launch point for tubing and kayaking with Bear Paw Adventures (see *Paddling*). Closed Sun.

St. George Island

The **Blue Parrot Cafe** (850-927-2987; blueparrotcafe.net), 68 W Gorrie St, offers the island's only oceanfront dining; feast on oyster and grouper while the sea breeze blows in your face. I loved the fact that I could have gumbo instead of fries with my sandwich, but watch out for the tropical drinks—they're potent! Serving lunch and dinner; entrées are $15–25 and under.

✴ Entertainment

Apalachicola

The beautifully restored **Dixie Theatre** (850-653-3200; dixietheatre.com), 21 Ave E, hosts musicals, plays, jazz and folk concerts, and ballroom dancing. There's hardly a week when there isn't an event going on; check their website for the upcoming schedule.

Carrabelle

Catch the spirit of the Gulf at **Harry's Bar** (850-697-3420), 306 Marine St, an old-time fisherman's hangout; shoot some pool and shoot the breeze 7 AM–10 PM daily. Across the water, the **Tiki Hut** on Carrabelle Island is a favorite hangout at the Carrabelle River Marina, 275 Timber Island Rd.

Marianna

Chipola Junior College (850-718-2301; chipola.edu), 3094 Indian Circle, sponsors an annual performing arts series that includes Broadway shows, musicians, choral groups, and opera.

✳ Selective Shopping

Apalachicola

At **All That Jazz** (850-653-4800), 84 Market St, I love the local arts and crafts, especially the clever coin catchers—socks topped with open-mouthed ceramic faces. Crème brûlée coffee tempts, too.

🐾 Satisfy your sweet tooth at the **Apalachicola Chocolate Company** (850-370-6937), 15 Ave E, where you can try a tupelo honey walnut caramel, bourbon pecan truffles, fresh divinity, or dozens of other tasty creations. Too hot for sweets? Cool down with their homemade gelato.

Sponges from the Gulf of Mexico—harvested just like in olden times from offshore beds—are the heart of the **Apalachicola Sponge Company & Smokehouse Antiques** (850-653-5564; apalachspongecompany.com), now at 29 Ave E. Select one for scrubbing, or a few to heighten your nautical decor. Handmade olive oils and soaps also hark to the Greek influence on this port city, and you'll find plenty of decor items for your home.

Inside the historic Sponge Exchange building, **Charming Comforts** (850-653-2777; charmingcomforts.com), 16 Ave E, has stylish decor for home and garden.

Step through the back door into busy **Downtown Books & Purl** (850-653-1290), 67 Commerce St, which features an excellent range of literary fiction, Florida books, and a small newsstand; they've branched out into yarn and knitting supplies as well.

On the waterfront, the renovated **J. E. Grady & Co. Market** (850-653-4099), 76 Water St, Apalachicola's ship's chandlery circa 1884, is now a department store with tin ceilings and its original wooden floor. Browse for everything from dressy apparel and classic reproduction toys to "Wild Women" gear.

I'm an outdoorsy gal, but **Riverlily** (850-653-2600), 78 Commerce St, reawakened my feminine core with the wedding gown of my dreams and other delightful items—dresses, scarves, purple satin slippers, aromatherapy, incense, and candles—to uplift a woman's spirit. Need mermaids? You'll find them in every shape and size here.

At the **Southern Sage** (850-323-0599), 82 Market St, classy Apalachicola T-shirts, portable works of art with designs harking back to the city's heyday as purveyor of fish to the world, come shrink-wrapped on Styrofoam trays. Piles of antiques and memorabilia fill the store, which was once home to the local newspaper.

Inside **The Stuffed Owl** (850-653-8960), 75 Commerce St, are gourmet goodies and everything you need to set the perfect table.

Looking for nautical antiques? You're in the right city. The **Tin Shed** (850-653-3635), 170 Water St, has everything from portholes and ship's bells to lobster traps and even a ship's binnacle or two. Be sure to step out back, where the collection of buoys is quite the artistic show. At **Wefing's Maritime Village** (850-899-3618), 252 Water St, they've been "serving the marine line since 1909" as the first-ever distributor of Johnson outboard motors in one of the oldest commercial buildings in Florida. Inside this low brick building you'll find art and antiques mingled, including antique outboard motors, cast nets, lures, and a blacksmith bellows from the 1890s next to fine art photos and wood carvings.

Blountstown

Miss Me Jeans, fashion jewelry, flashy handbags, and classy sundresses at small prices are what you'll find at

NAUTICAL DECOR AWAITS AT TIN SHED ANTIQUES, APALACHICOLA

Cold Creek Boutique (850-674-1535; coldcreekboutique.com), 20725 Central Ave E.

Frazier's (850-674-3302), 20693 Central Ave E, has a little bit of this and little bit of that, a jumble shop of antiques and flea market items.

🛥 **Golden Pharmacy** (850-674-4557), 17324 Main St N, is one of those old-fashioned drugstores you'll find in a small town—they used to have a soda fountain, and folks still rest on seats while waiting for their prescriptions. You'll find local art and cute gifts, soy candles, great greeting cards, and tasty treats like slushies and tupelo honey made just down the road in Wewahitchka (see the *Panama City* chapter).

At **Rivertown Antique Mall** (850-674-1000), 20693 Central Ave E, look for movie posters, tables laden with trays, glassware, and candlesticks, a fair selection of books, and many odds and ends in the dealer booths.

Carrabelle

At the **Beach Trader** (850-653-7635; beachtraderpam.com), 781 US 98, ALL OUR DUCKS ARE IN A ROW says the yellow sign with concrete ducks beckon-ing you into this collection of driftwood art, lawn ornaments, seashells, and more. Open Thu–Sat.

Inside **Two Gulls** (850-697-3787), corner of US 98 and Marine St, you'll find nautical gifts, inspirational items, toys, candles, and local art—a little bit of everything. Closed Sun.

Cottondale

At **The Ivy Cottage** (850-352-2083), 3093 Main St, rummage through fine consignments like vintage hats, classy glassware, and retro dresses.

You've seen the signs along I-10—$20 BONSAI! Now go take a peek at **Bonsai by Dori** (850-352-4390), 3089 Main St, purveyor of diminutive trees along US 231, to fall in love with a miniature forest of your own.

Graceville

♿ This little town along FL 77 is home to **Factory Stores of America** (factorystores.com), 950 Prim Ave, the only factory outlet mall I know of in a truly rural area. Why here? It's halfway between Dothan, Georgia, and Panama City Beach. Merchants include Corningware, Van Heusen, Bon Worth, Easy Spirit, and many more. Open daily.

Hosford

Stop in the **Bargain Barn** (850-379-3000), 21521 NE FL 20, for folksy furniture and antiques—butter churns, glass, bottles, stoneware, and jugs—as well as glittery, pretty things, like an oversized sequined dragonfly I now keep around the house. Closed Sun.

Marianna

At **Chipola River Book & Tea** (850-526-5040; chipolariverbookandtea.com), 4402 Lafayette St, browse through local history books, take a peek at the children's book collection—where I found one of my own—and generally relax with a cup of coffee or tea while being surrounded by stacks and shelves of literature. Closed Sun.

Our Secret Garden (850-482-6034; secretgardenrareplants.com), US 90 E and Turner Rd, has been in business for more than 35 years selling both native and unusual plants, including bonsai, water gardens, ferns, and bog plants. Mon–Sat 8–5.

St. George Island

Sometimes It's Hotter (888-468-8372; sometimesitshotter.com), 37 E Pine St. Showcasing spicy, unusual foods, including boutique beers, private-label hot sauces, and their own award-winning seasonings. Open daily.

Journeys of St. George Island (850-927-3259; sgislandjourneys.com), 240 E 3rd St, is part outfitter (see *Eco-tours*) and part beach shop, with kayaks for sale under one roof and sarongs, teeny dresses, and Hawaiian shirts in the next room. Closed Sun.

PRODUCE AND SEAFOOD MARKETS

Apalachicola

At **13 Mile Seafood Market** (850-653-1399; 13milebrand.com), 227 Water St, three generations of Buddy Ward's family have worked the waters here bringing the fine taste of the coast to you. Coolers available.

Blountstown

On Saturday mornings, the **Downtown Farmer's Market** (along FL 20, adjoining Wakulla Bank) brings in the rural goodness of the surrounding area, including fresh cheese and milk from Ocheesee Creamery (see *Dairy Farm*), succulent barbecue, in-season produce, and creative crafts.

Eastpoint

Grab your oysters right along the bay at **Lynn's Quality Oysters** (850-670-8796; lynnsqualityoysters.com), 402 US 98, where today's catch comes direct off the boats—it doesn't get any fresher! Open daily 9–6.

Marianna

Operating May–Aug, the **Jackson County Farmers Market** (850-592-5848), 2896 Madison St, is an open-air fete of fresh produce starting every Tue, Thu, and Sat at 7 AM.

Sneads

Buddy's Picked Fresh Produce (850-593-9977), 8082 US 90, stand offers farm-fresh fruits and vegetables all year long.

Two Egg

This tiny town amid the cotton and cane fields of northern Jackson County has a dozen explanations for its very odd name; take away a piece of its history from **Robert E. Long Cane Syrup**, a roadside stand along CR 69 selling fresh cane syrup by the quart and gallon. If you stop in at the crack of dawn on the first Saturday of December, you'll catch the crew grinding cane and cooking up a big breakfast for visitors.

✳ Special Events

April: **Apalachicola Classic & Antique Boat Show** (850-653-9419; antiqueboatshow.org), held at the Apalachicola Maritime Museum at the end of the month.

Carrabelle Riverfront Festival (850-697-2585), last weekend, features arts and crafts, lots of fresh seafood, and an open house at the FSU Turkey Point Marine Lab along US 98 near Alligator Harbor. Now that there's a beautiful riverfront walkway in Carrabelle, it's a great venue for the event!

The **Marianna Arts Festival and BBQ Cook-Off** (mariannaartsfestival .com) brings plenty of people out to Citizens' Lodge Park (see *Parks*) for fabulous eats and the skilled works of local artists. Mid-month.

Panhandle Folk Life Days (850-674-3050). Demonstration of traditional arts and crafts at the Panhandle Pioneer Settlement (see *Museums*). First weekend, 9–3. Free.

May: ✍ Since 1996, the **Big River Roundup Flathead Catfish Tournament** (blountstownrotary.com) has offered up prizes for landing the big cats (see *Fishing*).

On the **Apalachicola Annual Spring Tour of Historic Homes** (850-653-9550), tour up to 20 historic private homes on a guided walking tour; $15 donation.

August: Sponsored by Apalachicola Riverkeeper and celebrating filmmaking along the Apalachicola River and other wild places, the **Wild & Scenic Film Festival** (apalachicolariver keeper.org) goes on for two weeks through the region, moving from Carrabelle to Apalachicola and Marianna at various venues; check the website for details.

October: Centered in Eastpoint, the **Franklin County Oyster Festival** (850-927-7744), first weekend, celebrates the humble oyster with a shucking tournament, educational displays, kids' activities, and, of course, lots of eating.

Learn about the biggest mammal in the region at the **Forgotten Coast Black Bear Festival** (defenders.org), held mid-month at Sands Park in Carrabelle and with field trips into Tate's Hell State Forest to learn more about bear habitat.

November: **Florida Seafood Festival** (888-653-8011; floridaseafoodfestival .com), Apalachicola. The granddaddy of seafood festivals is now nearly 50 years old and simply shouldn't be missed—from oyster shucking to the annual blessing of the fleet, it's a *huge* event.

🐾 ✍ Luminaries and Christmas lights settle holiday magic on Apalachicola during the **Historic Apalachicola Christmas Celebration** (apalachicola bay.org), for the Thanksgiving weekend. Costumed docents in historic finery bring a touch of history to town, and Santa will arrive on a shrimp boat at 4 PM at the City Dock to kick off the celebration.

TALLAHASSEE & THE BIG BEND

JEFFERSON, LEON, TAYLOR, WAKULLA & EASTERN GADSDEN COUNTIES

On March 4, 1824, Florida's politicos decided on a meeting place half-way between the thriving cities of Pensacola and St. Augustine, and dubbed it **Tallahassee**—a corruption of the Creek word for "abandoned village." A log cabin served as the first capitol, replaced by a more grandiose structure completed just in time for Florida's induction into the Union in 1845. Tallahassee's classy downtown, a mix of old brick buildings and modern architecture with side alleys just wide enough for a horse and carriage, has incredible hills for a Florida city—you'll think you're in New England.

Atop the tallest hill in **Monticello**, the Jefferson County Courthouse evokes déjà vu: It's a replica of Thomas Jefferson's famous home. The namesake of **Havana** is indeed Cuba, as the Red Hills region supplied the Cuban cigar industry with tobacco until Fidel Castro came to power. The old tobacco-drying barns and downtown infrastructure now make up the region's top antiquing town. Several generations ago folks in the nearby tobacco community of **Quincy** invested in a young company called Coca-Cola, and their dividends show in the Victorian homes that dominate this artistic town.

As you head toward the Gulf of Mexico, red clay hills give way to the densely forested Woodville Karst Plain, a wonderland of sinkholes and springs defining **Wakulla County**. It's a green, wet place, with lushly canopied roads edged by floodplain forests and salt marshes. The medicinal qualities of the sulfur and magnesium springs near **Panacea** led to its unusual name, but this coastal town is best known for its seafood. Buy it roadside direct from the fishermen, or have it fried or broiled at one of the local eateries. Also renowned for seafood, the fishing village of **St. Marks** sits along the St. Marks River and the vast estuaries where it meets the Gulf of Mexico. The U.S. Congress created this town in 1830 as a port of entry to the United States before Florida's first major railroad, the Tallahassee & St. Marks, joined the two cities in 1837.

Continuing along the sweep of the Big Bend southward, **Perry**, the seat of Taylor County, grew up around farming in the 1860s, but the economy shifted to lumber and turpentine after Reconstruction. Timber companies removed vast tracts of

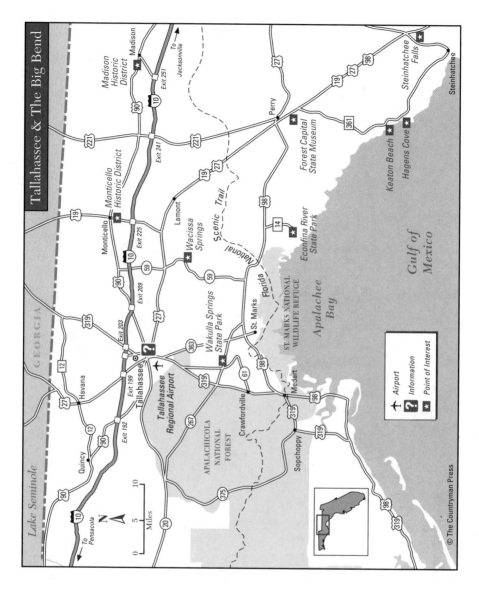

virgin pines and cypress, and processed the harvest in two enormous timber mills. Along this coastal puzzle of swamp forests and estuary you'll find the small communities of Adams Beach and **Keaton Beach**, and the more well-known **Steinhatchee** along the Steinhatchee River, founded by settlers looking for cedar to feed the pencil factories in the Cedar Keys (see *Lower Suwannee*). In the 1940s Greek sponge divers moved into the area to work the vast sponge beds in the Gulf of Mexico, and the fishermen followed. Although the sponge divers are long gone, you can see reminders of Greek culture in the offerings on local menus.

GUIDANCE For an overview of the region's natural wonders and history, the collaborative multi-county **Natural North Florida** (877-955-2199; naturalnorth

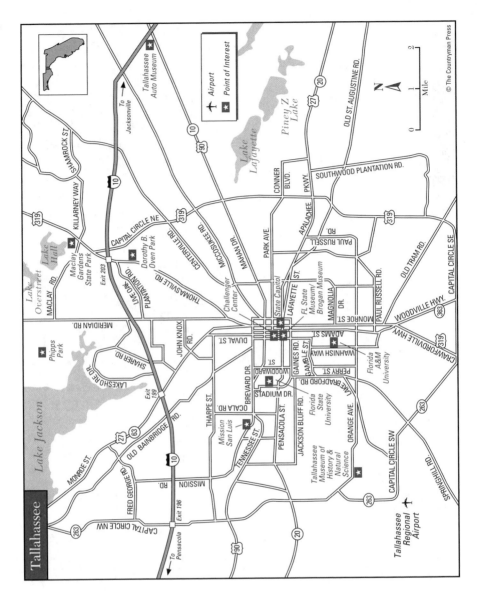

© The Countryman Press

florida.com) provides visitor information and links to all local visitors services. **Visit Tallahassee** (visittallahassee.com) has a prominent Downtown Visitor Information Center (800-628-2866 or 850-606-2305), 106 E Jefferson St, with a wall of brochures and a gift shop serving free iced tea, Mon–Fri 8–5. Street parking may be tricky, so head to nearby Kleman Plaza. Stop in the **Gadsden County Chamber of Commerce** (850-627-9231; gadsdencc.com), 208 N Adams St, Quincy, when you're exploring downtown Quincy.

Along US 98 in Panacea, the **Wakulla County Welcome Center** (visitwakulla .com) sits across from Panacea Mineral Springsand has exhibits about local history and nature in addition to general travel information. **Jefferson County** (visit jeffersoncountyflorida.com), which stretches from the Georgia border to the Gulf of Mexico, provides planning information online, as does **Taylor County** (taylor florida.com).

GETTING THERE *By air:* **Tallahassee Regional Airport** (850-891-7800; talgov .com/airport), 3300 Capital Circle SW, has commuter service on Atlantic Southeast, Continental, Delta, Northwest, and US Airways.

By bus: **Greyhound** (850-222-4240; greyhound.com) pulls into 112 W Tennessee St, downtown Tallahassee.

By car: **I-10** is the major east–west corridor through Florida's Panhandle, with **US 98** providing the scenic route connecting coastal communities between Panacea and Perry, and **US 90** running through the northerly Red Hills region from Monticello through Tallahassee to Quincy. US 27 connects Havana and Perry with Tallahassee.

GETTING AROUND *By car:* With its many one-way streets, downtown Tallahassee can be a bit confusing; watch for signs that direct you to points of interest. Roads radiate out of Tallahassee like spokes on a wheel: **US 27** leads northwest to Havana, southeast to Perry; **US 319**, north to Thomasville, Georgia, and south to Crawfordville; **FL 363** south to St. Marks; **US 90** northeast to Monticello, northwest to Quincy. **Capital Circle** defines the wheel's rim. From Monticello, **US 19** heads south through Perry to pass by Steinhatchee on its way to the towns of the Lower Suwannee.

By bus: Weekdays, catch a free ride between downtown Tallahassee points of interest on the **Old Town Trolley,** every 20 minutes, 7–6. **StarMetro** (850-891-5200; talgov.com/starmetro), the public bus service, runs routes to suburban neighborhoods; fares $1.25, or $3 for a one-day pass.

By taxi: **City Taxi** (850-562-4222) and **Yellow Cab** (850-580-8080).

THE KEATON BEACH HOT DOG STAND

PARKING Havana, Monticello, and Quincy have free street parking for shopping. But in busy Tallahassee, metered on-street spaces have time limits from 30 minutes to 10 hours. If you're visiting a museum or restaurant, it's best to pop into a parking garage. **Kleman Plaza**, between Bronough and Duval, is roomier than the Eastside Parking Garage on Calhoun and offers easy access to museums and downtown historic sites. Weekday rates range from $2 for one hour to $8 per day, and only $1 for all day on weekends.

MEDICAL EMERGENCIES **Tallahassee Memorial Hospital** (850-681-1155; tmh.org), 1300 Miccosukee Rd, Tallahassee, **Capital Regional Medical Center** (850-325-5000; capitalregionalmedicalcenter.com), 2626 Capital Medical Blvd, Tallahassee, and **Doctor's Memorial Hospital** (850-584-0800; doctorsmemorial .com), 333 N Byron Butler Pkwy (US 27), Perry. Call 911 for all major emergencies. In outlying areas, it may take up to an hour to reach an emergency room.

GOODWOOD

A corn-and-cotton plantation dating back to the 1830s, **Goodwood** (850-877-4202; goodwoodmuseum.org), 1600 Miccosukee Rd, is the most accessible of the region's grand antebellum plantations. It was originally established in the 1830s by Hardy Bryan Croom, a botanist who explored the Apalachicola River basin and discovered and named *Toreya taxifolium*, the torreya tree. While he was en route with his family to Florida to make a life at Goodwood, their ship sank and all were lost. His brother took over the estate, and legal squabbles continued for many years before the property passed through several hands until it landed in the lap of Senator William C. Hodges, whose wife so admired a bed in the house that he, as the story goes, bought the whole estate. With period furnishings, including many European antiques, dating back to the Hodgeses' ownership of the home, its classy interior is beautiful to behold. Crystal chandeliers dangle from the ceilings, velvet drapes add a touch of Europe, and the ornate ceiling in the salon is considered the oldest existing fresco in Florida. Traditional dogtrot architecture is broken up by a half-curved stairway in the center of the building leading up to the bedrooms, which are extremely roomy for their period. An ornate canopied alabaster bed frame sports an original lace bedspread; the medallion above the master bed is painted with delicate roses, as is the bath. It is a place of romance and history, where Granny slyly smiles like Mona Lisa from the picture frame. Step inside, and touch a Florida long gone. Sixteen buildings and extensive historic gardens make up the complex, but the main house is truly the crown jewel. Mon–Fri 10–4, Sat 10–2, reservations recommended for tours; fee.

ANTEBELLUM PLANTATIONS Most of Florida's remaining antebellum plantations are found in the Capital Region—the visitors bureau lays claim to 100 plantations between Tallahassee, Thomasville, and Perry, many still working farms, some owned by folks like Ted Turner. Although specifically noted for its formal gardens, the grounds of **Alfred B. Maclay Gardens State Park** (see *Gardens*) encompass an antebellum quail-hunting plantation.

In 1896 the Hickory Hill Plantation encompassed 2,800 acres along the Georgia border. Architect Henry Beadel designed a grand home overlooking Lake Iamonia, now known as the **Beadel House**. With four rooms upstairs, and four downstairs decked out in original furnishings, this unique plantation home reflects the sensibilities of its New York owners, who added an Adirondack-style hunting lodge in 1923. A skilled photographer and painter (whose watercolors are signed with the number of minutes it took to complete each piece), Henry Beadel was an avid sportsman who felt that the lack of controlled burns of plantation fields limited quail populations. In 1958 Beadel founded the **Tall Timbers Research Station** (850-893-4153; ttrs.org), 13093 Henry Beadel Dr, which occupies much of the original plantation and serves as a facility for the study of fire to regenerate habitats. Tall Timbers, with walking paths above Lake Iamonia, is open daily; the plantation home opens for docent-led tours once monthly on the third Sun (except on holidays). Fee.

Evoking *Gone with the Wind*, the **Brokaw-McDougall House** (850-891-3900), 329 N Meridian Ave, shows off its 1850 Classical Revival charm with its balcony and verandas behind the Corinthian columns. Nearby, **The Grove**, home of Florida's first territorial governor, Richard Keith Call, isn't open for tours, but you can drive by (100 E 1st Ave) and admire this 1825 beauty, dubbed the finest Greek Revival building in Florida. Adjacent to The Grove, the **Governor's Mansion** (850-488-4661; floridagovernorsmansion.com) is not an antebellum plantation, but it looks like one—it's patterned after Andrew Jackson's Hermitage and is open for free tours; see their website for dates and times.

ARCHAEOLOGICAL SITES Two extraordinary earthen temple sites in the region are at **Lake Jackson Mounds Archaeological State Park** (850-922-6007; floridastateparks.org/lakejackson), 3600 Indian Mounds Rd, and **Letchworth/ Love Mounds Archaeological State Park** (floridastateparks.org/letchworth) off US 90 west of Monticello. On the north shore of Lake Jackson, the temple complex of Lake Jackson Mounds consists of six earthen temple mounds and a burial mound, part of an AD 1200–1500 village. At Leitchworth Mounds you can walk around the base of the tallest and most complex ceremonial mound in Florida, 46 feet high, from the Woodland Period circa AD 500.

ART GALLERIES

Havana
First Street Gallery (850-539-5220), 204 NW 1st St NW, is a local fine arts co-op with sculpture, paintings, and photography by area artists. Open Fri–Sun.

Quincy

Gadsden Arts Center (850-875-4866; gadsdenarts.org), 13 N Madison St, show-cases fine visual arts in a historic 1910 hardware store; this is one of North Florida's top collections. Massive wood sculptures by Mark Lindquist dominate the lobby. Climb upstairs to see the Bates Children's Gallery, with the fine works of local schoolchildren, and don't miss the gift shop, with its one-of-a-kind works of art. Open Tue–Sat 10–5.

Tallahassee

The **Le Moyne Art Foundation** (850-222-8800; lemoyne.org), 125 N Gadsden St, encompasses a complex of three major buildings connected with a sculpture garden, where fine arts from local, regional, and national artists fill the galleries and gardens. Closed Mon and major holidays; fee. Near Florida State University, **Railroad Square Art Park** (850-224-1308; railroadsquare.com), 567 Industrial Dr, contains a cluster of art galleries and gift shops surrounding a sculpture garden and a diner inside a railroad caboose. The **Museum of Fine Arts Florida State University** (850-644-6836; mofa.fsu.edu), 250 Fine Arts Bldg, features changing exhibits from students and national artists, and the **Foster Tanner Fine Arts Gallery** (850-599-3161; famuart.com) at Florida A&M focuses on world art, with an emphasis on African American artists.

One of the highlights of **The Mary Brogan Museum of Art and Science** (see *Family Activities*) is the third-floor gallery space, where fine art is frequently a focus of exhibitions presented here. During my last visit, an enchanting array of baroque artworks—Italian masterpieces spanning from the end of the Dark Ages through the Renaissance—were on display.

DOWNTOWN TALLAHASSEE

Visit Tallahassee

GHOST TOWNS There isn't much left of **Port Leon**, founded in 1838 as the terminus of Florida's first railroad, the Tallahassee Railroad. Located southeast of San Marcos de Apalache (see *Historic Sites*), scattered bricks and the outlines of streets are all that remains in the salt marsh. In 1843, soon after Port Leon became the seat of the newly formed Wakulla County, a hurricane obliterated the town; water covered the streets up to depths of 10 feet. The survivors decided not to rebuild and moved inland to establish the village of Newport.

HISTORIC SITES

Crawfordville

Built in 1892, the original **Wakulla County Courthouse** (850-926-1848), two blocks west of US 319 along High St, houses the chamber of commerce, open Mon–Fri 9–noon and 1–4. Across the street, the **Old Jail** (850-926-1110), circa 1949, has a small regional history museum and gift shop, Thu–Fri 10–4.

Monticello

A Florida Heritage downtown, **Monticello** has more than 40 historic buildings, including the 1908 county courthouse that mimics Thomas Jefferson's grand home. Since 1890, the **Monticello Opera House** has dominated the town square. Peer in the windows of the office to see historical artifacts, including a 1928 Greta Garbo poster found under the stage. Built in 1852, **Monticello High School**, west on US 90, is Florida's oldest brick school building. Walk around downtown to enjoy other residential and business structures with fine Classical and Greek revival architecture, including the 1833 **Wirick-Simmons House**.

Perry

Visit downtown Perry for a look at the historic district, centered on the **Taylor County Courthouse** and the railroad depot.

Quincy

Quincy has an extraordinary number of historic buildings in excellent condition. All are privately owned but can be viewed from the sidewalks. Stop by the **United Methodist Church** to see the handiwork of Louis Comfort Tiffany, who also installed windows in homes around town. Around the corner, the **White House**, constructed in the early 1840s, became the home of Pleasants Woodson White, chief commissary officer for the Confederate army in Florida. Both the **Allison House** and **McFarlin House** (see *Bed & Breakfasts*) offer glimpses into Quincy's storied past; many more structures are explained in the walking tour handbook available at the Gadsden Arts Center (see *Art Galleries*).

St. Marks

Significant as the site of the first coastal fortress along Florida's Panhandle, **San Marcos de Apalache Historic State Park** (850-922-6007; floridastateparks .org/sanmarcos), 148 Old Fort Rd, protects several generations of battlements, from the faint tracings of the original wooden stockade fort completed by the Spanish in 1679 at the confluence of the St. Marks and Wakulla rivers to the remains of the masonry structure occupied up through the Civil War. Visit the museum before walking the interpretive trail along the rivers. Fee for museum.

Tallahassee

There are more than 100 historic sites in the Tallahassee area; pick up information from the visitors center (see *Guidance*) to start your exploration. The downtown contains many historic treasures, including some narrow old brick alleyways reminiscent of those in New England cities. Tallahassee's two universities, Florida A&M and Florida State, also merit their own historic districts, and both the Park Avenue and Calhoun Street historic districts are lined with antebellum and early-1900s homes.

At **The Columns** (850-224-8116), 100 N Duval St, the Greek Revival columns say it all: It was built for the first president of the Bank of Florida, William Williams.

The **First Presbyterian Church** (850-222-4504; oldfirstchurch.org), 102 N Adams St, built in 1838, is Tallahassee's only church remaining from territorial days, complete with frontier accoutrements like rifle slits in the basement. The massive pipe organ was built to fit the building, and the North Gallery served as a segregated congregation for plantation owners' slaves.

The 1843 **Knott House** is one of several houses in town built by George Proctor, a free Black man (see *Museums*).

&. The **Old Capitol Building** (flhistoriccapitol.gov), 400 S Monroe St, dates back to 1845 and has been restored to how it looked when the legislature met in 1902. With extensive historic exhibits on two floors, it is open daily for tours (see *Museums*).

&. Site of the first Spanish mission in Northwest Florida, **Mission San Luis** (850-487-3711; missionsanluis.org), 2020 Mission Rd, once oversaw the operation of more than 100 missions throughout Spanish Florida from 1656 to 1704. Managed by the Department of State, this is Florida's only fully reconstructed Spanish mission, complete with fortress, church with living quarters, tradesmen, and village homes where you'll find occupants grinding corn or working on corn husk dolls. Atop one of the highest hills in Tallahassee, this was also the home of a thriving Apalachee village, which is why the Jesuit priests settled here among them. The most notable feature in the village is the mighty Apalachee council house, a full-sized replica complete with palm thatch. From the outside, it looks like a wooden volcano with smoke curling skyward from its center. When you duck inside, take in the proportions—the enormous original could hold up to 3,000 people, one of the

RECONSTRUCTED SPANISH MISSION AT MISSION SAN LUIS

largest indigenous structures in the southeastern United States. Archaeological digs continue on a regular basis, so stop and take a look at what's new. A nature trail zigzags down steep slopes to the only natural spring in the area. A new entrance along Tennessee Ave (US 90) guides you through a visitors center showcasing artifacts found on the property, including carved figurines and pottery. Tue–Sun 10–4; fee.

Woodville

Natural Bridge Historic State Park (850-922-6007; floridastateparks.org /naturalbridge), 7502 Natural Bridge Rd. An important site in Florida's Civil War history, Natural Bridge speaks to a time when the Confederacy was close to collapse. On March 6, 1865, Union troops marching north from their landing point at the St. Marks Lighthouse met the Florida 5th Cavalry and cadets from the West Florida Seminary (now Florida State University). The Confederate troops routed the Union attack and are credited with keeping Tallahassee the only Confederate capital east of the Mississippi that did not fall into Union hands during the war—although some historians surmise that the Union objective was to capture the key port of St. Marks rather than invade the capital city, and they came to this spot to utilize the Natural Bridge, a place where the St. Marks River dives underground at a river sink and reemerges less than a quarter mile south at a spring. Free.

LIGHTHOUSE One of the most photographed structures in the region is the **St. Marks Lighthouse** (fws.gov/saintmarks/lighthouse.html) built in 1842. It's at the end of the road in St. Marks National Wildlife Refuge (see *Wild Places*) and looks over its own little beach. During the Civil War, the Fresnel lens was removed and hidden in the salt marsh to make the lighthouse useless to the Union Blockading Squadron. Lighthouse keepers and their families lived in the structure until 1960, when the U.S. Coast Guard automated the beacon. It remains a working lighthouse, opening for visitors to explore on Florida Lighthouse Day (floridalight houses.org) and during other special events at the refuge.

MARINE CENTER ✐ An oil spill. A delicate estuary. A coastal community that thrives on fresh shrimp. Operation Noah's Ark was born during the chaos of the *Deepwater Horizon* oil spill, a clever plan to protect and cultivate a reproducing colony of Gulf shrimp to preserve the genetic material of local shrimp to reseed the Gulf waters. Part aquarium, part scientific lab, at the **Gulf Specimen Marine Lab** (850-984-5297; gulfspecimen.org) off US 98, Panacea, you can interact with the native marine life of the Gulf estuary—and see the efforts in place to preserve them, such as Operation Noah's Ark. The aquarium has a special focus on the small side of Florida sea life—scallops and crabs, snails and lobsters, sea fans and sea urchins, shrimp and oysters, and other tiny denizens of the coastline. Mon–Fri 9–5, Sat 10–4, Sun noon–4; fee.

MUSEUMS

Perry

✐ ᕐ **Forest Capital Museum State Park** (850-584-3227; floridastateparks.org /forestcapital), 204 Forest Park Dr, Perry. In Florida's heart of forestry, this lively museum focuses on the importance of Florida's timber, particularly its pine forests. In addition to a diorama on the historic turpentine and naval stores industries, there are life-sized replica habitats and a talking tree to teach the kids about the life cycle of Florida's trees. A wooden map of Florida showcases the variety of native trees in the state (314 kinds), with each county made out of a different type of wood. The jewel of the complex, however, is its reconstructed Cracker homestead. These pioneer homes and farm outbuildings came from a variety of locations. Decorated with period furnishings, the dogtrot home evokes the hardship of life on the farm in early Florida. Thu–Mon 9–noon and 1–5; fee.

PIONEER HOME AT THE FOREST CAPITAL MUSEUM STATE PARK

Tallahassee

In addition to commemorating the former senator's accomplishments, the **Claude Pepper Center** (850-644-9309; claudepeppercenter.fsu.edu), 636 W Call St, contains research materials dating back to the New Deal era and an art gallery with a focus on political activism. A true believer in liberalism, Senator Pepper received the Presidential Medal of Freedom while working to improve life for his fellow Americans. Open Mon–Fri 8:30–5; free.

At the **Knott House** (850-922-2459; museumoffloridahistory.com), 301 E Park Ave, step into 1928 and learn about the lives of William Knott, a former state treasurer, and his wife, Luella, a temperance advocate and whimsical, published poet who wrote about and attached short poems to virtually every piece of the home's original furnishings, earning the home the nickname "The House that Rhymes." The home was designed by George Proctor, a free Black man, in 1843, commissioned as a wedding gift for Catherine Gamble from her husband-to-be, attorney Thomas Hagner; on May 20, 1865, the Emancipation Proclamation was read from its front steps. Tours on the hour Wed–Fri 1–3, Sat 10–3; free, donations appreciated.

✐ ✤ At the **Museum of Florida History** (850-245-6400; museumoffloridahistory.com), 500 S Bronough St, prepare to have your eyes opened about Florida's rich and colorful past. It's one of the most immersive places to learn about the state. In addition to rotating thematic exhibits, the state's official history museum includes a climb-aboard replica of an early steamboat, tales of buried treasure, a citrus-packing house from the 1930s, information on Florida's role in the Civil War, and much more—interactive exhibits that'll keep the kids hopping. The adjoining History Shop contains classy reproductions and a great selection of Florida books. Open Mon–Fri 9–4:30, Sat 10–4:30, Sun noon–4:30. Free, donations appreciated.

✤ **Old Capitol Museum** (850-487-1902; flhistoriccapitol.gov), 400 S Monroe St. Construction began in 1839 to replace the old log cabin used as a meeting place for Florida's first legislators. Although the new capitol opened in 1845, a hurricane damaged it in 1851. Restoration and expansion followed; the building continued to sprawl until the 1970s, when the state replaced it with a tall modern structure next door. Saved from the wrecking ball by public support, the Old Capitol, restored to its 1902 Classical Revival glory, is now a museum devoted to Florida's legislative history. Mon–Fri 9–4:30, Sat 10–4:30, Sun noon–4:30; free, donations appreciated.

The **Riley House** (850-681-7881; rileymuseum.org), 412 E Jefferson St, is home to the **John G. Riley Center and Museum of African-American History & Culture.** In this 1890 home designed by John G. Riley, a Black architect, you'll find a museum of regional African American history from Reconstruction through the civil rights movement, with a special focus on historic cemeteries. Mon–Fri 10–4, Sat 10–2; fee.

✇ ᣗ At **Tallahassee Antique Car Museum** (850-942-0137; tacm.com), 6800 Mahan Drive at I-10 exit 209A, prepare to disappear into this cavernous two-story space for hours, memories trigged by thousands of antique objects placed together in thematic collections. It's way more than automobiles, although you'll find the spread of wheels on the ground floor—from the first steam-powered car ever built (the 1894 Duryea) to prop vehicles from several Batman movies—a car collection to put Jay Leno to shame. It's the top antique-car collection in the nation, right here for you to see. Museum owner, entrepreneur Devoe Moore, is a collector of collections, which is most evident on the second floor. Toy trucks. Cash registers. Sports memorabilia. Comics. Motorcycles. Pedal cars. Brass fans. The finest collection of antique outboard motors in the world. A huge room devoted to a massive model train layout (designed and run by a local club) is flanked by railroad memorabilia, from brass buttons to fine china, on every wall. The sheer amount of items in this museum is mind boggling. Visit with a friend or your family, so you can share "Remember when . . ." stories as you browse. Mon–Fri 8–5, Sat 10–5, Sun noon–5; $13.50–16 adults, $10.75 students, $7.50 ages 5–8.

✇ ᣗ **Tallahassee Museum of History & Natural Science** (850-575-8684; tallahasseemuseum.org), 3945 Museum Dr, isn't at all what you'd expect from a museum. Gentle footpaths and boardwalks blend into the natural surroundings, winding through Florida habitats alive with native wildlife like bald eagles, alligators, Florida panthers, and river otters. I looked up in a tree and saw a gray fox peering calmly down at me. In the Discovery Center, interactive natural science exhibits change every four to six months. Kids were busy in a fossil dig as I continued on to the Big Bend Farm, a living history area that shows Florida as it used to be: Workshops demonstrate shucking corn and pressing cane for sugar. On the opposite side of the main building (with a gift shop full of fun toys for the kids) are several historic structures, including the 1897 Concord School, the first post-Reconstruction school where Blacks were taught, and Catherine Murat's 1850s manor home, moved here from the Bellevue cotton plantation. To further enjoy the historic exhibits on display, rent the audio tour, which lets you plug codes into a cell-phone-like device to get audio clips from the

A PARADE OF ANTIQUE AUTOS AT THE TALLAHASSEE ANTIQUE CAR MUSEUM

Florida State Archives—oral histories, music, interviews, and narrations. What impressed me the most? Inside the 1924 Florida East Coast Railroad caboose, I pressed a button and heard a recording from the 1940s of Zora Neale Hurston singing a railroad lining chant. Now, that's connecting with the past. Mon–Sat 9–5, Sun 12:30–5; $9 adults, $8.50 seniors/students, $6 ages 4–15.

RAILROADIANA In Tallahassee, addition to **Railroad Square** (see *Art Galleries*) near FSU, be sure to see the **railroad exhibit** at the Tallahassee Museum of History & Natural Science and the **model railroad** at the Tallahassee Antique Car Museum (see *Museums*). The **Tallahassee–St. Marks Historic State Trail** (see *Greenways*) traces the route of Florida's earliest lengthy railroad, circa 1837.

For classic depots, downtown Perry has a beautifully renovated **passenger station** from the Live Oak, Perry & Georgia Railroad, now housing shops and restaurants. In downtown Sopchoppy, the classic wooden **Sopchoppy Railroad Depot** has been restored to its former glory.

WINERY Monticello Vineyards & Winery (850-294-WINE; monticellowinery .com), 1211 Waukeenah Hwy, is a small operation at Ladybird Organic Farm on CR 259 south of Monticello. All wines are certified organic, processed from muscadine grapes grown on site. Sat–Mon 10–6; during harvest months, Aug–Sept, visitors can pick fresh grapes.

✳ To Do

BICYCLING The **Tallahassee–St. Marks Railroad State Trail** (see *Greenways*) is the region's longest bike trail, ideal for overnight trips. At its south end, rent bicycles from Shields Marina (see *Boating*). Follow **FL 12** through Gadsden County on the North Florida Art Trail; signs lead the way. In the Apalachicola National Forest (see *Wild Places*), the **Munson Off-Road Bicycle Trail** attracts mountain bikers from around the region to ride the rolling sandhills. Mountain bikers have fun inside city limits, too. Winding mountain bike paths on rugged terrain can be found in the **Lake Overstreet Trails** portion of Alfred B. Maclay Gardens State Park and at **Phipps Park** (see *Parks*).

BIRDING With hundreds of excellent birding spots throughout the region, it's tough to just pick a few. **St. Marks National Wildlife Refuge** (see *Wild Places*) can't be beat for the number of species to spot during the winter migration. Stop by the **Henry M. Stevenson Memorial Bird Trail** at Tall Timbers Research Station (see *Antebellum Plantations*), open Mon–Fri 8–4:30, for prime birding along Lake Iamonia. You'll have excellent opportunities to see bird behavior while on the tour boat at **Wakulla Springs State Park** (see *Springs*). Hang out at **Hagens Cove** (see *Beaches*) to watch flocks of shorebirds, including black skimmers.

BOATING Shields Marina (850-925-5612; shieldsmarina.com), 95 Riverside Dr, in St. Marks is the largest marina along the Big Bend, well sheltered from the sea up the St. Marks River. With a well-stocked ship's store, fuel, dockage, mechanics on site, and rentals—boat, kayak, and bike—it's a must-visit if you want to take a pontoon ($125–175) out into the estuaries. In Steinhatchee you can rent boats and pontoons at **Sea Hag** (352-498-3008; seahag.com). Marinas provide dockage and storage (including dry dock) at varying rates. A public boat ramp is located at the end of CR 358 on the north side of the river; turn right at the end of the bridge.

ECOTOURS With the launch of the **Florida Green Guides** (fgga.us) program in this region almost a decade ago, the region has many guides who'll take you out on well-interpreted adventures through the many wild places that make up more than 70 percent of Wakulla County. Among those I've met over the years are birding expert **George Weymouth** (850-962-9092) and coastal expert **Captain Jody Campbell** (850-926-1173), who also leads light tackle sport-fishing trips. Others who specialize in personalized trips are paddler **David Morse** (850-962-2446), based in Sopchoppy; charter captain **James Hodges** (850 421-3555; stmarks charters.com), who runs wildlife and birding trips from the water; and **Russ Peters** (850-926-4348; cypressrunfarm.com), who runs eco-friendly trail rides. Each can customize a tour to your interest and budget. One of the tours that everyone who visits the region does is the boat tour at **Wakulla Springs State Park** (see *Springs*), an excellent introduction to the beauty and wildlife of the Wakulla River.

FAMILY ACTIVITIES ✍ ⅋ **The Mary Brogan Museum of Art and Science** (850-513-0700; thebrogan.org), 350 S Duval St, Tallahassee, an associate of the Smithsonian Institution, offers an interesting mix—science for the kids, art for you. And it works! Rotating first-floor exhibits feature colorful hands-on play stations; the second floor showcases permanent science exhibits such as the Ecolab (check out the Florida watershed map), the WCTV weather station, and the Early Childhood Area for the smallest of small fry. Third-floor exhibits celebrate the merging of art and science; I enjoyed a stroll through the History of Photography, which kicked off with Matthew Brady's classic photo of Abraham Lincoln. Special stations focused on the science behind photography. Stop in the Museum Store for a delightful selection of creative gifts to spark any budding artist. Open Mon–Sat 10–5, Sun 1–5, closed major holidays; fee.

✍ ⅋ At the **Challenger Learning Center and IMAX Theatre** (850-644-IMAX; challengertlh.com), 210 S Duval St, Tallahassee, most folks are there for the big-screen IMAX with 20,000 watts of sound and the incredibly crisp digital planetarium in its 50-foot dome, where dazzling graphics immerse you into space like no other planetarium show I've ever seen. But with reservations, your kids can also spend three hours taking over Mission Control and become astronauts on a space station mission to collect data on a comet in two realistic training laboratories (minimum age 10). This collaborative effort between the FSU College of Engineering and NASA is a living memorial to the *Challenger* crew. Open daily, varying hours; fee.

✍ At **Cross Creek Driving Range** (850-656-GOLF; crosscreekgolfandrange .com), 6701 Mahan Dr, Tallahassee, practice your putts on the driving range, or challenge the kids to a round of par-3. Open daily at 8 AM.

✍ **Tallahassee Rock Gym** (850-224-ROCK; tallyrockgym.com), 629-F Industrial Dr, Railroad Square, Tallahassee, offers a popular climbing wall in a historic railroad warehouse; take lessons, or practice your skills!

FISHING With more than 60 miles of wilderness coastline, the Big Bend has always attracted a steady clientele of saltwater anglers in search of grouper, cobia, and trout. Toward that end, you'll find plenty of fishing guides, especially around **Steinhatchee**. Ask around at the marinas (see *Boating*) regarding specific captains' specialties, and expect a day's worth of guided fishing (which includes your license) to cost $400–800, depending on what you're after. **Captain Tommy Thompson** (888-843-9949 or 352-284-1763; flanaturecoast.com/capttommy), who's literally written the book on fishing this region, offers nearshore fishing from a flats skiff out of Steinhatchee. Captain Chuck Simpson of **Big Bend Fishing** (850-544-5713; bigbendfish.com), leads nearshore from the other end of the Big Bend, Panacea and St. Marks. At **Keaton Beach**, a lengthy fishing pier provides a quiet place to drop a line.

Around Tallahassee, saltwater anglers head for St. Marks, the nearest launch point into the Gulf of Mexico; ask after guides at **Shell Island Fish Camp** (see *Fish Camps*) and **Shields Marina** (see *Boating*). Inland, **Lake Talquin**, a hydroelectric reservoir on the Ochlockonee River, has plenty of speckled perch, sunfish, and tantalizing, trophy-sized largemouth bass for the patient angler. There are numerous fish camps off FL 267 and several off FL 20 on the Upper Ochlockonee River, along with many boat ramps around the lake.

GAMING Greyhound racing is the focus of the **Jefferson County Kennel Club** (850-997-2561; jckcgreyhounds.com), US 19 north of Monticello, but I'm told their dining room offers good old-fashioned southern hospitality; dress for the occasion!

GENEALOGICAL RESEARCH & You'll hit the jackpot for all sorts of historical research at the **Florida State Archives** (850-245-6700; dlis.dos.state.fl.us /archives), 500 S Bronough St, but most folks who quietly sit at the long tables inside are digging through their ancestors' roots. Tip: Use their online resources first, and then come to Tallahassee to look through manuscripts and letters you couldn't otherwise view.

GOLF Playing a round on the gently rolling greens at the par-72 **Wildwood Golf Club** (850-926-GOLF; clubatwildwood.com), 3870 Coastal Hwy, Crawfordville, is like taking a walk in the woods, with each fairway fringed with a forest of oaks and pines. Great blue herons patrol the edge of water features in search of their next meal, and foxes slink across the back nine. The club includes a driving range, pro shop and 19th hole, The Bistro at Wildwood. Non-member fees include cart and green fee. A stay at the Wildwood Resort (see *Lodging*) includes a free round of golf.

In Tallahassee, enjoy a round at **Hilaman Golf Course** (850-891-3935; hilaman golfcourse.com), 2737 Blair Stone Rd, a municipal course with 18 holes and driving range. **Jake Gaither Golf Course** (850-891-3942; talgov.com/parks/golf/jake .cfm), 801 Tanner Dr, is a city course with nine holes, reservations on weekends. Owned by FSU, the **Don Veller Seminole Golf Course and Club** (850-644-2582; seminolegolfcourse.com), 2550 Pottsdamer St, is an 18-hole course with lighted driving range, reservations required.

HIKING The **Florida Trail** (see *What's Where*) winds its way from St. Marks National Wildlife Refuge through the entire width of the Apalachicola National

Forest. One of the trail's wildest and most remote sections is through the Bradwell
Bay Wilderness, a watery swamp forest with ancient trees. Two other particularly
scenic segments in this region are Goose Pasture and the Aucilla River Sinks
(see *Wild Places*). In Tallahassee, the day-hiking loop at Phipps Park (see *Parks*)
is a must, as are the trails just south of town at Leon Sinks Geological Area in
the Apalachicola National Forest (see *Wild Places*). West of Tallahassee toward
Quincy, **Lake Talquin State Forest** (see *Wild Places*) has several excellent hiking
trails. Along the Big Bend, don't miss **Steinhatchee Falls** (see *Waterfall*), with its
6-mile round-trip trail along the Steinhatchee River. Two short hiking trails in the
Tide Swamp Unit of Big Bend WMA lead through coastal pine flatwoods along the
tidal marshes near Hagens Cove; **Dallus Creek** is the more scenic.

HUNTING Hunt camps are sprinkled throughout the **Apalachicola National
Forest** (see *Wild Places*) and are very busy during deer hunting season, which is
big sport between Thanksgiving and Christmas in the thousands of acres of natural
lands throughout the region, including the **Aucilla Wildlife Management Area**
and **Big Bend Wildlife Management Area**. Check with the Florida Fish and
Wildlife Conservation Commission (myfwc.com) for hunt locations and dates.

PADDLING With the **Sopchoppy**, **Aucilla**, **Ochlockonee**, **St. Marks**, **Steinhatchee**, **Wacissa**, and **Wakulla** rivers sluicing through this region (and goodness
knows, I've forgotten others I haven't yet explored), paddlers will find plenty of
challenges. The Aucilla offers rapids, the Steinhatchee a waterfall, and the Sopchoppy is a twisting, winding, blackwa-
ter river. The Ochlockonee, St. Marks,
and Wakulla rivers pour out into the
Gulf of Mexico through a mazy meander of salt marshes, much fun for
kayakers. **The Wilderness Way** (850-
877-7200; thewildernessway.net), 3152
Shadeville Rd, is an outfitting shop that
offers paddling instruction and guided
tours throughout the region. I've paddled with the folks at **TnT Hideaway**
(850-925-6412; tnthideaway.com), 6527
Coastal Hwy, to explore hidden springs
and watch for manatees along the
Wakulla River. **Shields Marina** (see
Boating) offers kayak rentals on the St.
Marks River. For a trip on the beautiful and little-known Wacissa River,
Wacissa River Canoe Rentals (850-
997-5023; wacissarivercanoerentals
.com), 290 Wacissa Springs Rd, is just
up the road from the springs and rents
canoes daily.

For a tiny taste of whitewater thrills,
head to **Steinhatchee** with your kayak

HIKERS AT LEON SINKS

to leap the Steinhatchee Falls (see *Waterfall*). The 8-mile trip from the falls to Steinhatchee along this obsidian-colored waterway winds through dark river hammocks and forested residential areas before meeting the tidal basin, offering several Class I rapids. Rent kayaks from Steinhatchee Outpost (see *Camping & Cabins*); take-out is at Fiddler's Restaurant (see *Dining Out*).

Estuary dominates the central and most remote portion of a rough but scenic 91-mile saltwater paddle attempted by a handful of people every year: the **Historic Big Bend Saltwater Paddling Trail** (a segment of the Florida Circumnavigational Trail; see *The Lower Suwannee* chapter). Paddlers on this segment can find services at Steinhatchee, Keaton Beach, and Econfina, where sea kayakers put in at Econfina River State Park (see *Wild Places*) for easy access to the Gulf of Mexico. On US 98 you'll find picnic tables and a boat ramp on the Econfina River, a jungle-like paddling route that heads south 6 miles to the state park. A little farther west, paddlers can also put in at the Aucilla River and head upstream along the Wacissa River Canoe Trail into Jefferson County; the Aucilla quickly peters out as it disappears through its famed sinks.

SCALLOPING For many years the estuaries of the Big Bend have been the only place where enough scallops naturally breed to be harvested; their estuarine nurseries in other parts of the state had been overcollected and poisoned by runoff. Although more counties along the Gulf Coast have had their waters reopened for an annual scalloping season, **Steinhatchee** remains the destination of choice for serious shellfish harvesters. Your success is in direct proportion to the weather: Too much rain and the scallop population suffers. The season runs Jul 1–Sept 10, and you must abide by state-mandated limits of 2 gallons of whole scallops per person per day. If you snorkel from your own boat, you must have a saltwater fishing license and display a DIVER DOWN flag. Many local marinas arrange charters; **Big Bend Charters** (352-498-3703; bigbendcharters.com) specializes in scalloping trips. No fishing license is required when you scallop with a charter, nor if you head for **Hagens Cove** (see *Beaches*), where you can wade into the Gulf and collect to your heart's content.

AT STEINHATCHEE, PREPARING FRESHLY GATHERED SCALLOPS IS AN ART

SCENIC DRIVES The 220-mile-long **Big Bend Scenic Byway** (floridabigbendscenicbyway.com) creates a network of scenic roads throughout the region, and extends west to the Apalachicola River (see the *Apalachicola River* chapter).

In addition to cruising Tallahassee's many "official" canopy roads, such as **Meridian Road**—which is wonderful in late March when azaleas and wisteria are in bloom—you'll want to pick up the *North Florida Art Trail* brochure and follow rural FL 12 and FL 269 across Gadsden County from Havana through Quincy, Greensboro,

Visit Tallahassee

CAPITOL FOUNTAIN, TALLAHASSEE

and Chattahoochee to enjoy the rolling farmland and stops for art aficionados along the way. **The Loop** in Taylor County is a nearly 100-mile circuit taking you through the scenic fishing villages along the Gulf Coast, via US 19, FL 51, and CR 361 through the heart of the "Forest Capital of Florida."

SWIMMING At **Wakulla Springs State Park** (see *Springs*), dive into Florida's deepest spring and paddle back to the sandy shoreline; stay within the ropes, since the 'gators cruise just outside them! For an old-fashioned swimming hole, head to wild **Wacissa Springs** (see *Springs*), where a rope swing tempts over the spring boil where the river begins. You can also swim at the beaches (see *Beaches*) in the region.

WALKING TOURS In Tallahassee, grab a map at the visitors center and hit the bricks for a self-guided walk around more than **60 historic sites downtown**. You can watch the Florida Legislature at work by hooking up with a **walking tour at the capitol**; don't miss the view from the 22nd-floor observation deck! Quincy has a self-guided walking tour booklet of 55 historic homes and churches; drop by the Gadsden Arts Center (see *Art Galleries*) for a copy. Monticello offers a historic walking tour following numbered posts in front of significant buildings; drop in at the chamber of commerce for a guide.

✳ Green Space

BEACHES The Big Bend isn't noted for its beaches—it's an estuary. But these vast salt marshes along the Gulf of Mexico do yield to some remote beaches accessed from US 98 or, in Taylor County, off CR 361. Some of the better-known spots are **Mashes Sands Beach** at Panacea and near Spring Creek, **Shell Point**

Beach and **Wakulla Beach**. My favorite slender strands are on **Dickerson Bay** at the end of Bottoms Rd, and behind the **St. Marks Lighthouse** (see *Lighthouse*).

🐚 Down near Steinhatchee, families will enjoy a soft white strand at **Hodges Park** in Keaton Beach, complete with picnic pavilion and playground. Between Steinhatchee and Keaton Beach on CR 361 in the Tide Swamp Unit of Big Bend WMA, **Hagens Cove** is a prime destination for scalloping, especially for families with small children. Don't expect a beautiful white-sand beach here. It's an accessible piece of shoreline along an infinite stretch of mudflats, a beautiful place to sit and watch the sunset.

GARDENS ♿ 🐚 Walk through the iron gate at **Alfred B. Maclay Gardens State Park** (850-487-4556; floridastateparks.org/maclaygardens), 3540 Thomasville Rd, and up the brick path—the azaleas are in bloom, and the air is strong with their sweet fragrance; a thousand shades of green march down the hill to Lake Hall. It's spring, and it's just as New York financier Alfred Maclay envisioned—his retirement home surrounded by blooms. When Maclay purchased an antebellum quail hunting lodge in 1923, he turned his landscape design skills to the surrounding hills. Several years after he died, his widow opened the formal gardens as a tourist attraction, turning it over to the state a decade later. The flow of form is subtle: As you approach the house, the grounds yield from wild woodlands to formal Italianate walled gardens, with burbling fountains and stands of cypress. Prime blooming months run from December to early summer, but the gardens are a joy to

GATHERING SEA CREATURES FOR STUDY FROM DICKERSON BAY

HODGES PARK AT KEATON BEACH

explore any time of year; adjacent Lake Overstreet is a wild, wooded addition to the park with miles of hiking and biking trails. The antebellum home, furnished in antiques bought and used by the family, is open for tours 9–5 Jan–Apr. Fee.

&. ♂ A hidden gem owned by the city of Tallahassee, **Dorothy B. Oven Park** (850-891-3915; talgov.com/parks /cc/oven.cfm) 3205 Thomasville Rd, has a series of formal gardens, including extensive azalea and camellia plantings, surrounding a manor house designed by Alfred Maclay. Located on an original 1824 land grant within the city, its quiet niches offer spaces to relax, walk, or read.

GREENWAYS Tallahassee–St. **Marks Historic Railroad State Trail** (850-922-6007; dep.state.fl.us/gwt/state /marks), 1022 Desoto Park Dr, Tallahassee. Although the trail runs up into the southern suburbs of Tallahassee, the trailhead along FL 363 provides ample parking, restrooms, picnic tables, and a historic marker that explains it all: The Tallahassee–St. Marks Railroad began operation in 1837 with mule-drawn cars and switched to steam locomotives in 1839, connecting ships coming into Port Leon with Tallahassee. This paved bike trail runs through wilderness areas along its 23-mile route to its southern terminus in St. Marks, so take plenty of water and ride with a friend if possible. An equestrian trail runs parallel to the forested right-of-way.

The **Miccosukee Canopy Road Greenway** parallels Miccosukee Rd, with four entrances offering bicyclists, hikers, and equestrians 6 miles of canopied trail and open spaces. The **J. R. Alford Greenway**, 2500 S. Pedrick Rd, covers 800 acres with rambling trails.

PARKS Lake Jackson, the largest lake in Tallahassee, is one of those oddball geological mysteries: Every 25 years or so, the lake's waters vanish "down the drain" into a sinkhole, and it takes a few years for the lake to brim with water again. Bordering Lake Jackson's east shore on Meridian Rd, **Elinor Klapp-Phipps Park** (850-891-3975; talgov.com/parks/parks/phipps.cfm) has an excellent hiking loop as well as biking and equestrian trails. On the west shore of Lake Jackson, **J. Lee Vause Park** (850-606-1470), 6024 Old Bainbridge Rd, has a boardwalk along the lake and nature trails as well as picnic shelters. There is also a small pull-off along US 27 for access to Lake Jackson.

Off to the west along FL 20, **Lake Talquin State Park** (850-922-6007; florida stateparks.org/laketalquin) gives you a scenic panorama of Lake Talquin with a fishing dock and nature trail; fee. In downtown Tallahassee, folks like to stroll around Lake Ella in **Fred O. Drake Jr. Park**, Monroe St, where you can picnic under the pines.

In Panacea the **Otter Creek Unit** of **St. Marks National Wildlife Refuge** (see *Wild Places*) has a boat launch, fishing area, hiking trail, and shady picnicking along the shores of Otter Lake. **St. Marks River City Park**, with restrooms, picnic tables, a fishing pier, and a boat ramp on the St. Marks River, marks the southernmost terminus of the Tallahassee–St. Marks Historic Railroad Trail (see *Greenways*).

Ochlockonee River State Park (850-962-2771; floridastateparks.org/ochlockonee river) sits just south of Sopchoppy on US 321 and has hiking trails, camping, and plenty of waterfront for fishing the estuary. The riverfront trail is especially scenic for an afternoon stroll, and all of the picnic pavilions come with a cool river breeze.

SPRINGS ✎ ♿ Showcasing Florida's deepest spring, where the water is so clear you can see the bones of mastodons and giant sloth resting at the bottom of the 180-foot pool, **Edward Ball Wakulla Springs State Park** (850-224-5950; florida stateparks.org/wakullasprings), 550 Wakulla Park Dr, Wakulla Springs, offers swimming facilities (69 degrees year-round) with a high diving platform, more than 10 miles of shaded nature trails and hiking trails, and daily boat tours where you're bound to see dozens of alligators and innumerable waterfowl. At the center of it all is the classic Wakulla Lodge (see *Lodging*); don't miss the marble-topped soda fountain in the gift shop! Fee.

Lesser-known **Wacissa Springs** [30.340389, -83.991268], end of Wacissa Springs Rd in Jefferson County, has the expansive feel of Wakulla Springs without any development of the spring basin. It's rustic—there's a dirt parking lot, boat ramp, and ladder out of the water where you can jump into the spring. Canoe rentals are available just up the road (see *Paddling*). But it's a gorgeous and wild place, especially from the water.

WATERFALL Steinhatchee Falls [29.74635, -83.342608] rates as Florida's broadest and most interesting waterfall. This limestone shelf along the Steinhatchee River served as a crossing point for wagons as settlers pushed their way south along the Gulf Coast, and the wagon ruts are still visible in the limestone on both sides of the river. A riverside park has interpretive information, picnic tables, and a boat launch; a hiking trail starts just outside the gate. The trailhead and falls are off CR 51, 2 miles west of US 19/27.

WILD PLACES The **Apalachicola National Forest** (850-643-2282; fs.usda.gov /apalachicola) is one of the wildest places in Northwest Florida. Sweeping around the southern and eastern sides of Tallahassee, it's also Florida's largest national forest. Some of its special spots include Leon Sinks Geological Area; Bradwell Bay, a wild and lonely wilderness area along the Florida National Scenic Trail; and the cypress-lined Sopchoppy River, a great paddling route. Its full-hookup recreation areas are located on the western side of the forest (see the *Apalachicola River* chapter), but simpler camping can be found at many designated primitive sites along its creeks.

Encompassing more than 16,000 acres, **Lake Talquin State Forest** (850-627-9674; fl-dof.com/state_forests/lake_talquin.html) is spread across 10 tracts on the shores of the Ochlockonee River and Lake Talquin. You can hike through forests of magnolia and beech along trails on the Fort Braden Tract and Bear Creek Tract, or ride horses on the equestrian trails. Bicycling is permitted on forest roads, numerous boat ramps allow access for anglers, and there is seasonal hunting on some of the tracts.

Established in 1931 to protect the fragile Gulf estuaries, **St. Marks National Wildlife Refuge** (850-925-6121; http://saintmarks.fws.gov), 1255 Lighthouse Rd, St. Marks, spans three counties. Monarch butterflies rest here in October on their annual migration to Mexico, carpeting the saltbushes in shades of orange and black. Although the refuge is broken up into several units, most folks arrive at the visitors center south of Newport off US 98. Browse the exhibits and learn about this mosaic of habitats before setting off down the road. The Florida Trail crosses the entire width of the refuge. Shorter nature trails give you a taste of the salt marshes, pine flatwoods, and swamps. Drive to the end of the road to visit the historic St. Marks Lighthouse (see *Lighthouse*).

During hunting season, you'll see plenty of pickups pulling into **Aucilla WMA** and **Hickory Mound WMA** between Newport and Perry along US 98, and the **Big Bend WMA** surrounding Steinhatchee. Off-season, Hickory Mound's extensive dike trails are great for birding and alligator-watching. Off US 98 east of the Aucilla River bridge, the **Aucilla River Sinks** and **Goose Pasture** provide access to one of the strangest rivers in Florida—after rushing across rapids, it vanishes beneath the limestone bedrock and pops up time and again in "windows" in the aquifer, deep sinkholes with water in motion. Use the Florida Trail (see *What's Where*) to explore this unique area. At the end of CR 14, **Econfina River State Park** (850-584-3026; floridastateparks.org/econfina_river) gives paddlers and boaters a put-in to the vast Gulf estuary, and offers loop trails through uplands along the marsh.

STEINHATCHEE FALLS IS FLORIDA'S BROADEST WATERFALL

❋ Lodging

BED & BREAKFASTS

Monticello 32344

♂ (((•))) A visit to the **Avera-Clarke House** (850-997-5007; averaclarke .com), 580 W Washington St, made me fall in love with southern hospitality all over again. The main house is a 1890 Victorian with four elegant bedrooms. Lounging in the yard with lemonade, I asked about The Cottage, across the lawn, clearly occupied by happy honeymooners. It's thought to be the oldest building in Jefferson County, circa 1821, moved here in 2006 and renovated as a romantic hideaway. Rates $79 and up.

🐾 ♂ (((•))) The **John Denham House** (850-997-4568; johndenhamhouse .com), 555 Palmer Mill Rd, is a classic piece of history, built by a Scots immigrant in 1872. Luxuriate in the silky sheets under a down comforter, or relax in a clawfoot tub. Each of the five large rooms has a fireplace accented with candles. $85–125; children and pets are welcome in a safe, family-friendly environment.

Quincy 32351

🐾 ♂ (((•))) **Allison House Inn** (888-904-2511; allisonhouseinn.com), 215 N Madison St. The former home of General A. K. Allison, who stepped into office as governor of Florida at the end of the Civil War, this 1843 Georgian-style house is one of the oldest in North Florida. Extensive renovation in 1925 added a story to the house and gave it an English country look. Step into Florida's genteel past and enjoy one of the six spacious guest rooms and fine crumpets and orange marmalade offered by innkeepers Stuart and Eileen Johnson; many of the rooms have multiple beds in this family-friendly inn. $95–140.

♂ (((•))) **McFarlin House** (877-370-4701; mcfarlinhouse.com), Love St.

Decorated with Tiffany windows original to the home and 11,000 square feet of imported Italian tile, this century-old Queen Anne Victorian showcases the good life that Quincy's well-to-do gentry enjoyed. With renovations completed in 1996, this was a finalist for an award as one of the top homes in the United States. The three-story mansion has nine elegant rooms, each unique in size, shape, and decor, offering romantic amenities such as Jacuzzi and fireplace; $99–229.

St. Marks 32355

🐚 **The Sweet Magnolia** (850-925-7670; sweetmagnolia.com), 803 Port Leon Dr, offers an interesting meld of old-fashioned charm and updated facilities; it's a former railroad boardinghouse from 1923, but the interiors are sparkling new. Of the seven roomy bedrooms ($85–185), five offer a Jacuzzi for two. I especially like the beautiful water gardens behind the home, a perfect place to settle in and read a book, and the comfy back porch for just hanging out. Gourmet breakfasts served; dinner on request.

HOTELS, MOTELS & RESORTS

Crawfordville 32327

🐚 🐾 ♿ ♂ ✈ (((•))) For a getaway in the heart of the region's outdoor recreation, head to **Wildwood Resort** (800-878-1546 or 850-926-4455; innat wildwood.com), 3896 Coastal Hwy. Art reflects nature in details throughout the common areas, from the etched-glass doors to the large breakfast area with fireplace in wood and stone. Each of its comfortable guest rooms ($89 and up) features a writing desk (with free high-speed Internet access), luxury linens, and coffeemaker. Certified a "green" accommodation for its energy-efficiency and reuse practices, the inn offers deals with local outfitters so you can get out and play and return and relax—from paddling and guided photography trips to golf packages. Included in your room rate is access to the pool and tennis courts at the adjacent golf course (see *Golf*). A gazebo out back is popular for small weddings.

Keaton Beach 32348
In this little fishing community on the Gulf of Mexico, **Keaton Beach Marina Motel & Cottages** (850-578-2897; keatonbeachmarina.com/motels and cottages.html), 20650 Keaton Beach Dr, is a small family motel with spacious rooms; the unit I checked out had a glassed-in porch overlooking the channel. It's an older building, with uneven floors, but that just adds to its charm. $69 for motel rooms, $99 for cottages, which are two-bedroom efficiencies and require a two-night stay.

Perry 32348
From the pre-interstate days when Perry was a bustling junction of major US highways, the **Chaparral Inn** (850-584-2441), 2519 S Byron Butler Pkwy, has aged gracefully. Each modest room ($45 and up) includes cable TV, phone, and air-conditioning; enjoy the pool or sit in a porch swing on the well-manicured grounds.

✔ ♿ (☊) The **Hampton Inn** (850-223-3000; hamptoninn.hilton.com), 2399 S Byron Butler Pkwy, has been ranked among the top in the nation for its chain. In addition to an expanded continental breakfast, look for cookies and chocolate-dipped strawberries in the dining area every afternoon; families crowd the swimming pool on weekends. Rates start at $90; reservations recommended, especially during football season, when they catch the spillover of fans from Tallahassee.

Steinhatchee 32359
Condos converted to motel rooms in 2002, the **Pelican Pointe Inn** (352-498-7427; pelicanpointeinn.com), 1306 SE Riverside Dr, offers a riverfront view and dockage in front of your room, adjacent to Fiddler's Restaurant (see *Dining Out*). Amenities vary, but all of the spacious rooms have cable TV and screened balcony; $130–175.

🦟 ☂ ✔ ♿ ♂ **Steinhatchee Landing Resort** (352-498-3513; steinhatchee landing.com), 203 Ryland Circle off FL 51, is a magical place, with the feel of a turn-of-the-20th-century village on the shores of the Steinhatchee River, where ancient live oaks shade Old Florida and Victorian gingerbread homes that melt into the landscape. When owner Dean Fowler came to Steinhatchee from Georgia in the 1970s to fish, he saw a need for a place where the whole family could come and relax while the family angler was out on a fishing trip. The 31 tasteful, old-fashioned homes come with modern interiors: a step from Florida Cracker into a page out of *House Beautiful*, with hardwood and tiled floors, high ceilings, gleaming modern kitchens, and inviting overstuffed beds. Most of the homes are owned privately and leased for rental through the 35-acre resort, where guests are free to roam and enjoy the riverside pool, health center, petting farm, children's playground, and miles of walking trails; canoes and kayaks, guided pontoon tours, and bicycles are available for a nominal fee. In addition to a conference center accommodating 60 guests, the Dancing Waters Chapel provides a lovely natural non-denominational setting for weddings and other special events. This family-friendly venue hosts many reunions, including get-togethers of the Carter clan of Plains, Georgia, and caters to newlyweds with romantic Honeymoon Cottages, each with fireplace and hot tub. Rates start at $119 off-season for a one-bedroom, one-night stay in one of the Spice

Cottages, modeled after old Florida seaside village homes; discounts apply to stays of weekends and longer.

🐾 ♂ (ỵ) ↝ **Steinhatchee River Inn** (352-498-4049; steinhatcheeriverinn .net), Riverside Dr, has 17 large and tidy suites on a hillside above the river, offering a variety of room configurations (most are two-room suites) for $79 and up. The swimming pool—and the entire motel—overlooks the river.

🦐 At **The Sunset Place** (352-498-0860; thesunsetplace.com), 115 1st St SW, a condo resort, every condo has a full kitchen and sweeping view of the Gulf estuary along the Steinhatchee River; watch the sunset from your balcony or at the pool. $84–189.

Tallahassee
& (ỵ) As the hub of regional activity, Tallahassee boasts a large number of hotels and motels, primarily major chains such as **Hampton Inn** (850-574-4900; hamptoninnandsuitestalla-hassee.com), 3388 Lonnbladh Rd; **Homewood Suites** (850-402-9400; homewoodsuites1.hilton.com), 2987 Apalachee Pkwy; and the **Doubletree Hotel** (850-224-5000; doubletree1 .hilton.com),101 S Adams St. Despite the many choices, it can still be hard to find a room in town—lobbyists and football fans often book the place full. Your best bet is to call Visit Tallahassee (see *Guidance*) for recommendations when rooms are tight.

& ↝ (ỵ) I've stayed many times for business at the **Cabot Lodge** (850-386-7500; cabotlodgethomasvilleroad .com), 1653 Raymond Diehl Rd, and appreciate both the warm, welcoming lobby—with its backwoods-lodge feel, comfortable spaces for a business chat, evening happy-hour cocktails for guests, and hot breakfast in the morning—and the spacious rooms upstairs, which have the desks and other amenities

that business travelers need. $99 and up.

(ỵ) & An intimate boutique hotel, **The Governors Inn** (800-342-7717 or 850-681-6855; thegovinn.com), 209 S Adams St, created in the heart of a historic warehouse and stable in the shadow of the capitol, showcases the finest that Tallahassee has to offer, with complimentary valet parking, breakfast, and cocktail hour. Learn a little history, too—each room is named for one of Florida's former governors. The refined atmosphere extends from the common spaces into the rooms, where you'll enjoy a large bath, writing desk, and terry robe for lounging. Rooms and suites, $139 and up.

& (ỵ) ↝ At the **Hotel Duval** (866-957-4001 or 850-224-6000; hotelduval .com), 415 N Monroe St, each spacious room has a sleek, modern feel, the perfect meld of function and beauty. Nestled in this downtown boutique hotel for a conference, I didn't want to leave. The modern bathroom, with a clear sink and pebbled shower room, was a work of art. An easy chair adjoining the bed had perfect ambience for reading; the desk felt just right, and the upstairs lounge had a bustling bar with a killer view of the city. Big bonus: Since they're part of the Marriott chain, I picked up plenty of points that week. Rooms and suites, $125 and up.

Wakulla Springs 32305
🦐 ♂ ↝ Dating back to 1937, **Wakulla Lodge** (850-224-5950), 550 Wakulla Park Dr, overlooks the fabulous springs at Wakulla Springs State Park (see *Springs*). This is Florida's only state park lodge, a true step back in time, with gleaming Tennessee marble floors and period furnishings in each of the 27 rooms ($99 and up), and no television—except in the lobby, where guests mingle as they enjoy checkers,

cards, and conversation at the marble tables in front of "Old Joe," an 11-foot alligator shot by a poacher in 1966. Look up and take in the artistic beauty of the hand-decorated wooden beams, completed by a Bavarian artist, or thumb through the album of clippings that spell out the history of the lodge. As night falls, a soft mist rises from the springs, and alligators crawl up onto the beach as you peer from the windows of The Ball Room (see *Dining Out*) during dinner. In the morning head out on a boat tour or a hike, or hit the 33-foot diving board for a jump into Florida's deepest spring.

CAMPING & CABINS

Monticello 32344

🐾 ♂ (⬤) Accessed from US 19 south of Monticello, the **Tallahassee East KOA** (800-562-3890 or 850-997-3890; koa.com/campgrounds/tallahassee) offers shady spots in a forested campground visible from I-10. Tent spaces, RV pull-throughs, and both small and large cabins available, $26–90.

Panacea 32346

🦐 🐾 ♂ (⬤) **Holiday Campground** (850-984-5757; holidaycampground .com), US 98 at the Panacea Bridge, is a large family campground with a steady breeze off Ochlockonee Bay; great views from many of the sites. They can accommodate anything from a tent to a big rig and offer full 30- and 50-amp service, nice bathhouses, a playground, a 200-foot pier for fishing the bay, a swimming pool, and a camp store. Dump station available. $29–38, weekly and monthly rates available.

Perry 32348

♂ 🐾 (⬤) **Perry KOA** (850-838-3221; perrykoa.com), 3641 US 19 S, provides a mix of shady and sunny pull-through sites with full hookups or tent sites and cabins and cottages with bath, $26–90.

Amenities include a swimming pool and hot tub.

Sopchoppy 32358

🦐 ♂ Set along the Sopchoppy River, the **Myron B. Hodge Sopchoppy City Park** (850-962-4611) has campsites ($15) with hot showers at the bathhouse, nature trails, a boat ramp, and fishing docks, and is a great put-in for explorations of the river.

🦐 ♂ At **Ochlockonee River State Park** (see *Parks*), the well-shaded campground (800-326-3521; florida stateparks.reserveamerica.com) catches a nice persistent breeze off the river, and you can walk right down and fish along the river from your campsite; $18.

St. Marks 32355

🦐 **Newport Recreation Area** (850-925-6171), US 98, Wakulla, with picnicking, playground, and deeply shaded campsites ($15) in the forest along the St. Marks River, sits just outside St. Marks National Wildlife Refuge (where camping is not permitted).

Steinhatchee 32359

🐾 **Steinhatchee Outpost** (800-589-1541; flrvoutpost.com), junction of US 19 and FL 51, adjacent to the Steinhatchee River, offers open and shaded sites for tents and RVs ($15–20), as well as a private pond for paddling, and canoe and kayak rentals for trips on the river.

(⬤) On the Jena side of the river in Dixie County (see the *Lower Suwannee* chapter), **Nature Coast RV Resort** (352-498-7344; naturescoast rvresort.com), 4802 CR 358, has RV sites right with 30/50-amp service right along a waterway connecting to the river. Lounge around their pool or meet with friends around the fire pit while relaxing after a day of fishing or scalloping. Seasonal rates $16–30.

Tallahassee

🐾 📶 **Big Oak RV Park** (850-562-4660; bigoakrvpark.com), 4024 N Monroe St 32303, offers shady spaces under grand old oaks just north of Tallahassee, perfect for antiquing excursions and a favorite for legislators living on a budget, offering a mix of back-in and pull-through 50-amp full-hookup sites for self-contained RVs only, $39.

🐾 📶 **Tallahassee RV Park** (850-878-7641; tallahasseervpark.com), 6504 Mahan Dr 32301, has azalea-lined roads with shaded spaces, picnic tables and full hookups at each site, and a swimming pool, $43.

FISH CAMPS Six fish camps cluster around Lake Talquin off FL 267, offering anglers a place to retreat from busy Tallahassee. The busiest is **Whippoorwill Sportsman's Lodge** (850-875-2605; fishthewhip.com), 3129 Cooks Landing Rd, Quincy 32351, which has cottages, two rooms in the lodge, a campground, and a marina.

For saltwater fishing, visit **Shell Island Fish Camp** (850-925-6226), 440 Shell Island Rd, St. Marks 32355, on the Wakulla River. They offer basic, clean motel rooms with a small fridge, cable TV, no phones, $65; cabins and park models also available. Ramp and dockage available; fee.

✳ Where to Eat

DINING OUT

Panacea

🦐 **Angelo & Sons Seafood Restaurant** (850-984-5168; panaceaseafood .com), US 98 at the bridge, stretches out over Ochlockonee Bay into the next county, providing gorgeous waterfront views while you dine on sumptuous seafood dishes with a Greek flair. They've been in business since 1945;

I've been stopping here for 20 years and have never been disappointed by my selections. Fresh Florida lobster is a highlight on the menu, as well as grouper, charbroiled mullet, oysters prepared several ways, and local shrimp. Greek Night on Thu. Entrées $10–28.

Spring Creek

🦐 Do go out of your way to visit **Spring Creek Restaurant** (850-926-3751; springcreekfl.com), 33 Ben Willis Rd, end of CR in Wakulla County, one of Florida's finest down-home seafood restaurants. Tended by the Lovel family since 1977, this off-the-beaten-path seafood restaurant is filled with artifacts recounting history along the Forgotten Coast. The crab chowder is superb, but that's just the beginning of your meal. Fresh, locally caught seafood on the menu includes grouper, mullet, shrimp, and soft-shell crabs. Tue–Fri 5–9 PM, Sat–Sun noon–9.

Steinhatchee

Fiddler's Restaurant (352-498-7427; fiddlersrestaurant.com), 1306 SE Riverside Dr, is set in a giant fishpond (complete with koi) overlooking the river. Kick back and enjoy the view out the picture windows as you feast on specialties like grilled grouper with caper sauce, caprice chicken, seafood gumbo, and Greek shrimp with feta over linguine. The steaks are fantastic: Delmonico, prime rib, and filet mignon. Entrées $16–market price. At lunch, they morph into Cackleberry's, "Home of the famous Steinhatchee Sabertooth Sandgnat Sandwhich," with soft-shell crab, pecan chicken salad, Alfredo shrimp, and burgers, $7–9. Stop in the lobby on your way out and look over the great selection of Guy Harvey T-shirts. Open daily.

Tallahassee

Andrew's 228 (850-224-2935; andrews downtown.com/andrews228.html), 228 S Adams St. The upscale big brother to Andrew's Capital Grill & Bar (see *Eating Out*) presents a very different face than its neighbor, featuring fine continental cuisine, with entrées $15–36.

Melding Chinese and Thai cuisine, **Bahn Thai Restaurant** (850-224-4765), 1319 S Monroe St, presents a wide array of fresh Asian food for discriminating palates in an unassuming locale. Nothing is precooked, save the items on the nightly all-you-can-eat buffet, and there are more than 126 menu options, including 15 different soups and an extensive selection of vegetarian dishes; entrées $12 and up. The convivial staff can be caught breaking into traditional song and dance in honor of their patrons' birthdays. Open for lunch on weekdays, dinner daily.

Chez Pierre (850-222-0936; chez pierre.com), 1215 Thomasville Rd, is French, as the name indicates—but with a southern twist. Chalk paintings greet you along the walk, and flamboyant modern impressionism dresses up the tasteful maroon walls, setting a festive mood that spills over to Chef Eric's parade of fresh French cuisine—hors d'oeuvres ($8–14) include escargots and bacon-wrapped dates stuffed with blue cheese, sandwiches and a quiche du jour are available, and entrées ($19–32) feature mussels marinière and duck breast tapenade. Save room for a selection from the elegant pastry tray! The wine selection, of course, is broad, and Le Piano Bar hosts jazz weekends. Stop in on Bastille Day and find yourself surrounded by festivity—more than 1,000 people show up for dancing, arts and crafts booths, and wine tastings.

Always reserve ahead at the **Cypress Restaurant** (850-513-1100; cypress restaurant.com), 1350 W Tennessee St, as it's a favorite of the local politicos—and can you blame them? Chef-proprietor David Gwynn serves up creations like grilled beef hanger steak with cheesy Gorgonzola red potatoes and Florida shrimp and grits with country ham, tomatoes, carrots, and shiitake mushrooms; entrées start around $18. Open Mon–Sat at 5.

Just a few steps from Kleman Plaza, **OneOOne Restaurant & Lounge** (850-391-1309; 101tallahassee.com), 215 W College Ave, has a lunch menu that leans toward tapas. Not wanting a heavy meal, I went for the crabcakes with fruit salad; my dining companion tried the shrimp. Both were delectable. This snazzy bistro appeals to the professional crowd—especially with their social-lubricating $4 martini and wine specials—and features a slightly daring menu, entrées $15–26. Get together with friends at 101 and enjoy a late night on the town.

Wakulla Springs

Large windows open out onto a view of the Wakulla Springs as you settle back into a fine-dining experience at ♿ 🍴 **The Ball Room** at Wakulla Lodge (see *Lodging*) where they've served guests since 1937. With backlit photos of the park, it feels a little like an interpretive center, although well-dressed wait staff wheel your food over on carts laden with vintage dishes. And what food! Breakfast brings fluffy stacks of pancakes and eggs with grits, and after you spend a day out on the water it's tough to choose between the fresh-as-can-be Apalachicola fried oysters (light, salty and slightly crisp, breaded in crushed crackers with a dusting of flour) for lunch or dinner, and the traditional "Old South" fried chicken, a patrons' favorite since 1946. Their world-famous navy bean soup is a must. Open daily, entrées $14 and up. Reservations requested.

EATING OUT

Crawfordville

🍴 ✎ At **Myra Jean's Restaurant** (850-926-7530), 2669 Crawfordville Hwy, you can feed the whole family for a small price and keep them entertained with the suspended G-scale model railroad running way up over the tables. Breakfast comes as cheap as $1.49 for the "El Cheapo"—one egg, grits, and a fluffy biscuit—but I prefer ordering anything where their home fries come as a side, cooked up with peppers and onions. For more than 20 years, they've been feeding folks down here with comfort food, and their "Economic Stimulus Menu" (all under $6.95) keeps the prices low. Don't forget the ice cream counter—grab a chocolate shake on your way out.

Havana

Ah, the temptations inside **Joanie's Gourmet Market And Fabulous Cafe** (850-539-4433; joaniesgourmet market.com), 102 W 8th Ave. Fine wines. Fresh chocolate. Sweets and treats. Gorgeous cheeses. When I walked in, owner Joanie Lauther was just finishing up lunch; the aromas, heavenly. Enjoy a glass of wine and a muffuletta wedge or a ham-and-Brie for lunch, $8–10, or show up for the Friday or Saturday Night Dinner Party; reservations required for dinner. Dining Tue–Sat 11:30–6:30, with Sunday brunch 11:30–2.

Monticello

A little hometown diner, **The Rare Door** (850-997-3133), 329 N Cherry St, serves up country dinners under $7 like meat loaf with mashed potatoes and gravy and green beans, plus lunch subs, salads, and burgers and soft-serve ice cream. Their menu is up on a chalkboard; the big bay windows let the sunshine stream in, overlooking the outdoor seating area. Open daily for breakfast 5:30–11 AM, lunch 11–2, and for dinners Mon–Fri until 8 or 9.

Panacea

Posey's Steam Room & Oyster Bar (850-984-5243), 1506 Coastal Hwy. I stopped here for dinner late one day and ate a mess of shrimp and a slice of key lime pie, yum. Serving up sandwiches, steamed shrimp and snow crab, or baskets of fried seafood including grouper fingers, oysters, and jumbo lump crabmeat (the best crab-cake ever!), $6–18. Their old location in St. Marks has been reborn along the Panacea waterfront, just down the road, as **Posey's Dockside** (850-713-0014), 99 Rock Landing Rd, a delightful place to savor fresh seafood and a view of Dickerson Bay. Fresh seafood dinners in both locations for under $20.

Perry

((ᵠ)) At **Goodman's Real Pit Bar-B-Que** (850- 584-3751), 2429 S Byron Butler Pkwy, I was immediately delighted at the selection and the speed of service for smoky, succulent pork on a platter. I took half the piled-high food home in a take-out box, and it cost me less than $10 for everything, tip included.

I popped into **Pouncey's** (850-584 9942), 2186 S Byron Butler Pkwy, on a trip through Perry, and wow, what a flashback—it's a real 1950s family restaurant serving up comfort food that feels so good after a long trip. Their burgers are exactly what they claim: the best. Dinners under $15, cash only.

St. Marks

Riverside Cafe (850-925-5668; riversidebay.com), 69 Riverside Dr, is the epitome of Old Florida waterfront dining—open air, the breeze coming right in off the river. Chow down on a variety of sandwiches from oyster to BLT, or savor a dinner of stone crab claws in-season, or any of several vegetarian specialties. They rent canoes as well; ask at the front counter. Breakfast served daily 9–11, lunch and dinner thereafter, $14 and up.

Sopchoppy

Backwoods Bistro (850-962-2220; thebackwoodsbistro.com), 106 Municipal Ave. You won't miss the full-sized gorilla outside, nor the barnacle-encrusted bicycle in the front window of this classy pizza parlor, housed in the renovated 1912 drugstore that served this once bustling railroad town. Choose from specialty pizzas like the Extreme, Veggie Garden, or Carnivore, $11–21, or try a gourmet Greek or Mexican pizza; sandwiches, salads, and lasagna, too, with a side of music on Fri evening. Ask about canoe and kayak rentals via Sopchoppy Outfitters.

Steinhatchee

Everyone raves about **Roy's** (352-498-5000; roys-restaurant.com), 100 1st Ave SW, a fixture since 1969 with a killer view of a Steinhatchee sunset. Their mashed potato salad goes down smooth as silk, and the barbecue attracts folks from several counties. Offering a wide variety of steaks and seafood, Roy's is a place for fresh locally caught specialties, including bay scallops, shrimp, oysters, and tender mullet. Entrées $11 and up; open for lunch and dinner.

Tallahassee

At **Andrew's Capital Grill & Bar** (850-224-2935; andrewsdowntown.com/capitalgrill.html), 228 S Adams St, the sandwiches come named for Florida politicos—try the "Jeb" or the "Bob Gra-HAM" burgers for lunch, $10. Looking for something more substantial? Entrées include cedar-planked salmon, fresh Florida grouper, and filet mignon, $11–30. Open daily at 11:30.

Big-band music drifts into the **Black Dog Cafe** (850-224-2518), 229 Lake Ella Dr, from the adjoining American Legion, filling this hangout where friends chat and singles tap on their laptops, hoping to be noticed. Be the scene: Order up a latte and settle into a comfortable chair. Anywhere that hosts Scrabble Nights is all right by me! Open until midnight most nights.

When you're done walking through the downtown museums, grab a bite at **Fat Sandwich** (850-425-8303), 500 S. Bronough, inside the R. A. Gray Building, home of the Florida State Museum and Florida State Archives. Grilled Reubens, quesadillas, homemade sides—it's a perfect lunch pick, $6–8.

❀ **Metro Deli** (850-224-6870; metrodelis.com), 1041 S Monroe St. Since 1942, this tiny downtown sub shop has been packing 'em in at lunchtime with its full slate of deli sandwiches, hot subs, melts, and grinders, $4–7. The aroma of cheddar bacon soup will draw you in!

& Tuck into gluten-free pizza at the **Mellow Mushroom** (850-575-0050; mellowmushroom.com/tallahassee), 1641 W Pensacola St, one of the few places I know that serves it. This college-town favorite has spread across the Southeast, and their Tally outlet is right on the edge of FSU. The pizza menu puts all others to shame, with options for vegans and vegetarians, too. $8 and up, depending on toppings.

☙ At **Riccardos** (850-386-3988; riccardostallahassee.com), 3305 Capital Circle NE, they're still in love with Lucy, with an *I Love Lucy* shrine by the kitchen piled in lunchboxes, mugs, photos, and ornaments. But the menu is neither Irish nor Cuban—it's Italian, and delicious. My eggplant Parmesan came with a very light breading, and the tiramasu was delicate. Entrées are very reasonable, $8–12. It's a busy family restaurant, so you might want to call ahead for weekend reservations.

Paradigm Restaurant & Lounge (850-224-9980; paradigmrestaurant lounge.com), 115 W College Ave, draws in the late-night crowd by serving chicken & waffles—and chicken & pancakes—after midnight. Open for lunch and dinner, entrées $10–12.

Po'Boys Creole Cafe (850-224-5400; poboys.com), 224 E College Ave, dishes up more than 20 types of po'boy sandwiches (from crawfish to tuna salad) and authentic Creole favorites like crawfish roll and southern pork for dinner ($8–12). Stop in on Sunday for the Bayou Brunch, 10–2, with omelets stuffed with crabmeat and shrimp, soufflés with andouille sausage, and more.

☙ Tucked into an urban Tallahassee strip backing up on FSU, **Pitaria** (352-412-PITA; thepitaria.com), 617 W Tennessee St, is a grill shop serving up souvlaki, pita, dolmades, and other Greek standards in veg and non-veg versions (make mine lamb!), $5–8. Around for nearly 20 years, it's obvious it's an FSU tradition as the back-to-college crowd files in. Falafel, hummus, and fava beans accent the menu. Opa!

San Miguel (352-385-3346), 200 W Tharpe St. Authentic Mexican in a comfortable atmosphere, with à la carte items $2 and up, and entrées under $10, like the tasty enchiladas verde, smothered in spicy green

tomatillo sauce. Murals brighten the intimate spaces; I couldn't help but notice the Aztec warrior carting off a maiden toward a raging volcano!

☙ **Shell Oyster Bar** (850-224-9919), 114A Oakland Ave, is a hot spot for the capitol crowd, where the raw and steamed oysters are the talk of the town. It's a small, family-owned business focused on fresh seafood—and I enjoyed a heaping plate of peel-and-eat on my last visit. All fish, lunch and dinner, $8 and up, with sides like cheese grits and homemade onion rings. No credit cards.

☙ The **Soul Vegetarian Restaurant** (850-893-8208) is a weekday lunchtime pushcart on Kleman Plaza that's served up vegan specialties to busy downtowners for more than a decade. Try a spicy jerk tofu platter, lentil soup, or a slice of sweet potato pie.

Since Ted Turner owns a massive plantation down by Lamont, it's no surprise that **Ted's Montana Grill** (850-561-8337; tedsmontanagrill.com), 1954 Village Green Way off Capital Circle NE, popped up in Tallahassee recently. Turner's own steak house chain, drawing on his cattle ranches out west, serves up fresh juicy Angus beef or bison steaks and burgers, entrées $15 and up.

Uptown Cafe (850-218-9800; uptown cafeandcatering.com), 1325 Miccosukee Rd, moved away from downtown but still serves breakfast and lunch ($3 and up) made from scratch, including buttermilk biscuits and hearty blueberry pancakes.

Woodville

No matter the hour, **The Seineyard** (850-421-9191; theseineyard.com), 8159 Woodville Hwy, is a busy dining spot—I have friends who'll drive two hours to have dinner here. Fresh Gulf shrimp is featured prominently on the menu; have your seafood fried, broiled, or blackened to taste. Entrées run $12–27, including combination platters. This is one of the rare places where you can have a mullet sandwich for lunch.

✳ Entertainment

Watch your representatives at play: Legislators hang loose at **Clyde's and Costello's** (850-224-2173), 210 S Adams, a city pub with pool tables. But Tallahassee has a classy side, too: More than 25 years old, the annual **Tallahassee Bach Parley** (tallahasseebach parley.org) features classical music in venues like Goodwood; the **Tallahassee Symphony Orchestra** (850-224-0461; tsolive.org), 1345 Thomasville Rd, has a decade of concert series behind them, playing Sept–May. The **Big Bend Community Orchestra** (850-893-9934; bbcorch.org) offers Sunday-afternoon classical and "pops" in area parks, and the **Artist Series of Tallahassee** (850-224-9934; theartist series.com), 1897 Capital Circle NE, brings in philharmonic orchestras and soloists from around the globe. **Theatre A La Carte** (850-224-8474; theatrealacarte.org) bills itself as North Florida's premiere musical theater company, putting on two musicals each year, and the **Tallahassee Film Society** (850-386-4404; tallahasseefilms .com) shows indie, art, and retro films twice monthly at the All Saint Cinema, 918½ Railroad Ave.

More off the beaten path, you'll find live music (bluegrass, country, and classic rock) on the waterfront at the **Riverside Cafe** in St. Marks on Fri and Sat nights (see *Eating Out*) and at the **Sopchoppy Opera**, a country music and bluegrass jam venue along US 319 where country legend Tom T. Hall has been sighted. The Apalachee Blues Society meets at the **Brad-**

fordville Blues Club (850-906-0766; bradfordvilleblues.com), 7152 Moses Ln off Bradfordville Rd, where you can catch live blues concerts on Fri and Sat evenings.

✳ Selective Shopping

Centerville
A drive up Centerville Rd from Tallahassee will take you to **Bradley's Country Store** (850-893-1647; bradleyscountrystore.com), 10655 Centerville Rd, a general store in continuous operation since 1927. Stop in for their signature country-smoked sausage and milled grits, tasty coffee, local history books, and country-themed gifts.

Crawfordville
My Secret Garden (850-926-9355), 3299 Crawfordville Hwy. This little Cracker home has fine home decor, pretty pottery and garden statues, and all the little (and big) things you need to plan a fancy 'do or wedding outdoors.

Havana
Havana is the region's antiques hub, with more than 20 shops filling the downtown buildings, old railroad station, and tobacco barns to overflowing with a little bit of everything country.

♪ **Little River General Store** (850-539-6900), 308 N Main St, is a page from the past, where kids gaze at the penny candy while Mom picks up a bar of Fels-Naptha soap; mixed in are comfy throws, old-fashioned toys, and gourmet foods.

Mirror Image Antiques (850-539-7422), 303 1st St NW, is a sprawling complex with an eclectic selection of items—it's not just antiques. You'll find an art gallery, a gourmet food room stocked with British imports, rooms filled with books, and intriguing items from the Far East, like a Vietnamese

Buddha. Since it's all in the family, they absorbed a great deal of the Beare's Historical Bookshelf, and these antiquarian tomes are offered along with the Peterson Asian Collection and other vintage items.

A rambling building along the railroad tracks, **The Planters Exchange** (850-539-6343), 204 NW 2nd St, sweeps you back through the last century in a series of dealer booth settings that'll have you thinking about your next home decorating project, with everything from vintage glass, games, books, and art to very fine furnishings.

With a female backpacker gracing their sign, how could I not visit **Wanderings** (850-539-7711; thewanderings .com), 312 1st St NW. This roomy shop, part of the 1906 Havana depot, deals in exotic home decor and primitives—arts, crafts, and furnishings.

Medart
Just Fruits & Exotics (888-926-7441; justfruitsandexotics.com), 30 St. Francis St. Along US 98 east of Medart, this sprawling native plant and exotic fruit emporium has everything from ferns and *Sarracenia* (carnivorous pitcher plants) to persimmon and guava trees. A must-stop for the serious gardener.

Monticello
It feels like the '50s inside **Jackson's Drug Store** (850-997-3553), 166 E Dogwood, where local art spruces up the walls along the corridor off Jefferson St.

At the **Old Bank Antique Mall** (850-997-8163), 100 N Jefferson St, look for collectibles and not-so-antiques along with classic items.

Perry
You'll find both old and new books at the **Book Mart** (850-584-4969; book mart.blogspot.com), 1708 S Byron Butler Pkwy, where I was enthralled with the collection of Florida books out front and was pointed toward an essential book for learning about this region, *Along the Edge of America* by Peter Jenkins.

Michelle's Bull Pen (850-584-3098), 3180 S Byron Butler Pkwy, is a great western wear shop with moccasins, boots, hats, and jewelry as well as tack for your steeds.

Perry Flea Market (850-838-1422), 3609 S Byron Butler Pkwy, held Fri–Sun, is a good old-fashioned flea market featuring antiques, collectibles, and tools.

Sopchoppy
🌸 **George Griffin Pottery** (850-962-9311), 1 SunCat Ridge Rd. It's a rough road back to George's place, a little cabin in the woods where he's practiced his craft for more than 35 years, where wind chimes echo through a Florida stewardship forest administered by the artist. But you'll be glad you made the detour to his tin-roofed gallery, as George's pottery is a wonderful, fluid thing; it's natural sculpture in a very natural setting, reflective of his inherent love of the craft. Stroll the shaded grounds and enjoy the outdoor art; sculptures rise along the fishpond, looking like the pitcher plants that grow in the surrounding forest. Little sheds contain earth-toned treasures, and inspirational quotes (along with Polaroids of folks who've come to learn at the studio) are interspersed among pieces with form and function inside the main gallery. Open Tue–Sun, varying hours; call or look for the sign out front.

The **Petunia Patch** (850-567-2100), 118 Municipal Ave, showcases the creative output of the Sopchoppy Arts Association, including watercolors and ceramics, amid a good array of antiques and collectibles like playbills, matchbooks, and fine china. Stop here

GEORGE GRIFFIN POTTERY, SOPCHOPPY

for your official Worm Grunting T-shirts (see *Special Events*).

The scent of clean fills the air at **Rose's Botanicals** (850-962-7830; rosesbotanicals.com), 434 Pullback Rd, where their soaps, medicinal creams, and salves are made in small batches, by hand, from local herbs. In addition to their mainstays, they offer gourmet foods, gift baskets, and vitamins and supplements. Open Wed–Sat.

Tallahassee

Artzania (850-222-8411; artzania .com), 110 N Monroe St, offers the finest in local art on consignment from artists creating original oils, dichroic glass and glass bowls, sculpture, and literature.

It's fun to browse the historic tourist cottages that now make up the **Cottages at Lake Ella**, 1650 N Monroe St. My favorites include **Quarter Moon Imports** (850-222-2254; quarter moonimports.com), filled with exotica like lush tapestries from India, sensu-

ous sushi platters, and Moroccan tea sets; **Barb's Southern Style Gourmet Brittles** (850-385-9839; barbs brittles.com), for a sweet treat; and **Glasswork by Susan** (850-222-5095), a stained-glass studio with supplies and original art.

✐ Mix toys with candy making and an ice cream fountain, and **Lofty Pursuits** (850-521-0091; loftypursuits.com), 1415 Timberlane Rd #410, is just plain fun. You can buy a kite, a yoyo, or a board game, or just stop in for an ice cream cone.

✐ At the Mary Brogan Museum of Art and Science (see *Family Activities*), the **Museum Shop** offers creative and fun science toys, a great selection of children's books and art books, and beautiful works of art—art glass tables, bowls, limited-edition baskets, and more.

✐ **Native Nurseries** (850-386-8882; nativenurseries.com), 1661 Centerville Rd, is a nursery for nature lovers, a shop where you'll learn about native plants and animals as you browse. Be sure to check out the Children's Nature Nook and the Wren's Nest Nature Shop, and if you're in town for a while, sign up for one of the many free workshops on native creatures and gardening.

Offering both new and used titles, the **Paperback Rack** (850-224-3455), 1005 N Monroe St, has been around for more than 20 years and shines with an incredible diversity of titles (I found Alison Lurie, Gerald Durrell, and Jack Kerouac all in a few minutes' search), with an especially deep selection in fine literature but also a great variety in travel, Black studies, and children's books. An extensive genre paperback section fills the front of the store.

Simply Entertaining (850-668-1167; simplyentertainingtallahassee.com), 1355 Market St. A fun stop for culinary items: gourmet foods and wines, plus kitchen accessories that would make a chef proud.

Something Nice (850-562-4167), 206 E 6th Ave, is a collection of gallery shops filled with antiques, collectibles, and handcrafted children's furniture; they also hold a flea market the first Sat monthly.

The Tallahassee **Visitor Information Center** (see *Guidance*) has its own shop featuring art, books, and CDs from Tallahassee artists, including photo cards, primitives, bold acrylics, fiber arts, paintings on slate, and more.

With more than 35 years serving Tallahassee, **Trail & Ski** (850-531-9001; trailandski.com), 2748 Capital Circle NE, is the shop where backpackers and campers head when they're gearing up for a trip. The store features a fine selection of outdoor guidebooks, travel items, and technical clothing; rental gear available.

FARMER'S MARKETS, FRESH SEAFOOD, AND U-PICK

Lamont
A 1960s-style roadside stand, **Pecan House** on US 19 (south of I-10 at Monticello) sells fresh fruit, jumbo pecans, and country-smoked sausage.

Monticello
A century farm, **Turkey Hill Organic Farm** (850-216-4024; home.igc.org /~divine), 3546 Baum Rd, has organically grown veggies on an 89-acre family-run farm; it holds an annual open house but otherwise sells produce every Sat at Market Square Shopping Center, Timberland Rd. Get your blueberries, strawberries, blackberries, and grapes in-season at **Windy Hill Vineyard** (850-894-1511; windyhillvineyard.com), 1 mile west of FL 59 on US 90.

Newport
Where FL 267 meets US 98, you'll find "**The Tupelo Honey Man**," Preston Bozeman, a longtime local vendor selling tupelo honey, mayhaw jelly, and cane syrup out of the back of his pickup truck on weekends year-round.

Panacea
Known for its fresh fine seafood, the fishing village of Panacea boasts the largest number of roadside seafood stands in Wakulla County. In addition to folks selling shrimp and oysters out of the backs of their trucks, some of the old standbys with storefronts on US 98 include **D. L. Thomas Seafood**, the oldest outlet in town; and **My Way Seafood**.

Quincy
Davis Farm Fresh Fruits & Vegetables, a large farm stand on FL 65 S, sells direct from this family grower; you'll always find green boiled peanuts and vine-ripe tomatoes in-season.

PICK UP A JAR OF TUPELO HONEY FROM THE TUPELO HONEY MAN ALONG US 98

St. Marks

Lighthouse Seafood Market (850-925-6221), 720 Port Leon Dr, features fresh fish caught daily.

Steinhatchee

Ocean Fresh Seafood Company (850-672-0070), 1313 2nd Ave NE, has fresh seafood you can't do without, direct from their boat to you. Visit in-season for fresh stone crabs and scallops.

Tallahassee

✵ Don't miss the **Downtown Marketplace** (850-980-8727; downtownmarket .com) in Ponce de Leon Park (Park Ave between Monroe and Adams), where vendors haul in the freshest of local produce while local musicians play on stage, poets and authors offer readings under the grand live oaks, and kids can join in fun activities like pumpkin carving, sidewalk chalk art, and other hands-on arts and crafts. Sat 8–2, Mar–Nov; free.

A community co-op, **New Leaf Market** (850-942-2557; newleafmarket .coop), 1235 Apalachee Pkwy, is more than 30 years old and invites the public in to shop for organic produce, eco-friendly household goods, alternative diet foods, and more.

✳ Special Events

March: **Natural Bridge Civil War Re-enactment** (850-922-6007), first weekend at Natural Bridge Historic State Park, Woodville (see *Historic Sites*).

✵ **Red Hills Horse Trials** (850-893-2497; rhht.org), Elinor Klapp-Phipps Park, Tallahassee. A nationally recognized equestrian competition with Olympic riders, educational exhibits, and special activities for the kids. Fee.

April: Now more than 20 years running, the **Tallahassee Jazz and Blues Festival** (tallahasseemuseum.org/jazz -and-blues) brings together the finest

Dixieland, swing, big band, and smooth jazz musicians in the region, second weekend.

◊ **Sopchoppy Worm Grunting Festival** (850-962-5282), first Sat. If you didn't know how to grunt an earthworm out of the ground, you will by the end of this festival, which also features live bluegrass, arts and crafts, and the annual worm grunters' ball. No jokes, folks—this is an honest profession in the Apalachicola woods!

The annual **Wakulla Wildlife Festival** (wakullawildlifefestival.com) gets you into the woods and out on the waters of Wakulla County on guided expeditions for birding and wildlife-watching.

May: **Panacea Blue Crab Festival** (850-227-1223; bluecrabfest.com), first weekend. A parade and craft booths are an adjunct to seafood, seafood, and more seafood from the folks who know crabs!

October: ◊ Celebrated at St. Marks National Wildlife Refuge (see *Wild Places*), the **Monarch Butterfly Festival**, last weekend, offers guided naturalist tours to view butterflies along hiking trails, environmental exhibits (including a great butterfly tent for the kids), arts and crafts, and the opportunity for you to volunteer to tag butterflies for research. (I couldn't believe it was possible until I saw it done!)

During the same weekend, the **St. Marks Stone Crab Festival** (stmarksstonecrabfest.com) draws visitors to the riverside restaurants with massive fixed price feeds, live bluegrass, and a small arts and crafts festival.

November: ◊ The **North Florida Fair** (850-878-3247; northfloridafair.com), Tallahassee, is the Red Hills region's largest agricultural fair, featuring major country music acts, midway rides, agricultural competitions, and food vendors over the span of two weeks. Fee.

North Florida 2

GAINESVILLE & VICINITY

ST. JOHNS RIVER

THE UPPER SUWANNEE

THE LOWER SUWANNEE

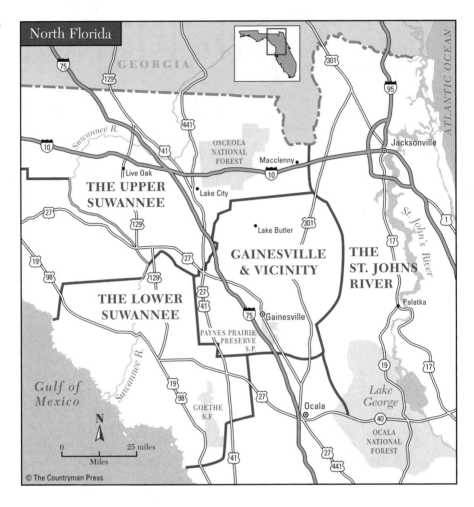

GAINESVILLE & VICINITY

ALACHUA, BRADFORD & UNION COUNTIES

In 1765, botanist William Bartram described a visit to the village of Cuscowilla, on the edge of a vast prairie, where he met with the great chief Cowkeeper. Cowkeeper's descendants, the Seminoles, were pushed south off their ancestral lands by settlers eager to claim the rich prairies, oak hammocks, and pine flatwoods as their own. After Florida became a U.S. territory in 1821, Congress authorized the construction of the Bellamy Road, a wagon route from St. Augustine to Tallahassee, leading settlers to this region. But it was not until the establishment of the University of Florida in 1853 that **Gainesville**, now the largest and most vibrant city in the region, became a major population center. All three counties maintain their rural roots, where farming and ranching surround small historic communities.

Gainesville started out as Hogtown, an 1824 settlement of 14 inhabitants on a creek that snaked its way into the vast prairie south of town. Named for General Edmund Gaines, commander of U.S. Army troops in Florida during the Second Seminole War, Gainesville won out over Lake City for the location of the newly formed University of Florida, becoming the county seat in 1854. Civil War skirmishes in downtown streets added a touch of excitement in the 1860s, but it wasn't enough to dissuade a steady stream of settlers. Gainesville incorporated as a city in 1869.

Historic but hip describes the towns north along US 441, mingling old and new, with historic structures reinvented into cafés, art galleries, and theaters. Settlers coming down the Bellamy Road moved into **High Springs** on the Santa Fe River as early as the 1830s; Florida's phosphate boom accelerated the town's growth in the 1870s, and it retains that turn-of-the-century feel. The Bellamy Road also brought settlers to the pastoral town of **Alachua**, founded in 1905. Blink and you'll miss the turnoff from US 441 to Alachua's Main Street, just a mile south of I-75. But it's worth the stop. Although only a few blocks long, downtown Alachua is crammed with unique shops and restaurants.

In Bradford County, the county seat of **Starke** lives in infamy as the home of the Florida State Prison and its electric chair, but downtown Call Street shows the genteel side of this historic city. South of Starke on US 301 is **Waldo**, founded in

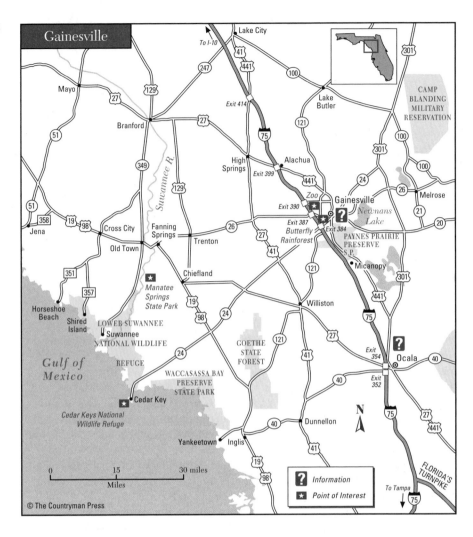

Gainesville

1858 as a railroad town. In the 1960s Waldo became infamous for its speed traps along US 301, so much so that a former officer wrote a book about it. *Waldo* remains a synonym for *speed trap* in Florida, so watch that gas pedal when you drive through!

The railroads also ran through **Hawthorne**, established in 1880 as a junction for trains from Gainesville to Ocala and Waldo. The Lake District continues in a sweep southward past Newnans Lake and the historic village of **Rochelle** down to Lake Lochloosa and Orange Lake, where Pulitzer Prize–winning author Marjorie Kinnan Rawlings put the fishing village of **Cross Creek** on the map. Nearby **Evinston**, established in 1882 on the Marion County border, was a major citrus center until the deep freezes of the 1890s killed the groves. And **Micanopy**, founded in 1821 near Paynes Prairie, is one of Florida's top destinations for antiques shopping, its downtown a snapshot of the late 1800s. In western Alachua

County, history buffs will appreciate tiny **Archer** for its railroad museum and Civil War history. Florida's 1870 phosphate boom built the town of **Newberry**, where workers dug deep pits to extract the black nuggets used for fertilizer. In more recent times paleontologists have had a field day in Newberry's phosphate pits, pulling out fossilized crocodiles, turtles, and other creatures whose bones are on display at the Florida Natural History Museum in Gainesville.

GUIDANCE Stop in at the **Gainesville/Alachua County Visitors & Convention Bureau** (352-374-5260; visitgainesville.com), 30 E University Ave, Gainesville 32801. For points east and north of Gainesville, visit the **North Florida Regional Chamber of Commerce** (904-964-5278; northfloridachamber.com), 100 E Call St, Starke 32091.

GETTING THERE *By air:* American, Delta, and US Airways provide daily commuter service to the **Gainesville Regional Airport** (352-373-0249; gra-gnv.com), located east of town off FL 20.

By bus: **Greyhound** (352-376-5252), 516 SW 4th Ave, Gainesville.

By car: **I-75** runs through the heart of Gainesville and Alachua County, paralleled by **US 441**; **US 301** passes through major towns in Bradford and Union counties.

GETTING AROUND *By bicycle:* Gainesville is one of Florida's most **bicycle-friendly** cities, with rail-trails, dedicated urban bike paths, and bike lanes connecting the city core and the University of Florida with the suburbs. **FL 20**, **24**, and **26** radiate out of Gainesville to reach points east and west in Alachua County, and **US 41** provides an often-canopied scenic rural route between High Springs, Williston, and Archer. **FL 121** connects Gainesville with Lake Butler to the north.

By bus: Given the University of Florida's large student population, local bus service via **Regional Transit System** (352-334-2600; go-rts.com) is frequent and comprehensive. Adults $1.50; half fare for students, seniors, military; children and disabled free.

By taxi: **A1 Yellow Cab** (352-374-9696), **Gator Taxi Cab** (352-336-8484), **Commuter Taxi & Shuttle** (352-256-1086).

PARKING Although there are some free parking spaces in downtown Gainesville (two-hour limit), it's mostly **metered parking, two-hour limit** in most places. **Two parking garages** serve the downtown district, one along University Ave and the other near the Hippodrome Theatre. At the University of Florida, if you can't find metered parking along the edge of campus, it's essential to pick up a visitors pass (free) at one of the staffed parking permit kiosks off University Blvd or SW 13th St. Park only in **permit areas** that match the color of your pass—even in metered areas—or you'll face a parking ticket, payable immediately at the main parking office on North-South Rd. In all other communities, you'll have no problem finding free street parking within easy walking distance of shops and restaurants.

PUBLIC RESTROOMS You'll find public restrooms in High Springs in a replica train depot housing the chamber of commerce at the south end of the antiques district.

MEDICAL EMERGENCIES In Gainesville, **Shands HealthCare** (352-265-0111; shands.org), 1600 SW Archer Rd, is one of the nation's top medical facilities; you also have the option of **North Florida Regional Medical Center** (352-333-4000; nfrmc.com), 6500 W Newberry Rd.

✳ To See

ARCHAEOLOGICAL SITES Thanks to the archaeologists of the University of Florida–Gainesville, many significant sites have been identified throughout Alachua County. Some, like the **Law School Burial Mound**, are open to public inspection. Located on the University of Florida campus near Lake Alice, this burial mound dates back to AD 1000. It contains the remains of the ancestors of the Potano culture, also known as the Alachua Tradition peoples. The **Moon Lake Villages** were a series of Alachua Tradition villages on the site now occupied by Buchholz High School in Gainesville. Accessed by the trails in Gum Root Swamp Conservation Area (see *Wild Places*), villages along **Newnans Lake** were occupied as early as 3000 BC, and more recently by the Seminoles, who called the lake Pithlachocco, the place where boats are made. More than 100 aboriginal canoes were unearthed from the lake in 2000, the largest such find in Florida. Most remain buried in the mud. Another Paleo-Indian site has been identified near the boardwalk along US 441 in the middle of Paynes Prairie. At **San Felasco Hammock Preserve State Park** (see *Wild Places*), one of the first Spanish missions in North America was established in 1608 and occupied until 1706. Its exact location is not marked, but you can walk through the woods around the mission along the Old Spanish Way trail, where Alachua County's original seat, Spring Grove, vanished under the thick cover of hardwood forest. The rim of **Paynes Prairie** (see *Wild Places*) is also dotted with village sites.

ART GALLERIES

Gainesville

🖉 ♿ **Samuel P. Harn Museum of Art** (352-392-9826; harn.ufl.edu), SW 34th St and Hull Rd, Gainesville, showcases thematic exhibits of fine arts from their extensive collections as well as rotating traveling exhibits. The tall, open rotunda provides access to the main galleries. In the Richardson Gallery, you might encounter an exhibit of fine turn-of-the-20th-century American oils, but you'll always find the museum's masterpiece on display—Monet's *Champ d'Avoine*. Take a seat and enjoy some quiet time studying this impressionistic masterpiece. Looking for more to aid your art appreciation? Stop in the Bishop Study Center to peruse their library of fine art books, or examine the computers for exhibits from virtual galleries. In addition to books, jewelry, and fine art reproductions, the Museum Shop carries artsy games and toys for kids, and the artistic works of several local artisans. Tue–Fri 11–5, Sat 10–5, Sun 1–5. Closed on state holidays. Free; donations appreciated.

Santa Fe Art Gallery (352-395-5621; dept.sfcollege.edu/vpa/GALLERY), 3000 NW 83rd St, Building P, Room 201, Gainesville. Approved for loans of high-security exhibits from the National Gallery of Art and the Smithsonian Institution, Santa Fe College displays rotating exhibits of contemporary art in their galleries. Mon–Fri noon–4. Free.

Thomas Center Galleries (352-334-5064; gvlculturalaffairs.org), 302 NE 6th Ave, Gainesville. Serving the community as the Hotel Thomas from 1928 to 1968,

THE HARN MUSEUM OF ART, GAINESVILLE

this is now a cultural center housing a small history museum, two art galleries with rotating exhibits, and the city's Department of Cultural Affairs. Roam the galleries and enjoy the beautiful surrounding gardens. Mon/Wed/Fri 8–5, Tue 8–7, Sat 1–4; free.

A commercial gallery with an outstanding collection of Florida artists, **Thornebrook Gallery** (352 378-4947; thornebrookgallery.com) is one of the cornerstones of Thornebrook Village (see *Selective Shopping*). Fine art glass and sculptures are displayed as well as original and limited-edition oils, acrylics, and photography. Closed Sun.

University of Florida Galleries (352-392-0201; arts.ufl.edu/galleries), Gainesville, include the University Gallery (Tue–Sat) in Fine Arts Building B, with contemporary national and regional art displays; the Focus Gallery (Mon–Fri) in Fine Arts Building C, featuring student art and emerging artists; and the Grinter Gallery (Mon–Fri) in Grinter Hall, with its international art displays. Free.

Micanopy

My friend Jeff Ripple returned to his roots with the **Ripple Effect Studio & Gallery** (352-398-3375; jeffrippleart.com), 112 NE Hunter Ave behind the Old Florida Cafe (see *Eating Out*). Displaying both his outstanding outdoor photography and his plein air interpretations of Florida scenes in oils, it'll get your heart stirring to see nature the way Jeff does in the field—and yes, he does offer workshops.

HISTORIC SITES

Archer

In 1865 David Levy Yulee, U.S. senator and head of the Florida Railroad, stashed the personal effects of Confederate president Jefferson Davis at his **Cottonwood**

Plantation while Davis attempted to flee to Florida after the surrender of the Confederacy. Yulee's servants led Union soldiers to the prize, and Yulee was jailed for treason. A plaque near the old **Archer Depot** (see *Museums*) tells the story; the plantation house burned in 1939.

Cross Creek

At **Marjorie Kinnan Rawlings Historic State Park** (352-466-9273; florida stateparks.org/marjoriekinnanrawlings), CR 325, house tours take you through the living and working space of this Pulitzer-winning novelist beloved by regional historians for her accurate depictions of rural North Florida. Set in what remains of her original orange grove from the 1940s, this dogtrot Cracker home offers some quirks specific to its northern resident, including the "liquor cabinet" with firewater on top and firewood on the bottom, as well as her use of inverted mixing bowls as decorative fixtures for lights. Cary Grant, Spencer Tracy, and many other legends stayed in Marjorie's guest room. Costumed guides explain what life was like in Cross Creek when Marjorie sat on the front porch and typed the drafts of her novels, including *The Yearling*. Fee.

Gainesville

Several historic districts surround the city core of downtown Gainesville, where the original **Courthouse Clock** (circa 1885) resides in a new housing at the corner of University and 1st St in front of the new courthouse. B&Bs (see *Lodging*) stake a claim in the historic **Southeast Residential District**, Gainesville's earliest suburb, settled in the 1880s. Wander through these streets for some fine examples of Victorian and Cracker architecture. In the lushly canopied **Northeast Historic District**, covering a few blocks around the Thomas Center, 12 historic homes show off their Victorian charm beneath the live oaks and magnolias. Start your tour there at the **Thomas Center** (see *Art Galleries*). Built in 1906, this restored Mediterranean Revival hotel began as the home of Major William Reuben Thomas, the man instrumental in attracting the University of Florida to Gainesville. Founded in 1853, the **University of Florida** boasts its own historic center. In 1989 the **Pleasant Street District** was placed on the National Register of Historic Places, the first predominantly African American community in Florida to gain that designation. Comprised of a 20-block area to the northwest of downtown, it contains 35 points of historical interest, including the **St. Augustine Day School**, 405 NW 4th Ave, an 1892 mission for African Americans, and the **Dunbar Hotel**, 732 NW 4th St, a favorite of jazz musicians and the only Gainesville lodgings available to African American travelers from the 1930s through the 1950s.

High Springs

High Springs itself is a historic downtown; many of its buildings date back to the late 1800s. A remnant of the original wagon road that brought settlers to this region, the **Old Bellamy Road** can be accessed from US 41 north of High Springs: Follow the Bellamy Road east to the interpretive trailhead. Just south on US 41 is the **De Soto Trail monument**, commemorating the route of explorer Hernando de Soto and his men as they traversed the Florida peninsula in 1539.

Kanapaha

Established in 1855, the **Historic Haile Homestead** (352-336-9096; hailehome stead.org), 8500 SW Archer Rd, provides a glimpse into the life of Florida's territorial settlers on a 40-acre remnant of the original 1,500-acre Sea Island cotton plantation. Open Sat 10–2, Sun noon–4; fee.

Micanopy

More than 35 historic sites crowd Micanopy's small downtown, best enjoyed as a self-guided walking tour (see *Walking Tours*). Some don't-miss stops include the **Old Presbyterian Church**, built in 1870; the 1890 **Thrasher Warehouse**, housing the Micanopy Historical Society Museum (see *Museums*); the 1880 **Calvin Merry House**, the oldest home on the east side of the street; the Victorian Gothic Revival **Powell House**, from 1866; the 1895 **Brick School House**; the 1875 **Simonton-Herlong House** (see *Lodging*); and the **Stewart-Merry House**, built around the 1855 log cabin where Dr. James Stewart practiced medicine. None of the homes are open for public inspection, although many of the historic business buildings now house the town's shops.

Newberry

For a ramble through a preserved homestead, visit ✪ **Dudley Farm Historic State Park** (see *Farms*), where rangers in period costume take you through a day in the life of a turn-of-the-20th-century Florida farmer. The museum at the visitors center interprets the several generations of family who lived here, and how farming changed over the years; the tour will open your eyes to how difficult life was for Florida's early settlers.

Starke

The historic **Bradford County Courthouse** anchors the west end of Call St to US 301; the **Gene Matthews Museum** (see *Museums*) marks the east end of the historic district. A restored theater shows first-run movies. As renovation of the historic district continues, expect to see more of the storefronts fill in.

MUSEUMS

Archer

Housed in the former railroad depot, the **Archer Historical Society Museum** (352-495-9422; afn.org/~archer), Magnolia and Main streets, displays local history and railroad memorabilia, including a lab-model Edison phonograph, an original telephone and telegraph from the depot, and the curator's antique camera collection. Open Sat 9–1; donation.

Gainesville

Alachua County Historic Trust and **Matheson Museum** (352-378-2280; mathesonmuseum.org), 513 E University Ave. In addition to its interpretation of Alachua County's history, the museum houses a historical library and archives, with an extensive collection of Florida history books and documents. Closed Mon. Free. The trust also administers the historic **Matheson House**, the second-oldest residence in Gainesville, and the **Tison Tool Museum**, both open by appointment only. Fee.

✪ ♿ Interactive and engaging, the **Florida Museum of Natural History** (352-846-2000; flmnh.ufl.edu), SW 34th St and Hull Rd, continues to evolve with picture-perfect new 3-D dioramas and hands-on activities. Kids and adults love the walk-through Florida cave, which now funnels you into the permanent exhibit called Northwest Florida's Waterways and Wildlife, showcasing everything from karst topography and carnivorous plants to indigenous peoples and the creatures of the salt marsh. In the South Florida People and Environments gallery, shrink down to the size of a killifish to explore the world beneath the mangroves, and

walk into the home of a Calusa chief-
tain. Dinosaurs never walked Florida's
soil, but we've had saber-toothed
tigers, mastodons, and shoveltuskers;
learn more about them in the dynamic
Florida Fossils exhibit. One of the
museum's top attractions is the Butterfly Rainforest, a separate (fee-based)
exhibit that will surround you with
these winged wonders (see the *Butterflies* sidebar). Don't miss the Collectors
Shop, a must for picking up educational toys and books for the kids. Mon–
Sat 10–5, Sun 1–5. Free; donations
encouraged.

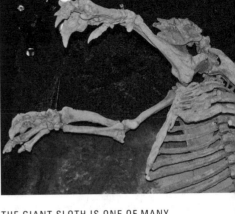

THE GIANT SLOTH IS ONE OF MANY
IMPRESSIVE FLORIDA FOSSILS AT THE
FLORIDA MUSEUM OF NATURAL HISTORY

The **Institute of Black Culture** (352-
392-0895; multicultural.ufl.edu/ibc),
1510 W University Ave, exhibits African, African American, and Caribbean art on
the University of Florida campus. Mon–Thu 9–9, Fri 9–5; free.

Hawthorne

Hawthorne Historical Museum (352-481-4491; hawthorneflorida.org/museum
.htm), 7225 SE 221st St, is housed in a restored 1907 church; artifacts, exhibits,
and primitive arts illustrate the long history of this rural village.

Micanopy

Micanopy Historical Society Museum (352-466-3200; afn.org/~micanopy), corner of Cholokka and Bay streets. Housed in the Thrasher Warehouse (circa
1890)—the "Home Depot of its day," says volunteer Paul Oliver, built along the
railroad tracks—this small but comprehensive museum gives an overview of life in
and around Micanopy, from the ancient Timucua and William Bartram's visit to
Cuscowilla in 1774, through the town's settlement as a trading post in 1821, and on
into this century, with special exhibits of historical railroad items, relics from the
Thrasher Store (now Tyson Trading Company), and period pieces from the Simon
H. Benjamin Collection. There's also a small gift shop and bookstore with historical tomes on the region. Open 1–4 daily. Donation.

Starke

Boat Drain School Museum, 581 N Temple Ave. In 1893 this one-room pine
board schoolhouse served the needs of Bradford County's small population; today
it's a small museum dedicated to the history of Bradford High School. The **Gene
Matthews Bradford County Historical Museum** (904-964-4606), 201 E Call
St, showcases Bradford County's history, with a special emphasis on turpentine,
logging, and railroads. Open Tue–Sun 1–5; free.

RAILROADIANA At Magnolia and Main in Archer, the Archer Historical Society
Museum (see *Museums*) occupies the **old railroad depot**; across the street at the
Maddox Machine Works, a gleaming **Seaboard Air Line steam engine**, circa
1910, is on display. Visit the Micanopy Historical Society Museum (see *Museums*)
for historical information and relics from the **Gainesville, Rocky Point &**

Micanopy Railroad, circa 1895. After it became the Tampa & Jackson Railroad, locals called the T&J the "Tug & Jerk." It stopped at Thrasher's Warehouse, which now houses the museum.

High Springs grew up around Henry Plant's Seaboard Air Line; the man credited with putting Tampa on the map selected High Springs as his distribution center. On Railroad St (south of Main), look for the original **passenger depot**, a historic site now housing the Station Bakery & Cafe (see *Eating Out*). To the west of the station, vast rail yards, roundhouses, and engine shops kept busy with mighty steam engines; the only reminder of their passing is a bright red **Seaboard Coast Line caboose** tucked behind city hall.

Railroads shaped the towns of Starke, Waldo, and Hawthorne as well. You'll find a working **railroad depot** at E Brownlee St (FL 16) in Starke at the railroad crossing just west of US 301, and a retired **caboose** sitting on a siding southwest of the junction of US 301 and FL 20 in Waldo.

ZOO ✍ & **Santa Fe College Teaching Zoo** (352-395-5604; sfcollege.edu/zoo), 3000 NW 43rd St, Gainesville. For more than 20 years, this unique, hands-on zoo has taught generations of animal technicians (once known as zookeepers) how to create exhibits and handle animals. Ramble the walkways and boardwalks of this deeply forested complex and spend time in front of the enclosures, watching squirrel monkeys swing, turtles sun, and guanacos browse. Actively involved in the international Species Survival Plan, the zoo has endangered species from exotic locations, including Matschie's tree kangaroo and Asian small-clawed otters. A new playground provides a place for small children to let off steam. While you visit, you may see students at work, learning how to care for their charges. Open daily 9–2, except for special events; fee.

✴ To Do

ALLIGATOR SPOTTING In 2002 artists created alligator sculptures that were placed throughout Gainesville, and then auctioned off as a fundraiser for the arts. To track down the remaining whimsical pieces, ask around for a *Gator Trails* brochure, or look it up online on the *Gainesville Sun* website (gainesvillesun.com). To spot hundreds of live alligators, visit **Alachua Sink** in Paynes Prairie Preserve State Park (see *Wild Places*) or visit the University of Florida campus, where a network of nature trails surrounds **Lake Alice**. Visitors get up close and personal with the university's real-life namesakes—but don't ramble down the pathways after dark! The daytime sightings of 10-foot alligators sunning themselves along the trail are thrill enough. Parking areas on Museum Rd are restricted to student use until 3:30 PM.

BICYCLING Gainesville is a city for serious bicycling; many residents use bikes as their sole means of transportation. For a map of the urban bikeway network, contact the **Gainesville Bicycle/Pedestrian Program** (352-334-5074; cityof gainesville.org), 306 NE 6th Ave, Gainesville. The **Gainesville-Hawthorne State Trail** (see *Greenways*) starts at Boulware Springs Park in southeast Gainesville and runs to downtown Hawthorne, providing riders with a 34-mile round-trip. An extension continues into downtown Gainesville from Boulware Springs to Depot St. **San Felasco Hammock Preserve State Park** (see *Wild Places*) has more

BUTTERFLIES

Butterflies float like autumn leaves across a backdrop of tropical forest at
ᚻ ✿ **Butterfly Rainforest** (flmnh.ufl.edu/butterflies), a permanent conservatory
at the Florida Museum of Natural History (see *Museums*). Bright blossoms and
the constant movement of color through the air make this a magical place to
stroll, best enjoyed on weekdays when the crowds are lighter. The conservatory is part of the McGuire Center for Lepidoptera and Biodiversity, hosting the
world's second-largest collection of mounted specimens amid 39,000 square
feet of research labs. What will catch your eye from the museum floor and
draw you into this space is the Wall of Wings, with thousands of colorful and
unique specimens. Outdoors, enjoy the Florida Wildflowers & Butterflies Garden. Open Mon–Sat 10–5, Sun 1–5; closed Thanksgiving and Christmas. Adults
$10.50, Florida residents $9, students/seniors $8, ages 3–17 $6.

In Earlton, near Melrose, visit native Florida butterflies at the ✿ **Great-
house Butterfly Farm** (866-475-2088; butterflyfarm.com), 20329 FL 26 E, where
tours of this working butterfly farm lead you through gardens and greenhouses and into the Butterfly Barn, a magical experience. Tours at 10 AM
daily; $12 adults, $6 children, under 4 free. Gift shop on premises open
Mon–Sat.

BUTTERFLIES AND BLOOMS AWAIT AT THE BUTTERFLY RAINFOREST

than 12 miles of shady, rugged mountain biking routes. Check on bike rentals at **Gator Cycle** (352-373-3962; gatorcycle.com), 3321 SW Archer Rd, Gainesville, and **Santa Fe Bicycle Outfitters** (352-454-BIKE; santafebicycle.com), 10 N Main St, High Springs.

BIRDING At **Paynes Prairie Preserve State Park** (see *Wild Places*) birders head for open ground—look for overlooks from Bolen's Bluff and the La Chua Trail, and along US 441. Encounter dozens of trilling species around the water gardens at **Kanapaha Botanical Gardens** (see *Botanical Garden*). Any spot with a marsh is a major haven for birds; check the *Green Space* section for ideas.

DIVING Northwestern Alachua County lies along the spring belt, offering openwater and cave diving at **Poe Springs** as well as underwater adventures in adjacent Gilchrist County at **Ginnie Springs** and **Blue Springs** (see *Springs*). At High Springs check in at **Extreme Exposure Adventure Center** (800-574-6341; extreme-exposure.com), 15 S Main, for rental equipment, instruction, and pointers on the area's best dives. At **Lloyd Bailey Scuba and Watersports** (352-332-0378; lloydbaileysscuba.com), 3405-B NW 97th Ave, Gainesville, go with a pro with nearly 40 years of training experience; classes and guided trips are offered.

ECOTOURS Author and river rat Lars Anderson runs regular guided kayaking trips out of his **Adventure Outpost** in High Springs (see *Paddling*). At the **Lubee Bat Conservancy** (352-485-1250; batconservancy.org) north of Gainesville, researchers care for endangered fruit bats under the auspices of the Lubee Foundation, formed by rum magnate Louis Bacardi. Group tours are offered on Thu by reservation only, donation required.

FISHING While there are many lakes in the region, two stand out as fishing destinations—**Lake Lochloosa** and **Orange Lake**, linked by Cross Creek. Cast for bass, bluegill, and speckled perch by slipping your boat into the water at busy **Lochloosa Park**, a favorite launch point in the tiny town of Lochloosa along US 301, or from one of the fish camps along the lake (see *Fish Camps*). **Newnans Lake** is just east of downtown Gainesville between FL 20 and 26. A boat ramp and pier at **Earl P. Powers Park**, 5902 SE Hawthorne Rd, provide direct access for fishing; if you're in need of a boat or some fishing advice, head just down the road to **Kate's Fish Camp** (see *Fish Camps*).

GOLF Ironwood Golf Course (352-334-3120; cityofgainesville.org), 2100 NE 39th Ave, is a city-owned public course with PGA pro Bill Iwinski on staff; 18 holes, par 72, on an Audubon-approved natural course established in 1962. West of I-75 on FL 26, the West End Golf Course (352-332-2721; westendgolf.com), 12830 W Newberry Rd, features the world's longest fully lighted course (18 holes, par 60), along with a driving range.

HIKING Home to the state office of the **Florida Trail Association** (877-HIKE-FLA; floridatrail.org), 5415 SW 13th St—where you can stop in and pick up hiking information and hiking-related gifts—Gainesville is ringed with dozens of excellent opportunities for hikers, including more than 20 miles of trails at **Paynes Prairie Preserve State Park** and another 12 miles of trails at **San Felasco Hammock**

FISH ON NEWNAN'S LAKE AT EARL POWERS PARK, GAINESVILLE

Preserve State Park (see *Wild Places*). Or opt for an easier stroll at one of the nature centers, county preserves, or wilderness areas. With both the Alachua Conservation Trust and the county's Alachua Forever program setting aside lands for public use, the amount of hiking in the area has grown significantly since I wrote *50 Hikes in North Florida*. Some of the new hikes I recommend include **Mill Creek Preserve**, CR 241 and CR 236, Alachua, where you can explore the southernmost beech forest in the United States; **Split Rock Conservation Area** off SW 20th Ave, with its limestone outcrops and sinkholes; and **Sweetwater Preserve**, accessible from Boulware Springs Park following the Gainesville-Hawthorne Trail west.

PADDLING Two outfitters in High Springs can get you in the water and down the Santa Fe or the nearby Ichetucknee in Columbia County. At **Santa Fe Canoe Outpost** (386-454-2050; santaferiver.com), US 441 at the Santa Fe Bridge, rent a canoe (shuttle included) or take a guided trip (including overnights) on the Santa Fe or Ichetucknee rivers. In addition to their "menu" of guided trips and a selection of canoes and kayaks for sale or rent, the **Adventure Outpost** (386-454-0611; adventureoutpost.net), 18238 NW US 441, High Springs, has technical clothing, camping equipment, and a nice selection of regional guidebooks. Owners Lars and Patsy keep the shop well stocked: You'll even find pottery and other gift items from local artists. Kick back and thumb through a book, or relax at the picnic tables outside under the trees.

PRAIRIE OVERLOOK Paynes Prairie Overlook, I-75 rest area southbound. Notice the DANGEROUS SNAKES warning signs around the rest area, intimidating visitors from getting too close to the edge of Paynes Prairie, North Florida's largest prairie. Reflecting this theme, the Florida Department of Transportation built a snake-shaped walkway out to an observation deck overlooking the prairie. To northbound travelers, the walkway and deck look like an enormous snake, complete with a ribbon of concrete creating a forked tongue.

SCENIC DRIVES The **Old Florida Heritage Highway** (scenicus441.com), a Florida Scenic Highway, circles the Gainesville area, using US 441, CR 346, CR 325, and CR 2082 to create a beautiful drive around Paynes Prairie and along canopied roads. Along CR 234, from FL 26 south through Rochelle to Micanopy along the east side of Newnans Lake, you'll cruise past historic homes under a canopy of ancient live oaks.

WALKING TOURS Check with the Thomas Center (see *Art Galleries*), the Gainesville CVB (see *Guidance*), or the Matheson Museum (see *Museums*) for brochures outlining walking tours of historic Gainesville, such as the **Pleasant Street Historic Walking Tour** and **Historic Gainesville: A Walking Tour**, which covers the Northeast Historic District around the Matheson Museum. Stop in at the Micanopy Historical Society Museum (see *Museums*) to purchase an inexpensive walking tour booklet that details the history and location of 38 significant sites in the historic district.

✴ Green Space

BOTANICAL GARDEN 🐾 ❀ ♿ With more than 14 distinct garden areas spread across 62 acres bordering Lake Kanapaha, **Kanapaha Botanical Gardens** (352-372-4981; kanapaha.org), 4700 SW 58th Dr, provides a peaceful retreat on the western edge of Gainesville. One of the top gardens in America for bamboo species, they're known for their annual bamboo sales. In late winter, trillium—at the southernmost point of its range—fill hillsides with blooms. By spring, you can revel in the aromas of azalea and camellia. Come anytime to walk more than a mile of pathways between the burbling water gardens, the palm hammock, and the woodland gardens, where you can pause and sit on a bench next to a reflective pool, lose yourself in a Celtic labyrinth, or watch an artist at work painting one of the many lovely garden scenes. Plant identifications add to your understanding of native plants and popular botanicals. Kids will appreciate the expanded children's garden, as well as the many places to duck beneath bowers of plants. Art glass aficionados should note the collection assembled in the gift shop; you'll always find fine art on display in the Summer House, and plants available from the on-site nursery. Managed by the North Florida Botanical Society, this is one of Florida's little-known beauty spots. Dogs on leash permitted. Closed Thu; fee.

FARMS ❀ Two carrots is the admission to the **Mill Creek Farm Retirement Home for Horses** (386-462-1001; millcreekfarm.org), 20307 NW CR 235A in Alachua, open Sat 11–3. In the 1840s farmstead at **Morningside Nature Center** (see *Nature Centers*), kids learn what life in Old Florida was really like during living history demonstrations on weekends. Let them visit with the barnyard animals and join in on a cane-grinding session.

GREENWAYS The paved **Gainesville-Hawthorne State Trail** (352-336-2135; floridastateparks.org/gainesville-hawthorne) runs along a 17-mile section of the old railroad line between the two towns, with termini at Boulware Springs Park in southwest Gainesville (although the trail extension continues into downtown to Depot St) and in downtown Hawthorne, with additional parking areas at all major road crossings. Enjoy biking, hiking, or horseback riding along the adjoining grassy strip. Passing through Hampton on US 301, the new **Palatka–Lake Butler State Trail** (dep.state.fl.us/gwt/state/palatka), when completed, will connect these towns on a ride through rural Putnam, Bradford, and Union counties, crossing the New River to ride right through the middle of downtown Lake Butler. The Florida Trail (see *What's Where*) follows its route from Keystone Heights north to Lake Butler.

NATURE CENTERS At **Paynes Prairie Preserve State Park** (see *Wild Places*), the nature center has hands-on exhibits, a theater with a film introducing you to

DUDLEY FARM HISTORIC SITE STATE PARK

Stepping off the sidewalk and onto the historic highway, a dirt road through the Dudley Farm, you feel a sense of slipping through a time warp. Tobacco is drying in a small barn by the cow pasture; a cheerful woman in a gingham skirt whisks the yard outside the family farmhouse. Turkeys gobble in the backyard. You hear children giggling. Behind the back porch, in modern T-shirts and jeans, kids are putting clothes through the wringer. "Monday was wash day," said the park ranger, wiping her hands on her skirt. "It took *all* day." A little girl's eyes grew wide.

A trip to **Dudley Farm Historic Site State Park** (352-472-1142; floridastateparks.org

KIDS LEARN HOW TO DO THE WASH THE OLD-FASHION WAY AT DUDLEY FARM HISTORIC STATE PARK

/dudleyfarm), 18730 W Newberry Rd, is one of the best ways to let the kids—or grandkids—learn about life before electricity, city water, and motorized vehicles. The working 19-century Florida farm belonged to the Dudley family, who

the habitats of the preserve, and extensive interpretive information about the park. The popular observation tower is a short walk away.

🦋 **Morningside Nature Center** (352-334-2170; natureoperations.org), 3540 E University Ave. Preserving 278 acres of forest on the eastern edge of Gainesville, the Morningside Nature Center provides a living history farm, interpretive exhibits, and a network of hiking trails through longleaf pine flatwoods and sandhills. Free except during special events.

PARKS As befits a large town with a lot of greenery, Gainesville has an extraordinary number of small parks with picnicking, playgrounds, and other fun family activities. One of the more unusual parks in the area is the **Devil's Millhopper**

settled here in the 1880s, building an entire complex to keep daily life going—canning shed, smithy, smokehouse, syrup house, barns and sheds, and even a general store along the highway, where folks stopped to pick up mail, swap stories, and buy household items. Each of the rooms in the well-preserved farmhouse gives a glimpse into the family's daily lives. On weekends and during special events, park rangers in period costume present living history demonstrations of sugarcane harvesting and daily farm chores. Farm open Wed–Sun 9–5, grounds 8–5. Guided tours available. Fee.

A 16-MILE BIKE PATH, THE GAINESVILLE-HAWTHORNE STATE TRAIL PROVIDES A SCENIC RIDE

Geological State Park (352-955-2008; floridastateparks.org/devilsmill-hopper), 4732 Millhopper Rd, where you can walk down 232 steps to the bottom of a 120-foot sinkhole lush with vegetation. In the rainy season, tall waterfalls cascade down its sides.

For spring blooms, ♫ **Alfred Ring Park** (352-334-3326), 1801 NW 23rd Blvd, lets you ramble through a ravine lined with trout lily and false Solomon's seal; a small public garden is the center of attention with its camellias and azaleas. At **Bivens Arm Nature Park** (352-334-3326), 3650 S Main St, nature trails and boardwalks circle a willow marsh. **Palm Point Nature Park** (352-334-3326), 7401 Lakeshore Dr, is a pretty city park that doesn't feel like

PIONEER CABIN AT THE MORNINGSIDE NATURE CENTER

city—it's a deeply shaded breezy peninsula into Newnan's Lake, and bank fishing is permitted—just watch for those alligators!

🐾 Dogs are welcome to roam off-leash at **Squirrel Ridge Park**, 1603 SW Williston Rd, a city park with an open fenced area for dogs to play. For a theme park for your dog, visit **Dog Wood Park** (352-335-1919; dogwoodpark.com), 5505 SW Archer Rd, where Fido can romp and play across a 15-acre preserve, a true doggy delight with swimming ponds, a walking trail, and doggy playground equipment. Open to non-members on Sun only; per-dog fee.

♫ Along the Santa Fe River, **Chastain-Seay Park**, US 121 in Worthington Springs just north of the bridge, protects the original Worthington Springs, which you can look at but can't enter. However, the park has rambling nature trails and boardwalks

IT'S A LONG CLIMB IN AND OUT ON THE 232 STEPS OF DEVIL'S MILLHOPPER

that lead down to sandy beaches along the river, where you can fish or swim or swing into the water. The city of **Lake Butler** has a pretty community park along the edge of cypress-lined Lake Butler, downtown at the end of N Lake Ave, with playground, picnic area, and a walkway out over the lake for swimming and fishing.

SPRINGS On CR 340 outside High Springs, there are three major parks centered on the region's largest springs. **Blue Springs** (386-454-1369; bluespringspark.com) forms the centerpiece of a county park with picnicking, nature trails, and camping, but most visitors dive and snorkel in the springs. Open 9–7 daily. $10 adults, $3 children 5–12; no pets. Just over the line in neighboring Gilchrist County, **Poe Springs Park** (386-454-1992; week-endadventures.com/Poe_Springs_Park.html) is a 197-acre county park with rolling hills and steep bluffs along the Santa Fe River, with canoe launch, picnic pavilions, and swimming in the spring; fee. At nearby **Ginnie Springs** (386-454-7188; ginniespringsoutdoors.com), overnight campers can swim in the springs until midnight; it's a mecca for cave divers. Tube and canoe rentals available; open 8–sunset. $12 adults, $3 ages 7–14 (see also *Springs* in the *Lower Suwannnee* chapter).

Gainesville once pulled its municipal water supply from **Boulware Springs** (gru.com/OurCommunity/ParkProjects/boulwaresprings.jsp), 3300 SE 15th St, where you can visit the historic waterworks and see the spring pumping. Boulware Springs Park is also a major access point for the Gainesville-Hawthorne Trail (see *Greenways*).

WATERFALLS Visit **Devil's Millhopper** (see *Parks*) during the rainy season, and you'll see cascades dropping more than 100 feet down the walls of this steep sinkhole, creating an atmosphere much like a tropical rain forest for Florida's southernmost natural waterfall.

WILD PLACES For sheer scale of an open landscape, nowhere else in North Florida can compare to **Paynes Prairie Preserve State Park** (352-466-3397; floridastateparks.org/paynesprairie), 100 Savannah Blvd, a 22,000-acre wet prairie defining the southern edge of Gainesville. Herds of bison and wild horses roam the vast open spaces, while alligators collect en masse in La Chua Sink at the north end of the prairie. With more than 20 miles of hiking, biking, and equestrian trails and a beautifully shaded campground (see *Camping & Cabins*), it's one of the best places in the region for wildlife-watching. Open 8–sunset daily; fee.

Enjoy many miles of rugged mountain biking and hiking trails through the hills of **San Felasco Hammock Preserve State Park** (386-462-7905; floridastateparks .org/sanfelascohammock) on Millhopper Rd, a lush preserve with Appalachian-like landscapes formed by Florida's limestone karst. Open 9–5 daily; fee.

Conservation areas are some of the wilder spots around the region's lakes, where hikers, bikers, and equestrians can roam miles of old forest roads and developed trails through floodplain forests. Visit **Gum Root Swamp Conservation Area** on FL 26 for a glimpse of Newnans Lake; the **Newnans Lake Conservation Area** (with three tracts: Hatchet Creek, North, and South) off CR 234 and FL 26; and the **Lochloosa Conservation Area**, where you can hike out to an observation platform on Lake Lochloosa from a trailhead adjoining the fire station in Cross Creek. All are managed by the St. Johns Water Management District (386-329-4483; sjrwmd.com).

ALONG THE LA CHUA TRAIL AT PAYNES PRAIRIE PRESERVE STATE PARK, ALLIGATOR SIGHTINGS ARE GUARANTEED

✴ Lodging
BED & BREAKFASTS

Gainesville 32601

♿ ♂ (ᵩ) One of the anchors of the bed & breakfast district of Gainesville, the **Laurel Oak Inn** (352-373-4535; laureloakinn.com), 221 SE 7th St, is a place to unwind. Sit on the spacious porches of the roomy 1885 Queen Anne and watch the owls from the comfort of your rocking chair, or enjoy the pampering afforded by the soft robes, fragrant lotions, and candles that accompany your in-room hydro-jet massage tub. It's a hit with honeymoon couples, and business travelers appreciate Internet access in every room ($140–199). You won't go away hungry, as innkeepers Monta and Peggy Burt ensure that a steady parade of artfully presented gourmet treats appears on your breakfast plate. A ground-floor room accommodates wheelchairs with an appropriately sized wheel-in shower.

🐾 ✂ ♂ (ᵩ) At the **Magnolia Plantation Inn** (800-201-2379; magnolia bnb.com), 309 SE 7th St, relax in a private tropical oasis. In 1991 Joe and Cindy Montalto opened the Baird House, an 1885 Victorian painted lady, as the first B&B in Gainesville. In addition to the five lavish rooms in the main house, each with private bath ($135–165), their plantation now encompasses nine lovingly restored cottages ($175–225) connected by lush, shaded gardens developed by Joe, a landscape architect. Full breakfast served where you'd like it, whether in the lovely Baird House dining room, or outdoors on a porch or gazebo. Pets and children welcome in some of the cottages; call ahead for details.

♂ (ᵩ) Cornelia Holbrook's complex of historic homes just outside downtown, **Sweetwater Branch Inn** (800-595-7760; sweetwaterinn.com), 625 E University Ave, provides a selection of tastefully themed rooms ($99–185) in two Victorian homes plus six cottages ($125–240). The Honeymoon Cottage is popular with newlyweds who take their vows at McKenzie Hall, the Victorian-style banquet room on site. Sit on the broad, breezy veranda to enjoy complimentary wine and hors d'oeuvres each evening, or stroll the lush gardens and listen to the burble of the fountains.

Hampton 32091

🦐 (ᵂⁱ-ᶠⁱ) **Hampton Lake B&B** (800-480-4522; hamptonlakebb.com), US 301. On Lake Hampton, this massive winged A-frame with a native stone fireplace and pecky cypress walls is the dream home of Freeman and Paula Register; the antique gas pumps were handed down from Grandpa, who was the local Gulf Oil distributor in the 1930s. This is a retreat for those who love the outdoors, with fishing tackle and a pedal boat waiting at the pier, walking trails winding through 18 acres of pines, a porch swing and rockers overlooking the lake, and a hot tub for relaxing after play. Outdoorsy decor accentuates the spacious Wade Room, big enough for an entire family. Four rooms of varying sizes, $99–159. Full breakfast provided; dinner prepared for an additional fee with notice.

High Springs 32643

(ᵂⁱ-ᶠⁱ) Enjoy spacious accommodations in a romantic setting at the **Grady House** (386-454-2206; gradyhouse .com), 420 NW 1st Ave, a charming two-story mansion from 1917 with intimate formal gardens in the backyard. The aroma of home-cooked muffins wafts through the dining room; settle down by the fireplace and read a book. Chose from five rooms, $115–175; or Skeet's Cottage with two bedrooms sleeping four, $230–280 (two-night minimum).

🦐 Set on a 7-acre mini ranch, the **Rustic Inn** (386-454-1223; rusticinn.net),

3105 S Main St, is where Tom and Wendy Solomon offer relaxation in six modern rooms ($79–149) with nature themes, from the Everglades to sea mammals; settle into a rocking chair on the porch or take a lap around the pool. A continental breakfast basket is left at your room each evening so you can set your own pace in the morning.

Micanopy 32667

(ᵂⁱ-ᶠⁱ) ♂ When guests come to the **Herlong Mansion** (800-HERLONG; herlong.com), 402 NE Cholokka Blvd, a neoclassical 1875 mansion, they take to the verandas, where comfortable chairs overlook the expansive lawns. Of the four suites, five rooms, and two private outbuildings, sisters and girlfriends traveling together will especially appreciate Pink's Room, with its two antique cast-iron beds and a daybed; brothers will like the masculine Brothers' Room, with a double bed and a daybed. The mansion features private baths, classy antiques, and original push-button electric switches throughout. For a touch of history, settle back in the Music Room and watch *The Yearling* or any of several other movies filmed in the region. If the house looks vaguely familiar, have you perhaps

RELAX IN OLD-FASHIONED COMFORT AT THE HERLONG MANSION, MICANOPY

seen *Doc Hollywood*, which was filmed on site with Michael J. Fox? Micanopy now celebrates with Doc Hollywood Days (see *Special Events*), centered on the mansion. Ah yes, and there are ghosts, although I didn't hear any bumps in the night when I enjoyed a quiet evening here. Full breakfasts on weekends; continental breakfasts weekdays; no special orders. No children, no pets, no smoking on premises. $119–189.

HOTELS, MOTELS & RESORTS

Gainesville 32601

As a university town—and a sports town—Gainesville has pretty much every major chain hotel up and down the four exits of I-75, plus a handful around downtown. My top picks from the pack include the & ⊸ **Hampton Inn & Suites Downtown** (352-240-9300; hamptoninnandsuitesgainesville .com), 101 SE 1st Ave, which blends in nicely into the downtown historic district and is right in the heart of nightlife and the arts, and the & ⊸ **Country Inn and Suites** (352-375-1550; countryinns.com), 4015 SW 43rd St, by I-75 with easy access to state parks and Kanapaha Botanical Gardens. Other properties are listed below.

🦎 🌀 & ((ᵠ)) After another comfortable stay at the **Cabot Lodge** (352-375-2400; cabotlodgegainesville.com), 3726 SW 40th Blvd, I'm ready to recommend them all over again. The spotless, spacious rooms invite a good night's sleep and have the amenities a business traveler expects; when in town to meet with friends, it's a big plus that Cabot Lodge believes in happy hour, serving up cocktails and snacks in a massive great room that reminds you of a Colorado lodge. An expanded continental breakfast is included in your stay. $99 and up.

🦎 🌀 & ((ᵠ)) ⊸ You gotta be a Gator—or know one—to book a room at the **Reitz Union Hotel** (352-392-2151; union.ufl.edu/hotel), Museum Rd at Reitz Union Dr, but having that in makes a comfortable stay all yours. Occupying the top two floors of the Reitz Student Union on the University of Florida campus, this under-the-radar student-run hotel offers ecofriendly rooms and suites with a bird's-eye view of the campus; $99–129. Reservations recommended.

& ((ᵠ)) ⊸ **University of Florida Hilton** (352-371-3600; www1.hilton.com), 1714 SW 34th Place. Top-notch chain hotel conference center with comfortable rooms ($109 and up) with free WiFi, fitness center, heated pool, and spa; visit **Albert's Restaurant** for fine dining, American-style, including a Sunday brunch with complimentary mimosas. Shuttle provided to airport.

High Springs 32643

🦎 ((ᵠ)) **High Springs Country Inn** (386-454-1565; highspringsinn.com), 520 NW Santa Fe Blvd. This newly refurbished 1960s family-run offering has cute landscaping outside its period rooms ($42–60), which vary in size from small to suite; each is sparkling clean, with small tiled bathroom, fridge, microwave, and cable TV.

CAMPING & CABINS

Cross Creek 32640

Next to the Yearling Restaurant (see *Dining Out*) along Cross Creek, **Secret River Lodge/Yearling Cabins** (352-466-3999), 14531 S CR 325, is an eclectic collection of restored fish camp cabins providing a quiet venue for relaxing in a sleepy little town. Each cabin is named for a book by Marjorie Kinnan Rawlings, and varies in amenities from a simple bed and bath to a two-bedroom cabin with full kitchen. $89–129.

High Springs 32643

⚘ Camp near a spring! Both Blue Springs Park and Ginnie Springs (see *Springs*) offer camping as well as day use, and campers, of course, get to splash in the spring for many more hours than other visitors do. At **Blue Springs Park** (386-454-1369) campsites are first come, first served and can handle tents or RVs; 30/50-amp service available for $12. Camping fees are per person: $15 adults, $6 ages 5–12, which includes park admission. **Ginnie Springs** (386-454-7188) has plenty of tent camping space—sites have grills and picnic tables—all first come, first served, plus 90 sites with hookups for $7 a night. Per-person camping fees are $20 adults (senior discount), $6 ages 7–14, free for younger guests. A three-bedroom, two-bath cottage is also available for $175 for up to four adults, minimum two-night stay.

⚘ **High Springs Campground** (386-454-1688; highspringscampground .com), 24004 NW Old Bellamy Rd, provides camping in a family-oriented atmosphere, with playground, swimming pool, tent sites, and full hookups, $18–28.

⚘ (((ᴘ))) **River Rise Resort** (352-318-4602), 252 SE Riverview Circle. With horseback riding, camping, canoeing, swimming, and nearby hiking trails, it's a centrally located mecca for outdoor recreation along the Santa Fe River. $38–48, discounts for Passport America members.

Micanopy 32667

🐾 ⚘ If you're visiting Gainesville, the closest campground to town is at **Paynes Prairie Preserve State Park** (see *Wild Places*). Deeply shaded and within walking distance of a nice new playground, boat ramp, and boardwalk along Lake Wauberg, the spaces in the **Puc Puggy Campground** (800-326-3521; floridastateparks.reserveamerica .com) accommodate tents, trailers, or RVs, $18.

Starke 32091

☀ (((ᴘ))) **Starke KOA** (904-964-8484; starkekoa.com), 1475 US 301. Large campground, partially shaded, with exceptional amenities like free wireless Internet and wide, grassy 70-foot pull-through spaces ($39–46). Heated swimming pool, playground, one-room camping cabins with no bath ($48); no tents.

FISH CAMPS I sat around a campfire many years ago at **Kate's Fish Camp** (352-372-1026; katesfishcamp .com), 6518 Hawthorne Rd, as J. T. Glisson told tale after tale of being a young boy growing up in Cross Creek when "Miss Rawlins" was around. There's something about a fish camp that brings on this sort of camaraderie, and Kate's has been sparking that magic since the 1950s. With access to Prairie Creek, Newnan's Lake, and the Gainesville-Hawthorne Trail just off FL 20, Kate's is a piece of Old Florida that locals cherish. Stop here to rent a boat ($45) or a canoe or kayak ($20), or just camp on the property ($10) and explore the local wilds.

Once owned by Wade Boggs, **Lochloosa Harbor Fish Camp** (352-481-2114; lochloosaharbor.com), 15008 SE US 301, Hawthorne, has the best views of and access to Lake Lochloosa. Bring your RV ($25), full-hookup, a tent, or rent a cabin ($62) so you can head out before daybreak on this placid lake and land your own lunkers at this tournament destination.

Right on historic Cross Creek, **Twin Lakes Fish Camp** (352-466-3194; twinlakesfishcamp.com), 17105 S CR 325, lets you settle in and enjoy the two best lakes to fish in the area. Rent a boat or pontoon, $45–110, or a canoe, $10–20, to explore the lakes—Lochloosa tends to hold more water than Orange Lake in a dry year—camp for $24, or rent one of their cabins (satellite TV provided), $76–81.

✳ Where to Eat

DINING OUT

Cross Creek

Although the outside looks like an old shack along Cross Creek, **Yearling Restaurant** (352-466-3999; yearling restaurant.net), 14531 E CR 325, has a dining room that features dark, rich wood and windows on the creek. If you're lucky enough to end up in the overflow section, it's an antiques shop replete with a fishing skiff, booths from the original restaurant, and shelves lined with classic books like the sci-fi thriller *Thuvia, Maid of Mars* by Edgar Rice Burroughs. This is a funky place celebrating the legacy of their neighbor Marjorie Kinnan Rawlings, where you're as likely to rub elbows with the poet laureate of Tennessee as you are with local fishermen. Cheese and crackers kick off each meal, which you can supplement with an appetizer like the large portion of freshly battered fried mushrooms. "Cross Creek Traditions" include crawdads, alligator, frog legs, venison, soft-shell crab, catfish, and pan-fried quail, as well as a variety of steaks and combination platters. Coated in a light breading, the fresh venison medallions are surprisingly tender and juicy; the stuffed flounder contains a mass of succulent buttery crabmeat. Lighter fare is available before 5, including a unique "Creek Boy" sandwich served up with your choice of fried shrimp, oyster, or alligator with coleslaw and Jack cheese. For dessert, try the sour orange pie, a tiger-striped creation with the taste of a chocolate orange truffle. Entrées $13 and up. Thu noon–9, Fri–Sat noon–10, Sun noon–8; Live music Fri and Sat.

Gainesville

🍴 Gainesville's top pick for fine Italian cuisine, **Amelia's Restaurant** (352-373-1919; ameliasgainesville.com), 235

FISHING LAKE LOCHLOOSA FROM THE LOCHLOOSA HARBOR FISH CAMP

S Main St, Ste 107, entices you off the street with the aromas of fresh sauces bubbling in the kitchen, ready to become part of your Penne alla Sorrentino or Capellini Puttanesca. It's Italian dining at its finest, with extensive seafood and chicken options. Top off your dinner with a gorgeous dessert like their bittersweet chocolate torte. Entrées $13–24. Lunch Tue–Fri 11:30–2, dinner Tue–Sun starting at 5.

Bistro 1245 (352-378-2001; leonardos gainesville.com), 706 W University Ave, a tiny speck of a café near the busiest corner in Gainesville serves fabulous lunches in a classy atmosphere. I was impressed by my choice: portobello mushroom with apple jam, smoked Gouda, and red pepper aioli on fresh bread. Sandwiches run $7–11, dinner $9–20; wine tastings and live jazz on Fri.

Make mine sushi at the famed **Dragonfly Sushi & Sake Company** (352-371-3359; dragonflysushi.com), 201 SE 2nd Ave. Purple walls and velvety black and red chairs accentuate the op-art feel of sushi served up by Gainesville's only certified sushi chef. Lunch and dinner entrées; sushi served à la carte and as rolls ($3–14) and platters ($12–35). Consider the delicious Mango Tango, a roll with smoked salmon, cream cheese, avocado and mango strips, topped with tempura flakes and sweet potato curls, and served with a plum and apricot sauce.

With a daily selection of Spanish tapas, Cuban and Caribbean sandwiches, and Cuban entrées in a setting with a special Spanish-Caribbean flair, **Emiliano's Cafe** (352-375-7381; emilianos cafe.com), 7 SE 1st Ave. provides Gainesville's best choice for fine Latin cuisine. Try tapas for lunch ($3–9) or a hearty sandwich, served Tue–Sat; dinner ($12–20) every day but Mon; Sun brunch.

Dining with a vegetarian friend at **Liquid Ginger** (352-371-2323; liquid gingergainesville.com), 101 SE 2nd Place #118, we had no problem finding tasty creations to please both our palates. Having arrived straight from the Harn, I was delighted to settle into this hip, artsy space and order up tea and tastings, including edamame, garlic eggplant, and Buddha rolls. Entrées come grilled or sautéed, with veggie selections like Thai red curry tofu and the vegetable sauté, with mixed vegetables and tofu stir-fried in a vegan coconut cream sauce. $14–28 for entrées, or make a meal of the tastings for a spin through Asia. Lunch Mon–Fri 11:30–2:30, Sun noon–5; dinner nightly 5–10.

Winner of numerous awards, **Mildred's Big City Food** (352-371-1711; mildredsbigcityfood.com), 3445 W University Ave, is a hot spot for those who enjoy good food beyond café fare. Sandwiches at lunchtime include beef brisket with beer-cheddar sauce and a sloppy tempeh-joe with fried onions; creative salads and a quiche of the day. Dinner starts at 5, with three perfect courses to select from: perhaps fresh sardines with a roasted shallot custard, followed by a carrot ginger bisque with carrot salad, and hanger steak with a leek-mushroom tartlet, paired with the perfect wine. $7–24.

❦ **Panache Bistro** (352-372-8446), 113 N Main St. Part of the Wine & Cheese Gallery (see *Selective Shopping*), this upscale lunch spot (11–2:15) serves up unusual daily specials, such as the sweet potato quesadilla, a hot blue cheese and green apple sandwich, or the cheeseboard with three cheeses, French loaf, and fruit du jour; lunch offerings $6 and up. For atmosphere, sit out in the shaded patio garden to sip your choice (4 to 10 options daily) from the wine bar. My lunch companions gave the Florida Sunshine Cake "delightful" and "scrumptious" ratings for the orange-rich flavor, delicate frosting, and white chocolate garnishes.

Paramount Grill (352-378-3398; paramountgrill.com), 12 SW 1st Ave. In this sophisticated downtown, European-style bistro, chef-owner Clif Nelson draws on more than 25 years of local experience to create provocative fusion food. I enjoyed my chilled cucumber, yogurt, and almond soup du jour and artfully presented salad with four types of farm-fresh berries and baby asparagus over baby greens. Their menus change often; entrées when I visited included such creative gems as spicy Thai-style prawns with Asian vegetables, linguine, fresh basil, and coriander; seared garam-masala-spiced tuna steak served over green onion hummus with tomato cucumber chutney, grilled papadam, and vindaloo vinaigrette; and pan-roasted prime Angus fillet served over garlic mashed potatoes with shiitake mushroom sherry wine sauce, poached asparagus, puff pastry, and white truffle oil. Entrées $14–27, with salads à la carte. Lunch weekdays 11–2, dinner daily at 5; Sun brunch 10–3. Reservations suggested.

EATING OUT

Alachua

🍴 ✎ **Conestogas Restaurant** (386-462-1294; conestogasrestaurant.com), 14920 Main St, is one of those long-time institutions I'll go out of my way for, as do their other loyal customers. In this unpretentious, western-themed restaurant, you'll nibble on peanuts while waiting for one of the tender house sirloin steaks ($12–25), marinated in the family's secret marinade recipe. Burgers are the other big thing—fresh handmade burgers

($8–11) cooked the way you want them. The Main Street Monster Burger ($21) challenges *Guinness Book of World Records* appetites with 48 ounces of beef on an extremely over-sized bun; free T-shirt and a slice of key lime pie if you eat it, sides and all. Open for lunch and dinner; closed Sun.

Gainesville

Tucked inside busy Books Inc., the **Book Lovers Cafe** (352-384-0090; thebookloverscafe.com), 505 NW 13th St, serves creative vegetarian and vegan salads and entrées ($7 and up), going well beyond tofu burgers and sprouts. Check the artsy menu board for the day's offerings, which may include gourmet salads such as Thai cucumber, with crunchy fresh cucumbers in rice vinegar, and red beans in walnut sauce, a tasty combination of textures in olive oil. If you can't make up your mind, try the 3 Salad Sampler. Savor a cup of authentic Indian chai, or enjoy freshly squeezed lemonade. Seating is scattered throughout the bookstore, but if you sit near the kitchen, you'll smile at the young chefs singing along to mellow music behind the counter as they prepare your meal. Themed dinners showcase macrobiotic and ethnic foods. Open daily.

🍴 **Burrito Brothers Taco Company** (352-378-5948; burritobros.com), 16 NW 13th St. A Swedish chef serves up Mexican take-out, and the burritos are out of this world. The new digs feature a garden patio dining room. It's a popular student stop just off campus with vegetarian and vegan choices; don't miss the excellent fresh guacamole. $4–11; order from the website—they ship!

🍴 **Chop Stix Cafe** (352-367-0003; chopstixcafe.com), 3500 SW 13th St. Vietnamese noodle bowls, Thai and Chinese entrées, a sushi bar, and a wide variety of vegetarian choices, all presented in a soothing Asian atmosphere with giant carp and a sweeping view of the alligators cruising Bivens Arm. Fabulous food—$6 and up for everything from giant noodle bowls to combination platters. Closed Sun.

David's Real Pit BBQ (352-373-2002; davidsbbq.com), 5121 NW 39th Ave. Cheap, fast, and good: It's not supposed to be possible, but this award-winning barbecue place pulls it off. Plates of barbecued ribs, chicken, beef, turkey, and pork run $8–13, hearty sandwiches $4–5, and you can choose your sauce from the "wall of fire." They even do omelets and pancakes for breakfast, $3–7. The surroundings are nothing fancy, but the food is sublime.

Harvest Thyme Cafe (352-384-9497; harvestthymecafe.com), 2 W University Ave. It's somewhere to kick back and read the morning paper while sipping coffee, tea, or chai. Enjoy shakes and smoothies, fresh fruit, sandwiches, soups, salads, and wraps, $7–8. The menu is posted on a colorful chalkboard over the kitchen. Mon–Sat 8–8, Sun 8–5.

Setting a mood with gleaming chrome, dark wood, and snappy 1940s jazz, the **New Deal Cafe** (352-371-4418; newdealcafegainesville.com), 3445 W University Ave, provides quick-stop diners with delicious organic food, including goat cheese and beet salad, eggplant panini, and Artie's Tempeh Burger (lunch $6–10). Don't walk out without a slice of cake. I couldn't resist the chocolate mocha ganache, but it was a tough choice stacked up against a raspberry whipped cream torte, a French silk torte, and the decadent Chocolate Fudge Corruption. Mon–Thu 11–10, Fri–Sat 11–11.

I stopped at **The Swamp** (352-377-9267; swamprestaurant.com), 1642 W University Ave, and enjoyed a great lunch with friends in this renovated 1915 professor's home right across from campus. We ordered ahi tuna wontons, Bermuda salad, and my Parmesan-crusted grouper, and everyone went away happy. With a sports-bar atmosphere, it's a raucous place, but the meals are great; $8–16.

Think pop art and paint-by-number: **The Top** (352-337-1188), 40 N Main St, is a step back into the 1970s, with chairs like my 1976 high school cafeteria. But it's a hip young crowd that hangs here, with food to match: I loved the spinach salad with roasted peppers, onions, pecans, goat cheese, and a mango vinaigrette, and the speedy service made it possible to get back to my conference in record time. Lunch $7–11; dinner entrées like pecan-crusted tofu and ginger orange stir-fry show off the chef's creativity, $10–21.

High Springs

⊘ I'm glad to see the **Great Outdoors Restaurant** (386-454-1288; greatout doorsdining.com), 65 N Main St, not only back in business but thriving, named one of Florida's "top new restaurants" recently. An excellent place to kick back and chill out after a day of paddling, swimming, hiking, or diving, it feels like a comfortable lodge. Hang out with friends and enjoy the live music. Select a Nut n' Berry Salad for lunch, or a hearty Drunken Rib-Eye, $8–18; dinner, $15–29, requires a more relaxed pace to savor the standout on the menu, Naked Ed's Low Country Boil, with Gulf shrimp, snow crab legs, Georgia sausage, mussels, cobbed corn, and red-skin potatoes simmered in spices and Naked Ed's Pale Ale.

⊘ In the old railroad depot, the **Station Bakery & Cafe** (386-454-4943), 20 NW Railroad Ave, offers great sandwiches on fresh-baked bread ($3–6), including the classic "fluffernutter," as well as salads, ice cream, and fresh-baked goods. Open for lunch daily.

Micanopy

For flatbread and antipasto, it's worth the drive to **Blue Highway** (352-466-0062; bluehighwaypizza.com), 204 NE US 441, a bistro evoking a French country kitchen with its bold colors and bright local artwork. Their hand-crafted pizzas come with creative but sensible combination toppings like Rustica, Greek, and BBQ Chicken, but I love their Blue Highway Salad, crunchy with toasted pecans and feta, the best. Open Tue–Sun for lunch and dinner; $4–20.

⌁ Aunt Sherry's chicken salad is the usual for me at **Coffee N Cream** (352-466-1101; micanopycoffeeshop .com), 201 Cholokka Blvd, where you can sit out on the shaded porch and enjoy the sunshine or plop back into a couch with your coffee cup. Other favorites from the chalkboard menu include the Micanopy Salad and Frito Pie. The café is an ice cream parlor and a coffeehouse that I frequent on every trip to Micanopy—a good selection of ice cream and fresh lemonade guarantees a steady customer. The owner, Cliff, is a rodeo cowboy, so you'll see ephemera from his adventures around the shop. Grab breakfast, lunch, or a treat, $2–10.

A funky antiques-shop-*cum*-lunch-spot under the shade of giant live oaks, the **Old Florida Cafe** (352-466-3663), 203 NE Cholokka Blvd, provides tasty homemade soup, black beans and rice, and chili as well as a gamut of "generous sandwiches," hot Cubans and Reubens, and fabulous thick BLTs ($4 and up). Browse the shelves while waiting for your order, or stake out a place on the front porch and watch the world wander past. Don't miss out on their desserts, especially the piquant McIntosh wild orange pie. Open 11–4; closed Mon.

On the outside, it looks like your basic convenience store. But step inside **Pearl Country Store** (352-466-4025), US 441 and CR 234, and you'll be treated to down-home breakfast sand-wiches, hotcakes, French toast, and omelets served 6–11 AM, followed by a parade of barbecue ($5 and up): sand-wiches, dinner platters, and barbecue-by-the-pound, as well as daily dinner specials. It's all tucked away in David Carr's eclectic country store, where local baked goods, organic veggies, and books on natural Florida share the floor with more traditional conven-ience store fare. Barbecue served Sun–Thu 11–7, Fri and Sat 11–8.

✴ Entertainment

Gainesville

Check with the **Gainesville Cultural Affairs Office** (352-333-ARTS; gvl culturalaffairs.com) for their latest slate of free public concerts downtown on Fri night, presented year-round. Since this is a university town, the place to see and be seen is downtown, of course, on the patio bars and cafés surrounding Sun Center and the **Hip-podrome State Theater** (352-375-4477; thehipp.org), 25 SE 2nd Pl, where vibrant live productions take the stage. For those into student-driven nightlife, nightclubs line Main and University.

Dance aficionados enjoy the **Gaines-ville Ballet Theatre** (352-372-9898; gainesvilleballettheatre.org), 1501 NW 16th Ave, a 30-year-old nonprofit regional ballet company. **Dance Alive!** (352-371-2986; dancealive.org), 1325 NW 2nd St, presents modern works and classic ballet as the State Touring Company of Florida. After 20 years, the **Gainesville Chamber Orchestra** (352-336-5448; gcomusic.org), per-forming at a variety of venues around the city, continues to delight its fans.

One of those venues, the **Philips Center for the Performing Arts** (352-392-2787; phillips.centerperforming arts.org), 100 34th St, can be counted on for a wide variety of shows.

High Springs
The Priest Theater (386-454-SHOW; facebook.com/priesttheater), 15 NW 1st St, is Florida's oldest movie theater, built in 1926 as a minstrel and vaudeville venue. Movies are shown here on vintage X-16 projectors from the 1940s, on Mon, Fri, and Sat evenings for $3–5.

✷ Selective Shopping

Alachua
Little Hearts Desire (386-462-7706), 14925 Main St. A sweet little shop with local country crafts and ceramics accenting an array of consignment antiques. Closed Sun.

Inside a lovely little pink cottage, **Pink Porch Books** (386-462-9552; pink porchbooks.com), 14720 Main St, boasts more than 7,000 "previously loved books" that'll take you hours to browse. Stop in and sit a spell!

Evinston
Wood & Swink (352-591-1334), 18320 SE CR 225. Built in 1884 of heart pine, this general store and local post office is one of the few remaining historic post offices in the United States, complete with original decorative postboxes. It's a welcoming place with a jumble of antiques, crafts, groceries, fresh produce, books on local culture and history, and gift items. Stop by and say hello!

Gainesville
Brasington's Adventure Outfitters (888-438-4502; brasingtons.com), 2331 NW 13th St. If you're headed out to the trail or to one of the pristine nearby rivers, stop in and get outfitted at Brasington's, one of only a handful of outdoor adventure outfitters in Florida where you can pick up backpacking gear. With paddling equipment, camping supplies, technical clothing, and a wide variety of travel and outdoor adventure guides, you'll find everything you need for outdoor recreation in North Florida.

Harold's Frames & Gallery (352-375-0260; haroldsframes.com), 101 SE 2nd Place. Showcases stunning images of natural Florida by local photographers, including some of my favorites by John Moran.

Paddiwhack (352-336-3175; paddi whack.com), 4128 NW 16th Blvd. "Art for Life" is the theme of this most eclectic of art shops, where creativity molds colorful, playful, vibrant pieces ranging from mirrors and wall hangings to large pieces of furniture, each signed by one of the many artists represented.

Thornebrook Village (352-378-4949), 2441-6D NW 43rd St. A trendy and popular collection of galleries and boutiques at the north end of Gainesville. Among them you'll find Gainesville's standout antiques shop, **The Painted Table** (352-371-1555), full of delightful vintage collectibles, pottery, furnishings, and books; **Thornebrook Chocolates** (352-371-0800; thornebrookchocolates.com), where it's hard to walk out of the heavenly scented shop without a bagful of fresh truffles or melt-in-your-mouth treats; **McIntyre Stained Glass Studio & Art Gallery** (352-372-2752; mcintyrestudio.com), for all your stained-glass needs; and **Thornebrook Gallery** (see *Art Galleries*), showcasing the work of fine Florida artists.

Wild Iris Books (352-375-7477; wild irisbooks.com), 802 W University Ave. It's loud, it's proud, and it's feminist. The merchandise at Wild Iris runs the gamut from raunchy greeting cards and comics to tomes on Zen Buddhism, Wicca, and artistic inspiration. The back room houses used books, while culturally sensitive children's books rate their own special corner, and the main section contains a special emphasis on strong female voices in fiction and nonfiction.

The **Wine & Cheese Gallery** (352-372-8446; wineandcheesegallery.com), 133 N Main St. More than 4,000 types of wine line the floor-to-ceiling shelves at this 30-year-old fixture in downtown Gainesville, a necessary stop for the discriminating gourmand. In addition to the perfect wine, you'll find imported chocolates, microbrew beers, and a wide array of gourmet food items. Lunch served in their Panache Bistro (see *Dining Out*).

High Springs
High Springs Emporium (386-454-8657; highspringsemporium.net), 660 NW Santa Fe Blvd, has a heavy focus on beautiful Asian- and African-import home decor items: sculptures and carvings, jewelry, wall hangings, and trinkets. But the real reason to stop here is to check out their collection of rocks and minerals, with everything from New Age quartz points to assemblages of crystals that will impress the most serious mineral collector—as will the owner, who knows her stuff about geology.

High Springs Art Co-op (386-454-1808; highspringartcoop.blogspot.com), 115 N Main St. Representing works from more than 700 artists (with at least 30 percent local content), this gallery soars with art with a natural feel, from the playful painted metal flowers and creatures of Sarasota artist Brian Meys to the large amount of art glass on display.

Main Street Antique Mall (386-454-2700), 10 S Main St, is chock-full of

small items like saltcellars, antique glassware, and kitchen items.

Wisteria Cottage (386-454-8447), 225 N Main St. A true period piece, this tin-roofed Cracker home with bead board walls and ceilings has numerous spacious rooms filled with country crafts and collectibles, a kitchen filled with gourmet foods, and an Americana room.

Micanopy
One of the top antiquing towns in Florida, downtown Micanopy dates back to the 1820s. Enough shops crowd Cholokka Blvd (Micanopy's "Main Street") to allow you to spend the entire day shopping. Some of my favorites include:

Dakota Mercantile (352-466-5005; dakotamercantile.com), 110 Cholokka Blvd, evokes feminine bonding over fine linens and toddler clothes, fragrant soaps and perfumes, and a quiet garden shop out back.

The Garage at Micanopy, Inc. (352-288-8485), 212 Cholokka Blvd. Fun ephemera fills the booths in this 1920s garage, from figurines and postcards to toys and glassware at reasonable prices.

House of Hirsch Too (352-466-3744), 209 Cholokka Blvd. High-end antique furnishings, modern quilts, and home decor items.

The **Mosswood Farm Store** (352-466-5002; mosswoodfarmstore.com), 703 NE Cholokka Blvd, is a must-stop on my trips to Micanopy for guilt-free gluten-free baked goods, but they have so much more than food. Within this rambling country home, stacks of books invite you to learn about organic gardening and living the simple life; homemade soaps are stacked up next to organic shampoos; you can even buy a clothesline and clothespins. Featuring a regular fresh garden market and nursery items out back, plus a place to savor a coffee in the breeze, it's a friendly, relaxing place.

O'Brisky Books Inc. (352-466-3910), 112 NE Cholokka Blvd. Bursting with books, O'Brisky deals mostly in used nonfiction and features an excellent Florida section in the front of the store. Bring your want list—I've been surprised at the gems I've discovered in the stacks, and manager Gary Nippes runs a free search service for those tough-to-find items.

I've picked up many a gift at the **Shady Oak Gallery & Art Glass Studio** (352-466-3476; shadyoak.com), 201 Cholokka Blvd, where in addition to selling the whimsical creations of local artists, they teach hands-on art glass courses at very reasonable prices. Check their website for full details.

The Shop (352-466-4031), 210 Cholokka Blvd. Every nook and cranny of this rambling maze of nooks is a haven for home decor, where you'll also find crafts, antique glassware and furnishings, and quilts.

Smiley's Antique Mall (352-466-0707; smileysantiques.com), CR 234 and I-75 (Micanopy exit). With more than 200 booths, this mini mall of antiques will keep you browsing for hours. Open daily 9–6.

Starke

When I was a kid, US 301 was Main Street for tourists headed down to Central Florida, and the shops and attractions along the way were geared to wide-eyed northerners. Signs proclaimed RARE 16 FOOT ALBINO ALLIGATOR!, SEE THE WALKING CATFISH!, and FREE ORANGE JUICE! Most of those old-time tourist traps (and I say that with affection) are now gone, but the stretch of US 301 north from Starke to Lawtey hosts a few hangers-on. At **Textile Town** (904-964-4250), housed

in an old Stuckey's, you can nab chenille bedspreads, towels by the pound, and T-shirts at three for $10. And a former Horne's restaurant hosts **Florida Souvenir Land**, with pecans and candies, T-shirts and towels, and all sorts of ticky-tacky ephemera that the kids will love. Downtown, **Scarlett's Custom Framing and Gallery** (904-964-9353), 139 E Call St, deals in antique advertising and sheet music, as well as a fine selection of quilts. Open Thu–Sat.

Waldo

Waldo Antique Village (352-468-3111), US 301. Adjoining the flea market, this big barn full of antiques has been around for more than 20 years— the large farm implements outside are just a sample of the primitives and country items you'll find here. Bargain hunters can browse for hours through nearly 80 dealer booths with everything from classic rock albums to Vaseline glass glowing under fluorescent lamps. With multiple staircases running up and down the two floors inside the 24,000-square-foot building, it's a destination. Open daily.

GRAB GREAT ANTIQUE BARGAINS AT WALDO ANTIQUES

Waldo Farmer's and Flea Market
(352-468-2255; waldofarmersandflea
market.com), US 301. The reason to
stop in Waldo: a sprawling complex of
more than 800 vendors across 40 acres
on both sides of the highway, showcasing the best produce that North Florida has to offer. Sat and Sun 7–4.

**FARMER'S MARKETS, PRODUCE
STANDS, AND U-PICK** One thing
the Gainesville area is known for is
blueberries. I have friends who make
their annual pilgrimages every May
to pick their own at farms totaling
more than 700 acres of these tasty
natural treats. Much of this area is
rural, so you'll often see farmers selling
fruits and vegetables in-season at tem-
porary stands and off the backs of their
trucks.

Earlton
Growing their blueberries the organic
way, **Berry Bay Farm** (352-468-
2205), 20256 NE 114th Ave (CR
1469), is open for U-pick and pre-
picked blueberries from mid-May
through mid-June; call for directions.

Gainesville
Alachua County Farmer's Market
(352-371-8236; 441market.com), 5920
NW 13th St, corner of US 441 and FL
121. Fresh produce straight from local
farmers, Sat 8:30–1 or until everything
is sold.

Union Street Farmer's Market
(352-462-3192; unionstreetfarmersmkt
.com), downtown at the Hippodrome.
Local produce, baked goods, candles,
plants, and live acoustic music. Wed
4–7:30 PM.

Hawthorne
Brown's Farm (352-475-2015), FL 26
east of US 301. A permanent roadside
stand selling straight from the farm;
stop in for fresh honey, veggies, and
fruits, including strawberries, peaches,
and onions in-season.

Cross Creek Groves (352-481-2000;
crosscreekgroves.com), 6609 SE US
301, has grove-fresh oranges and
grapefruit in season—which they'll
ship anywhere for you—and tropical
fruits and wines year-round.

Run by a family who's grown citrus
locally since the Civil War ended, **The**

ROADSIDE AMERICANA AT THE WALDO FLEA MARKET

Orange Barn (theorangebarn.com), US 301, is one of the northernmost places in Florida to grab a big bag of fresh citrus.

High Springs
High Springs Farmer's Market (386-454-8145; farmersmarket.high springs.com), 25 SE Railroad St next to the railroad tracks downtown, has local vendors with seasonal fresh produce. Thu 2–6 PM.

Starke
In addition to the massive **Starke State Farmers' Market** (382-329-3713; florida-agriculture.com/market ing/markets/starke_market.htm), 2222 N Temple Hwy (US 301), and **Wainwright's Pecans, Produce, and Seafood** (904-964-5811), 302 N Temple Hwy, the bountiful produce of Bradford County (well known for its excellent strawberries) fills fruit and vegetable stands all along US 301 from Starke north to Lawtey. Some are permanent locations, like **Kings Kountry Produce** (904-964-2552), 18079 US 301 N, open daily; others are transient stands that show up during the growing season.

✳ Special Events
February: ♪ **Hoggtown Medieval Faire** (352-334-ARTS), at the Alachua County Fairgrounds, 39th Ave, Gainesville. The largest and longest-running (26 years in 2011) Renaissance Faire in Florida, the Hoggtown Medieval Faire spans two weekends each February with active participation by the Society for Creative Anachronism, a playful bunch that usually keep their events off-limits to the public. At Hoggtown more than a third of the crowd dresses in medieval drag; it's a place to get in touch with your inner knight (or princess), where wandering minstrels strum on mandolins; fairies, dwarves,

and witches roam the streets; and the vendors take "Lady Visa and Master Card." Kids will have a blast with street theater, magic shows, medieval carnival games, and manually powered amusement rides you won't see anywhere else, like the Barrel of Bedlam and the Hippogriff. Vendors include an alchemist with real charms, tarot readers and other mediums, and artisans crafting in fiber, wood, and wax. Even the food court is a little different: You'll see knights fresh off the battlefield toasting one another with cobalt bottles of frothing cherry ale. Daily events include jousting, live chess battles, and the court processional through the streets of Hoggtown. Fee.

March: **Spring Garden Festival**, Kanapaha Botanical Gardens (see *Botanical Garden*), Gainesville. A weekend's worth of gardening tips, landscaping tricks, and environmental awareness set in the beauty of this region's largest garden.

April: Remembering the movie filmed in Micanopy—and raising funds for Parkinson's research—**Doc Hollywood Days** (micanopychamber.com /doc_hollywood8.htm) includes a formal dinner, a crazy "Squash Festival" parade based on the movie, craft vendors, music, good food, and a health fair.

♪ **Farm & Forest Festival**, Morningside Nature Center (see *Nature Centers*), Gainesville, features cane grinding and other pioneer crafts, displays of fire engines, and hands-on activities for the kids.

May: **High Springs Pioneer Days** (386-454-3120; highsprings.com). Annual celebration of local history, arts and crafts, held the first weekend of the month.

Commemorate a noble vegetable at the **Windsor Zucchini Festival** (afn.org/~windsor/page2.htm), second weekend, Windsor.

June: **Yulee Day,** Archer, second Sat. Celebrating the birthday of David Levy Yulee, Florida's first U.S. senator and founder of the Florida Railroad, the town that was his home hosts exhibits, crafts, and vendors at the historic railroad depot.

October: Drift into the **Florida Butterfly Festival** (flmnh.ufl.edu/butterfly fest), Florida Museum of Natural History (see *Museums*), second weekend, for live native butterfly exhibits, a photography contest, lectures, field trips, and on-site vendors.

November: **Alachua County Fair** (352-372-1537), first week, at the fairgrounds on NE 39th Ave, Gainesville. A traditional county fair attracting farmers from around the region, showing off their cattle, chickens, vegetables, and more in friendly competition. Top country music acts and exhibitions from vendors; fee.

Micanopy Fall Harvest Festival (352-466-7026; micanopyfallfestival .org), Micanopy. Since 1973, this celebration of harvesttime brings together artisans, craftspeople, and musicians with more than 200 display booths throughout town.

ST. JOHNS RIVER

GREEN COVE SPRINGS, PALATKA, ORANGE PARK/CLAY & PUTNAM COUNTIES

T he St. Johns is one of only 14 rivers designated an American Heritage River. This top fishing spot covers 70 square miles of rivers and lakes, with many towns settled along its banks, most notably Jacksonville at the shallow ford closest to the river's mouth. Farther south on this north-flowing river, things get rustic and rural. Where the Timucua Indians once built villages on the riverbanks, anglers now slip past looking for quiet coves to spend the morning. Where settlers headed upriver to find suitable homesteads, there are now farms. Where steamboats once chugged upstream guiding tourists to Silver Springs and Sanford, Spanish moss sways from the branches of ancient cypress trees. Things are pretty quiet on this part of the St. Johns.

With its county seat of **Palatka** its prime destination, Putnam County spans both sides of the river at the southern end of North Florida, while Clay County hugs the western shore just south of Jacksonville, where **Orange Park**—founded in 1877 by developers from Boston atop plantations that, before the Civil War, flourished atop a Spanish land grant from 1780—is now a bustling suburb of Jacksonville along I-295. The rural communities of the region have long and storied histories, from Palatka's role in the Civil War to **Green Cove Springs**—a destination for wealthy northerners who wanted to "take the waters" for their health. On Lake Santa Fe, **Melrose** was established along the Bellamy Road in 1887, and you won't find a better place to study early Florida architecture: There are nearly 80 buildings in town on the National Register of Historic Places. At the north end of Lake Santa Fe, **Keystone Heights** shows off its 1920s charm.

GUIDANCE Clay County Tourism (claycountygov.com/Tourism) can help you with your travel planning for Orange Park, Green Cove Springs, Penney Farms, and Middleburg. In Palatka stop by the **Putnam County Chamber of Commerce** (386-328-1503; putnamcountychamber.org), 1100 Reid St, Palatka 32178.

GETTING THERE *By air:* **Jacksonville International Airport** (see the *Jacksonville* chapter) or **Gainesville Regional Airport** (see the *Gainesville & Vicinity* chapter) are the nearest major airports.

By bus: **Greyhound** (800-231-2222; greyhound.com).

By car: From Jacksonville, take **US 17** south of I-295. From the St. Augustine area, take **FL 16** from I-95 to Green Cove Springs. **FL 207** connects St. Augustine and Palatka.

By train: The **Amtrak** station in Palatka (800-872-7245; amtrak.com), 220 N 11th St, is one of the few remaining active passenger stations in North Florida. It's served by the Silver Service/Palmetto, which runs from New York City and Washington DC, to Jacksonville, Orlando, Tampa, and Miami.

GETTING AROUND US 17 runs from Orange Park south along the St. Johns River past Green Cove Springs into Palatka, where it crosses to the east side of the river and continues south through Crescent City, passing Welaka. **FL 19** heads south from Palatka along the west side of the St. Johns River to reach the Ocala National Forest. **FL 16** runs east–west from Green Cove Springs past Penney Farms and Camp Blanding in Starke to the Bradford county line. Take **FL 21** from Orange Park south to reach Middleburg and Keystone Heights. **FL 100** connects Palatka with Keystone Heights, or branch off onto **FL 26** to reach Melrose.

MEDICAL EMERGENCIES Orange Park Medical Center (904-276-8500; orangeparkmedical.com), 2001 Kingsley Ave, Orange Park. **Putnam Community Medical Center** (386-328-5711; pcmcfl.com), 611 Zeagler Dr off FL 20 W, Palatka.

✳ To See

ARCHAEOLOGICAL SITES Mount Royal Indian Temple Mound, along Mount Royal Rd (CR 309), Welaka, is believed to be the largest shell mound in the state. The 100-foot-high site of the Timucua Indian ceremonial ground dates back to AD 1200–1600. **Bubba Midden** is located on the east bank of Black

ALONG THE ST. JOHNS RIVER, GREEN COVE SPRINGS

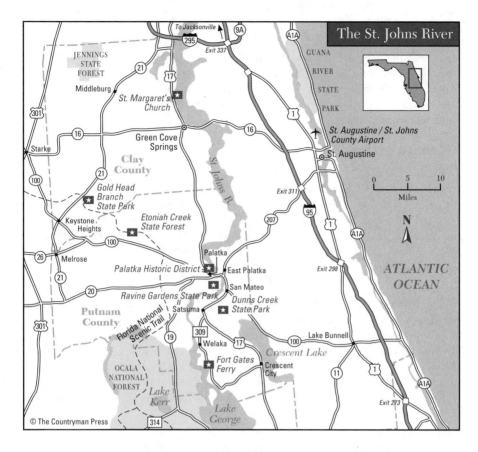

Creek, 2 miles north of its confluence with the St. Johns River in the vicinity of Hibernia, near Fleming Island.

ART GALLERIES Embracing performing and visual arts, the **Florida School of the Arts** (386-328-1571; floarts.org), 5001 St. Johns Ave, has gallery space showcasing local artists in its downtown location, Palatka.

Serving as a public library until the 1980s, the **Larimer Arts Center** (386-328-8998; artsinputnam.org/gallery.html), 216 Reid St, Palatka, is now the home of the Arts Council of Greater Palatka and the council's monthly exhibits. The gallery is open Thu and Fri 1–5, Sat 10–2. **Melrose Bay Gallery** (352-375-3866; melrose bayartgallery.com), 103 FL 26, Melrose, represents fine regional artists in a variety of media. Open Sat 10–6, Sun noon–5 or by appointment.

FOLKLORE While traveling through the small community of Bardin off FL 100, peer into the piney woods and look closely; you might just catch a glimpse of the **Bardin Booger**. Local legend has it that a giant, shaggy-haired creature, much like the elusive Sasquatch, was first sighted in the mid-1980s. Said to smell much like rotting cabbage and stand 13 feet tall, the ape-like creature has been touted as

Northeast Florida's Bigfoot. The Bardin Booger was immortalized in the late Billy Crain's "Bardin Booger" song, which is still played at many festivals and events along with the occasional appearance of the Booger itself. The curious and disbelievers can view a scrapbook filled with news clippings and illustrations at **Bud's Store** (386-328-4257), 341 Bardin Rd, the Bardin community gathering spot. You'll also find Jody Delzell's 1995 book *The Enigmatic Bardin Booger* at Andrea's Book Store in Palatka.

HISTORIC SITES

Crescent City
Charles & Emily Cheatham House, 102 Main St. Emphasizing horizontal planes and wide eaves, this Prairie-style home showcases the American architectural style of Frank Lloyd Wright. Henry G. Hubbard, who was the first to bring the camphor tree and Japanese persimmon to Florida, built the **Hubbard House**, 600 N Park St. Now a private residence, the circa-1879 dwelling is surrounded by elaborate gardens.

Hibernia
A long drive down a narrow dirt road is richly rewarded when you reach the quaint **St. Margaret's Episcopal Church** (904-284-3030; stmargaretsfl.org), Old Church Rd. George Fleming emigrated from Ireland and established Hibernia (Latin for "Ireland") Plantation on the 1,000 acres now known as Fleming Island. The church, a gift for his wife, Margaret Seton Fleming, was completed in 1878. With only 50 seats, the Gothic-style sanctuary requires three services on Sun. The annual Tour and Tea (see *Special Events*) re-creates the Civil War era with guided tours of the plantation grounds; high tea is served.

Interlachen
The quaint 1892 **Interlachen Town Hall** (386-684-3811), 311 Atlantic Ave, on the National Register of Historic Places, was the social center in the early 1900s, holding such town hall activities as dances, ladies' society meetings, and voting—events it hosts to this day.

HISTORIC ST. MARGARET'S EPISCOPAL CHURCH, HIBERNIA

Keystone Heights
Keystone Beach (see *Swimming*) dates back to 1928, with its historic bathhouse and dance hall perched on Lake Keystone.

Melrose
Boasting one of the highest concentrations of historic sites in Florida, with 79 classic homes and businesses, **Melrose** is a town where history is part of everyday life. Many buildings are more than a century old but remain well kept and occupied as residences; see *Walking Tours* for how to explore local history.

GREEN COVE SPRINGS

Green Cove Spring and Swimming Pool, Magnolia Ave & Walnut St, a popular tourist destination in the late 1800s, is thought to be Florida's first therapeutic mineral springs. A decorative railing surrounds the clean and clear spring, about 20 feet in diameter, set amid tall oaks and palm trees. You can look down about 31 feet, where it tapers to a narrow entrance into the cavern. This section is out of sight, but it opens to 25 feet wide and descends another 150 feet before flowing toward the St. Johns River. The spring keeps the neighboring 50-by-100-foot swimming pool at a constant 72 degrees year-round, then overflows down a stream about 300 feet to the St. Johns. You'll note the sulfurous odor, but the water is safe for swimming and at one time was bottled as drinking water. The spring is open year-round; swimming in the pool is allowed only during summer months. The centerpiece of downtown, the spring and pool are now part of Spring Park (see *Parks*), which surrounds the stream and outflow.

SOAK IN A SPRING-FED POOL AT HISTORIC GREEN COVE SPRINGS

Middleburg

Middleburg Methodist Church Cemetery and the 1847 **Middleburg United Methodist Church** are next to the Middleburg Historical Museum (see *Museums*).

Orange Park

The grounds of **Club Continental** (see *Lodging*) evoke an era when travel to Florida meant settling in for the season. Built in 1923 as Mira Rio, a grand estate for the heir of the Palmolive Soap Company, it morphed into classy accommodations a

BRONSON-MULHOLLAND HOUSE

Just the grounds of the 1854 **Bronson-Mulholland House** (386-329-0140), 100 Madison St, whisk your thoughts back to the Civil War and its complexities along the St. Johns River, but ah, if walls could talk. Inside this grand antebellum plantation home, the finery of the past—including exquisite furnishings and art—is full of tales, as is your docent. The Greek Revival mansion sat upon a land grant, a plantation known as Sunny Point that encompassed what is now Palatka, and was one of the first residences built in the region, with a once-sweeping view of the St. Johns River. Built for Judge Isaac Bronson, one of Florida's first circuit judges, it is where the city of Palatka was born, prompted by Judge Bronson's request. Abandoned during the Civil War, it was occupied by both sides as a command post at different times. In 1866, it became a school for freed slave children, and during both world wars it served as a Red Cross center. Now owned by the city of Palatka and beautifully restored, it is open for tours thanks to the efforts of the Putnam County Historical Society, who ensured the home was saved. Their museum (see *Museums*) sits next door. Open Tue, Thu, and Sun 2–5.

THE BRONSON-MULLHOLLAND HOUSE, AN ANTEBELLUM PLANTATION HOME IN PALATKA

generation later. Next door, their wedding venue, **Winterbourne**, is one of the oldest remaining homes in the area, built in 1870.

Since 1921, the Loyal Order of Moose at **Moosehaven** (904-278-1210; moose haven.org), 1701 Park Ave has been a part of the Orange Park community. The fraternal organization dedicated to bettering the lives of children and the elderly, along with helping their communities, donated many sites and buildings, which are now the town hall, fire station, and library, to the town of Orange Park. The retirement community resides on 63 acres along the St. Johns River and has its own chapel, library, and a state-of-the-art assisted-living health care center.

Palatka

Built by the Atlantic Coast Line in 1908, the **Historic Union Station** (see *Railroadiana*) showcases the architectural style of H. H. Richardson with its random window openings and hexagonal dormered bays.

The Georgian-style **Tilghman House** (386-325-8750), 324 River St, built around 1887, now operates as the home of the Palatka Art League. Note the half-gabled veranda supported by Greek Doric columns and the Palladian window in the gable dormer. Open Mon–Fri 9–5.

Penney Farms

Founded as a retirement community "for Christian people whose lives had been devoted to Christian service" by businessman J. C. Penney, **Penney Farms** dates back to 1927. It is centered on the **J. C. Penney Memorial Church** (904-529-9078), which at the time was surrounded by 98 cottage apartments. Southern magnolias were planted in rows along FL 16; they now form a spectacular canopy as you drive through Penney Farms, which still thrives under its original mission.

MURALS Pick up a map at the Putnam County Chamber of Commerce (see *Guidance*) and stroll through the "Mural City of Northeast Florida" seeking out the murals scattered throughout the downtown historic district. These building-sized, breathtaking murals beautifully depict the history, landscape, and culture of **Palatka**. Among them, you'll find a cattle drive, a St. Johns River steamboat, sailboats from the annual Mug Race, and a collection of identified wildflowers. Look for the tiny gray church mouse in the Billy Graham mural (it's on the church porch).

MUSEUMS

Crescent City

The Crescent City Women's Club takes on a labor of love filling the **Little Blue House Heritage Museum and Art Center** (386-698-4711), 602 N Summit St, with pieces of the past. The former home, dating back to 1871, showcases the history and art of South Putnam. Open Tue–Sat 2:30–5.

Green Cove Springs

& Local history is well documented at the **Clay County Historical Museum** (904-284-9644), 915 Walnut St. And with the addition of the Railroad collection you'll enjoy the collection of photographs, fine china and silverware, timetables, bells and whistles, step boxes, and baggage tags once part of the Clay Street Hill Railroad. Look for Phantom Train ACL 76. Open Sun 2–5 or by appointment. Free, donations appreciated.

Keystone Heights

On 170,000 acres of sand pine and scrub oak in the heart of the Florida wilderness, Camp Blanding was home to 800,000 World War II soldiers from 1940 to 1945. Nine infantry divisions prepared for conflict in ankle-deep sand on arguably one of the toughest training grounds anywhere. The **Camp Blanding Museum**

and Memorial Park (904-682-3196; campblanding-museum.org), Starke, is dedicated to these soldiers but also honors all who served in Korea, Vietnam, and Desert Storm. The newest addition is the Black Soldiers Memorial Park, dedicated in 1998. Life at Camp Blanding during the 1940s is depicted in the museum through colorful displays of weaponry, photos, memorabilia, and even a life-sized bunkhouse. In the Memorial Park, monuments honor the original nine army infantry divisions and the 508th Parachute Infantry Regiment; several World War II aircraft and vehicles are on display. Actors Demi Moore and Viggo Mortensen worked long hours in the harsh environment during the filming of *GI Jane*, and real military drill instructors put 16 civilians through basic training for TV's *Boot Camp*. The current site, now reduced to about 73,000 acres, continues to train members of the U.S. National Guard, Active Army, and Army Reserves from all over the United States. The museum gift shop has a fine selection of books, pins, and patches. Open noon–4 daily.

Middleburg

The **Hilltop Black Heritage Education Center** (904-282-7658), Longmire Ave at Hunter-Douglas Park, is a sensitive and thought-provoking view of Black culture during the late 1800s displayed in a one-room schoolhouse.

Photographs and displays of the early turpentine, timber, and phosphate industries depict one of the oldest continuous communities in Florida at the **Middleburg Historical Museum** (904-282-5924), 3912 Section St. Open Sun 2–4. Donations appreciated.

Palatka

Originally part of Fort Shannon during the Seminole Indian Wars (1832–1845), the **Putnam Historic Museum** (386-325-9825), 100 Madison St, is the oldest dwelling in the Palatka area. Open Tue, Thu, and Sun 2–5.

RAILROADIANA All aboard at the **Historic Union Station** (386-329-5538) and *✍ **David Browning Railroad Museum** (386-328-0305; railsofpalatka.org), 222 N 11th St, Palatka, managed by the Palatka Railroad Preservation Society at the corner of 11th and Reid. The Union Depot is open daily with railroad memorabilia, historical documents, and photographs of the Palatka area. But you'll want to plan your visit when all the members run their trains at the Browning Museum—on the first Sun and third Sat of the month. Look for the 31-foot HO-scale model train, one of the longest in the world, chugging along the tracks for the enjoyment of young and old. The museum is open daily. Stop in the **Clay County History Museum** (see *Museums*) to see their extensive display of railroad ephemera from the Atlantic Coast Line.

✳ To Do

AGRICULTURAL TOURS Working with Jacksonville's sister city of Masan, Korea, **Jaxma Orchids** (904-284-4442; jaxma.com), 6440 US 17 S, south of FL 16, grows and distributes six different types of orchids, including *Phalaenopsis* and *Dendrobium*. Their 110,000-square-foot greenhouses are open for public viewing Mon–Fri 8–5, Sat 10–4; free.

Learn about warm-water fish production and native Florida fish conservation at the **Welaka National Fish Hatchery** (386-467-2374; fws.gov/welaka), CR 309,

THE WELAKA FISH HATCHERY

Welaka. The facility, built in 1926, now focuses on breeding and restoration of Gulf Coast striped bass. Open daily 7–4; guided group tours. Free.

BICYCLING No matter whether you normally ride city streets or rough and rural, several great off-road touring and mountain bike paths can be found throughout the county. The Northeast Regional Planning Council (904-363-6350; nefrpc.org /publicationsSub/bike.htm) produces **Bikeways of Northeast Florida**, Clay and Putnam counties, which can be picked up at parks in the region or downloaded from their website. Near Fleming Island, there is a nice **paved bicycle path** paralleling US 17 from Doctors Lake south about 7 miles; or you can veer off onto Pine Ave for views of the St. Johns River. For off-roaders, head to the rolling sandhills of **Gold Head Branch State Park** (see *Parks*), then down FL 21 to CR 352 for a leisurely lakeside ride. For a challenge, start at the Maintenance Building on Putnam County Blvd in East Palatka and head west on FL 207A, traveling 17.8 miles through riverfront farmlands and neighborhoods reflecting rural Florida. The trail ends at Federal Point Rd.

If you're up for a ride being your vacation this year, Gainesville-based tour operator **Bike Florida** (bikeflorida.org) leads multiday guided, supported tours on the vast **St. Johns River-to-Sea Loop**, a 260-mile bike route from Palatka to St. Augustine and points as far south as Titusville, with many Old Florida communities to visit along the way.

BIRDING Hundreds of osprey nests top the trees and beacon markers along the St. Johns River. Great blue herons and snowy egrets are a common sight along the banks, especially around the fish camps. The roadside observation tower at the **Welaka National Fish Hatchery** (see *Agricultural Tours*) provides excellent viewing, in winter and spring, of sandhill cranes, southern bald eagles, and a variety of egrets and herons. The **Welaka State Forest** (see *Wild Places*) Mud Trail is a good place to see woodpeckers, Osceola turkeys, and owls. Thousands of azaleas bloom in spring, making **Ravine Gardens State Park** (see *Garden*) a great place to view cedar waxwings, cardinals, hummingbirds, and a variety of butterflies. View limpkins, gallinules, anhingas, and white ibises at the Rodman Recreation Area off US 19 in the **Ocala National Forest** (see *Wild Places*), which is home, in its vast strands of longleaf pine between Rodman and Lake Delancy, to colonies of endangered red-cockaded woodpeckers.

BOATING Dock Holiday Boat Rentals (904-215-5363; dockholidayboatrentals .com), 3108 US 17 S, Fleming Island, provides weekend-long rentals for fishing boats and pontoon boats at $185 for half a day. Want to try out a houseboat? They have them, too, 41-foot Gibson houseboats complete with air-conditioning and bedding for eight, starting at $750 for a mini weekend. Be sure to reserve well in advance of your trip.

& **River Adventures** (866-OUR-BOAT; riveradventuresinc.com), Crystal Cove Marina, Georgetown. Motor down the St. Johns River while living on board a 60-foot luxury houseboat. Stretch out on the sundeck, then slip down the waterslide for quick refreshment. These large houseboats sleep 8 to 10 comfortably. Take it out for a weekend or a week, $1,775 and up. Just want to try one on for size? You can stay overnight, docked at the marina, for a different kind of accommodation, $50 per person (four-person minimum) per night.

Welaka Charters (386-559-1957; welakacharters.com) 10 Boston St, Welaka, focuses on boat rentals for your exploration of the St. Johns, either by pontoon or with a fishing boat—with a Triton bass boat available for the enthusiast. Reserve for a half or full day, $100–200.

On Doctors Lake, **Whitey's Fish Camp** (see *Eating Out*) rents 14-foot boats for fishing on the lake—$15–20 without a motor, $45–65 with one.

THE KIRKPATRICK DAM AT RODMAN RECREATION AREA IS A MAJOR DESTINATION FOR ANGLERS

DRIVING TOURS Fans of Lynyrd Skynyrd will want to find **Brickyard Road** in Green Cove Springs, where Ronnie Van Zant lived before his untimely death. Unfortunately, other fans kept stealing the sign, so the county erected a concrete pillar with the street name painted on it.

Pick up *A Driving Tour of Putnam County* to explore the scenic byways in the area; the brochure does a great job of linking together sites of cultural and historical interest. See *Scenic Drives* for more ideas.

FISHING While the **St. Johns River** is well known for its bass fishing, and the **Rodman Reservoir** draws a

FERRYBOAT

A narrows in the St. Johns River attracted settlers back to the area of Fort
Gates, a Seminole War outpost, in 1856, where a cluster of historic homes
sits beneath the canopy of ancient oaks on the western shore. A crossing
was needed to the eastern shore, and so the ferry began. The **Fort Gates
Ferry** is a one-of-a-kind experience, a classic 1910 Sharpie sailboat piloting
a 1930s barge, its route saving nearly 60 miles of driving. It can hold up to
two cars side by side, and drifts softly across the cypress-lined river as
ospreys wheel overhead and you slip back in time. I'll warn you—the roads
to the ferry through the Ocala National Forest are not kind to your car; however, now that the ferry is part of the Florida Black Bear Scenic Byway (see
Scenic Drives), I'd imagine upkeep of the clay and sand roads will be more
frequent. Ferry crossings are on demand, 7–5:30, closed Tue, $10 per car. It
operates out of the Gateway Fish Camp (see *Fish Camps*) on the eastern
shore. If you arrive and the ferry is on the other side of the river, pull up on
the loading ramp and turn on your headlights.

FLORIDA'S OLDEST FERRYBOAT, THE FORT GATES FERRY

crowd daily at the George Kirkpatrick Dam outflow, don't pass up the deep waters
of **Crescent Lake**. Often neglected by anglers, this 12-mile body of water quickly
drops from the 3-foot shoreline flats to depths reaching 14 feet. You may want a
depth finder to locate the 12- and 13-pound bass lurking under the tea-stained
water, or catch them as they move to the shallows to feed in such places as Shell
Bluff and Sling Shot Creek. When fishing Crescent Lake, stop by **Leonard's
Landing/Lake Crescent Resort** (386-698-2485; lakecrescentfl.com), 100 Grove
Ave, Crescent City (see *Fish Camps*), for all your bait, tackle, and marine needs.

Off CR 309 several marinas and fish camps (see *Fish Camps*) lead down to the St. Johns River; bait and tackle is plentiful, and you can rent boats and find local guides.

GAMING Live greyhound racing and poker rooms are at the **Jacksonville Kennel Club** (904-680-3647; jaxkennel.com), 20455 Park Ave, Orange Park.

GOLF Adjoining Ravine Gardens State Park (see *Garden*), the **Palatka Golf Club** (386-329-0141; palatkagolfclub.com), 1715 Moseley Ave, is a Donald Ross–designed gem from 1925. Tee off with a sense of history as you enjoy 9 or 18 holes on rolling terrain, $15–30.

HIKING With so many wild places (see *Wild Places*) throughout the region, this is an excellent area for backpackers and day hikers to roam during hiking season, Oct–Apr. The common thread through many public lands is the **Florida Trail** (see *What's Where*), as the 1,400-mile National Scenic Trail slips through forests and swamps on its way between the Ocala National Forest and the Suwannee River. My favorite segments include hiking through a cathedral of longleaf pines between Lake Delancy West (see *Camping & Cabins*) and Rodman Reservoir (see *Fishing*); walking beneath ancient cypress along Rice Creek; standing on the bluffs above Etoniah Creek; and taking the trail across Gold Head Branch State Park (see *Parks*). Both Rice Creek Conservation Area and Etoniah Creek State Forest offer screened camping shelters for backpackers. For day hiking, don't miss the beautiful Fern Loop at the bottom of the ravine in Gold Head Branch State Park, the stroll to Mud Spring in Welaka State Forest, and the rugged, botanically diverse loop around Black Creek Ravines (see *Wild Places*).

OFF-ROADING With more than 125 miles of designated off-road trails looping through the northern part of the Ocala National Forest (see *Wild Places*), the **Ocala North OHV Trail System** is a major destination for ATV enthusiasts. The system is made up of the Motorcycle Loops, 14 miles for off-road dirt bikes only; 35 miles more just for unlicensed vehicles less than 50 inches wide; and 76 miles where jeeps and other all-terrain licensed vehicles can snake through the woods on narrow tracks. A three-day pass is $10, $5 for drivers under 15; annual pass $75.

PADDLING **Black Creek** meanders through Middleburg for many miles from Jennings State Forest toward the St. Johns River at Hibernia, with put-ins at Black Creek Park along US 17 at Hibernia and at Master Sergeant John E. Hayes Memorial Park along Main St in Middleburg [30.072775, -81.852475] beyond the historic district. One of the wildest scenic waterways in the region, the **Ocklawaha River** will take you back to a time when steamboats puffed their way up the St. Johns to visit Silver Springs. Cypress-lined and winding, it can be accessed at two points in the northern part of the Ocala National Forest—a dirt ramp on the west side of the George Kirkpatrick Dam at Rodman Reservoir, Kirkpatrick Dam Rd, and at the bridge farther along FL 19 south.

SCENIC DRIVES Paralleling the St. Johns River, FL 13 and CR 13 are designated the William Bartram Scenic Highway, passing through farmland and river bottom between Hastings and Jacksonville. Although most of its route is south of

Putnam County, the **Florida Black Bear Scenic Byway** (floridablackbearscenic byway.org), a national scenic byway, extends up into the Ocala National Forest to Buckman Lock and across the Fort Gates Ferry (see *Ferryboat*) to loop back down through Welaka to Volusia County.

SWIMMING Revive yourself in a chemical-free community pool: The constant 72-degree water of **Green Cove Springs** (see *Historic Sites*) feeds directly into the pool and then out to the St. Johns River, ensuring clean, mineral-rich water at all times. The pool is open only during summer months. Step back in time at **Keystone Beach** (352-473-7847; keystoneheights.us), 565 S Lawrence Blvd, Keystone Heights. Established in 1924, it's a place where you can splash around on a sandy beach outside the historic bathhouse on Lake Geneva, and has one heck of a wooden playground for the kids to lose themselves in. Fee.

WALKING TOURS The Clay County Historical Society (904-284-3615; clay countyhistoricalsociety.org) provides guided tours through two historic districts on the National Register of Historic Places. You'll find 85 structures in the **Green Cove Springs Historic District**, mostly around Walnut St and bounded by Bay St, the CSX railroad tracks, Center St, Orange Ave, St. Elcom St, and the St. Johns River. There are a dozen buildings in the Middleburg Historical District along Main and Wharf streets.

The *Historic Melrose 125 Years: A Celebration Tour* brochure outlines a walking tour of the 79 historic sites in town, from businesses to private homes, churches, and cemeteries, in the **Melrose Historic District**. I found the brochure while visiting the Micanopy Historical Society Museum (see the *Gainesville & Vicinity* chapter), but you may want to write to Historic Melrose (afn.org/~mbca/hmi .html), P.O. Box 704, Melrose 32666, for a copy. Or just explore on your own: Amble down the narrow back streets (many unpaved) along the Lake Santa Fe chain of lakes on foot or by car to see genteel homes set in lush landscaping under ancient live oaks.

The "Golden Age" is beautifully represented in **Crescent City**, whose streets are lined with ornately decorated Victorian architecture under a generous canopy of live oaks. A brochure, detailing the location of 20 of these historical homes (see *Historic Sites* for two examples), churches, and commercial buildings, is available from Crescent City (904-698-2525; crescentcity-fl.com), 115 N Summit St, with a virtual tour online.

Seek out the many murals (see *Murals*) and extensive Victorian architecture in historic downtown Palatka. The city boasts several historic districts, including the **North Historic District**, where the Bronson-Mulholland House (see *Historic Sites*) is located; the **South Historic District**, which includes residences that once served as hotels; and the **Central Business District**, where you'll see fine commercial architecture. Pick up *Palatka and Putnam County Through the Ages*, a detailed walking and driving tour brochure, at the Putnam County Chamber of Commerce (see *Guidance*).

✳ Green Space

BEACHES The sandy beach and crystal-clear water at ❧ **Keystone Beach** (see *Swimming*) make this a great inland spot for swimming, snorkeling, and catching some rays. You'll also find a swimming beach on **Little Lake Johnson** at Gold Head Branch State Park (see *Parks*) and on spring-fed **Lake Kingsley** (see *Camping & Cabins*) at Camp Blanding.

GARDEN Home of the Florida Azalea Festival, ✍ & **Ravine Gardens State Park** (386-329-3721; floridastateparks.org/ravinegardens), 1600 Twigg St, Palatka, is one of Florida's finest places to see spring put on a show. Constructed in and around a steephead ravine by the Civilian Conservation Corps in 1933 with 250,000 ornamental plants and 95,000 azaleas, it was Palatka's first and foremost tourist attraction. Drive 1.8 miles around the rim of the ravines through canopies of live oaks surrounded by thick blankets of tropical and subtropical flora, or stroll the walkways through the 182-acre park, where the kids will love bouncing across the swaying pedestrian suspension bridges. A rose garden and a collection of unusual plants, including endemic East Palatka holly and a double-trunked cabbage palm, are at the top next to the visitors center and parking areas. Open daily 8 AM–sunset; fee.

GREENWAY A segment of the **Cross Florida Greenway** (dep.state.fl.us/gwt/cfg) straddles Buckman Lock on the Cross Florida Barge Canal and continues down toward Rodman Reservoir, hugging both shores of the reservoir and the Upper Ocklawaha River. On the south side of the canal, the Florida Trail (see *What's Where*) connects Buckman Lock with the George Kirkpatrick Dam area before heading deep into the Ocala National Forest. Rodman Campground (see *Camping & Cabins*) along Kirkpatrick Dam Rd is a popular campground for exploring the north end of the forest.

PARKS A relatively wild place, **Dunns Creek State Park** (386-329-3721; florida stateparks.org/dunnscreek), 320 Sisco Rd, Pomona Park, protects sandhills and scrub along a sharp bend in the St. Johns River. Stop for a picnic, or follow the 1.5-mile nature trail to Blue Pond.

Mike Roess Gold Head Branch State Park (352-473-4701; floridastateparks .org/goldhead), 6239 FL 21, Keystone Heights, centers on an incredible ravine dripping with ferns, from which the sand-bottomed Gold Head Branch is born. Nature trails let you climb down into the deep ravine and follow the stream's course to Little Lake Johnson, where you can grab a canoe and paddle across the expanse. Three miles of the Florida Trail (see *What's Where*) pass through the park, with a primitive campsite along the way; developed camping and cabins from the Civilian Conservation Corps era are also available.

SPRINGS The spring and pool are the focal point of this pretty little park on the edge of the St. Johns River, but the view from the spring at **Spring Park** (904-529-2200), **Green Cove Springs**, looks out over the St. Johns River, making this a great place for picnics. Gentle breezes blow through the shady canopy of tall and graceful live oaks covering the children's play area. A truly wild place, **Mud Spring** in Welaka State Forest (see *Wild Places*) shimmers like an underwater garden, an aquatic pool teeming with life.

WILD PLACES This region is a place for wilderness, with vast tracts of public land protecting the watersheds of tributaries feeding the St. Johns River. The granddaddy of them all is the **Ocala National Forest** (352-236-0288; fs.usda .gov/ocala), occupying the southwest end of Putnam County south of Palatka and providing recreation of all types. Covering more than 400,000 acres, the forest extends across four counties. In this region, popular recreation sites include the Rodman Reservoir and Kirkpatrick Dam (see *Fishing*); the Florida Trail (see *Hiking*); the Ocklawaha River (see *Paddling*); and a vast system of OHV trails stretching from Rodman Reservoir to Salt Springs, with trailheads at Rodman and along FL 19 south.

Bayard Point Conservation Area (904-529-2380), FL 16, Green Cove Springs. Access this 10,000-acre preserve from the John P. Hall Sr. Nature Preserve entrance off FL 16 near the St. Johns River Bridge to follow the trails through pine flatwoods and scrub out to a beautiful campsite on the banks of the St. Johns River. It's a popular place for trail riding and fishing, and it's used for environmental education classes for the local school district. Free.

If you've always wanted to see pitcher plants in bloom, stop at **Black Creek Ravines Conservation Area** (904-269-6378), Green Rd north of CR 218, Middleburg, and walk the trails out to the vast bogs beneath the high-tension lines. The reason for this preserve, however, is the rugged terrain—bluffs up to 90 feet above sea level, deeply cut with ravines that channel rainwater down to Black Creek. Primitive camping, biking, and horseback riding are permitted; bring your camera for the showy parade of spring wildflowers! Free.

Dunns Creek Conservation Area (386-529-2380), off FL 100 south of San Mateo, has a splendid array of bog wildflowers along its trails in spring; there's one primitive campsite.

Etoniah Creek State Forest (386-329-2552), FL 100 N, Florahome, protects one of Florida's most beautiful ravines at Etoniah Creek, where hikers can look down a 40-foot bluff to see tapegrass waving in the current of the stream at the bottom; visit in springtime, when the azaleas and dogwoods put on a show. The Florida Trail (see *Hiking*) runs through the state forest, with designated campsites and a screened-room camping shelter at Iron Bridge. Fee.

Jennings State Forest (904-291-5530; fl-dof.com/state_forests/jennings.html), 1337 Long Horn Rd, Middleburg. Popular with equestrians for its dozens of miles of riding trails, this high-and-dry forest amid the sandhills outside Jacksonville also offers several hiking trails; try out the Fire & Water Nature Trail for an interpretive introduction to the habitats found here, including seepage slopes with pitcher plants. The North Fork Black Creek Trail offers primitive camping within a stone's throw of the waterway. Fee.

Murphy Creek Conservation Area (386-329-4883), CR 309-B, is a two-part preserve with a loop trail through floodplain forest off Buffalo Bluff Rd, near Welaka, and a loop trail on Murphy Island, leading to rare high bluffs above the St. Johns River, accessible only by boat; camping permitted. Free.

Rice Creek Conservation Area (386-329-4404) is a very special preserve off FL 100 N, 3 miles west of Palatka. From the new trailhead, follow the main road back to the T-intersection and turn right to find the Florida Trail (see *Hiking*). A 2-mile blue-blazed loop follows impoundments built in the 1700s by British settlers who scraped an indigo and rice plantation from the floodplain forest; dozens of bridges carry you across blackwater waterways between ancient cypresses. Free.

Welaka State Forest (386-467-2388; fl-dof.com/state_forests/welaka.html), CR 309 south of Welaka, is one of the best places in the area for an overnight camp-out. Grab your backpack and walk 4 miles along the Johns Landing Trail to one of two spectacular primitive campsites right on the St. Johns River. Or take the kids on an easy stroll through the floodplain forest on the nature trail at the fire tower, or along the short Mud Spring Trail to see Mud Spring, a crystal-clear garden of aquatic plants. Fee.

✳ Lodging

BED & BREAKFASTS

Green Cove Springs 32043

Take in the cool river breeze of the St. Johns while sitting on the veranda of an 1887 inn on the National Register of Historic Places. Just across from the Green Cove Springs (see *Historic Sites*) is the **River Park Inn Bed & Breakfast** (904-284-2994; riverparkinn .com), 103 S Magnolia Ave. During its heyday in the late 1800s and early 1900s, the spring was a mecca for wealthy tourists. This three-story Frame Vernacular home is just one of the "cottages" built to accommodate the well-heeled crowd. Five guest rooms, all with private bath, feature vintage decor. The Master Suite has a two-person Jacuzzi and sitting room. A part of the historic district, the inn is within easy walking of the fishing pier, antiques shopping, dining, and movies. Rooms with breakfast $94–210.

HOTELS, MOTELS & RESORTS

Palatka 32177

🐾 🐕 ♿ (⌖) There aren't a lot of hotel choices in Palatka, but the **Sleep Inn & Suites** (866-538-0187; sleepinn.com /hotel-palatka-florida-FL906), 3805 Reid St, comes highly recommended from friends looking for a good night's sleep after days of backpacking in the Ocala National Forest. Located along FL 19 on the west side of town, it provides easy access to nearby natural lands. It's a newer property with the typical amenities, including deluxe continental breakfast, mini fridge, microwave, and coffeemaker. Add in the swimming pool, laundry room, popcorn in the lobby, and DVD player in your room (with free DVDs from the front office), and you might just get those non-campers in your family down here to enjoy the outdoors. $80–99.

CAMPING & CABINS

Keystone Heights 32656

🐾 🐕 ♿ ↝ One of North Florida's top getaways for camping is **Gold Head Branch State Park** (see *Parks*), thanks to two expansive campgrounds, lots of trails to roam, paddling and swimming on Little Lake Johnson, and their proximity to the eager-to-get-outdoors Jacksonville crowd. Campsites and cabins (800-326-3521; floridastate parks.reserveamerica.com), including some original CCC beauties, range $20–100; some cabins are wheelchair-accessible.

Lake Kingsley 32091

🐕 Fish, swim, or just lounge around at **Kingsley Beach RV Park Camp-ground & Resort** (904-533-2006), 6003 Kingsley Lake Dr, off FL 16. There's a lot to do at this family-oriented 30-acre park. Scuba lessons, banana boat rides, paddleboats, and Jet Skis are just some of the water amenities on this clear blue lake. If you don't want to cook, the restaurant serves all three meals. Bait-and-tackle shop, game room, and live outdoor entertainment. RV sites and furnished cabins.

IN ORANGE PARK

🦐 ♂️ 📶 While it bills itself as a bed & breakfast, the **Club Continental and River Suites** (800-877-6070 or 904-264-6070; clubcontinental.com), 2143 Astor St 32073, is so much more. Walk amid the splendor of the carefully manicured gardens and fountains set in intimate courtyards. Towering centuries-old live oaks bend to frame the three swimming pools. The tropical courtyard invites you to step inside and soak in the elegance of the past. Still owned by the same family after several generations, this historic 27-acre estate centers on a top-notch private, members-only dining club that you get to enjoy as an overnight guest. There are seven rooms in the former Mira Rio, a Mediterranean Revival gem built in 1923 for Palmolive Soap Company heir Caleb Johnson at the cost of more than $700,000, an extravagant retirement retreat. In the 1940s the family rented out rooms to airmen at the nearby Jacksonville Naval Air Station, including Joe Kennedy. It was Fredrica Massee, however, along with her husband, Jon, who oversaw the restoration of the property, opened the private dining club—where executive chef Sheldon Harris now presides over an ever-changing menu featuring the freshest seafood, meats, and local produce—and added the River Suites, 15 spacious suites directly on the St. Johns River, each with a European flair. The original rooms, upstairs from the dining club, are themed around classic travel destinations that guests in the 1920s might have visited on their grand tours, such as Spain, France, and Mexico, with antiques and decor to suit. Wedding parties are a specialty, with an 1870 home, Winterbourne, used for weddings and receptions. Rooms include continental breakfast, $99 and up.

A STAY AT CLUB CONTINENTAL EVOKES THE ROARING 20S ALONG THE ST. JOHNS RIVER

Palatka 32134

On Lake Delancy in the Ocala National Forest (see *Wild Places*), two campgrounds cater to different camping crowds. Open year-round, **Lake Delancy West** is a launch point for ATVs onto the Ocala North OHV Trail System through the forest, and sits within an easy walk of the Florida Trail (see *Hiking*). Shaded sites look out onto the lake. No hookups, small campers and tents only, 30 sites at $6 per site plus $6 day-use fee; portable toilets. On the east side of the lake, the seasonally open (Oct–June) **Lake Delancy East** has no nearby trails, so it's focused on fishing, boating, and relaxing. There are 29 sites at $10 per site, no hookups, portable toilets; small trailers and tents only. Both are accessed off FL 19; watch for signs south of the Ocklawaha River.

On the Cross Florida Greenway, **Rodman Campground** (800-326-3521 or 386-326-2846), Kirkpatrick Dam Rd, has 43 full-hookup campsites tucked under the pines and oaks not far from Rodman Reservoir. Tent campers can choose a primitive site; there's a bathhouse nearby. Long-distance hikers on the Florida Trail (see *Hiking*) often leave cars here for safekeeping; call the local number for rules and cost.

San Mateo 32187

Set along the St. Johns River, **Lynchs Landing** (386-546-0546; lynchslanding rvpark.com), 129 Troupe Rd off US 17, has a place for you to park your trailer under the trees and walk over to their dock to fish; 30-amp hookups, free cable TV included, $30 night/$330 month.

FISH CAMPS

Crescent City

Quiet and rustic, the **Gateway Fish Camp** (386-467-2411), 229 Fort Gates Ferry Rd 32139, is located in the heart of bass fishing country, between Little Lake George and Lake George. Stay in the air-conditioned cottages, complete with stove, where you can fry up your catch of the day. Fish off the private boat ramp or take to the river in a rental boat. Cottages $35–50 daily, $210–300 weekly. Rental boats $35 a day. You can also pitch your tent for $10. It's also the gateway to the Ocala National Forest via the Fort Gates Ferry (see *Ferryboat*), which they operate.

Leonard's Landing/Lake Crescent Resort (386-698-2485; lakecrescentfl .com), 100 Grove Ave 32112, sits on the west side of the largely undeveloped Crescent Lake (see *Fishing*). It's here you'll find black crappie, bream, black and striped bass, and catfish. Fish from the pier or put in and explore the lake's hidden depths. The camp features efficiency rooms with cable TV and full kitchen (one has a fireplace), suites, RV sites, covered marina slips, a swimming pool with a beautiful view of the lake, recreation room, and bait-and-tackle store. Rooms $75–100, RV sites $30–35, marina slips $7–10.

Orange Park 32003

An angler's getaway since 1963, **Whitey's Fish Camp** (904-269-4198; whiteysfishcamp.com), 2032 CR 220, has 44 RV sites with full hookups ($40), a restaurant (see *Eating Out*), boat rentals, and, of course, fishing.

Satsuma 32189

Leave the cell phone at home, and don't even think about a Jet Ski—the vintage **Stegbone's** (386-467-2464; stegbones.com), 144 Norton Fish Camp Rd, will have none of that. This 1946 retreat on the St. Johns River near Marker 41, the wilds of the Ocala National Forest on the opposite shore, offers quiet accommodations in one of five classic Florida cabins, the upscale three-bedroom Riverfront Getaway cottage, or a single-wide trailer ($85–260).

Welaka 32193
Sunset Landing (386-467-8430; sunsetlanding.net), 110 River Bend Rd, has old-fashioned fish camp cabins ($45–60) set under a canopy of oaks along the St. Johns River as well as 10 sites for RVs or trailers, full hookups with cable TV, $20.

✳ Where to Eat
DINING OUT
Melrose
🐟 With a formal dining room in shades of oceanic blue, the classy **Blue Water Bay** (352-475-1928), 319 FL 26, pulls in patrons all the way from Gainesville and Jacksonville with entrées ($13–40) like lemon-steamed snow crab legs, Cajun étouffée, and their famous seafood platters. French night is Tue; buffets on Fri and Sat at 5. Their sushi and desserts are some of the best I've ever sampled.

EATING OUT
Crescent City
What a treat to find **3 Bananas** (386-698-2861; 3bananas.com), 11 S Lake St. This tropical paradise, just off the lake, offers up a large chicken Caesar salad, Caribbean jerk chicken, lightly fried Crescent catfish, and a half-pound paradise burger. Sit on the outside deck and look for the sunken pirate ship while drinking Rum Runners and piña coladas. Live island music on weekends. Closed Tue.

East Palatka
🐟 The fresh and friendly **Mussel-white's Seafood & Grill** (386-326-9111; musselwhiteseafood.liveonatt.com), 125 US 17 S, serves up such dishes as Florida alligator tail with a tangy twist; tangerine tuna marinated

with citrus, soy, ginger, and honey; and New York strip cut and grilled to your liking. Entrées $10–17, plus some market price, like the fresh catch of the day. Save room for dessert: Key lime pie and chocolate peanut butter pie are only $3. Open Thu–Sun, serving dinner only on Sat.

Green Cove Springs
On a drive up to Jacksonville in the early morning, I was glad to grab breakfast at **Cousins Cafe** (904-284-8475), 206 Orange Ave S, tucked away in a strip mall downtown. A quick breakfast of eggs-over-easy and I was on the road again. Good prices, friendly service, and all for under $5. Serving breakfast and lunch; call ahead for take-out.

Keystone Heights
Johnny's Bar-B-Q Restaurant (352-473-4445; johnnysbbqcatering.com), 7411 FL 21. Eat in, walk up, or drive through at this busy local icon, where families gather for great barbecue and burgers. The waitresses know everyone by name, and service is in a snap, even during the lunch rush. Historic photos and memorabilia from Keystone Heights line the walls. Lunch ($4–8) and dinner plates ($9–13) pack in the crowds; salads (with your choice of barbecue meat) appeal to the lighter palate.

Orange Park
Catfish with Florida flair is the specialty at **Whitey's Fish Camp** (904-269-4198; whiteysfishcamp.com), 2032 CR 220. All-you-can-eat catfish ($16) is only for those with a big appetite. Petite eaters can order a basket with slaw, fries, and hush puppies. If you're not into catfish, then there's just about any other type of fish you can think of—and you can choose grilled, blackened, broiled, fried, or pecan-crusted. Seafood platters include shrimp, oysters, scallops, and grouper. Fear not,

landlubbers: You can get a 16-ounce rib eye or marinated chicken breast. Sandwiches and baskets around $8, entrées $12–30. The outdoor terrace has live music on the weekends.

Melrose

I love the little **Melrose Cafe** (352-475-2626), 888 N FL 21—blink and you miss it—because they serve real blueberry pancakes. A popular breakfast and lunch spot for the locals, it's a place to grab good eats at small-town prices.

Palatka

You can't visit Palatka without a stop at **Angel's Diner** (386-325-3927), 209 Reid St, Florida's oldest operating diner, opened in 1932. Crowded at breakfast and lunch—yes, it's a tight squeeze inside—you'll want to come during the lulls between. Their signature fountain drink is the Pusalow, made with chocolate milk over ice laced with a dash of vanilla syrup. Serving up standard southern diner fare, from scrambled eggs and hash browns in the morning to fried catfish and big burgers in the afternoon, it's a place to stop with an appetite, say, after a hike. Meals under $7.

Welaka

Adjoining its namesake campground (see *Fish Camps*), **Sunset Landing** (386-467-8430; sunsetlanding.net), 110 River Bend Rd, serves up breakfast, lunch, and dinner right on the St. Johns River—gotta love the view from these picnic tables on the porch. I could be tempted by the Sunrise at Sunset, with two eggs-over-easy atop hash browns spread over a biscuit with sausage gravy, then topped with bacon, but my doctor would probably have something to say about it. Fried seafood baskets at lunch and dinner plus lighter options like grilled chicken or whitefish. Most meals under $10; breakfast $2–5. Open Wed–Sun, 7:30 AM–9 PM.

✳ Entertainment

Thrasher Horne Center for Performing Arts (904-276-6815; thcenter .org), 283 College Dr, Orange Park. This state-of-the-art 84,666-square-foot theater is fully equipped with a multiuse theater and two art galleries. Performances include professional theater, dance, and music, along with visual arts exhibits.

✳ Selective Shopping

East Palatka

Stop by **County Line Produce** (904-692-9400), 848 FL 207 near the Putnam–St. Johns line for fresh produce from this potato-producing area.

Melrose

Ann Lowry Antiques (352-475-2924), 1658 SE 5th Ave, housed in a historic church under a canopy of ancient live oaks, showcases classy home decor items and furnishings.

In the Hilton-Brinson House, an 1886 landmark, **Bellamy Road Fine Arts, Literature, and Film** (352-475-3435; bellamyroadarts.com), 5910 Hampton St, offers a nod to the region's history and combines the interests of its owners to offer an antiquarian bookstore and art gallery featuring artists that capture the soul of Florida, as well as film screenings. Hours are limited; call ahead.

Find an excuse to stop in **Chiappini's** (352-475-9496), corner of FL 21 and FL 26, just because. The heart of town since 1935, they dispense bait and beer, gasoline and Dom Pérignon, and a sense of a time gone by.

Middleburg

Country Charm Mercantile (904-282-4512), 4544 Alligator Blvd. Handcrafted quilts bulge from the shelves; wind chimes dangle from the ceiling. This five-room home is jam-packed with gift items and home decor, from

Heritage Village miniatures to Yankee Candles, gourmet foods, and Beanie Babies. Closed Sun.

Palatka

At **Elsie Bell's Antique Mall** (386-329-9669), 111 N 4th St, I was looking for a music stand—and they'd just sold out. Drat! Filled with vintage furnishings that would look good in any home, it's a collection of dealer spaces with a little bit of everything, including old-fashioned candy that your kids will love.

For Christmas shopping, don't miss the open house at the **Palatka Art League**, when the Tilghman House (see *Historic Sites*) is filled with cheery Christmas crafts and fine pieces by local artisans.

ELSIE BELLS ANTIQUES, PALATKA

San Mateo

Get buzzing and head to the self-serve **1947 Honey Stand** (386-749-3562), 303 E FL 100, San Mateo, where you'll find pure, raw Florida honey. Choose from orange blossom, gallberry, or wildflower in 1-, 2-, and 5-pound jars. Run by Barberville Produce, it's a local tradition.

✳ Special Events

January: The **Putnam County African-American Cultural Arts Festival** (386-325-9901), downtown Palatka, always on Martin Luther King Day, is a celebration of African American history, arts, and culture.

February: Taste a bit of Scottish culture at the **Northeast Florida Scottish Games & Festival** (904-725-5744; neflgames.com), last weekend, Clay County Fairgrounds, Green Cove Springs.

March: Ravine Gardens State Park (see *Garden*) and downtown Palatka host the annual **Florida Azalea Festival** (386-326-4001; flazaleafest.com), a local tradition since 1945. Always held the second weekend, with arts, crafts, music, and food, it's always an excellent reason to come to town.

You'll find traditional agricultural exhibits, entertainment, and midway rides at the ✿ **Putnam County Fair** (386-329-0318; putnamcountyfair.org), Putnam County Fairgrounds, East Palatka, celebrating its 85th year in 2011.

April: Keep the rural fun rolling with a visit to the ✿ **Clay County Fair** (904-284-1615; claycountyfair.org), 2493 FL 16 W, Green Cove Springs.

Best place to skin a catfish is at the **Florida Catfish Festival** (386-698-1666; floridacatfishfestival.com), Crescent City, run by the local Rotary Club. The championship catfish-skinning contest is one of many events, including the catfish run, a parade (led by King Catfish), a bluegrass concert, an antiques show, and an arts and crafts fair.

May: ৬ Not to be missed is the annual **St. Margaret's Tour and Tea** (904-284-3030; stmargaretsfl.org), Old Church Rd, Hibernia. The one-hour tour of Margaret's chapel (see *Historic Sites*) and the Fleming family plantation is followed by high tea. Civil War reenactments, Virginia reel dancing, period costumes, and southern hospitality are just some of what's on offer. A limited number of golf carts are available for the handicapped or those unable to walk the area. Fee.

One of this area's major events, the 42-nautical-mile **Mug Race** (904-264-4094; rudderclub.com/mug.html) is the world's longest river race. It sets sail from the Palatka riverfront and races to Jacksonville along the St. Johns River.

You'll find not only hot steaming blue crabs at the annual **Blue Crab Festival** (386-325-4406; bluecrabfestival .com), downtown Palatka, but also such delights as soft-shell crabs, shrimp, and alligator. Four days of entertainment, rides, and arts and crafts. Always on Memorial Day weekend.

June: Wake up early and head to the **Bostwick Blueberry Festival** (386-329-2658) for the blueberry pancake breakfast, where you can pick up blueberry-related foods, arts, and crafts.

August: Try some sweet potato pie at the **Soul Food Festival and Parade of Pride** (greencovesprings.com), Vera Frances Hall Park, Green Cove Springs.

October: Get your caboose to the **Palatka Railfest** (386-649-6137; rails ofpalatka.org), Union Station, corner of 11th and Reid, where you can learn about model and full-scale trains or enhance your HO, S, and N collection at the many railroad exhibits.

November: The Bronson-Mulholland House (see *Historic Sites*) is centerpiece to the **Fall Antique Fair** (386-329-0140), where local and out-of-town vendors display and sell several fine antique and estate pieces.

Relive the **Battle of Horse Landing** (386-328-1281), Rodeheaver Boys Ranch on the St. Johns River, with living history demonstrations including a Civil War reenactment and military ball.

December: Take a tour through **Crescent City**, where many of the grand and glorious homes are decorated in holiday splendor (386-649-4534).

During the **Clay County Historical Society Holiday Tour of Homes** (claycountyhistoricalsociety.org), walk through Green Cove Springs's authentic Victorian homes decorated for the holidays; fee.

THE UPPER SUWANNEE

LAKE CITY, LIVE OAK, MADISON, WHITE SPRINGS/BAKER, COLUMBIA, HAMILTON, LAFAYETTE, MADISON & SUWANNEE COUNTIES

A s the frontier territory of Florida opened for settlement in 1820, families migrating south found the red hills, deep ravines, and high bluffs along the Suwannee River and its tributaries reminiscent of the landscapes they'd left behind in Georgia and the Carolinas. Building farms and large plantations, they planted cotton, corn, and sugarcane and used the river for trade. Shallow-draft steamboats plied the waterway from the Gulf of Mexico up to White Springs, where the shoals of the Suwannee made further passage impossible.

The heart of the region was Alpata Telophka, or "Alligator Town," a Seminole village ruled by the powerful chief Alligator in the 1830s. To the north, settlers Bryant and Elizabeth Sheffield built a log hotel at White Sulphur Springs in 1835, entertaining the first tourists along the Suwannee River. The city of **Madison**, based on the Seminole village of "Hickstown," was founded in 1838, and has a core historic district of homes and churches built as early as the 1850s, with 50 historic structures on the National Register. **Fort White** grew up around a frontier fortress from the Second Seminole War.

As more settlers moved into the Suwannee Valley and traded with the Seminoles, the village of Alligator was founded between several lakes adjacent to the Seminole community. It became incorporated as **Lake City** in 1856. Lake City was the original site for the University of Florida, but the Gators were lured to Gainesville by supporters with political clout.

During the Civil War, nearby Ocean Pond became a massing ground for Confederate troops with a mission to protect the rail line leading west toward Florida's capital, Tallahassee. On February 20, 1864, a westward push of Union troops met the Confederate pickets near the town of **Olustee**. A full-scale battle erupted in the thick pine forest, with both sides utilizing the rail line to move cannons and troops. After four hours, more than 2,000 lay dead and dying; the Union troops retreated to Jacksonville.

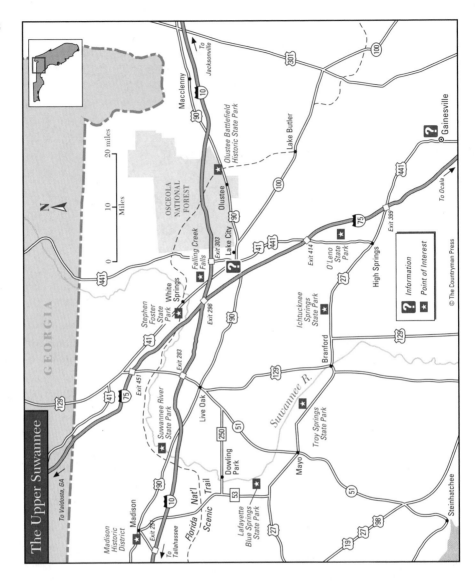

During the steamboat era, the region flourished. **White Springs** once had 14 hotels catering to tourists who came to "take the waters" at the springs. Along the banks of the Suwannee near one of the few bridges across the river, **Branford** was once an important steamboat-building town. Nearby **Mayo** became the county seat of agrarian Lafayette County in 1893. Covering only 1 square mile, **Lee** is one of the state's smallest incorporated towns. **Macclenny**, the seat of rural Baker County, dates back to 1886 and was once known as the horticultural capital of Florida; the Glen St. Mary Nursery, established 1907, was responsible for the citrus industry's standardization of orange varieties.

After Reconstruction, railroads crisscrossed the region. Full-scale logging of the surrounding pine woods brought prosperity to Lake City and **Live Oak**, with a building boom that set the tone for the feel of their downtowns today. But the end of the steamboat era left White Springs and others along the Suwannee behind the march of progress. Those that didn't vanish into ghost towns—like strategic Columbus, unearthed at Suwannee River State Park at the confluence of the Suwannee and Withlacoochee rivers—settled into a relaxed pace. Ongoing preservation efforts ensure the splendor of these classic old Florida small towns and of downtown Lake City and Madison. The youngster in the region is **Dowling Park**, established in 1913 along the Suwannee River as a retirement village by the Advent Christian Church for its members.

GUIDANCE At the upper end of the Suwannee River Valley, **Columbia County** (386-758-1397; springsrus.com), 263 NW Lake City Ave, is your top source of information. **Natural North Florida** (naturalnorthflorida.com) is a coalition that provides information for many of the other communities found in the region. Walk into the **Madison County Chamber of Commerce** (850-973-2788; madisonfl .org), 248 SW Range Ave, for walking tour brochures and more.

Several miles east off I-75 exit 439, right in the center of White Springs, the **State of Florida's Nature & Heritage Tourism Center** (386-397-4461; floridastateparks.org/findapark /natureandheritage.cfm), CR 136 and US 41, is Florida's official outdoor recreation tourism center. They provide a bounty of information on activities throughout the state. Browse their library of guidebooks, or pick up a handful of brochures and a state parks guide. Open daily 9–5.

If you're headed out on the Suwannee River, you'll want a map showing boating access and springs. Contact the **Suwannee River Water Management District** (386-362-1001; srwmd .state.fl.us), 9225 CR 49, Live Oak 32060; you can also download their recreational guide from the website.

GETTING THERE *By air:* The nearest commuter service comes into **Tallahassee** (see the *Tallahassee & the Big Bend* chapter) and **Gainesville** (see the *Gainesville & Vicinity* chapter); however, **Jacksonville International Airport** (see the *Jacksonville* chapter) provides a broader choice of carriers and is only a two-hour drive away via Interstate 10.

WAY DOWN UPON THE SUWANNEE RIVER, WHITE SPRINGS

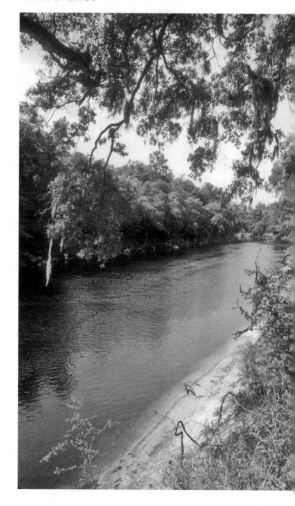

By bus: **Greyhound** (800-229-9424; greyhound.com) makes stops in Lake City, Live Oak, and Madison.

By car: **I-75** and **I-10** provide quick access to most of the region, but you'll want to wander the back roads to see the sights.

GETTING AROUND Heading north from High Springs, **US 41** passes through downtown Lake City before becoming Hamilton County's "Main Street," running through its three major towns—White Springs, Jasper, and Jennings. **US 129** also runs north–south, linking Branford, Live Oak, and Jasper. For the scenic east–west route, take **US 90** from Olustee west to Lake City, Live Oak, Lee, Madison, and Greenville; **US 27** takes a more southerly route, tying together High Springs, Fort White, and Branford on its way to Tallahassee. **FL 51** and US 27 meet at Mayo, the center of Lafayette County, passing through all of its major towns.

MEDICAL EMERGENCIES Regional hospitals include **Shands at Lake Shore Hospital** (386-755-3200; shands.org/hospitals/lakeshore), 560 E Franklin St, Lake City; **Shands at Live Oak** (386-362-1413; shandsliveoak.com), 1100 11th St SW, Live Oak; and **Madison County Memorial Hospital** (850-973-2271; mcmh.us), 309 NE Marion St, Madison.

✳ To See

DE SOTO TRAIL In 1539 Spanish explorer Hernando de Soto and his troops crossed Florida in pursuit of gold. Roadside markers along US 90 interpret his route.

EQUESTRIAN EVENTS Suwannee River Riding Club, Inc. (386-935-0447; srrcbranford.com), 9132 254th Terrace (US 129) north of Branford. Stop by their arena to watch team roping (first and third Fri) and speed events (first and third Sat) each month.

GHOST TOWNS The towns of **Columbus** and **Ellaville** vanished not long after steamboats stopped chugging up the Suwannee, supplanted by railroads. You'll find the Columbus Cemetery within Suwannee River State Park (see *Parks*). Directly across the Suwannee, the remains of Ellaville (primarily foundations and loose bricks) lie along the Florida Trail through Twin Rivers State Forest just north of the former site of the **Drew Mansion** off old US 90, on the west side of the Suwannee River bridge. An interpretive trail loops this historic governor's mansion site.

In 1870 **New Troy**, near Troy Springs, boasted busy steamboat docks and steady commerce. It was the seat of Lafayette County, but after an arsonist torched the courthouse in 1892, county residents voted to move the courthouse to Mayo; New Troy was abandoned soon after.

HISTORIC SITES

Falling Creek
First established as a Baptist congregation in a log cabin prior to 1866, the current **Falling Creek Methodist Church and Cemetery**, Falling Creek Rd, dates back to the 1880s, the land donated to the church after 1855 by heirs of one of the orig-

inal settlers of the area, Thomas D. Dicks from South Carolina. Wood frame weathered by age, original water glass, shaded by ancient live oaks and southern magnolias; the deep gorge of Falling Creek rings the property (see *Waterfalls*).

Jasper

Built in 1893, the **Old Jail** (386-792-1300), 501 NE 1st Ave, functioned as a prison until 1984 but now serves as the Hamilton County Historical Society Museum (see *Museums*) and gives a glimpse into what it was like on both sides of the bars—the sheriff and his family occupied living quarters connected to the jail. Visit the living quarters and walk through the creepy jail cells. Saved from the wrecking ball by a determined group of women, the structure is still undergoing restoration, as is the adjoining **Heritage Village** complex, and a cotton gin, a small church, and two shotgun houses await restoration.

Lake City

In downtown Lake City, check out the old **Columbia County Courthouse**, circa 1902. The Columbia County Historical Society (see *Museums*) sits in a neighborhood dominated by beautiful 1890s Victorian houses, including the **Chalker-Turner House**, 104 E St. Johns. Stop at the historical society for information on walking tours in the city's antebellum neighborhoods.

Live Oak

Take a look at that Wrigley's ad painted on the side of a building on W Howard St: It's been there since 1909. Glance at Sperring's Muffler and Lube, and you'll realize it's a **1960s Sinclair gas station**. That's the way history is in Live Oak: all around you, but transformed into something utilitarian, from the **1890s downtown block** filled with businesses to the pillared **Thomas Dowling house** on CR 136, renovated into a community center. There's plenty of interest for the history buff who's willing to poke around. Stop first at the Suwannee County Historical Museum (see *Museums*) to get your bearings for a walking tour of downtown.

Macclenny

Now serving as the town's library, the original **Baker County Courthouse** is an architectural landmark at the corner of 5th and McIver streets. The old **Baker County Jail**, built 1911–1913 (see *Genealogical Research*), is next door. The sheriff's family lived on site and prepared food for inmates. Stop in at the Macclenny Chamber of Commerce, 20 E Macclenny Ave, to browse through their book of historic sites and get directions to see the town's historic homes from the late 1800s, all privately owned. Located along the rail line, **Baker County Heritage Park** holds a collection of historic buildings from around the county as well as the historic depot and a caboose.

Madison

With more than 30 buildings from the 1800s and nearly 50 historic sites dating to 1936, downtown Madison has the highest concentration of historical architecture in the region. Start your walk by picking up the *Walking/Driving Tour of Madison County* brochure from the chamber of commerce; it contains a map and detailed information on each historic site. The **Wardlaw-Smith-Goza Mansion** (850-973-9432; nfcc.edu/community-programs/wardlaw-smith-goza-conf-center), 103 N Washington St, is a Classical Revival mansion built in 1860, once known as White-hall. North Florida Community College uses the mansion as a conference center, and tours are offered Tue–Thu 10–2 (closed mid-Dec to mid-Jan). Other historic homes of note include the **W. H. Dial House**, 105 E Marion St, a Victorian mansion circa 1880; the **J. E. Hardee House**, 107 E Marion St, a two-story Mediterranean villa from 1918 designed by Lloyd Barton Greer (who also designed the classy **Madison County Courthouse**); and the **Livingston House**, 501 N Range St, Madison's oldest home, from 1836. In continuous use for worship services since 1881, the small wood frame **St. Mary's Episcopal Church** (850-973-8338), 108 N Horry St, permits tours by appointment.

Dedicated in memory to Captain Colin P. Kelly Jr., a Madison resident and the first American casualty of World War II on December 9, 1941, at Clark Field in the Philippines, the **Four Freedoms Monument**, downtown, reflects on the "Four Freedoms" speech made by President Franklin Delano Roosevelt prior to the outbreak of the war.

Near the old Madison Depot, a giant steam engine sits along Range Rd at 109 W Rutledge. It's a relic of what was once the **largest cotton gin in the world**, combing through Sea Island cotton at the Florida Manufacturing Company in the 1880s.

Mayo

Steinhatchee Spring, a historic spa and the birthplace of the Steinhatchee River, is off FL 51 north of US 27. Dominating downtown Mayo, the **Lafayette County Courthouse** dates back to 1908.

White Springs

Behind the Nature & Tourism Center, follow the wooden staircase down to the original **White Sulfur Springs Spa**, built in the late 1800s. Standing on the balcony, you can look down into the spa, and down along the rapid flow of the Suwannee River. During World War II the spa and its grounds served as an internment camp for German prisoners of war. White Springs is a beautiful historic town; take the time to walk down River Street and its adjoining blocks to see many homes from the late 1800s.

MUSEUMS After you learn about Florida's most significant Civil War battle at the visitors center at Olustee Battlefield (see *Historic Sites*), stop in the **Olustee Visitor's Center and Museum** at the old railroad depot (off US 90) for an interactive walk through life in this logging and railroad community. In downtown Lake City, the **Lake City–Columbia County Historical Museum** (386-755-9096; lccchm .org), 157 SE Hernando Ave, offers exhibit rooms with furnishings that capture the period of this southern Italianate manor circa 1870, including artifacts from the Civil War. Wed 2–5, Sat 10–1.

Housed in the former Atlantic Coast Line freight depot from 1903, the **Suwannee County Historical Museum and Telephone Museum** (386-362-1776; suwannee museum.org), 208 Ohio Ave N, Live Oak, presents dioramas and an extensive collection of historic objects—including a working telephone switching station—to bring history alive. At the Old Jail in Jasper (see *Historic Sites*), the **Hamilton County Historical Society Museum** shows off historical documents, display cases with exhibits, and photos of historical structures throughout the county, along with a small gift shop with local art.

A repository of Madison County history, with information on long-lost historic sites like the San Pedro Mission and the Drew Mansion, is the **Treasures of Madison County Museum** (850-973-3661; treasuresofmadisoncounty.com), 194 SW Range Ave, in the beautiful W. T. Davis Building, one of only three metal-front commercial buildings remaining from its era. Open Tue–Fri 10–2, Sat 10–noon.

RAILROADIANA Many settlements of the Upper Suwannee started as railroad towns, so their railroad history remains. You'll find **turn-of-the-20th-century railroad depots** still standing in Fort White, Live Oak, and Madison, and restored

OLUSTEE

Olustee Battlefield Historic State Park (386-758-0400; floridastateparks .org/olustee), US 90, is the site of Florida's largest and bloodiest Civil War battle, a patch of hallowed ground beneath the pines, preserved as a memorial by the 1899 Florida Legislature to the men who fell during the four-hour conflict. Sparked by a push by Union general Truman A. Seymour, whose success at capturing Baldwin tempted him to send his troops toward the railroad bridge at Columbus without orders from his superiors, the Union forces were met by the largest Confederate buildup to defend Florida—thanks to Florida's crucial role as a beef supplier to the Confederate army. On February 20, 1864, more than 10,000 met in combat in these pine woods; casualties topped 2,000. An annual reenactment (third weekend of Feb, see *Special Events*) re-creates the battle and encampments; with nearly 10,000 participants, it's one of the South's largest encampments. It's an excellent educational experience, especially for those unschooled in Florida's Civil War history. Interpretive center open daily 9–5; an interpretive walk takes you through the battlefield stations. Free.

RE-ENACTORS AT THE BATTLE OF OLUSTEE

depots at **Olustee** (housing a beautiful national forest visitors center with regional railroad history) and **Macclenny** (with a red caboose outside the depot). A **historic iron boxwork bridge** crosses the Suwannee River at Dowling Park. The east–west main line paralleling US 90 through the region remains a busy thoroughfare (great train spotting for rail fans); its Suwannee River crossing (as seen from within Suwannee River State Park, or from the old US 90 bridge, now a walking trail—see *Hiking*) is fairly dramatic and has significant historic import—the military objective of the Union troops stopped at Olustee (see *Historic Sites*) was to blow up the original railroad bridge here, severing commerce between North Florida and the Panhandle. Stop in the **Suwannee County Historical Museum** (see *Museums*) for information on Live Oak's railroading history. Live Oak grew up around the Seaboard Air Line railroad, which came through in 1903, and the locally owned **Live Oak, Perry & Gulf Railroad**, affectionately known as the "Lopin' Gopher." Railroad shops in Live Oak once turned out steam locomotives and parts for the Plant System.

✷ To Do

BICYCLING Mountain bikers have a blast on rugged riverside trails built and maintained by the **Suwannee Bicycle Association** (386-397-2347; suwanneebike .org), P.O. Box 247, White Springs 32096. Stop by their office in downtown White Springs to pick up maps of local biking routes, including the popular Swift Creek, Gar Pond, Disappearing Creek, and Big Shoals routes. Each provides challenges to bikers with the undulating terrain along the Suwannee River and its tributaries; trails are posted for three levels of difficulty, from beginner to gung-ho. Perfect for beginning mountain bikers, the **Allen Mill Pond Bike Trail** runs 4.2 miles between Allen Mill Pond and Lafayette Blue Springs (see *Springs*) along the Suwannee River.

✍ For a tamer outing, the paved **Woodpecker Trail** at Big Shoals State Park (see *Wild Places*) is a gentle-enough ride for the kids through some beautiful river bluff forest. A paved rail-trail also runs along the **Suwannee River Greenway** (see *Greenways*) from Little River Springs County Park in Suwannee County to Ichetucknee Run in Columbia County, passing through the town of Branford. Madison County boasts **The Loop**, a 100-mile marked road biking route running down paved rural byways; pick up a map from the chamber of commerce (see *Guidance*).

BIRDING Top sites in the region include **Alligator Lake** (see *Parks*), where colonies of nesting egrets occupy the islands, and the ♿ **Nice Wander Trail** and **Mount Carrie Wayside** in the Osceola National Forest, where an early-morning visit lets you watch rare red-cockaded woodpeckers, marked with white bands, emerging from their holes in longleaf pines. Part of the Florida Trail (see *Hiking*), which also affords access to red-cockaded woodpecker colonies much deeper in the forest, the 2-mile accessible-with-assistance Nice Wander Trail starts at a trailhead at the Olustee Battlefield Historic State Park entrance. The Mount Carrie Wayside is along US 90. At the **Ladell Brothers Environmental Center** in Madison you can borrow a pair of binoculars from the Hamilton Library and go birding in this lush oasis of hardwoods in the middle of the North Florida Community College campus. **Cooks Hammock**, hidden in a maze of forest roads off FL

51 south of Mayo at the Lafayette Hunt Club, has a colony of white and glossy ibises.

BOATING Most of the rivers in this region have shallows, sandbars, and rapids. Unless your craft has a very shallow draft, don't take it any farther up the Suwannee River than its confluence with the Withlacoochee—snags and sandbars are very real hazards and have flipped many a Skidoo. See *Paddling* for details on the best river routes in the region.

DIVING Where the Santa Fe meets the Suwannee, the town of Branford calls itself the "**Spring Diving Capital of the World**." Stop in at the Steamboat Dive Inn (see *Dive Resort*) for information about open-water dive sites. Cave divers also flock here for both **spring diving in the Suwannee River** and the extensive underwater cave system at **Peacock Springs** (see *Springs*). For cold air, gear rentals, instruction, and a friendly chat with Cathy about cave diving, stop at the **Dive Outpost** (386-776-1449; diveoutpost.com), 20148 180th St, en route to the park.

Important note: Many open-water divers have died in this region while attempting cave diving. Do not enter an underwater cave or spring unless you are a certified cave diver. Most springs must be accessed by boat, and a DIVER DOWN flag is necessary while diving the river.

FAMILY ACTIVITIES 🕱 One of the favorite pastimes of local families is to get the kids in the van and head on down to Suwannee Springs (see *Springs*) for some freebie swimming and sunning on the **natural white-sand beaches of the Suwannee River**, or to the **water park at Jellystone Campground** (see *Camping & Cabins*) in Madison, where a 60-foot-tall, 300-foot-long spiral waterslide splashes down into a small lake lined with kids' activities, from playground equipment, boats, and water sprinklers to the nearby mini golf, tractor-train rides to a ghost town in the woods, and cartoons in the Yogi Theatre. $8 person for day use; water park and other kids' activities open weekends and for special events only.

FISHING From **Ocean Pond** at Olustee (see *Camping & Cabins*) to **Watertown Lake** [030.193332, -82.603032] on the edge of Lake City and Lang Lake Fish Management Area, a reclaimed phosphate pit north of Genoa on US 41, you'll find plenty of stillwater opportunities. Don't miss **Cherry Lake,** a WPA reservoir popular for bass fishing, north of Madison off FL 253. Looking for bream? Head for the **Aucilla River** west of Greenville. Anglers also enjoy **Koon Lake**, a 110-acre fish management area west of Mayo on US 27, where

ANGLERS TRY THEIR LUCK AT WATERTOWN LAKE, LAKE CITY

largemouth bass and bluegill provide spring sport. If you're fishing along the banks of the **Suwannee River**, target sunfish around the snags and channel catfish in the deep holes.

GENEALOGICAL RESEARCH Housed in the old Baker County Jail in Macclenny, the **Baker County Historical Society Family History Library** (904-259-0587), 42 W McIver, opens Tue 1–8 and Sat 1–4 for folks doing historical and genealogical research; you can also make an appointment to visit.

GOLF **Pineview Golf & Country Club** (904-259-3447), 1751 Golf Club Rd, Macclenny, offers golfing in an open, uncluttered environment with pleasing landscaping under the Florida pines. Eighteen holes $21–26, includes golf cart when available.

With three 9-hole, par-36 courses on their property, **Quail Heights Country Club** (386-752-3339; quailheightscc.com), 161 Quail Heights Terrace, Lake City, is a golfer's destination. Condos and efficiencies on site enable them to offer "Stay and Play" packages, $75–118.

HIKING Starting at Olustee Battlefield, you can backpack more than 100 miles of the **Florida Trail** (see *What's Where*), following the Suwannee River for nearly 70 miles from the southern shore of Big Shoals through White Springs to Mill Creek. To pass through sections of private land along the river, you must be a member of the Florida Trail Association (877-HIKE-FLA; floridatrail.org). One easily accessible public section is the **Big Oak Trail**, starting at the ranger station in Suwannee River State Park and crossing the old US 90 bridge to meet the main Florida Trail. You can also find excellent hiking at **Alligator Lake**, **O'Leno State Park**, and numerous other locations detailed in *50 Hikes in North Florida*. Don't miss the easy 2-mile round-trip to **Big Shoals** from Big Shoals Public Lands north of White Springs, where you can watch the rapids froth like cola, and the easy 0.25-mile walk down to **Falling Creek Falls** (see *Waterfalls*). Pursue your Florida State Forests Trailwalker patch with several qualifying trails in **Twin Rivers State Forest**, or take an easy amble along the Suwannee River waterfront on the **Milford Clark Nature Trail** at Dowling Park, a 4-mile round-trip starting behind the Village Lodge (see *Lodging*).

PADDLING The **Suwannee River** is one of the top paddling destinations in Florida, thanks to its length and lack of commercial boat traffic—it has enough shoals and sandbars to discourage most motorboats from heading any farther north than Ellaville. It takes two weeks to paddle the river from its headwaters in the Okefenokee Swamp in Georgia to the town of Suwannee on the Gulf of Mexico. With its broad sand beaches and beautiful springs, the Suwannee is a perfect choice for a long-distance canoe outing. To guide you down the river, the **Suwannee River Wilderness Trail** (800-868-9914; floridastateparks.org/wilderness) outlines the 170-mile route, providing river camps and numerous access points along the way.

Several outfitters provide rentals and shuttles along the Upper Suwannee. **American Canoe Adventures** (800-624-8081; aca1.com), 10315 SE 141st Blvd, can set you up with a canoe or kayak and shuttle service, $35–65 for a day trip, or arrange

CANOEING THE SUWANNEE RIVER WILDERNESS TRAIL

a multiday outing. Where US 129 crosses the Suwannee north of Live Oak, **Suwannee Canoe Outpost** (800-428-4147; suwanneeoutpost.com) provides canoe and kayak rentals and shuttles out of Spirit of the Suwannee Music Park (see *Camping & Cabins*); their day trips, $12–28, are set up to end at their take-out.

Canoeists putting in on the **Ichetucknee** and **Santa Fe** rivers near Branford can contact the **Santa Fe Canoe Outpost** (386-454-2050; santaferiver.com), US 441, for rentals and shuttles.

SWIMMING Swimmers have plenty of choices in the region: from the **water park at Jellystone Campground** in Madison (see *Camping & Cabins*) to the many **springs** open for swimming along the Suwannee River and its tributaries (see *Springs*).

TRAIL RIDING At **Windmill Ranch & Stables** (386-935-2278), 11300 NW 15th Ave, Branford, trail rides are offered daily in summer, weekends in winter, $30 per hour. Camping available. In Jasper, **McCulley Farms** (386-938-3011; mcculleyfarms.com), 6415 NE CR 143, a historic farmstead, holds the equestrian equivalent of RV rallies—guided group trail rides along the Withlacoochee River, with on-site camping and meals—several times a

TRAIL RIDING IN COLUMBIA COUNTY
VISIT FLORIDA

year. **R. O. Ranch Equestrian Park** (866-813-1617 or 386-294-1475; roranch .org), 10807 S FL 51, Mayo, has 14 miles of trails on their property plus more riding nearby, with a campground on site. Equestrian trails wind through **Big Shoals State Park**, **Twin Rivers State Forest** in Madison County, and crisscross the **Osceola National Forest** (see *Wild Places*), with opportunities for overnight camping.

TUBING The most popular tubing run in the state, the Ichetucknee River flows forth from **Ichetucknee Springs** (see *Springs*) to create a 6-mile crystalline stream that winds through deep, dark hardwood forests. Pick up a rental tube at any of the many small shops along US 27; Joanne's Tubes is the closest to the park's south entrance, off US 27. A shuttle takes you up to the north end of the park for launch; leave your rental tube in the tube corral at the end of the day for the outfitters to reclaim. Tubing season runs from the end of May through early September.

WALKING TOURS In Lake City, the **Lake Isabella Residential District** covers 30 blocks, and the downtown historic district encompasses another 15 blocks. Pick up a walking tour brochure at the Columbia County Historical Museum (see *Museums*). At **White Springs** grab a walking tour brochure at the State of Florida's Nature & Heritage Tourism Center (see *Guidance*); interpretive signs add to your understanding of the town's history as you walk. The **Madison County Chamber of Commerce** can also provide you with a walking tour brochure for their extensive historic downtown.

✳ Green Space

BEACHES While none of the counties in this region touches either the Atlantic or the Gulf, you'll find beautiful, if sometimes ephemeral, white-sand beaches suitable for sunning, swimming, and camping along the Suwannee River at **Suwannee Springs** (see *Springs*) and **Big Shoals** (see *Wild Places*), at **Spirit of the Suwannee Music Park** (see *Camping & Cabins*), and along the **Florida Trail** (see *Hiking*).

GARDENS O'Toole's Herb Farm (850-973-3269; otoolesherbfarm.com), Rocky Ford Rd (CR 591). Culinary herbs and flowers grown organically—that's the mainstay of Betty O'Toole's lovely gardens, and their greens garnish platters in fine restaurants around the region. Her beautiful 150-year-old family farm is now open by appointment or during their many festival weekends; check their website for the schedule.

GREENWAYS Running between Little River Springs County Park and Ichetucknee Run, the 12-mile **Suwannee River Greenway** (dep.state.fl.us/gwt/guide /regions/north/trails/suwan_river_greenway_bran.htm) provides a paved bicycle path with limited shade along an old railroad route; parking area in downtown Branford. Ten miles north of Madison, the 3-mile **Four Freedoms Trail** (madisoncountyfl.com/cd-recreation.aspx) starts at Pinetta and heads to the state border at the Withlacoochee River. Now unpaved but providing a pleasant hike, this new greenway project will eventually link the Georgia border to Madison with biking, hiking, and equestrian trails.

NATURE CENTER Tucked away in the middle of the North Florida Community College campus west of Madison, the ♪ **Ladell Brothers Outdoor Environmental Center** (850-973-1645; nfcc.edu/community-programs/nature-center), 1000 Turner Davis Dr, is a little hard to find: Park on campus near the Hamilton Library and walk between Building 5 (Biology) and the Student Success Center to reach the green space beyond. Follow the lakeshore to the trees, where you'll find the trailhead to this shaded network of hiking trails perfect for wildlife-watching.

PARKS

Branford
On the east shore of the Suwannee River at US 27, **Ivey Memorial Park** has a bait-and-tackle shop, a boat ramp, picnic tables with an expansive view of the Suwannee River, and a swimming hole at Branford Spring accessed via a boardwalk near the park entrance. It also provides parking for people using the Suwannee River Greenway.

High Springs
One of the oldest state parks in the system, **O'Leno State Park** (386-454-1853; floridastateparks.org/oleno), US 41, has two campgrounds with 64 spaces, and 17 stone-and-log cabins nestled along the Santa Fe River, which vanishes into a river-sink and flows underground for several miles. A network of hiking trails winds through shady hardwood forests, leading to the river rise.

Lake City
Alligator Lake Recreation Area (386-755-4100; columbiacountyfla.com/Parks andRecreation.asp), SE Country Club Rd. More than 6 miles of hiking trails surround Alligator Lake and its adjacent impoundments, where colonies of herons nest in the willows. Paddle a kayak across the placid water, or walk the gentle trails with your family.

Lee
Behind city hall, the historic **McMullen Farm House** forms the centerpiece of a small city park with a fishpond, picnic tables, and walking trail. Drive 10 miles east of Lee on US 90 to reach **Suwannee River State Park** (386-362-2746; florida stateparks.org/suwanneeriver), 20185 CR 132. Although this beautiful riverfront park boasts a pleasant campground, gentle and rugged nature trails, historic Civil War earthworks, and some of the best views you'll get of the Suwannee River, you're missing out if you don't visit its wild side along the north shore of the Suwannee, accessible only via the Florida Trail (see *Hiking*).

Macclenny
♿ Along US 90 west of town, **Glen St. Mary River Park** affords access for boaters and canoeists to the Little St. Mary River, with several fishing decks on a dredged channel out to the river.

Mayo
In downtown Mayo along US 27, ancient live oaks shade **Mayo Town Park**, which has a playground, picnic area, and historic Cracker home, and is home to the annual Pioneer Day Festival (see *Special Events*).

White Springs

The mission of ♿ **Stephen Foster Folk Culture Center State Park** (386-397-2733; floridastateparks.org /stephenfoster), US 41, is to preserve Florida's folk culture heritage, with the state folklorist on staff, a permanent craft village, and the Florida Folk Festival (see *Special Events*) as well as many folklore-oriented weekend events throughout the year. Exhibits in the park speak to the musical heritage of Stephen Collins Foster, a Pittsburgh songwriter who never set foot here. A towering carillon, one of only two in Florida, chimes frequently and plays old-time tunes that ripple across the waters of the Suwannee River at the base of the bluff. Camping in this park (see *Camping & Cabins*) is a delight, with its deeply shaded campground and quiet cabins perched above the river. The Florida Trail (see *Hiking*) passes right through the park, staying close to the river atop bluffs that burst into fragrant blooms of wild azalea each March.

THE FAMED CARILLION AT STEPHEN FOSTER FOLK CULTURE CENTER STATE PARK

SPRINGS Imagine a mirror-smooth surface of clear water reflecting hues of robin's-egg blue. That's Ichetucknee Spring, found at the north end of **Ichetucknee Springs State Park** (386-497-2511; floridastateparks.org /ichetuckneesprings), 8294 SW Elim Church Rd. In addition to swimming and diving at the spring, visitors grab tubes and float down the placid spring run (see *Tubing*) or take to the stream with canoes and kayaks for a serene trip down one of Florida's purest rivers.

Contact the Suwannee River Water Management District (see *Boating*) for a map of spring locations in the Suwannee River for diving and swimming; most can only be accessed by boat. In Suwannee County, small county parks provide access to **Charles Spring** (south of Dowling Park), **Little River Springs**, **Royal Springs** (north of Branford), and **Branford Spring** (at Ivey Park in Branford), all of which invite swimmers and divers to plunge into their chilly depths.

🐾 ♿ At **Peacock Springs State Park** (386-497-2511; floridastateparks.org /peacocksprings), 180th St (follow signs east from FL 51), a one-lane dirt road winds through deep woods past pull-offs leading to sinkholes that interconnect underground, forming a karst playground for cave divers. $10 dive fee. You must

WATERFALLS

Although Florida isn't known for its waterfalls, the Upper Suwannee boasts a high concentration of scenic spots with waterfalls along streams feeding the Suwannee River basin. Start your tour with a peek at **Falling Creek Falls** (386-758-2123) located north of Lake City off US 41 just north of I-10. Turn right on Falling Creek Rd (CR 131) and follow it 0.8 mile to the trailhead parking area. It's a 0.2-mile walk to the spectacular, root-beer-colored cascade, which plummets more than 10 feet over a deep lip of limestone and flows away over limestone boulders at the bottom of a ravine. Not far away as the crow flies, the new Bell Spring trailhead off Lassie Black Rd provides access to the Florida Trail (see *Hiking*) between Big Shoals and Little Shoals along the Suwannee River. Hike about a mile upstream to discover **Robinson Branch Falls**, a significant cascade that the trail traverses.

Following CR 25A north from White Springs, look for the small CAMP BRANCH sign on the left, and park at the trailhead. Follow the broad bike trail down to Disappearing Creek, where **Camp Branch** drops through a churning set of hydraulics before plunging down into a deep sinkhole. Feeling adventuresome? A blue-blazed trail of less than a mile leads up and around the creek to give you optimal views and a total hike of about 2 miles.

The Florida Trail crosses US 129 north of Live Oak, presenting two more waterfall-viewing opportunities. Park on the northbound shoulder of the road and follow the orange blazes east for less than 0.25 mile to **Sugar Creek**, which cascades a couple of feet between the cypress knees as it flows down to the Suwannee River. Members of the Florida Trail Association (floridatrail.org) can also take the trail west through private lands on a round-trip hike of 7 miles to visit **Mill Creek Falls**, which plunges in a double cascade of more than 15 feet over a limestone escarpment into the river.

ONE OF FLORIDA'S MOST ACCESSIBLE WATERFALLS, FALLING CREEK FALLS

be cave-certified to dive in these springs. No solo diving. Swimming is permitted in Orange Grove and Peacock Springs. A nature trail traces aboveground the route that divers are following below. Leashed dogs only.

Madison Blue Spring State Park (386-362-2746; floridastateparks.org/madison) provides visitors a cool natural pool along the Withlacoochee River at FL 6. $10 dive fee for cave divers. Along US 90 near Suwannee River State Park, **Falmouth Springs** creates a popular swimming area. ☙ At **Suwannee Springs** (north of Live Oak off US 129 before the river bridge), a warm sulfur spring pours into a turn-of-the-20th-century spa building before flowing out into the river. Expansive beaches make this a cool weekend hangout (see *Family Activities*).

At **Troy Springs State Park** (386-935-4835; floridastateparks.org/troyspring), 674 NE Troy Springs Rd off US 27 near Midway, the water is nearly 75 feet deep and contains the remains of the *Madison*, a steamboat scuttled in 1861 when her owner left to fight for the Confederacy in Virginia. Adjoining **Ruth Springs** is a third-magnitude spring open for swimming and diving. **Lafayette Blue Springs** (386-294-1617) along CR 350A has primitive camping, nature trails, picnic pavilions, and a boat ramp.

WILD PLACES Along CR 135 north of White Springs, **Big Shoals State Park** (386-397-2733; floridastateparks.org/bigshoals) encompasses river bluffs and uplands overlooking the roughest whitewater on the Suwannee River. Hike or mountain bike their rugged trails along the river bluffs, or put in your kayak or canoe for a paddle down to the shoals—yes, there is a portage around them, and you should use it if you're not experienced with whitewater, as many canoes have been ripped open on this rocky stretch of the river.

Osceola National Forest (386-752-2577; fs.usda.gov/osceola) is the smallest of Florida's three national forests. For an orientation to recreation in the forest, stop at the ranger station on US 90 at Olustee (open Mon–Fri 7:30–4) or at the Olustee Depot Visitors Center (open sporadically) at CR 231; the railroad depot (see *Rail-roadiana*) dates back to 1888. Walk the short nature trail at Mount Carrie Wayside for an introduction to the longleaf pine and wiregrass habitat, then head to Olustee Battlefield Historic State Park to follow the ♿ **Nice Wander Trail**, a 2-mile accessible loop along the Florida Trail through red-cockaded woodpecker habitat. Ocean Pond (see *Camping & Cabins*) is one of the most beautiful camping areas in North Florida, especially as the sun sets over the cypresses. To see the wildest side of the forest, visit the Big Gum Swamp Wilderness, where the Florida black bear roams. A new access point is from the Sanderson Rest Area on the westbound side of I-10, where the accessible-with-assistance ♿ **Fanny Bay Trail** leads you half a mile to a boardwalk into Fanny Bay, a floodplain forest with giant cypresses.

Spanning both sides of the Suwannee at its confluence with the Withlacoochee, **Twin Rivers State Forest** (386-208-1462; fl-dof.com/state_forests/twin_rivers.html) covers nearly 15,000 acres of thick hardwood forest and timberlands. In addition to seasonal hunting, it provides access to the Suwannee River for anglers and boaters, and hosts an extensive network of biking, equestrian, and hiking trails, including the Florida Trail.

❋ Lodging

BED & BREAKFASTS

Greenville 32331

🐾 🐕 The grand dame of Ray Charles hometown of Greenville, **Grace Manor** (888-294-8839 or 850-948-5352; grace manorinn.com), 117 SW US 221, is a romantic Victorian hotel circa 1898 with sweeping porches and an unexpected perk—a full-sized swimming pool! Expect the classic touches, too—flowers, candles, and teddy-topped beds, fireplaces and en suite baths. The extra-roomy Honeymoon Suite adds a bathroom as living space, with a whirlpool for two, while the Emerald and Rose Rooms have fluffy feather mattresses. Innkeeper Brenda Graham takes your needs into consideration as she plans each healthful gourmet breakfast. $85–125; pets are permitted in a two-bedroom cottage near the swimming pool and gardens, $135.

White Springs 32096

A 1901 boardinghouse, the **White Springs Bed & Breakfast** (386-397-4252; whitespringsbnb.com), 16630 Spring St, offers a casual getaway with historic touches, from the heart pine floors and pillared main fireplace to the restored 200-year-old antique German beds. Six eclectic rooms come in various shapes and shades; a favorite is the Magnolia Room, with its canopied bed and tiled fireplace. Dine on heart-shaped waffles during your candlelight breakfast, and relax on the wraparound porch with a book. Guests may borrow bicycles for a spin around town, or innkeeper Judith McClure will assist you in a shuttle up to the bike trails at Big Shoals. $85 and up.

HOTELS, MOTELS & RESORTS

Dowling Park 32060

🐾 ♿ In the Advent Christian Village, the **Village Lodge** (800-371-8381 or 386-658-5200; acvillage.net/village lodge.html) at Village Landing, CR 136 and CR 250, provides something I haven't found anywhere else on the Suwannee River—large, immaculate riverfront motel rooms in a tranquil setting. Rocking chairs outside each room await your arrival; sit and enjoy the view. Follow the walkways (where you can lounge in a porch swing and watch the river) to the Milford Clark Nature Trail, a gem of a hike along the river bluffs. Two rooms are enhanced for wheelchair use. No pets. Rooms and suite, $79 and up.

Greenville 32331

♂ 🛜 **Honey Lake Plantation Resort & Spa** (850-948-9911; honey lakeplantation.com), 1290 Honey Lake Rd, a new resort for the region, is set within the context of a historic quail hunting plantation in the hills between the Little Aucilla River and Honey Lake. Software entrepreneur Bob Williamson developed this private estate, which opened in 2011 into a resort centered on intimate but luxurious accommodations—two lodges, two houses, with multiple rooms within each $179 and up, plus the original Pansy Poe Cottage on Honey Lake. As a destination resort, Honey Lake Plantation offers its guests on-site activities such as trail riding, kayaking, hiking, sport shooting, and archery, plus a spa and fitness center.

Lake City 32055

Being a crossroads where I-10 and I-75 meet, Lake City has always had plenty of hotels and motels to choose from, and I've stayed there many times over the years. Virtually all of them are big-name major chains, with some of the top-quality options being the ♿ 🐾 **Hampton Inn & Suites** (386-487-0580; hamptoninn.hilton.com), 450 SW Florida Gateway Dr, $119 and up, and the **Country Inn & Suites** (386-754-5944;

countryinns.com), 350 SW Florida Gateway Dr, $99 and up. **Cabot Lodge** (386-755-1344; cabotlodgelakecity.com), 3525 US 90 W, whose style I'm generally fond of, took over one of the older motels and jazzed up the service, including adding their afternoon Happy Hour and expansive morning breakfast, starting at $70. If you're on a tight budget, there are many older properties in this area with rates under $70 per night.

Madison 32340

🐾 ♿ **Deerwood Inn** (850-973-2504; deerwoodinn.com), 155 SW St. Augustine Rd, just off I-75 at exit 258, has spacious rooms featuring a large work space for business travelers. $56 and up.

White Springs 32096

The **Historic Telford Hotel** (386-397-2000; telfordhotel.net), P.O. Box 407, on River Rd, dates back to 1903 and continues to welcome guests. Downstairs, enjoy a meal at the Telford Restaurant, renowned for its southern cooking (see *Dining Out*). The top floor is anchored by a long corridor on which all rooms open. They are high-ceilinged and sized for

A ROOM AT THE TELFORD HOTEL, WHITE SPRINGS

the period, reminiscent of railroad hotel rooms, each with antique furnishings and a washbasin; shared baths are down the hall. A breakfast room for guests sits at the end of the corridor, and there is a common area with books and games. Some of the rooms interconnect, and some offer multiple beds. $69 and up.

COTTAGES 🐾 ♂ A collection of six cottages, each with its own full kitchen and screened porch, the **Ichetucknee Hideaway Cottages** (386-935-0844; ichetuckneehideawaycottages.com), 22665 35th Dr, Lake City 32024, $70–100, provide a quiet, genteel retreat within a few minutes drive of Ichetucknee Springs State Park (see *Springs*) and O'Leno State Park (see *Parks*). Weekly and monthly rates available.

CAMPING & CABINS

Fort White 32038

Ichetucknee Family Canoe & Cabins (866-224-2064 or 386-497-2150; ichetuckneecanoeandcabins.com), CR 238, just west of the state park. Primitive cabins ($50–60) sleeping up to 6, and camping for tenters and RVs ($16–22) just upstream from one of the region's most beautiful springs; they provide tube rentals and offers float trip with pickup at take-out.

Lake City 32055

🐾 ♂ (((ϕ))) Not far north of I-10, **Lake City Campground** (386-752-9131; lakecitycampground.com), 4743 N US 441, is a former KOA with sites nicely tucked into the woods and family-friendly amenities like a pool, playground, nature trail, and fishing pond. With easy access to both downtown shopping and outdoor recreation in the Osceola National Forest, it's a nice choice for a getaway. Camping options include pull-through RV or tent sites,

$20–38; rustic cabins near the bathhouse, $38–40; cottages with bunk beds, $58; and lodges with full kitchen, $85.

Live Oak 32060

🏕 ♪ **Spirit of the Suwannee Music Park and Campground** (386-364-1683; musicliveshere.com), 3076 95th Dr, off US 129 at the Suwannee River. It's a campground. It's a concert venue. And it's so much more. Spread out across 700 thickly wooded acres along the Suwannee River, the Spirit of the Suwannee holds events that draw up to 20,000 people—and they still don't run out of space. You can pitch your tent ($20–25) anywhere, including the soft white-sand banks of the Suwannee River. RVs and campers have their choice of spaces along four separate loops ($30 and up), and a wide range of rentals (from the cozy but popular "Possum" trailer to the virtual skybox "Treehouse" overlooking the concert grounds) suit everyone's needs ($89 and up). There's even a special horse camping area with stables ($27–35 plus stable fee). Some visitors come for a weekend; others stay for six months. Canoe rentals, horseback riding, mini golf, swimming, pontoon boat rides, and a classy private floating dining room are just a few of the on-site offerings, along with the camp store and Heritage Village shops (weekends). Rates increase during special events.

Madison 32340

🏕 🐾 ♪ ♿ **Jellystone Park Campground** (850-973-8269 or 800-347-0174; jellystoneflorida.com), Old St. Augustine Rd. This family-oriented camping resort (see *Family Activities*) has a little something for everyone, with campsites and cabins to accommodate all needs and special events held almost every weekend. $35–45 for sites; $55–195 for cabins, which

range from a playful chuck wagon with bunk beds to comfortably refurbished portable classrooms with enough space for the entire family. No bathrooms provided in low-end cabins; nearby bathhouses are shared with campers. Pets permitted, but not in cabins.

Mayo 32066

🐾 (((⋅))) Under the canopy of live oaks along the river at **Suwannee River Rendezvous Resort & Campground** (386-294-2510; suwanneeriverrendezvous.com), 828 NE Primrose Rd, this expansive riverfront resort features a large playground, swimming area, canoe and kayak rentals, and a spring—Convict Spring—right on site. For lodging, take your pick from primitive tenting or full-hookup sites in the campground, $10–30, or rental cabins and basic rooms in the lodge, $60–125, including a riverside A-frame. Senior and military discounts provided.

↪ Along the Suwannee River Wilderness Trail, **Lafayette Blue Springs State Park** (see *Springs*) has cabin rentals (800-326-3521; floridastateparks.reserveamerica.com), $100.

Olustee 32072

Watch a picture-perfect sunset between the cypress trees at **Ocean Pond Campground** (386-752-2577) at Osceola National Forest (see *Wild Places*). The primary full-service campground inside the national forest, Ocean Pond has a special appeal thanks to its perch on its namesake lake, great for fishing, kayaking, and even a little swimming. The campground has both tent sites with a nearby bathhouse and RV sites, all situated in the shade of tall pine trees, $8–18. Osceola National Forest also has limited-facility and primitive campgrounds scattered throughout the forest; see their website for locations.

White Springs 32096

🌸 **Kelly's RV Park** (386-397-2616; kellysrvpark.com), 142 NW Kelly Ln, off US 41 south of town, has sites for RVs and tents ($28), and roomy rental cabins ($55) with screened porch, air-conditioning, and heat set in a deeply shaded park with nature trails that lead to the adjoining Gar Pond Tract.

🐾 **Lee's Country Campground** (386-397-4132; leescountrycamp ground.com), I-75 and CR 136, has more than 30 sites in an open field, suitable for RVs and vans; tent camping is in a nicely shaded patch of woods. Dump station; hot showers and laundry facility, $25.

🐾 ✒ ♿ ✈ **Stephen Foster Folk Culture Center State Park** (800-326-3521; floridastateparks.reserveamerica .com), P.O. Drawer G, US 41. Set up your tent at one of 45 sites under the ancient live oaks, $16, or rent one of their beautiful two-bedroom cabins with screened porch, $100. Leashed pets welcome in campground, not in cabins.

DIVE RESORT (ᵰ) Cave divers visiting Branford stay at the **Steamboat Dive Inn** (386-935-2283; steamboat diveinn.com), corner of US 129 and US 27, Branford 32008, which provides basic motel accommodations and suites ($50–80) with dive instructors and "ice cold air" on site.

✳ Where to Eat

DINING OUT

White Springs
Inside the beautiful historic Telford Hotel (see *Lodging*), the **Telford Restaurant** (386-397-2000; telford hotel.net), 16521 River St, is a great place to gather with friends and family. They dish up a mean catfish and hush puppies, fried chicken and mac-and-cheese, and other southern favorites on their daily buffet. But it's their sweet tea that always steals my heart,

KICK BACK ON THE SCREENED PORCH OF A FLORIDA STATE PARK CABIN AT STEPHEN FOSTER FOLK CULTURE CENTER STATE PARK

just perfect. Lunch buffet $7, dinner $10; entrées including steaks and seafood, $9–15.

EATING OUT

Branford
Nell's Country Kitchen (386-935-1415), 403 Suwannee Ave. Serving up good southern cooking for more than 30 years, Nell's is a regional favorite with breakfasts under $5 and big buffet spreads. Dinner buffet $9.

Grab an ice cream at **Sprinkles** (386-935-6637), 102 Suwannee Ave, where they also serve up burgers, hot dogs, salads, and sandwiches.

Dowling Park
The Village Cafe (386-658-5777) at Village Landing serves breakfast 7–11; lunch and dinner options range from hot dogs to crabcakes. Meals under $10, open until 8 most evenings.

Fort White
Heaping helpings wait at the buffets at the **Goose Nest Restaurant** (386-497-4725; thegoosenest.net), 8877 US 27, where I stopped for some cinnamon French toast one morning. Mon–Sat brings their lunch buffet, $7, where there's always fried chicken; Sat–Sun breakfast buffets, $7, and the Grand Buffet for lunch on Sun, $11.

Lake City
Chasteen's (386-752-7504), 204 N Marion Ave. Sandwiches, salads, and daily lunch specials; don't miss the homemade pimiento and cheese spread! Mon–Fri 7:30–2.

Order a chocolate malt at one of Florida's last remaining authentic drugstore soda fountains, **DeSoto Drug** (386-752-9958), 405 N Marion Ave. Hearty salads and lunch counter favorites in their On the Way Cafe bring this old-fashioned soda fountain into the 21st century—but you can still order a real vanilla Coke or an egg cream with your

meal, $4–10. Tue–Thu 10–6, Fri 10–10.

Ken's Barbecue (386-752-6725), US 90. Mmmm . . . barbecue. This regional chain offers simply the best. Additional locations at South Oak Square on US 129, Live Oak; FL 100 in east Lake City; S 1st St in Lake City; and US 90 (near the college) in Madison. Closed Sun.

For breakfast, enjoy a fresh orange muffin at **Ruppert's Bakery and Cafe** (386-758-3088), 134 N Marion Ave, served up in a former drugstore soda fountain on the square downtown. Tempting bakery items include coconut macaroons, fruit turnovers, and a chocoholic's selection of brownies. Serving up lunch favorites, frozen cappuccino slush and old-fashioned fountain drinks, too!

Live Oak
🦪 **Dixie Grill & Steer Room** (386-364-2810), 101 Dowling Ave. With mouthwatering pies on display when you walk in, you know you'll save room for dessert. This is the in place in Live Oak, where the politics of Suwannee County get resolved over coffee. Daily specials ($6 and up) offer heaping helpings of home-cooked favorites like fried chicken and meat loaf. Daily 5:30 AM–9 PM.

Live Oak Sub Shop (386-362-6503), 511 S Ohio Ave. Boasting "World Famous Subs," this Live Oak landmark piles it on with massive sandwiches good for a picnic on the Suwannee River.

Mayo
At 3 PM on a Monday, the parking lot at the **Mayo Cafe** (386-294-2127), 850 Main St (US 27), is packed. That's because everyone in the tri-county area knows Belinda Travis and Shirley Watson, and knows that these ladies dish up great home cooking, buffet-style.

Try the tempting salads at the salad bar, and southern comfort foods like fried chicken, fried okra, and collard greens. Breakfast served 5–10:30; lunch and dinner until 9 (10 on weekends).

Macclenny
Pier 6 Seafood & Steak House (904-259-6123), 853 S 6th St, has a loyal clientele devoted to their heaping seafood platters for two: Order fried, which comes with a lot of 'gator tail, or steamed, my preference, with shrimp, crabs, and clams. Lunch and dinner daily, $9–15.

Madison
🍴 Now, this is an all-you-can-eat. **O'Neal's Country Buffet** (850-973-6400), 904 W Base St, offers a spread under $10 that boggles the mind with great southern cooking. Start with ribs, catfish, whitefish, or fried chicken and pile on the creamed corn, yams, cheese grits, sour cream potatoes, and baked beans. Your waitress will bring you crystal-clear homemade lemonade or perfect sweet tea, and you can finish up with cherry cobbler or banana pudding. There are dozens of other choices, too, but come early or late—this place is packed at noon!

White Springs
🍴 Moving down the street a bit, the Stormant family still serves up good southern fare as **Fat Belly's** (386-397-2040), 16750 Spring St. Barbecue is the mainstay here but they open early for breakfast—5 AM—for folks headed out early to enjoy the outdoors, and make great pancakes, eggs, and grits. Stop by and fill yourself up!

✳ Entertainment
Hosting everything from the Suwannee River Gospel Jubilee to the Further Festival, the **Spirit of the Suwannee Music Park** (musicliveshere.com), Live Oak, is a massive music venue with concerts on an ongoing basis in both indoor and outdoor locations. Check their website for the current schedule of events, which also range to antique car shows, national trail riding meetings, and other large gatherings.

At **Thayer's Grove** (904-755-9035; southwestfloridabluegrass.org/fljams .html), Mikesville, enjoy free bluegrass and folk music jams on Wed at 1 PM, off FL 18 just west of I-75.

✳ Selective Shopping
Dowling Park
In the shops of Village Landing on CR 136, the **Rustic Shop** (386-658-5273) stands out with its mix of antiques, import items, and crafts, including fine quilts, pillows, and crocheted baby sets

BARBECUE AND GOOD SOUTHERN BREAKFAST AWAITS AT FAT BELLY'S IN WHITE SPRINGS

FRANKLIN MERCANTILE, GLEN ST. MARY

174 N Marion Ave, where I discovered intricately carved and inlaid pelicans and parrots as well as fine gemstones cut and awaiting your choice of setting.

Nana's Antiques & Collectibles (386-752-0272), 327 N Marion Ave. Lovely antique oak china cabinets, country gifts and antiques, collectible Heritage Lace, and Boyds Bears—a little bit of collectibles, a lot of home decor.

Rowand's Mall (888-904-9045 or 386-752-3350), 261 N Marion Ave. A bit of everything in this multidealer mall, from collectible coins, stamps, baseball cards, and postcards to minerals, matchbooks, Depression glass, and a smattering of books.

Webb's Antique Mall (386-758-5564; webbsantiquemalls.com), US 441/41 and I-10. With 300 dealer booths to roam, you can get lost in here for days, checking out items from vintage tools and golf clubs to fine china, collectible Barbies, and church pews. Plan a day—you'll need it to absorb everything!

Macclenny
Rachel's Farmhouse (904-259-2990), 238 E Macclenny Ave. Step inside this old-time mercantile set in a historic home to browse primitives, local crafts, and old-time farm implements. Antique furniture in various stages of restoration is scattered throughout the house and the porches. Open Wed–Sat.

Madison
For summer fun, **Madison Antiques Market & Interiors** (850-973-9000), 197 SW Range Ave, had an entire tableau of water-skiers in vintage swimsuits filling their front window. This large downtown store is chock-full of treasures, including vintage clothing, fine antique furnishings, and classy glassware.

made by local residents. Open 10–5; closed Sun.

Glen St. Mary
Franklin Mercantile (904-259-6040), CR 125 S, is an old-time general store and post office in this once thriving citrus town. Step back a century as you browse through antiques, local crafts, and gifts. Open Fri–Sat 10–5.

Lake City
A Company of Angels (386-752-5200), 313 N Marion Ave. Uplifting gifts, from spiritual books, candles, and New Age music to wind chimes, custom-recipe aromatherapy, and, of course, angel-themed items.

Antiques North-South Connection (386-758-9280), I-75 and US 441, exit 414. Five thousand square feet. One owner. Loads of antiques. Literally: A new truckload comes in every week. Look for beaded Victorian lamps, quilts, milk bottles and country kitchen implements, Christmas decor, and, my favorite, row upon row of funky saltcellars.

For fine art in stone, visit **Lake City Lapidary & Jewelry** (386-755-9665),

Bring your life list! Heavily stocked with out-of-print fiction, especially vintage paperbacks, **The Old Bookstore** (850-973-6833), 115 W Pinckney, is a bibliophile's dream, a place to spend hours browsing the narrow aisles. Their Florida section includes both used and new books. Record collectors—ask about 78s and other vinyl.

White Springs

Cousin Thelma's is the gift shop at Stephen Foster Folk Culture Center State Park (see *Parks*), and thanks to the focus of the park, it's a shop full of Florida folk music and craft. There are turquoise-inlaid fine wood turnings by Tony Cortese, pine needle baskets, painted window folk art, and quilts by "Artist Lady" Ann Opgenorth. I find new treasures here on every visit!

FARMER'S MARKETS AND U-PICK

Lake City

K. C.'s Produce (386-752-1449), 2275 SE Baya. The most popular spot in Lake City to pick up a bunch of bananas or a pound of peppers—a great selection of fresh fruits and vegetables sold wholesale and retail. Closed Sun.

Live Oak

Suwannee County Farmer's Market (386-776-2362), 1302 SW 11th St. Fresh produce from local farms every Sat 9–1, Apr–Sept, at the Railroad Station in Live Oak, year-round.

Wellborn

Scott's Blueberry Farm (386-963-4952), 4984 124th St off US 90. Watch for the sign that says FOLLOW THE YELLOW DIRT ROAD and do just that to one of the region's most popular U-picks. In-season mid- to late May.

✳ Special Events

February: The **Battle of Olustee** (battleofolustee.org/reenactment.html), Olustee, third weekend. It's the largest Civil War reenactment in the Southeast, featuring living history encampments, a large sutlers' (period shopping) area, and battle reenactments on Sat and Sun.

"Just Because" Herb Festival, O'Toole's Herb Farm (see *Gardens*), brightens up a winter's day betwixt the solstice and equinox. Come out for live music, workshops, and vendors; fee.

March: **Wild Azalea Festival** (386-397-2310), third Sat, White Springs. Celebrate the fragrant blossoms that usher in spring on the Suwannee with arts, crafts, music, and food.

Suwannee County Fair (386-362-7366; suwanneecountyfair.com), 1302 11th St, at the Suwannee County Fairgrounds, held the last week of March/beginning of April. A traditional, old-time county fair with judged livestock and vegetables, quilting, fine arts, and other crafts; commercial and educational exhibits, a popular midway, talent show, and the "politician bake off" (this, I've gotta see!).

April: **Lee Days**, Lee, first Sat. A celebration of the heritage of this tiny Florida town, with arts and crafts and food vendors at the park.

May: More than 40 years running, the **Hamilton County Rodeo** (386-792-1415) is held the first weekend, Hamilton County Arena, Jasper.

Step back to pioneer days in downtown Madison at **Down Home Days** (madisonfl.org), Madison, third weekend, with traditional crafts and foods.

June: ✐ The **Wellborn Blueberry Festival** (386-963-1157; wellborn communityassociation.com) celebrates the fruits of the harvest with a parade, talent content, live entertainment, and, of course, a blueberry bake-off. Free wholesome family fun!

October: **Alligator Festival**, O'Leno State Park (see *Parks*), mid-month,

FLORIDA FOLK FESTIVAL

(877-6FL-FOLK; floridastateparks.org/folkfest), Memorial Day weekend, Stephen Foster State Folk Culture Center, White Springs. If you truly want to know Florida and its people, plan your vacation around this incredible Memorial Day weekend extravaganza of folk music and Florida culture, now more than half a century old. The Folklife Area brings together Florida's melting pot of cultures, and 14 concert stages scattered throughout the park host more than 250 concerts daily. Each evening the spotlight shifts to the main stage, where Florida troubadours continue the tradition of Will McLean and Gamble Rogers with their haunting ballads of our state, its history, its beauty, and its troubles. Nationally acclaimed folk acts perform on Saturday evening, and the Florida State Fiddle Contest brings on a hoedown atmosphere Sunday night. As the weekend unfolds, follow the orange blazes in search of the Seminole Camp and homemade churned-on-site ice cream, or join in one of the 75 music, dance, and storytelling workshops. And don't forget the ethnic-food vendors! It's your annual opportunity to touch the soul of Florida. Daily admission costs $20–25 adults, $4 ages 6–16; weekend pass $40–50 adults. For optimum comfort, bring your own folding chair.

celebrates the heritage of Columbia County, where the first settlement (now Lake City) was called Alligator Town. The three-day Columbus Day weekend event includes a reenactment of the 1836 Seminole War Battle of San Felasco Hammock and a Native American gathering with foods and crafts.

Pioneer Day Festival (lafayette countychamber.com/pioneerday.htm), Mayo, second Sat. This pioneer-themed event mixes up history and fun: Southern belles drift through town as staged gunfights rage; the crowd whoops and hollers at the rodeo while more sedate visitors amble through hundreds of craft booths and an arts show.

Stephen Foster Quilt Show & Sale, Stephen Foster Folk Culture Center State Park (see *Parks*), held last weekend. A top southeastern quilt show.

Late October–early November:
Columbia County Fair (386-752-

8822; columbiacountyfair.org), a traditional agricultural fair.

December: The forest sparkles during the **Christmas Festival of Lights**, Stephen Foster Folk Culture Center State Park (see *Parks*), held month-long. From dusk through 9 PM, take a horse-drawn carriage through the wonderland of more than four million Christmas lights, or ride in a slow line of vehicles along the park's looping road and wish you'd taken the carriage ride. Shops in the Craft Village will be open and selling their wares.

Festival of Lights, Live Oak. A drive-through wonderland of light in Spirit of the Suwannee Music Park (see *Camping & Cabins*), including a miniature Victorian Christmas Village and Santa's workshop. $5 per car.

Greenville Country Christmas, Greenville, is held mid-month with a parade and live entertainment.

THE LOWER SUWANNEE

CEDAR KEY, CHIEFLAND, AND TRENTON/DIXIE, LEVY & GILCHRIST COUNTIES

I f you've come to Florida for peace and quiet, you'll find it "way down upon the Suwannee River" in the Pure Water Wilderness, a region known best for its rivers, springs, and estuaries, part of the laid-back western shore of Florida known as the Nature Coast. Settlers trickled into the region in the 1850s when state senator David Levy Yulee (son of Moses Levy, founder of Levy County) ran his Florida Railroad from Fernandina Beach to **Cedar Key,** providing the first shipping link across Florida. In 1867 naturalist John Muir followed the path of the Florida Railroad on his 1,000-mile walk to the Gulf of Mexico. Arriving at the Cedar Keys, he fell ill with malaria and spent several months living in the village, which had a booming pencil industry. The fine southern red cedars and white cedars growing on scattered islands throughout the Gulf made the perfect housing for pencil leads. The original settlement on Atsena Otie Key included several houses and the Eberhard Faber Pencil Mill. After the island was devastated by a tidal surge in 1896, business shifted to Depot Key, today's downtown Cedar Key.

Cedar Key sits between the mouth of the Withlacoochee River, on which the towns of **Yankeetown** and **Inglis** sprang up, and the mouth of the Suwannee River, home to the fishing village of **Suwannee**. The railroad line (now the Nature Coast State Trail, a rail-trail) connected **Fanning Springs**, where Fort Fannin was built along the river in 1838 as part of a chain of forts during the Seminole Wars, with the turpentine and lumber towns of **Chiefland**, **Old Town**, and **Cross City**.

On the southern shore of the Steinhatchee River, the fishing village of **Jena** grew up around the abundant mullet and crab, with packinghouses shipping out seafood to distant ports. Dixie County boasts the lowest per-capita population in the state, and Gilchrist County has only a single traffic light, at the crossroads in the county seat of **Trenton**. Sleepy riverside hamlets and end-of-the-road fishing villages like **Suwannee** provide a natural charm found only in rural Florida.

GUIDANCE Pure Water Wilderness (352-486-5470; purewaterwilderness.com), P.O. Box 779, Cedar Key 32625, is the primary contact for the region, which comprises six distinct chambers of commerce in the three-county area.

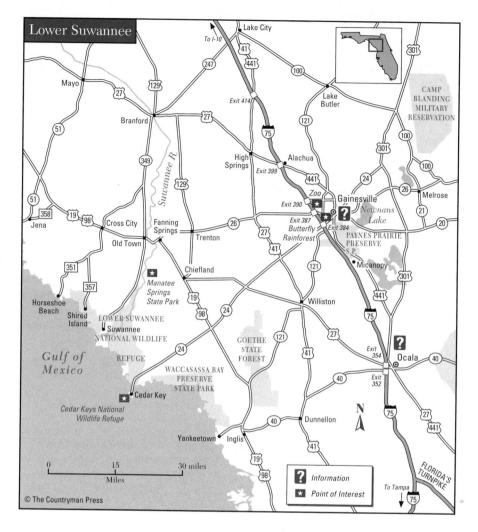

Lower Suwannee

© The Countryman Press

GETTING THERE *By air:* **Gainesville Regional Airport** (352-373-0249; gra-gnv
.com; see *Gainesville & Vicinity* chapter) provides the only "nearby" commuter
access, an hour or more from most points on the Nature Coast.

By bus: **Greyhound** stops along US 19 in Cross City and Chiefland.

By car: **Alt US 27**, **US 129**, and **US 19** are the major north–south routes through
this trio of rural counties. To reach them from **I-75**, use **US 27** from Ocala or
High Springs, or **FL 24** or **FL 26** west out of Gainesville.

GETTING AROUND This is a large rural area with many dead-end roads to the
coast and to the Suwannee River. Make sure you have adequate gas in your tank
before heading down the long roads to Suwannee, Shired Island, and Horseshoe
Beach. **Driving is a must** between points, unless you're **paddling** the coastline on
the Historic Big Bend Saltwater Paddling Trail (a segment of the Florida Circumnavigational Trail; see *Paddling*) or **bicycling** the trails of the region (see *Bicycling*).

ADVENTURE AWAITS AT CEDAR KEY

MEDICAL EMERGENCIES **Nature Coast Regional Hospital** (352-528-2801), 125 SW 7th St, Williston. Call 911 for serious emergencies; the nearest major hospitals are **Seven Rivers Community Hospital** (352-795-6560; sevenriversregional .com), 6201 N Suncoast Blvd in Crystal River (10 miles south of Levy County on US 19) or in Gainesville (see the *Gainesville & Vicinity* chapter), 40 miles east. Important: Cell phone coverage may be sporadic to nonexistent off the main highways.

✳ To See

ARCHAEOLOGICAL SITES At the end of CR 347 in the **Shell Mound Unit** of Lower Suwannee NWR (see *Wild Places*), a short trail takes you to the most significant archaeological feature in this region, a 28-foot-tall shell midden created between 2500 BC and AD 1000 by the ancestors of the Timucua who once inhabited this coastline. Just off CR 351 at Old Railroad Grade in Dixie County, the **Garden Patch Archaeological Site** at Horseshoe Beach has several burial and ceremonial mounds and two large middens.

A PARK FOR THE ARTS IN DOWNTOWN CEDAR KEY

ART GALLERIES Intrigued by the stacks of driftwood outside **Catch the Drift** (352-542-7770), 410 US 19 S, Old Town, I stopped to take a look and was glad I did. C. Emery Mills's decade-old gallery is all about nature as art, with 10 local artists creating sculptures from wood, shells, and coral.

Adjoined by a whimsical art park created by its members, the **Cedar Keyhole** (352-543-5801; cedarkeyhole .com), 457 2nd St, Cedar Key, represents more than 20 local artists and a handful of consignments. Their gallery tempts with art in virtually every medium. Fused art glass captures the motion of ocean waves, and Cindy's gourd handbags add a touch of humor. Despite ceramic slugs and hand-painted dresses, the art reflects island themes. Ongoing gallery events, including nationally juried exhibits, occupy the second floor.

HISTORIC SITES **Atsena Otie Key**, abandoned by most of its settlers after an 1896 hurricane-driven storm surge, is now part of the Cedar Key NWR (see *Wild Places*), only accessible by boat (see *Ecotours* and *Paddling*). Buried under cover of maritime hammock along the short hiking trail from the dock are reminders that this was the original town of Cedar Key. Bricks scattered around a deep hole are all that's left of the Eberhard Faber Pencil Mill. The deep hole contained the machinery of the mill, driven by water flowing through a sluice. Workers sawed cedars into the small slats required for making pencils. In an ironic twist of nature, a grand cedar now crowns the spot. The trail ends at the town's cemetery, set on a bluff overlooking the salt marshes. The marble tombstones date back to 1882, some fallen, some as clean as the day they were erected. A wrought-iron fence cordons off one tiny corner, a private family plot under the windswept oaks. **Seahorse Key**, part of the island chain, has a small cemetery with Union soldiers who died while occupying the Seahorse Key Lighthouse. The island can only be visited on open-house days during the fall seafood festival (see *Special Events*).

In Fanning Springs, **Fort Fanning Park** marks the site of the original fort just north of US 19 on the Suwannee River. Back in 1838, U.S. Army troops built and manned a small wooden fortress at the river crossing, Palmetto, as part of a string of defenses during the Second Seminole War. It was renamed Fort Fannin in honor of Colonel Alexander Fannin; the name became corrupted over time to Fanning. As the war raged on and Fannin attempted to round up Seminoles for deportation to the West, the garrison grew from a dozen men to nearly 200 in 1843. Yellow fever ravaged the troops. Abandoned in 1849, the remains of the fort vanished back into the forest.

MUSEUMS

Cedar Key

&. **Cedar Key Historical Society Museum** (352-543-5549; cedarkey museum.org), 609 2nd St. Exhibits and artifacts trace the history of this coastal town from its founding through Civil War occupation, the rise and fall of the pencil industry, and current advances in aquaculture; an excellent resource for researchers and amateur historians in understanding Florida's Gulf Coast. Open Sat 11–5, Sun–Fri 1–4; donation.

✍ &. **Cedar Key Museum Historic State Park** (352-543-5340; floridastate parks.org/cedarkeymuseum). Follow the signs out through the residential

FORT FANNING PARK

area to this large compound established in 1962 as the first museum to capture Cedar Key's long history as presented by St. Clair Whitman, a colorful local man who started his own personal museum of artifacts and seashells. Whitman's house is under restoration on the property; a small trail leads along the edge of the estuary. Thu–Mon 10–5; fee.

Levyville

& Amid the farms and fields of Levy County, quilting is one of the favored pastimes. At the **Levy County Quilt Museum** (352-493-2801), 11050 NW 10th Ave, quilters come together to perfect their craft. The modern log structure contains plenty of space for active quilting while displaying prizewinning quilts (and other related handicrafts) around the rooms.

RAILROADIANA Although the railroad no longer carries cypress logs through Chiefland, Trenton, and Bell, these **train depots** along US 129 are put to good use. In Chiefland, the depot houses the chamber of commerce and is the centerpiece of a small park that's the southern terminus of the Nature Coast Trail (see *Greenway*). When the chamber is open, you can tour the new **Chiefland Historic Train Museum**, a collection of railroad ephemera and artifacts in this 1913 station. The 1906 **Trenton Railroad Depot** serves as another trail terminus in a city park, while the **Bell Trail Depot**, built in 1905, serves as Bell Town Hall. On US 19 in Cross City, the old **railway freight station** marks another end of the Nature Coast Trail near Barber Ave. At Cedar Key the **depot** marking the historic western terminus of the Florida Railroad is still on Railroad St, but the trestle leading to the coast has been obliterated by condos. You can walk along the old railroad line on the **Cedar Key Railroad Trestle Nature Trail** off Grove St [29.144801, -83.032668]. Along US 19, watch for "3 Spot," a **steam engine circa 1915** in a small wayside park just north of the blinker at Gulf Hammock. One of the few pieces of original rolling stock displayed in Florida, it pulled logging cars to the Patterson-McInnes sawmill.

WINERY & **Dakotah Winery & Vineyards** (352-493-9309; dakotahwinery.com), 14365 NW US 19, Chiefland. Established in 1985, this premier Florida winery features wines and other products produced from cultivated muscadine grapes. It's a unique place with a touch of the romantic: Antique windmills stand tall over the vineyard, and visitors relax under an arbor overlooking the vines and a duck pond. Inside the tasting room, owner Rob Rittgers buzzes around, answering questions and pouring wine for each new group of guests. Art fills the spacious room, from hand-painted wine bottles with Florida scenes to woodcraft, paintings, quilts, and sketches by local artists. Mon–Sat 10–5.

✱ To Do

BICYCLING On the **Nature Coast Trail** (see *Greenway*), enjoy a 32-mile paved bike path connecting the communities of the Lower Suwannee. Mountain bikers frequent the trail system at **Manatee Springs State Park** (see *Springs*).

BIRDING You'll always see pelicans at the **Cedar Key dock**—just beware of getting too close! At **Cedar Key NWR** (see *Wild Places*), each island has colonial bird rookeries and beautiful beaches; watch out for the high snake population in forested areas. **Seahorse Key** is off-limits to all visitors Mar–June due to its fragile pelican rookery. **Lower Suwannee NWR** (see *Wild Places*) offers great birding opportunities along the trails at the **Shell Island Unit**, where you'll see Louisiana herons, willets, and other wading birds in shallow saline ponds near Dennis Creek, and belted kingfishers along the hammocks in the **California Swamp** (see *Scenic Drives*). In spring follow the **Road to Nowhere** (see *Scenic Drives*) through the **Jena Unit of Big Bend WMA**, and take the side roads (if wet, only navigable by four-wheel drive or on foot) west to the Gulf hammocks to see seaside sparrows, clouds of migratory birds (from robins to vireos and warblers), and nesting pairs of black rails. At any time, you'll see wading birds roadside in the salt marshes.

BOATING For a map of boat ramps along the **Suwannee River**, contact the Suwannee River Water Management District (386-362-1001; srwmd.state.fl.us); one of the easiest to access is off US 19-98 at the Gilchrist–Dixie county line in the old roadside picnic area. Recreational boaters enjoy playing on a segment of the **Cross Florida Barge Canal** accessed at Inglis, off US 19. In Cedar Key parking gets tight around the **public marina** (downtown) on weekend mornings. **Island Hopper Tours** (352-543-5904; cedarkeyislandhopper.com), City Marina, rents boats and provides guided tours and drop-offs (see *Ecotours*) on the Gulf of Mexico. At Suwannee marinas, including **Miller's Marina** (see *Houseboating*) and **Suwannee Marina** (352-542-9159), provide access to the Suwannee River and the Gulf of Mexico.

DIVING Scuba divers have several unique venues to try out their skills. At **Devil's Den** near Williston (see *Dive Resort*), a shimmering pool of 72-degree ice-blue water fills an ancient cave. As you descend stone steps to access the open water underground, a chandelier of ivy dangles down through the sinkhole, with rays of sunlight filtering through the opening. It's a surreal and beautiful scene. Divers delight in discovering prehistoric fossils on the limestone bottom. Dive fee $37, additional $10–15 for night dives, gear rental $35 for full kit. Cave certification not required. Full dive shop and instruction on site. General admission, $9, lets you snorkel or just watch.

At nearby **Blue Grotto Springs** (352-528-5770; divebluegrotto.com), 3852 NE 172nd Court, cave-certified divers can descend up to 100 feet into the Floridan Aquifer, dropping down into a cave system from the bottom of a sinkhole; dive shop with rentals on site. Daily 8–6, $38 per diver.

The many **springs of the Suwannee River** are open to open-water diving, but *only* cave-certified divers should venture into the crevices from which the waters pour. Wreck diving is a popular pastime, as divers can visit sunken steamboats such as the *City of Hawkinsville* (flheritage.com/archaeology/underwater). Built in 1896, it was the very last of the Suwannee River steamboats, sunk just south of Fanning Springs in 1922. It's a designated underwater archaeological preserve. See **Suwannee River Scuba** (352-463-7111; suwanneeriverscuba.com), 17950 NW 90th Court, for guided trips, cold air, rentals, and instruction. In addition to open-water dives, they'll take you out into the Gulf of Mexico to dive sponge beds that few people ever see.

ECOTOURS ✐ Catch a ride out to the outer islands of the Cedar Keys with **Island Hopper Tours** (see *Boating*), offering island drop-offs (perfect for exploring Atsena Otie or Seahorse Key), one-hour scenic cruises, and sunset cruises. $25 adults, $15 children under 12.

Captain Doug's Tidewater Tours (352-543-9523; tidewatertours.com), Cedar Key, takes you out from the City Marina on a catamaran for an interpretive cruise of Cedar Key from the water, followed by your choice of tours, including a cruise up the Suwannee River or through the islands that make up the Cedar Keys. $26–45 with discounts for ages 10 and under.

Paddle with knowledgeable local guide Brack Barker at **Wild Florida Adventures** (877-WILD-WAV; wild-florida.com), where you'll explore the region's estuaries and waterways at a leisurely pace on a custom-tailored trip. Destinations include Cedar Key, Steinhatchee, Waccassa, and Suwannee, $35–45.

FISHING For recommended fishing guides and charters in Cedar Key, check with the Cedar Key Chamber of Commerce (see *Guidance*). ❦ **Lady Pirate Island Tours** (352-486-4413; ladypirateboattours.com), Slip 16, City Marina, will take you out on their 22-foot pontoon for half a day of inshore fishing, $55 per person—or you can rent the whole boat and crew for the day. Bait and tackle are available at **Fishbonz** (352-543-9222), 509 3rd St, Cedar Key. In Suwannee the full-service **Suwannee Marina** (352-542-9159; suwanneemarinainc.150m.com), 219 Canal St, has a boat ramp, charters, dry dock, gasoline, bait and tackle, and mechanics on site. At Inglis, **Lake Rousseau** is a hot spot for bass anglers; check in at the fish camps (see *Fish Camps*) along CR 40 for guides.

HIKING Hiking in the region is limited to short day hikes leading out to scenic points along the Suwannee River and the Gulf estuaries, mainly in the **Lower Suwannee National Wildlife Refuge** (see *Wild Places*) and state parks. I especially enjoy the nature trails at **Manatee Springs State Park** (see *Springs*). At **Andrews Wildlife Management Area** (see *Wild Places*), trails lead past state and national grand champion trees. The **Cedar Key Railroad Trestle Nature Trail** (see *Railroadiana*) offers great views and birding with a different take on Cedar Key. One constant about hiking anywhere near the Suwannee River—ticks are a common problem except in the dead of winter. Use big doses of insect repellent before you hit the trails.

HOUSEBOATING **Miller's Suwannee Houseboats** (800-458-BOAT or 352-542-7349; suwanneehouseboats.com), CR 349, Suwannee, rents houseboats for cruises up the 70-mile meander of the Suwannee River from Suwannee to Fanning Springs— head out for an overnight, a few days, or a week. You have all the amenities of home, minus the yard, as you drift past shorelines crowded with red maple and sweetgum, and sight a manatee or two. Rates vary by season and number of days, starting at $599 for two days and going up to $1,495 for a week; special deals for active military personnel on leave. Millers now also offers local lodging (see *Lodging*).

HUNTING Off US 19 in Fanning Springs, **Andrews Wildlife Management Area** (see *Wild Places*) is a popular fall hunting ground for deer and wild hogs on more than 3,500 acres of uplands and swamp forest.

PADDLING Two major paddling trails meet in this region defined by estuary and swamp forests. The lower Big Bend section of the **Florida Circumnavigational**

Trail (dep.state.fl.us/gwt/paddling/saltwater.htm) stretches 101 miles from Steinhatchee to Yankeetown. If that sounds like a lot of paddling, you're right. Like the Wilderness Waterway in Everglades National Park, this is an extraordinarily remote paddling trip. Don't set out unless you have appropriate maps and navigational aids, camping gear, and an adequate supply of fresh water and food. Maps and details are provided on their website, including information on which sections require a free permit for camping.

Along the **Suwannee River Wilderness Trail** (800-868-9914; floridastateparks .org/wilderness) it's 55 miles from Gornto Spring (see *Springs*) to the mouth of the Suwannee alone. En route, five sites provide a place for you to launch from or camp overnight. Canoe liveries can help you get out on the Suwannee at Manatee Springs, Fanning Springs, Otter Springs, and Hart Springs (see *Springs*). **Suwannee Guides** (352-542-8331; suwanneeguides.com), based in Suwannee where the two trails meet, can help you with rentals, logistics, and shuttles for any length of paddling expedition. **Suwannee River Tours** (352-450-6892; suwanneerivertours .com), based just outside Manatee Springs State Park, provides kayak and canoe rentals and sets up multiday paddling trips along this section of the river.

Easy paddling trips can be started and ended at any of the springs and campgrounds along the Suwannee River that rent canoes. But if you'd like to explore the vast Gulf estuary, there are several good options. **Kayak Cedar Keys** (352-543-9447) rents kayaks you can launch from the City Beach in downtown Cedar Key to explore the estuary or paddle over to Atsenie Otie Key. The **Faraway Inn** (see *Hotels, Motels & Resorts*) rents kayaks as well. Or go with a guide. Brack Barker with **Wild Florida Adventures** (see *Ecotours*) leads personalized guided trips all along this coast and the rivers that feed it.

If you've brought your own kayak, there are public launches along the **Suwannee River** (see *Boating*) and at various points along the estuary, such as the end of CR 40 in Yankeetown and at **Shell Mound** (see *Archaeological Sites*). Between Suwannee and Shired Island, you can launch into the creeks off the **Dixie Mainline Trail** (see *Scenic Drives*), but be sure you find somewhere to park that isn't blocking the road. Or to really get away from it all, put your kayak in at the Cow Creek Bridge in **Big Bend WMA**, where a maze of estuarine waterways cuts through the plain of black needlerush out to the Gulf. On a day trip into any of these watery wilds, carry a GPS and make sure you mark a waypoint at your launch point so you can find it again.

SCENIC DRIVES Showcasing the remote southern fringe of Dixie County in Lower Suwannee Wildlife Refuge (see *Wild Places*), the **Dixie Mainline Trail** is a one-of-a-kind scenic drive, a 9-mile one-lane hard-packed limestone road through the wilds of the cypress-and-gum floodplain of the California Swamp, with one short stop at Salt Creek for a walk out on a boardwalk. Don't expect to drive more than 20 mph, and watch for oncoming traffic. There are pull-offs every mile to allow vehicles to pass. Check with the refuge before utilizing the drive to ensure it's not flooded.

Imagine, if you will, a lengthy paved road in the wildest and most inaccessible portion of a generally wild and inaccessible part of Florida, ending abruptly in the salt marshes of the Big Bend Aquatic Preserve: the **Road to Nowhere**. This highway didn't access a single home or a fishing pier: It was a clandestine airstrip. During the 1970s and 1980s smugglers landed planes as big as a DC-9 on this highway to drop off loads of marijuana destined for points north. The operation was shut down by law enforcement, but its legacy remains—a ribbon of pavement with unparalleled views of the salt marshes, now used by anglers and paddlers, bikers and birders. One warning: If you drive down the Road to Nowhere, there are two short unpaved sections. Don't go too fast on the second one, or you'll miss the end of the road and end up in the salt marsh! The Road to Nowhere runs through the Jena Unit of Big Bend WMA (see *Wild Places*) and is most easily accessed from CR 358 from the Steinhatchee Bridge (see the *Tallahassee* chapter).

SWIMMING For refreshing plunges into cool, fresh water, try the swimming area at **Fanning Springs State Park** and the open springs at **Hart Springs**, **Manatee Springs**, **Otter Springs**, and **Blue Spring** (see *Springs*). At Cedar Key City Park, a small waterfront park adjacent to the City Marina provides the village's only public beach on the Gulf of Mexico. Several motels in the area have their own private beaches, but the best ones are found on the outer islands, accessed only by boat. Shallow Gulf waters invite at **Shired Island** (end of CR 357) and **Horseshoe Beach** (end of CR 351), accessible via Cross City.

TRAIL RIDING Circle B Ranch (352-450-6892; suwanneerivertours.com/Circle BRanch.html), at the entrance to Manatee Springs State Park, Chiefland, offers equestrians the opportunity to ramble through the dense river forest on half-hour trail rides.

Goethe State Forest (see *Wild Places*) is a favorite, with more than 100 miles of equestrian trails. Look for trailheads at the Black Prong, Apex, and Tidewater Units along CR 336. Camp across the street from the Apex trailhead with your horse at **Trailhead Ranch** (see *Camping & Cabins*) or **Black Prong Equestrian Center** (see *Hotels, Motels & Resorts*), or arrange a guided trail ride with Roberta Cogswell from **North Star Acres** (352-489-9848; dunnellonbusiness.com/north star.htm) in nearby Dunnellon.

With your own horse, you can ride alongside the paved **Nature Coast Trail** (see *Greenway*) connecting Chiefland, Trenton, and Cross City.

At **Two Hawk Hammock** (see *Lodging*), Williston, take a gentle trail ride through the forests on their property and at adjoining Devil's Den (see *Dive Resort*), either on horseback or in a horse-drawn buggy. $50 per rider, discount for additional riders.

WALKING TOURS Stop in at the Cedar Key Historical Society Museum (see *Museums*) for the official **walking tour of Cedar Key**, which leads you past sites in the old town and explains the history of the outlying islands.

✳ Green Space

GREENWAY From its start in Dixie County at Cross City, the 32-mile **Nature Coast Trail** (352-493-6072; dep.state.fl.us/gwt/guide/regions/crossflorida/trails /nature_coast_trail.htm) forks in Fanning Springs. One prong heads east to Trenton, ending at their historic train depot; the other heads south to end at the Chiefland railroad depot. Equestrians may use the grassy strip parallel to the paved biking trail.

SPRINGS

There's a big reason they call this the Pure Water Wilderness. Fresh water abounds! Especially along the Suwannee River, where more than 200 springs can be found. Here's some of the more popular for outdoor recreation. Contact the Suwannee River Water Management District (see *Boating*) for a map of spring locations in the Suwannee River for additional diving and swimming choices.

North of Old Town, **Gornto Springs**, off CR 349 and Rock Sink Church Rd [29.779457, -82.940365] is a Dixie County Park, an old-fashioned swimming hole with a platform where folks jump into the 10-foot-deep water, which flows down a short run and into the Suwannee.

✍ **Hart Springs Park** (352-463-3444; hartsprings.com), 4240 SW 86th Ave, is a family-oriented Gilchrist County Park with swimming, hiking, and camping (see *Camping & Cabins*); the crystalline Hart Spring pours out 62 million gallons each day. Fee.

Fanning Springs State Park (352-463-3420; floridastateparks.org /fanningsprings), 18020 NW US 19, has a well-developed swimming area around the main spring, plus canoe rentals and cabins (see *Camping & Cabins*). **Manatee Springs State Park** (352-493-6072; floridastateparks.org /manateesprings), NW 115th St, outside Chiefland, has swimming in the beautiful but chilly spring, boating, fishing, hiking and biking trails, and a large campground (see *Camping & Cabins*).

Otter Springs (352-463-0800; ottersprings.com), 6470 SW 80th Ave, Trenton, is a second-magnitude spring along the Suwannee. In addition to swimming in the 73-degree water, you can ramble the hiking trails or relax in their campground (see *Camping & Cabins*).

At the end of CR 339A off Alt US 27 between Bronson and Chiefland, **Blue Springs Park** (352-486-3303), 4550 NE 94th Place, in Devil's Hammock creates a natural 72-degree pool as it feeds the Waccasassa River. Spend an afternoon picnicking and swimming under the shady oaks at this Levy County Park; fee. South of Bronson, **Blue Grotto Springs** and **Devil's Den** cater to cave divers (see *Diving*).

In addition, **Blue Springs** (386-454-1369; bluespringspark.com), **Ginnie Springs** (386-454-7188; ginniespringsoutdoors.com), and **Poe Springs Park** (386-454-1992) are in Gilchrist County along the Santa Fe River. However, these parks are very close to High Springs and far from the rest of the region. See the *Gainesville & Vicinity* chapter for more details.

WILD PLACES Encompassing more than 40,000 acres, the **Lower Suwannee National Wildlife Refuge** (352-493-0238; fws.gov/lowersuwannee), 16450 NW 31st Place, protects the floodplain of the Suwannee River as it reaches the Gulf of Mexico. Most of it is inaccessible except by boat, although there are short hiking trails at Shell Mound and the park headquarters. In Fanning Springs, **Andrews Wildlife Management Area** (386-758-0531; myfwc.com/viewing/recreation/wmas /lead/andrews) off US 27 is notable for the number of national and state champion trees in its dark riverside forests, reached by dirt roads and short hiking trails.

Near Blue Spring, **Devil's Hammock WMA** (myfwc.com/viewing/recreation /wmas/cooperative/devils-hammock) off Alt US 27 is crisscrossed with old logging roads usable for hiking, biking, and horseback riding; be mindful of hunting season for your own safety.

Extending through most of southern Levy County, **Goethe State Forest** (352-447-2202; fl-dof.com/state_forests/goethe.html), 8250 SE CR 336, has three large tracts for recreation and a new visitors center, plus a showcase cypress tree at Big Cypress.

At **Cedar Key Scrub State Reserve** (386-758-0531; floridastateparks.org/cedar keyscrub) off FL 24, hikers meander through a coastal scrub, rare in this wetland region.

Hunters make much use of the **Jena Unit of the Big Bend WMA** (myfwc.com /viewing/recreation/wmas/lead/big-bend/visitor-information), a massive preserve in Dixie County along the Road to Nowhere (see *Scenic Drives*), where rugged side roads reach pristine beaches along the grassy shores of the Gulf estuary.

Boaters and paddlers have an extensive watery wilderness to explore. In addition to the backwaters of the Lower Suwannee NWR and the 90-mile **Big Bend Aquatic Preserve** (dep.state.fl.us/coastal/sites/bigbend) to the north of Suwannee (see *Paddling*), they can visit the islands making up **Cedar Key National Wildlife Refuge** (352-493-0238; fws.gov/cedarkeys), off Cedar Key. And at **Waccasassa Bay Preserve State Park** (352-493-0238; floridastateparks.org/waccasassabay), 31,000 acres between Cedar Key and Yankeetown, boaters have the place all to themselves—it's a wet wilderness suitable for paddling and fishing, with primitive campsites available to paddlers.

✴ Lodging

BED & BREAKFASTS

Cedar Key 32625

🐾 ✎ ♂ (ᵠ) At the **Cedar Key Bed & Breakfast** (877-543-5051 or 352-543-9000; cedarkeybandb.com), corner of 3rd and F streets, P.O. Box 701, innkeepers Bill and Alice Philips take you back to Cedar Key's heyday as an exporter of fine cedar for buildings and pencils. Built in 1880, this home was used as a boardinghouse by the daughter of one of Florida's first senators, David Levy Yulee. Within an easy walk

of shopping and the docks, it's an ideal place to unwind under the paddle fans with a good book. Six romantic rooms with TV, two suites, and a Honeymoon Cottage, each decked out with period antiques, $105–240.

Don't look for right angles in the **Island Hotel** (800-432-4640 or 352-543-5111; islandhotel-cedarkey.com), 2nd and B streets, a historic tabby-and-oak hotel, built just before the Civil War—it's the place in town to sleep with history. Each room ($80–135) has a private bath; full breakfast in the restaurant downstairs is included with your stay.

Inglis 34449

☗ ♪ ((ᵗ)) ⤳ **Pine Lodge Country Lodge** (352-447-7463; pinelodgefla .com), 649 CR 40 W. Enjoy lazy days and quiet nights amid romantic decor in Old Crackertown, with a selection of four rooms inside the main house or five nearby cottages, $110–156. A beautiful sunset is just steps away on the antique porch rockers, and a hearty country breakfast awaits you in the morning. Elvis fans will appreciate being immersed in part of the set of *Follow That Dream*, which was filmed along this highway out to the Gulf.

Williston 32696

The pretty guest rooms at **Two Hawk Hammock** (352-528-0885; twohawk hammock.com), 17990 NE 53rd Ln, let you roll out of bed and head out for a trail ride—or a dive at adjacent Devil's Den (see *Dive Resort*). Each room sleeps up to four people, $75–85, with mini fridge and coffeemaker. Hot breakfast prepared for an additional $10-per-person fee. Stable your horse on the property for $15–25.

HOTELS, MOTELS & RESORTS

Bronson 32621

☗ A haven for horse lovers, **Black Prong Equestrian Center** (352-486-1234; blackprong.com), 450 SE CR 337, is surrounded by Goethe State Forest (see *Wild Places*). In addition to being a playing and training ground for your favorite steed, it's also a secluded getaway with modern, well-appointed one- and two-bedroom apartments ($88–110), all manner of campsites ($20–30), and stalls for your horses ($32–40).

Cedar Key 32625

♠ ☗ ♿ Although it's one of the older lodges on Dock Street, **Dockside**

Motel (800-541-5432), 491 Dock St, delivers with large well-kept suites overlooking either the marina or the Gulf ($55–60). Open up those massive picture windows and let the sea breeze pour through. Ten units; small pets accepted.

☗ ⤳ Harking back to childhood vacation memories, the rooms and cottages at the **Faraway Inn Motel & Cottages** (352-543-5330; farawayinn.com), 3rd and G streets, sweep you back into the great age of Florida tourism—the funky beach cottage of the 1940s. $75–120 for rooms, $140–160 for cottages, with weekly rates a great deal. Small pets accepted.

♠ ☗ Located at the very end of FL 24, the 1950s-era **Gulf Side Motel** (888-543-5308; thegulfsidemotel.com), 552 1st St, sits right on the Gulf, enabling visitors to kick back and relax on the fishing pier, porch swing, or Adirondack chairs overlooking the water. Neat and recently redecorated after extensive renovations, all rooms are nonsmoking. Choose from efficiencies or standard rooms ($75–140) and be sure to check out Room 8, with its great Gulf view. Nine units; small pets accepted.

♠ **Harbour Master Suites** (352-543-9146; cedarkeyharbourmaster.com), 390 Dock St. Settling in for an extended stay? Here's luxury for you— a choice of six suites with apartment-style amenities, available by the night, week, or month, $90–145. Each suite features tastefully furnished rooms with large windows; two provide full kitchen.

☗ ((ᵗ)) ⤳ **Seahorse Landing** (877-514-5096; seahorselanding.com), 4050 G St, provides a fabulous view of sunset over the Gulf from newer large condo units (1,024 square feet, sleeping four or six) equipped with washer and dryer, dishwasher, microwave, full

CAPTURING THAT PELICAN MOMENT, CEDAR KEY

dishes and linens, television and VCR; DSL available in some units. $160–175.

🐾 **Sunset Isle Motel & RV Park** (800-810-1103; cedarkeyrv.com), FL 24. Along the estuary, this pleasant family motel has rooms with refrigerator, microwave, and coffeemaker ($50) but is primarily a waterfront RV park, $25–39; tent campers welcome.

Chiefland 32626
🐾 ♿ (ᵠᵖ) **Best Western Suwannee Valley Inn** (352-493-0663; bestwestern .com/suwanneevalleyinn), 1125 N Young Blvd, has the feel of a small family motel, with a coin laundry and soda machines in the breezeway and a pleasant pool out front. Central to everything, they have 60 large rooms, many with desk and dataport, some with microwave and refrigerator; $71 and up.

Cross City 32628
Carriage Inn (352-498-3910; carriage -inn-motel.com), 16872 SE US 19. At this family motel, the wrought-iron railings remind me of the French Quarter. Enjoy well-kept, reasonably sized 1960s-style rooms, $45–57, with

a swimming pool, shuffleboard court, and adjacent restaurant; across the road from the Nature Coast Trail.

COTTAGES

Cedar Key 32625
🐾 My friends love to stay at **Mermaid's Landing** (877-543-5949; mermaidslanding.com), 12717 FL 24, an easy stroll from town and a great place to launch a kayak. Set in a funky beach atmosphere, each cottage, $54–110, comes with an equipped kitchen, cable TV, and air-conditioning. Kayak rental on site.

🐾 (ᵠᵖ) At **Pirates Cove** (352-543-5141; piratescovecottages.com), FL 24, each cottage ($69–95) comes fully equipped with dishes and linens; free use of bicycles for exploring Cedar Key, or fishing equipment to settle back on the shore and cast a line.

CAMPING & CABINS

Bell 32619
🛶 **Hart Springs Park** (see *Springs*) on SW CR 344 west of Trenton offers both primitive tent and full-hookup sites, dump station, grills, picnic tables,

and hot showers, $24, or rental of the Hart Springs House, a beautiful three-bedroom home up on piers and not far from the river, sleeps eight, $125, two-night minimum.

Branford 32008

🐾 ♪ ((ᵠ)) **Ellie Ray's River Landing Campground** (386-935-9518; ellie raysriverlanding.com), 3349 NW 110th St. A high canopy of oaks shades this expansive campground along the Santa Fe River, a great place for river rats to hang out. You've got swimming in a horseshoe-shaped spring on the river, canoeing and kayaking down to the Suwannee, boating, fishing, plenty of springs nearby for divers, canoe and paddleboat rentals, and an on-site lounge. $25–35; weekly and monthly rates available. Leashed pets only.

Cedar Key 32625

Shell Mound County Park (352-543-6153; wxtoad.com/campgrounds/shmo.htm), CR 326, on the edge of Lower Suwannee NWR, provides basic tent and camper sites cooled by breezes off the salt marsh; many of the sites are in the shade, $5–15. Ideal for hikers, paddlers, and anglers who like to get an early start; boat ramp, picnic tables, and privies.

Chiefland 32626

Along Alt US 27 halfway to Bronson, **Breezy Acres Campground** (352-493-7602), 10050 NE 20th Ave, is a welcome sight, its grassy pine-shaded spaces beckoning. Full hookups, can handle RVs up to 50 feet, $20, with weekly and monthly rates available

&. The campground at **Manatee Springs State Park** (see *Springs*) is wonderfully shady, keeping things cool as you pitch your tent within walking distance of the springs and the Suwannee River. Campsites (800-326-3521; floridastateparks.reserve america.com), $20.

Fanning Springs 32693

&. ↪ At **Fanning Springs State Park** (see *Springs*), choose from several modern cabins (800-326-3521; florida stateparks.reserveamerica.com), tucked into the woods above the swimming area, $100, sleep six.

Jena 32359

((ᵠ)) Closer to Steinhatchee (see the *Tallahassee* chapter) than the rest of Dixie County, **Nature Coast RV Resort** (352-498-7344; naturescoastrvresort.com), 4802 CR 358, has RV sites right with 30/50-amp service right along a waterway connecting to the river. Lounge around their pool or meet with friends around the fire pit while relaxing after a day of fishing or scalloping. Seasonal rates $16–30.

Old Town 32680

With campsites tucked in the deep shade of the river forest, the **Original Suwannee River Campground** (352-542-7680), 28872 SE US 19, is one

CAMPING AT BREEZY ACRES, CHIEFLAND

beautiful hideaway set above the Suwannee River. Choose from tent sites or pull-through sites with full hookups, $20 and up. There are also camping cabins. Swimming pool, boat ramp, and fishing dock.

🐾 ((ᵞ)) **Old Town Campground** (352-542-9500), 2241 SE CR 349, provides a quiet place to tuck your tent or RV under the trees and dream Suwannee dreams, with easy access to the river and free shuttle service if you show up with your own kayak or canoe, $20–28.

Suwannee River Hideaway Campground (352-542-7800; riverhideaway .com), CR 346-A. You're greeted by a cute replica of an old general store at check-in at this new campground along the Suwannee, with pretty full-hookup spaces under the pines and oaks. Tenters get the primo access to the river; a boardwalk leads from the bathhouse area down to the water. Sites $15 and up; closed July–Oct.

🏵 The only area campground with a significant amount of river frontage, the **Yellow Jacket Campground** (352-542-8365; yellowjacketcamp ground.com), 55 SE 503rd Ave (FL 349), blends well into its natural surroundings. A rope swing with a grand view of the Suwannee River hangs off an ancient live oak tree next to shady riverside campsites; guests enjoy a beautiful swimming pool and spa area. $32 tents, $44–49 riverbank RV sites, $120 for their pleasant cottages.

Shired Island

It's the epitome of rustic. But if you really want to get away from it all, pitch your tent or bring your trailer to **Shired Island County Park** (352-498-1240), the most remote campground on the Nature Coast, at the end of CR 357 right on the Gulf. Launch your sea kayak from the beach, and enjoy a sunset that's all yours. Self-serve $10; nearby boat ramp.

Trenton 32693

Otter Springs Park & Campground (352-463-0800; ottersprings.com), 6470 SW 80th Ave, not only provides an excellent spot to swim along the Suwannee River, but has lodging as well. Relax in a nice new cabin, $65 (bring your own linens and cleaning supplies), or a stilt house, $85, that sleeps eight. Full-hookup 30/50-amp sites for RVs and tent campers, $24; longer stays available for all facilities.

Yankeetown 34498

🐾 ((ᵞ)) **B's Marina and Campground** (352-447-5888; bmarinacampground .net), 6621 Riverside Dr. Campsites ($25) along the pine-and-palm-lined Withlacoochee River, with paved pads and picnic tables. Bring your boat and take advantage of the dock, or come by boat and arrange overnight dockage. It's a great place to launch a kayak and head out to the Gulf, with rentals available.

DIVE RESORT

Williston 32696

Surrounding its world-renowned dive venue (see *Diving*), **Devil's Den** (352-528-3344; devilsden.com), 5390 NE 180th Ave, provides a full-service dive resort with 30 RV sites ($22), 20 tent sites ($8), and three kitchenette cabins ($85, sleeping four) perched on the rim of a large sinkhole. Campers enjoy use of bathhouses and a heated pool on site. In addition to the must-dive grotto, enjoy swimming, snorkeling, and scuba in spring-fed Ray's Fish Pond, ranging up to 22 feet deep, and picnicking in the covered pavilions or open tables under the forest canopy. No pets permitted.

FISH CAMP

Suwannee 32692

Plan your next fishing expedition on the Gulf at **Bill's Fish Camp** (352-

542-7086; billsfishcamp.com), 63 219th St, where you can settle into a basic motel room ($65), bring in your RV ($30, full hookups), or pitch a tent. Fish-cleaning room available and a cookhouse. Bill's also maintains the adjacent river camp on the Suwannee River Wilderness Trail (see *Paddling*), Anderson River Camp.

✳ Where to Eat
DINING OUT
Cedar Key
The island's dressiest restaurant, **The Island Room Restaurant at Cedar Cove** (352-543-6520; islandroom .com), 10 2nd St, serves up proprietor-chef Peter Stefani's specialties, like grouper Savannah (pecan-crusted, served with a sherry beurre blanc) and New Zealand rack of lamb; entrées $12–28. Reservations suggested.

Williston
The Ivy House (352-528-5410; ivy housefl.com), 108 NW Main St. Featuring recipes handed down through the Hale family for more than 50 years, The Ivy House presents gourmet southern cooking in a 1912 Victorian home; five differently themed rooms provide unique backdrops to

THE IVY HOUSE, WILLISTON

the main attraction, the food. From southern-fried scallops to baked crispy chicken to a Big South sampler of a Delmonico steak, friend shrimp, and cod, you'll find something to fit every appetite, served up with roasted vegetables, corn bread, yeast rolls, and their trademark baked potato with cheese. Entrées $12–24. Leave some room for a homemade dessert, like their classic milk cake. Open for lunch and dinner; closed Sun. Their upstairs gift shop boasts an array of feminine gift items.

EATING OUT
Bell
If you're in the mood for mounds of food, stop by **Akins Bar-B-Q & Grill**, (352-463-6859), US 129, where the locals gather for heaping helpings of country cooking; the last time I stopped in, I couldn't find an empty table at 2 PM on a weekday. Mon–Thu 5:30 AM–9 PM, Sat 5:30 AM–10 PM, meals under $10.

Bronson
Barbecue with attitude is the key to **BubbaQues** (352-486-4126; bubbaques bbq.com), 830 E Hathaway Ave (Alt

HEARTS OF PALM SALAD IS A CEDAR KEY SPECIALTY

US 27), with menu items like Redneck Nachos (made with fries instead of corn chips), Fried Green Beans (yep, it's a southern thing), and the Mother-clucker: "Smoked chicken breast topped with Tractor Grease . . ." This small Florida chain—I've also eaten at their locations in Chiefland, 116 N Main St (US 19), and Cross City, 16368 SE US 19—pushes the redneck theme pretty hard but the food's dang good, and that's what matters most. Kick back and suck those ribs off the bone. Lunch and dinner, $4–19, plus smoked meat to go.

Cedar Key

🍴 I've always loved breakfast at **Annie's Cafe** (352-543-6141), FL 24 and 6th St, a quiet little place down by the clam farms with that pop of protein you need in the morning, like omelets and French toast, under $6. Cash only.

For a taste of what Cedar Key does best—raising clams—stop in **Big Deck Raw Bar** (352-543-9992), 331 Dock St, for local clams, oysters, and fresh Gulf shrimp steamed and grilled. Live music Thu–Sun.

You must try the clam chowder at **Tony's Seafood Restaurant** (352-543-0022; tonyschowder.com), 597 2nd St, since Tony's the king of chowder makers and his ingredients can't get fresher. Savor a Low Country boil with all the fixin's, or try shrimp or steamed clams Tony's way and you won't be disappointed. Open for lunch and dinner, under $20.

Chiefland

🍴 **Bar-B-Q Bill's** (352-493-4444), US 19 and FL 320, is always packed, and it took but one meal to understand why: fine barbecue that even impressed my friends from Texas. Served with traditional fixings, barbecue comes as sandwiches ($3 and up) and plates ($7 and up), with optional salad bar. Daily lunch specials served 11–3; open lunch and dinner.

It looked like a truck stop, but I was famished, so I gave **Bett's Big T Restaurant** (352-490-4906), 12351 NW US 19, just north of town, a try one Sunday night. Inside, it's a real contrast to the exterior. I saw fresh Cedar Key mullet on the menu and had to go for it. Served up with southern sides, it was perfect, as was their sweet tea, just the way I like it—not too sweet. Entrées include southern fried chicken, fried shrimp, and steak, $8–15; lunches under $7.

Cross City

🍴 **Cypress Inn Restaurant** (352-498-7211), US 27 and CR 351-A. Since 1928, they've been serving up heaping helpings of southern cooking in this beautiful pecky cypress building; sit down and make yourself at home. Pick from the prime rib special, seafood dinners (including fresh mullet and grouper), and much more, $10 and up, and everything comes with your choice of home-style sides like fresh acre peas, baby limas, fried okra, and corn nuggets. Open 5–9:30; cash or debit cards only.

Fanning Springs

Always packed for dinner, the **Lighthouse Restaurant** (352-463-2644), 7600 N US 19 across from the state park, serves fresh Gulf seafood and thick steaks that folks come for from miles around. Try the Swamp Thing, with 'gator tail bites, catfish strips, and golden-fried deviled crab, or the Dinghy for small appetites, with flounder, shrimp, crab, and oysters. Entrées $10 and up; open 11–11 daily.

Suwannee

Salt Creek Restaurant (352-542-7072), 23440 SE CR 349, is a spacious restaurant with seating overlooking the

Gulf estuary. It's worth the drive to the end of the road for their succulent seafood, including fresh oysters, mullet, bay scallops, and their steamer pots (six choices of seafood, $9 and up) cooked with veggies and red potatoes. Entrées, including a Fisherman's Platter with blue crab, run $12 and up.

Trenton

Inside the spacious Suwannee Valley Quilt Shop (see *Selective Shopping*), the **Suwannee Rose Cafe** (352-463-3842; suwanneeshops.com) offers delightful daily specials like crab salad on croissant and the quiche of the day, sweet little gourmet meals under $10. You'll be tempted by slices of pie—like cashew, sawdust, and tin roof—displayed prominently in a bakery case on the edge of this garden-like space inside the historic Coca-Cola bottling plant. Open Mon–Sat 10–5.

Williston

🍴 **Driftwood Restaurant** (352-528-5074), 515 E Noble Ave. Enjoy a heaping helping of comfort food in this comfy down-home cafe, where a plateful of pancakes with your choice of toppings (blueberry, chocolate chip, or peaches and cream) will run you less than $4; southern-style lunches and dinners $3–15.

✳ Selective Shopping

Cedar Key

Every little town needs an independent bookstore, and none so much as Cedar Key, being an enclave of artists and writers. **Curmudgeonalia** (352-543-6789; curmudgeonalia.com), 598 2nd St, fills the niche, with an excellent selection of tomes on Florida and by Florida authors, and a children's section that caters to inquisitive outdoorsy kids.

Dark woods accent the nautical theme at the **Dilly Dally Gally** (352-543-

DRIFTWOOD RESTAURANT, WILLISTON

9146; dillydallygally.com), 390 Dock St, with wooden signs, wood carvings, and antique ephemera tucked away in the back rooms. The front desk also serves as the check-in for the Harbour Master Suites (see *Lodging*).

Haven Isle Gifts & Glass (352-543-6806), 582 2nd St. Dating back to 1884, this little white gingerbread cottage houses the usual gift items found in small tourist towns, but with a twist—the owner is a well-respected stained-glass artist, and the back of the shop serves as his studio. Look high up

THE DILLY DALLY GALLEY

TRENTON

A complex of artsy shops that's grown in downtown Trenton, **Suwannee Valley Shops** (352-463-3842; suwanneeshops.com), 517 N Main St is now a destination all its own. It all started with the **Suwannee Valley Quilt Shop**, which isn't just a quilt shop; it's a piece of history, the former Coca-Cola bottling plant. Inside you'll find the Suwannee Rose Cafe (see *Eating Out*) and the most amazing array of fabrics you've seen in years. Poke around the many rooms and you'll find great bargains, too. Next door, the renovated Crystal Ice House is now the **Suwannee Valley Antique Gallery**, filled with fine furnishings, antique sewing machines, classic glass, and, of course, beautiful quilts on the tall walls. Walk to the far back of the building to see the only long-arm machine for quilting that I've ever encountered. The tempting aroma of chocolate won't let you walk by **Linda's Simply Delightful Confections**, where you can watch Chef Linda making her exquisite creations. If you miss her, not to worry—her chocolates are for sale up front. On the other side of the historic railroad station (see *Railroadiana*), the **Suwannee Valley Stained Glass Works**, 409 N Main St, offers classes in stained-glass art on Saturday mornings; experts can stop in and select from the full array of colors and textures of more than 20,000 pounds of stained glass. The entire complex is open Mon–Sat 10–4.

QUILTS, ART, AND ANTIQUES ARE ALL AT THE SUWANNEE QUILT SHOP, TRENTON

on the walls for original art in glass, wood, and metal by local artists.

Chiefland

At the **Chiefland Farmers Flea Market** (352-493-2022; chieflandflea market.com), 1206 N Young Blvd (US 19); comb through the stalls for country bargains! Sat and Sun 8–4.

Magnolia Mist Unique Gifts & Antiques (352-493-7877), 711 N Main, stands out along US 19 in downtown Chiefland with a good selection of antiques and gift items.

With wagon wheels piled outside a pecky cypress building, **Manatee Antiques** (352-493-4043), 121 S Main St, draws your attention with a porchful of farm implements and country fare.

Williston

Cedar Chest Antiques (352-528-0039), 48 E Noble Ave. Modern home decor items like carved hope chests share space with beaded Victorian lamps, Vaseline glass, and collectible dolls in a virtual showroom of antique furniture.

Dixie's Antiques (352-528-2338), 131 E Noble Ave, is a mini mall overflowing with antiques and collectibles, with a heavy emphasis on kitchenware and dishes—look for your missing Fenton glass, Fiestaware, and enamelware here. But you'll also find country crafts, western home decor, rustic wooden furniture, and ironworking by a local blacksmith in among the stacks of paperbacks, Hardy Boys mysteries, and soda pop bottles—a little something for everyone. Closed Sun. The produce stand in the parking lot carries seasonal fresh fruit and vegetables.

R&S Produce (352-528-0100), sells fresh fruit and vegetables out of a permanent, canopied fruit stand just west of US 41 on FL 121, south of Williston.

Williston Peanut Factory Outlet (352-528-2388), 1309 US 41. Small outlet with offerings of peanut goodies made on site, from roasted peanuts to peanut butter and peanut brittle; open during production hours.

✳ Special Events

March: More than 50 years running, the **Suwannee River Fair** (352-486-5131; mysrf.org) is the combined county fair for the three-county region, with livestock and vegetable judging, rides and crafts, and more. Suwannee River fairgrounds.

April: Started in 1963, the **Cedar Key Arts Festival** (352-543-5600; cedar keyartsfestival.com) lets you enjoy the works of local artists, with a taste of seafood for good measure.

May: **Red Belly Day** (352-463-3310), Fanning Springs State Park. One of the most amusing Memorial Day weekend celebrations in Florida,

SEAHORSE KEY LIGHTHOUSE

centered on the town's favorite member of the bream family (which makes for a great fish fry), with families participating in sack races, melon chunking, and the ever-popular belly-flop contest.

October: **Cedar Key Seafood Festival** (352-543-5600; cedarkey.org), third weekend. Thousands converge on this tiny village for samplings of local seafood and a large arts and crafts show, as well as special tours of the Cedar Key lighthouse.

The Atlantic Coast

3

JACKSONVILLE

AMELIA ISLAND

ST. AUGUSTINE

FLAGLER COUNTY

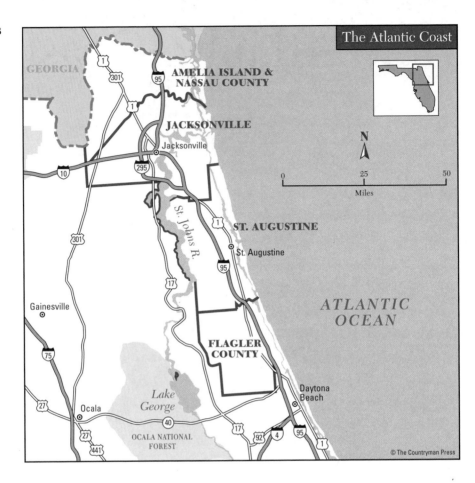

JACKSONVILLE

The place known as "Cowford" by early Florida settlers who drove their cattle across the shallows of the St. Johns River has grown up into **Jacksonville**, one of the financial centers of the Southeast. The heart of the region, its lifeblood, has always been the St. Johns River. One of the nation's only north-flowing rivers, it springs from the marshes of Central Florida, its 310-mile length lying two dozen miles or less west of the Atlantic Ocean's shoreline. By the time the St. Johns reaches Mandarin Point, Jacksonville's southernmost outpost on the river, it widens to a mighty channel, perfect for commercial shipping.

The earliest human habitation along the river, indicated by the massive shell middens (prehistoric oyster-shell landfills) along the St. Johns, came from the Timucua and their forefathers more than a thousand years before the first Europeans set foot in Florida. On May 1, 1562, three years before the founding of the Spanish colony at St. Augustine, French Huguenots landed along the shores of "the River of May"; their leader, Jean Ribault, claimed this land for France and began a small colony at what is now Fort Caroline. In 1564 more than 200 soldiers, artisans, and civilians settled on the St. Johns' bluff in the protection of the new fort. But just a year later, Pedro Menendez de Aviles, founder of St. Augustine, marched here with 500 troops and massacred most of the French settlers; the colony was abandoned.

The region stood under many flags. British loyalists settled here during the American Revolution, and American patriots sent them packing. But the Spanish held on to this portion of Florida for nearly 200 years before ceding it to the United States in 1821. "Cowford" was then christened "Jacksonville" in honor of territorial governor General Andrew Jackson in 1822.

A thriving commercial center by the time the state of Florida was established in 1845, Jacksonville saw a great deal of action during the Civil War, with both Union and Confederate forces taking, abandoning, and retaking the city. When in federal hands, Jacksonville was a launching point for Union raids up the St. Johns River and along the Florida Railroad west to Olustee. By the late 1800s, the city became a place for northerners to escape the cold and convalesce. Author Harriet Beecher Stowe once held court on her front porch along the St. Johns River in **Mandarin**, where passing steamboats would point out her house to passengers and sometimes stop for a visit. **Jacksonville Beach** blossomed into a turn-of-the-20th-century tourist destination. With bustling business districts on opposite sides of the same

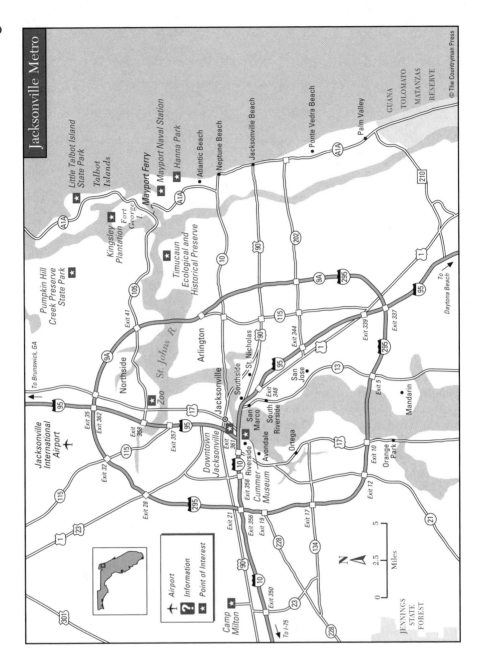

Jacksonville Metro

© The Countryman Press

street (Atlantic Blvd), **Atlantic Beach** and **Neptune Beach** have long been a destination for the region's beach lovers.

The Great Fire of 1901 marked a turning point. In less than eight hours, it wiped out 2 square miles of wooden buildings, destroying Jacksonville's downtown in what was the largest-ever city fire in the South. With 10,000 people homeless and 2,600 buildings gone, the city immediately began to rebuild. More than 20 distinct communities emerged, graced with homes and businesses designed using new architectural styles in stone and brick, not wood. Today the historic districts highlight classic architecture of the 1920s, '30s, and '40s.

All of Duval County is within the city of Jacksonville's jurisdiction, a point it's tough to believe as you're driving on US 301 on the county's western rural fringe or along the salt marshes paralleling Heckscher Drive north of the St. Johns River. For that reason, destinations within this chapter are broken out under their neighborhoods or traditional community names.

GUIDANCE The primary source of tourism information for the region is **Visit Jacksonville** (800-733-2668 or 904-798-9111; visitjacksonville.com), 208 N Laura St, St. 102, Jacksonville 32202. **Walk-in visitor information centers** are located on the lower levels of the Jacksonville Landing (904-791-4305), 2 Independent Dr, open Mon–Thu 11–3, Fri–Sat 10–7; Jacksonville International Airport baggage claim area, open daily 9 AM–10 PM; and the Beaches Visitor Center, 380 Pablo Ave, Jacksonville Beach, open Tue–Sat 10-4:30.

GETTING THERE *By air:* **Jacksonville International Airport** (904-741-4902; jaa.aero), 2400 Yankee Clipper Dr, Jacksonville, is the region's major airport, with a full schedule of flights by major carriers.

By bus: **Greyhound** (904-356-9976; greyhound.com) takes you into downtown Jacksonville, where transfers to city buses and JTA Skyway are nearby.

By car: **I-95** runs north–south through the heart of Jacksonville, with **I-10** coming in from the west to meet **I-295**, the beltway around the west side of the city.

By train: **Amtrak** (904-766-5110; amtrak.com), 3570 Clifford Ln on the north side of Jacksonville, 7 miles from the downtown area.

GETTING AROUND *By public transportation:* **JTA Skyway**, **JTA Trolley**, **Community Shuttles**, and **City Bus** (904-743-3582 or 904-RIDE-JTA; ridejta.org). The automated Skyway peoplemover weaves through the downtown area from Kings Avenue Garage to the FCCJ campus and the Convention Center on Bay St, Mon–Fri 6 AM–9 PM and on weekends for special events only. During peak

DOWNTOWN JACKSONVILLE'S NORTHBANK RIVERWALK—HOME TO MANY FESTIVALS AND THE JACKSONVILLE LANDING

Ken McCray

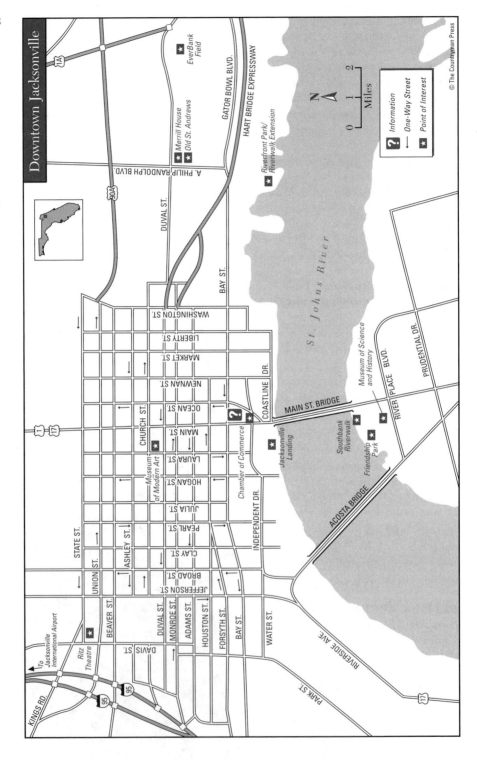

Downtown Jacksonville

St. Johns River

EverBank Field

Merrill House
Old St. Andrews

Riverfront Park/
Riverwalk Extension

Museum of Science
and History

Southbank
Riverwalk

Friendship
Park

Jacksonville
Landing

Chamber of Commerce

Museum
of Modern Art

Ritz
Theatre

To
Jacksonville
International Airport

GATOR BOWL BLVD.

HART BRIDGE EXPRESSWAY

A. PHILIP RANDOLPH BLVD.

DUVAL ST.

BAY ST.

WASHINGTON ST.

LIBERTY ST.

MARKET ST.

NEWNAN ST.

OCEAN ST.

MAIN ST.

LAURA ST.

HOGAN ST.

JULIA ST.

PEARL ST.

CLAY ST.

BROAD ST.

JEFFERSON ST.

DAVIS ST.

CHURCH ST.

COASTLINE DR.

INDEPENDENT DR.

MAIN ST. BRIDGE

ACOSTA BRIDGE

RIVER PLACE BLVD.

PRUDENTIAL DR.

STATE ST.

UNION ST.

ASHLEY ST.

BEAVER ST.

DUVAL ST.

MONROE ST.

ADAMS ST.

FORSYTH ST.

HOUSTON ST.

BAY ST.

WATER ST.

RIVERSIDE AVE.

PARK ST.

KINGS RD.

Miles
0   1   2

N

? Information
→ One-Way Street
★ Point of Interest

© The Countryman Press

hours it runs every three minutes; off-peak, every six. It connects with the JTA Trolley, which runs through downtown on weekdays and is free. Buses take you east to the beach or southwest to Orange Park for $1 and up, depending on distance; discounts for disabled, seniors, and youth. JTA's Community Shuttles act like regular bus routes but focus on small neighborhood areas. Exact fares are required, but fare cards can be bought in advance at automated machines

By car: There are four main highways that take you from Jacksonville's neighborhoods east to the coast. North of the St. Johns River, follow **Heckscher Dr** (FL 105) east to A1A, which comes north on the Mayport Ferry and continues north to the Talbot Islands. From downtown, follow **Atlantic Blvd** (FL 10) to Atlantic Beach/Neptune Beach. US 90, **Beach Blvd**, connects downtown with Jacksonville Beach. From the Southside, follow **J. Turner Butler Blvd** (FL 202) to Ponte Vedra. I-95 and US 1 head north–south through the heart of the city, with I-295 forming a beltway out to Orange Park, I-10, and the airport. In town, **Roosevelt Blvd** (US 17) parallels the west side of the St. Johns River south from downtown past Riverside, Five Points, Avondale, and St. Johns Park to I-295; **San Marco Blvd** (US 13) does the same on the east side of the river from downtown through San Marco and San Jose to Mandarin.

By boat: **S.S. Marine River Taxi** (904-724-9068; jaxwatertaxi.com). Northside at Jacksonville Landing; Southside at Riverwalk. $3 one-way, $5 round-trip. Sun–Thu 11–9, Fri–Sat 11–11.

PARKING **Metered street parking** is the norm throughout the city, so bring lots of quarters. Rates vary widely, and flat lots are infrequent, although there are parking garages in the heart of downtown. Most meters allow two to four hours of time for shopping.

A WATER TAXI TRANSPORTS VISITORS DOWNTOWN

Visit Jacksonville

MEDICAL EMERGENCIES For general emergencies, visit **Memorial Hospital Jacksonville** (main number 904-399-6111; emergency 904-399-6156; memorial hospitaljax.com), 3625 University Blvd S. A medical destination within the city is the world-renowned **Mayo Clinic Jacksonville** (904-953-2000; mayoclinic.org /jacksonville), 4500 San Pablo Rd.

✳ To See

ART GALLERIES Set in the oak-shaded shopping district, **The Avondale Gallery** (904-389-6712; theavondalegallery.com), 3545 St. Johns Ave, Avondale, showcases paintings of estuarine and beach scenes by local artists as well as palm tree pop art.

My weakness is art glass, and **Eclectic Galleries** (904-247-3750; eclecticgalleries .com), 2405 3rd St S, Jacksonville Beach, knows exactly how to press those buttons with aquatic life scenes in art glass that evoke the fluid motion of the sea. From milliflora paperweights to fine glass sculptures, this is a place an art glass aficionado will stare for hours.

Emerging artists thrive at **Gallery 1037 at Reddi Arts** (904-398-3161; reddiarts .com/gallery.html), 1037 Hendricks Ave, San Marco, which presents bimonthly shows of local artists launching their careers. Open daily.

Featuring top contemporary and modern artists, the **J. Johnson Gallery** (904-435-3200; jjohnsongallery.com), 177 4th Ave N, Jacksonville Beach, provides a unique venue to showcase the works of sometimes-controversial but well-known names such as Robert Mapplethorpe, Henri Matisse, and Pablo Picasso. Open during special exhibitions and by appointment.

In an elegant, classical setting, **Stellers Gallery** (904-396-9492; stellersgallery .com), 1409 Atlantic Blvd, San Marco, is one of Jacksonville's oldest galleries representing local fine artists, many of whom draw inspiration from the wild places along this coast. Tue–Fri 10–5, Sat 10–3.

Founded in 1924, the **Museum of Contemporary Art** (904-366-6911; moca jacksonville.org), 333 N Laura St, was the first institution in the city devoted to

THE MUSEUM OF CONTEMPORARY ART (MOCA)

Visit Jacksonville

visual arts. It displays a fine selection of modern and contemporary works by locally and nationally acclaimed artists. Ongoing changing exhibitions highlight photography as well as paintings, sculpture, and printmaking. A very special place is the ArtExplorium loft, with lots of family interaction and education in the 16 interactive stations. Open Tue–Wed/Fri–Sat 10–4, Thu 10–8, Sun noon–4. $8 adult, $5 seniors and students, free for active military and UNF students. Free on Sunday for families and on Wednesday evening for Artwalk, 5–9.

ART MUSEUMS

CUMMER MUSEUM OF ART AND GARDENS

🌊 ♿ (904-356-6857; cummer.org), 829 Riverside Ave, Riverside. Arguably one of the best fine art museums in the state and certainly North Florida's largest, the Cummer displays a permanent collection of art from the Middle Ages to the present. Walking through the expansive gallery spaces, it's awe inspiring to reflect on original works, from Glakens to Rubens, not often seen in Florida. One of their more important pieces is Thomas Moran's oil painting *Ponce de Leon in Florida* (1878), which depicts the Spanish conquistador in the company of native Floridians deep in the mystical forests around the St. Johns River. Thirteen formal galleries are centered on the Reinhold Courtyard and its adjacent loggia. One of the more surprising finds, in the large Lovett Gallery, was the extensive Wark Collection of Early Meissen Porcelain, with pieces more than 250 years old donated to the museum over 20 years ago. Artwork displayed in the galleries ranges from contemporary pieces to 19th-century American landscapes, and Renaissance, baroque, rococo, and impressionist works. One arm of the museum houses working studio space and a special children's section, an immersion into art known as Art Connections. Here, hands-on activities rule. Walk a time line through how art history pairs up with the history of the Jacksonville area from ancient times to modern, or pop into a room where you create computer art projected on the wall simply by moving your body. Between the museum and the St. Johns River are this attraction's other major feature, formal landscaped gardens dating back to 1903 (see *Gardens*). Natural works of art guided by the talents of two noted landscape architects, the gardens are partially shaded by one of the oldest live oaks in the region. $10 adults, $6 seniors/military/students, 5 and under free. Open Tue 10–9, Wed–Fri 10–4, Sat 10–5, Sun noon–5; admission is free on Tue 4–9.

BREWERY TOUR Anheuser-Busch Budweiser Brewery Tour (904-751-8116; budweisertours.com), 111 Busch Dr, Jacksonville. Take this open-air tour overlooking the Brew Hall, where golden beers and amber ales are bottled and canned; then sample the popular American beer. Great gift shop of logo items. Mon–Sat 9–4; free.

FERRY In continuous operation since 1948, the **St. Johns River Ferry** (904-241-9969; stjohnsriverferry.com),

THE HOSPITALITY ROOM AT THE BUDWEISER BREWERY TOUR

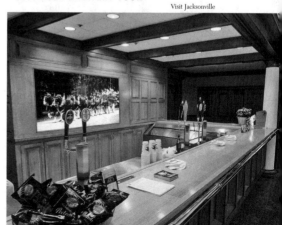
Visit Jacksonville

one of Florida's last (and certainly largest) ferryboats, connects from Mayport across the St. Johns River to Heckscher Dr on the Northside at Fort George Island. It's the official route of FL A1A. Mon–Fri 6 AM–7 PM; Sat–Sun 7 AM–8:30 PM. $5 car, $3 motorcycle, $1 pedestrian.

FOOTBALL Fall and winter, catch North Florida's only NFL team, the **Jacksonville Jaguars** (904-633-2000; jaguars.com), 1 ALLTEL Stadium Place, near the Hart Bridge, downtown.

HISTORIC SITES

Arlington

☠ ✎ Fort Caroline National Memorial (904-641-7155; nps.gov/foca), 12713 Fort Caroline Rd. A replica of Fort Caroline, the first colony in Florida, sits along the St. Johns River inside this deeply wooded preserve, its size and shape based on the paintings of 1500s French settler and artist Jacques Le Moyne. Clamber up the battlements and peer over the sides. In 1565 the founder of St. Augustine, Pedro Menendez, marched here with 500 troops to roust the French from Florida under the orders of King Phillip II. Taking the fort by surprise, they murdered 140 settlers, sparing only the women and children. Nearly 50 settlers, including Le Moyne, escaped by boat and returned to France. An interpretive center tells the story, and signs along the nature trails invoke the interaction between the French and Timucua. Open daily 9–5; free.

A short drive to the end of Fort Caroline Rd takes you to the **Ribault Monument** on St. Johns Bluff, commemorating where the French first landed; it is a replica of the stone erected by Jean Ribault in 1562.

Midtown

Now home to the Jacksonville Historical Society, **Old St. Andrews Episcopal Church** (904-665-0064; jaxhistory.com/headquarters.htm), 317 A. Philip Randolph Blvd, was constructed in 1887 and was the largest house of worship in the city prior to the Great Fire of 1901. Designed by architect Robert S. Schuyler, with a brick exterior, Gothic spires, and Florida yellow pine interior, it was considered one of the "most satisfying pieces of architecture in the South" in 1889. Dilapidated by the 1990s, it was on land purchased by the city for their new football stadium and given to the historical society under the provision it be restored. Restoration completed in 1998, it is now on the National Register of Historic Places. Open Mon–Fri 10-5. The adjoining **Merrill House** (see *Museums*), a 1903 Victorian home, was also preserved.

SLAVE CABINS AT KINGSLEY PLANTATION

Northside

☠ Kingsley Plantation (904-251-3537; nps.gov/timu/historyculture/kp

.htm), 11676 Palmetto Ave. Established in 1791 by John McQueen, who sought his fortune under a policy of the Spanish government of Florida that invited Americans to homestead on land grants throughout eastern Florida, this Sea Island cotton plantation passed into the hands of Zephaniah Kingsley, a slave trader, in 1812. Zephaniah Kingsley lived here with his wife, Anna Madgigine Jai, a slave he had bought in Senegal and later freed, and their children. He strove to establish liberal policies for the freeing of slaves, and to ensure the rights and privileges of free Blacks in Florida, but failed, and moved his family to Haiti in 1837. Tour the plantation home (a limited portion of it has been renovated) and the slave cabins; walk the waterfront along the St. George River. Open Mon–Sun 9–5; home tours offered on weekends at 11 and 3, call ahead for reservations. Free.

☙ There's not much to **Yellow Bluff Fort Historic State Park** (904-251-2320; floridastateparks.org/yellowbluff), New Berlin Rd [30.399745, -81.55564], save its storied history. The deep gouges in this hillside above the St. Johns River (now hidden by a screen of trees) were earthworks used by both Confederate and Union troops during the Civil War, an encampment from which big guns were trained on the river below. Some cannons remain, and a picnic spot. Free.

Northwest Jacksonville

☙ ✐ ♿ A significant Civil War historic site, **Camp Milton Historic Preserve** (see *Parks*) has an educational center with artifacts and interpretive information about Camp Milton, one of the Confederacy's largest encampments in the region. Trails lead to defensive earthworks and McGirts Creek Bridge, a replica of a "Campaign Bridge" of the era.

Jacksonville Beach

✐ Learn about the history of the railways and beaches at **Pablo Historical Park** (904-246-0093; beachesareahistoricalsociety.com), 425 Beach Blvd. Highlights on the free guided tour include the relocated Mayport railroad depot; Florida East Coast house #93, serving as a museum; and a Cummer and Sons locomotive from the cypress logging days, fresh off the old Mayport & Pablo Railway, which ended here at the beach in the late 1800s. Open Mon–Sat 10–3; fee.

On the beach, the landmark **American Red Cross Volunteer Life Saving Corps Building** dates back to 1947. Established in 1912, the corps provides volunteer lifeguards for the beaches, and historically provided rescue teams in lifesaving boats for ships in distress.

Riverside/Avondale

Thanks to its vibrant business districts, this part of Jacksonville is well traveled and well known. Get a block or two off the busier roads to see some of the architectural marvels of its residential areas. The **Riverside/Avondale Historic District** (riversideavondale.org), which also includes the **St. John Quarter**, is heavily influenced by the bungalow style, but you'll also find Mediterranean Revival, Tudor Revival, and even Art Moderne.

Springfield

Established in 1869, the northerly neighborhood of Springfield didn't suffer from the Great Fire of 1901—in fact, it grew as residents exited the charred city and built uptown homes. The **Springfield Historic District** (sparcouncil.org) covers a square mile between Hogan's Creek, Ionia St, and 12th St, created to inspire and assist residents to maintain the architectural glory of this residential district. While no homes are open for tours, you can drive around and see Queen Anne Victorians, Craftsman bungalows, Prairie School structures, and other magnificent architectural styles.

MUSEUMS ✍ The Great Fire of 1901 brought immediate attention to the need for Jacksonville's buildings to be sturdy brick and stone. At the **Jacksonville Fire Museum** (904-630-0618; jacksonvillefiremuseum.com), 1406 Gator Bowl Blvd, Midtown, learn about the history of firefighting in Jacksonville inside a historic firehouse, complete with a 1902 American LaFrance horse-drawn fire engine. Open Mon–Fri 9–4.

From Jean Ribault's discovery of the "River of May" to modern naval operations at Mayport, discover the rich heritage of seafarers at the **Jacksonville Maritime Heritage Center** (904-355-1101; jacksonvillemaritimeheritagecenter.org), 2 Independent Dr at the Jacksonville Landing, downtown. Model ships, photography, and artifacts tell the tales. Open Tue–Sun 1–5.

Researchers will appreciate access to the **Karpeles Manuscript Library Museum** (904-356-2992; rain.org/~karpeles/jaxfrm.html), 101 W 1st St, Springfield, part of the world's largest private collection of important *original* manuscripts and art. Holdings across this library system include the writings of Sir Arthur Conan Doyle, The Lawrence Williams Presidential Collection of portraits, the Bill of Rights, Roget's *Thesaurus*, Einstein's *Theory of Relativity*, and many other treasures. Open Tue–Fri 10–3, Sat 10–4, closed holidays.

Not far from where Harriet Beecher Stowe waved to steamboats from her porch, the **Mandarin Museum** (904-268-0784; mandarinmuseum.net), tucked within Walter Jones Historical Park (see *Parks*), is in a farmhouse dating back to 1873. Guided tours through the home and farmstead, restored to reflect daily life at the turn of the last century, are offered Sat 9–4; peek in the original Mandarin Post Office on the first and third Sat, 1–3. Free, donations appreciated.

Learn about life in Jacksonville circa 1903 at the **Merrill House Museum** (904-665-0054; jaxhistory.com/tours.htm), 317 A Philip Randolph Blvd, Midtown. Inside this Victorian house museum, a docent will guide you through the life of the James Merrill family and its intersection with important events in Jacksonville. Presented by the Jacksonville Historical Society, Thu 1:30–3:30; fee.

✍ ♿ The extensive **Museum of Science and History** (904-396-7062; themosh .org), 1025 Museum Circle, downtown, brings together science and local history into an entertaining and educational package that will take you most of a day to explore. Walk the Currents of Time, learning about local history through artifacts and interpretation, including Jacksonville's former role as the top silent movie producer of that era—yes, Laurel and Hardy hung out here along with hundreds of other early screen stars. Discover life beneath the St. Johns River and the Atlantic Ocean in Water Worlds. Play in the Universe of Science, launching a rocket or discovering magnetic attraction. Tots can explore the tree house in KidSpace, or you can settle in for a scientific lecture with the MOSH After Dark series. Listen to music in the starry night with Cosmic Concerts at the Alexander Brest Planetarium for an additional charge. Open Mon–Thu 10–5, Fri 10–8, Sat 10–6, Sun 1–6; $10 adults, $8.50 seniors, $8 ages 3–12. Limited free parking.

Learn about the lifestyle and culture of the antebellum South at the **Museum of Southern History** (904-388-3574; museumsouthernhistory.com), 4304 Herschel St, Avondale. While largely focused on the Civil War, exhibits and artifacts cover politics, fashion, home life, and military memorabilia of the day, as well as prehistoric Florida. Open Tue–Sat 10–4; donation.

The silver screen was the silent screen at the beginning of its life, and Jacksonville was the "Winter Film Capital of the World," thanks to Henry Flagler's railroad. In 1920 Richard Norman of nearby Middleburg founded Norman Studios, the first film studio to feature African American actors in non-stereotypical roles. The **Norman Studios Museum** (904-212-0105; normanstudios.org), 6337 Arlington Rd, Arlington, encompasses the historic studio complex, the remaining of hundreds that thrived in the region between 1901 and 1928. The complex is under restoration but should open soon; efforts are under way to have it become part of the National Park System.

The history of African American life in Jacksonville is depicted at the beautifully restored **Ritz Theatre and Museum** (904-632-5555; ritzjacksonville.com /museum), 829 N Davis St, in the heart of the century-old LaVilla district near downtown, once known as the "Harlem of the South." The 400-seat theater (see *Entertainment*) is home to exciting musicals and theatrical performances. Inside the 11,000-square-foot museum, learn from brave men and women who made a difference during a time of institutionalized racism, their stories told through artifacts, displays, and animatronic figures. Open Tue–Fri 10–5, Sat 10–2. $8 adults, $5 seniors and children.

ZOO ♿ ✒ At the **Jacksonville Zoological Gardens** (904-757-4463; jacksonville zoo.org), 8605 Zoo Pkwy, Northside, nothing ever stays the same. New habitats,

STINGRAY BAY AT THE JACKSONVILLE ZOOLOGICAL GARDENS

Scott A. Drake

new animals, new gardens give you a reason to keep coming back. On this site along Trout Creek since 1925, today's zoo looks nothing like the past. Entering the 92-acre complex through the Main Safari Camp Lodge, with a hand-thatched roof created by 24 Zulu craftsmen from South Africa, you'll find a good showing of African wildlife in the Plains of East Africa, including Cape buffalo and Grevy's zebras. In Wild Florida, discover the Florida panther, Florida black bear, boar, eagles, and alligators in a wetlands environment. Kangaroos, wallabies, and koalas are in the Australian Adventure, and the Range of the Jaguar exhibit showcases the tropical rain forest with four jaguars, along with golden lion tamarins, tapirs, capybaras, giant river otters, anteaters, and reptilians, including the anaconda. Komodo dragons lurk in the Asian Bamboo Gardens, and the latest addition, Tuxedo Coast, showcases Magellanic penguins. Let the kids run in the Play Park, 2½ acres with life-sized models of Florida's coastal animals, a splash zone, maze, climbing decks, and a forest play area. An animal care facility shows children how otters and squirrel monkeys are cared for. My favorite stop? The River Valley Aviary, with free-flying rare birds like the turaco and the whitebellied bustard. Daily 9–5; $14 adults, $12 seniors, $9 ages 3–12.

✳ To Do

BICYCLING The **Jacksonville-Baldwin Rail Trail** (dep.state.fl.us/gwt/guide) comprises 14.5 miles of an old CSX railway line through a dense canopy of forests, wetlands, and fields between Imeson Rd and CR 121. There are three separate paths: one for walking, jogging, and in-line skating; one for mountain bikers; and one for horseback riding. This historic route was the path taken by Union soldiers en route to and in retreat from the Battle of Olustee (see the *Upper Suwannee* chapter). Mountain bikers can play on the wiggling, winding singletrack at **Hanna Park** (see *Beaches*), with rides ranging from easy to difficult. **Ray Greene Park** (904-252-9923; coj.net), 1946 Ray Greene Dr, Northside, managed by Jacksonville BMX (jacksonvillebmx.com), lets you bring your own bike for **BMX** action or rent a bike and helmet on the spot. Your first practice and race is free. Open 5 AM–10 PM; members only on Tue and Fri evenings.

Off-road opportunities are also available at **Tillie K. Fowler Regional Park** and the **Theodore Roosevelt Area** (see *Parks*). Rent beachgoing bicycles at **Rent Beach Stuff** (904-305-6472; rentbeachstuff.com), 11 1st St N, Jacksonville Beach.

BIRDING Birding sites are plentiful along the wild estuarine shorelines where the St. Johns River meets the sea. From the bluffs at **Pumpkin Hill Creek** (see *Wild Places*) and the **Theodore Roosevelt Area** (see *Parks*), watch herons, ibis, and other wading birds in the tidal creeks and mudflats along with ospreys overhead. **Castaway Island Preserve** (see *Parks*) is busy with bird life along the Intracoastal Waterway, even in the heat of the day. Songbirds echo through the forest at the **Sawmill Slough Preserve** (see *Parks*) on the University of North Florida campus. See *Green Space* for many more locations.

BOATING Have a party on the water with **Jacksonville River Cruises** (904-306-2200; jaxrivercruises.com), 1501 Riverplace Blvd, where you can sign up for a public cruise, $40, offered monthly, or rent the whole boat for your own shindig. In Jacksonville Beach, **Atlantic Watersports** (904-270-0200; atlantic-watersports

.com), 2327 Beach Blvd at the Intracoastal Waterway, has 19-foot Cobias for fishing, 19-foot Bowriders for zooming, and a 20-foot Hurricane Deck boat for relaxing; rentals $79 per hour.

ECOTOURS When you can't hike—or would rather try something completely different—head out on wheels. **Ecomotion Tours** (904-251-9477; ecomotion tours.com), 11255 Fort George Rd, Northside, has all-terrain **Segway Tours** at Fort George Island State Park (see *Parks*) down the nature trails and through the coastal hammocks to major points of interest, including Kingsley Plantation, $65–85. Reservations required.

A 14-person canoe headed down the St. Johns? That would be the crew at **Nautical Escapes Tours** (nauticalescapes.com), whose artful canoe never escapes notice as you scan for dolphins in the creeks of Timucuan Preserve. Depending on the needs of the group, you'll head out with your guide in the canoe or on sit-upon kayaks. Trips start at $30 adult, $25 child; they offer rentals and shuttles for paddlers as well. See *Paddling* for more outfitters that offer guided interpretive trips on the water.

FAMILY ACTIVITIES ✐ **Adventure Landing** (904-246-4386; adventurelanding.com/jaxbeach), 1944 Beach Blvd, Jacksonville Beach. Get wet at **Shipwreck Island Water Park**, and then compete with the kids on go-carts, miniature golf, and laser tag. Fee.

✐ Eat, drink, and play at **Dave & Buster's** (904-296-1525; daveandbusters.com), 7025 Salisbury Rd, Jacksonville Beach. Interactive games, simulators, arcades, and food and drink. Daily. After 10 PM on Fri and Sat, the facility is reserved for the grown-ups. Fee.

SHIPWRECK ISLAND WATERPARK AT ADVENTURE LANDING, JACKSONVILLE BEACH

Visit Jacksonville

✑ Inside a cute castle that seems incongruous on this busy boulevard, the **Hands On Children's Museum** (904-642-2688), 8580 Beach Blvd, Southside, offers hands-on adventures for small children. They can make a deposit at the Mini Bank, be cashiers at the Winn-Dixie Little Grocery, or play with the puppets. Tiny tots have their own adventure room to explore, and everyone gets soapy in the Bubble Room. Fee.

✑ You'll have a great time at the nicely landscaped **Mandarin Mill Family Golf** (904-262-7888), 10910 San Jose Blvd, Mandarin. Fee.

✑ A shady oasis in this urban area, **Tree Hill Nature Center** (904-724-4646; treehill.org), 7152 Lone Star Rd, Arlington, is a place for families to explore together, with more than 53 acres to roam on nature trails and boardwalks. Enjoy the butterfly garden and explore their natural history museum, with its interactive exhibits on native wildlife, energy, and more; fee.

FISHING Deep-sea fishing is an option when you head offshore from the mouth of the St. Johns River, and there are charters to make your adventure a pleasurable one, such as **King Neptune** (904-220-6363) and the **Mayport Princess** (904-241-4111; mayportprincessfishing.com), 4378 Ocean St, both launching from Mayport, rates starting around $300. Head out with **Big River Fishing Charters** (904-866-8054, bigrivercharters.com) for trips upriver to the quieter spots where the river-banks get a little wild and you can catch some serious bass, $300–400 for up to two people. **Captain Dave Sipler** (904-642-9546; fish-jacksonville-fishing.com) will take you up into the inlets and tidal creeks for trips starting at $400; he runs non-fishing scenic cruises, too. For pier fishing, head to the **Jacksonville Beach Pier** (jaxbeach-pier.com).

THE JACKSONVILLE BEACH PIER

GOLF While golfers tend to cast an eye southward to the notable offerings around Ponte Vedra (see the *St. Augustine* chapter), Jacksonville has its own charming courses. Rated as one of the top golf courses in Florida by *Golf News*, **Windsor Parke Golf Club** (904-223-4653; windsorparke.com), 13823 Sutton Park Dr N, Southside, is an 18-hole course designed by Arthur Hills, considered the only beginner-friendly course in the area. Run by the city of Jacksonville, **Bent Creek Golf Course** (904-779-0800; golfbentcreek.com), 10440 Tournament Ln, Jacksonville Heights West, is a 6,620-yard par 71 with meandering fairways edged by pine flatwoods. Offering the best tee times and rates, **Florida's First Coast of Golf** (800-530-5248; florida-golf.org/teetimes) can book you into any of the major courses between Amelia Island and St. Augustine.

HIKING In this urban area, Jacksonville's preserves, along with state and federal lands, shine as destinations for hikers. None of the hikes is especially lengthy, but scenic vistas are the norm. One of my favorites is the **Island Hiking Trail** at Little Talbot Island State Park (see *Beaches*), a 3.8-mile loop through coastal habitats and up and over sand dunes to end as a beach walk back to the main part of the park. For a surprising bit of urban quiet that's perfect for the kids, check out **Castaway Island Preserve** (see *Parks*) on the way to Jacksonville Beach. In town, **Tree Hill Nature Center** (see *Family Activities*) has extensive trails to roam, and the **Theodore Roosevelt Area, Timucuan Ecological & Historic Preserve** (see *Parks*), offers great views from its bluffs above the St. Johns River. Explore a surprising variety of habitats at **Sawmill Slough Preserve** (see *Parks*) on nearly 5 miles of trails on the University of North Florida campus.

PADDLING The extensive saltwater creeks and tidal marshes of the St. Johns River can only be seen by kayak. Paddle these remote, scenic waterways with **First Coast Outfitters** (904-502-7733; firstcoastoutfitters.com), 616 12th Ave N, Jacksonville Beach, in search of ospreys and pelicans. Now part of Kayak Amelia (see the *Amelia Island* chapter), they collaborate on many tours throughout the region, including up the Fort George River, along Julington Creek, and even paddling through downtown Jacksonville. Rates are typically around $55 adult, $35 child for guided trips of up to three hours. Check **Black Creek Guides** (blackcreekguides.com), a spin-off of local outfitter Black Creek Outfitters (see *Selective Shopping*), for their list of guided tours; beginning trips start at $65. **Rent Beach Stuff** (904-305-6472; rentbeachstuff.com), 11 1st St N, Jacksonville Beach, offers **sit-upon kayaks** among its rental inventory; it's a quick trip over the bridge to Castaway Island Preserve (see *Parks*) to launch into the winding tidal creeks along the Intracoastal Waterway, and they will deliver, $50 per day.

KAYAKING IS POPULAR IN JACKSONVILLE'S CREEKS AND MARSHLANDS

Wes Lester

✴ Green Space

BEACHES Wildly popular with the younger set, **Jacksonville Beach**, **Neptune Beach**, and **Atlantic Beach** all offer broad, sunny strands on which to nourish a tan; parking fee. ♿ ✍ **Oceanfront Park** is a small access point (with parking) along 1st St S, Jacksonville Beach, with beachfront access centered on a variety of sculptures that children love to play on, including a manatee and sea turtle. Interpretive information explains the creatures' roles in the local habitat.

✍ At **Kathryn Abbey Hanna Park** (904-249-4700; coj.net), 500 Wonderwood Dr, Mayport, boardwalks lead through gnarled forests of sand live oaks and over tall, windswept dunes topped with cabbage palms and sea oats to strands of white sand that attract sunbathers from all over the region. The park also includes fishing ponds, separate hiking and biking trails, and two campgrounds—developed and primitive; fee.

North of the St. Johns River, beachgoers flock to **Huguenot Park** (904-251-3335; coj.net), 10980 Heckscher Dr, Northside, a shifting sandbar at the mouth of the St. Johns River with a campground (see *Camping & Cabins*). It's considered one of the best places in the region to catch a wave.

GARDENS At the **Cummer Museum of Art & Gardens** (see *Art Museums*), the formal gardens now complement one of Florida's finest art collections, but are much older than the museum itself. Having made their fortune in logging Florida's cypress, the Cummer family built a grand home on the St. Johns, with gardens landscaped to impress. The first garden, started in 1903, was the English Garden. In the 1930s both William Lyman Phillips and Ellen Biddle Shipman were hired—

TALBOT ISLANDS
North of Fort George Island, A1A runs through **Little Talbot Island State Park** (904-251-2320; floridastateparks.org/littletalbotisland), 12157 Heckscher Dr, Northside, and **Big Talbot Island State Park** (floridastateparks.org/big talbotisland), N A1A. These adjoining barrier islands provide an immersion into the wilds along two undeveloped Florida shorelines—estuary and oceanfront—a rare and glorious experience. The beachfront at Little Talbot is a 5-mile-long swath of dunes and wilderness; walk north to stake out your own private piece of waterfront for the day. On Big Talbot, a short hiking trail leads out to one of Florida's most unusual beaches, Blackrock Beach. With offshore sandbars and black rocks in the foreground, it looks like a scene from Hawaii, but the lava-like "rocks" are made of naturally eroded peat and sand. The Bluffs Picnic Area provides a promontory at the north end of the island and is frequented for surf fishing; a new multiuse trail is in the works. The campground on Little Talbot Island (see *Camping & Cabins*) sits in a shady bowl created by the dunes of the maritime forest; canoe rentals available. Fee.

EXPLORE CASTAWAY ISLAND WITH THE KIDS FOR WILDLIFE-WATCHING

by different family members—to redesign the garden space. Those designs persist today, with Shipman's Italian Garden using arches to direct your gaze out over the St. Johns River. One of the oldest live oaks in the region, a landmark from the river, was incorporated into the design of the Upper Garden. Open in concert with the museum, the gardens are included in the admission price and are accessed via the loggia.

☀ One of the more unusual arboretums in Florida is the **Camp Milton Historic Tree Grove** at Camp Milton Historic Preserve (see *Parks*). Located west of the city along the rail corridor where Camp Milton—an important Confederate encampment during the Civil War—was located, this grove of 58 young trees serves as a memorial to that difficult time. Each tree was propagated directly from trees that existed during the Civil War, from the Gettysburg Address honeylocust to the Fredrick Douglass White Oak.

PARKS The city of Jacksonville has many parks and preserves; these are some highlights. For more places to explore, see their website at coj.net.

☀ ✔ ♿ One of the most pleasant coastal parks in the region, **Castaway Island Preserve** (floridahikes.com/castawayisland), 14548 San Pablo Dr N, offers a gentle, paved nature trail with boardwalks for birding along the Intracoastal Waterway. At the end of a residental bike path, it's a place you can slip a canoe in the water, stop at the playground, or visit the nature center before communing with wildlife along the well-interpreted loop trail.

☀ ✔ ♿ In addition to its Civil War history, **Camp Milton Historic Preserve** (904-255-7912; coj.net), 1175 Halsema Rd N, northwest Jacksonville, offers recreational facilities as a stop along the Jacksonville-Baldwin Trail (see *Bicycling*), including nature trails and an 1800s Florida farm to explore.

✒ On a hot summer day, catch the mist off the world's first high-spraying fountains at **Friendship Park & Fountain** (jaxfountain.com), 1015 Museum Circle, Southbank Riverwalk, downtown, on the St. Johns River. Refurbished in recent years to its former glory, it's the site of evening light and music shows.

☙ The site of numerous periods of human habitation and the highest hill on the southeastern Atlantic coast, **Fort George Island Cultural State Park** (904-251-2320; floridastateparks.org/fortgeorgeisland), 12157 Heckscher Dr, Northside, shows signs of the human touch—the former golf greens of the historic Ribault Club are being reclaimed by coastal forest. Opened in 1928, the Ribault Club attracted affluent guests with a yacht basin, lawn bowling courses, and nine-hole golf course. The island's human history dates back tens of thousands of years, however; explore it along the Saturiwa Trail driving tour; free. A new way to see the loop is on a cross-terrain Segway with Ecomotion Tours (see *Ecotours*).

At **Jesse Ball DuPont Treaty Oak Park**, Prudential Dr at Main St (FL 13), downtown, the ancient live oak that canopies much of the park boasts a spread of more than 160 feet. In 1907 the tree was festooned with electric lights as electricity came to Jacksonville for the first time.

Between Riverside and Avondale, **Memorial Park** (904-630-2489; coj.net), 1620 Riverside Ave, was the city's first major park, dedicated in 1924. Designed by the prestigious Olmsted Brothers firm, it offers a broad open green space overlooking the St. Johns River, a gathering place for locals and a quiet place to read amid a neighborhood of stately 1920s homes. A central piece of art to the park is the bronze sculpture *Life* by Charles Adrian Pillars.

♿ More than 300 acres of upland and floodplain habitats are protected as **Sawmill Slough Preserve**, University of North Florida (904-620-2998), 4567 St. Johns Bluff Rd, Southside. An extensive, well-marked trail system guides you through the preserve, with a portion of it a wheelchair-accessible boardwalk through the heart of a cypress swamp. Deeper into the woods, one of Florida's more ancient cypresses can be seen from an overlook. A parking pass is required on weekdays; fee.

☙ **Theodore Roosevelt Area, Timucuan Ecological & Historic Preserve** (904-221-5568; nps.gov/timu), 13165 Mt. Pleasant Rd, Arlington, is both a wild shore and a preserve of archaeological and historic importance due to its massive Timucuan middens and a trail on which the Spanish trod en route to Fort Caroline. This deeply shaded park encompasses coastal scrub, freshwater wetlands, shady oak hammocks, and saltwater marshes, with several miles of biking and hiking trails. Open daily 9–4:45; free.

☙ ✒ ♿ Covering 509 acres across US 17 from the Jacksonville Naval Air Station, **Tillie K. Fowler Regional Park** (904-573-2498; coj.net), Ortega, is a park you can get lost in. Its extensive trail system includes an off-road bicycle trail loop, an easy walk from the park's nature center to an observation tower overlooking the Ortega River floodplain, and the Island Trail, which heads out to an island in the river swamp and has so many side trails you'll need a map or GPS to stay on track. Playgrounds and picnic area sit beneath the pines. Open 5 AM–7 PM/9 PM during Daylight Saving Time.

♿ With a boardwalk along the St. Johns River and access to a fishing pier and ramp adjacent, **Walter Jones Historical Park** (904-268-0784; coj.net), 11964 Mandarin Rd, Mandarin, is an interesting stop any time of year, but especially in

February and March when the azaleas are in bloom. The 1873 homestead of
Major William Webb and later Walter Jones, Mandarin's postmaster, the park
centers on the homestead, home to the Mandarin Museum (see *Museums*). Open
5 AM–10 PM.

WILD PLACES On a peninsula between Julington and Durbin Creeks, tributaries of the St. Johns River, **Julington-Durbin Preserve** (386-329-4404; sjrwmd
.com/recreationguide/julington-durbin/index.html), Bartram Park Blvd, Mandarin,
covers more than 2,000 acres of wild on the south border of the county. Trails
meander through pine forests, sandhills, and floodplain swamp, and can be hiked
or biked.

Within city limits yet certifiably wild, **Pumpkin Hill Creek Preserve State Park**
(904-696-5980; floridastateparks.org/pumpkinhill), 13802 Pumpkin Hill Rd, Northside, lies north of the St. Johns River off a maze of roads off Heckscher Dr (follow
the signs). More than 4,000 acres are protected along the Nassau River, encompassing tall bluffs, scrub, and salt marshes. I've hiked out to the bluffs and along
some of the multiuse trails, which are popular with the equestrian crowd. Free.

✳ Lodging

BED & BREAKFASTS Note: A
change in local regulations has caused
some B&Bs to open for only part of
the year. Be sure to reserve in advance
over the phone or online.

Jacksonville 32204
The gorgeous 1912 Colonial-style
House on Cherry Street (904-384-
1999), 1844 Cherry St, Avondale, is
directly on the St. Johns River, within
easy walking distance of the shopping
district. You'll instantly relax once
surrounded by the elegant period
antiques and Oriental rugs, and in the
nurturing hands of friendly innkeepers
Victoria and Robert Freeman. The inn
is grand and elegant, but not stuffy or
fussy. You won't want to miss evening
conversations while sipping wine and
sampling hors d'oeuvres on the spacious screened-in back porch, dis-
cussing everything from politics to the
latest novel. Take a stroll on the large
lawn overlooking the St. Johns, where
you'll discover secret gardens and hidden treasures, then rest on the Crone's
Bench and watch the dolphins play in
the river. Breakfast is equally elegant,
with kayaker's quiche, fresh fruit, and

baked goods. The small pecan grove
and blueberry patch produce just
enough to make fresh muffins for
the occupants of the guest rooms.
$105–115.

🐾 (ᵖ) One of the grandest homes in
Riverside, **The Inn at Oak Street**
(904-379-5525; innatoakstreet.com),
2114 Oak St, is a 1902 Frame Vernacular with heart pine floors and original
fireplaces. Constructed soon after the
Great Fire of 1901, it was converted to
apartments in the 1980s. A major renovation effort prior to its unveiling as a
bed & breakfast in 2002 re-created the
exterior of the home, including the
wraparound porch. The tasteful, spacious rooms cater to business travelers as
well as vacationers, offering amenities—
such as large flat-screen televisions and
ironing boards—that work for both. Of
the six rooms, Hemingway's Hideout
has a natural appeal that speaks to
every writer, especially with its writing
desk alcove and balcony in the trees.
The spacious 1854 Room with gold
walls and rich bed linens has a king-
sized four-poster bed, an 8-foot-tall
French armoire with amber glass

doors, and a wine refrigerator. Spa services, concierge services, and a private chef available. Children over 10 welcome. Rates include gourmet breakfast and evening libations, $105–185, plus special corporate rates available to solo travelers on weekdays.

((ᵞ)) ⋺ A 1925 Prairie School brick home, the **Jenks House** (904-387-2092; thejenkshouse.com), 2804 Post St, Riverside, still contains many original furnishings owned by the Jenks family and passed down to Ila Rae and Tom Merten, who've resided in and lovingly cared for this home for several decades. Two rooms invite you in: the Mission Room, with a cane-back headboard and modern 1920s flair, and the Live Oak Room, awakening your sense of style with classic art deco furnishings. $95–110, including gourmet breakfast.

🐾 ((ᵞ)) In the romantic **Riverdale Inn** (904-354-5080; riverdaleinn.com), 1521 Riverside Ave, Riverside, a dash of period furnishings as part of the soothing decor of each room adds to the appeal of leaving the everyday world behind and cozying up in this 1901 Shingle-style mansion along "The Row," where turn-of-the-20th-century wealth built stately homes. This is one of only two remaining. With 10 guest rooms and suites, including accommodations in the mansion's Carriage House, an on-site restaurant and pub open for guests (and their friends), and a policy of permitting small dogs, the inn attracts a regular clientele. Jacuzzi tubs are featured in some of the larger rooms, and the Petit Lancaster room has two twin beds, perfect for sisters traveling together. $110–220.

((ᵞ)) Built in 1914, the **St. Johns House** (904-384-3724; stjohnshouse.com), 1718 Osceola St, Riverside, is an elegant Prairie School home that offers views of the river from its sunporch as you enjoy your breakfast. Innkeepers Joan Moore and Dan Schafer live on site, attentive to your needs. Three spacious guest rooms provide amenities that business travelers will appreciate, including coffeemaker, hair dryer, ironing board, alarm clock, and WiFi. The beautiful Barnett Room provides a writing table and a strong dose of natural light to get you going in the morning. Open Nov–May, $99–125.

Jacksonville Beach 32250

🍷 🐾 🔑 ((ᵞ)) Perched in the Bird Room of the **Fig Tree Inn** (877-217-9830 or 904-246-8855; figtreeinn.com), 185 4th Ave S, I can see right down the avenue. A willow bed frame highlights this cozy nest, its walls and surfaces accented with avian tchotchkes—lamps, birdhouses, prints, pillows, and a handmade quilt. The room radiates southern beach charm, with its bead board ceilings and walls, and rustic doors and furnishings, yet it includes modern amenities: small television with VHS, coffeepot, phone, and wireless Internet. Out front, the scent of honeysuckle greets you as you enter the house through the arbor and gardens. Built in 1915 as a summer beach cottage, it's now the proud possession of Dawn and Kevin Eggleston, who renovated for eight years before they opened the home to guests. On weekdays, guests enjoy a continental breakfast; on weekends, it's a sumptuous feast whipped up by your innkeepers and served on the screened porch. The courses keep coming—fresh fruit and yogurt, homemade pumpkin bread, stuffed French toast, hash browns, sausage—so come hungry! After breakfast, grab your favorite novel and a beach chair and walk down to the end of the street to the beach; you can borrow bicycles and coolers, umbrellas and towels, too. Most guests can't help but return here every year for their beach vacation, so book early! There are six uniquely appointed rooms; two of them (the Coral and Palm) adjoin, perfect for families. Small pets permitted. $99–175.

HOTELS, MOTELS & RESORTS

As a financial center with many business travelers, Jacksonville has multiple locations of every major chain hotel scattered across the region.

Atlantic Beach 32233

♂ ♂ ((ŋ)) ⊱ Walk into **One Ocean Resort** (904-249-7402; oneoceanresort.com), 1 Ocean Blvd, and you'll immediately feel the touch of class. Stay in an oceanfront room or suite to be left breathless at the perfection of an Atlantic sunrise. It's the Sea Turtle rejuvenated and pushed up the high society ladder, with appealing modern decor and a new sense of style. Some of the unique amenities include your own docent and guest historian, a personalized refreshment cabinet, complimentary snacks and beverages, iPod docking stations, ocean sound machines, 42-inch LCD televisions, and heat sensors that tell housekeeping whether you're in or out so you aren't disturbed by a knock on the door. WiFi is included, but a resort fee is charged atop your base room fee. Aspiring novelists, note: Each room has a writing desk. Read John Grisham's *The Brethren*, which he wrote here when this was the Sea Turtle Inn, and discover your inspiration, too. $150–299.

🍴 ♂ ((ŋ)) Go retro at **The Palms Retro** (904-241-7776; palmsretro.com), 28 Sherry Dr, a colorful beach hotel reborn from a classic 1950s motor court. With 10 pop-art rooms paying homage to celebrities from your childhood (if you're a boomer), this boutique hotel encourages you to relax

by the sea, the beach just a couple of blocks away. Chat with friends over drinks outdoors on the patio at the tiki bar. Big flat-screen TVs with DVD player and hotel amenities including on-site parking—a big plus in this area—makes this a delight for business travelers and vacationers. $99–109.

Jacksonville 32202

((ŋ)) From the **Hyatt Regency Jacksonville** (866-613-9330 or 904-633-9095; jacksonville.hyatt.com), 225 Coast Line Dr E, downtown, you can stroll the Riverwalk to the Landing, downtown's hot gathering spot. Rooms come in two flavors: Riverview or Cityview. Suites are available on the Regency Club Level, where guests enjoy a private breakfast. The 19th floor has a rooftop fitness center, hot tub, and pool overlooking the river. There are two restaurants and two bars in the massive complex, which is a favorite for major conventions. $135–230.

Jacksonville Beach 32250

♂ **The Casa Marina Hotel** (904-270-0025; casamarinahotel.com), 691 N 1st St, opened on June 6, 1925, to great fanfare, the same day that Pablo Beach was rechristened Jacksonville Beach. The well-to-do flocked to this new Spanish Mediterranean hotel in droves. A parade of famous folks has stayed here through the years, from Al Capone to Harry S. Truman. And like many of Florida's historic hotels, it was commandeered for the war effort during World War II to house troops. Not until 1991 did it reopen as a hotel with the elegance of its former glory, with 24 individually decorated rooms and suites providing a taste of the regal past. A member of the Historic Hotels of America, it's a destination that no classic-hotel buff should miss. $99 and up.

Neptune Beach 32266

All rooms face the ocean at the **Sea Horse Oceanfront Inn** (800-881-2330 or 904-246-2175; jacksonville oceanfronthotel.com), 140 Atlantic Blvd, its exterior distinctively decorated with blue neon seahorses. Inside your room, savor the view, or better yet head down to the famous Lemon Bar, an oceanside tiki bar that gets rolling well after dark. Standard rooms offer refrigerator and coffeemaker; suites and a penthouse are available. $109–179.

CAMPING & CABINS

Jacksonville 32226—Northside

🐾 ✿ Just across the St. George River from Little Talbot Island, perched at the mouth of the St. Johns, **Huguenot Memorial Park** (904-251-3335; coj .net), 10980 Heckscher Dr, is one of the region's more popular remote beaches but is extra-special because it offers camping. Bounded by water on three sides, the size of the park expands and contracts with the tides, but the three campgrounds (inlet, river, and woods) remain the same—88 sites total. There are no hookups, but it's one heck of a bargain—$10–15 per night. Tents and RVs welcome.

✿ ♿ At **Little Talbot Island State Park** (see *Beaches*), the campground (800-326-3521; floridastateparks .reserveamerica.com) is across the street from the beach but in a perfect place, well hidden from the sun by a thick canopy of sand live oaks. Walk down to the Intracoastal and fish from the bank or explore the nature trail; canoe rentals are available at the boat ramp. There are 36 sites to choose from, $24.

Jacksonville 32218—Northlake

🐾 ✿ ((ᵞ)) Rally the wagons around the lake! Or the RVs, if you will. **Flamingo Lake RV Resort** (800-782-4323;

flamingolake.com), 3640 Newcomb Rd, is just off I-295 at Lem Turner Rd. With 288 full-hookup sites, WiFi included, this is one monster of an RV destination, complete with its own dog park. Kids will enjoy splashing into the lake at its little beach, or fishing at the other end. Located next to the playground, a pool is open during the summer months. The on-site Sunrise Cafe whips up breakfast, lunch, and dinner. Sites $42–65, depending on location and surface; rental cabins with kitchen equipment and linens included, $70–120.

✳ Where to Eat

DINING OUT

Atlantic Beach

"Delicious ambience" awaits at the intimate **Ocean 60** (904-247-0060; ocean60.com), 60 Ocean Blvd, where the experience starts in the Martini Room, with its infinite array of elegant delights and live music Thu–Sat. Move along to the main dining room to savor the menu by owner and executive chef Daniel Groshell, which might offer Togarashi seared diver scallops, whole fried pompano, or Ocean 60 Shrimp Scampi made with Mayport shrimp. Entrées are $14–31, but you won't want to stop there, not with oh-so-special salads and mouthwatering desserts to bookend your meal. You can drop a bundle with your date, but call it an education in epicurean. Reservations strongly recommended.

Avondale

Biscotti's Expresso Cafe (904-387-2060), 3556 St. Johns Ave, is a foodie hot spot where the creative cuisine ($8 and up) matches the trendy coffee that comes in 20 different flavors. The "cafe bites" are exquisite, from grilled shrimp with roasted tomatillo salsa to crab and artichoke fondue. It's hard to pick a favorite, but at a minimum come for coffee and their to-die-for chocolate desserts. The cozy tables inspire intimate conversations, especially over a glass of wine from their extensive wine list.

🍲 For relaxed dining, grab an early dinner at the **Brick Restaurant** (904-387-0606; brickofavondale.com), 3585 St. Johns Ave, a local favorite where the bistro-inspired menu resonates well inside the restored 1926 Perkins Building. Entrées ($18–27) include shrimp-stuffed tilapia and New York strip; for a real treat, try the Seafood Tower Salad, featuring lobster, shrimp, scallops, and guacamole.

Under the deep shade of a live oak tree, guests partake in makdous and the hubble-bubble of a hookah pipe at **The Casbah** (904-981-9966; thecasbah cafe.com), 3826 St. Johns Ave, where the ambience transports you to a secret hideaway deep within a Moroccan souk, complete with pillows on the floor and a belly dancer. Billing itself as "Florida's Original Hookah Lounge," it's quite the draw for the late-night crowd. The food is pure Middle Eastern, and as my vegetarian friends and I did, order the mezze and share: Hummus, stuffed grape leaves, tabouleh, and baba ghanoush (with a side of kibbe for the carnivores) make an interesting meal (three-mezze combo, $15).

Downtown
Known nationwide as one of the top steak house chains, **Morton's, The Steakhouse** (904-399-3933; mortons .com/jacksonville), 1510 Riverplace Blvd, doesn't disappoint in their Jacksonville location. Choose from nearly a dozen cuts and preparations of fine aged USDA beef from Chicago, or consider a whole baked Maine lobster. Save room for their legendary Hot Chocolate Cake topped with Häagen-

Dazs vanilla ice cream, and expect a bill of at least $50 per person.

Sit and watch the river traffic at **River City Brewing Co** (904-398-2299; rivercitybrew.com), 835 Museum Circle, where the five-star meals are as much a draw as the location. In casual but elegant surroundings, the restaurant's menu relies heavily on fresh seafood, starting with steamed tiger clams and calamari and moving on to jambalaya, tempura shrimp, and traditional gumbo, thick with oysters, shrimp, crab, crawfish, scallops, and andouille sausage. Local Mayport shrimp are featured as well, but landlubbers will appreciate the grilled New York strip and other beef and chicken choices. Salads and vegetables are à la carte, so dinner for two (before the wine) will run at least $75. It's well worth it.

Neptune Beach
Settle into a Mediterranean trattoria at **Mezza Luna** (904-249-5573; mezza lunaneptunebeach.com), 110 1st St, a place to relax over tempura shrimp (drizzled with sirachi aioli) or a goat cheese pizza with truffle sauce, and watch the world drift by. Entrées ($12–28) include "create your own pasta" from fresh ingredients and delicious creations like Hawaiian mako with potato hash and Meyer lemon oregano jam. Save room for executive chef Tony Pels's handmade desserts!

Of course you'd expect seafood in Neptune Beach, and if you like it raw, **Tama's Fine Japanese Cuisine and Sushi** (904-241-0099), 106 1st St, showcases this fine art. In addition to sushi, enjoy udon noodle soups, gyoza, tofu, katsu, and more, $7 and up.

San Jose
Since 1985, **Sorrento Italian Restaurant** (904-636-9196), 6943 St. Augustine Rd, has consistently delighted

diners with fresh presentations of Neapolitan favorites such as sausage with peppers, veal rustica, and eggplant Parmesan. The trattoria atmosphere is perfect for an evening out with family, $19–30.

San Marco

Creative cuisine is what you'll find at **bb's** (904-306-0100; bbsrestaurant .com), 1019 Hendricks Ave, where sandwiches include crispy crabcake and grilled swordfish to complement their signature soup, a rich shrimp bisque. Savor the selections, starting at $12, with a wine pairing from their extensive list. Prix fixe menu Mon–Thu 5–10, $25 for three courses, or choose from ever-changing entrées like cumin-dusted vermillion snapper with seared polenta, or char-grilled filet with bacon shallot potato gratin, $21–30.

♠ Rated one of Jacksonville's best by its patrons, **Bistro Aix** (pronounced *X*, like the city in France) (904-398-1949; bistrox.com), 1440 San Marco Blvd, melds French and Mediterranean influences for the best of both worlds. The 1940s brickwork and plush leather seats offer comfortable surroundings as you savor grilled tuna over whipped potatoes or a mushroom and Fontina wood-fired pizza; entrées $13–29, with half portions of pasta available. At lunch, try the warm lamb "French dip" or salmon tartare, and don't miss the crispy homemade potato chips with warm blue cheese. It's a culinary experience you won't soon forget. Gluten-free eaters rejoice: Wine and food selections await.

EATING OUT

Avondale

A retro diner with booths and counter service, the **Fox Restaurant** (904-387-2669), 3580 St. Johns Ave, should be your lunch stop for comfort food, from hand-patted hamburger patties to meat loaf and chicken potpie. Breakfast for under $10 means a line out the door for hearty morning fare.

Atlantic Beach

♠ Savor the aromas flowing from **Al's Pizza** (904-249-0002; alspizza.com), 303 Atlantic Blvd, a local chain found all over the city. Settle into the snazzy bistro digs and order a to-die-for BLT pizza—I couldn't have believed how good it was until we polished one off. Al Mazur is the quintessential immigrant-makes-good success story, and he means a lot to the local community. The New York–style pies run $10 and up, and the menu includes other Italian faves as well.

♣ Since 1956, **Joseph's Pizza** (904-270-1122; josephsitalian.com), 30 Ocean Blvd, home of the homemade crust, has fed a steady stream of satisfied customers. Bring Fido to the pet-friendly side patio to share your pizza pie, and leave a little room for the nightly gelato specials. Pizzas $9 and up. Three locations, including Southside and downtown.

By day, the **Sun Dog** (904-241-8221; sundogjax.com), 207 Atlantic Blvd, is a funky neighborhood diner with sandwiches and burgers. By night, local bands transform the place into a pulsing dance floor with steak and seafood sides. Pick your mood, and arrive at an appropriate hour to enjoy this local favorite. Dinner entrées kick off with meat loaf (finished on the grill), $11–19.

Downtown

The elegance of the marble-and-glass lobby of the Hyatt Regency (see *Hotels, Motels & Resorts*) spills over to set the ambience of the **Trellises Restaurant**, which looks out across the lobby to the St. Johns River. The menu features fresh veggies and local fish. Their "famous grouper sandwich" stands up to its name, with fish so fresh it melts in your mouth; try it blackened for just a touch of spice. Breakfast, lunch, and dinner; entrées $15–30.

Five Points

Dining with a friend at **Cozy Tea** (904-329-3964; cozyt.com), 1029 Park St, it was tough to choose "just the right tea" from their four-page menu of teas from around the world, served hot or iced. Entrance to this little café is through a corridor of fine china and antiques. We met early for lunch, when it's tough to choose from "Hot Savories" like the Zesty Cheeses & Tomato Tart or Curried Chicken Pastry, or go with tea sandwiches or salads. Later in the afternoon, they switch to formal teas, with several options that'll have you salivating over fresh-baked scones and whipped cream. Speaking of salivating, you must draw close to a case of handcrafted chocolate truffles as you go to pay your bill, each a tempting little work of art. Lunch under $12. Open Mon–Fri 11–4, Sat 11–5.

Jacksonville Beach

Take in the view from the rooftop open-air bar at the **Beachside Seafood Market & Restaurant** (904-241-2702; beachsideseafood.info), 120 3rd St S, or just stop by and grab a pound of fresh Mayport shrimp to steam back at the rental. Lunch is the busy time here, with their signature "shrimp burger" a perennial favorite.

❧ Grab a quick bite at **Lubi's Hot Subs** (904-642-3800; lubis.com), 500 N 3rd St, home of "The Famous Lubi" ($6). Piled high on a steamed hero roll, it's like a Philly but has a Jacksonville twist—seasoned ground beef with mayo, mustard, American cheese, and a dash of hot pepper sauce. Wash it down with fresh-made cherry limeade!

LaVilla

For more than 50 years, **Jenkins Quality Barbecue** (904-353-6388; jenkinsqualitybarbecue.com), 830 N Pearl St, has served up the most succulent barbecue in the city. Now under the third generation's care, this institution features meats smoked over a wood-fired pit and smothered in secret sauces; it'll have you coming back again and again. $5–26 (for a huge slab of ribs).

Mandarin

Savor a slice of Floridiana at a funky fish camp—**Clark's Fish Camp Seafood Restaurant** (904-268-3474; clarksfishcamp.com), 12903 Hood Landing Rd. With a menagerie of critters looking over your shoulder, you'll savor southern favorites like fried green tomatoes and fried dill pickles, or choose an off-the-wall appetizer like fried antelope, smoked eel, or charred kangaroo (I just couldn't, but you might). Their "house special" oysters are the cream of the crop. Open daily for lunch and dinner, with an extensive menu ($12–30)—try the big Low Country boiled platter for two if you have a sweetie to share that heap of steamed seafood.

For comfort food, **Famous Amos** (904-268-6159; famousamos.bz), 10339 San Jose Blvd, can't be beat. It reminds me of the Howard Johnson's of the 1960s, but with a southern twist. Think breaded pork chops, ham and pinto beans, gizzards . . . you get the picture. Each home-style entrée comes with your choice of three veggies or a slice of pie—you'll have a tough time deciding between chocolate cream pie and broccoli, right? Breakfast served 24 hours, including southern fare like pecan waffles and fried tomatoes and grits. No matter what time of day, you'll walk out full for under $15.

❦ Dinner with friends is always a fond memory, and I enjoyed one such dinner at **Santioni's Cucina Italiana** (904-262-5190), 11531 San Jose Blvd #6, after a charity fund-raiser. The atmosphere is old-school Italian with traditional Neapolitan entrées, $7 and up—the lunch buffet is a steal.

Neptune Beach

Dine outdoors on picnic tables under a canopy or indoors in the cozy booths at the ever-popular **Sliders Oyster Bar** (904-246-0881), 218 1st St, where folks gather for the super-fresh and inexpensive seafood (especially the oyster specials) and cheap beer. Try their Shrimp Dip, made with fresh Mayport shrimp, or a fish taco, with classic southern sides like collard greens, pepperpot vegetables, and cheese grits; chase that hunger away for $7 and up.

San Jose

❦ A landmark 1938 filling station has become a place where the whole neighborhood hangs out—and lucky me, I know the neighbors! Established in 1992, the **Metro Diner** (904-398-3701; metrodinerjax.com), 3302 Hendricks Ave, caters to eclectic and southern palates with breakfasts like shrimp and grits, grilled three-cheese sandwich, and their specialty, the Breakfast Pie, packed with eggs, cheese, mushrooms, onion, bell peppers, red-skin potatoes, and herbs. Enjoy lunch or brunch favorites like the Metro Pot Roast or chicken potpie. Most meals are under $12, and beverages run the gamut from fresh-roasted coffee and lattes to Key West limeade. Open 7–2 daily.

San Marco

Lunchtimes are busy at the **San Marco Deli** (904-399-1306; sanmarco deli.com), 1965 San Marco Blvd, where it's a pleasure to dine alfresco with the sound of the Three Lions fountain as a backdrop. The menu includes your typical run of deli delights. $5–9 for sandwiches, salads, and burgers.

Southside

Southern comfort food will keep you sated at the **Secret Garden Cafe** (904-645-0859; secretgardencafe.net), 10095 Beach Blvd, a spiffy bistro with down-home roots. Try the fried green tomatoes, stacked with goat cheese and served with roasted red pepper mayonnaise and red onion marmalade—a real tasty twist on the original, or an aromatic Italian grilled cheese with mozzarella, fresh basil leaves, tomato, and roasted red pepper. Salads and sandwiches $7–12, breakfast $7–14, closed Mon.

St. Nicholas

❦ **Beach Road Chicken Dinners** (904-398-7980; beachroadchicken dinners.com), 4132 Atlantic Blvd, is one of those places that if I could still eat fried chicken, I'd move in. It's been here since 1939, and it's just plain good southern cooking—mashed potatoes and creamed peas, soft biscuits, and sweet tea to go with your done-just-right chicken.

✳ Entertainment

Atlantic Beach/Neptune Beach

On a Friday night, the in place to be is **Atlantic Blvd**, with parties on both sides of the street where Atlantic Beach and Neptune Beach meet at the shore. With a few dozen places to hang out until all hours, it's easy to find a nightspot to fit your mood, or try a pub crawl—there's one every few doors. Jazz lovers flock to **Ragtime** (904-241-7877; ragtimetavern.com), 207 Atlantic Blvd, a New Orleans–style establishment that goes on and on and on down the street. Featuring handcrafted beers, it's not a bar but a series of intimate spaces (each with its own bar) evoking the French Quarter, and it offers a full dinner menu and plenty of appetizers till late. Bouncers guard the doors at the **Lemon Bar** (904-246-2175; lemonbarjax.com), the famous tiki bar at the Sea Horse Oceanfront Inn (see *Lodging*), and the place is wall-to-wall people late into the night. History buffs note: **Pete's Bar** (904-249-9158), 117 1st St, was the first bar in Florida to reopen after Prohibition. You expect Mickey Spillane to step out of the shadows in this smoky noir setting with its dark booths and busy pool tables—"a serious bar for serious drinkers." For a more sedate experience, walk down to the next block to **200 First Street** (200firststreet.com) for "Music in the Courtyard" every Friday and Saturday evening Apr–Oct, 7–10 PM. Local artists kick up the jams amid gleaming chrome at the **Sun Dog** (see *Eating Out*), and upstairs at Caribee Key, go for a taste of the Virgin Islands and some island rhythms at their tropical Cruzan Rum bar beneath bright Caribbean pastels; be sure to sample the avocado salsa and coconut shrimp!

In a classic playhouse—the Adele Grage Cultural Center, 716 Ocean Blvd, built in 1932—the **Atlantic Beach Experimental Theatre** (ABET) (904-249-7177; abettheatre .com) acts out Sept–May. In their 20th season in 2011, they stage classics like *Little Shop of Horrors* as well as edgy, experimental pieces. Visit their website for schedule and tickets.

Downtown

One of Florida's last remaining 1920s Mediterranean Revival fantasy theaters, the beautifully refurbished **Florida Theatre** (904-355-5661; floridatheatre.com), 128 E Forsyth St,

takes center stage as the venue for summer movies, top-name concerts—remember the national stir over Elvis and his on-stage gyrations in 1956? it started here!—and community events.

Expect live entertainment on the riverfront stage at the **Jacksonville Landing** (see *Selective Shopping*) every Fri–Sun in addition to what the restaurants have to offer.

& At the **Times Union Center for the Performing Arts** (904-633-6110;), 300 W Water St, see major traveling shows like *Sesame Street Live*, *Dancing with the Stars*, and more. It is the home of the **Jacksonville Symphony Orchestra** (904-354-5547; jaxsymphony.org), with concerts year-round.

Five Points

Catch indie films and midnight movies at the **5 Points Theatre** (904-359-0047; 5pointstheatre.com), 1028 Park St, a restored 1927 beauty that was one of the first theaters in Florida to show "talkies," signaling the end of Jacksonville's golden age as a silent film production mecca.

The trendy underground scene is underground, literally, at **Underbelly** (904-354-7002; jaxunderbelly.com), 1021 Park St, a modern speakeasy with local indie performers beneath the floors of Anomaly (see *Selective Shopping*).

Jacksonville Beach

✔ Bring your beach chair or blanket and join the locals for **Moonlight Movies on the Beach** (jacksonvill ebeach.org/visitors/special-events) offered at Jacksonville Beach at the Sea Walk Pavilion; free. Check their website for nights and films. The Sea Walk Pavilion is also home to the **Summer Jazz Series** (904-247-6100; jaxbeachjazz.com).

LaVilla

The vibrant **Ritz Theatre** (904-632-5555; ritzjacksonville.com/theatre), 829 N Davis St, celebrates the richness of African American music and culture with stage shows, concerts, storytelling, theater, and dance. Home to both the Ritz Jazz Society and the Ritz Jazz Orchestra, it's a venue where you'll find something new going on every weekend. Check their website for upcoming programs; box office open Mon–Fri 10–4.

Riverside

Bringing world-class music to Jacksonville year-round, the **Riverside Fine Arts Series** (904-389-6222; riversidefinearts.org) is based in the sanctuary of the Episcopal Church of the Good Shepherd, 1100 Stockton St, a venue that seats 550. See their website for events.

San Marco

An art deco treasure, the **San Marco Theater** (904-396-4845; sanmarco theatre.com), 1996 San Marco Blvd, designed by Roy A. Benjamin in 1938, is an elegant place to take a date as the centerpiece of an evening out on the town. The theater shows both art films and cult classics, and in addition to popcorn, they serve up beer and wine. Call ahead for showtimes. Just down the street, the art deco **Harold K. Smith Playhouse** (904-396-4425; theatrejax.com), offers a slate of live theater Sept–June—and they're approaching their 90th season!

Southside

For more than 40 years, the **Alhambra Dinner Theatre** (904-641-1212; alhambradinnertheatre.com), 12000 Beach Blvd, Jacksonville, has given Broadway-style performances like *Phantom of the Opera* coupled with a nice home-style dinner. Tue–Sun, with matinees on weekends, $42–49, $35 children.

✳ Selective Shopping

Atlantic Beach

Patina (904-242-4990), 40 Ocean Blvd, showcases appealing home decor with upscale beach flair.

The scent of vintage paper envelopes you at **Tappin Book Mine** (888-246-1399 or 904-246-1388; tappinbook mine.com), 705 Atlantic Blvd, a libraryesque collection of used books where you can lose yourself for a few hours browsing hundreds of volumes, sheet music, and maps. The rarest items are under lock and key, but don't be afraid to ask.

Avondale

Reminiscent of the flower stalls in London's Covent Garden, **Anita's Garden Shop** (904-388-2060; avon daleboutiques.com/anitas.html), 3637 St. Johns Ave, beckons you through its white gates flanked with blooms bursting from containers into a floral shop with garden extras.

Avondale Antique Mart (904-384-8787), 3651 Park St, isn't in the main shopping district but is worth the detour for antiques hounds who enjoy a browse through dealer booths.

A collector's destination, **Avondale Gift Boutique** (904-387-9557; avon dalegiftboutique.com), 3650 St. Johns Ave, is distinguished by its fountain out front and elegant collectibles inside. Look for Lladro figurines, pottery, and glass art; don't miss the Christmas room.

The danger in reviewing shopping districts is the amount of money you can spend when you find the perfect store for gift shopping. **Cowford Traders** (904-387-4557; cowfordtraders.com), 3563 St. Johns Ave, was just that kind of place. It's what you wished Woolworth's was like when you were little— a department store full of fun. Complementing a fabulous children's toy section are games and puzzles for adults, cards, and small knickknacks. Outside along the sidewalk, you'll find a pet-friendly water trough.

✐ Find plenty of fun for the kids inside **The Green Alligator** (904-389-3099; thegreenalligator.com), 3581 St. Johns Ave, where they sell toys, toys, and more toys, many of them science-based, and elaborate European playsets. The kids will be so busy playing, they won't realize they're learning, too.

Downtown

Locals just call it "The Landing," and it's *the* place to hang out downtown. **Jacksonville Landing** (904-353-1188; jacksonvillelanding.com), 2 Independent Dr, sits right along the river in the thick of things. In all, there are 14 shops and 17 restaurants in the riverfront complex, ranging from **The Toy Factory** (904-353-4874; thetoyfactory.net), a one-of-a-kind toy store with the weirdest things, to **Koja Sushi** (904-350-9911; kojasushi.com), one of Jacksonville's top sushi restaurants. The Landing is also home to the Maritime Heritage Center (see *Museums*).

Five Points

Duck into **Anomaly** (904-354-7002; anomalyfivepoints.wordpress.com), 1021 Park St, to browse their hip clothes and accessories—including designer bags made here in Jacksonville—and you might just stumble across the secret of their success, the Underbelly. This virtual speakeasy is beneath the floor of the shop, so hiding beneath those chic little dresses are some jamming local bands and the crowd that gathers, over drinks, to hear them. Shhh . . .

Get your crystals, gems, and lapidary supplies at **Bead Here Now** (904-475-0004; beadherenow.org), 1051 Park St, where you can not only take

beading classes but arrange for black-smithing classes (off site) as well!

Explore the nooks and crannies of **Fans & Stoves Antique Mall** (904-354-3768), 1059 Park St, and it may take you a while. These dealer booths are crammed to the hilt with cool stuff like paint-by-number kits, saltcellars, lobby cards, and Fiestaware. Someone walked past me with a huge L&N Railroad sign. There are literally thousands of items to sift through in this maze of a store.

You can surely plump out your gift list at **One of Each Gifts** (904-389-9360), 1026 Park St, where trinkets and candles sit side by side with puzzles, magnets, and jewelry. Filled with stocking stuffers that'll keep your friends smiling, it's worth a browse.

Midnight Sun (904-358-3869; themidnightsun.net), 1055 Park St, is the local center of imported exotica—fabrics, wind chimes, mobiles, gemstones, and other New Age offerings, including yoga instruction.

Jacksonville Beach

Since 1973, **Aqua East Surf Shop** (904-246-9809; aquaeast.com), 696 Atlantic Blvd, has been Surf Central for Northeast Florida, with surf, wave, and skate gear.

A vision in white, **Ashes Boutique** (904-270-0220; ashesboutique.com), 332 2nd St S, evokes heavenly thoughts as you browse their delicate children's and ladies' clothing. Artist Dana Roby's charcoal sketches are the perfect complement, and they can be transferred onto any clothing or tote. Bring your daughter for a cozy afternoon tea in their tearoom, open Mon–Sat.

At **Black Sheep Surf and Sport** (904-241-6612), 237 5th Ave S, stop in for kayak and Hobie Cat rentals, beachwear, and surfboards; open daily.

Just a peek in the window caught my curiosity at **Cats MEOW Boutique** (904-242-2560), 328 9th Ave N, where you'll find fine contemporary clothing that's just purr-fect.

As befits its name, **Cottage by the Sea** (904-246-8411; cottagebythesea online.com), 401 3rd St S, has rambling rooms with nautically themed glass: hand-painted folk art windows, stained glass, and art glass. It's not just about sea glass, however; wander from room to room and notice the richly embroidered pillows, handmade mermaids, and furnishings fit for a seaside retreat.

Pineapple Post Gift Shop (877-757-7678; pineapplepostgifts.com), 2403 3rd St S, offers great gifts and home accessories with southern hospitality; complimentary gift wrap.

Sugarfoot Antiques (904-247-7607; sugarfootantiques.com), 1013 3rd St N, is a classic fine antiques store, specializing in European and Victorian furniture. But poke around a little and you'll find smaller treasures as well—dolls, fine china, children's books from the 1940s, and a year-round Christmas room.

Mandarin

An eclectic two-story gallery, **Bamboo Global Art & Home Accessories** (904-292-0230), 9165 San Jose Blvd, features art and home decor items in natural fiber, wood, stone, and metal.

With more than 100 booths, **Sugar Bear Antique Mall** (904-886-0393), 3047 Julington Creek Rd, provides a place to search stacks of memorabilia, collectibles, and fun retro items.

Neptune Beach

Set your sights on **200 First Street** (904-241-1026; 200firststreet.com) for a fun collection of shops centered on a courtyard with live music (see *Entertainment*). Among them are **Boutique**

Unique (904-241-7109), 216A 1st St, which features beach and casual wear, but what caught my eye were the brightly painted beach totes. The temptation to indulge was overwhelming at **First Street Gallery** (904-241-6928; firststreetgalleryart.com), 216 1st St, where intricate mosaics evoke ancient Crete and stained-glass windows offer a view into undersea worlds. Florida photography, turned wood, fine ceramics, fiber art, paintings of the beaches—you name it, you'll find a piece of art to call your own. **The Red Daisy** (904-339-0137) mixes old and new, antique and vintage decor items with candles, soaps, and books. **Bali Cargo Company** (904-270-2254) imports items from Indonesia; once you see them, you'll want to take them home.

Riverside

🐾 Pet lovers! Look for the pet boutique inside the **Primrose Antique Mall** (904-384-7671), 2730 Park St.

San Jose

Fine furnishings shine inside **The Antique Market of San Jose** (904-733-1968; theantiquemarketofsanjose .com), 5107 San Jose Blvd. If you're looking for something more rustic, check out their Consignment Barn next door.

San Marco

Gifts for the garden are at **Edwards of San Marco** (904-396-7990; edwardsofsanmarco.com), 2018 San Marco Blvd, where you'll find resin critters, garden flags, wind chimes, and collectibles like Lampe Berger. They began in 1969 as a tobacco shop, and still sell fine cigars.

Local artists showcase landscapes and city scenes at **Gallery Framery** (904-398-6255; galleryframery.com), 1718 Hendricks Ave.

Enjoy a convivial evening of sampling fine wines at **The Grotto** (904-398-0726; grottowine.com), 2012 San Marco Ave, where a wine bar complements the luxe wine shop.

Fine glass and pottery take center stage at **Mimi's of San Marco** (904-399-1218; mimisonline.com), 1984 San Marco Blvd, where I found a unique garlic-shaped bottle stopper amid the antique glass, table linens, and pewter.

Indulge at **Peterbrooke Chocolatier** (904-398-2489; peterbrooke.com), 2024 San Marco, where the cocoa aroma fills the store and you can pick up free samples or enjoy delights like chocolate-dipped potato chips and vanilla cream truffle eggs.

Upscale gifts abound at **Underwood Jewelers** (904-398-9741; underwoodjewelers.com), 2044 San Marco Blvd, a San Marco institution since 1928. It's considered by some to be the finest fine jewelry store in Florida. In addition, think bridal registry—the most elegant china, crystal, and glass are showcased.

Southside

At **Avonlea Antique Mall** (904-636-8785; avonleamall.com), 8101 Philips Hwy, browse through more than 200 dealer booths with a little something for everyone. This is a massive cache of vintage goods, 40,000 square feet strong, and in its aisles you'll find fine art and art glass, advertising ephemera, furniture, vintage books, and more.

Headed out on a hike or a kayaking trip? Stop first at **Black Creek Outfitters** (904-645-7003; blackcreekoutfitters.com), 10051 Skinner Lake Dr, an outfitter with the goods to get you on the trail and in the water. Open since 1984, it's the region's only substantial destination for outdoor gear and one of the most complete outfitters in Florida, with a full line of kayaking, surf, hiking, mountaineering, and climbing equipment.

IN ST. JOHNS PARK

In all of my travels around the world, I have never seen a bookstore with more books. **Chamblin Book Mine** (904-384-1685; chamblinbookmine.com), 4551 Roosevelt Blvd, boggled my mind. You can lose yourself all day in here, winding through a labyrinth of narrow passageways stacked floor-to-ceiling with books. No wonder they call it a mine—you could dig through it for years and never see it all. It's so comprehensive that the stacks are numbered like a library and authors broken out into their own sections. The staff claim there are more than a million books in stock, 95 percent used, and they've been accumulating inventory for 30 years. Bursting at the seams inside a former appliance store, this bookstore is one of the United States' top destinations for bibliophiles—even the obscure stuff is on the stacks. Serious researchers will revel in the finds in the nonfiction section. For fiction, bring your life list! I found my whole library of books on Nepal echoed on their shelves, and some of my collection came straight from Kathmandu! Open Mon–Sat 10–6, trades welcome.

U-PICK Rural Duval County is a hot spot for blueberry farming, thanks to the acidic soil. In June, pick your own at the **Dowless Blueberry Farm** (904-772-1369), 7010 Ricker Rd, 2 miles south of 103rd St off I-295, and **Sellers Blueberry Farm** (904-781-7739), 10229 Old Plank Rd, off I-10.

✳ Special Events

For a full roster of major events held in Jacksonville, see the **City of Jacksonville Office of Special Events** (makeascenedowntown.com) website.

March: During **Garden Week at the Cummer** (904-355-0630; cummer .org), mid-month, expect an array of talented artists and speakers riffing off the beauty of these formal gardens, with special art exhibitions also keyed to the floral displays.

Chow down on the fruits of the sea at the **Great Atlantic Seafood Festival** (jaxbeach-pier.com/foodfest.php), Jacksonville Beach, mid-month.

April: Kick off spring with the **Springing the Blues Festival** (jaxbeach-pier .com/springingtheblues.php), three days of free blues concerts by the sea by top-name artists.

On the **Spring Tour of Homes** (river sideavondale.org), mid-month, a tradition in Riverside/Avondale, join a two-day self-guided tour of some of the area's finest architectural marvels—on the inside. Advance tickets $15

The **Mandarin Art Festival** (904-268-1622; mandarincommunityclub .org), 12447 Mandarin Rd, third weekend, showcases local artists in a juried exhibition.

The multicultural **World of Nations Celebration** (904-630-3690; coj.net) in Metropolitan Park, downtown, serves up exotic foods and fun from more than 30 participating countries, last weekend.

May: The **Jacksonville Beer & Food Festival** (904-394-7196; beerfestjax .com), 100 Festival Park Ave, features more than 130 exotic beers and food, third Sat.

Enjoy free jazz performances on multiple downtown stages during the **Jacksonville Jazz Festival** (904-630-3690; coj.net), packing the city over Memorial Day weekend to hear major performers like Herbie Hancock, Natalie Cole, and Boney James.

October: Follow the stories at the **Jacksonville Film Festival** (904-355-5661; jacksonvillefilmfestival.com), mid-month.

November: The **Greater Jacksonville Agricultural Fair** (904-353-0535; jacksonvillefair.com) features livestock, a petting zoo, arts and crafts, midway rides, and live entertainment.

December: The **Holiday by the Sea Festival** takes place at the Seawalk Pavilion (jaxbeach-pier.com) in Jacksonville Beach.

AMELIA ISLAND

FERNANDINA BEACH, CALLAHAN, HILLIARD, YULEE/NASSAU COUNTY

With its long, rich history, Amelia Island—the southernmost of the Sea Island chain and home of the colonial-era city of Fernandina Beach—has borne the rule of eight flags. In 1562 the French claimed this land, attempting to establish a colony along the St. Johns River to the south. The Spanish massacred most of the colonists in 1565 and divided the land into land grants. But because of its deep-water port at the mouth of the St. Marys River, Fernandina Beach always was up for grabs by anyone who wanted to challenge the authority of Spain.

By 1763 **Fernandina Beach** was a port of operations for the British, who had an uprising—the American Revolution—on their hands. When Britain passed control back to Spain, local patriots seized the deep-water port several times, hoisting three different flags (Patriots, Florida Green Cross, and Mexican Rebel) but never hanging on to control for more than a few years. In the wake of Thomas Jefferson's Embargo Act of 1807, all U.S. ports were closed to foreign shipping—but not Fernandina Beach. Its Spanish governor looked the other way as the port slid into the ribaldry echoed throughout lawless ports of the Caribbean, where smugglers met, pirates plotted, racketeers reconnoitered, and the seamy side of life stayed close to the surface. The city officially became part of the United States when Florida became a territory in 1821.

When the War Between the States broke out, Fort Clinch was considered a prime defender for the port of Fernandina Beach and the St. Marys River, the dividing line between Georgia and Florida. The Confederate flag rose above the fort, and Senator David Yulee came to town. He bankrolled Florida's first significant railroad system, the Florida Railroad, to move export goods from the deep-water port to the Cedar Keys, a shortcut for ships serving the ports of Mobile, New Orleans, and Havana. On March 3, 1862, the town and its Home Guard evacuated as Union troops arrived to take over the fort. A few years after Florida rejoined the Union, naturalist John Muir arrived and walked the railroad route west as part of his "Thousand-Mile Walk to the Gulf."

The railroad, too, shaped the destiny of this city; when Henry Flagler bypassed Yulee's stronghold, Fernandina Beach became a sleepy backwater in an otherwise robust new tourist industry along Florida's Atlantic Coast. A new industry came to

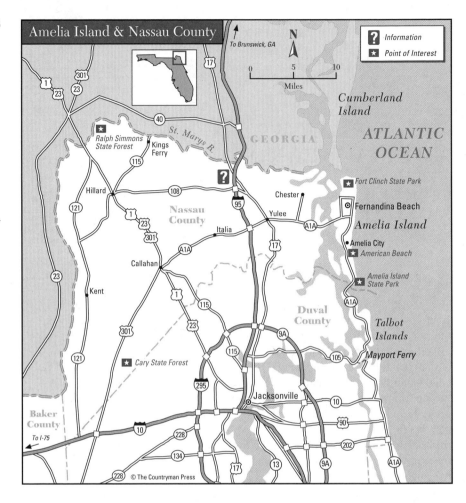

Amelia Island & Nassau County

the forefront—shrimping. Employing fishermen from Sicily, Portugal, Greece, and Germany, all of whom rowed boats while trawling their handmade nets, the shrimping industry grew quickly after 1900. The S. Salvador Company added refrigeration and better nets to motor-powered vessels, creating the first shrimp boats. Standard Marine (known locally as the Net House) started out making nets for the shrimp boats; now they also provide the nets used for Major League Baseball backstops.

As the city of Fernandina Beach grew, the population expanded farther south into the wilds along Amelia Island. Established in 1933 as a benefit for employees of the Afro-American Life Insurance Company, **American Beach** was Florida's first African American beach resort during segregation, boasting its own swinging nightclubs and hotels.

With the Intracoastal Waterway defining the western shore of Amelia Island, Amelia Island's wild side is showcased in its vast acreage of natural preserves, with Fort Clinch and St. Johns Aquatic Preserve offering protection to the seemingly unending stretches of estuarine marsh fringing the island. Inland, you'll find Sim-

DOWNTOWN FERNANDINA BEACH

mons State Forest along the languid St. Marys River, and Cary State Forest, with its pitcher plant bogs amid the wet flatwoods. Western Nassau County remains a rural outpost, with farming and forestry its primary economy, its largest towns **Hilliard** and **Callahan** along US 301.

GUIDANCE Stop by the **Amelia Island–Fernandina Beach–Yulee Chamber of Commerce and Welcome Center** (904-261-3248; islandchamber.com), 961687 Gateway Blvd Ste 101G (at A1A and Amelia Island Parkway), for information and recommendations. Or plan your trip ahead of time on the **Amelia Island Tourist Development Council** website at ameliaisland.org.

GETTING THERE *By air:* **Jacksonville International Airport** (see the *Jacksonville* chapter) is the nearest major airport, just 30 minutes south along I-95.

By car: **I-95** runs north–south through the region, connecting all major highways; FL A1A passes through all coastal communities, including Fernandina, and connects to US 301 to reach interior communities.

GETTING AROUND *By car:* From **I-95**, take **FL A1A** east to Amelia Island. A1A loops north through the Fernandina historic district, then turns east again to the beach. Head south on **Fletcher Ave** (FL A1A) through Fernandina Beach; the road turns west at Amelia City and connects with FL 105. The **Buccaneer Trail** (FL 105) continues past the roads leading to American Beach and then on to the Talbot Islands, turning to follow the St. Johns River, where you can take the Mayport Ferry to continue on A1A. **US 1** also connects Fernandina to Jacksonville. A1A continues west from Fernandina to **US 301**, which is the route from Folkston, Georgia, south through Hilliard and Callahan.

MEDICAL EMERGENCIES You'll find emergency services available at **Baptist Medical Center Nassau** (904-321-3500; community.e-baptisthealth.com/bmc /nassau), 1250 S 18th St, Fernandina Beach.

✳ To See

ART GALLERIES In Fernandina Beach, art galleries and studios showcase their works on **Artrageous Second Saturdays**, an art walk involving more than a dozen art studios and galleries open 5:30–8:30 PM in historic downtown Fernandina Beach. Some of the usual participants include the **Slightly Off Centre Gallery** (904-277-1147), 218C Ash St, with unusual collections of ceramics, paintings, and glass, plus funky clothing; **Gallery C** (904-583-4676), 218B Ash St, Carol Winner's working studio and gallery; and the **Blue Door Artists** (904-556-7783), 205½ Centre St, with nine studios under one roof. **Island Art Association** (904-261-7020; islandart.org), 18 N 2nd St, is a co-op for more than 200 local artists to showcase their work, open daily.

The **Plantation Artists Guild** (904-432-1750), 94 Village Circle, Amelia Island, presents the work of artists who live in Amelia Island Plantation, with sculpture, fine art, and photography.

> ✍ ☖ Dating back to 1842, **Fort Clinch**, the centerpiece of Fort Clinch State Park (see *Beaches*), is one of the largest brick structures in Florida and a must-see for architecture buffs. Designed as a Third System fortress, it utilizes some snazzy masonry tricks for roof support, including flying buttresses, vaulted archways, and hexagonal archway systems, with bricks facing downward in the ceilings in some of the tunnels. You'll even find a Gothic pentagonal ceiling inside the bastion, echoing the fortresses of Europe. Built to defend the important Fernandina port, Fort Clinch has a two-wall fortification: one masonry, one earthen. Batteries stand on the masonry walls. While construction started in 1842, it did not end until 1867. The fort was garrisoned during the Civil War and the Spanish-American War before the U.S. government sold it in 1926. Thankfully, it was not torn down by the developer who bought it, and instead came into state ownership in 1935. Laborers from the Civilian Conservation Corps worked for six years on its renovation.
>
> All year long, the park rangers make a visit to Fort Clinch a very special experience. Any day you visit, you'll be treated to someone in uniform—and character—from the fort's storied past, be it inside the blacksmith shop or kitchen, the jail or the laundry. On the first weekend of each month, reenactors command a Union garrison of the fort. There are many living history events and special tours offered throughout the year, including guided candlelight tours. A new and well-thought-out museum at the fort's entrance interprets local history as well. Admission to Fort Clinch is an extra small fee atop the state park admission.

HISTORIC SITES With its **50-block historic district**, the city of Fernandina Beach is one giant historic site, a treasure trove for architecture and history buffs. More than 400 of the city's homes and shops predate the 1920s building boom. Victorian mansions are concentrated in the **Silk Stocking District**, and they come in all flavors—from Florida vernacular to Queen Anne. For a guided immersion into the past, take a walking tour down Centre St, or a ghost tour beginning at St. Peters Cemetery; check with the Amelia Island Museum of History (see *Museums*), located in the historic **Nassau County Jail**, for details.

At **Fernandina Plaza State Park** [30.688624, -81.456447] civilizations have made their mark for more than 4,000 years, with the Spanish touch reaching these shores in the mid-1600s. This unassuming open space marks the spot of Plaza San Carlos, a parade ground for the fortress that protected a fledgling city known as Fernandina. From this bluff, you have a clear view of the St. Marys River and Cumberland Island.

In the original settlement of Fernandina—now known as **Old Town**—explore the side streets to see historic homes that are part of the town that moved off the bluff at the urging of railroad magnate and Florida senator David Yulee in the mid-1800s, as he wanted his railroad to end at not just a deep-water port, but a thriving commercial center. It's found along N 14th St [30.688624, -81.452038].

MUSEUMS & Stop by the old Nassau County Jail, home to the **Amelia Island Museum of History** (904-261-7378; ameliamuseum.org), 233 S 3rd St, to learn about why Amelia Island is the only location in America to have been ruled under eight flags. The immersive displays walk you through vast swaths of history starting with the Timucua, with interpretive information and artifacts to tell the stories of the growth of Fernandina Beach as an important port along the eastern seaboard. Open Mon–Sat 10–4, Sun 1–4; fee.

✤ Inside the **West Nassau Museum of History** (904 879-3406; wnhsfl.org), 45383 Dixie Ave, a historic depot that is home of the Railroad Days festival (see *Special Events*), railfans will rejoice at the extensive displays of railroad memorabilia and artifacts from local railroad history, plus an extensive collection of HO, O, and G model railroad cars. Open "every other Saturday" 9–2; free, donations welcome.

RAILROADIANA As the eastern terminus of the **Florida Railroad**, one of Florida's first railroads, the region is steeped in railroad history. Responsible for bringing the railroad to this deep-water port, Senator David Yulee also was one of people fleeing the city by rail as the Union Blockading Squadron bombed the trestles between Fernandina Beach and what is now the town of Yulee.

You can walk along a segment of that **old railroad bed** and learn more

OLD TOWN, THE ORIGINAL FERNANDINA SITE

HISTORIC RAILROAD DEPOT AND MUSEUM IN CALLAHAN

about its history at the John Muir Ecological Park (see *Parks*), along A1A just west of Yulee. But the place to immerse yourself in this early railroad history is during the annual **Railroad Days** festival (see *Special Events*) at the **Historic Callahan Depot** (904 879-3406), 45383 Dixie Ave, Callahan. The depot is a don't-miss, beautifully restored to serve as the West Nassau Museum of History (see *Museums*), with a **Seaboard Air Line caboose** outside.

✷ To Do

BICYCLING ✐ I think it's a necessity to arrive at **Fort Clinch State Park** (see *Beaches*) with your bike, since you have two lengthy rides to enjoy—the **Fort Clinch Bicycle Trail**, an undulating 6-mile singletrack over ancient dunes beneath a tight-knit canopy of windswept oaks, and the park road itself, enjoying that same shady canopy but perfectly flat and easy for road bikes. A ride on the **Egans Creek Greenway** (see *Greenway*) lets you savor views across the estuaries.

BOATING When you arrive at **Fernandina Harbor Marina** (904-491-2090; fhmarina.com), 1 S Front St, the view is fabulous in any direction—for boaters, the panorama of the historic downtown; for landlubbers, the sweep of the St. Marys River meeting the Atlantic Ocean as it laps the shores of Cumberland Island. Facilities, including a welcome center, open daily 6:30 AM–8:30 PM. An adjoining boat ramp lets you head out into the river for exploration of the near islands.

CARRIAGE TOURS ♘ **Old Towne Carriage Company** (904-277-1555; amelia carriagetours.com), Amelia Island. Take a 30- to 40-minute ride in a horse-drawn carriage through the Fernandina Beach historic district while your narrator points out the history and culture of sites on the National Register of Historic Places in a 50-block area. Tour rates start at $15 adult, $7.50 ages under 13 for 30 minutes.

ECOTOURS **Amelia River Cruises** (904-261-9972; ameliarivercruises.com), 3 S Front St, departs from the Fernandina Harbor Marina (see *Boating*) and offers a wide variety of tours, from daily Sunset Cruises and trips along Cumberland Island and Cumberland Sound to full-day expeditions to St. Augustine and Jekyll Island by water. Rates start at $20 adult, $14 child.

✐ For adventures by bicycle and kayak, check in with **Kayak Amelia** (see *Paddling*) for guided trips through the coastal estuary and along the bicycle trails of Fort Clinch. Rates $45–55 and up; family kayak trips available.

FISHING Fishing guides can be found at the Fernandina Harbor Marina (see *Boating*) for oceangoing and nearshore trips. For pier fishing, head to **Fort Clinch State Park** (see *Beaches*) or the **George Crady Fishing Pier State Park** (904-251-2320; floridastateparks.org/georgecradybridge), made up of the former A1A bridge connecting Amelia Island with Big Talbot Island. It's open 24 hours.

At **St. Marys River Fish Camp & Campground** (see *Camping & Cabins*), you're so close the Georgia border you can cast your line across it. Take a ride down the black waters of the St. Marys in a small bass boat as it curves past white sandbars, cypress trees, and alligators, then under a train trestle. Fish or just enjoy the view. The river winds along a 130-mile path from the Okefenokee Swamp to the Atlantic. Given the connection to the ocean, tides play a role most of the way upriver. Watch for shallow and narrow areas during low tide when sandy banks are displayed, especially in the narrower sections.

HIKING You can hike for hours on the back roads of **Simmons State Forest** (see *Wild Places*), which lead to scenic views of the St. Marys River and past some of the rarest plants in Florida. You'll see pitcher plant bogs at **Cary State Forest** (see *Wild Places*) with a walk on their short but pleasant Cary Nature Trail in the pine flatwoods. At Fort Clinch State Park (see *Beaches*), the **Willow Pond Trail** loops around freshwater ponds in the middle of a peninsula jutting into saltwater.

LOADING UP FOR A SUNSET CRUISE AT THE MARINA

PADDLING Learn the correct way to kayak at **Kayak Amelia** (904-251-0016; kayakamelia.com), 13030 Heckscher Dr, in the saltwater marshes between Big and Little Talbot Islands. Jody Hetchka shows you safety first, and then carefully fits you with top-of-the-line paddles and kayaks. Head out into the saltwater marshes while your guide explains the history of area and local wildlife. You'll take a break and pull up on a pristine sandbar, where you can go for a refreshing swim. Special treats are warm chocolate chip cookies in summer and hot cider in winter. A single kayak runs $32 for a half day, $47 for a full day. A tandem kayak or canoe costs $47 or $62; they run a wide array of ecotours, too (see *Ecotours*).

Rent a canoe or kayak from the folks at St. Marys Canoe Country Outpost (see *Camping & Cabins*), Hilliard, and then explore the **St. Marys River**, cypress-lined and sinuous, defining the state line. Don't forget to pack a lunch, since you'll want to stop for a relaxing break on its sandy banks.

SAILING Sail off the beaches of Fernandina with Charlie and Sandra Weaver on ***Windward's Child*** (904-261-9125; windwardsailing.com), Fernandina Harbor Marina. Dolphins swim alongside the 34-foot Hunter sloop as you pass horses running on the beach on Cumberland Island. See Fort Clinch from the water, just as the Civil War blockade-runners saw it. Move under the power of the wind with the quiet sounds of a warm sea breeze. Half-day, full-day, and sunset cruises, starting at $200 for two hours.

ONE OF THE MANY PIRATES ON CENTRE STREET

SPAS After a long day of hiking, it was a delight to unwind at the **Spa at Amelia Island** (877-843-7722; spaamelia.com), 6800 First Coast Hwy, where treatments include many types of massages, wraps, facials, and the vigorous Vichy shower.

TRAIL RIDING Jim Kelly holds the coveted Horseman of Distinction designation, so it's no wonder that his horses are in class-A shape and well trained to ride through the salt marshes, white sand, and frothy surf of Amelia Island State Park (see *Beaches*). At the **Kelly Seahorse Ranch** (904-491-5166; kellyranchinc.com) you start out in a wooded area, and then ride along miles of open beach next to dolphins just offshore. One-hour rides $60, adults and ages 13 and up only, departing at 10, noon, 2, and 4 Tue–Sun. Groups are limited to 10, so reserve in advance.

At **Country Day Stable** (904-879-9383), 2940 Jane Ln, Hilliard, take a one-hour trail ride through 40 acres of north woods past the owners' re-creation of a medieval castle. The Horse Discovery program lets small children groom their horse, followed by a hand-led ride. Reservations required.

✳ Green Space

BEACHES Protecting the southernmost sweep of Amelia Island, **Amelia Island State Park** (904-251-2320; floridastateparks.org/ameliaisland) spans from oceanfront to estuary, a popular spot for surf fishing and one of the few places in Florida for horseback riding on the beach (see *Trail Riding*).

 **Fort Clinch State Park** (904-277-7274; floridastateparks.org/fortclinch), 2601 Atlantic Ave, one of the oldest parks in the Florida State Park system, was acquired in 1935 when developers who planned to build along the peninsula couldn't pay their taxes; the state paid $10,000 with the "fort thrown in." Opened to the public in 1938, Fort Clinch State Park offers an array of seaside activities on its long swath of Atlantic beachfront, which has a popular fishing pier. Besides hiking, biking, picnicking, and fishing, you can tour the historic fort, constructed in 1842, or enjoy the salt breezes through either of its two campgrounds (see *Camping & Cabins*) on an overnight stay. Fee.

Beach access is available at many points along A1A, with one of the more popular options—because it's so close to lodging—**Main Beach Park** at the end of FL 200. Access become more limited the farther south you go along A1A through Amelia Island until you reach Amelia Island State Park. En route, look for the turnoff for historic **American Beach** (historicamericanbeach.com). If you've seen the John Sayles film *Sunshine State*, you know the story—half the residents sold out to developers, and now the historic beach is sandwiched between the Ritz-Carlton and Amelia Island Plantation. Local character, beloved "Beach Lady," and keeper of American Beach history MaVynee Betsch passed away in 2005. A memorial was raised to her on the dunes. A 2,500-foot strip of public beach remains for

MAIN BEACH, AT THE END OF FL 200

all to enjoy, and historic preservation efforts continue to protect structures with cultural significance.

GREENWAY A 300-acre strip that parallels Egans Creek, the **Egans Creek Greenway** (904-277-7350; ourgreenway.org) is a grassy multiuse trail that leads through salt marsh and upland hammocks, with boardwalks and bridges over the estuarine creeks. It's a fabulous spot for wildlife-watching—look for bobcats and deer in the uplands, and roseate spoonbills feeding on the salt flats. Access the greenway from trailheads at the Atlantic Recreation Center, 2500 Atlantic Ave; at Jasmine St; and at Citrona Dr. Open sunrise–sunset; free.

PARK John Muir Ecological Park (904-548-4689; nassaucountyfl.com), 463039 FL 200, Yulee, has boardwalks that zigzag through a swamp forest connecting picnic shelters together until the trail ends up at an elevated berm that was once the main line of the historic Florida Railroad (see *Railroadiana*).

WILD PLACES & Protecting pine flatwoods, cypress domes, and pitcher plant bogs, **Cary State Forest** (904-266-5021; fl-dof.com/state_forests/cary.html), US 301, Bryceville, has an extensive network of trails open to equestrians. The 1.4-mile Cary Nature Trail is a great short jaunt for kids and people of limited mobility—well graded, good for a stroller, and wheelchair-accessible with assistance. Families may wish to take advantage of the "primitive" campsites: tents only, but with showers and restrooms provided. Fee.

More than 4,000 acres in the **Ralph E. Simmons State Forest** (904-845-3597; fl-dof.com/state_forests/ralph_e_simmons.html), off US 301, Hilliard, offer some of the most beautiful wildflowers in the state, and several nice campsites with a view of Georgia across the St. Marys River. The forest roads are used for hiking, biking, and trail riding; take a map along or you will get lost! Fee.

✳ Lodging
BED & BREAKFASTS

Fernandina Beach 32034
((ɣ)) The **Elizabeth Pointe Lodge** (904-277-4851; elizabethpointlodge.com), 98 S Fletcher Ave, just drew me in. Calling to my coastal roots, the 1890s Nantucket shingle-style inn has a strong maritime theme. It's just steps from the ocean, and you can take in a breathtaking view from the porch or breakfast area. And even with 25 rooms, they are always booked—no wonder, as they're rated one of the top beachfront stays in America. Rooms with full breakfast, $215 and up.

♂ ((ɣ)) The well-manicured gardens of the **Fairbanks House** (888-891-9880 or 904-277-0500; fairbankshouse.com), 227 S 7th St, guide you in to a complex centered on the towering 1885 Italianate villa, where a sparkling pool invites you to relax. Breakfast delights like cinnamon orange pecan French toast come as part of the package with your room or private cottage, 12 options in all, tastefully decorated to set a mood. $175 and up.

♂ From the very Victorian 1905 **Hoyt House Inn** (800-432-2085; hoythouse.com), 804 Atlantic Ave, you need only walk out the door and up the street for all the shopping and dining options in the heart of historic Fernandina Beach. This bright and cheerful home was

THE FAIRBANKS HOUSE B&B

Fernandina Beach 32034

🏅 ✒ ♿ (((•))) Staying at **Amelia Hotel at the Beach** (ameliahotel.com), I was delighted by the sheer size of the room and the view of sunrise; the hotel sits right on the circle overlooking the ocean, the surf competing for your attention against the 42-inch flat-screen television and plush furnishings. This locally owned family property treats you like family, with a hearty better-than-continental breakfast, comfortable Tempur-Pedic beds (think about an afternoon nap after your beach walk), and mini fridge and microwave so you can nosh while watching an evening movie. Cool down with laps in the pool, or work out in the fitness center. Rooms and suites, $109 and up; packages available.

(((•))) If you've seen *Sunshine State*, you know the old-fashioned mom-and-pop motels have a hard time hanging in there when bigger properties come to town. One of the last of its breed, the **Beachside Motel Inn** (877-261-4236; beachsidemotel.com), 3172 S Fletcher Ave, is right on the beach. It's an older property, but nicely kept, and it'll bring back those childhood memories of

modeled after the Rockefeller Cottage on Jekyll Island, and makes you feel like you've joined that social circle for your stay. Between the exquisite three-course gourmet breakfast, featuring the Amelia Island Puff, their afternoon English Tea (open to non-guests as well, $11–23, not included in lodging fee), and their English Pub with full liquor license, you may never find time to go downtown after all. Ten sumptuous rooms, starting at $195.

♂ Relax on the veranda at the **Williams House** (800-414-9258 or 904-277-2328; williamshouse.com), 103 S 9th St, where this 1856 mansion will lull you into romantic musings on Fernandina's past. Scattered across three adjoining properties, 10 rooms provide an array of experiences, from the cozy Smuggler's Cove with its cantilevered window seat and big Jacuzzi to the velvety Isle of Santa Maria, with French doors onto the porch and a clawfoot tub in the spacious bathroom. Seasonal rates begin at $175, including gourmet breakfast, with packages available; two-night stay required most weekends.

THE HOYT HOUSE B&B

family vacations at the beach. The pool is perched on the dunes. Basic rooms and efficiencies starting at $86.

While this classic getaway is just across the St. Marys River on Cumberland Island, most visitors headed to the historic **Greyfield Inn** (904-261-6408; greyfieldinn.com) depart from the docks in Fernandina Beach, where their private ferry takes them across to a great escape from the hectic pace of the mainland. Guests stay in a private compound inside one of the wilder national seashores on the East Coast. A visit includes outdoor activities, including a three-hour guided wilderness tour with a staff naturalist in the comfort of a Land Rover vehicle, plus gourmet meals. Packages start at $395 per night with a two-night minimum.

✒ ♿ ⸜ᯤ⸝ ↔ One of the newer properties in town, the **Residence Inn Amelia Island** (904-277-2440; residenceinn ameliaisland.com), 2301 Sadler Rd, is tricked out for business travelers and accommodating for families, with suites the size of small apartments, complete with full kitchens. Relax during their evening social hour and grab the complimentary hot breakfast in the AM—you'll wonder what that kitchen is for! The beach is less than a block away, but the kids may prefer hanging out at the pool. $129 and up.

VACATION RENTALS If you're bringing a large family on vacation, ask **Amelia Island Vacations** (800-772-3359; ameliaislandvacation.com), 98 S Fletcher Ave, about rental properties like Katie's Light, a three-bedroom, two-and-a-half-bath oceanfront home shaped like a lighthouse. This unique structure, with a 360-degree deck, appeared in the movie *Pippi Long-stocking*; $380–485. Other beachfront properties and condos are also available by the night, week, or month.

For all vacation rentals, quality of accommodations can vary widely from unit to unit. Be aware that cleaning and maintenance fees may be added atop your room fee. Ask before booking.

CAMPING & CABINS

Fernandina Beach 32034

One of the more blissful state parks for enjoying a camping vacation, **Fort Clinch State Park** (see *Beaches*) offers two campgrounds (800-326-3521; floridastateparks.reserveamerica .com) ruffled by sea breezes along the peninsula that the park occupies. Choose from the shady River Campground or the sunnier Beach Campground, $26. Be sure to bring your bicycles, since the ride down the park road is well shaded, letting you easily connect with other amenities inside the state park, like the beach and the park's namesake fort (see *Historic Sites*).

Hilliard 32046

✒ ♿ Down a dirt road in a quiet corner of the Ralph E. Simmons State Forest (see *Wild Places*), you come to **St. Marys River Fish Camp & Campground** (866-845-4443 or 904-845-4440; stmarysriverfishcamp.com), 28506 Scotts Landing Rd. Steve Beck's family-oriented environment provides a great getaway place for safe, clean fun. You'll often see the kids up late at night playing basketball with him at the basketball court, just off the porch of the community store. Everyone hangs out here, and the sense is of community, caring, and southern hospitality. Take to the water in fishing or pleasure boats to catch bream, catfish, or bass. Pull up on a sandy beach for a swim or picnic. Learn how to water-ski. Search for the elusive goats on Goat Island. On weekends, watch a movie in the outdoor amphitheater, hike the many nature trails in the nearby state forest, or just relax and enjoy the beautiful solitude of the area—you'll run out of time before you run out of things to do. RV sites $25 daily, $120 weekly, $300 monthly. Primitive tent sites $12 daily.

Yulee 32097

🐾 ((ᵞ)) Nearly on the Georgia border, the **Osprey First in Florida** (800-628-9953), 77219 Hance Pkwy (US 17), is a pet-friendly RV and trailer campground, no tents.

✳ Where to Eat

DINING OUT

Amelia Island

The signature restaurant of the Ritz-Carlton, **Salt** (904-277-1100; ritz carlton.com/en/Properties/Amelia Island/Dining), 4750 Amelia Island Pkwy, connects the ocean with its artful preparations through the use of salts from around the world. In ancient times, salt was worth more than gold, and Salt awakens you to the world of salt as seasoning. Enjoy a Painted Hills Filet Mignon dressed with Pure Ocean Horseradish Salt, or Scottish salmon with chickpeas, heirloom tomato, feta cheese, and serrano. In addition to their exquisite entrées, $25–42, you may select from the Natural and Infused Salts menu to take your own exotic taste of the world home, from Aguni, harvested from a small island in Japan, to Adriatic Citrus Salt, blending rich salt from the northernmost salt pan in Croatia with Florida citrus peels.

Fernandina Beach

From the outside, the **Beech Street Grill** (904-277-3662; beechstreetgrill .com), 801 Beech St, entices before you even learn about their food. The 1889 home features two stories of highly ornamented Chippendale-style

balustrades along its verandas. Inside, the dining room is abuzz. Your evening's delight might be seared U-10 sea scallops with sherry vinegar cream over roasted garlic mashed potatoes with white truffle oil, fresh arugula, and fried leeks; or grilled toasted cumin, thyme, and black pepper rubbed veal loin chop with black truffle butter over tasso hash and a lemon thyme veal sauce. Save room for their delicious ice-cream-puff creation, Profiteroles, for dessert. Entrées, $18–34. Dinner nightly, reservations recommended.

🦐 ✎ No visit to Fernandina Beach is complete without a meal at **The Crab Trap** (904-261-4749; crabtrapamelia .com), 31 N 2nd St, a downtown fixture for more than 30 years. First, the seafood is fresh and delicious, with quality overseen by executive chef Max Wohlfarth. Blackened shrimp just don't come any better, with just the right touch of blackening on the outside, the shrimp crisp and fresh, as is the slaw. My key lime pie was a tart, thick slab. But there's a quirk at this restaurant that the kids (and yes, many grown-ups) will love: the hole in the table. When you're peeling fresh shrimp, or pulling apart crab legs, it saves a big mess for the waitress when you can

LUSCIOUS SHE-CRAB SOUP AT THE CRAB TRAP

drop all the shells and peelings into the hole. Entrées, primarily seafood, $10 and up. Opens at 5 PM nightly, casual atmosphere but reservations recommended.

You'd think you were in New Orleans at **Joe's 2nd Street Bistro** (904-321-2558; joesbistro.com), 14 S 2nd St, dining inside a home more than a century old or in the courtyard, surrounded by gardens. Visually appealing and tasty, their creations blend cuisines from many cultures, such as the almond and pepper crusted tilapia with mango jicama slaw and mimosa sauce sharing a menu with sautéed pork Schnitzel with German-style spaetzle and braised red cabbage. Entrées $16–28.

Enjoy the charm of **Le Clos** (904-261-8100; leclos.com), 20 S 2nd St, while dining by candlelight in an intimate 1906 cottage. The creatively prepared French dishes by Cordon Bleu– and Escoffier-trained chef-owner Katherine Ewing are partnered with equally fine wines. Dinner nightly except Sun, $15–28.

EATING OUT

Callahan
Smoky, succulent barbecue awaits at **Callahan Barbecue** (904-879-4675), 45007 FL 200, one of the busiest restaurants in town. It's no wonder, since the aroma will draw you in. Choose from beef, pork, or chicken or grab a plate of ribs; and while it's not my cup o' tea, they do serve fried gizzards. Lunch and dinner under $10.

Fernandina Beach
Have a hearty southern comfort meal at **Barbara Jean's** (904-277-3700; barbarajeans.com), 960030 Gateway Blvd, with crabcakes to write home about, tasty shrimp and grits, classic meat loaf, chicken-fried chicken, and chicken-fried steak. Opens at 11 for lunch and dinner, with breakfast served starting at 8 on weekends and holidays.

🦐 Delightful deli sandwiches and salads at **FernanDeli** (904-261-0008; fernandeli.com), 17-B S 8th St, will have you stopping in more than once during your stay. Grab a Big BLT or Craig's Bayou Dog and chase those munchies away. $5–10, with breakfast served every morning, too! Mon–Fri 7–7, Sat 8–7, Sun 8–4.

For a jolly time, you'll always find your way to an Irish pub, and **O'Kanes** (904-261-1000; okanes.com), 318 Centre St, is extra friendly. The Davis Turner Band has been playing here for over a decade, every night Wed–Sat. Dine on great Irish fare like steak and Guinness pie, Shannon seafood au gratin, and fish-and-chips in the pub or the dining room, $9–20.

If you visit only one bar in Florida, make it the **Palace Saloon** (904-491-3332; thepalacesaloon.com), 117 Centre St, Florida's oldest. Opened in 1878, it boasts a 40-foot-long mahogany bar, handcrafted caryatids, and lush hand-painted murals—you can imagine pirates plotting (or are those Vanderbilts whispering?) in the dark corners.

🐟 A family favorite, **Sliders Seaside Grill** (904-277-6652; slidersseaside .com), 1998 S Fletcher Ave, has both a tiki bar and a playground with sandbox overlooking the beach—how smart is that? Being within walking distance of several recommended lodgings ensures steady traffic, too. Plenty of salad and sandwich options, and their entrées include their most excellent crabcakes as well as "The Biggest & Best Platter in North Florida" with shrimp, scallops, grouper, and crab, $9–28.

The Surf Restaurant (904-556-1059; thesurfonline.com), 3199 S Fletcher Ave, serves up lunch, dinner, and late-night snacks with live music on the huge outdoor sundeck. The menu ranges from deli delights to cheeseburgers, salads, fried seafood baskets, crab burgers, and creative wraps, $4–24. Catch their weekly specials, like Sunday $6.99 lobster night.

🍴 **T-Rays Burger Station** (904-261-6310), 202 S 8th St, open for breakfast and lunch, is one of a kind. You'll mistake it for an actual Exxon (I did, and had to circle the block), except for the picnic tables between the pumps. Grab your own drinks and utensils and settle down to a grilled-onion-smothered beauty of a burger, served up on mismatched plates in the ambience of a gas station. Biscuits are only a buck, but ask for jelly and you'll pay $8.75, or so the signs say. In reality, you can pick up a hearty lunch for under $10.

✴ Selective Shopping

Amelia Island
Whether you're fishing or dreaming about the coast, **Orvis Tidewater Outfitters** (904-261-2202), 40 Amelia Village Circle, can feed your need. Stop in for fly rods, technical apparel, paintings by local artists, and gift items.

Callahan
Find the freshest strawberries, tomatoes, melons, and cucumbers at **Hildebrand Farms** (904-845-4254), 1210 Patsy Ln.

Fernandina Beach
Centre Street is the heart of the shopping district—find a parking spot and start roaming. Don't forget to peek down the side streets, where more boutiques and galleries are tucked into quiet corners.

The elder statesman of local bookstores, the **Book Loft** (904-261-8991), 214 Centre St, has a decidedly collectible bent. Find Floridiana—including many of my books—downstairs near the front window, or head upstairs to curl up with a good book amid vintage tomes.

🔖 You'll think you're on the boardwalk at **Books Plus** (904-261-0303; booksplusamelia.com), 107 Centre St, where a wooden walkway winds among 3,800 square feet of shiny new tempting tomes in this one-of-a-kind independent bookstore, complete with its own indoor gazebo for kids to sit in and read. Owners Don and Margo Shaw started the successful Amelia Island Book Festival and are respected contributors to national Book Sense picks.

The Irish-owned **Celtic Charm** (904-277-8009), 306 Centre St, inspires thoughts of the Emerald Isle with traditional silver Celtic knots, sweaters, and even postcards in all the shades of green; lots of golfing gifts, too.

Not since Mackinac Island have I watched, enraptured, as fudge was poured on a marble slab and worked over into a delectable treat. But you can do that at **Fernandina's Fantastic Fudge** (904-277-4801; fantasticfudge.com), 218 Centre St, and the overpowering aroma of chocolate will guarantee you walk out with more than a sample.

You can't get shrimp any fresher than at the **Fernandina Seafood Market** (904-491-0765), 315 N Front St. Pay by the size and by the weight.

Harbor Wear (904-321-0061), 212 Centre St, has a great assortment of Life is Good women's quality sun and fun clothing, including Amelia Island logo items.

Dress up the tots at **Pineapple Patch** (904-321-2441), 201 Centre St, where they feature Flap Happy and Fresh Produce kids' clothing.

Take the **Last Flight Out** (904-321-0510), 114 Centre St, and learn the history behind the name. The small shop offers a variety of gift and logo items and apparel.

Need a fishing net, or a ship's flag? How about a pirate statue, of which this city has no lack? Try **Ship's Lantern** (904-261-5821), 210 Centre St, for nautical decor items.

🐾 Pets on leash are welcome at the **Bark Avenue Pet Boutique** (904-261-BARK; barkavenuepetboutique.com), 1008 Atlantic Ave, an upscale shop for pets carrying everything from doggy dresses and pet armoires to holistic pet food.

Carrying all major brands of technical outdoor apparel, **Red Otter Outfitters** (904-206-4122; redotteroutfitters.com), 1012 Atlantic Ave, is also your stop for biking and kayaking gear, Crocs, travel necessities, and guidebooks.

Yulee

At the crossroads in Yulee, **Old Flood Store Antiques** (904-225-0902; oldfloodstore.com), 463085 FL 200, is a browser's paradise for fine antique furniture, plates, and glassware plus collectible ephemera. Fri–Sun.

✳ Special Events

February: The **Amelia Island Book Festival** (ameliaislandbookfestival.com) in Fernandina Beach features book signings, readings, and workshops. Have "lunch with an author" or go on a "beachwalk with an author." Mid-month.

March: **Amelia Concours d'Elegance** (904-636-0027; ameliaconcours.org), Amelia Island, is one of the nation's largest classic car shows, with hundreds of rare cars from private collections on display. A four-day soiree of seminars, gala dinners, charity auctions, and road tours, it's a must for serious car collectors.

⚘ **Railroad Days**, Callahan. Held at the Historic Callahan Depot (see *Railroadiana*) this community celebration centers on the railroad history of the region, featuring a parade with model steam trails, model railroad layouts

AMELIA ISLAND CONCOURS D'ELEGANCE

Visit Jacksonville

that the kids can operate, food, music, and lots of family fun. Last weekend.

May: **Isle of Eight Flags Fernandina Shrimp Festival** (904-277-7274; shrimpfestival.com), in downtown historic Fernandina Beach, has celebrated the shrimping industry for the past 50 years with music, fine arts and crafts, antiques, pirates, and shrimp, shrimp, shrimp. Festivities include the Blessing of the Fleet (yes, shrimping is still a viable way of life here), the Shrimp Boat Parade, Family Fun Zone, fine arts and crafts show, a 5K run, food and vendor booths, and more. The festival kicks off with the solemn laying of a memorial wreath at the Shrimpers' Memorial, traditionally done by a member of the fleet.

Get your reservations well in advance for the **Amelia Island Chamber Music Festival** (904-261-1779; aicmf.com), 1890 S 14th St. World-renowned musicians perform chamber music at venues throughout the island in this fabulous annual event, which extends into June.

December: ✪ **Christmas at the Ritz-Carlton Amelia Island** (800-241-3333; ritzcarlton.com/AmeliaIsland) is *the* event of the year for the whole family. Santa and Mrs. Claus arrive in a horse-drawn carriage, giving the reindeer a rest before the big night. Enjoy a bonfire on the beach with hot chocolate and s'mores, campfire music, and storytelling. For the kids, there's an afternoon tea and storybook performances, and Santa will even tuck your little one in at night. And as for the 17-foot-tall gingerbread pirate ship in the lobby? That's not just a rumor.

Amelia Island Annual Holiday Cookie Tour (ameliaislandinns.com /cookie-tour). Not sure which B&B to stay at next time? Or just want to see the beautiful architecture decked out in holiday splendor? Then make this favorite trek. Fresh-baked cookies leave you warm all over as you explore local B&Bs filled with holiday music and Christmas decor. Tickets $25.

ST. AUGUSTINE

ST. AUGUSTINE, PONTE VEDRA & THE BEACHES

The breezy coastal city of **St. Augustine** invites the weary traveler to sit and stay awhile, to soak in its Old World charm. Victorian houses sprout along narrow streets lined with palm trees. Coquina walls, made from seashell conglomerate quarried by the Spanish, hide small gated gardens and patios. Each home, built with defense in mind, on orders of the king of Spain, has its main entrance off a courtyard brimming with greenery. Many of the city's oldest buildings are of coquina quarried from Anastasia Island, including St. Augustine's defining landmark, the Castillo De San Marco, an enormous Spanish fortress that dates from 1695 and commands the seaward side of the nation's oldest city. Founded in 1565 by Spanish explorer Pedro Menendez de Aviles, St. Augustine is the oldest continually occupied European settlement in the United States, a little slice of the Old Country on Florida's shores.

St. Augustine is a melting pot of cultures, a concentration of history in layers thicker than any other city in the United States. A thriving Greek community grew from Minorcan settlers who escaped the tribulations of a colony farther south at New Smyrna and sought refuge in the city. The oldest free Black settlement in the United States—Fort Mose, established in 1738—sat just north of the Spanish settlement. Thirty years later, Sir Francis Drake, a pirate sanctioned by the British government, set the Spanish city aflame, blazing the way for British rule through 1784. Most of the colonial homes you see today were built during the second Spanish Colonial Period, just before Florida became a U.S. territory in 1822. St. Augustine is the only U.S. city with street patterns and architecture reflecting the Spanish colonial ambience commonly seen in Caribbean and Latin American cities.

To its north, the seaside community of **Ponte Vedra** has gained fame as a golfer's paradise, thanks to nearly a dozen courses flanking TPC Sawgrass, a world-class golfing destination. While primarily residential, this portion of the coast has its local destinations worth seeking out, like relaxing waterfront restaurants in **Palm Valley**, established in 1908 with a heritage of fish camps, and quiet stretches of beach north of **North Beach**. St. Johns County, of which St. Augustine is the

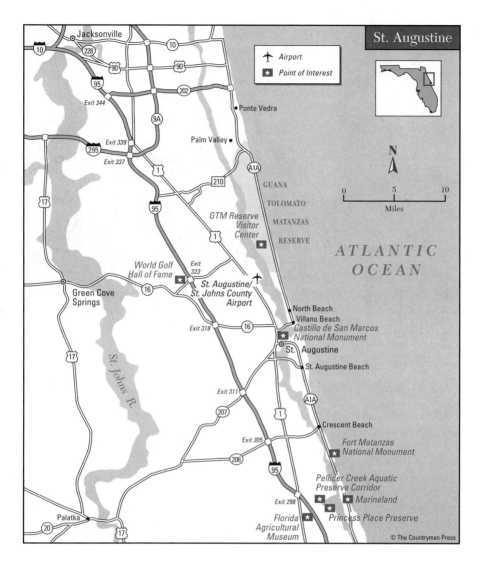

St. Augustine

Airport

Point of Interest

Jacksonville

Ponte Vedra

Palm Valley

Exit 344

Exit 339

Exit 337

GUANA

TOLOMATO

MATANZAS

RESERVE

GTM Reserve
Visitor
Center

World Golf
Hall of Fame

Exit
323

Green Cove
Springs

St. Augustine/
St. Johns County
Airport

Exit 318

North Beach

Villano Beach

Castillo de San Marcos
National Monument

St. Augustine

St. Augustine Beach

Exit 311

Crescent Beach

Exit 305

Fort Matanzas
National Monument

Pellicer Creek Aquatic
Preserve Corridor

Marineland

Exit 298

Palatka

Florida
Agricultural
Museum

Princess Place Preserve

St. Johns R.

ATLANTIC
OCEAN

N

0   5   10
Miles

© The Countryman Press

county seat, stretches to the St. Johns River, and along that freshwater coastline
you'll rediscover the charm of old Florida fish camps, campgrounds, and quiet
canopied roads. The western and southern portions of the county are rural, known
for their potato and cabbage farms. South along A1A across the Bridge of Lions is
Anastasia Island, where the Spanish oversaw the cutting of massive coquina
stones from quarries to build the impenetrable walls of the Castillo. The St.
Augustine Lighthouse towers over the island. While Anastasia State Park wins my
pick as best beach in the area—an unsullied sweep nearly 5 miles long—there is
no lack of beachfront for every taste. Busy **St. Augustine Beach** has plenty of
accommodations within walking distance of the shoreline, and while **Crescent
Beach** is residential, beach access is assured for all. Fort Matanzas was the scene
of a bloody massacre of shipwrecked French explorers who'd founded a colony

THE CITY GATES OF ST. AUGUSTINE

along the St. Johns River at Fort Caroline (see the *Jacksonville* chapter) and lost the struggle for regional dominance with the Spanish in St. Augustine. At the southern mouth of the Matanzas River, **Summer Haven** began in the 1890s as a summer getaway for well-to-do northerners who came to St. Augustine on Henry Flagler's trains and continued on by boat to create their own fishing and hunting camps in the wilds.

St. Augustine is the birthplace of Florida tourism, thanks to Henry Flagler's grand hotels and railroad, built in the 1890s, which drew the first northern tourists to Florida "for their health," and that's part of why there is so much to see and do here. It is a city infused with history and art, timeless and yet chic. It's also my favorite Florida city, in my humble opinion the most vibrant and charming destination Florida has to offer.

GUIDANCE St. Augustine, Ponte Vedra, & The Beaches Visitors & Convention Bureau (800-653-2489; floridashistoriccoast.com), 29 Old Mission Ave, has a website where you can plan your entire trip online, from reservations to ordering tickets. You also have the option of stopping in at the prominent **St. Augustine Visitor Information Center** (904-825-1000), 10 S Castillo Dr, off San Marcos Ave near the city gates or the **Downtown Visitor Center** (904-825-5079) 48 King St, at the Government House Museum. At the San Marco location, you can grab brochures, on-the-spot reservations, and an introduction to the area via exhibits and a video presentation. Right in front of the center, you'll discover the first of a series of downtown maps that lead you through the Historic District.

GETTING THERE *By air:* **Jacksonville International Airport** (See the *Jacksonville* chapter).

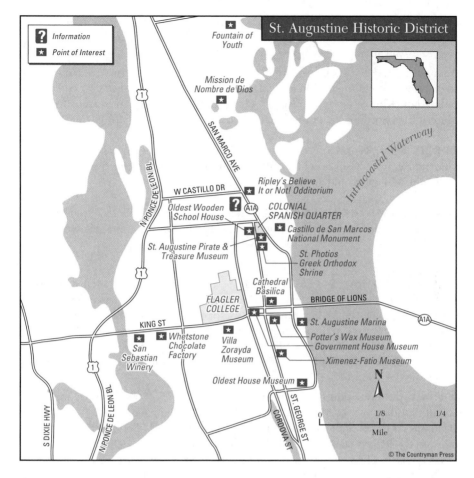

St. Augustine Historic District

- ? Information
- ★ Point of Interest

Fountain of Youth ★

Mission de Nombre de Dios ★

Ripley's Believe It or Not! Odditorium ★

Oldest Wooden School House

COLONIAL SPANISH QUARTER

Castillo de San Marcos National Monument ★

St. Augustine Pirate & Treasure Museum

St. Photios Greek Orthodox Shrine

Cathedral Basilica

FLAGLER COLLEGE

BRIDGE OF LIONS

KING ST

St. Augustine Marina

Whetstone Chocolate Factory

Villa Zorayda Museum

Potter's Wax Museum
Government House Museum
Ximenez-Fatio Museum

San Sebastian Winery

Oldest House Museum ★

Intracoastal Waterway

0   1/8   1/4
Mile

© The Countryman Press

By car: **Interstate 95** runs west of St. Augustine; exit at **FL 16** and head east, or follow **US 1** south from Jacksonville, north from Bunnell. For the beach route, follow **A1A** south from Jacksonville Beach to reach Ponte Vedra, Vilano Beach, St. Augustine, Anastasia Island, St. Augustine Beach, Crescent Beach, and Summer Haven.

GETTING AROUND I-95 forms the spine for travel through St. Johns County, with **FL 16** and **FL 207** major east–west connectors between FL 13 (which runs along the St. Johns River) and US 1/A1A (along the coast). Old St. Augustine (the historic downtown) is a place to park and **get out on foot**: The ancient streets are narrow, with loads of pedestrian traffic. If you're planning to spend a day or more and aren't staying in the Historic District (free parking is a great perk that comes with your room), ditch the car in one of the many **flat-fee lots**, which typically run $5 a day except during special events and holiday weekends A new **2,500-space parking garage** now looms behind the visitors center; fee. There is **free two-hour street parking** along the waterfront and in residential neighborhoods, if you can find it; there are some **short-term metered spaces** downtown along King St. Numerous **tour operators run trams through the city** (see *Sightseeing Tours*) with on/off privileges, making it easy to get around. They let you park in their lots as part of the package deal, which makes it especially worthwhile if you're not up for heavy walkabout.

Addresses listed in this chapter are in St. Augustine unless otherwise noted. Districts referenced in town include the **Historic District** (the Oldest City core), **San Sebastian** (King St between Flagler College and US 1), and **San Marcos** (San Marcos Blvd north of the visitors center and south of the bridge to Vilano Beach).

PUBLIC RESTROOMS There are several sets of public restrooms along **St. George St**, at the visitors center on **San Marcos Ave**, in the courtyard of the **Lightner Museum**, and at the **marina**.

MEDICAL EMERGENCIES Flagler Hospital (904-819-5155; flaglerhospital .com), 400 Health Park Blvd, St. Augustine. Call 911 for major emergencies.

✳ To See

ARCHAEOLOGICAL SITES The city of St. Augustine is one big archaeological site, so much so that any new construction requires a team of archaeologists to assess the site before building, since pottery shards, pieces of clay pipes, and the remains of 1800s yellow fever victims have routinely been discovered around town. The **Tolomato Cemetery** on Cordova Street, circa 1777, was formerly a Tolomato Indian village. It's the first place I'd encountered one of the famed ghosts of St. Augustine (see *Ghost Tours*).

🐾 ✐ ♿ At the **Fountain of Youth Archaeological Park** (800-356-8222; fountain ofyouthflorida.com), 11 Magnolia Ave, amble around the pleasant natural grounds at the site of the Timucuan village of Seloy, where Ponce de Leon stepped ashore on April 3, 1513, to claim the land of La Florida for Spain. In 1952 archaeologists discovered the Christian burials of Timucua here circa 1565, proving the site was the first Catholic mission in the New World. A dripping rock spring is reverentially referred to as Ponce's Fountain of Youth, and you're invited to take a sip—I did so back in the 1960s, and everyone tells me I look 20 years younger than I am, so who knows? Judge for yourself; of course, you can take home bottled water from the spring for a small fee. The expansive grounds hold many secrets, which archaeological teams continue to unearth in active digs. Stop by and watch them at work and ask questions. You'll also encounter living history as conquistadores and soldiers roam the grounds and the Timucua work in their village. Museum exhibits, a planetarium, and the ever-present peacocks add to the colorful display in this waterfront setting.

ANCIENT URNS AT THE FOUNTAIN OF YOUTH ARCHAEOLOGICAL PARK

As you wander the streets of Old St. Augustine, be on the lookout for new **interpretive signs at archaeological**

FORT MOSE

&. A little-known chapter in Florida history is that of Fort Mose, the first free Black settlement in the southern United States. Founded in 1738 under the direction of the Spanish as Gracia Real de Santa Teresa de Mose, this segregated community of emancipated slaves constructed a log fortress around their village along the salt marsh. In 1740 British invaders from Georgia overran the fortress; its inhabitants escaped to the Castillo de San Marcos in St. Augustine, where they joined a Spanish force to retake the strategic point. Visit the site at **Fort Mose Historic State Park** (904-461-2000; floridastateparks.org/FortMose), at the end of Saratoga Blvd off US 1 north of St. Augustine, where you can amble through a museum in the visitors center that tells the story, complete with artifacts unearthed on the site. Follow an interpretive boardwalk to an overlook of the location of the original fort in the salt marsh. Visitors center open Thu–Mon 9–5; fee. The grounds are open for exploration daily, 8–sunset; free.

sites in open lots between historic buildings. I found one such at the corner of Cuna and Spanish streets. The Florida Museum of Natural History provides an **online archaeological gallery** (flmnh.ufl.edu/staugustine/timeline.asp) highlighting sites in their historical content along with images of the artifacts removed from the sites.

ART GALLERIES St. Augustine is North Florida's cultural center, with more than 20 galleries showcasing local art. For ongoing arts events, check in with the **St. Augustine Art Association** (904-824-2310; staaa.org), 22 Marine St, and the **Art Galleries of St. Augustine** (AGOSA) (904-829-0065; artgalleriesofst augustine.com), which holds **Artwalks** the first Fri of each month, 5–9 PM, showcasing the galleries in a moving festival. For those who aren't up for walking, the St. Augustine Sightseeing Trains (see *Sightseeing Tours*) offer free rides along the art route. **Uptown Saturday Night** is the gala monthly art walk through the San Marco Arts District, held 5–9 PM the last Saturday of each month. Pick up the *Art Galleries of Saint Augustine Guide* for the full scoop, and see *Selective Shopping* for additional galleries more strongly focused on retail sales.

St. Augustine—Historic District

Splashy American pop art pops at **Absolute Americana Art Gallery** (904-824-5545; absoluteamericana.com), 77 Bridge St, where advertising art—the original Absolut campaign and other pop-sensation libations—includes lithographs from Andy Warhol and Leroy Nieman.

At the **Brilliance in Color Fine Art Gallery** (904-810-0460), 25 King St, I found entrancing scenes of the Florida coastline glowing in giclee from Peter Pettegrew, and street scenes of Old St. Augustine from Arthur Fronckowiak. Representing local fine artists, the gallery showcases paintings, fine glass art, sculpture, and more.

Bold art will catch your eye at the **Crooked Palm Fine Art Gallery** (904-825-0010), 75 King St at the Lightner Museum Courtyard, such as the tropical fantasies in wavy frames by Steve Barton, Caribbean dreams by Dan Macklin, and strongly defined portraiture by Tim Rogerson.

The **High Tide Gallery** (904-829-6831; thehightidegallery.com), 51 Cordova St, features local artists in watercolors, acrylics, pottery, and more. Brenda Flynn's bright acrylics jump off the walls, and Brenda Phillips creates oils on canvas with colors that'll jazz up any space.

On the first level of the Casa Monica Hotel (see *Hotels, Motels & Resorts*), the **James Coleman Signature Gallery** (904-829-1925; tropicart.com), 65 King St, catches your attention with playful fish and birds, art glass alligators, and brightly popping acrylics of tropical scenes.

Savor the wonder of swirled glass creations inspired by earth, wind, and fire at **Natural Reflections Glass Gallery** (904-217-3685; naturalreflectionsglass.com), 11F Aviles St.

The **P.A.S.T.A. Fine Art Gallery** (904-824-0251; pastaartgallery.com), 214 Charlotte St, has more than 200 original pieces of art on display and changing monthly exhibits.

Dating back to 1924, the oldest gallery in town is the **St. Augustine Art Association** (904-824-2310), 22 Marine St, with competitive shows and permanent exhibits Tue–Sat 10–4, Sun 2–5.

Tripp Harrison Signature Gallery (800-678-9550 or 904-824-3662; trippharrison .com), 22 Cathedral Place. In addition to historical paintings by this renowned national artist with a distinctive and popular style, the gallery includes works by

HYPOLITA STREET

other sculptors and two-dimensional artists; I fell in love with the vivid blue hues
of *Manatee Sunrise*, a giclee by Victor Kowal.

St. Augustine—San Marco
Managed by the St. Johns Cultural Council, the **Art Advocate Gallery** (904-826-4116; stjohnsculturalcouncil.org), 76B San Marco Ave, is a small gallery showing local member artists in visual and performing arts.

WB Tatter Studio Gallery (904-823-9263; wbtatter.com), 76A San Marco Ave, featuring Wendy's beautiful batik art, offers an inviting gallery with marine-inspired pillows, fine framed batik art, cards, and sculptures.

St. Augustine—San Sebastian
The neon sign outside the **Butterfield Garage Art Gallery** (904-825-4577; butterfieldgarage.com), 137 King St, will catch your attention—stop inside for a blast of "high-octane art" from this multi-artist co-op. It has large open spaces accommodating huge canvases, and you'll find many different media on display, like Estella J. Fransbergen's raku elephant ear leaves.

The heart of the arts district is **Rembrandtz Gallery** (904-829-0065; rembrandtz .com), 131 King St, the gallery that inspired all others back in 1995. Lovingly tended by Lynne Doten and Kimberly Hunt and representing more than 75 artists, this funky gallery shows off art glass, fabric arts, paintings, photography, pottery, and more; my eyes were drawn to Ray Brilli's colorful scenes of St. Augustine.

HISTORIC SITES

Anastasia Island
✎ Dating back to 1874, the **St. Augustine Lighthouse & Museum** (see *Lighthouse*) encompasses the entire light station complex. The light keeper's house is now a fun interactive museum with period items (including the original first-order Fresnel lens from the original tower, 1855–1871) and exhibits showcasing the history of light tending along the coast.

St. Augustine—Historic District
No other U.S. city can boast the number of centuries spanned by historic sites than can downtown St. Augustine—homes, hotels, churches, and more. You'll find additional sites under *Museums* and *Archaeological Sites*.

✎ ♿ Along Matanzas Bay, the imposing **Castillo de San Marcos** (904-829-6506; nps.gov/CASA), 1 S Castillo Dr, completed in 1695 of coquina rock quarried from Anastasia Island, provided the city's coastal defense. Although the wooden town was burned several times by invaders, residents survived by taking refuge behind the fortress walls; the sedimentary rock absorbed cannonballs. Now a national monument, the Castillo offers interpretive tours, a fabulous bookstore, and excellent views of the bay, 8:45–5:15 daily; fee. From the outer walls of the Castillo, a wood-and-stone rampart enclosed the city; visitors entered through the City Gates, which still stand at the entrance to St. George St.

✎ Built before 1763, the **Oldest Wooden Schoolhouse** (904-824-0192; oldest woodenschoolhouse.com), 14 St. George St, is indeed the oldest wooden school structure remaining in the United States. It's fun to take the kids through and a favorite stop for school groups. Mon–Thu 9–5, Sat 9–8, Sun 9–6; fee.

THE COLONIAL SPANISH QUARTER

Passing beneath the grape arbor, the chickens squawking as they parted from our path, we could see and smell wood smoke rising from a small, rustic building. My sister Sally and I found the source—the blacksmith's pile of glowing coals and the blacksmith himself, pushing hard on the bellows. On a chilly January day, we were glad for the warmth. A little farther along the path, past the garden, we stopped at a thatch-roofed house and peeked inside. "This looks like where I lived in Greece!" Sally said, marveling at the simplicity of the whitewashed bedroom and kitchen in the de Hita House.

✍ The **Colonial Spanish Quarter** (904-825-6830; historicstaugustine.com), 29 St. George St, immerses you in the sights, smells, and sounds of what St. Augustine used to be, a Spanish outpost on the other side of a very large ocean, where residents had to make do or do without. This living history museum includes original buildings such as the **Mesa-Sanchez House**, where a formal tour leads you through kitchen, sleeping, and living quarters expanded from an original home built in 1740, and the **Taberna del Gallo**, an authentic Spanish tavern serving up fresh sangria and live music—open later than the rest of the complex, with no entrance fee. Ducking inside one building, we encountered a Spanish scribe who asked us to sit while he did a piece of calligraphy, gleefully noting that our family name was a "stinking English name" and we might need to be "interrogated as spies" forthwith. School groups keep the place hopping on weekdays. The Colonial Spanish Quarter is open daily for self-guided tours—well enhanced by the in-character docents you meet—from 9 to 5:30 daily except Christmas; fee.

LIVING HISTORY AT THE COLONIAL SPANISH QUARTER

BRIDGE OF LIONS

🖋 Along US 1, you'll see the **Old Jail** (see *Museums*), which looks like an 1890s hotel—Henry Flagler had it built in 1891 to move the undesirables away from his hotels to the edge of town, and it served its purpose until 1953. Flagler's Gilded Age also brought the stately **Bridge of Lions** on FL A1A, connecting St. Augustine with Anastasia Island. Residents have successfully fended off efforts to replace the bridge with a more modern structure, despite the traffic delays caused when the bridge opens to let ships through. If you're stuck on the bridge, grin and bear it—it's a small price for historic preservation of such a grand structure! I'm glad to report that the bridge has now been completely restored and is even better than before, but still as narrow.

Take a boat ride out to **Fort Matanzas National Monument** (904-471-0116; nps.gov/foma), 8635 A1A S, Crescent Beach. Along the way you may encounter dolphins or manatees in the Mantanzas River. Although the small but impressive fortress wasn't built until 1740 to protect Spanish St. Augustine from British encroachment, the site of the fort was where, at the command of St. Augustine founder Pedro Menendez de Aviles, the French survivors of Fort Caroline (see the *Jacksonville* chapter) were slaughtered. Open 9–5:30 daily except Christmas; fee for tour.

FORT MATANZAS

CASTLE OTTTIS

Vilano Beach

As you drive along FL A1A north of Vilano Beach, you'll notice an Irish castle peeping above the saw palmetto. **Castle Otttis** (904-824-3274) was built in 1988 by Rusty Ickes as a landscape sculpture in "remembrance of Jesus Christ." The castle is an impression of one built more than 1,000 years ago and was created under the guidance of the Catholic diocese to replicate the atmosphere of an Irish abbey. Amazingly, just two people, without outside aid, did all the masonry work. True to the castles of the period, the building is open to the environment. A privately owned structure, it is occasionally open for church services.

HISTORIC HOMES With the discovery of coquina came solid buildings of stone. The **Gonzales-Alvarez House** (904-824-2872; staugustinehistoricalsociety.org /oldhouse.html), 271 Charlotte St, is the city's oldest house, its tabby floors laid in the early 1700s; during the British period in 1776, the house served as a tavern. **Oldest House** tours hosted by the St. Augustine Historical Society interpret the lives and times of its visitors and residents and include admission to the full historic complex, including the Manucy Museum, filled with artifacts and dioramas that capture moments in the history of St. Augustine; the Page L. Edwards Gallery, featuring ever-changing historical exhibits on a specific topic at a time; an 18th-century

ON THE GROUNDS OF THE OLDEST HOUSE MUSEUM

detached kitchen; and the lovely gardens that surround these homes. Daily 9–5 except Christmas; fee.

The nearby **Sequi-Kirby Smith House** (904-825-2333; staugustinehistorical society.org/library.html), 6 Artillery Ln, houses the St. Augustine Historical Society Research Library (open Tue–Fri 9–4:30) and was the family home of Confederate general Edmund Kirby-Smith; the house dates back to the Second Spanish Period. The library's holdings include translations of church documents from 1594, copies of official Spanish and British colonial documents (1513–1821), and detailed genealogical information for the region, especially for those of Minorcan descent. Tue–Fri 9–4:30 and the third Sat, 9–12:30; free.

Built in 1798, the **Ximenez-Fatio House** (904-829-3575; ximenezfatiohouse.org), 20 Aviles St, is open as a house museum with guided tours Tue–Sun 11–4; fee. In the 1800s it was a boardinghouse, so a walk through the home gives you a unique peek into the city's tourist past. One of the treasures found here during an archaeological dig was a detailed bronze Caravaca Cross believed to date back to the 1560s.

St. George and its cross streets are notable for homes dating back to the late 1700s—look for historical plaques with names and dates on each home. The **Pena-Peck House**, circa 1750, was the residence of the royal treasurer from Spain; it's managed as a house museum by a nonprofit, the Woman's Exchange (see *Selective Shopping*). Fee.

HISTORIC HOTELS When railroad magnate Henry Flagler built his destination hotels in the 1880s, he kicked off Florida tourism as we know it today. Stand at the corner of Cordova and King, and you can visually compare all three. Only one, the **Cordova**, remains a hotel, renovated in the 1990s into the elegant Casa Monica (see *Hotels, Motels & Resorts*). The others are open to the public but serve different uses. The **Alcazar** is now city hall and the Lightner Museum (see *Museums*), where a café is tucked into the giant indoor swimming pool (the largest of its time in the 1880s), and visitors can wander through the original ballroom and baths. Flagler bequeathed his grand **Hotel Ponce de Leon** to become Flagler College (flagler.edu), a liberal arts college that started out as a women's school. Public access is limited, but you can join a walking tour (see *Walking Tours*) to immerse in the grandeur of Flagler's vision, as executed by interior decorator Louis Comfort Tiffany. The **Villa Zorayda**, built in 1883 by Franklin Smith as a one-tenth-scale replica of the Alhambra in Spain, became a casino in 1922 and then an attraction, Zorayda Castle, in 1936, recently restored and reopened (see *Museums*). Another quirky former hotel was the **Castle Warden Inn**, now better known as the Ripley's Believe It or Not Museum (see *Family Activities*). Built in 1887 for Standard Oil magnate William G. Warden, it was purchased in 1941 and run as a hotel by Ocala hotelier Norton Baskin, who relocated to Crescent Beach; his wife, novelist Marjorie Kinnan Rawlings, soon followed.

HISTORIC CHURCHES When Father Francisco Lupez de Mendoza Grajales offered the first Mass in St. Augustine, he did so at the **Mission Nombre de Dios** (904-824-2809), 27 Ocean Ave, more than four centuries ago. On the grounds of the ancient mission, a modern 208-foot stainless-steel cross marks the founding of

INSIDE THE ST. PHOTIOS SHRINE

St. Augustine in 1565; the statuette within the ivy-covered **shrine of Our Lady of La Leche** dates back to 1598 and was the first memorial to the Virgin Mary in the Americas. At St. George and Cathedral streets, the **Cathedral Basilica**, the first Catholic parish in the New World, was built in 1797 with stones from the ruins of the original mission. The **St. Photios Greek Orthodox National Shrine** (904-829-8205; stphotios.com), 41 St. George St, is the only Greek Orthodox shrine in the United States. Henry Flagler and his wife are buried in a tomb within the **Memorial Presbyterian Church,** 32 Sevilla St, built in 1889 by Flagler.

LIGHTHOUSE ✍ ♿ The **St. Augustine Lighthouse & Museum** (904-829-0745; staugustinelighthouse.com), 81 Lighthouse Ave, Anastasia Island, isn't just a working historic lighthouse but an entire light station complex. Built in 1871, it is outfitted with a first-order Fresnel lens, a beehive-shaped work of art, 370 hand-cut glass prisms towering 12 feet tall. Damaged by a vandal's bullets, it was repaired in 1986 and became the focal point of local efforts, spearheaded by the Junior Service League of St. Augustine, to preserve and protect this historic site. The 165-foot lighthouse is the second permanent tower to stand along this coastline. After peeking in the exhibits on the bottom floor, climb the steep spiral staircase (219 steps with landings) for a 35-mile view of the coast on a clear day, including a panorama of the Historic District on the other side of the Matanzas River. Look down and you can catch flocks of ibises in flight between their roosts at the St. Augustine Alligator Farm and their feeding grounds on the mudflats of Anastasia Island. The museum in the light keeper's house serves as a museum recounting the maritime history of St. Augustine, complete with artifacts of local life and various types of lenses used for bringing sailors home. Open daily 9–6, closed Thanksgiving, Christmas Eve, and Christmas Day. Admission $9.50 adults, $7.50 seniors and ages 12 and under. Children must be 44 inches tall to climb the lighthouse; if they're shorter, admission is free. Special events and exclusive behind-the-scenes tours let you explore by moonlight and sunrise; check their website for details.

MUSEUMS

St. Augustine—Historic District
The **Government House Museum** (904-825-5033), corner of King and Cathedral, exhibits St. Augustine's finest collection of historical artifacts, with more than

300 colorful displays recounting life from Timucuan times through the founding of St. Augustine, the Seminole Wars, and the Flagler era. Open Tue–Sat 10–4; fee.

✦ ♿ Otto C. Lightner, founding editor of *Hobbies* magazine, was a collector of collections. I remember the **Lightner Museum** (904-824-2874; lightnermuseum.org), 75 King St, which opened in 1948, when it showcased its treasures in a way a kid could understand—open a hotel room door, and you'd find a room full of postcards. Or a room full of buttons. Or a room full of teacups. Then city hall moved into the Hotel Alcazar in 1971, saving the financially struggling museum but squeezing it into one segment of the hotel. Befitting its opulent setting, the museum shifted its emphasis to its upscale objets d'art—oil paintings, carvings, fine glasswork, and antique furnishings—although you can still find the button and matchbook collections tucked away in nooks, and one portion of the museum is devoted to the sciences, with minerals, archaeological specimens, and an Egyptian mummy. As you stroll past the hotel's grand indoor swimming pool (the world's largest in 1888) and spa, you'll feel a part of the Gilded Age. Open 9–5 daily except Christmas; $10 adults, $5 ages 12–18, under 12 free with adult.

The **Spanish Military Hospital** (904-827-0807; spanishmilitaryhospital.com), 3 Aviles St, provides a glimpse into 18th-century medical treatments at the Royal Hospital of Our Lady of Guadalupe on a narrated tour through this haunted building, with dioramas and artifacts like porcelain bedpans and scary-looking period medical instruments. As with many St. Augustine buildings, it comes with its own haunts. Fee.

If you think the visual fantasy of **Villa Zorayda** (904-829-9887; villazorayda.com), 83 King St, is something from the outside, wait until you step inside. Built in 1883 by Franklin Smith as a one-tenth-scale replica of the Alhambra, a Moorish castle built for Muslim rulers during the 14th century in Granada in Spain, it sparked a Moorish Spanish revival in St. Augustine that both inspired the look of Henry Flagler's hotels (see *Historic Hotels*) and created a demand for the building technique of using crushed coquina mixed with concrete, a local take on tabby (normally done with oyster shells). The interpretive handheld audio tour guides you from

VIEW FROM THE ST. AUGUSTINE LIGHTHOUSE

ST. AUGUSTINE PIRATE & TREASURE MUSEUM

✆ ♿ (877-GO-PLUNDER; thepiratemuseum.com), 12 S Castillo Dr. The newest addition to St. Augustine's museum scene delves into its oldest stories with an interactive "wow" factor that'll have you asking, "This is a museum?" The rollicking Pirate & Treasure Museum appropriately looks out over the Castillo de San Marcos. Once you're inside, you're immersed in the world of pirating from a St. Augustine perspective. Skillful lighting, well-crafted interpretive displays, and the sounds and smells of the waterfront and the sea tell tales of pirates' plunder along these shores and others. When owner Pat Croce amassed his collection of more than 800 pirate artifacts, including Captain Tew's Treasure Chest, the only known authentic treasure chest in the world, a Jolly Roger flag, and rare books on pirating, he originally opened his museum in Key West. Here in St. Augustine, it's found an appropriate home. With the help of the Florida Division of Historical Resources, doubloons and gold bars are a part of the scene, and you can actually lift a gold bar to feel how heavy it is. Inside a tavern where a rogue's gallery of St. Augustine pirates graces the walls, lose yourself in the fascinating stories of notable pirates in the interactive Book of Pirates at each table. Feel the deck tremble underfoot as you let loose a cannon blast on the Gun Deck, and feel the fear Below Deck as Blackbeard fights his last battle all around you in a surround-sound chamber designed by Disney Imagineers. Including every perspective on pirating, from an homage to pirate movies to a hilarious translation of pirate-speak piped into the restrooms, this museum is a don't-miss. Open daily 9–8, $13 adults, $7 ages 5–9, under 5 free.

ST. AUGUSTINE PIRATE & TREASURE MUSEUM

room to room with stories of how the home became a private club, and then, under the ownership of Abraham S. Mussallem, importer of fine arts and rugs from the Mideast, the most fashionable casino in the region. Some of the gaming equipment and much of the fine art and furnishings that Mussallem acquired are showcased in each room, including a 2,400-year-old Sacred Cat Rug, woven from Egyptian cat hair. Mon–Sat 10–5, Sun 11–4, closed Easter, Thanksgiving, Christmas. Self-guided audio tours, $10 adult, $8 students, $4 ages 8–12; docent-led tours $14 adult, $6 ages 8–13, free for younger ages. Free flat-lot parking for the day (until the lot is full) is included with your admission, which is a nice bonus.

St. Augustine—San Marco

⚓ ♿ **Florida Heritage Museum,** Old Jail Complex, presents an excellent introduction to the region's long and storied past, from exhibits of Florida's First Peoples to the tale of Fort Mose (see *Archaeological Sites*), the Spanish and British settlements, and the tale of Henry Flagler and his Model Land Company, the first snowbird real estate scheme in Florida history. 10–5 daily; fee.

⚓ A hulking re-creation of a wooden fortress along San Marcos Ave, **Fort Menendez at Old Florida Museum** (800-813-3208 or 904-824-8874; oldfloridamuseum .com), 259 San Marco Ave, was quite the surprise inside. Waiting at the gate (in the gift shop) with your letter of passage, you are met by a tour guide who ushers you back in time through the bastion, sharing stories of life in St. Augustine when the first Spanish settlers and the Timucua shared the land. The hands-on complex includes much for the kids to do, from trying out ancient games to learning how to use a mortar and pestle or pump a water pump. The re-created thatch-roofed buildings, including a Colonial Hacienda, Timucuan Council House, and Chief's Hut enable you to immerse in what the past looked, felt, and smelled like. A natural sulfurous spring bubbles out of the ground and creates a small marsh in the middle of it all. Hands-on and perfect for families, it teaches Florida history by doing; fee. Open daily 9–5, $11 adults, $8 ages 3–18. Discounts for Florida residents.

⚓ Step into the somewhat scary history of justice in frontier St. Augustine at the **Old Jail** (904-829-3800; historictours.com), 167 San Marcos, where characters—and I do mean characters—in swaggering character walk you through the means of justice in these here parts from the Gilded Age through the 1950s. Henry Flagler had this fancier-than-normal jail built in 1891, and for a significant chunk of time it was Sheriff Joe Perry who kept the peace here in town. On your tour, you'll visit the sheriff's quarters, walk under the hanging tree, and linger awhile in cells once packed with prisoners. Open daily 8:30–5; fee.

St. Augustine—World Golf Village

♿ At the **World Golf Hall of Fame** (904-940-4000; wgv.com), 1 World Golf Place, the museum takes you from the birth of the game in St. Andrews, Scotland, all the way through to today's champions by showcasing historical artifacts related to the game and its players. In Shell Hall, a stunning crescent of acrylic pedestals honors Hall of Fame members. The second floor is set up as 18 holes, with the front 9 covering the historical game, where you can walk across a replica of the famed St. Andrews Swilcan Burn Bridge, and the back 9 covering the modern game, where you'll see President Eisenhower's golf cart and discover the elements of golf course design. Test your swing at the virtual-reality exhibit. Open Mon–Sat 10–6, Sun noon–6. $12 adults, $7 ages 5–12.

WINERY ᕪ At **San Sebastian Winery** (888-352-9463; sansebastianwinery.com), 157 King St, enjoy a tour of the processing plant in the arts district (the vineyards are off site at a sister winery) with a complimentary wine tasting thereafter. A wine and jazz bar offers a laid-back place to chat with friends, or browse the Wine Shop for gourmet foods, kitchen items, and the signature wines of San Sebastian. Mon–Sat 10–6, Sun 11–6; free.

ZOO ⌗ ᕪ It was a family favorite when I was a kid, with alligator wrestling and snake stunts, and now that the **St. Augustine Alligator Farm** (904-824-3337; alligatorfarm.com), 999 Anastasia Blvd, Anastasia Island, is a fully accredited zoological park, it still hasn't lost its funky charm. Dating back to 1893, it's one of Florida's oldest tourist draws, and yes, there are plenty of alligators. Marvel at the many reptilian species represented here, including albino alligators from Louisiana, endangered Nile crocodiles, caimans, and gharials that share their space with tiny muntjac deer. My favorite part of the park has always been the Alligator Swamp Nature Trail and Native Bird Rookery, where more than a dozen species of birds (including wood storks, green-backed herons, and least bitterns) build their nests in early March and raise their young in the trees, protected from predators like egg-stealing raccoons by the alligators cruising below. It's the only place I know of where you can get close enough to photograph fledgling roseate spoonbills without disturbing them. As you walk along the shaded walkways between exhibits of crocodiles and Australian creatures, the rope-and-wood bridges hanging in the trees will catch your attention—they're a part of the park's newest attraction, Crocodile Crossing (see *Zipline*). Themed sections, like the Great Down Under, Birds of Africa, and Land of Crocodiles, will appeal to every member of the family. Daily wildlife shows focus on interpretation of species behavior. Open 9–5 daily, $22 ages 12 and over, $11 ages 5–11 and guests in wheelchairs.

CROCODILE CROSSING CANOPY BRIDGES AT THE ST. AUGUSTINE ALLIGATOR FARM

BIRDING One of the best spots in Florida for birding and bird photography is the **Native Swamp & Rookery** (rookery.alligatorfarm.com) at St. Augustine Alligator Farm (see *Zoo*), where the long-term presence of so many alligators assures the nesting colonies of egrets, herons, and wood storks that raccoons won't steal precious bird eggs. It's always raucous there during nesting and especially fledging season, Feb–July. Along FL A1A in **Crescent Beach**, watch for nande conures, a variety of chartreuse parrot that has naturalized along the Intracoastal Waterway. Wading birds are a common sight along the lagoon at **Anastasia State Park** (see *Beaches*), and I've watched many a flock of skimmers or brown pelicans on the beach there. **GTM Reserve** (see *Wild Places*) offers birding opportunities right at the dam along the Guana River. Walk deep into the preserve along its trails for songbirds in the oak hammocks; the preserve is on the flyway used by migrating painted buntings.

BICYCLING All along this coastline, from Ponte Vedra to Summer Haven, A1A is designated a road route for the **East Coast Greenway** (greenway.org/fl.aspx), a national bike route spanning from Maine to Key West. **Bike Florida** (bikeflorida .org) leads multiday guided, supported tours on the vast **St. Johns River-to-Sea Loop**, a 260-mile bike route linking Palatka, St. Augustine, Flagler Beach, and points as far south as Titusville, with many Old Florida communities to visit along the way. For off-road fun, head to **GTM Reserve** (see *Wild Places*), where more than 9 miles of double-track is shared with hikers; a pedal out to the Tolomato River will net you some easy dolphin-watching from the shoreline.

BOATING Rent or charter your own boat at the marina from **Bay Ray** (904-826-0010; bayrayrentals.com), 240 Vilano Rd, Vilano Beach, which has miniature speedboats, pontoon boats, ocean kayaks, fishing charters, and a 33-foot sailing sloop. At **Devil's Elbow Fishing Resort** (see *Fish Camps*) in Crescent Beach, rent a 16-foot Carolina Skiff or a 20-foot pontoon to enjoy your own nature cruise along the Matanzas River, $95–300.

The **Schooner *Freedom*** (904-810-1010; schoonerfreedom.com), 111 Avenida Menendez, St. Augustine's one and only tall ship, takes guests out on relaxing three- and four-hour cruises on Matanzas Bay daily. This replica of a blockade-runner is a 34-ton clipper, a family operation that lets guests take

SAILING ON THE SCHOONER *FREEDOM*

the wheel after passing through the Bridge of Lions—ride this, and you can be the one who holds up bridge traffic instead of waiting in it. Starts at $35.

Sailing in to St. Augustine? You'll find plenty of slips at the **St. Augustine Municipal Marina** (904-825-1026; staugustinemarina.com), 111-E Avenida Menendez; hail the harbormaster on VHF channel 16. Dockage (including use of showers and water) runs $4–5 per hour, weekly and monthly rates available. Of course, it's a blast to pull in at the **Conch House Marina** and settle into a tiki hut overlooking the water. Vessels from 20 to 120 feet can dock at this 194-slip marina; call ahead (800-940-6256; conch-house.com) for availability and rates, which vary seasonally. North of the Historic District, the **Camachee Cove Marina** (800-345-9269 or 904-829-5676; camacheeisland.com), 3070 Harbor Dr, is off A1A N just before it crosses the Vilano Bridge. It has 250 slips and hosts **St. Augustine Sailing** (904-829-0648; sta-sail.com), 3076 Harbor Dr, where you can charter bareboat or with a captain to ply the waters of Matanzas Bay, $195 and up; sailing lessons available.

CHOCOLATE FACTORY TOUR Who can ignore the siren call of chocolate? Not I. So I was pleased to discover **Whetstone Chocolates** (904-217-0275; whetstone chocolates.com), 139 King St, in its new digs, with a stylish gift shop, coffee bar, and chocolate factory tour. On this informative tour, you'll learn about chocolate and how it's made, the history of Whetstone Chocolates, started here in St. Augustine in 1966, and taste fresh-made treats, too. Tours offered Tue–Sat and limited to 25 people; reservations suggested. Fee.

ECOTOURS **Ripple Effect Ecotours** (904-347-1565; rippleeffectecotours.com) provides a full menu of kayak tours to explore the estuaries of GTM Reserve (see *Wild Places*). Guided trips in the region start at $50 and include all equipment and entrance fees.

⌔ Cruise with **St. Augustine Eco Tours** (904-377-7245; staugustineecotours .com), 111 Avenida Menendez, to see the best that St. Augustine has to offer in its wild places and watery deeps. Their 90-minute Dolphin & Nature Tours get you out on the Matanzas River for birding and spotting dolphins and manatees, $40 adult, $35 ages 3–12; or you can arrange a customized tour of the same duration to fit your specific interests for one to six guests, $175. Learn about the little critters of the sea on a estuary exploration with your family on their two-hour Beach Comber Tours, reaching isolated beaches by boat, $50 adults, $40 children. Guided paddling tours are also provided.

⌔ Go dolphin-watching with **Scenic Cruises of St. Augustine** (800-542-8316; scenic-cruise.com), 4125 Coastal Hwy, a narrated trip on the *Victory III* that departs from the St. Augustine Marina up to five times daily, $17 adults, $10 ages 13–18, $8 ages 4–12.

FAMILY ACTIVITIES ⌔ A fixture in St. Augustine, the **antique carousel** at Davenport Park, corner of San Carlos and San Marco Ave, still costs only a dollar for a ride. ⌔ ⌔ Davenport Park itself contains a **handicapped-accessible playground** and picnic area.

⌔ Get in the SWING—*St. Augustine's Wish for Its Next Generation*—at Francis Field, between Castillo Dr and Orange St behind the St. Augustine Visitors Center

THE ST. AUGUSTINE CAROUSEL

parking garage. This **23,000-square-foot wooden playground** will keep the tots busy for hours while you relax in the picnic area after a long day of sightseeing.

✍ Love **miniature golf**? There are courses perfect for the entire family, including **Anastasia Mini Golf** (904-825-0101), 701 Anastasia Blvd, dominated by a big hill flanked by a wrecked pirate ship and a pioneer cabin. At St. Augustine Beach, **Fiesta Falls Miniature Golf** (904-461-5571), 818 A1A Beach Blvd, has 18 holes of fun surrounding a Spanish galleon. For a course that's simply focused on technique, not flash, try your hand at **Bay Front Golf** (904-829-1673), 111 Avenida Menendez, the mini golf course between the marina and Bridge of Lions in the Old City. For serious play, head to **World Golf Village** (see *Golf*) and try your hand at the 18-hole putting course in front of the World Golf Hall of Fame (see *Museums*).

✍ At **Potter's Wax Museum** (800-584-4781; potterswax.com), 17 King St, the 160 stiffs don't move (mostly); in addition to the usual suspects (politicians and movie stars), there are lesser-known faces from history and art, including Voltaire, Sir Francis Drake, St. Augustine founder Menendez, Rembrandt van Rijn, and Gainesborough. And what wax museum would be complete without a horror chamber, in this case direct from Vincent Price's House of Wax? You'll bump into Harry Potter and Dobby, too. Open Fri–Sat 10–8, Sun–Thu 10–5; $10 adults, $9 seniors, $7 ages 6–12.

✍ Looking like an escapee from a Charles Addams cartoon, the original **Ripley's Believe It or Not Museum** (904-824-1606; ripleys.com/staugustine), 19 San Marco Ave, believe it or not, was once the Castle Warden Inn, a fine hotel managed by novelist Marjorie Kinnan Rawlings's husband (see *Historic Hotels*). It's full of weird stuff from cartoonist Ripley's travels and the most authentic location of the ever-growing chain, but has enough funhouse components thrown in that the kids will absolutely love it. Oh, and yes—it's haunted. $15 adults, $12 seniors, $8 ages 5–12.

FISHING ✦ Fish for redfish and snook along the shallow estuaries of the region with Captain Tommy Derringer of **Inshore Adventures** (904-377-3734; inshore adventures.net), $350–450 for up to two anglers, licenses, gear, bait and tackle, and photos of your trip included. Families welcome.

For outfitting and access to the Matanzas River, visit **Devil's Elbow Fishing Resort** (see *Fish Camps*), 7507 FL A1A S. A local landmark, Devil's Elbow provides everything from bait to guide service and boat rentals, and has a handful of fish-camp-style rentals on site.

For pier fishing, the **St. Johns County Ocean Pier** (904-461-0119), 350 Beach Blvd, provides access for saltwater anglers to try their stuff at St. Augustine Beach. Bait and tackle on site, fishing passes $3 adults, $1 children, open 6 AM–10 PM. The **Vilano Fishing Pier**, 260 Vilano Rd, is free.

While saltwater is the primary focus along this coast, don't forget that the *other* coast for the region is the **St. Johns River**, with its renowned bass fishing. Access for boaters is off FL 13, the Bartram Scenic & Historic Highway (see *Scenic Drives*) at **Trout Creek Park** (see *Parks*), **Riverdale Park** [29.824343, -81.553062], and **Palmo Road Boat Ramp** [29.967409, -81.567439], 8698 Palmo Fish Camp Rd. Bank fishing is possible by the FL 16 bridge across the St. Johns River as well as at **Alpine Groves Park** (see *Parks*), and the **Shands Pier** [30.006482, -81.614492], end of Shands Pier Rd north of the FL 16 bridge, provides anglers a place to drop a line. If you want to settle in for a long stretch of fishing along the St. Johns, head for **Pacetti's** (see *Fish Camps*), established in 1929 as an angler's getaway with full services—guides, bait and tackle, camping and motel, and boat ramp.

In quiet Palm Valley, stop in at **Valley Life** (904-285-1700), 337 S Roscoe Blvd "under the bridge," for bait and tackle and kayak rentals to slip yourself into the quiet coves of the Tolomato River inside GTM Reserve to the south of their put-in for some great fishing in one of the area's most secret spots.

VALLEY LIFE, PALM VALLEY

GHOST TOURS ⚘ Standing atop the seawall, her scarf and 1790s attire fluttering in gusts of wind spawned by a distant hurricane, Amanda spun the tale of Jean Ribault's failed attack on St. Augustine and his armada's untimely demise. "For three days, the bay ran red with blood . . . the fishermen say to beware, when looking into the water after dark, of the faces of the slaughtered Huguenots . . ." Around her, the audience stood rapt with attention. Wrapping legend around history and serving it up as entertainment, St. Augustine's many ghost tours do a bang-up job of spinning spooky stories that'll have your hair standing on end. Amanda's outfit, the granddaddy of ghost tours, is **A Ghostly Experience** (888-461-1009; ghost toursofstaugustine.com), which was founded to provide visiting school groups with something to do after dark. Each walk is different, touching on a handful of the thousands of stories that permeate this city. On one such expedition with my sister, a visit to the Tolomato Cemetery revealed a ghostly presence in a photo I took with my iPhone, surprising the heck out of both of us. Reservations are generally recommended for any of the ghost tours, which vary in length and price and type, the combinations too varied to list here. Just for this operator, their offerings include traditional walks, a ride on the "Trolley of the Doomed," and the "Ghosts of the Matanzas" sailing tour. Tours begin after dark, of course, and start at $14 per person, ages 7 and up. A few of the many other companies presenting ghost tours in St. Augustine include **Ghost Tours St. Augustine** (888-OLD-1565; ghostaugustine.com), with their Haunted Pub Tour, Hearse Ride, and Paranormal Investigative Tours; **A Ghostly Encounter** (904-827-0807; staugustine ghosttours.net), 3 Aviles St, the after-dark arm of Ancient City Tours (see *Walking Tours*); and **St. Augustine Ghost and Pirate Tours** (904-501-7508; staugustine ghostandpiratetours.com), 27 San Marco Ave.

GOLF The go-to region for golf in North Florida, St. Augustine and Ponte Vedra offer some of the state's top courses, including one that is home to one of the world's biggest championship tournaments, **The Players Championship** (pgatour .com/theplayers). **TPC Sawgrass** (904-273-3235; tpc.com/tpc-sawgrass), 110 Championship Way, Ponte Vedra Beach, was built specifically to challenge the pros—if you've ever watched a golf tournament, you've probably seen the infamous 17th hole Island Green—but you can experience the challenges of these courses, too, which are owned by the players of the PGA Tour. Designed by Pete Dye and former PGA Tour commissioner Deane Beman, **The Players Stadium Course** was built with spectators in mind. The newer **Dye's Valley Course** is a collaboration with Bobby Weed. This crown jewel of courses is surrounded by numerous private golf communities, including the Plantation at Ponte Vedra and Sawgrass Country Club.

Two major courses are the highlight of the **World Golf Village** (904-940-6088; golfwgv.com), 2 World Golf Place, a golfer's destination itself as home of the World Golf Hall of Fame (see *Museums*) and a shopping/dining complex centered on golf. Arnold Palmer and Jack Nicklaus collaborated on the design of the **King & Bear**, an 18-hole course for serious drivers. Its greens edges by pine forests and cypress domes provide natural beauty as well as tricky challenges; Palmer picks hole 15, Stone Reflection, as one of his "Dream 18" of all time. The **Slammer & Squire**, their second 18-hole course with two distinct nines, is a Bobby Weed design with inputs from Sam Snead and Gene Sarazen.

At the **Royal St. Augustine Golf & Country Club** (904-824-GOLF; royalst augustine.com), 301 Royal St. Augustine Pkwy, 18 holes are carved out of pine forests and wetlands.

Offering the best tee times and rates, **Florida's First Coast of Golf** (800-530-5248; florida-golf.org/teetimes) can book you into any of the major courses in the area.

HIKING For one of the best day hikes in the region, head to **GTM Reserve** (see *Wild Places*) and hike the 9-mile perimeter loop for exploration of a landscape where hidden Timucuan middens and the remains of an ancient Spanish mission are buried deep beneath expansive forest canopies. With a good dozen different habitats along the way, it's one of my all-time favorites. Many more local day hikes are covered in *50 Hikes in North Florida*, but some easy family destinations that aren't in the book include the nature trail boardwalk at **Fort Matanzas** (see *Historic Sites*) and the nature trail at **Faver-Dykes State Park** (see *Parks*).

PADDLING With its dozens of uninhabited islands on which to stop and lunch or camp, the **Matanzas River** is a popular paddlers' getaway. You'll see manatees and dolphins cruising along this saline inland waterway, which runs between St. Augustine and Summer Haven. While the Northeast Florida Blueway is still under development, access points are many, and a navigational chart will help you chart your course among the many public lands that border the waterway. At the south end of the **GTM Reserve** (see *Wild Places*), most paddlers put in at **Faver-Dykes State Park** or at an access point in Summer Haven. Near Crescent Beach, canoe and kayak rentals and put-in are available at **Devil's Elbow Fishing Resort** (see *Fish Camps*). At the north end, where the **Tolomato** and **Guana** Rivers work their way to Matanzas Bay, GTM Reserve provides direct access to the Guana River at two sites off A1A; fee. To explore the Tolomato River's wild shores south of Ponte Vedra, you can rent a kayak from **Valley Life** (904-285-1700), 337 S Roscoe Blvd, in Palm Valley "under the bridge." For guided paddling opportunities, see *Ecotours*.

One of the more wild and offbeat places to paddle is **Deep Creek** (see *Wild Places*), a tributary of the St. Johns River in Hastings. Bald eagles are known to nest along this waterway and cypress swamp.

PARASAILING If you've noticed a giant smiley face cruising overhead, here's why: **Smile High Parasail Inc.** (888-300-0812 or 904-819-0980; smilehighparasail.com), 111 Avenida Menendez #C, St. Augustine, offers crew-supported soars above the Matanzas River; up to three can fly together in flights from 700 to 1,400 feet above the waves.

SCENIC DRIVES Few highways in the northern Florida peninsula match the beauty of the **Historic A1A Scenic Byway** (scenica1a.org), particularly in sections where the dunes remain preserved and free of development—as they do within GTM Reserve between Ponte Vedra Beach and North Beach. Check their website for driving route details. Sites of interest along the byway are included in an audio tour you can access from your cell phone; just look for the markers when you stop. Along the St. Johns River, FL 13 is designated the **William Bartram Scenic & Historic Highway** (bartramscenichighway.com). Canopied in many spots, the highway parallels the river route that the famed naturalist paddled when St. Augustine was more than a century old, leading you through rural and wild lands and communities established nearly 300 years ago.

SIGHTSEEING TOURS Besides ghost tours and walking tours, St. Augustine offers some of the state's oldest narrated tram tours. Choose your color: The red

trains are the **St. Augustine Sightseeing Trains** (800-226-6545 or 904-824-1606;
sightseeingtrains.com), 170 San Marco Ave, in operation since 1953 and offering
complimentary pickup and drop-off at city motels as well as a truly educational
tour of the city, with on/off privileges at all stops for three days. $22 adults, $9 ages
6–12, for the standard historic tours, which run continuously daily 8:30–5 except
Christmas. Additional themed tours are offered, including Ghost Tours, Black History Tours, and the Big Red Christmas Train.

In shades of green and orange, **Old Town Trolley Tours** (904-829-3800; trolley
tours.com/st-augustine), running out of a depot at the Old Jail (see *Museums*), covers more than 100 points of interest with 20 stop-offs and reboarding privileges for
three days on your ticket. $23 adult, $10 ages 6–12, includes access to their Beach
Bus, a shuttle to St. Augustine Beach, the St. Augustine Alligator Farm (see *Zoo*),
and the St. Augustine Lighthouse (see *Lighthouse*), plus admission to the Old
Florida Museum (see *Museums*). In-character guides often accompany the tours,
and all have live narration. In addition to the standard history tour, they provide a
Ghosts & Gravestones tour and the city's only Chocolate Tour, visiting not just the
Whetstone Chocolate Factory (see *Chocolate Tours*) but sites of culinary interest
as well.

🐾 For a truly romantic tour, hop on board one of the sightseeing carriages along
the bayfront near the Castillo de San Marcos, from **St. Augustine Transfer
Company** (904-829-2391; staugustinetransfer.com), 23 Avenida Menendez, which
has been providing rides for horse-drawn passengers since 1877. Join a shared tour
for $20 adults, $10 children 5–11, at 10, noon, 5, and 7 daily, or take over a carriage on your own for $85. Walking tours, romance tours, and paranormal tours are
also a part of their schedule.

Ride in style in a 1929 Model A or 1955 Chrysler Imperial on an **Antique Car
Tour**; check with the Casa Monica Hotel (see *Hotels, Motels & Resorts*) for details.

SPA The Spa at Ponte Vedra Inn & Club (see *Hotels, Motels & Resorts*) provides a perfect haven for relaxation after a long day on the golf course or exploring
neighboring St. Augustine. Wrap yourself in an elegant spa robe and sit with a light
beverage while awaiting your treatment in the relaxation room or in the 2,000-
square-foot Cascada Garden with oversized Jacuzzi and cascading waterfall. Then
move on to your own private room for treatments like a reflexology massage, a
deep-cleaning facial or men's skin care treatment, or a honeysuckle-alga scrub.
Treatments start at $65, with partial and full day packages available up to $534.

WALKING TOURS In addition to leading ghost tours (see *Ghost Tours*),
costumed guides from **Tour St. Augustine** (800-797-3778 or 904-825-0087;
staugustinetours.com), 4 Granada St, lead walking tours touching on many different themes, from architectural history to the Victorian era, as do the folks at
Ancient City Tours (904-827-0807; ancientcitytours.net), 3 Aviles St, based in the
Spanish Military Hospital (see *Museums*). Tours at **Flagler College** (904-823-
3378; flagler.edu), May–Aug, offer a look at the grandeur of Henry Flagler's flagship, the Hotel Ponce de Leon (now the college campus); fee. Or pick up a free
Walking Tour Map at the visitors center to take your own 32-stop self-guided
tour of the Oldest City.

WHALE-WATCHING Each winter, **right whales** migrate from sites near New-foundland to the shores of St. Johns County and their ancestral calving ground, where they give birth and raise their young. The right whale is the most endan-gered whale on earth, with only about 350 members of the species remaining. During the calving season, volunteer whale-watchers take up positions along beaches in Crescent Beach, Summer Haven, and Marineland to record whale sightings. Each whale has a unique pattern of spots, making it easier to positively identify specific individuals. Check with Marineland's Right Whale Project (aswh .org/whale/main.html) to become an official whale-watcher during the winter calv-ing season.

ZIPLINE Head for the trees at the **St. Augustine Alligator Farm** (see *Zoo*) on the new Crocodile Crossing, a set of two zipline and canopy walk trails where you swing, sway, and fly above alligators and crocodiles and other creatures in the zoo's enclosures. From the ground, it looks like a crazy obstacle course, complete with zigzag and crisscross wooden steps attached to guy wires, a basic training course in the air. The Sepik River Course is the lower of the two aerial adventures; the Nile River Course is higher and faster, for bigger thrills. Open daily with a separate admission from the park, $25–40 per course, takes one or two hours each.

✹ Green Space

BEACHES **Vehicles are permitted on the beach** in Vilano Beach (which has two ramps) and from St. Augustine Beach south through Matanzas Inlet, with access ramps off A1A at A Street, Ocean Trace, Dondanville, Matanzas Ave, Mary St, Crescent Beach, and Fort Matanzas. North of North Beach, only 4x4s are allowed. Fees are $7 per day or $50 for a season pass, residential discount. Please follow posted speed limits, be cautious of beachgoers, and don't disturb flagged areas set aside for hatching sea turtle nests. Driving is at your own risk: I've seen many a driver stranded due to soft sands or rising tides down near Matanzas Inlet. From May 1 to Oct 31, vehicular traffic on the beach is allowed between 8 AM and 7:30 PM; after 7:30 PM no vehicles are allowed on the beach. During the rest of the year, you can drive on the beach at night.

WOOD STORK ALONG THE LAGOON AT ANASTASIA STATE PARK

Anastasia State Park (904-461-2033; floridastateparks.org/anastasia), 1340A FL A1A S, Anastasia Island. It's my favorite place to take a walk on the beach—an 8-mile unsullied round-trip to the tip of the island, right along Matanzas Pass, where you can sit and watch the sailboats come into the har-bor at St. Augustine. Birding is superb along the shoreline and the lagoons, and the campground (see *Camping & Cabins*) in the coastal hammock can't be beat. Swimmers and surfers flock to these shores every summer, so it gets pretty busy on weekends. The park also includes the historic coquina quarries used by the Spanish to quarry blocks for the Castillo de San Marcos and other structures in the Oldest City, and paddlers—stand-up boards being the hot new thing—like to explore the lagoon. Fee.

🐾 Historic **Butler Beach** was established by Frank B. Butler, a St. Augustine grocer and real estate developer, as one of Florida's few African American seaside destinations during segregation. You'll find it along A1A north of Crescent Beach and north of Fort Matanzas, with beach-ramp access at Mary St.

🐾 **Crescent Beach** has direct access for motorists in the little community area around the intersection of A1A and FL 206. This beach was a favorite getaway for novelist Marjorie Kinnan Rawlings in the 1940s, as she had a beach home here, a private residence that locals will gladly point out. Her husband, Norman Baskins, ran the Castle Warden Inn (see *Historic Hotels*) in St. Augustine.

🐾 **GTM Reserve** (see *Wild Places*) contains the wildest stretch of shoreline in the county, with no residences in sight, which makes it a popular getaway. There are three parking areas with beach access inside the reserve; fee.

🐾 **Matanzas Beach**, A1A just north of Matanzas Inlet, Crescent Beach, was a favorite destination for my family when I was a teen. This quiet strand near the inlet can be accessed from a parking area and dune crossover immediately north of the bridge, or by a beach ramp (fee), a little farther north. Parking on the west side of the highway is mainly used for bank and bridge fishing into the inlet, but at low tide a broad beach appears and you'll see many people walking their dogs up toward Fort Matanzas, which is around the bend in the waterway.

🐾 In addition to being the only public access point for Ponte Vedra Beach, **Mickler's Beachfront Park** (904-209-3740), 1109½ Ponte Vedra Blvd off A1A, has parking for horse trailers—yes, you can ride your horses on the beach here, but a permit is required from the county; call ahead.

🐾 **Nease Beachfront Park** (904-209-0655), 3201 Coastal Hwy, Vilano Beach, provides beach parking next to a historic home owned by Florida's first forester. You'll find restrooms and a shaded picnic spot behind the building. Gnarled oaks reach out over the dunes, and a boardwalk leads to an open view of the Tolomato River marshes, an excellent spot for birding. Beach access is across A1A down a boardwalk—mind the high-speed traffic when you cross.

🐾 🐶 **North Beach Park** (904-209-0655), 3721 Coastal Hwy, North Beach, has a large parking area and playground on the west side of A1A, along with a picnic grove under the windswept trees. A pedestrian bridge makes this a safe access point for families to cross over to the beach.

🐾 🐶 **St. Augustine Beach** is a long strand with many accommodations, including campgrounds, within walking distance of the beach. For day-trippers, there are small lots at the ends of some of the roads, plus beach ramps for access with your vehicle. One of the more popular access points is the St. Johns County Ocean Pier (see *Fishing*), which has restrooms and a playground and walk-in access to Anastasia State Park (pedestrian fee charged for access to the state park).

PARKS 🐾 🐶 Along the St. Johns River, the original Spanish land grant of Francis Philip Fatio, who founded Switzerland, Florida, in the 1700s, is preserved as **Alpine Groves Park** (904-209-0382), 2060 FL 13, Switzerland. Shaded by old-growth oaks and pines, this county park has a playground, trails, and access to the river for bank fishing.

✎ **Bird Island Park** (904-209-0346), 101 Library Blvd, Ponte Vedra, is just off US 1. Designed especially for families with children, it's a landscaped park featuring a sea turtle maze, a storytelling area, boardwalks around the pond, and a play area for the kids. Open daily dawn–dusk.

Nestled in oak hammocks along Pellicer Creek, **Faver-Dykes State Park** (904-794-0997; floridastateparks.org/faver-dykes), 1000 Faver Dykes Rd off US 1, Dupont Center, offers camping (see *Camping & Cabins*), nature trails, and some of the best paddling along the coast. Bring your kayak or rent a canoe (reservations required) to enjoy the Pellicer Creek Trail, gliding through mazes of needlerush as you paddle out to the Matanzas River. Mellon Island in the Matanzas River is accessible only by boat and open to primitive camping. Fee.

✎ Along Salt Run in the shadow of the St. Augustine Lighthouse (see *Lighthouse*), **Lighthouse Park** and the J. Edward "Red" Cox Recreation Facility on Anastasia Island have a playground and picnic area tucked under the windswept oaks and a boat ramp with access to the run.

☀ ✎ **Trout Creek Park** (904-522-1573), 6795 Collier Rd, Orangedale, is just off FL 13/16. Slip your boat down the ramp into the creek for easy access to bass fishing along the creek and the nearby St. Johns River. Picnic pavilions, playground, and nature trails.

WILD PLACES Launch a canoe into **Deep Creek Conservation Area** (386-329-4404; sjrwmd.com/recreationguide/deepcreek), FL 207 south of FL 206, Hastings, a preserve accessible only by boat, to explore a wild bottomland cypress swamp that drains to the St. Johns River [29.724166, -81.483888].

Guana-Tolomato-Matanzas (GTM) Reserve (904-825-5071; gtmnerr.org), 505 Guana River Rd. Most visitors come here for the beaches—they go on forever, it seems, paralleling FL A1A for several miles, with two large parking areas at either end. But I like the hidden treasure on the Intracoastal side of the park at the dam, the hiking and biking trail system that loops for 9 miles through a variety of habitats and provides fresh salt breezes as you walk under the oaks lining the Tolomato River. Fishing is superb in the Guana and Tolomato rivers, and a popular activity at the dam. Expect a beach parking fee during peak seasons and weekends. A 21,000-square-foot Environmental Education Center interprets this 60,000-acre reserve; stop in and see a 12-minute video; learn about the indigenous whales, stingrays, and fish; or stand on the back deck and watch flocks of birds coast over the grand estuary that surrounds the River of Palms. A gift shop offers scientific toys and books. Fee.

Located just south of FL 206, **Matanzas State Forest** (386-446-6786; fl-dof.com), 6840 US 1 S, offers access to nearly 5,000 acres along the Matanzas River. Outdoor recreation opportunities include wildlife- and bird-watching along the network of walkable roads, and hunting in-season.

At **Moses Creek Conservation Area** (386-329-4404; sjrwmd.com/recreation guide/mosescreek), FL 206, Dupont Center, where you backpack or ride your horse to a distant campsite with a sweeping view of the Matanzas River salt marshes [29.757224, -81.27556].

Just north of St. Augustine, the 274-acre **Stokes Landing Conservation Area** (386-329-4404; sjrwmd.com/recreationguide/stokeslanding), Lakeshore Dr, provides an outdoor classroom for local schools and beautiful panoramic views of the salt marshes along the Tolomato River for hikers [30.0, -81.361104].

Swamps are a central feature of the aptly named **Twelve Mile Swamp Recreation Area** (386-329-4404; sjrwmd.com/recreationguide/twelvemileswamp), International Golf Pkwy west of US 1. Part of a larger commercial pine plantation, this ridge defines the watershed between the St. Johns and Mantanzas rivers. Hike or bike the forest roads; seasonal hunting is permitted [30.01, -81.40028].

✳ Lodging

BED & BREAKFASTS

St. Augustine 32084— Historic District

With 26 B&Bs at last count, St. Augustine provides a wide range of choices for the history-minded traveler. Check the **St. Augustine Historic Inns** website at staugustineinns.com find the best B&B to suit your needs. Here's a handful I've visited or stayed in myself:

🐾 🐾 ⚘ ♿ ((ᵠ)) Delightfully classy, recently redecorated, and in the midst of the historic downtown, the **Agustin Inn** (904-823-9559; agustininn.com), 29 Cuna St, is a 1903 Victorian with 18 guest rooms, most with Jacuzzi tubs and one (the Greensboro) with private entrance and wheelchair ramp. Your breakfast may include homemade Belgian waffles or house-recipe quiche; dietary needs can be accommodated. Hurricane-prepared, the inn can run off a generator for up to three weeks. Children over 12 are welcome. $109–249.

⚘ ((ᵠ)) It's wonderful when travelers bring their experiences back to their own establishment, and you'll find that at the B&B known as **At Journey's End** (888-806-2351 or 904-829-0076; atjourneysend.com), 89 Cedar St, where the late-1800s Victorian is a backdrop for exotica—bedrooms themed after China, Egypt, and African safaris, as well as Key West

and summer, with elegant beds and original art. The Key West suite is family-friendly and can handle a family of six; its own veranda overlooks the garden. Rooms include cable TV and wireless Internet. A full breakfast is served every morning, with snacks and drinks available all day. $129–289.

((ᵠ)) Built more than 128 years ago by a master carpenter, the **Carriage Way Bed & Breakfast** (800-908-9832 or 904-829-2467; carriageway.com), 70 Cuna St, has been, over the course of its life, a private home, apartments, and now a delightful option for lodging in a quiet part of the Historic District. With Victorian charm reflected in its decor and the big porch out front, the complex includes nine rooms in the main house, with two that have multiple beds for friends and relatives traveling together. Brandy and schnapps await in a cozy parlor along with a large flat-screen TV. Expect a big breakfast with recipes straight out of their cookbook, *Cooking with Carriage Way*. $109–349 (for the two-bedroom Diane's Cottage).

♿ ((ᵠ)) When I arrived at **Casa de Solana** (888-796-0980 or 904-824-3555; casadesolana.com), 21 Aviles St, the courtyard was abuzz with guests enjoying their breakfast. Built in the early 1800s, the historic main home is constructed of coquina stone and retains many of its original features, including handmade bricks. The adjacent de Palma house is now part of the complex. The decor reflects colonial St. Augustine with modern updates such as whirlpool tubs, cable TV, and wireless Internet. Gregarious guests will appreciate the evening social and desserts; those looking for a more intimate time will find it on the balconies and in the corners of the garden. Ten rooms, each uniquely decorated, $129–259.

& **Casa de Suenos** (800-824-0804; casadesuenos.com), 20 Cordova St, is the "House of Dreams," a 1920s Mediterranean Revival home where guests can watch the world drift by from the vibrant sunporch or settle down for a read in the parlor. A chandelier sparkles over the whirlpool tub, funky black-and-white furnishings dress up the common areas, and each room uplifts the soul. Each of the five rooms is a relaxing retreat, with comfy robes, fine literature, and a decanter of sherry on the dresser; two rooms boast a whirlpool. Enjoy a gourmet breakfast each morning. $159–299.

🐾 (ᵞᵖ) Perfectly located—just a block off busy St. Georges on a quiet back street—**44 Spanish Street** (800-521-0722 or 904-826-0650; 44spanishstreet .com), 44 Spanish St, has rooms that are chic and bright, with luxurious linens, cable TV, irons, and hair dryers. The eight rooms come in several configurations with some connecting rooms and some with extra beds, making it great for girlfriend/sister getaways. Rosewood is especially appealing for those getaways, since it has its own private entrance from the street and a spare bed. I found my perch in Jasmine, at the back of the building, especially quiet and relaxing when I needed to unwind with a hot bath and a good book after walking around the city. A separate breakfast room sits in an intimate tropical garden in the backyard, where you recharge in the morning with coffee and a hot breakfast prepared especially for you. A big perk is free parking in a lot down the street with all-day in-and-out privileges. $95–199.

🐾 🐾 (ᵞᵖ) **The Kenwood Inn** (800-824-8151; thekenwoodinn.com), 38 Marine St, dates back to the 1860s, when it served as a boardinghouse. This Queen Anne Victorian has that wonderful feel of an old-time hotel, with narrow corridors, low ceilings, and mismatched floors. Each of the 14 spacious rooms has its own particular character; many are two-room suites. I enjoyed my stay in the Blue Porcelain Suite, with walls the color of Wedgwood china, where I could sway in a hammock on the balcony and listen to the carriages go by. All guests enjoy use of a private pool and secluded garden courtyard, where you can borrow a bicycle for a ride around town or settle back and meet your fellow guests during the evening social hour. Hot entrées are served along with lighter fare at breakfast, and on weekends they break out the Mimosas and Bloody Marys. Children over 8 welcome; pet-friendly rooms available. $129–259.

🐾 An 1899 Victorian with classic charm, the **Old Powder House Inn** (800-447-4149; oldpowderhouse.com), 38 Cordova St, entices with its second-floor veranda, ideal for people-watching from the porch swing. From the frilly Queen Ann's Lace to The Garden, a three-bed girls' getaway, each of the nine elegant rooms offers a perfect 1900s ambience. Breakfast brings out the culinary talents of your hosts, with delights like Katie's five-cheese breakfast casserole and stuffed French toast. You won't leave hungry! $105–275.

(ᵞᵖ) In a residential neighborhood behind the San Marco Ave antiques district, **Our House** (904-824-9204; ourhouseofstaugustine.com), 7 Cincinnati Ave, is a two-story Victorian with a snazzy urban feel befitting its owner, former *USA Today* editor Dave Brezing. Three spacious rooms—Greenhaven, Morningview, and Fern Garden—are featured in the main house, where bold monochrome walls set off the restored heart pine floor, art and literature accent each room, and a piano stands at the ready in the parlor. Across the secluded garden courtyard in a neighboring Victorian are two garden studio apartments, Jasmine and Azalea. Each features a queen-sized bed; sitting area; a kitchenette supplied with dishes and cutlery; a large bath with whirlpool tub; private entrance; and porch. Azalea, with a convertible sofa, can accommodate up to four people. Guests in the main house enjoy Dave's excellent gourmet breakfast. No pets; not suitable for children under age 12. $129–189, breakfast not included with studio rentals.

St. Francis Inn (800-824-6062; stfrancisinn.com), 279 St. George St. With not a straight angle in the place, this is a three-story home with charm—how many B&Bs in the United States date back to 1791? Every room has its own unique shape, size, and furnishings befitting the character of Senor Gaspar Garcia; I'm drawn to Margaret's Room, in their adjoining Wilson House, with its private balcony with garden view. A small swimming pool sits off the lush garden courtyard, and guests can enjoy the peace of St. Francis Park next door. Beyond the chef-prepared gourmet breakfast, many extra-extra amenities are included, like free admission to the St. Augustine Lighthouse (see *Lighthouse*) and day use of the innkeepers' beach cottage with restroom, shower, cold drinks, and beach toys. $129–299.

Southern Wind (800-781-3338; southernwindinn.com), 18 Cordova St, is a beautiful 1916 Victorian home with one key feature—a wraparound veranda that's the perfect place to hang out and relax. Period furnishings and antiques add to the Gilded Age ambience of the inn's 10 rooms, ranging from cozy nooks to spacious suites, and little touches like bottled water, bathrobes, and hair dryers make you feel pampered. Breakfast is served buffet-style but always features one hot entrée like macadamia French toast. $99–169.

St. Augustine Beach 32080

The **Beachfront Bed & Breakfast** (904-461-8727; beachfront bandb.com), 1 F Street, is indeed right on the beach. A complex of three rooms in a cottage and a beach house with five rooms, the rooms are more "coastal elegance" than beachy, with the fine decor a reminder for you to wipe the sand off your feet before you walk inside. The nicely landscaped grounds with a heated swimming pool, big shared porch, and a hot tub, all within sound of the surf, make this an ideal gathering place for friends. A gourmet breakfast is served every morning, and beach toys and bikes are yours to borrow. $159 and up, packages available.

HOTELS, MOTELS & RESORTS

On Anastasia Island, just across the Bridge of Lions, you'll find small non-chain motels with rates in the $60s. Poke around the northern fringe of St. Augustine for similar bargains, but do check their online ratings before you pick one. You'll also find top-name national chains along San Marco Ave, at St. Augustine Beach, and at I-95 and FL 16, where the factory outlet malls are located.

Crescent Beach 32080

🦐 🐾 An Old Florida motor court, the **Crescent Silver Sands Motel** (904-471-1406), 8448 A1A S, hides so well behind a screen of sand dunes and saw palmetto that you pretty much only see it heading northbound. This is how beach motels were when I was a kid, simple rooms with kitchenettes, porch chairs and shuffleboard outside, and an easy walk over the dunes to your own quiet stretch of beach. $60–100 for motel rooms, $100–180 for cottages; weekly rentals available.

Ponte Vedra Beach 32082

🐚 ♂ (ᵖ) ✣ Rediscover the 1920s at the **Ponte Vedra Inn & Club** (904-285-1111; pontevedra.com), 200 Ponte Vedra Blvd, where you'll experience all the grandeur of a famed winter resort for the wealthy and famous. Generations of guests continue to come back, and generations of staff continue to cater to their every need. The main inn opened in 1938 and has retained much of its original grandeur. The oceanside rooms are larger and feature two queen poster beds in a beautiful honey-blond finish. The European turndown service was new to me; bedcovers are removed, and two soft sheets surround your blanket for a much softer and more hygienic sleep. In the bathroom you'll find the television piped in so you won't miss the morning news. This resort is all about the little details, from intimate corner nooks to friendly personal service, and there is a full-service spa on site (see *Spa*). $199–250.

St. Augustine 32084— Historic District

♿ ♂ (ᵖ) ✣ **Casa Monica** (800-648-1888; casamonica.com), 95 Cordova St. Stride into the Turkish-inspired lobby and take a step back into Henry Flagler's Gilded Age in this grand hotel, with its beaded Victorian lamps and painted beams, where the white-gloved staff usher you to your private abode. This is what Florida tourism meant in 1888, when the Casa Monica (built by Flagler's partner, Franklin Smith) first opened its doors. After four months, Flagler bought the hotel and renamed it the Cordova. Restored to its original lavish glory by hotelier Richard Kessler, the hotel offers rooms in many shapes and sizes, from cozy to spacious, as well as opulent suites, all with modern appointments. They are a member of the Historic Hotels of America and part of the Marriott Autograph Collection. $169 and up.

🐚 ♿ (ᵖ) ✣ I was upset to see my favorite old waterfront motel disappear to redevelopment until I didn't see new **Hilton St. Augustine Historic Bayfront** (904-829-2277; hiltonhistoricstaugustine.com), 32 Avenida Menendez, for the first time. Yep, that's right—I drove right past it, did a double take, and came back around the block for another look. The hotel's facade fits in perfectly with the row of homes overlooking the bay, and that's a pleasure to behold. You'll find the usual Hilton attention to detail within the 72 rooms inside, but the best part is that you're within walking distance of all of the Historic District. $112–269.

🦐 🐚 ♿ (ᵖ) In the heart of the Historic District, the **St. George Inn** (904-827-5740 or 888-827-5740; stgeorge-inn.com), 4 St. George St #101, blends in seamlessly with the shops and restaurants of St. George Street at the City Gates. Large, well-appointed rooms boast killer views of the downtown area; 25 units in four buildings, with some very roomy suites ideal for families. My favorite is Room 25, with a balcony that looks out on the Castillo and Matanzas Bay. An elevator provides access to the upper floors, and a coffee shop is in the courtyard. $129–199; suites, $219–229.

St. Augustine 32084

♦ ♥ 🐾 🍸 ♿ (((•))) During a stay at **The Cozy Inn** (888-288-2204; thecozyinn.com), 202 San Marco Ave, where friends were joining me for local explorations, it was great to be able to share the space and entertain in their like-new two-story town houses, each with a small kitchen. This Superior Small Lodging is sparkling on every visit I've made. Their standard old-fashioned motor court rooms are certainly cozy, brightly decorated with a Florida coastal theme, and sport queen beds and 1940s bathrooms. Cozy rooms, $77–87; big suites and town houses, $137–197.

♥ 🐾 🍸 (((•))) In a surprisingly offbeat yet central location, the **Inn at Camachee Harbor** (800-688-5379 or 904-825-0003; camacheeinn.com), 201 Yacht Club Dr, can have you cruising up the coast to Ponte Vedra or toward downtown in no time. Better yet, step outside and meet a fishing guide for a cruise up the Tolomato River. Located at the Camachee Cove Marina (see *Boating*), the rooms face waterfront or the garden, and are tastefully decorated with a coastal appeal. Continental breakfast is included. $99–159.

St. Augustine 32092

♿ (((•))) ⤷ Adjacent to the World Golf Hall of Fame (see *Museums*) is the **Renaissance Resort at World Golf Village** (888-236-2427 or 904-940-8000; worldgolfrenaissance.com), 500 S Legacy Trail. The resort borders the village's original championship course, at which hotel guests have full privileges, and offers guests preferred tee times to the Slammer and the Squire. The European-accented hotel includes such amenities as an outdoor pool, professional golf simulators, a 24-hour health club and sauna, a billiards room,

a cigar room, and a gift shop—plus complimentary parking (or valet service, your choice) and free shuttles to the Oldest City. They'll also book your airport shuttles to and from Jacksonville International. Drink in the beautiful views from your room, $109 and up, many package deals available.

St. Augustine Beach 32080

♿ (((•))) ⤷ **Castillo Real** (866-941-7325 or 904-471-3505; castilloreal.com), 530 FL A1A (Beach Blvd), is the new kid on the beach, a boutique hotel that's part of the Clarion chain. It feels nothing like its cousins, however, with its Moorish theme extending from the vaulted lobby with fountain to fine wood furniture and luxe linens in the guest rooms. Choose from standard, Jacuzzi, and oceanfront rooms. $109–199.

🍸 ♿ (((•))) ⤷ The Mediterranean-themed **La Fiesta Ocean Inn & Suites** (800-852-6390; lafiestainn.com), 810 FL A1A (Beach Blvd), has spacious rooms decorated in local artwork, tile entries, and great landscaping with a palm-lined pool. The beach is just a stroll down the boardwalk over the dunes. Rooms 216–219 have a beautiful sunrise view. Continental breakfast included. $113–299.

HOUSE RENTALS ♥ 🍸 (((•))) **The Beach Cottages** (888-963-8272; beach-cottages.com). Large families and friends traveling together often find house rentals an economical way to visit the beach. To enjoy the charm of 1890s Summer Haven, stay at **The Lodge**, a restored five-bedroom dogtrot cottage sandwiched between the Summer Haven River and the Atlantic Ocean, with breezy wrap-around porches and gorgeous beadwork walls and ceilings, or **The Hut**, an adjacent funky little historic beach cottage with plank floors, lots of natural light, and a constant sea breeze. Specializing in family reunions, agent Win Kelly also represents another 13 beach cottages along the coast. Rentals range from $200 a night (three-night minimum) upward, depending on the season, with weekly rentals preferred; cleaning fees and pet fees apply.

CAMPING & CABINS

Anastasia Island 32080

&. At **Anastasia State Park** (see *Beaches*), you couldn't ask for a more perfect setting for a campground (800-326-3521; floridastateparks.reserve america.com). Protected by the dunes, deeply shaded by wind-sculpted sand live oaks, the 124 sites are so close to the sea you'll be lulled to sleep by the waves. The best reason to camp here is to have the park to yourself before and after hours, for moonlight walks on the beach and sunrise over the Atlantic. $28 and up.

North Beach 32084

🐾 🦈 You'll find a shady campsite with a salt breeze at **North Beach Camp Resort** (904-824-1806; northbeach camp.com), 4125 Coastal FL A1A. Nestled on a barrier island between a remote stretch of A1A and the North River, it features beautifully land-scaped sites shaded by mature trees. Tent campers enjoy sites within an easy walk of the river, so bring your fishing tackle! Newly added are rental cabins tucked under the forest canopy. Facilities include a convenience store, playground, pool, Jacuzzi, and fishing pier; weekly rates available. Sites $45–80, cabins $110–150.

St. Augustine 32086

Indian Forest Campground (800-233-4324), 1505 FL 207. Tuck your camper into the shady forest, or choose a sunny pull-through space. RV spaces with gravel pads, each with pic-nic table; bathhouses scattered throughout the campground. Tent campers welcome but must check in before 6 PM. $25 and up.

🦈 &. Settle into a campsite under the pines at **Faver-Dykes State Park** (see *Parks*), the campground (800-326-3521; floridastateparks.reserveamerica .com) cooled by breezes off Pellicer Creek and the Matanzas River. A favorite of paddlers and anglers, it has easy and direct access to the estuary, and distances by water aren't as far to nearby preserves as they are by land. $18 and up.

St. Augustine Beach 32080

🦈 **Bryn Mawr Ocean Resort** (904-471-3353; brynmawroceanresort.com), 4850 FL A1A S. Just over the dunes from the Atlantic (with direct beach access), this campground has a mix of park models, permanent residents, and RV spaces, many with adjoining decks with picnic tables. Some sites are tucked in the maritime hammock, but most are out in the open along the ocean; the swimming pool is next to a nicely shaded playground area. Sites $53–71, park models $102–119.

🦈 (ᵱ) **Ocean Grove Camp Resort** (800-342-4007; oceangroveresort.com), 4225 FL A1A S. Set in a remnant maritime hammock with a grove of tall pines on Matanzas Bay, this campground with natural appeal has shady spaces, luxury park models, and tent spaces with beautiful views across the salt marsh. Dock with boat launch, fish-cleaning station; a camp store has marine items. Bicycle, canoe, and kayak rentals on site. Sites $50–60, park models $300 for three nights, $600 per week plus $50 cleaning fee.

FISH CAMPS Snuggle up next to the Matanzas River in a funky little cottage at **Devil's Elbow Fishing Resort**

(904-471-0398; devilselbowfishing
resort.com), 7507 FL A1A S, Crescent
Beach. It's been here since the 1950s,
providing easy access for anglers to the
long stretch of saltwater lagoon connecting the Oldest City and Summer
Haven.

It started as a fish camp in 1929, and
the family-owned **Pacetti's Marina,
RV Campground and Fishing
Resort** (904-522-1374; pacettirv.com),
6550 FL13 N, is still a popular retreat
for anglers, with dockage, a boat ramp,
and easy access via Trout Creek to the
St. Johns River. With an annual Fishing Tournament each February, guide
services, a tackle shop, and live bait,
you can settle into the motel or set
up your tent or RV—full hookups available—and enjoy a fine week of fishing.
Camping $22–45, weekly and monthly
rates available; motel rooms $65.

✱ Where to Eat

DINING OUT

Anastasia Island
Decked out in Caribbean pastels on
the outside and with a jazzy New York
bistro feel on the inside, the award-
winning **Gypsy Cab Company** (904-
461-8843; gypsycab.com), 828
Anastasia Blvd, dishes out "urban Italian" treats like seafood fra diablo with
spinach (one of the weekday lunch
specials served 11–3). Of the soup
selections, the wild mushroom bisque
delivers with a velvety texture and
just the right amount of mushrooms;
sandwiches and salads $7–9, dinner
entrées $16–22. Top off your meal
with tiramisu, or go for the choco-
holics' favorite, their rich and creamy
chocolate mousse.

North Beach
🦐 A rockin' 1920s fish camp gone
upscale, **Cap's On The Water** (904-
824-8794; capsonthewater.com),
Myrtle St, is hidden back in a
neighborhood along the Intracoastal
Waterway. Boaters can find it easily
enough; you'll have to follow the signs.
With the doors thrown wide open and
the whole place shaded by giant live
oak trees, it blurs the line between
indoors and outdoors—with a killer
view of the Tolomato River estuary
thrown in for good measure. Try some
vanilla grouper, a nut-encrusted fresh
catch with a sweet vanilla rum sauce;
pear ravioli; or pineapple pecan
shrimp, seared and served over
pepper-pimiento rice. Stopping here
for a late lunch, I nibbled on shrimp
vilano, a fiery little concoction melding
fresh local shrimp with a garlic-chile
sauce, set on a bed of crispy spinach
with Asiago crumbles. Just writing
about it makes me want a snack.
Despite how well it's hidden, this is a
busy, busy place on weekends—come
at an off-hour if you don't want a long
wait. The restaurant faces west across
the water, making it a perfect place to
savor a sunset. Entrées $13–25.

Dining at **The Reef** (904-824-8008;
thereefstaugustine.com), 4100 Coastal
Hwy, soak in the ambience of the
dunes while looking out over the
Atlantic and savoring dilled shrimp
salad, made with the local catch, or
crab Florentine, with thick chunks of
blue crab. The extensive menu
includes regional favorites like shrimp
and grits, Florida rock lobster, and
jambalaya, $14–29. Open for lunch and
dinner daily, but Sunday brunch is
their forte—for $32, the extensive
spread includes crab legs and eggs
Benedict made to order, and you'll
enjoy jazz or classical guitar in accom-
paniment to the strum of the waves
outside.

St. Augustine—Historic District

ও Settle back into that comfortable chair and savor St. Augustine's most upscale dining experience, **95 Cordova** (904-810-6810; 95cordova.com), 95 Cordova St, at the Casa Monica (see *Hotels, Motels & Resorts*). Experience the grandeur of the 1880s, when Henry Flagler's railroad brought the crème de la crème of New England society to this very place; although evening attire isn't required, you'll want to be dressy for this occasion. The menu is a changing palette of entrées ($18–44) of the caliber of coriander-crusted sea scallops and roasted duckling. Winner of the *Wine Spectator* "Award of Excellence"; reservations recommended. ও ((ᵠ)) Insider tip: **The Cordova Cafe**, at the corner of King St and Cordova St, serves gourmet food in a more casual atmosphere, with a bakery and fudge shop to tempt passersby.

🦴 🐾 At the **Floridian** (904-829-0655; thefloridianstaug.com), 39 Cordova St, expect to be dazzled by both the artful presentation and the taste of your handcrafted meal. Featuring the freshest Florida produce, meats, and fish, this foodie delight serves up southern-style dishes with a hip twist. I ordered a daily special, a riff on their Southern Belle Salad with leeks and fennel, and was delighted by both taste and texture. Relax out on the patio with your pooch, or hang out with friends in the big room with a painted pine floor, church pew bench seats, and a rowboat on the ceiling. Hidden in the back of the restaurant, the County Line is a small bar featuring Florida beers and wines. Menu items incorporate vegan and gluten-free choices. Lunch and dinner $8–21; closed Tue.

ও I was glad a friend steered me toward **Pizzalleys Chianti Room** (904-825-4100; pizzalleyschiantiroom .com), 60 Charlotte St, because I never would have suspected from their pizza joint on St. George St that there'd be a fine restaurant attached on the other side. Feeling like a Tuscan tavern, the restaurant offers eight types of Chianti plus other fine wines, and diners sit within the sight and sound of the open kitchen and its busy pizza oven. You can order pizza, of course, but in this setting the Italian entrées seemed most appropriate. My Charlotte Street chicken had thinly sliced fillets smothered in crab Alfredo and pepper sauce. From the heaping entrées around me, I assume no one else went home hungry, and I had twice as much food as I needed. Entrées $13–22.

St. Augustine—San Marco

Le Pavillion (904-824-6202; lepav .com), 45 San Marco Ave. In a grand old home in the antiques district, this elegant French restaurant remains one of St. Augustine's top dining experiences. For lunch, enjoy the special oyster platter and salad, or crêpes stuffed with seafood, beef, spinach, or chicken, $11–12. Dinner entrées include filet mignon, half roast duckling, fresh trout sauté amandine, and their famous rack of lamb for one, $19–28. Top it all off with a luscious crème de menthe parfait.

Tucked into an 1879 Victorian home under the trees along the avenue, it's as inconspicuous as it is delicious. For more than 20 years, the **Raintree Restaurant and Steakhouse** (904-824-7211; raintreerestaurant.com), 102 San Marco Ave, has delighted diners with its award-winning entrées and extensive wine list. Choose from lamb shank osso buco, grilled portobello napoleon, beef Wellington, and more. Don't miss the dessert bar, where the chef creates bananas Foster and crêpes tableside. Entrées $20–30, with seasonal dinner specials $12–18. Open for dinner; reservations suggested.

St. Augustine
🍴 **Creekside Dinery** (904-829-6113; creeksidedinery.com), 160 Nix Boatyard Rd. Set off the mainstream of US 1, this gabled replica Cracker house looks like someone's home—until you step inside. The vast open rooms and wraparound porches along Oyster Creek blur the line between indoors and out. Imagine toasting marshmallows tableside as the crickets buzz at twilight under the magnolia trees: You can do that at Creekside on an open tabby grill pit. The focus of the menu is seafood, with fresh grouper, plank-cooked salmon, and other specialties presented on fish platters. Ask for the piquant and spicy house dressing on your salad, and if the squash casserole is available as the night's vegetable, don't miss it! The grilled fish will leave you with a smile—I recommend the Crock a' Shrimp for shrimp lovers. Entrées $9–21.

St. Augustine Beach
Cafe Eleven (904-460-9311; cafe eleven.com), 501 FL A1A (Beach Blvd), is a snazzy combination of bistro and performance space, with live music on weekends. Breakfasts include funky treats like a feta, spinach, and cheese croissant and praline French toast, but I gravitate to the enormous fresh salads—pear and berry, bruschetta, tomato mozzarella—and big sandwiches; $6 and up. The pastry case will tempt you, too. Open Mon–Fri 7:30 AM–10 PM, Sat–Sun 7:30 AM–3 PM.

🍴 **Saltwater Cowboys** (904-471-2332; saltwatercowboys.com), 299 Dondanville Rd. Good luck finding a parking space at this wildly popular seafood house on the Matanzas River; your best bet is arriving for lunch or a very early dinner. It's all about fish, of course—fried, broiled, baked, blackened, and steamed—but they've got killer Florida barbecue as well. Try a Florida Cracker specialty like frog legs or cooter, or the hot and spicy jambalaya. Entrées $9–21.

EATING OUT
Anastasia Island
🍴 They say fried shrimp was invented in St. Augustine, and **O'Steen's Restaurant** (904-829-6974), 205 Anastasia Blvd, has been the local hot spot for fried shrimp and pilau (pronounced *per-loo*)—a classic regional dish of seasoned rice, shrimp, and Minorcan sausage—since 1965. The lines get long here, so sign up at the window and browse next door in the antiques shop while you listen for your name on the loudspeaker. Open Tue–Sat for lunch and dinner ($15–20); cash only.

Crescent Beach
South Beach Grille (904-471-8700; southbeachgrill.net), 45 Cubbedge Rd. It's a surreal scene: 1940s music spills across the dunes as you sip a margarita and watch the waves crashing on the beach. With a full complement of beach drinks, from the Goombay Smash to Blue Island Ice Tea, the South Beach Grill is the hot spot in Crescent Beach. Choose the open-air back porch for best effect and enjoy steamed shrimp with datil-pepper corn bread, or the thick seafood jambalaya. Entrées run $10–35, but you can opt for wraps or burgers for a lighter meal. My suggestion: Stop by for a drink and a bowl of their outstanding roasted corn and blue crab corn chowder, a crunchy, buttery concoction that will have you ordering seconds.

North Beach

For more than a century, the Usina family has been quietly serving up fresh seafood to boaters along the Tolomato River. It all started with Henry Flagler sailing by in 1900 and stopping to ask Catherine and Frank Usina if they'd roast some oysters for him and his friends. The family finally opened up a restaurant in 2009, **Aunt Kate's** (904-829-1105; aunt-kates.com), 612 Euclid Ave. Open daily, they're perched on the river and continue the family tradition of providing their patrons fresh seafood, from St. Augustine–style shrimp to pilau and a Low Country boil. And yes, you can get those famed steamed oysters. Entrées $10–20; open daily for lunch and dinner.

Orangedale

🐾 Watch for seaplanes as they land and take off by **Outback Crab Shack** (904-522-0500; outbackcrabshack.com), 8155 CR 13 N at Six Mile Marina on the St. Johns River (take FL 16 west—it's worth the drive). You'll get your money's worth, as they dish out enormous platters of fried scallops, alligator, and catfish. Lobster, crawfish, blue crab, and clams are steamed to perfection. They'll even blacken or stir-fry your meal. Get your daily requirement of veggies with the steamed Low Country tender potatoes, onions, corn, broccoli, mushrooms, and sausage for $12. Open daily for lunch and dinner, $13–25, with massive steamed or fried seafood family platters $34–70, that feed four hungry people.

Palm Valley

Relax along the Intracoastal at **Lulu's Waterfront Grille** (904-285-0139; luluswaterfrontgrille.com), 301 N Roscoe Blvd, Ponte Vedra Beach, a fine family place with a funky Old Florida feel inside the bar and out on

CRAB LEGS ARE A DELIGHT AT THE OUTBACK CRAB SHACK

the expansive deck, where you can sit and watch the boaters putter past. Dockage means you might meet a few. Despite the down-home appearance, the food is upscale. Entrées include lemon basil soft-shell crab, portobello grouper, and crab au gratin. Entrées $12–22. Open for lunch, when they have "baskwiches," and dinner. Just for fun, take a putt in the side yard—you're within driving range of one of the world's top golf courses. Add live music and waterside wine tastings, and you might want to stay awhile.

Ponte Vedra Beach

Sprung from the old seafaring merchant business that started the worldwide thirst for rum, **Pussers Caribbean Grille** (904-280-7766; pussersusa.com), 816 FL A1A N, is the first I've seen outside Tortola in the British Virgin Islands. Their menu is distinctly Caribbean, with fiery firecracker shrimp, pressed Cuban sandwiches, coconut-encrusted grouper, and seasoned pulled pork among the tasty appetizers and entrées. The extensive drink menu has a heavy focus on rum, of course. Weekday lunch specials for $5, sandwiches and entrées $9–28, with vegetarian options.

St. Augustine—Historic District

🎗 **A1A Ale Works** (904-829-2977; a1aaleworks.com), 1 King St. With its upstairs dining area overlooking Matanzas Bay and jazzed up with fish tanks and snazzy nautical decor, this is a place for funky fusion seafood like a delicious blue crab BLT, Caribbean-style jerk scampi, and shrimp and grits. The extensive drink menu means the party goes on for hours. Lunch and dinner, entrées $15–25.

🎗 **Acapulco's** (904-804-9933; acabay .com), 12 Avenida Menendez, offers Mexican dishes like carne asada, pollo colorado, and mole poblano in the shadow of the Castillo de San Marcos, with a stellar view of Matanzas Bay from their upper floor. Savor it all with a pitcher of margaritas. Serving lunch and dinner in a comfortable atmosphere, $11–17.

Decorated with murals depicting the founding and settlement of St. Augustine, **Athena Restaurant** (904-823-9076; athenacafe.com), 14 Cathedral Place, provides a unique setting for classic Greek dishes like pastitsio, moussaka, and saganaki, but the big deal here are the desserts (baklava, napoleons, and more) that beckon from the front bakery case. Open for breakfast, lunch, and dinner, entrées $12–21.

A great spot for people-watching, the **Bunnery Bakery & Cafe** (904-829-6166), 121 St. George Ave, opens early to offer breakfasts ($4–7) like southern eggs—laid atop fluffy biscuits with

home-style sausage gravy and grits. Lunches include burgers, sandwiches, and salads, $4–8. Open 8 AM–3 PM.

The little **City Perks Coffee Co** (904-819-1644; citycoffeeco.com), 6 St. George St, is full of goodness. We popped in there early on a Sunday morning for breakfast and found tasty mocha cappuccino and muffins.

🎗 Stopping in for a cold drink at the **Gourmet Hut** (904-824-7477), 17 Cuna St, I found myself gravitating back on a daily basis after an unexpectedly delicious platter of Mexican scrambled eggs I had for dinner, served outside the kitchen hut. A green space with seating divided by two small cottages—one for the creative drinks and coffees, the other for creations like tropical fish wrap, sky-high spinach bake, and eggs Benedict, $3–10—it's kissed by a salt breeze and blessed with a view of Fort Matanzas.

🎗 Miss not **The Hyppo** (904-217-7853; thehyppo.com), 5 Hypolita St, if you seriously want to be blown away by weird, delicious icy creations. Their popsicles are like nothing I've ever tried before, with flavors ranging from pineapple cilantro to mango habenero and Mexican hot chocolate. Delicious!

If you love omelets, don't miss **Mary's Harbor View Cafe** (904-825-0193), 16A Avenida Menendez, where 11 choices await along with an extensive breakfast and lunch menu. It's a small but bustling bargain breakfast bistro, opening at 7 AM.

For an touch of the Irish, relax along the bayfront at **Meehan's on Matanzas** (904-810-1923; meehansirishpub .com), 20 Avenida Menendez, home of the local Celtic Fest. Irish pub fare and a splash of the Old Country—including Harp, Smithwick's, Kilkenny, and Magner's Cider—are their mainstay, but I couldn't ignore the fresh seafood choices like Shrimp Floridian, with spicy whole Florida shrimp, garlic, grape tomatoes, and onions served up over fettuccine in a paella pan, one massive meal. Irish clam chowder is on the menu, or choose from the raw bar. Open for lunch and dinner, entrées $15–26.

🦞 Catering to the British palate, the **Prince of Wales Restaurant** (904-810-5725; theprinceofwalesstaugustine .com), corner of Spanish and Cuna streets, is the place for mushy peas and Yorkshire pudding as sides with your entrée, and sticky toffee and treacle as a treat. Have a classic bangers and mash, "curry of the day" with an authentic Kingfisher beer, or a ploughman's lunch, $9–15.

Art and a bagel—it's an early-morning wake-up. **Schmagel's Bagels & Deli** (904-824-4444), 69 Hypolita St, is in the heart of the shopping district. Choose from 10 different types of freshly baked bagels topped with everything from lox to hummus (my fave: green olive cream cheese). Deli sandwiches and panini for lunch, all selections under $8. The deli connects to the High Tide Gallery through a courtyard (see *Art Galleries*).

Since 1976, the **Spanish Bakery** (904-471-3046; thespanishbakery.com), 42½ St. George Ave, has served up tempting treats from the historic Salcedo Kitchen. Stop in for empanadas, cinnamon cookies, and rolls and munch down on your goodies under the shade of an old cedar tree. Open daily at 9:30 AM.

St. Augustine
The **Kings Head British Pub** (904-823-9787), 6460 US 1 N, looks like it dropped out of an Elizabethan painting: an ivy-covered cottage with bright red British phone booth (à la Dr. Who)

outside; inside, real Brit food from bangers and mash to Scotch eggs, ploughman's platter, various meat pies, and fish-and-chips, $10–18. Lunch and dinner, closed Mon.

A delightful restaurant with many vegetarian choices, **The Manatee Cafe** (904-826-0210; manateecafe.com), 525 FL 16, Westgate Plaza, offers breakfast goodies ($5 and up) like veggie burritos, fruit-topped pancakes, and omelets, and main dishes ranging from tofu chili to Cajun-style chicken. Herbal teas, carrot juice, and other "good for you" foods, too! Serving breakfast and lunch; a portion of all sales goes to manatee preservation funds.

St. Augustine— World Golf Village
You'll say "I'm all right" at the **Murray Bros Caddyshack** (904-940-3673; murraybroscaddyshack.com), 455 S Legacy Trail. Tee up with nachos with chili or chicken wings, tour the greens with the Wedge Salad, and check out the back nine with the Caddyshack Classic—a 12-ounce USDA strip steak. The 19th Hole has domestic and imported beers. Sandwiches, salads, and entrées with a Chicago flair, $8–24.

St. Augustine Beach
Right on the beachfront, **Beachcomber Restaurant** (904-471-3744), A Street, is a local favorite with classic American fare—burgers, sandwiches, salads—for lunch. Local seafood figures in with their spicy homemade Minorcan clam chowder, fried gator tail, shrimp dip, and fried shrimp and scallops, $10 and up. Open for breakfast, too, except Tue.

♿ Viva la Mexico! **Casa Maria** (904-342-0532; casamariajax.com), 1001 FL A1A, made my sister and I smile with perfect margaritas and authentic options like enchiladas suizas, chilaquiles, and fish tacos. With many different options and combinations, it was hard to choose! Lunch and dinner, $5–16.

Breakfasts come hearty at the **Sea Oats Caffe** (904-471-7350), 1073 FL A1A, tucked away in the Publix plaza. For less than $10 you can fill up on their pancakes (bacon, cheddar-filled, chocolate chip, banana, blueberry); or try out the homemade cheddar grits (I loved 'em) with a shrimp, cheese, and tomato omelet. This was the only non-hotel breakfast spot open along the beachfront on a Sunday morning, and I'm glad I found it.

Sunset Grille (904-471-5555; sunset grilleA1A.com), 421 FL A1A (Beach Blvd). Enjoy the "world's best" coconut-crusted shrimp with piña colada dipping sauce and the smoothest margaritas along the beach in this casual, award-winning local favorite. Half orders available on their massive pasta plates. Lunch and dinner, $7–22.

✳ Entertainment

Anastasia Island

&. After extensive renovations, the historic **St. Augustine Amphitheatre** (904-471-1965; staugamphitheatre .com), 1340 S A1A, is now a hopping venue for serious concertgoers. Built in 1965 and set in a beautiful coastal hammock adjacent to Anastasia State Park (see *Beaches*) and encompassing some of the historic Spanish-era coquina quarries, it was the home of the *Cross & Sword*, the official Florida state play depicting the founding of the city, for 30 years. Entirely revamped to be a top-notch performing arts venue, it hosts concerts virtually every weekend by artists like Duran Duran, Peter Frampton, Incubus, and the Oak Ridge Boys. Tickets available online or

at the box office; the grounds are open daily and worth a stroll to see the ancient quarries, now ponds with observation decks to watch the fish and turtles.

Ponte Vedra Beach

&. For indoor concerts, film series, and stage shows, check the schedule for the **Ponte Vedra Concert Hall** (904-209-0399 pvconcerthall.com), 1050 A1A N, a cultural arts facility that opened in April 2011. Recent events included a screening of *Tommy* as part of the WJCT public broadcasting film series, concerts by Wanda Jackson and Queensryche, and a one-man stage show, *An Evening with Ralph Stanley*, with weekly events scheduled. Tickets available online or at the box office.

St. Augustine—Historic District

Between Memorial Day and Labor Day, families gather at Plaza de la Constitucion for free weekly **Concerts in the Plaza** (904-825-1004; plaza concerts.com), Thu evening 7–9, with jazz, blues, folk, and country artists keeping the crowd swinging. Catch live music 5–8 and 9–close nightly at the **Tropical Trade Winds Lounge** (904-829-9336; trade windslounge.com), 124 Charlotte St, where the house band Matanzas plays Jimmy Buffett and a jammin' collection of their own home-grown St. Augustine–style tunes, or settle back with a beer on the rooftop of the **Old Mill House** on St. George St for breezy acoustic music. For a real immersion into history, stop in at the **Taberna del Gallo**, one of St. Augustine's original watering holes, at the Colonial Spanish Quarter (see *Historic Sites*) to raise a tankard to the Bilge Rats as they draw you back to 1734 with their repertoire of seafaring tunes. Open Thu–Sat 2–9:30, Sun noon–7.

The play's the thing at the **Limelight Theatre** (866-682-6400; limelight -theatre.org), 11 Old Mission Ave, with year-round performances that include professional productions like *I Hate Hamlet* and *The Diary of Anne Frank.*

St. Augustine— World Golf Village

✍ ♿ Experience first-run movies like never before at the **World Golf Hall of Fame IMAX Theater** (904-940-4133; worldgolfimax.com), 1 World Golf Place. After a day spent chasing down pirates all over the Oldest City, I settled in for a 3-D showing of *Pirates of the Caribbean: On Stranger Tides*— an appropriate choice for the city of the Fountain of Youth—and felt more immersed in a movie than I've ever been, and no wonder, since this is the largest IMAX screen in the Southeast. In addition to Hollywood blockbusters, they show documentary films you're more likely to identify with IMAX theaters around the country. Open daily, $8.50 adults, $7.50 seniors/military, $6 ages 3–12 for documentaries; $13 adults, $12 seniors/military, $10 ages 3–12 for box office "special engagements."

✳ Selective Shopping

Anastasia Island

Known well to locals as the place to browse while you're waiting for your seat at O'Steen's, **Anastasia Antique Center** (904-824-7126), 201 Anastasia Blvd, offers dozens of dealer booths within a broad, open space. You'll find Blue Mountain pottery, ruby and Vaseline glass, guitars, and books. Closed Sun.

Filled with my kind of fun, flamboyant art, **Simple Gestures Art & Gifts** (904-827-9997), corner of White St and Anastasia Blvd, gets the nod not just because of their copious supply of

funky stuff by local artists—including Roadside America kitsch, Story People, art sets for kids, mosaics, and garden art—but also because they unearthed part of a local mystery in their front yard, the rails to the old streetcar line that ran from downtown to the beach nearly a century ago. How cool is that? Ask for their "free phantasmagorical gift wrap" for the treasures you're bound to pick up.

Near the corner of A1A and Alternate A1A, explore a Florida roadside classic—**Tom's Souvenirs & Sea Shells** (904-471-2355), 1812 A1A S, a roadside stand filled with all that said "Florida vacation" in my childhood, from seashells to corals and sponges, nautical decor, Florida candies, gator heads, and kitschy Florida gifts.

Ponte Vedra

Offering flirty, fun fashions, **5 Sisters Boutique** (904-399-1004; 5sisters boutique.com), 330 A1A N, has racks filled with clothes from trendy designers like Marisa K and Three Dot.

St. Augustine—Historic District

Anastasia Books (904-824-0648; anastasiabooks.com), 81 King St #C, has a good selection of Floridiana (new and used) as well as plenty of children's books and textbooks for homeschoolers. Large used-book section, including the area's largest selection of science fiction and fantasy. Closed Sun.

Satisfy your need for acquiring old stuff in the Oldest City at **Antiques & Uniques Collectibles** (904-829-0960; antiquesanduniquescollectibles.com), 5 Aviles St, where you'll find Civil War artifacts, movie star memorabilia, nautical decor items, and funky salt and pepper shakers.

Around the World Marketplace (904-824-6223), 21 Orange St. The burble of fountains makes browsing a pleasant experience as you poke through colorful imports—Tavalera porcelain, onyx chess sets, masks, statues, mirrors, and wall art.

Bouvier Maps & Prints (904-825-0920), 11-D Aviles St. If you're looking for a map to go with St. Augustine's history, this is the place to visit. Dealing in original antique maps and prints, this shop is as rare a find as its incredible inventory. Closed Tue–Wed.

Stop in **Claude's Chocolate** (904-808-8395; claudeschocolate.com), 15 Hypolita St, where French chef Claude Franques whips up memorable bonbons, truffles, and chocolate bark. You can grab homemade ice cream here, too.

Earthbound Trading Company (904-824-6283; earthboundtrading.com), 108 St George St, is a fun new addition importing interesting locally sourced goods from the third world—I saw my India block print tablecloths there! You'll find Balinese figurines, star lamps from India, minerals, smarmy bumper stickers and magnets, and flowing clothing.

Grover's Gallery (904-824-5738), 14B St. George St. Big pieces, low prices: That's the philosophy of artist Grover Rice, who has spent more than 30 years carving wood into art such as life-sized sea turtles and pelicans, tikis made from palm trunks, and model villages.

A Michigan chain, **Kilwins** (904-826 0008), 140 St. George Ave, tempts you inside with display cases filled with chocolate goodies; they sell ice cream as well.

For historic tomes, stop in at **La Libreria** on St. George St, the official bookstore of the Colonial Spanish Quarter (see *Historic Homes*).

It's one of the most interesting locations I've ever seen for an antiques store, so I suggest you go out of your

way to the **Lightner Antique Mall** (904-824-9948), 25 Granada St, located inside the original swimming pool of the historic Alcazar Hotel, now the Lightner Museum (see *Museums*). Go around the back of the museum to enter.

Think gifts with attitude at **Materialistic** (904-824-1611), 125 St. George St, where even the T-shirts are smarmy. Pick up a punching rabbi, a dashboard hula dancer, or a Brahman lunch box.

At **Metalartz** (904-824-6322; metalartz.net), 58 Hypolita St, mobiles and glass balls dangle from the ceiling, and lizards and dragonflies cling to a tree that rises from the floor. With art glass, paintings, metal sculptures, and much more, this kaleidoscope of artistry represents 15 local artists and their very creative expressions.

St. Augustine Art Glass (904-824-4916), 54 St. George St, isn't just about glass—check out the raku art sculptures and playful metal sculptures in the tranquil garden behind the building.

Second Read Books (904-829-0334), 51 Cordova St, keeps a brisk business going with used books for sale or trade just a block from Flagler College. Look for a good local section, fine literature, and a broad young-adult selection.

The granddaddy of sweet stuff in the Oldest City is **Whetstone Chocolates** (904-825-1720; whetstonechocolates.com), 42 St. George St, a local fixture since 1967. Their newest location, at 139 King St, is also their factory, where they give tours (see *Chocolate Factory Tour*).

The **Woman's Exchange** (904-829-5064; staugustinewomans-exchange.com), 143 St. George St, is a volunteer organization dating back to 1892 that manages tours through the historic Peck Pina House (circa 1700) in order to run a consignment outlet for top-quality home crafters. Their motto is "Creative need is as important as the financial need," and their creativity runs the gamut from watercolor note-cards and cookbooks to clothespin dolls, hand-smocked dresses, hand-crafted soaps, and hand-painted glass.

St. Augustine—San Marco

A huge selection of beads and necklaces waits at **The Bead Chick** (904-829-8829; beadchickstaugustine.com), 78B San Marco Ave. Sit and create your own strands of beauty.

A historic two-story home now beckons as **Eden** (904-829-2122), 82 San Marco Ave, with "temptations for the home." Inside, look for beaded dresses and jackets, chic lamps, gifts, and large pieces of antique furniture.

I spent quite of bit of time browsing **Jena's Antiques & Art** (904-806-4274), 56 San Marco Ave, turning up treasures like classic wooden toys, Tiffany glass, a dry sink, vintage mirrors, and hand-painted fruit.

St. Augustine Antique Emporium (904-829-0544), 62 San Marco Ave, features 22 dealer booths in a refreshingly open setting, making it easy to keep track of the rest of your group as you browse through the art glass, jewelry, postcards, saltcellars, stained glass, and other ephemera.

Fine glassware, lamps, furnishings, and home decor are the tip of the iceberg at a **Step Back in Time** (904-810-5829), 60 San Marco Ave.

Gleaming diving helmets set the tone at **SOS Antiques** (904-823-0008), 74 San Marco Ave, where a pirate greets you as you walk in to explore classic nautical decor such as glass diver balls, ship's wheels, and, of course, treasure chests.

At **Uptown Antiques** (904-824-9156), 63 San Marco Ave, look through the mini mall of dealer booths and you'll unearth treasures like historic postcards of St. Augustine, movie memorabilia, posters, and books.

Wolf's Head Books (800-521-5061 or 904-824-9357; wolfsheadbooks.com), 67B San Marco. I walked in here to look around and walked out with a rare book in my favorite field of study, Florida natural history. This is a true antiquarian bookseller. You will find books here you can't even find on the Internet, especially in the Florida section, with great prices and a superb selection. Open daily.

St. Augustine Beach

✍ Out at the beach, you'll find all the usual surf, swimming suit, and T-shirt shops you've come to expect from every beachfront town. Drive FL A1A to explore, and you'll find gems like **Sunburst Trading Company** (904-461-7255), 491 FL A1A (Beach Blvd), the shell shop for the region, with a selection of shell crafts, burbling Mexican fountains, Latin imports, and, of course, shells. Bring the kids: The incredible selection starts at 20¢, and there are fossils and coral to choose from, too. An additional location is at 146 St. George St in the Old City.

FARMER'S MARKETS Wednesday Market at St. Augustine Beach (904-347-8007; staugbchcivicassoc.com/market.html). Now, here's a twist—a farmer's market that's also an art gathering, where you can peruse the works of local sculptors and painters while picking up the perfect peck of potatoes. Every Wed 8–12:30 at the St. Johns County Ocean Pier (see *Fishing*).

At the **Old City Farmer's Market** (staugustinefm.com), stop in for fresh food straight from the farms in the southwest corner of St. Johns County. Every Sat 8:30–12:30 at the St. Augustine Amphitheater (see *Entertainment*).

☀ Special Events

February: **Menendez Birthday Festival**. A weekend's worth of parades, music, and heritage celebrations commemorating the founder of St. Augustine, with events throughout the Oldest City.

March: During **Searle's Sack of St. Augustine** (searlesbucs.com/searles .html), first Sat, pirates camp out near the Fountain of Youth (see *Archaeological Sites*) and stealthily make their way to the city gates, reenacting the sacking and burning of the Historic District in 1668, with swordfights, brawls, and general mayhem through the streets.

April: **Florida's Birding & Photo Fest** (floridasbirdingandphotofest .com), St. Augustine Amphitheatre. A nature-based festival offering workshops, seminars, and field trips throughout the region on birding, native wildlife, and enjoying the outdoors. Last week.

May: ♪ Join the "Potato Capital of the World" in celebrating their **Annual Potato and Cabbage Festival**, Hastings Recreational Field, 150 Main St, Hastings, first weekend. Expect a Spud Run, mouthwatering potato stew and cabbage soup, potato cupcakes and potato fudge, hot-air balloon rides, live music, and fun for the whole family.

Gamble Rogers Folk Festival (904-794-0222; gamblerogersfest.org), Historic District, last weekend. One of Florida's top folk music weekends, with dozens of performers honoring one of the strongest voices in Florida folk music, and vendors and craftspersons with Florida art. Performance venues and vendors will be scattered throughout downtown. Three-day weekend pass $60, evening pass (one major performance), $30.

The Players Championship (pgatour .com/theplayers) is one of the top golfing events in the nation. It descends on TPC Sawgrass (see *Golf*), Ponte Vedra Beach, mid-May for three days, bringing tens of thousands of golfing fans to the region.

June: **Drake's Raid** (searlesbucs.com /drakes.html), first Sat. I love the poster I saw for this one: "the largest 16th-century reenactment in the United States." As if there could be another? Only the most studious of history lovers (and the locals, of course) know that swashbuckling pirate Sir Francis Drake came ashore and set fire to St. Augustine in 1586, sacking the city.

September: **St. Augustine Founder's Day Festival**. Founded on September 8, 1565, this city has plenty to party about, with reenactments and live entertainment. Join the countdown to the half millennium! Held the Saturday after Sept 8.

October: **Colonial Folk Arts and Crafts Festival**, Colonial Spanish Quarter. Browse 17th-century arts and crafts—everything from weaving to blacksmithing—in one of the most interesting living history festivals in Florida. First Sat.

Kick off Hispanic Heritage Month at the **Hispanic Heritage Festival** (904-806-7001), held the first Sat at the Palencia Club, 600 Palencia Club Dr, St. Augustine near World Golf Village.

The **Feast of San Gennaro** (904-461-8449; staugustineitalianfest.com), first weekend, celebrates the Italian heritage of St. Augustine with food, carnival rides, and entertainment at the St. Augustine Beach Pier Park Pavilion.

At the **Annual Greek Festival** (904-829-0504; stauggreekfest.com), now in its 15th year, enjoy fine food, music, and dancing at Francis Field behind the visitors center parking garage, second weekend.

Discover the hottest thing to come out of St. Augustine at the annual **Datil Pepper Festival** (904-209-0430), St. Johns County Agriculture Center, 3125 Agriculture Center Dr, third Sun.

Plunder awaits at **The Pirate Gathering** (904-824-4997; pirategathering .com), an annual assemblage of ne'er-do-wells and their followers in the streets of St. Augustine. Visit the Thieves' Market, learn how to handle a sword, and avoid getting shanghaied onto a pirate crew. Francis Field, last weekend.

December: During much of the month, the Brits take over the Oldest City during the **1770s British Encampment** (britishnightwatch.org), with Colonial Market Days, daily military drills by the British Redcoats, magicians, and more. Opens 9 AM daily at Francis Field; free.

For nearly 50 years, the Garden Club of St. Augustine has hosted the **Annual Garden Club Christmas Tour of Homes** (gardenclubofstaugustine.org), a walking tour that gets you behind the coquina walls and Victorian porches into the beautiful historic homes of the Historic District. First Sun, noon–5. $20 per person.

Watch the waterfront light up during the annual **Regatta of Lights** (904-824-9725; sayc2000.com), Avenida Menendez, with a holiday parade of boats judged for their creativity. Held along the bayfront, second Sat, starting 6 PM.

Artists and craftspeople strut their talents in an after-Christmas fine arts show, the **Old Town Art & Craft Show** (holidayartshows.com/old-town -art-craft-show.html), last weekend at Francis Field, 10–5; free.

FLAGLER COUNTY

PALM COAST, BUNNELL, FLAGLER BEACH, BEVERLY BEACH

I t's one of the first Florida places etched in my memory, the wind whipping through our 1955 Ford as Dad drove with the windows open down A1A, the Atlantic Ocean spreading off to the horizon. I remember a day spent at Marineland, a soft plastic toy as a souvenir, and holding my nose at the smell of the sulfur springs at Washington Oaks. South of St. Augustine, north of Daytona Beach, Flagler County has been a quiet place—until recently. Now condos rise from the dunes south of old Marineland and at the edge of the jungle-like forests of **Hammock**, and **Palm Coast** continues to spread. Yet there are still many corners of the county where you can immerse in the wild that has always been, along its placid creeks and salt flats, beneath the towering oaks, and beside tidal pools on the shore.

Spanish land grants shaped this region, where the first plantations were carved out along the coast and rivers in the late 1700s. Some have continued on as preserves and historic sites, such as Washington Oaks Gardens State Park, Princess Place Preserve, Bing's Landing, and Bulow Plantation Ruins State Park, which was the site of Florida's largest sugar mill circa 1821. Carved out of neighboring St. Johns and Volusia, Flagler County was established in 1917 with **Bunnell** as the county seat, but most of the action centered on **Flagler Beach**. While incorporated in 1925, this seaside community got its start in 1920 as "Ocean City" when the first bridge opened from the mainland; a casino, bars, and hotels soon followed.

GUIDANCE The **Flagler County Chamber of Commerce Visitor's Center** (866-736-9291 or 386-437-0106; visitflagler.org), 20 Airport Rd Ste C, Palm Coast, is off FL 100 between Flagler Beach and Bunnell. You'll also find a walk-in visitors center inside the **Flagler Beach Historical Museum** (386-517-2025; flaglerbeach museum.com), 207 S Ave, Flagler Beach, open Mon–Sat 10–4, where you can ask about local accommodations and pick up brochures and maps.

🐾 Of all of Florida's coastal communities, Flagler County is one of the most pet-friendly. Dogs are welcome on nearly every public and some private beaches, and most mom-and-pop lodgings allow you to bring your best friend along. Some of

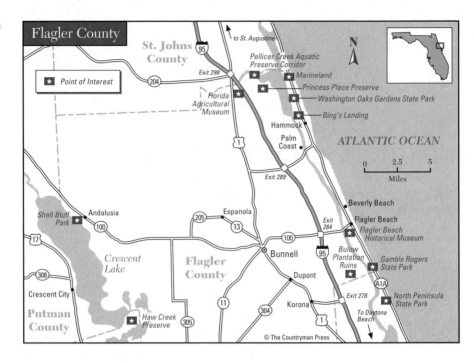

the eateries are dog-friendly, too. If your dog has never romped in the surf, this is the destination for you!

GETTING THERE *By air:* From the north, fly into **Jacksonville International Airport** (see the *Jacksonville* chapter), or from the south, fly into **Daytona Beach International Airport** (386-248-8069; volusia.org/airport).

By car: **Interstate 95** provides access to the highways that lead to Flagler's back roads and bridge to A1A and US 1, paralleling to the east and west. Exit at Dupont Center, US 1, Palm Coast, and Flagler Beach.

GETTING AROUND A car is necessary to make your way around the county. **FL A1A** and **US 1** are the major north–south routes, with **FL 100** connecting Flagler Beach and Bunnell.

MEDICAL EMERGENCIES Florida Hospital Flagler (386-586-2000; florida hospitalflagler.com), 60 Memorial Medical Pkwy, Palm Coast.

✳ To See

ARCHAEOLOGICAL SITES ✍ �&. Beneath the deep shade of ancient live oaks, the remains of buildings on the **Mala Compra Plantation** can be found at Bings Landing (see *Parks*). The former home of Brigadier General Joseph Martin Hernandez stretched over 724 acres; in the early 1800s he grew Sea Island cotton, corn, and oranges. Purchased in 1816 for the then-tidy sum of $1,500, the plantation was burned to the ground in 1836 by Seminoles during the Second Seminole

Indian War. Under cover of an open-air roofed building, the well-interpreted archaeological dig explains Hernandez's role in early Florida, with artifacts like buttons, stoneware shards, and boot spurs displayed with a backdrop of the foundations of plantation buildings. General Hernandez was Florida's first delegate to the U.S. Congress, and also its first Hispanic member. Free.

Set along Pellicer Creek, a **water-powered sawmill** built by John Hewitt was one of the first in the region, built in 1770. This interpretive site can be accessed from a trail starting at a gated parking area off US 1 [29.642776, -81.286058]; it's managed by and a part of the Florida Archaeological Museum (see *Museums*). Free.

ART GALLERIES

Palm Coast
Tucked beneath the live oak canopy of Hammock, **The Baliker Gallery** (386-446-0069; paulbaliker.com), 5928 N Oceanshore Blvd, beckons you to stop with its larger-than-life driftwood sculptures. Step inside to surround yourself with vivid acrylics of Florida forests and estuaries, and delicate bronze statuettes. The creative spirit of Paul Baliker hums through this open space, where the figures of sailfish, sea turtles, and sprites emerge from the natural curves of driftwood. Open weekends.

In the City Marketplace, **Hollingsworth Gallery** (386-871-9546; hollingsworth gallery.com), 160 Cypress Point Pkwy, represents area artists in a broad variety of mainly two-dimensional media, with a special emphasis on members of the Southeast Coalition of Contemporary Artists. Mon–Fri noon–6 or by appointment.

Flagler Beach
At the **Gallery of Local Art** (386-439-6659; galleryoflocalart.com), 208 S Central Ave, you might wander in to look at watercolors and acrylics of coastal scenes and hear a buzz from the back, where classes go on inside a studio space. The gallery also interconnects with several other shops, but the focus here is on art created and shared by members of the local community.

HISTORIC SITES

Bunnell
The **Bunnell State Bank Building** (circa 1917), 101–107 N Bay St, was the only bank in Flagler County from 1917 to 1932. Today the two-story Mason Vernacular is known Citizens Bank of Bunnell.

Built in 1915 using convict labor, the **Old Dixie Highway** was the first paved road through the region. A narrow, 9-foot-wide segment of the original road can be driven through the towns of Hastings, Espanola, and Bunnell between Flagler and St. Johns counties.

Flagler Beach
❀ At **Bulow Plantation Ruins Historic State Park** (386-517-2084; floridastate parks.org/bulowplantation), CR 2001 south of FL 100, your immersion into the ancient history of Bulowville begins once you get beyond the new subdivision at the entrance and settle into the long drive down a one-lane dirt road buried deep in the primordial forest of Bulow Hammock. It was here that Major Charles Wilhelm Bulow established a sugar plantation in 1821, using slave labor to clear, plant,

and maintain more than 2,200 acres of sugarcane; his son took over operations after his death. Planted in January and February, the cane would be harvested in October and brought to this mill on the plantation. As you walk through the ruins of the oldest and most extensive colonial-period sugar works in Florida, interpretive signs point out how the process worked. A steam boiler ran the rollers that crushed the cane, which rode up on a conveyor belt to the second floor to be pressed flat between the rollers. Cane juice ran down to the bottom floor into kettles, which were ladled out into troughs for cooling. After processing, the raw sugar and molasses would be floated on flatboats down Bulow Creek to the Halifax River and on to Mosquito Inlet in New Smyrna, where ships sailed out to the Caribbean and the East Coast with Bulow's products. It was a busy enterprise, and a town, Bulowville, grew up around the mill. In 1836, Seminole warriors burned the town and the plantation, which never recovered. By the age of the trees around the old sugar works, it seems longer. Interpretive information and artifacts are in a small adjoining museum. Fee.

Paralleling US 1 and I-95 you'll find segments of the **Old Kings Road**, Florida's first highway. Before the American Revolution, Colonel James Grant, governor of British Florida, sought to connect plantations along the East Coast by following an old Indian trail, and he put his lieutenant governor, John Moultrie, in charge. He eventually achieved the objective: connecting St. Augustine to Andrew Turnbull's New Smyrna plantation. By 1774 the shell-surfaced road had pine logs for crossing the swampy sections and numerous bridges, and it was used by settlers and military patrols.

MARINE LAB At **Whitney Laboratories** (904-461-4000; whitney.ufl.edu), managed by the University of Florida, scientists and students delve into the secrets of

---

PALM COAST

One of the most beautiful places on this coast is the oldest homestead in Flagler County, **Cherokee Grove**, now protected as a part of Princess Place Preserve (see *Parks*). Established as land grant in 1791 from the king of Spain and planted in orange groves, it was purchased by Henry Cutting in 1886. Making it his winter home, he constructed an Adirondack-style hunting lodge using local materials—pink coquina, cedar trunks, and cabbage palm trunks. He also built Florida's first in-ground pool, fed by an artesian spring, and a nearby stable for carriages. Overlooking the Matanzas River and accessible by boat from St. Augustine, Cherokee Grove became a popular stop for Henry's circle of New England socialites. Several years after he died, his widow Angela married an exiled Russian prince, Boris Scherbatoff. Together they lived in Cherokee Grove, entertaining royalty in a royal setting. In private hands until 1993, the homestead then became a Flagler County Park. Tours are provided Fri–Sun at 2 PM, and the grounds are open daily 8–6. Sit on the porch in a rocking chair and breathe in the salt breeze to feel the slower pace of life enjoyed on these grounds.

the deep to apply to biomedical and biotechnical research. "Marine invertebrates are great models for human beings," said Maureen Welch as she showed me recent studies that used sea slugs to model the neurological problems of Alzheimer's patients. In addition to some permanent exhibits across the street at Marineland (see *Dolphin Encounters*), the lab holds an open house each spring. Groups can arrange private tours. A free monthly lecture series provides informative background on marine topics, 7 PM; see their website for schedule.

MUSEUMS

Bunnell

Home to the Flagler County Historical Society, the **Holden House Museum** (386-437-0600), 204 E Moody Blvd (FL 100), was originally built in 1918 for Ethel and Tom Holden by her father. The couple lived there until the 1970s. The rooms reflect the home's use in the 1920s, with period furnishings and decor. It was one of the first buildings in the area with indoor plumbing. Each gable is inset with pieces of apothecary bottles, antique colored glass, and bits of dishes. Open Wed 10–1.

At the **Earth Wonders Geological Museum** (386-679-4353; earthwonders.org), 1769 Moody Blvd, treasures from the earth gleam, sparkle, and even glow under fluorescent lamps. Learn about the beauty of minerals and how they are cut and polished into jewelry and art by using lapidary techniques. Mon–Fri 10–4, Sat by appointment; free.

Built in 1938, the **Little Red Schoolhouse** (386-437-7533), 800 Howe St, a brick structure on the campus of Bunnell Elementary School, showcases the period of the single-room schools that once dotted the county. Originally constructed as the FFA classroom, it was the only survivor of a fire that burned down Bunnell High School in 1970. Call ahead to request a tour.

Flagler Beach

A Sea Hunt comic book. A brochure for Florida Animal Land and Marine Studios. A 1950s booklet titled *Atomic Attack! How to Protect Yourself*. Walking through the exhibits in the **Flagler Beach Museum** (386-517-2025; flagler beachmuseum.com), 207 S Central Ave, I had that sense of touching childhood memories, looking at things foreign yet familiar, like the "Food and Water 14 days for One Person" box and its contents, remembering both the visceral fear of atomic attack and

THE FLAGLER BEACH MUSEUM

the joy of dashing down the curved halls of the aquatorium at Marineland. Of course, the museum delves much deeper into local history, covering the founding of Flagler Beach in the 1920s and archaeological finds from the earliest coastal civilizations, but seeing local history intersect with childhood memories made a deeper impression. Open Mon–Sat 10–4.

✳ To Do

BICYCLING

While the longest and most obvious place to bike, the sea breeze with you all the way, is the **East Coast Greenway** (greenway.org/fl.aspx) paralleling A1A, there are other trails to explore. Parking at Bing's Landing along this route, you can slip into the shady coastal hammock on the **Mala Compra Plantation Greenway** (386-437-7490; flaglercounty.org), 115 Malacompra Rd, between Hammock and Painters Hill. More routes, including ones from 50 to 78 miles long, are suggested on the Historic A1A Scenic Byway website (scenica1a.org/Ridingroutes.aspx). If you're up for a long ride being your vacation this year, Gainesville-based tour-operator **Bike Florida** (bikeflorida.org) leads multiday guided, supported tours

---

PALM COAST

✐ A 300-acre living history museum, the **Florida Agricultural Museum** (386-446-7630; myagmuseum.com), 7900 Old Kings Rd off US 1 just south of I-95, lets you touch, smell, and feel the agricultural heritage of Florida. This is no stuffy place. It's an open-air ramble amid a collection of historically significant buildings brought together to provide a peek into Florida's growth as a grower's powerhouse. Part of the Division of Agriculture and Consumer Services, the museum's prime mission is education, so it was no surprise, when I arrived, to see a large group of students headed out into the woods on a trailer pulled by a tractor. A walk through the complex at the front of the park lets you visit a massive dairy barn, once owned by Governor Millard Caldwell and now used for special events, and a 1930s citrus-sorting house. Then it's on to the tractor-led tour, chugging through the sandhills deeper into Florida's past. Step onto the porch of an 1890s farmhouse and watch the cows graze beyond the garden. Pop into a former schoolhouse now serving as a museum of African American cowboy heritage in Florida. Walk the squeaking floorboards of a cavernous dry goods store. Trundle past a display of vintage farm equipment and wave to the passing equestrians—you can join them later on a trail ride (see *Trail Rides*). The complex also includes the remains of an old sawmill (see *Archaeological Sites*) across US 1, accessible along a short hiking trail. Open Wed–Sun 9–5, with tours starting at 10. $8 adults, $6 children, or $25 for the entire family (if it provides a savings).

on the vast **St. Johns River-to-Sea Loop**, a 260-mile bike route linking Palatka, St. Augustine, Flagler Beach, and points as far south as Titusville, with many Old Florida communities to visit along the way.

The **Lehigh Trail**, running between Colbert Rd and Belle Terre along Old Kings Rd, is one of two paved trails in Palm Coast; the other, the **Palm Coast Linear Park**, connects with it at Colbert and meanders through the heart of Palm Coast toward the Intracoastal. Between Boardman Pond (see *Birding*) and Bulow Plantation Ruins (see *Historic Sites*), the **Bulow Creek Trail** is open for mountain biking; the northerly route is an old forest road and less technical. **Bike rentals** are available from Tropical Kayaks (see *Paddling*) for $5 hour, $20 day, or $50 week.

BIRDING One of my favorite spots for birding is **Boardman Pond** [29.406077, -81.126873] just north of the Volusia County line. Park your car along Walter Boardman Rd and watch from the bank, or wander down the Bulow Creek Trail (see *Hiking*), also accessible from the road, to a blue-blazed trail leading to the Audubon observation deck.

Next to the Flagler Beach Library off S Flagler Ave, there is a beautiful walkway leading into the marshlands of **Betty Steflik Memorial Preserve** (see *Parks*). Some locals come here for artistic inspiration, others to watch the ospreys and wading birds along the mangrove-lined tidal creeks and mudflats. Shaded benches provide a morning perch for birding.

DOLPHIN ENCOUNTER ⚓ **Marineland Dolphin Adventure** (888-279-9194 or 904-460-1275; marineland.net), 9600 Oceanshore Blvd, is on the site of the world's oldest marine park, opened in 1938. But it's not your grandpa's Marineland—the iconic three-story-tall Marine Studios tank gave up the ghost, and along with it went the original buildings and most of the aquatic life. The focus now is on the state-of-the-art Dolphin Conservation Center built atop the old Whitney Park. Make advance reservations to swim and otherwise interact with the dolphins, reinforcing behaviors such as playing ball and jumping, starting at $26 to touch and feed the dolphins or $199 for 30 minutes in the water. Daily 9–5, general admission $8.50 ages 13 and up, $7.25 seniors, $4 children.

WATCHING DOLPHIN INTERACTION AT MARINELAND

ECOTOURS While based in St. Augustine, **Ripple Effect Ecotours** (904-347-1565; rippleeffectecotours .com) provides a full menu of kayak tours to explore the estuaries between the Guana-Tolomato-Matanzas National Estuarine Research Reserve and Pellicer Creek (see *Wild Places*). In partnership with Marineland Dolphin Adventure and the Florida Agricultural Museum, tours that involve water-based and land-based components are also offered. Guided trips in the region start at $50 and include all equipment and entrance fees. Based in Palm Coast, **Tropical Kayaks** (see *Paddling*) also offers guided trips, customized to your own pace and the best wildlife-watching for the season, starting at $40.

FAMILY ACTIVITIES ♂ Take the kids bowling at **Coquina Lane**s (386-445-4004; coquinalanes.com), 11 Old Kings Rd N, Palm Coast, where all 24 lanes have bumpers available. Open daily 9:30 AM–2 AM; $2.75–3.50 per person.

FISHING A popular spot with saltwater anglers, the **Flagler Beach Pier** (flagler beachpier.net) is a great place to get a line wet or just to get a great view of the beach; fee. For a morning in the shallows on a flats skiff with an expert captain, contact Captain Chris at **Palm Coast Fishing** (386-437-2545; palmcoastfishing .com). Captain Rob at **Osprey Fishing Charters** (386-439-2636; flaglerfishing charters.co), 46 Bulow Woods Circle, offers inshore light-tackle fishing for redfish, snook, and more. If you're looking for bass, head for **Crescent Lake,** which is most easily accessed from Shell Bluff Park (see *Parks*) in Andalusia off FL 100.

HIKING ♂ My first Florida hike was along the **Mala Compra Trail** at Washington Oaks Gardens State Park (see *Garden*) as a youngster—it's short and fun for kids to explore. The park's **Bella Vista Trail** loops through an incredible variety of habitats in only a mile, including a deeply shaded oak and pine forest with enormous pine trees, a breezy coastal scrub, and a mangrove-lined shoreline. The many trails of **Princess Place Preserve** (see *Parks*) will keep you busy all day exploring along the salt marshes of Pellicer Creek and the pine flatwoods in the uplands. **Haw Creek Preserve** (see *Wild Places*) has a boardwalk that winds along its namesake creek, an excellent spot for birding. An even lengthier boardwalk is at **Betty Steflik Preserve** (see *Parks*) in Flagler Beach, slipping through mangroves into dark coastal hammocks. The **Coastal Strand Trail** at North Peninsula State Park (see *Beaches*) works its way for more than 2 miles around Smith Creek and behind the line of dunes. But my favorite hike in the region is the **Bulow Creek Trail**, which connects Bulow Plantation Ruins Historic State Park (see *Historic Sites*) with Bulow Creek State Park in Volusia County. This slender ribbon, nearly 8 miles one way, guides you through some of the most primeval forest you'll see on this coast, ancient southern magnolias and oaks shading the grand Bulow Hammock, where coontie grows in profusion and giant leather ferns along the sluggish creek make you feel like you're in the Land of the Lost.

PADDLING Tropical Kayaks (386-445-0506; tropicalkayaks.com), 200 Club House Dr, at the Palm Coast Golf Resort Marina, Palm Coast. Take an ecotour (see *Ecotours*) past historical treasures or rent a kayak or paddleboard to explore the inlets for manatees, dolphins, and jumping mullet. Kayak rentals $20 per person, $40 per day, tandems and deliveries available.

To explore wild and wonderful **Bulow Creek**, rent a canoe at Bulow Plantation Ruins State Park (see *Historic Sites*). Sea kayaks are available for paddling the **Intracoastal Waterway** at Gamble Rogers Memorial State Park (see *Beaches*).

Toting your own kayak? Put in at **Princess Place Preserve** (see *Parks*) or **Guana-Tolomato-Matanzas Reserve** (see *Wild Places*) to paddle for miles through the

BULOW CREEK IS A POPULAR CANOEING DESTINATION

coastal estuaries, enjoying dozens of uninhabited islands on which to stop and lunch or camp. For freshwater exploration, head to **Shell Bluff Park** (see *Parks*) or **Haw Creek Preserve** (see *Wild Places*) for wild waterways and cypress-lined shores.

SCENIC DRIVES Few highways in the northern Florida peninsula match the beauty of the **A1A Scenic and Historic Coastal Byway** (904-596-0029; scenic a1a.org), particularly in sections where the dunes remain preserved and free of development. Designated a American Byway, this two-lane highway stays close to the ocean and connects the beachfront communities of Flagler County. A cell phone audio tour gives background on scenic stops along the way.

One of my personal favorite loop drives in Florida is to follow A1A south from Flagler Beach to North Peninsula State Park (see *Beaches*) and turn right on **High Bridge Road**. This narrow, winding road provides vistas across landscapes of salt marsh and cabbage palms, places where you'd expect a giant sloth or woolly mastodon to lumber along. At the T-intersection with **Walter Boardman Lane**, turn left to drive beneath a dense canopy of oaks past Boardman Pond (see *Birding*). At the next T, make a right onto **Old Dixie Highway** for more canopied road, and a right again when you reach **Old Kings Road** to pass by the entrance of Bulow Creek Plantation Ruins State Park (see *Historic Sites*), whose park road is a unique scenic dirt road through a deep, dark forest. Continue up to **FL 100** and turn right to return to Flagler Beach.

SURFING When the surf gets rolling, you'll want to be ready! Check in at **Z Wave Surf Shop** (386-439-9283; zwavesurfshop.com), 400 S Oceanshore Blvd, for tips on local hot spots and the latest gear. Open daily, offering surf lessons and rentals. The folks at **Si Como No Inn** (see *Lodging*) also run regular Surf Camps and give private surfing sessions.

TRAIL RIDES Equestrian trails connect **Princess Place Preserve** (see *Parks*) and its equestrian campground with neighboring **Pellicer Creek Conservation**

Area (see *Wild Places*) and, across a land bridge visible south of the US 1 exit on I-95, the **Florida Agricultural Museum** (see *Museums*), where you can saddle up for a guided trail ride.

WHALE-WATCHING The **calving ground of the right whale** can be seen from both the River to Sea Preserve (see *Beaches*) and neighboring Summer Haven and Crescent Beach in St. Johns County; check with Marineland's Right Whale Project (aswh.org/whale/main.html) to become an official whale-watcher during the winter calving season.

✳ Green Space

BEACHES 🐾 ♿ Sunbathers enjoy the strand at the **River to Sea Preserve** (386-313-4020; flaglercounty.org), 9805 N Oceanshore Blvd, where dolphin cutouts in the boardwalk echo memories of Marineland past, and interpretive information clues you in about this history of the grand aquarium and film studio no longer along this shore. On the north side of Marineland, the same preserve enables access to the strip of beach on a slender peninsula.

Just a few miles south, the **Coquina Beach** at Washington Oaks Gardens State Park (see *Garden*) is one of Florida's true geological treasures, a natural sculpture created by the sea digging into an outcropping of the shell-laden Anastasia limestone of the Atlantic Coastal Ridge. You can't swim here, but it's worth a visit to take a walk on the beach and marvel at the incredible rock formations and tidal pools sculpted from coquina. Fee.

🐾 ✎ A gem of an oceanfront park, **Malacompra Park** (386-313-4020; flagler county.org),115 Malacompra Rd in Hammock, is nestled in an expanse of saw pal-

SEASIDE BOARDWALK AT THE RIVER TO SEA PRESERVE

COQUINA BEACH AT WASHINGTON OAKS GARDENS STATE PARK

metto along the shoreline. Nature trails lead to the north and south through the dunes, while a boardwalk carries you over to the quiet strand. The coquina shelf found at Coquina Beach extends down here, too, but under the water, so this beach is for strolling, sunbathing, and shelling. Open dawn–dusk.

🐾 ♿ In Beverly Beach, **Varn Park** (386-313-4020; flaglercounty.org), 3665 N Oceanshore Blvd, has always been a family favorite since it's just far enough north of Flagler Beach to not be as busy. In **Flagler Beach**, beach parking and access surrounds the pier downtown.

🐾 ♿ With soft sands tinted orange by coquina shells and an expansive 144-acre beachfront, **Gamble Rogers Memorial State Recreation Area** (386-517-2086; floridastateparks.org/gamblerogers), 3100 S FL A1A, Flagler Beach, is a park for relaxing and catching some rays. Home to the annual Gamble Rogers Folk Festival (see *Special Events*), the park is named for the famed Florida folksinger who lost his life trying to save a drowning man at this beach. Rip currents are an issue here, so stay closer to shore. Stretching from the Atlantic to the Intracoastal, the park has a gentle nature trail through a diminutive forest of windswept oaks, and boater access to the waterway. Rentals of bicycles, kayaks, and canoes are available at the ranger station. Fee.

Although parking is limited, the beach certainly isn't at **North Peninsula State Park** (386-517-2086; floridastateparks.org/northpeninsula), S FL A1A, Flagler Beach, stretching 2 miles along the coast. Overlapping into Volusia County, this preserve immerses you in dunes covered with saw palmetto as you drive south on A1A, and stretches west to the vast marshlands along Bulow Creek. An access point at Smith Creek Landing off High Bridge Rd [29.409675, -81.099383] provides a place to take a hike, slip a kayak into the marshes, or just settle back and fish from the shoreline. Free.

FAMILY FUN AT GAMBLE ROGERS MEMORIAL STATE PARK

GREENWAYS A segment of the **East Coast Greenway** (greenway.org/fl.aspx), a route under development to enable bicyclists safe passage from Maine to Key West, runs through Flagler County paralleling A1A. You'll notice that the paved bike path start just south of Marineland, and it continues much of the length of the county. In Hammock, the **Mala Compra Plantation Greenway** (386-437-7490; flaglercounty.org), 115 Malacompra Rd, lets bicyclists and pedestrians make their way from Bing's Landing (see *Parks*) through this preserve. Inside residential Palm Coast, **Palm Coast Linear Park** (palmcoastgov.com/City/Attractions/PCG), 31 Greenway Court, a 57-acre greenway, is home to trails and kayak launch points, open 7–7 daily.

PARKS ✦ **Bings Landing Park** (386-437-7490; flaglerparks.com/bings/preserve .htm), 5880 N Oceanshore Blvd (FL A1A), Hammock, on the shores of the former Mala Compra Plantation (see *Archaeological Sites*), is deeply shaded by a canopy of ancient live oaks. Picnic under the oaks or fish from the pier. On weekends you can rent kayaks for a gentle paddle on the Intracoastal. Bings Landing Park is located on the west side of A1A, approximately 2 miles north of the Hammock Dunes Bridge.

At the confluence of the Matanzas River and Pellicer Creek, **Princess Place Preserve** (386-313-4020; flaglercounty.org), 2500 Princess Place Rd, Palm Coast, is one of the county's largest and most beautiful parks. At its heart is historic Cherokee Grove (see *Historic Sites*), established in 1886; the iconic lodge is open for tours Fri–Sun at 2. Encompassing 1,500 acres of pine flatwoods and salt marsh, the preserve has a bounty of outdoor recreation opportunities, including a beautiful, deeply shaded campground (see *Camping & Cabins*). Open daily 8–6; free.

Shell Bluff Park (386-313-4020; flaglercounty.org), FL 100, Andalusia, is the westernmost park in the county and the only place where you can directly access Crescent Lake, one of the region's best destinations for inland boating and bass fishing. Launch your canoe, kayak, or boat, use the picnic grounds, or take a walk on the nature trail. Open dawn–dusk; free.

☙ ✿ ♿ Hidden right below the SR 100 bridge, **Betty Steflik Preserve** (386-313-4020; www.flaglercounty.org), 815 Moody Ln, Flagler Beach, is missed by most passersby, but locals know it as their own hidden treasure for birding and manatee-watching. At dusk, sunset plays across shallows wrapped in a mangrove fringe. Extensive boardwalks make this a gentle walk for all. Open dawn to dusk daily.

WILD PLACES The headwaters of Bulow Creek rise in the cypress swamps of **Graham Swamp Conservation Area** (386-437-7490; sjrwmd.com/recreation guide/grahamswamp), along Old Kings Rd just south of Palm Coast [29.508334,

GARDEN

✿ **Washington Oaks Gardens State Park** (386-446-6780; floridastateparks.org /washingtonoaks), 6400 N Oceanshore Blvd. On the site of the first Spanish land grant in the region, these formal gardens were lovingly cultivated between 1936 and 1964 by Owen D. Young, chairman of the board of General Electric, and his wife. Meandering pathways lined with azaleas and camellias make a maze through a hammock of ancient live oaks, past benches set in scenic spots for quiet contemplation. On the wilder side of the park, walk the short Mala Compra Trail to explore mangroves and needlerush along the Matanzas River en route to a popular picnic area; hike the 1.7-mile Bella Vista Trail to see coastal scrub, maritime hammock, and dense hardwood forests. Across the street is an otherworldly strand of shoreline along the Atlantic called Coquina Beach, stones and tidal pools sculpted by the sea (see *Beaches*). Fee.

IN THE GARDENS OF WASHINGTON OAKS GARDENS STATE PARK

-81.161392]. This preserve protects a freshwater floodplain that creates a barrier against saltwater intrusion from the Atlantic Ocean; a mile-long trail lets you explore the swamp by hiking or mountain biking. Fishing is welcome in the lakes.

Protecting sensitive lands along the Matanzas River, **Guana-Tolomato-Matanzas Reserve** (904-825-5071; nerrs.noaa.gov/gtm) is home to the northernmost stands of mangrove on the Atlantic coast as well as rich oyster beds that can wreak havoc with your boat if you don't heed the tides. Straddling both sides of the waterway and including pristine islands such as **Mellon Island** [29.668951, -81.218349], a palm hammock reached by kayak offshore from Summer Haven, this southern segment reserve offers endless waterways for kayakers to explore. The primary public access point for the preserve is the county-managed River to Sea Preserve (see *Beaches*).

At **Haw Creek Preserve** (386-313-4020; flaglercounty.org), 2007 CR 2007, Bunnell, there's a boat ramp and canoe put-in to slip your craft into the cypress-lined waters. By the number of alligators I saw here, a walk on the boardwalk is the reason to come, as you wander along—safely off the shores—the edge of the creek with numerous observation decks along the way.

Pellicer Creek Conservation Area (386-329-4404; sjrwmd.com/recreationguide /pellicercreek) off US 1 south of I-95 [29.6375, -81.257776] protects almost 4,000 acres of wetlands, pine flatwoods, and upland hammocks between Faver-Dykes State Park and Princess Place Preserve. Access its trails from Princess Place Preserve (see *Parks*) or the Florida Agricultural Museum (see *Museums*) as well as from a point along Old Kings Hwy that leads back to a fishing pier and put-in along the creek.

✷ Lodging

HOTELS, MOTELS & RESORTS

Palm Coast 32137

🔸 🐾 ✒ ⚹ One of Florida's more unique pieces of roadside history, **Palm Coast Villas** (386-445-3525; palmcoastvillas.com), 5454 N Oceanshore Blvd, is the rebirth of a longtime landmark along A1A in Hammock. Once known as the Rock Lodge, the complex includes the original motor court and newer additions of larger rooms and suites. Inside the original rooms, you'll feel like you stepped into a national park lodge. The walls are pure, thick coquina, quarried in this region, and the crisp, simple decor is just enough not to show up their natural beauty. Even the bathrooms, 1940s in size, have rock walls! All rooms include an efficiency kitchen, and all have tile floors and windows that let you look out on the lush hammock of ancient oaks and palm trees behind the building. The newer rooms and suites are modern and spacious and also include kitchen facilities. Continental breakfast is provided with your stay. Trails lead through the woods back to the Intracoastal Waterway, where you can borrow a canoe and paddle upstream, or just take burgers out to the grill and enjoy them at a picnic table with a breeze. The original pool sits out near the road, fenced in for children's safety. Borrow a bicycle to explore Hammock along the East Coast Greenway, or take a drive down the street to Malacompra Park (see *Beaches*). Rooms and suites, $59–99, available by day, week, or month.

✒ ⚹ ⭕ ((•)) **Hammock Beach Resort** (866-841-0287; hammockbeach.com),

PALM COAST VILLAS

200 Ocean Crest Dr, is an all-encompassing luxury resort and conference center towering over the dunes. Built as a condo resort and opened since the prior edition of this book, its suites—from one to four bedrooms in size—are sized right for a home-away-from-home, including full kitchens in multi-bedroom suites. With four eateries on site, however, including the Atlantic Grille and Delfinos (see *Dining Out*), you may never touch that stove. Two championship golf courses—The Ocean Course and The Conservatory Course—designed by Jack Nicklaus and Tom Watson provide oceanfront or wooded options. Kids will love the tropical water park with its lazy river, waterslide, and multiple pools while Mom slips away to the spa for a warm Coconut Stone massage. Rooms and suites starting at $200.

Flagler Beach 32136

 🚹 ♂ ((ɸ)) ⊷ An oasis for a romantic getaway, **Romantic Florida Rentals at Island Cottage Villas** (87-

ROMANCE-2 or 386-439-0092; romanticfloridarentals.com), 2316 S Oceanshore Blvd, is an island-inspired collection of spacious suites surrounding a courtyard with a heated pool. Relax along the water's edge or on your private balcony and listen to the strum

TAKE A DIP IN THE POOL AT ROMANTIC FLORIDA RENTALS AT ISLAND COTTAGE VILLAS

of the waves across the street, accessible via your own private beach during your stay. For innkeepers Toni and Mark Treworgy, creating a respite for romance is their top priority, which shows in the dreamy decor and well-appointed amenities, from plush towels and satiny sheets to fireplaces and Jacuzzi tubs. A hidden garden with a sunny deck and pond spans the space between their office and library/gift shop (where many of Toni's lithographs and original watercolors of coastal life are on display) to their intimate spa, perfect for couples massages. $600–1,600 weekly, $1,600–3,800 monthly.

🔧 🐾 ((ᵞ)) For artsy people like me, the **Si Como No Inn** (386-864-1430; sicomonoinn.com), 2481 N Oceanshore Blvd, is a special delight. Each room has its own funky decor, with original murals and other artistic touches. A real Old Florida find, it's a simple strip of retro motel rooms right across from the beach, some with kitchenettes. There's an old-fashioned tiki bar out front and a spring bubbling into a sometimes-open soaking pool and down into a salt creek out back, where you can launch a kayak into the mangroves. Borrow a bicycle and explore the town, take a private surf lesson, or just pad down to the beach with your pooch and relax. $89–135, weekly and monthly rates available.

🐾 ((ᵞ)) Built in the 1920s as the home of one of the city's most prominent citizens, the **Topaz Motel** (386-439-3301; topazflaglerbeachfl.com), 1224 S Oceanshore Blvd, is the central anchor of a complex that includes a modern motel and pool facing the beach. Inside the original home—open for tours—you'll find the reception desk and the Blue at the Topaz (see *Dining Out*), a restaurant and nightclub. With the beach right across the street and

kitchens or kitchenettes in many rooms, it's an affordable family option.

Treat yourself to luxury at the beachfront **White Orchid Inn & Spa** (800-423-1477 or 386-439-4944; white orchidinn.com), 1104 S Oceanshore Blvd. In the "Room with It All" you can enjoy a king-sized canopied bed, crisp white linens, a Jacuzzi big enough for two, and a poolside veranda. The "Courtyard and Lilac Green" room features a beautiful glass-block shower and covered lanai. You'll enjoy beautifully landscaped grounds, a swimming pool, and a heated mineral pool. The on-site holistic spa features a variety of massages, wraps, facials, and hand and foot care. $139–249.

CAMPING & CABINS

Beverly Beach 32136
You can't get any closer to the beach than at the **Beverly Beach Campground and RV Resort** (800-255-2706 or 386-439-3111; beverlybeach camptown.com), 2816 Oceanshore Blvd. With your RV parked facing the Atlantic Ocean, you'll greet each day with a stunning sunrise. RV sites $55–85, full hookup; slightly lower rates for camping on the other side of A1A.

Bunnell 32136
Well off the beaten path, **Bull Creek Campground** (386-313-4020; flagler county.org), 3861 CR 2006, is managed by Flagler County Parks and adjoins Haw Creek Preserve (see *Wild Places*). Its location is ideal for anglers looking to get out on the creeks and into Crescent Lake, a little-known destination for bass fishing (see the *St. Johns River* chapter). RV and tent sites, $15–35.

Set in piney woods along Hog Pond, **Thunder Gulch Campground** (800-714-8388 or 386-437-3135; thunder gulch-campground.com), 127 Lantana

Ave, is a peaceful place to settle in with your rig. Full hookup with 30-amp electric, $31–36; primitive campsites $29; surcharge for special events. Drop in next door at The Black Cloud (see *Eating Out*) for meals and entertainment.

Flagler Beach 32136

🎣 You'll love fishing in the ocean or the Intracoastal while at **Flagler By the Sea Campground** (800-434-2124 or 386-439-2124), 2982 N Oceanshore Blvd, where there's always something to do outside. Leashed pets okay. RVs only; full hookups with 30-amp electric, $50–70.

At **Gamble Rogers State Park** (see *Beaches*), the breezy campground (800-326-3521; floridastateparks .reserveamerica.com) has 34 sites out in the sun, directly overlooking the Atlantic Ocean. Although tents are welcome, this is primarily an RV getaway, with 30-amp hookups, hot showers, and a dump station, $28.

Palm Coast 32137

Equestrians will appreciate camping at the **Florida Agricultural Museum** (see *Museums*), $25 for primitive sites, $35 with electric because of their access to a vast network of trails both on their own grounds and across the land bridge over I-75 to Pellicer Creek Preserve and Princess Place. Paddocks and stalls available. Reservations required, call 386-446-7630.

At **Princess Place Preserve** (see *Parks*), the primitive campground run by Flagler County Parks (386-313-4020; flaglercounty.org) sits along the salt marsh, perfect for early-morning fishing or paddling expeditions. Equestrians have their own campground near the equestrian trailhead. These tents only sites do have privies and picnic tables nearby, $15–25. A camping permit is required in advance; call ahead.

DINING OUT

Flagler Beach

Inside **Blue at the Topaz** (386-439-4322; blueatthetopaz.com) at the Topaz Motel (see *Lodging*), expect to be dazzled by the creative choices on the menu, from wasabi horseradish honey crusted oysters to Parmesan-crusted double-cut pork chop and the tasty clams casino pasta. Being able to dine on the porch of a 1920s Victorian with a front-row view of the Atlantic Ocean is a nice perk. Sandwiches, salads, and dinners, $6–26.

Delicious fish is what you'll get at the **Flagler Fish Company** (386-439-0000; flaglerfishcompany.com), 180 S Daytona Ave, where you can pick up fresh seafood to go or relax and enjoy it prepared for you. Stop in for lunch and start off with a creamy lobster bisque; then move on to a sandwich like the Holy Mackerel BLT—topped with your choice of grilled fish—or fish tacos several different ways. Or settle in for dinner and choose directly from the fish case, plus sides like butter-fried noodles, savory grits, or Asiago potatoes. Burgers, steaks, and pasta too. Open Mon–Sat, $10–23.

Palm Coast

At Hammock Beach Resort (see *Lodging*), the **Atlantic Grille** (hammock beach.com) tickled my taste buds while I lunched with colleagues during a business conference. For a light meal, the Hammock Salad, with toasted pecans, dried cranberry, orange, and champagne vinaigrette, was perfect paired with a pass-around plate of their own Dirty Bleu Chips made with Stilton cheese. The views of the ocean were a nice break from the conference room. Open for breakfast, lunch, and dinner, lunches $13–19. Sister restaurant **Delfinos** (386-246-5650) focuses on contemporary Italian cuisine, with osso buco highlighting a slow-roasted pork shank, and scampi combining jumbo shrimp and diver scallops; entrées $17–34. Open at 5:30 each evening, reservations recommended.

EATING OUT

Bunnell

Step into **The Black Cloud** (800-714-8388), N US 1 at Thunder Gulch Campground (see *Camping & Cabins*) for an evening at the roadhouse. The dynamic sculpture outside will grab your attention, but so will the busy interior. The full bar stretches down one wall, four stages offer live entertainment five days a week, and a dance floor waits in the middle of the room. Add in billiards and munchies like Miss Kitty's Mussels, Cheyenne Chicken Wrap, and the Texas Burger, and you'll be here for the evening; lunch and dinner with daily specials, $7–14.

At **Woody's Bar-B-Que** (386-439-5010; woodys.com), 99 Flagler Plaza Dr, the Family Value Meal is your best bet, with a portion of chicken thighs and legs, ribs and sliced pork, and beef or turkey with four large sides. Open daily for lunch and dinner.

Flagler Beach

((ᵞ)) Beer, wine, and live music extend the hours of the **Beach House Beanery** (386-338-2484; beachhousebeanery .com), 202 S Central Ave, to add to evening nightlife in Flagler Beach. Stop in for a breakfast sandwich and a latte, have a vegan Jack and Lu Veggie Sandwich at lunch, or lounge with your drink out on the porch, drinking in the view of the ocean as you surf the 'net. Open daily.

♠ Sea shanties and windjammer ships decorate the walls of **The Fisherman's Net** (386-439-1818; thefishermansnet restaurant.com), 500 S Oceanshore

Blvd, where you get fresh seafood and fabulous service at a great price. It's a seafood market as well as an eatery, so take a gander at the goodies before taking a seat. Nightly early-bird specials, 4–6 PM, $10–13, include prime rib, mussels marinara, and their fried seafood platter (with many other options), plus a simple but nice wine list. Entrées $6–22, closed Mon.

It's always busy at **The Golden Lion** (386-439-3004; goldenlioncafe.us), 500 N Oceanshore Blvd, a funky beach bar and restaurant with ocean views. Join the perpetual party on the upper decks, or duck inside for their top-notch beer-battered fish-and-chips. Steak and chips is on the menu, too, along with a big broiled seafood platter and the Oceans 11 Seafood Boil, which'll fill you up. Lunch, dinner, and late-night bites, $7–24.

♠ Meeting up with a girlfriend at **High Tides at Snack Jacks** (386-439-3344; snackjacks.com), 2805 S Oceanshore Blvd, I was amazed how packed it was for a weeknight. Turns out this is an everyday occurrence for this old-time surfer hangout perched on the dunes, the parking lot so narrow and shoehorned that you have to let the fellows valet-park your car so they can stack them three and four deep. But hey, Snack Jacks was built in 1950 and there was a lot less width to the road (and more to the beach) back then. The breeze was pretty hefty out on the open deck so we went onto the screened porch and plunked down at a picnic table with a view of the Atlantic waves crashing. My shrimp came with a healthy dose of hot sauce, and between that, the margaritas, and some seafood platter shared, it was plenty and tasty. Open daily for lunch and dinner, and plenty of cold beer and icy drinks, $6–20.

🍧 For some of the funkiest popsicles you'll ever try, stop in **The Hyppo** (904-217-7853; thehyppo.com), 200 S Central Ave, a spin-off of the St. Augustine location. We're talking smooth, flash-frozen fruity combinations you'd probably never think of, like the pineapple cilantro that cooled me down on a hot day, a lavender lemonade, datil strawberry with those piquant hot peppers from the neighboring county, and a dozen more. If you're not so daring, go with a simple and tasty orange cream.

Breakfast at **Maggie's European Bakery & Cafe** (386-439-9990), 909 N Oceanshore Blvd, was simply magical. Bustling on a weekday morning, it's a refuge for locals loving their fine baked goods and a cozy, convivial atmosphere. Right out the wall of windows on the front wall, you can stare over your cup of coffee at the sea. Hues of lavender form a backdrop for European platters, paintings, and brochures. The specialty of the house is crêpes, and mine—apple rum raisin pie—came piled high with freshly whipped cream on the side. Breakfast and lunch, $5–11.

🐾 Right along A1A, the **Turtle Shack Cafe** (386-439-0331), 2123 N Oceanshore Blvd, is a pet-friendly lunch stop that boasts the "Best Burger in Flagler," but their seafood is what keeps the regulars happy. With creations like scallops St. Jacques and simple goodness in their crab dip and crabcakes, you won't miss with any selection. A "Lightning Lunch" is available for those in a hurry down the coast.

🍦 Grab cold, freshly made ice cream at **The Waffle Cone** (386-569-3153; thewafflecone.com), S 4th St, and take a walk down to the beach to savor it in the sea breeze. This little shop is always busy; sometimes you have to park blocks away to come grab a cone. Open daily noon–9:30 PM.

Hammock

🍦 After a morning at the beach, nothing's better than soft serve from the **Sea Breeze Sweet Shop** (386-446-

DINE OCEANFRONT AND OLD FLORIDA–STYLE AT HIGH TIDES AT SNACK JACKS

4231), 5861 FL A1A. Besides the cones, shakes, and sundaes, they can wet your whistle with burgers, dogs, subs, and homemade potato salad.

Palm Coast

At **High Jackers Restaurant** (386-586-6078; highjackers.com), 202 Airport Rd, they've got one of my favorites on the daily menu—Wisconsin beer cheese soup! Entrées are strictly steak and seafood, done up as kebabs and fried fish platters in the HoJo tradition. Located at the Flagler County Airport, they're a spin-off of High Tides at Flagler Beach. Give 'em a whirl!

✳ Entertainment

Cruise down A1A through Flagler Beach any night of the week and you'll find **live music** happening at restaurants along the way, especially those with outdoor patios or decks. Grab drinks and sing karaoke at **Finn's** (386-439-7755; finnsflagler.com), which has two stages. In Bunnell the hot nightspot is **The Black Cloud** (see *Eating Out*) at Thunder Gulch Campground. For upscale entertainment, try the **Piano Bar** or **Cigar Bar** at Hammock Beach Resort (see *Lodging*).

✳ Selective Shopping

Flagler Beach

Find fabulous gifts at **A Frame of Mind** (382-569-4429; christmascome true.org), 208B S Central Ave, and help others have a merry Christmas. Local artisans and writers sell their creative works in this colorful shop, with a portion of the proceeds going to Christmas Come True, a nonprofit run by artist Nadine King—whom you'll find staffing the store most days—to provide Christmas dinners and gifts for Flagler families in need.

Get your tropical groove on at **Bahama Mama's** (386-439-5678), 208 S Central Ave, where colorful prints on dresses and shirts compete for attention with jewelry, beachy souvenirs, and pirate stuff.

You'll find designer clothing along with a variety of works by local artisans at **Down By the Sea Boutique & Art Gallery** (386-439-2255), 208 S 3rd St.

She sells sea shells at **The Seaside Shoppe** (386-439-6322), 601 S Central Ave, along with wind chimes, T-shirts, and nautical decor.

FARMER'S MARKET Downtown Flagler Beach is abuzz on Friday mornings when the **Flagler Beach Farmer's Market** (flaglerbeach farmersmarket.com) and its customers swarm over all the green space where FL 100 and A1A meet. Since much of Flagler County is rural, the veggies are especially fresh off the farm. Open 7–2.

✳ Special Events

April: **Palm Coast Spring Art Festival** (386-871-8895; flaglercountyart league.com), City Marketplace, first weekend. Some of the region's finest artists are showcased at this juried exhibit and festival that includes artists' booths, storytelling, children's activities, and more.

Earth Day Celebration at Washington Oaks State Park (see *Garden*), third weekend. This long-standing outdoor celebration of Earth Day features reenactors with living history demonstrations of pioneer Florida, live entertainment by Florida folk musicians, hands-on activities for the kids, and local arts and crafts.

October: **Creekside Festival** (386-437-0106; flaglerchamber.org) at

Princess Place Preserve (see *Parks*), first weekend. This family-oriented outdoor extravaganza features Florida bluegrass and blues musicians boogying down along scenic Pellicer Creek. See artists in action, take kayak or walking tours of the preserve, visit the food booths, or check out the antique tractor displays.

November: **North Florida Folkfest** (nffolk.com) at the Florida Agricultural Museum (see *Museums*), mid-month, brings in classic Florida folk musicians from around the state.

INDEX